POVERTY AND UN-BRITISH RULE IN INDIA

POVERTY AND UN-BRITISH RULE IN INDIA

BY

DADABHAI NAOROJI

GYAN

Published by

Gyan Publishing House
5, Ansari Road
Daryaganj, New Delhi-110002
Phone: 011-47034999, 9811692060
E-mail: books@gyanbooks.com

Distribution Network
gyanbooks.com
India, USA, Canada, UK, Australia, France

ISBN: 978-81-212-8360-1 (PB)
First Published, 1901

2nd Impression 2023

Printed at: Gyan Press, Delhi.

POVERTY AND UN-BRITISH RULE IN INDIA
Author: DADABHAI NAOROJI

POVERTY AND UN-BRITISH RULE IN INDIA

BY

DADABHAI NAOROJI

LONDON
SWAN SONNENSCHEIN & CO., LIM.
PATERNOSTER SQUARE

1901

CONTENTS.

THE POVERTY OF INDIA.

THE CONDITION OF INDIA.

INTRODUCTION.

"BRITAIN'S SOLEMN PLEDGES."

ACT OF PARLIAMENT, 1833 (INDIA) :—

"That no Native of the said territories, nor any natural-born subject of His Majesty resident therein, shall by reason only of his religion, place of birth, descent, or any of them, be disabled from holding any place, office, or employment under the said Company." [The Company's duties were transferred to the Crown.]

THE QUEEN'S PROCLAMATION OF 1858 :—

"We hold ourselves bound to the Natives of our Indian territories by the same obligations of duty which bind us to all our other subjects, and these obligations, by the blessing of Almighty God, we shall faithfully and conscientiously fulfil.

"And it is our further will that, so far as may be, our subjects, of whatever race or creed, be freely and impartially admitted to offices in our service, the duties of which they may be qualified, by their education, ability, and integrity, duly to discharge.

"When, by the blessing of Providence, internal tranquillity shall be restored, it is our earnest desire to stimulate . . . . and to administer its government for the benefit of all our subjects resident therein. In their prosperity will be our strength, in their contentment our security, and in their gratitude our best reward. And may the God of all power grant to us and to those in authority under us strength to carry out these our wishes for the good of our people."

LORD LYTTON (the Viceroy), on the assumption of the title of Empress, 1st January, 1877, at the Delhi Assemblage :—

"But you, the Natives of India, whatever your race and whatever your creed, have a recognised claim to share largely with your English fellow-subjects, according to your capacity for the task, in the administration of the country you inhabit. This claim is founded in the highest justice. It has been repeatedly affirmed by British and Indian statesmen and by the legislation of the Imperial Parliament. It is recognised by the Government of India as binding on its honour, and consistent with all the aims of its policy."

LORD LYTTON (the Viceroy), as Chancellor of the Calcutta University, March, 1877 :—

"The Proclamation of the Queen contains solemn pledges, spontaneously given, and founded upon the highest justice."

JUBILEE of 1887. The Queen-Empress, in reply to the Jubilee Address of Congratulation of the Bombay Municipal Corporation :—

"Allusion is made to the Proclamation issued on the occasion of my assumption of the direct government of India as the charter of the liberties of the Princes and Peoples of India. It has always been and will be continued to be my earnest desire that the principles of that Proclamation should be unswervingly maintained."

IN order to give briefly some indication of the scope and object of this book, I make some introductory remarks.

The title of the book is "POVERTY AND UN-BRITISH RULE IN INDIA," *i.e.*, the present system of government is destructive and despotic to the Indians and un-British and suicidal to Britain. On the other hand, a truly British course can and will certainly be vastly beneficent both to Britain and India.

Before dealing with the above evil qualities of the present system of government I would first give a very brief sketch of the benefits which India has derived from British connexion, and of the immense importance of India to Britain for Britain's own greatness and prosperity.

The Benefits to India.

The present advanced humanitarian civilisation of Britain could not but exercise its humane influence to abolish the customs of *sati* and infanticide, earning the everlasting blessings of the thousands who have been and will be saved thereby.

The introduction of English education, with its great, noble, elevating, and civilising literature and advanced science, will for ever remain a monument of good work done in India and a claim to gratitude upon the Indian people. This education has taught the highest political ideal of British citizenship and raised in the hearts of the educated Indians the hope and aspiration to be able to raise their countrymen to the same ideal citizenship. This hope and aspiration as their greatest good are at the bottom of all their present sincere and earnest loyalty, in spite of the disappointments, discouragements, and despotism of a century and half. I need not dwell upon several consequential social and civilising benefits. But the greatest and the most valued of all the benefits are the most solemn pledges of the Act of 1833, and the Queen's Proclamations of 1858, 1877, and 1887, which if "faithfully and conscientiously fulfilled" will be Britain's highest gain and glory and India's greatest blessing and benefit.

Britain may well claim credit for law and order, which, however, is as much necessary for the existence of British rule in India as for the good of the Indian people; for freedom of speech and press, and for other benefits flowing therefrom.

The Immense Importance of India to Britain's Empire, to its Greatness and its Prosperity.

Lord Curzon, before he went out to India as Viceroy, laid great and repeated emphasis, two or three times, upon the fact of this importance of India to Britain. "India," he said, "was the pivot of our Empire. (Hear, hear.) If this Empire lost any other part of its dominion we could survive, but if we lost India, the sun of our Empire would be set" (*Times*, 3/12/1898).

Lord Roberts, after retiring for good from India, said to the London Chamber of Commerce :—

"I rejoice to learn that you recognise how indissolubly the prosperity of the United Kingdom is bound up with the retention of that vast Eastern Empire" (*Times*, 25/5/1893). He repeated "that the retention of our Eastern Empire is essential to the greatness and prosperity of the United Kingdom" (*Times*, 29/7/1893). And with still more emphasis he pointed out upon what essential condition such retention of the Indian Empire depended—not upon brute force; but "however," he said, "efficient and well-equipped the army of India may be, were it indeed absolute perfection, and were its numbers considerably more than they are at present, our greatest strength must ever rest on the firm base of a united and contented India."

I now come to the faults of the present un-British system of Government, which unfortunately "more than counter-balances the benefits."

Destructive and Despotic to the Indians.

The Court of Directors, among various expressions of the same character, said, in their letters of 17/5/1766 and others about the same time : "Every Englishman throughout the country . . . . exercising his power to the oppression of the helpless Natives. . . . . We have the strongest sense of the deplorable state . . . from the corruption and rapacity of our servants . . . by a scene of the most tyrannic and oppressive conduct that ever was known in any age or country!" Such unfortunately was the beginning of the connexion between Britain and India—based on greed and oppression. And to our great misfortune and destruction, the same has remained in subtle and ingenious forms and subterfuges up to the present day with ever increasing impoverishment.

Later, as far back as 1787, Sir John Shore (subsequently Governor-General) prophesied the evils of the present system of the British Indian Government which is true to the present day.

He said in a deliberate Minute :—

"Whatever allowance we may make for the increased industry of the subjects of the State, owing to the enhanced demand for the produce of it (supposing the demand to be enhanced), there is reason to conclude that *the benefits are more than counterbalanced by evils inseparable from the system of a remote foreign dominion. . . . .*"[1]

Commonsense will suggest this to any thoughtful mind. These evils have ever since gone on increasing, and more and more counterbalancing the increased produce of the country, making now the evil of the "bleeding" and impoverishing drain by the foreign dominion nearly or above £30,000,000 a year in a variety of subtle ways and shapes; while about the beginning of the last century the drain was declared to be £3,000,000 a year—and with private remittances, was supposed to be near £5,000,000—or one-sixth of what it is at present. If the profits of exports and freight and insurance, which are not accounted for in the official statistics, be considered, the present drain will be nearer forty than thirty millions; speaking roughly on the old basis of the value of gold at two shillings per rupee.

Mr. Montgomery Martin, after examining the records in the India House of a minute survey made in 1807-1814 of the condition of some provinces of Bengal and Behar, said in 1835 in his "Eastern India":—"It is impossible to avoid remarking two facts as peculiarly striking—first the richness of the country surveyed, and second, the poverty of its inhabitants. . . . . The annual drain of £3,000,000 on British India has amounted in thirty years, at 12 per cent. (the usual Indian rate) compound interest to the enormous sum of £723,900,000 sterling. . . . . So constant and accumulating a drain, even in England, would soon impoverish her. How severe then must be its effects on India when the wage of a labourer is from twopence to threepence a day." He also calculates the result of the drain of £5,000,000 a year. What then must be or can be the effect of the unceasing drain which has now grown to the enormous amount of some £30,000,000 a year, if not famines and plagues, destruction and impoverishment!

Mill's "History of India" (Vol. VI, p. 671; "India Reform Tract" II, p. 3) says: "It is an exhausting drain upon the resources of the country, the issue of which is replaced by no reflex; it is an extraction of the life blood from the veins of national industry which no subsequent introduction of nourishment is furnished to restore."

Sir George Wingate has said (1859): "Taxes spent in the

[1] The italics are all mine, except when stated otherwise.

country from which they are raised are totally different in their effect from taxes raised in one country and spent in another. In the former case the taxes collected from the population . . . are again returned to the industrious classes. . . . . But the case is wholly different when the taxes are not spent in the country from which they are raised. . . . . They constitute . . . . an absolute loss and extinction of the whole amount withdrawn from the taxed country . . . . might as well be thrown into the sea. . . . . Such is the nature of the tribute we have so long exacted from India. . . . . From this explanation some faint conception may be formed of the cruel, crushing effect of the tribute upon India. . . . . The Indian tribute, whether weighed in the scales of justice or viewed in the light of our own interest, will be found to be at variance with humanity, with common sense, and with the received maxims of economic science" ("A Few Words on Our Financial Relation with India." London: Richardson Bros., 1859).

Lord Salisbury, as Secretary of State for India, in a Minute (26/4/1875) said—[C. 3086—1—(1884, p. 144)]:—

"The injury is exaggerated in the case of India, where so much of the revenue is exported without a direct equivalent. As *India must be bled* the lancet should be directed to the parts where the blood is congested or at least sufficient, not to those" (the agricultural people) "which are *already feeble from the want of it.*"

This was said twenty-six years ago, and those who were considered as having sufficient blood are also being brought lower and lower. The "want of blood" among the agricultural population is getting so complete that famines and plagues like the present are fast bleeding the masses to death.

Lord Lawrence, Lord Cromer, Sir Auckland Colvin, Sir David Barbour, and others have declared the *extreme poverty* of India.

But the drain is not all. All the wars by which the British Indian Empire is built up have not only been fought mainly with Indian blood, but every farthing of expenditure (with insignificant exceptions) incurred in all wars and proceedings within and beyond the frontiers of India by which the Empire has been built up and maintained up to the present day has been exacted from the Indian people. Britain has spent nothing.

There is the great injustice that every expenditure incurred even for British interest is charged to India. Under the recommendation of the late "Royal Commission on Indian Expenditure and Apportionment" the British Government has done a very small justice in refunding about £250,000 a year. Even for such trifle of justice we are thankful, and hope that this may lead to further justice. But it is necessary for us to have the help of the recognition and voice of the British public to ensure this.

The utter exhaustion and destruction from all these causes is terrific, and cannot but produce the present famines, plagues, etc. What would Britain's condition be under a similar fate? Let her ask herself that question. The Anglo-Indians always shirk that question, never face it. Their selfishness makes them blind and deaf to it.

Despotism.

I need only say that the people of India have not the slightest voice in the expenditure of the revenue, and therefore in the good government of the country. The powers of the Government being absolutely arbitrary and despotic, and the Government being alien and bleeding, the effect is very exhausting and destructive indeed.

Sir William Hunter has truly said:—

"I cannot believe that a people numbering one-sixth of the whole inhabitants of the globe, and whose aspirations have been nourished from their earliest youth on the strong food of English liberty, can be permanently denied a voice in the government of their country. I do not believe that races . . . . into whom we have instilled the maxim of 'no taxation without representation' as a fundamental right of a people, can be permanently excluded from a share in the management of their finances."

Un-British and Suicidal to Britain.

A committee of five members of the Council of the Secretary of State for India have declared the British Government to be "exposed to the charge of keeping promise to the ear and breaking it to the hope" (Report, 20th January, 1860).

Lord Lytton, as Viceroy of India, in a Minute referred to in the despatch of the Government of India of 2nd May, 1878, said: "No sooner was the Act (1833) passed than the Government began to devise means for practically evading the fulfilment of it. . . . . We have had to choose between prohibiting them and cheating them, and we have chosen the least straightforward course . . . . are all so many deliberate and transparent subterfuges for stultifying the Act and reducing it to a dead letter. . . . . I do not hesitate to say that both the Government of England and of India appear to me up to the present moment unable to answer satisfactorily the charge of having taken every means in their power of breaking to the heart the words of promise they had uttered to the ear." (First Report of the Indian National Congress.)

The Duke of Argyll has said: "We have not fulfilled our duty or the promises and engagements which we have made." (*Hansard*, 11/3/1869.)

Lord Salisbury, in reply to Lord Northbrook's pleading for the fulfilment of British solemn pledges, said it was all "political hypocrisy." (*Hansard*, 9/4/1883.)

SUICIDAL TO BRITAIN.

Sir John Malcolm says: "We are not warranted by the history of India, nor indeed by that of any other nation in the world, in reckoning upon the possibility of preserving an Empire of such a magnitude by a system which excludes, as ours does, the Natives from every station of high rank and honourable ambition. . . . If we do not use the knowledge which we impart it will be employed against us. . . . If these plans are not associated with the creation of duties that will employ the minds which we enlighten, we shall only prepare elements that will hasten the destruction of our Empire. The moral evil to us does not thus stand alone. It carries with it its Nemesis, the seeds of the destruction of the Empire itself."

Mr. John Bright: "I say a Government like that has some fatal defect which at some not distant time must bring disaster and humiliation to the Government and to the people on whose behalf it rules." (Speech in the Manchester Town Hall, 11/12/1877.)

The Duke of Devonshire pointed out that "it is not wise to educate the people of India, to introduce among them your civilisation and your progress and your literature and at the same time to tell them they shall never have any chance of taking any part or share in the administration of the affairs of their country *except by their getting rid in the first instance of their European rulers*."—(*Hansard*, 23/8/1883.)

Lord Randolph Churchill, as Secretary of State for India, has said in a letter to the Treasury :—

"The position of India in relation to taxation and the sources of public revenue is very peculiar, not merely from the habits of the people and their strong aversion to change, which is more specially exhibited to new forms of taxation, but likewise from *the character of the Government* which is *in the hands of foreigners who hold all the principal administrative offices, and form so large a part of the army*. The impatience of the new taxation, which will have to be borne *wholly as a consequence of the foreign rule imposed on the country*, and virtually to meet additions to charges arising outside of the country, would constitute a *political danger*, the real magnitude of which it is to be feared is not at all appreciated by persons who have no knowledge of or concern in the Government of India, but which those responsible for that Government have long regarded as of *the most serious order*." [1]

Lord George Hamilton candidly admits :—"Our Government never will be popular in India." Again, "our Government never can be popular in India."—(*Times*, 16/6/1899.)

How can it be otherwise? If the present un-British and suicidal system of government continues, commonsense tells us that such a system "can never" and "will never" be popular. And if so such a deplorable system cannot but perish; as Lord Salisbury truly says, "Injustice will bring the highest on earth to ruin." Macaulay has said, "The heaviest of all yokes is the yoke of the stranger." And if the British rule remains, as it is at present, a heavy yoke of the stranger and the despot, instead of being a true British rule and a friendly partner, it is doomed to perish. Evil is not, and never will be, eternal.

True British Rule.

True British rule will vastly benefit both Britain and India. My whole object in all my writings is to impress upon the British People, that instead of a disastrous explosion

[1] "Parliamentary Return" [C. 4868], 1886.

of the British Indian Empire, as must be the result of the present dishonourable un-British system of government, there is a great and glorious future for Britain and India to an extent unconceivable at present, if the British people will awaken to their duty, will be true to their British instincts of fair play and justice, and will insist upon the "faithful and conscientious fulfilment" of all their great and solemn promises and pledges.

Mr. John Bright has truly said: "The good of England must come through the channels of the good of India. There are but two modes of gaining anything by our connexion with India. The one is by plundering the people of India and the other by trading with them. I prefer to do it by trading with them. But in order that England may become rich by trading with India, India itself must become rich." Cannot British authorities see their way to such intelligent selfishness? Hitherto England has to some extent made herself rich by plundering India in diverse subtle and ingenious ways. But what I desire and maintain is that England can become far richer by dealing justly and honourably with India, and thereby England will not only be a blessing to India and itself, but will be a lesson and a blessing to mankind.

Macaulay, in his great speech of 1833, said: "I have no fears. The path of duty is plain before us; and it is also the path of wisdom, of national prosperity, of national honour. . . . . To have found a great people sunk in the lowest depths of slavery and superstition, to have so ruled them as to have made them desirous and capable of all the privileges of citizens would indeed be a title to glory all our own. The sceptre may pass away from us. Unforeseen accidents may derange our most profound schemes of policy. Victory may be inconstant to our arms. But there are triumphs which are followed by no reverses. There is an empire exempt from all natural causes of decay. Those triumphs are the pacific triumphs of reason over barbarism; that empire is the imperishable empire of our arts and our morals, our literature and our laws."

Sir William Hunter, after referring to the good work done by the Company, said: "But the good work thus commenced has assumed such dimensions under the Queen's government of India that it can no longer be carried on, *or even supervised*, by imported labour from England except at a cost which India cannot sustain. . . . . Forty years hereafter we should have had an Indian Ireland multiplied fifty fold on our hands. . . . . You cannot work with imported labour as cheaply as you can with Native labour, and I regard the more extended employment of the Natives not only as an act of justice but as a financial necessity." "The appointment of a few Natives annually to the Covenanted Civil Service will not solve the problem. . . . . If we are to govern the Indian people efficiently and cheaply we must govern them by means of themselves and pay for the administration at the market rates of Native labour." ("England's Work in India," pp. 118-9.)

The Duke of Devonshire has said: "If the country is to be better governed that can only be done by the employment of the best and most intelligent of the Natives in the Service."

Events are moving now at lightning pace, and it is difficult to say what tomorrow may bring, as forces evil or beneficent when once set in motion will move with accelerated speed to their natural results—evil out of evil, good out of good.

In the "faithful and conscientious fulfilment" of solemn pledges, India expects and demands that the British Sovereign, People, Parliament, and Government, should make honest efforts towards what the Bishop of Bombay described as the aspirations and necessities of India—"Self-government under British paramountcy" or true British citizenship.

This book contains a selection from my papers written from time to time as occasion arose, and I think giving them in the same order here will be the most intelligible form for a subject which is so complicated and whose important points are so much intermixed with each other.

POVERTY OF INDIA.

Papers

READ BEFORE THE BOMBAY BRANCH OF THE EAST INDIA ASSOCIATION OF LONDON

IN 1876.

POVERTY OF INDIA.

WHILE pointing out in these notes one of the unfavourable results of the present system of British administration, I do not for a moment mean to ignore the very bright side of British rule, and the many blessings of law and order which it has conferred on India. On the latter subject I have already expressed my sentiments on several occasions.

My object at present is to show in greater detail what I have already stated before, that, under the present system of administration, India is suffering seriously in several ways, and is sinking in poverty. In my humble opinion, this is the question, or rather the most serious question, of the day. Whether I am right or wrong will be for you to judge, after hearing what I have to say. If I am right, I shall have discharged a duty as a loyal subject to urge upon our rulers to remedy this most serious evil. If, on the other hand, I am shown to be wrong, none will rejoice more than myself; and I shall have equally done a duty, as a wrong feeling of a serious character will be removed.

These notes were written two to three years ago.[1] I lay them before you as they are. If necessary, I shall consider hereafter any modification that the light of subsequent events may suggest, either in confirmation or refutation of the views expressed in them. There will be a few repetitions from my former papers, but they are necessary in order to make these notes complete. I have endeavoured to avail myself as much as possible of the weight of official or other great authorities,

[1] These notes in their original draft were placed before the Select Committee on Indian Finance in 1873. They were taken, but not published with the Report, as they did not suit the views of the Chairman (Mr. Ayrton), and I was led to suppose, also of Sir Grant Duff, who was then the Under-Secretary of State for India.

and facts from official records; hence I shall have more quotations than might be thought suitable in an address before an audience; and my notes may prove dull, but I only hope they may be found of some importance to atone for such dullness. I may propose here that any discussion upon the notes may be deferred till they are all read, and my whole argument placed before you, or otherwise there will be confusion in the discussions.

Total Production of India.

In July, 1870, I made a rough estimate, in my paper on "The Wants and Means of India," placed before the East India Association, as follows:—

"The whole produce of India is from its land. The gross land-tax is put down for 1870-71 a little above £21,000,000. Now, I suppose I shall be within the mark if I say that Government takes for this land-tax, on an average, one-eighth of the gross produce, if not more. This gives for the gross production of the country, say, about £168,000,000; add to this—gross opium revenue about £7,000,000; gross salt revenue, £6,000,000; gross forest, £600,000. The total, thus, of the raw produce of the country amounts to under £182,000,000—to be on the safe side, let us say £200,000,000, to include the produce of half a million tons of coal, of alienation lands, or anything else there may be. Now, the population of the whole of British India is nearly 150,000,000; giving, therefore, less than 27s. a head for the annual support of the whole people."

I then further raised the production from £200,000,000 to £300,000,000, to include the value of manufacturing industries, excise on spirits, and a large margin for any omissions, making 40s. a head for the gross production of India as a high estimate.

Since then I have endeavoured to work out the same problem directly, as far as the official data I could get enabled me to do so.

Calcutta Statistical Committee.—Agricultural Tables.

Parliament requires a yearly report of the moral and material progress of India; and a Statistical Committee is formed at Calcutta to supply the necessary information. This Committee has prescribed certain tables to be filled up by the different Governments in their administration reports.

The Central Provinces and Burmah reports are the only two complete in their agricultural tables as far as practicable. Four others (Madras, North-West Provinces, Punjab, and Oudh) give them imperfectly. Bengal and Bombay gave the least, or none, up to 1869-70. For what I could not get from the reports I applied to the India Office, which naturally replied they could not give what they did not get from India. It will be seen, therefore, that I have been obliged to work out the production under much difficulty. Not only is the quantity of information insufficient, but the quality even of such as is given is defective. For instance, in the tables of prices of produce in the different districts of the Central Provinces, in order to get an average the prices are added up together, and the total is divided by the number of the districts. This principle is generally adopted by the returns made by all the Governments with respect to average of produce or prices. The principle, however, is altogether fallacious. In taking the average of prices, the quantities of produce sold at the different prices are altogether lost sight of. In the same way, in taking the average produce per acre, the extent of land yielding different quantities is overlooked.

Fallacy of its Statistics.

The result, therefore, is wrong, and all arguments and conclusions based upon such averages are worthless. Taking the instance of the Central Provinces in the administration report of 1867-8, the average price of rice is made out to be Rs. 2-12-7 per maund, when in reality the correct average will be only Rs. 1-8 per maund. Again, the table for the produce of rice per acre gives the average as 579 lbs., when in reality it is 759 lbs. Now, what can be the worth of conclusions drawn from these wrong averages? These averages are not only worthless, but mischievous. It is a pity that, with large Government establishments, more accurate and complete information should not be given. I sincerely trust that future reports will not only work averages upon correct principles, but also work out the total production of their respective provinces. *Then* only we shall know the actual condition of the mass of the people. All "I thinks" and "my opinions" are of no use on important subjects. The whole foundation of all administration, financial and general, and of the actual condition of people, rests upon this one fact — the produce of the country, the ultimate result of all capital, labour and land. With imperfect materials at command, and not possessed of the means to employ a staff to work out all the details as they ought to be, I can only give approximate results.

How Statistics should be Compiled.

On the question of taking proper averages and supplying complete information, I addressed a letter, in February, 1871, to the India Office, which I have reason to believe has been forwarded to the Governments in India. I hope that some attention will be paid to the matter. As a specimen of the correct principle of averages, I have worked out table A of the averages of price and produce of some of the principal productions of the Central Provinces. From this will be seen that the correct average price for rice is Rs. 1-8, instead of Rs. 2-12-7, as stated above; also that the correct average of produce is 759, and not 579 lbs. of rice per acre. I have explained, in the following calculations for the different provinces, the mode I have adopted for each. Though working with insufficient and defective materials, and without the means and time to work out details, I have endeavoured to calculate *above* the mark, so that, whatever my error, it will be found on the safe side, of estimating a higher produce than the reality.

The principle of my calculations is briefly this. I have taken the largest one or two kinds of produce of a province to represent all its produce, as it would be too much labour for me to work out every produce, great and small. I have taken the whole cultivated area of each district, the produce per acre, and the price of the produce; and simple multiplication and addition will give you both the quantity and value of the total produce. From it, also, you can get the correct average of produce per acre and of prices for the whole province, as in this way you have all the necessary elements taken into account.

Central Provinces.

The total area of cultivated land (Table 2 of Fiscal Report, 1867-8—an average *good season* year) is 12,378,215 acres. The price of produce per acre, as worked out in Table A for the important articles rice, wheat, other food-grains, oil-seeds, and cotton is Rs. 11-13-5—say Rs. 12.[1] The total value of agricultural produce will be acres 12,378,215 × Rs. 12 = Rs. 14,85,38,580. To this is to be added the produce of Sumbulpore; but the acreage of that district is not given. Making some allowance for it, I increased the produce to, say, Rs. 16,00,00,000, or £16,000,000, for a population of 9,000,000.

I have lately met with an unexpected confirmation of my views. The *Times of India* Summary of 6th June, 1873, takes from the *Englishman* some particulars from Mr. Pedder's reply to the Viceroy's circular on local funds. Mr. Pedder makes out, as the value of produce in the Nagpore district, about Rs. 8 per acre, and my estimate of the whole of the Central Provinces is Rs. 12 per acre. I do not know whether Mr. Pedder has avoided the wrong principles of averages—whether he calculates for an average good season, and whether any allowance is made for bad seasons.

PUNJAB.

The administration report of 1867-8 gives all the necessary agricultural tables, except one, *viz.*, the produce per acre of the different kinds of crops. I take this year (1867-8) as a better season, and with a larger extent of cultivation than that of 1868-9.

The chief crops are wheat and other inferior grains—the former nearly 20, and the latter 50 per cent., of the whole cultivation. The price of wheat is higher than that of other inferior grains; and as I take the prices of first-class wheat, I think the average price of the produce of one acre of wheat, applied to the whole cultivated acreage, will be very much above the actual value of the production, and my estimate will be much higher than it ought to be.

[1] The Table A is too large for insertion.

Summary.

	Acres.	Rs.
Rice	2,938,328	4,18,43,575
Wheat	3,313,677	3,51,77,956
Other Food Grains	4,197,516	4,70,63,760
Oil Seeds	697,100	1,04,42,854
Cotton	643,390	50,28,838
Total	11,790,011	13,95,56,983

Average, Rs. 11-13-5 per acre.

As the administration reports of both 1867-8 and 1868-9 do not give the produce of crops per acre, I ascertain it from other sources.

In the administration report of the Punjab for the year 1850-51 (published in 1854 by the Court of Directors), drawn up by Mr. (now Sir Richard) Temple, a detailed table, dated Jullundhur, 25th October, 1851, gives the produce per acre. The table gives fourteen instances of first-class lands, which, by the rough process of adding up and dividing by the number of instances, gives 14⅐ maunds = 1,160 lbs. (a maund equals 82 lbs.—Report 1855-6); for the *second class* from eight instances, I find the average 13½ maunds, or 1,107 lbs.; and for the third class from six instances, I find 11 maunds, or 902 lbs. From this table I have taken all at 10 maunds or upwards as representing irrigated land, and the second class, representing the bulk of it, as producing 1,100 lbs. per acre. For unirrigated land I have not sufficient data. I adopt 600 lbs. per acre, for reasons I have stated under heading "North-West Provinces."

After I had made my following calculations on the above basis, I was favoured with a loan from the Record Department of the India Office of the administration report for 1869-70. The produce per acre is given in this report, but the average is taken on the objectionable principle of adding up the produce of all districts and dividing by the number of districts, without reference to the extent of cultivation in each district. According to this, the average of the produce of wheat per acre of all the districts is given in the report as only 624 lbs. The highest produce in three districts included in this average is 1,044, 1,066, and 1,000 lbs.; so that my assumption of 1,100 lbs. per acre for *all* irrigated land is much above the mark. Again, even making allowance for the drought of the years 1868-9 and 1869-70, my assumption, of 600 lbs. of wheat per acre of all unirrigated land only, is also above the mark.

I take the calculated area of 1867-8, which is also the largest of the three years 1867-8, 1868-9, 1869-70; and I take prices for 1867-8, that having been an average good season. The prices of 1868-9 and 1869-70 are scarcity-prices. The year 1867-8 is a fair test for the produce of the Punjab in an average favourable season.

The report for 1867-8 does not give prices of produce for

all districts separately, but only of a few important towns, *viz.*, Delhi, Umballa, Lahore, Sealkote, Mooltan, and Peshawur (page ciii.); and as I take these prices to represent not only those of the whole of the districts of these towns, but of all the districts of the Punjab, I evidently assume a much higher price than actually must have been the case. My results, therefore, will be affected in a double way (*viz.*, firstly, in taking first-class wheat to represent all produce; and secondly, in taking the prices in the principal towns to represent all Punjab); and will show then the total value of the production of all Punjab much higher than the reality. I therefore think I shall not be unfair in deducting 10 per cent. as some correction of this double error; and even then I shall be above the mark. The prices given in the report for 1867-8 are as follows (111 E. J. Statement, showing the prices of produce in the Punjab for the year 1867-8) :—

	Price in Seers for One Rupee.					
	1st June 1866.	1st Jan. 1867.	1st June 1867.	1st Jan. 1868.	Average	
Delhi	21½	20	19½	25	21½	The Seer is 2 lbs.
Umballa	25	20	20¼	20½	21½	
Lahore	23	20	22	17	20½	
Sealkote	24	20	22	16	20½	
Mooltan	16	17½	16	13½	15¾	
Peshawur	24¾	22	20¾	15	20½	

I take the above averages of the towns to represent their whole districts, and then the average of the six districts to represent the whole of the Punjab in the following calculation (wheat first sort is taken to represent all produce) :—

Districts.	Irrigated Land.	Produce per Acre.	Total Produce.	For Re. 1.	Total Value.
	Acres.	lbs.	lbs.	lbs.	Rs.
Delhi	200,955	1,100	221,050,500	43	51,40,709
Umballa	96,328	,,	105,960,800	43	24,64,204
Lahore	447,295	,,	492,024,500	41	1,20,00,597
Sealkote	394,227	,,	433,649,700	41	1,05,76,821
Mooltan	505,750	,,	556,325,000	31½	1,76,61,111
Peshawur	249,144	,,	274,058,400	41	66,84,351
Total	1,893,699	—	——	—	5,45,27,793

The average value of produce per acre of the irrigated land of the six districts will, therefore, be Rs. 28-7-9.

I now apply this to all irrigated land of the Punjab.

Total irrigated acres are 6,147,038, which, at Rs. 28-7-9 per acre, will give Rs. 17,69,73,224 as the total value of the produce of irrigated land of the Punjab for 1867-8.

I now calculate the value of the produce of unirrigated land (wheat first sort is taken to represent all produce):—

Districts.	Unirrigated Land.	Produce per acre.	Total Produce.	For Re. 1.	Total Value.
	Acres.	lbs.	lbs.	lbs.	Rs.
Delhi . . .	307,690	600	184,614,000	43	42,93,348
Umballa . .	856,701	,,	514,020,600	43	1,19,53,967
Lahore . .	557,882	,,	334,729,200	41	81,64,126
Sealkote . .	425,440	,,	255,264,000	41	62,25,951
Mooltan . .	118,684	,,	71,210,400	31½	22,60,647
Peshawur. .	456,661	,,	273,996,600	41	66,82,843
Total .	2,723,058	....	....	..	3,95,80,882

The average value of produce of one acre of unirrigated land of the six districts is Rs. 14-5-3. Applying this to the unirrigated land of the whole of the Punjab, the result will be as follows:—Total unirrigated acres 14,810,697, at Rs. 14-5-3 per acre, will give Rs. 21,51,99,427 as the value of the produce of all unirrigated land of the Punjab for 1867-8.

Adding up the value of the produce of irrigated and unirrigated land, the total will be Rs. 39,21,72,651. From this I deduct 10 per cent. for reasons stated above, which will leave Rs. 35,29,54,800 for a population of 17,593,946, or say £36,000,000 for a population of 17,500,000.

North-West Provinces.

I take the figures of 1867-8, being an average good season. The subsequent ones, 1868-9 and 1869-70, have been bad.

The administration report does not give the distribution of chief crops, but I find in the Statistical Reporter of the *Indian Economist* (page 136) of 15th March, 1871, a table of the crops for 1868-9. From this it will be seen that, out of a total of about 22,000,000 acres, rice, jowari, bajri, wheat, and barley make up—

Rice	2,479,874
Jowari and Bajri . .	4,302,890
Wheat and Barley . .	7,257,873
Acres	14,040,637 or nearly ⅔

As I cannot get the prices of all the above kinds of produce, except wheat and barley, if I take wheat to represent all, I shall be above the mark.

In the administration report of 1868-9 there is a table given of prices of wheat and barley. I take the prices for the months of April, May, and June as those of the good season of 1867-8. The subsequent prices are affected by drought. I should have preferred to take the prices for January to June, 1868; but the table does not give the earlier months. These prices are of some of the chief markets only, so that, taking the prices to represent the whole of the respective districts, and then taking the average of these few districts to represent the whole of the North-West Provinces, the result will be much higher; so, as in the case of the Punjab, I deduct 10 per cent. as some correction for these errors of excess.

The prices given in the report of 1868-9, pages 29, 30, are as follows:—"The following table gives the prices at the close of each month for the year in the chief markets of the provinces. The figures denote seers and chittacks.

Districts.	Wheat.										My Remarks.
	April.		May.		June.		Average.				
	s.	c.	s.	c.	s.	c.	s.	c.	lb.	oz.	
Saharunpore	22	6	25	14	25	14	24	11	49	6	The report does not say which seer this is.
Meerut . .	26	0	27	0	27	8	26	13	53	10	Formerly 1 seer is given equal to
Moradabad .	26	10	25	10	24	0	25	8⅔	51	1	2·057 lbs. (Parliamentary
Bareilly . .	25	10	27	8	25	0	26	0	52	0	Return No. 29 of 1862, page 5.) I take this seer=
Muttra . .	24	0	....		24	0	24	0	48	0	2 lb. 16 chittacks = 1 seer.
Agra . . .	23	0	23	0	24	0	23	5	46	10	The report also does not say
Cawnpore .	23	0	23	0	22	0	22	11	45	6	whether these quantities were
Allahabad .	18	4	18	0	17	0	17	12	35	8	got for one rupee, but it evi-
Mirzapore .	18	0	18	0	17	0	17	10⅔	35	6	dently appears to be meant so.
Benares . .	17	5	18	5	18	0	17	15⅛	35	14	"

The administration reports give no table of produce per acre of different crops. I adopt the same scale as given in the case of the Punjab, for the following additional reasons:—[1]Captain Harvey Tuket's estimate in the year 1840, from 2,000 experiments, of which 512 were for wheat, made by the Government of the North-West Provinces, gives the average produce of wheat per acre at 1,046 lbs. The late Mr. Thornton, formerly Secretary to that Government, has recorded that, judging from his own experience, he should say that 1,200 lbs. per acre was a high average for irrigated land, and 700 lbs. for that of which a considerable portion is dry.[2] Mr. Maconochi, in his recent settlements of Oonah (Oudh), gives for irrigated land—

1st class	21	bushels	=	1,218 lbs. (at 58 lbs. per bushel.)
2nd ,,	16	,,	=	928 ,,
3rd ,,	9	,,	=	522 ,,

and for unirrigated land—

1st class	11	bushels	=	638 lbs.
2nd ,,	9	,,	=	522 ,,
3rd ,,	7	,,	=	406 ,,

Taking second class as representing the bulk, the average for irrigated land may be considered as 928 lbs., and for unirrigated 522 lbs. From all the above particulars it will be seen that the estimate I have adopted, of 1,100 lbs. per acre for irrigated and 600 lbs. for unirrigated land, is something above a fair average. A Settlement Officer of the North-West Provinces, in a letter to the *Indian Economist* of 15th February, 1871 ("Agricultural Gazette," page 171) sums up all that is known to him on the subject of the produce of wheat per acre in those Provinces. It will be too long an extract to insert here; but, making allowance for the "mischievous fallacy" of all official documents alluded to by this writer, about which I have already complained to the India Office, and which vitiates averages for a number of years or places, I think the average I have adopted above is something more than a reasonable one. When administration reports will give, as they ought, correct particulars for each

[1] The "Agricultural Gazette of India" of the *Indian Economist*, 15th August, 1870, No. 1.

[2] See also Parliamentary Return No. 999 of 1853, page 471.

district every year, accurate estimates of the actual produce of the Provinces could be easily made. I give the calculations below. The table of cultivated land, given at page 45 of the appendix to the administration report of 1867-8, does not give the irrigated and unirrigated extent of land separately for the Moradabad, Tarrae, Mynpoorie, Banda and Ghazipore districts.

I find that the totals of irrigated and unirrigated land bear nearly the proportion of two-fifths and three-fifths respectively of the whole total cultivated land. I assign the same proportion to the above districts in the absence of actual particulars.

Wheat.

Districts.	Irrigated Land.	Produce per Acre.	Total Produce.	For 1 Re.		Total Value.
	Acres.	lbs.	lbs.	lbs.	ozs.	Rs.
Saharunpore .	160,058	1,100	176,063,800	49	6	35,65,849
Meerut . . .	577,346	,,	635,080,600	53	10	1,17,26,444
Moradabad .	806,930	,,	787,623,000	51	1	1,73,83,069
Bareilly . . .	344,662	,,	379,128,200	52	1	72,82,174
Muttra . . .	332,542	,,	365,796,200	48	0	89,22,837
Agra	434,166	,,	477,582,600	46	10	1,02,43,058
Cawnpore . .	397,396	,,	437,135,600	45	6	96,33,842
Allahabad . .	345,624	,,	380,186,400	35	8	1,07,09,476
Mirzapore . .	198,823	,,	218,705,300	35	6	61,82,481
Benares . . .	238,971	,,	262,868,100	35	14	75,01,549
Total . .	3,836,518	...	......	...		9,31,50,779

The average value of the produce of one acre will be Rs. 24-2-8.

Applying the average of the above districts to the whole of the irrigated area of the North-West Provinces, the result will be—acres 10,045,050 × Rs. 24-2-8 = Rs. 24,38,93,814.

In a similar manner, the total value of the produce of unirrigated land, as represented by wheat, will be as follows :—

Districts.	Unirrigated Land.	Produce per Acre.	Total Produce.	For 1 Re.		Total Value.
	Acres.	lbs.	lbs.	lbs.	ozs.	Rs.
Saharunpore .	621,382	600	372,829,200	47	6	75,50,960
Meerut . . .	453,694	,,	272,216,400	53	10	50,76,288
Moradabad .	484,158	,,	290,494,800	51	1	56,88,992
Bareilly . . .	768,283	,,	460,957,800	52	1	88,53,920
Muttra . . .	406,153	,,	243,691,800	48	0	50,76,912
Agra	374,976	,,	224,985,600	46	10	48,25,424
Cawnpore . .	436,636	,,	261,981,600	45	6	57,73,696
Allahabad . .	644,594	,,	386,756,400	35	8	1,08,94,544
Mirzapore . .	614,658	,,	368,794,800	35	6	1,04,25,280
Benares. . .	202,818	,,	121,690,800	35	14	33,92,064
Total . .	5,007,352	...	...	...		6,75,58,080

The average value of wheat per acre of unirrigated land is, therefore, Rs. 13-4-9.

Applying this average to the whole unirrigated land of the North-West Provinces, we get — acres 14,132,111 × Rs. 13-4-9 = Rs. 19,06,42,177. The grand total of the value of the produce of irrigated and unirrigated land will be—

Irrigated . .	10,045,050	acres	Rs. 24,38,93,814
Unirrigated .	14,132,111	,,	,, 19,06,42,177
Total .	24,177,161	,,	,, 43,45,35,991

Deducting 10 per cent. for reasons stated above, the remainder will be Rs. 39,10,82,392 for a population of 30,086,898, or say £40,000,000 for a population of 30,000,000.

BENGAL.

The administration reports till 1869-70 give no information required by the Statistical Committee, except the area of districts in square miles and acres (report 1869-70). For information for cultivated area, distribution, produce of crops, and prices, I have to look out elsewhere, or make a rough estimate.

First with regard to the extent of cultivated land, I adopt the following plan as the best I can. The total area of the North-West Provinces is about 50,000,000 acres, of which about 25,000,000 are cultivated. The population of those Provinces is, by the late census of 1865, about 30,000,000, so we have the total area 5 acres to 3 persons, and of cultivated area five-sixths of an acre per head. Now, assuming Bengal to be at least as thickly populated as the North-West Provinces, and the total area, as given in the administration report of 1869-70 (appendix, page xxi), being about 105,000,000 acres, the population of Bengal will be about 63,000,000; and I am encouraged to adopt this figure instead of 36,000,000 of the report of 1869-70, as the *Englishman* of 25th June, 1872, states that the census of Bengal, as far as the figures are made up, leads to an estimate of about 65,000,000. Again, as in the North-West Provinces, I allow five-sixths of an acre of cultivated land per head, and take, therefore, 54,000,000 acres of cultivated land for a population of 65,000,000.

With regard to produce, coarse rice is the chief produce of Bengal, and in taking it to represent the whole produce, I shall be near enough the mark. For the produce of rice per acre, I take a table given in the report of the Indigo Commission (Parliamentary Return No. 72,1 of 1861, page 292), in which produce of paddy per beegah is given for a number of districts. The rough average, without reference to the quantity of land in each district, comes to about nine maunds per beegah.

The maund I take is the Indian maund of 82 lbs. The quantity of produce per beegah given in the table is evidently for rice in husk; for, though not so stated, this would be apparent by comparing the money values of these quantities given in the same table, with the prices for 1860 given in the table at page 291.

The beegah I find explained, at page lxi of the same return, at about one-third of an acre. Thacker's Bengal Directory for 1872, page 2, gives the following table for "Bengal square or land measure":—

1 chittack	= 45 square feet or 5 square yards.		
16 ,,	=	1 cottah =	720 sqr. ft. or 80 sqr. yds.
20 cottah	=	1 beegah =	14,400 ,, or 1,600 ,,

Thus gives a little more than 3 beegahs to an acre.

Mr. Cowasjee Eduljee, the manager of the Port Canning rice mills and lands, thinks, that for an average of all lands, or say for standard land, seven maunds of paddy per beegah will be a very fair calculation. I take eight maunds. Mr. Cowasjee further says, as the out-turn of his mills, that paddy yields 55 per cent. of rice at the outside.

For the price of rice I take the season 1867-8. I take the rough average of the weekly prices given in the Calcutta *Gazette* for the months of January to March, 1868, as fairly representing the effect of the season of 1867-8. This average is taken by simply adding up the prices and dividing by the number of districts, and not on the correct principle of taking the quantities of the produce of each district into account (as in specimen table A I have given for the Central Provinces). The average, therefore, which I have adopted, must be much higher than the actual one, and will require some reasonable deduction. I shall deduct only 10 per cent. as some correction for this, and to make up for any error in the produce per acre. Besides, the prices given in the *Gazette* are retail prices, and are therefore higher than the prices all over the country; so my deduction of 10 per cent. will be but a very small correction for all the errors of my rough calculation. I cannot get the extent of cultivated land for each district. I give below the calculations. Since writing these notes, I have seen the late census report, which gives the population as 66,856,859, or say 67,000,000. The approximate area of cultivated land will be, say, five-sixths of 67,000,000 or 56,000,000 acres. The produce per acre, taken as 24 maunds paddy per acre, will give about 13 maunds of clean rice, or 1,066 lbs., say 1,100 lbs. The total produce of 56,000,000 acres will be 616,000,000 lbs., which, at 58 lbs. per rupee (as obtained by the rough average of the weekly prices of the three months of January, February, and March, 1868), will give Rs. 1,06,00,00,000, or £106,000,000. Deducting 10 per cent. will give £95,400,000, or say £96,000,000, for a population of 67,000,000. This will amply cover the higher price of some of the articles, such as silk, indigo, cost price of opium, tea, etc., or any double crops, etc. The percentage of these products is a small one; the total value for all these will be under 10 per cent. of the whole produce, while the average of price I have taken for rice as representing the whole produce of the Presidency will be found much above the actuals. On the whole, I cannot help thinking that the total value of all productions of the Bengal Presidency will be found much under, than above, my estimate. It is very desirable, however, to get a correct result, and the Statistical Committee or Agricultural Department should give it.

MADRAS.

I take the administration report of 1868-9 as I have not been able to get an opportunity of studying that of 1867-8. Besides, as prices have not much altered, the later report is the better. I am obliged to ascertain the produce per acre from other sources: the report does not give the information. I take paddy to represent the produce of wet, and cumboo for dry land, as they form the bulk of the produce of the country.

Mr. H. Newill, the Director of Settlements for South Arcot, in his letter of 27th August, 1859 (Selections of the Madras Government, No. 14, of 1869, Appendix Y, from page 142), gives an elaborate table of produce per acre of the principal grains, as ascertained by a large number of experiments and general enquiry; and the result of his investigations gives, for the different classes of soils, the following produce, from which 5 per cent. is to be deducted for numerous ridges for regulating irrigation channels, exterior boundaries, etc. :—

Produce of Wet Land per acre for "Good Crop" first grade Land—

Description of Soils.	Value assigned for Good Crops per Acre H. C. (Bazar Huris Cullum).	Description of Soils.	Value assigned for Good Crops per Acre H. C. (Bazar Huris Cullum).
1	45	10	30
2	40	11	25
3	35	12	20
4	30	13	18
5	28	14 }	15
6	40	15 }	
7	35		—
8	30	Average . . .	30
9	28		—

Deducting 5 per cent. for ridges, etc., 30—1½ = 28½ H. C.

For second grade land, deduct 15 per cent., which will give 24¼ H. C. For third grade deduct 20 per cent., which will give 22·8 H. C. For bad seasons Mr. Newill deducts 10 per cent. more, which I do not; so that the produce calculated by me is for "good crop," or in "good season," as in all other cases. Taking second grade as the bulk of the land, I take 24¼ H. C. as the average of all wet land.

For dry land for cumboo (page 150), Mr. Newill gives the produce per acre as follows :—

Descriptions of Soil.	H. C.	Descriptions of Soils.	H. C.	Descriptions of Soils.	H. C.
1	21	6	17	11	12
2	18	7	15	12	10
3	17	8	13	13	10
4	16	9	12	14	9
5	14	10	14	15	8
				Average . .	$13\frac{11}{15}$
					say 14 H. C.

The next thing necessary is to ascertain the correct average price. I take the average price as given in the administration report (calculated on the wrong principle referred to by me before), bearing in mind that the correct average, as worked out according to specimen table A, would be very likely found lower. Again, taking the rough average of first and second-class paddy, the price comes to Rs. 180 per garce; and as second-class paddy must be the bulk of the produce, the correct average price in this respect also must be lower. In taking, therefore, Rs. 180 per garce, some reasonable allowance will have to be made. I shall make it only 10 per cent. for all kinds of excess. It is too much work for me to calculate as in table A.

Wet land under cultivation (except South Canara and Malabar, where areas under cultivation are not given), is, for 1868 9, 2,957,748 acres at $24\frac{1}{4}$ H. C. produce per acre (and $133\frac{1}{3}$ H. C. = 1 garce[1]) will give 511,490 garces, which, at Rs. 180 per garce, will give Rs. 9,68,53,500—the total value of the produce of wet land.

Dry cultivated land (except South Canara and Malabar) is 13,560,329 acres, and with produce at 14 H. C. per acre (and 133 H. C. = 1 garce), will give 1,427,403 garces. I take the rough average price as given in the table—Rs. 188 per garce—in the administration report of 1868-9. This will be an over-estimate, as quantities in each district are not taken into account. The total value will be—1,427,403 garces at Rs. 188 = Rs. 26,83,51,764. Total produce of wet and dry lands will be Rs. 36,52,05,264; adding 10 per cent.

[1] 24 Madras measures = 1 Huris Cullum.
$133\frac{1}{3}$ Huris Cullum = 1 Madras Garce.
(Selection of the Madras Government, No. XIV. of 1869, page 16.)

for South Canara and Malabar, the total for all the Madras Presidency will be a little above Rs. 400,000,000. From this is to be allowed 10 per cent. as a correction for errors of high averages, which will leave, say, £36,000,000 for a population of 26,539,052 (Parliamentary Return No. $\frac{C.\ 184}{1870}$), or say 26,500,000.

Bombay.

The season 1867-8 was a favourable one (Bombay administration report, 1867-8, page 59); that for 1868-9 unfavourable (report for 1868-9, page 65). I take the former to ascertain the produce of a fair good season. I am sorry that the administration reports give no agricultural information. I therefore take the necessary particulars from other sources. The Revenue Commissioner's reports for 1867-8 give the total area under cultivation for the Northern Division at 5,129,754 acres and 1,263,139 beegahs, in which are included for grass and fallow-land 611,198 acres and 226,708 beegahs. The actual cultivated land will, after deducting this, be 4,518,556 acres, and 1,036,431 beegahs = 609,842 acres, or total acres, 5,128,398. Out of this, bajri, jowari, rice, and cotton make up nearly two-thirds, or above 60 per cent., as follows:—

	Acres.	Beegahs.
Bajri	985,427	56,857
Jowari	676,377	224,210
Rice	616,802	94,306
Cotton	519,058	319,572
	2,797,664	694,945 = 408,791 acres,

or total acres 3,206,455.

Similarly for the Southern Division, out of the total acres, 13,985,892, jowari, bajri, rice, and cotton make up above 60 per cent. as follows:—

	Acres.
Jowari	4,906,073
Bajri	2,715,719
Rice	504,015
Cotton	704,629
	8,830,436

I take, therefore, these four articles to represent the produce of the whole Presidency, though this will give a higher estimate. Neither the administration nor the Revenue Commissioner's reports give produce per acre or prices. I take these two items as follows. From selections of the

Bombay Government, Nos. 10 and 11 of 1853, I get the following estimate of produce:—

Produce per Acre in Pounds.

Selections. No.	Selections. Page.	Districts Reported upon.	Bajri with Kuthole.	Jowari with Kuthole.	Sathi, or Coarse Rice.	Kupas, or uncleaned Cotton.	Remarks.
			lbs.	lbs.	lbs.	lbs.	
X.	15	Prant of Husore— Morassa & Bayar Pergunnah in Ahmedabad Collectorate ..	680	700 1,020 Jowari in fallow land.	1,020		Cleaned Cotton as per experiments made under order of Mr. Saunders, Resident of Hyderabad, in Bassein district of Berar —average of 8 acres giving $31\frac{3}{4}$ lbs. of clean Cotton and $83\frac{1}{2}$ lbs. of Seed. (*Agricultural Gazette of India* of 21st Aug. 1871, page 3.) This would give 82 lbs. for 305 lbs. of kupas.
	106	Duskroee Pergunnah—					
		Greatest ..	1,700	1,500	1,360	410	
		Least . .	270	210	410	200	
XI.	15	Dholka—					
		Greatest ..	1,700	1,500	1,360	410	
		Least . .	270	210	410	200	
		Rough average . . .	924	856	912	305	

The above averages belong to a fertile part of the Northern Division, so that if I put down 900 lbs. for bajri, jowari, and rice per acre, and 80 lbs. of cotton for the whole of that Division, I shall be making a high estimate.

The next thing to settle is the prices. I take them from the *Government Gazette* weekly prices for the months of January to May, 1868, as fairly representing the effect of the average favourable season of 1867-8. These are retail prices of the chief markets of the respective districts, and it will be necessary to deduct 10 per cent. to make a fair average for the whole of the Division. For cotton I take the export prices from the Prices Current of the Bombay Chamber of Commerce for January to May, 1868. This gives an average of Rs. 181 per candy. The export prices I have taken represent more than the average value of the whole crop of the

Presidency, as the above average is for Fair Dhollera and Bhownuggur, which necessarily give a higher figure than the average of all the different varieties. Again, the bulk of the cotton is not "fair," but "mid-fair"; so, to make a fair allowance for all these circumstances, I take the price for 1867-8 as Rs. 170 per candy of 784 lbs.

The Southern Division.—As a whole, this Division is not as fertile as the Northern. I shall take, however, only 50 lbs. less for bajri, jowari, and rice; and for cotton I take 60 lbs. per acre—a high average for the whole of the Division; for Mr. J. B. Smith, M.P., in his paper of 1857 read before the Society of Arts, quotes Mr. Vary, the then late Superintendent of Government Cotton Experiments in Sattara and Sholapore, to the effect that "40 lbs. of clean cotton per acre is considered a fair crop." For rice, I take Rutnagherry as exceptional in its produce. If I give 1,700 lbs. per acre for the whole district, it will be a high average.[1] I take the prices from the *Government Gazette* in the same way as for the Northern Division, and a similar reduction of 10 per cent. will have to be made. I give below a table worked out in the manner described above:—

[1] The Statistical Reporter of the *Indian Economist* of 22nd January, 1872, gives a table, on official authority, of the total produce of the Bombay Presidency. The figures given for Rutnagherry are evidently wrong. For 113,296 acres the produce of rice is given as 10,110,964 maunds of 82 lbs., which will be above 7,200 lbs. per acre. The best land may produce as much as 3,000, but 7,200 lbs. is simply out of the question. In the Pardy settlement (*Indian Economist* of 15th July, 1871, page 330, an acre of rice "in embanked land receiving full supply of water for a crop of rice," is put down as producing 3,400 lbs. Even in Bengal and Burmah—rice-producing countries—there is no such production as 7,000 lbs. per acre. For the rest of the Presidency (excepting Canara), the total produce is given as follows:—

	Acres.	Produce, maunds of 82 lbs.
Rice—	822,218	9,197,713, giving an average of 917 lbs.
Jowari and Bajri—	9,476,687	44,557,600, giving an average of 385 lbs.

Now, the year 1869-70 is reported to have been an average favourable season, in which case my adopting 900 lbs. for the Northern and 850 for the Southern Division for all grains, is very much higher than the real average. For cotton the figures are: acres, 1,937,375; maunds, 3,264,464, giving an average of 1·68 maunds, or 136 lbs. It is not stated whether this is cleaned or seed cotton. Anyway, this cannot be correct. It is, however, remarked by the official who supplies these statistics: "The figures in Table III., giving the weight of produce, are not, it is feared, very reliable, but now that attention is being given to the subject they will become more so every year." I earnestly hope that it will be so; correct statistics of this kind are extremely important.

Bajri.

Collectorates.	Cultivated Area.	Total Produce (at 900 lbs. per Acre).	Price per 1 Re.	Total Value.
	Acres.	lbs.	lbs.	Rs.
Ahmedabad . .	129,365[1]	116,428,500	33·6	34,65,134
Kaira	150,841	135,756,900	30·0	45,25,230
Surat	27,217	24,495,300	25·5	9,60,600
Khandeish . .	711,447	640,302,300	27·6	2,31,99,359
Tanna	......	......	....	....
Total . .	1,018,870	......	....	3,21,50,323
		(850 lbs. per Acre.)		
Poona	834,325	709,176,250	34·7	2,04,37,356
Admednuggur .	1,152,316	979,468,600	34·3	2,85,55,936
Kulladghee . .	240,165	204,140,250	64·4[2]	31,69,880
Rutnagherry. .	......	......	....	....
Belgaum . . .	76,228	64,793,800	59·2	10,94,489
Dharwar . . .	14,108	11,991,800	69·0	1,73,795
Sattara . . .	398,573	338,787,050	52·9	64,04,292
Total . .	2,715,715	......	....	5,98,35,748

Jowari.

Collectorates.	Cultivated Area.	Total Produce (at 900 lbs. per Acre).	Price per 1 Re.	Total Value.
	Acres.	lbs.	lbs.	Rs.
Ahmedabad . .	119,679	107,711,100	42·4	25,40,356
Kaira	44,536	40,082,400	42·4	9,45,339
Surat	178,839	160,955,100	27·1	59,39,302
Khandeish . .	465,198	418,678,200	40·4	1,03,63,322
Tanna	10	9,000	26·8	336
Total . .	808,262	......	....	1,97,88,655
		(850 lbs. per Acre.)		
Poona	1,487,816	1,264,643,600	49·5	2,55,48,355
Ahmednuggur .	852,232	724,397,200	45·6	1,58,85,903
Kulladghee . .	1,162,582	988,194,700	70·0	1,41,17,060
Rutnagherry. .	......	......	....	....
Belgaum . . .	426,542	362,560,700	66·0	54,93,344
Dharwar . . .	511,389	434,680,650	83·8	51,87,120
Sattara . . .	465,509	395,682,650	52·6	75,22,487
Total . .	4,906,070	......	....	7,37,54,269

[1] Gujerat, in Northern Division; the cultivated area is given partly in acres and partly in beegahs. The beegahs are converted into acres, as 1·7 beegahs = 1 acre.

[2] Bhagalkote price is taken.

Rice.

Collectorates.	Cultivated Area.	Total Produce (at 900 lbs. per Acre.)	2nd Sort, price per 1 Re.	Total Value.
	Acres.	lbs.	lbs.	Rs.
Ahmedabad	31,902	28,711,800	14·0	20,50,843
Kaira	51,443	46,298,700	12·2	37,94,975
Surat	108,348	97,513,200	11·27	86,52,458
Khandeish	12,081	10,872,900	20·1	5,40,940[1]
Tanna	468,499	421,649,100	20·1[2]	2,09,77,567
Total	672,273	605,045,700	...	3,60,16,783
		(850 lbs. per Acre.)		
Poona	108,643	92,346,550	22·2	41,59,754
Ahmednuggur	28,922	24,583,700	12·3	19,98,674
Kulladghee	5,496	4,671,600	20·9	2,23,521
Rutnagherry	130,403	221,685,100	27·0	82,10,559
		(1,700 lbs. per Acre.)		
Belgaum	70,889	60,255,650	29·0	20,77,781
Dharwar	91,840	78,064,000	27·1	28,80,590
Sattara	67,820	57,647,000	22·4	25,73,527
Total	504,013	539,253,600	...	2,21,24,406

Cotton.

Collectorates.	Cultivated Area.	Produce per Acre.	Total Produce.	Price per Candy.	Total Value.
	Acres.	lbs.	lbs.	Rs.	Rs.
Ahmedabad, Kaira, Surat, Khandeish, Tanna	707,041	80	56,563,280	170	1,22,64,997
Poona, Ahmednuggur, Kulladghee, Rutnagherry, Belgaum, Dharwar, Sattara	704,629	60	42,277,740	170	91,67,367

[1] Average of Tanna and Alibaug.
[2] Price at Dhoolia being not given, I have taken the same with Tanna.

SUMMARY.

Northern Division.

	Acres.	Rs.	Rs.	Rs.
Bajri .	1,018,870	3,21,50,323		
Jowari .	808,262	1,97,88,655		
Rice .	672,273	3,60,16,783		
			8,79,55,761—10 per cent. =	7,91,60,185
Cotton	707,041	......		1,22,64,997
Total .	3,206,446			Rs. 9,14,25,182

Average per acre . . . Rs. 28·51

Southern Division.

	Acres.	Rs.	Rs.	Rs.
Bajri .	2,715,715	5,98,35,748		
Jowari .	4,906,070	7,37,54,269		
Rice .	504,013	2,21,24,406		
			15,57,14,423—10 per cent. =	14,01,42,981
Cotton	704,629	......		91,67,367
Total .	8,830,427			Rs. 14,93,10,348

Average per acre . . . . Rs. 17.

Total Cultivated Area.

	Acres.			Rs.
Northern Division .	5,128,221	at Rs.	28·51 =	14,62,05,580
Southern " .	13,985,892	"	17 =	23,77,60,164
			Total . . . Rs.	38,39,65,744

This gives for the whole of the Bombay Presidency the total value as Rs. 38,39,65,744, or say £40,000,000 for a population of 11,000,000.

About two or three months ago I came across an unexpected confirmation of my calculations. I was able to get from my friend, Mr. Nowrojee Furdoonjee, a few notes from Colonel Prescott's reports on the settlement of Akleshwar Taluka—I suppose an average Gujerat taluka. Colonel Prescott has made the value of gross produce (excluding straw) about Rs. 24 per acre. Why, my estimate for the whole of the Northern Division is above Rs. 28 per acre.

OUDH.

The administration report does not give the agricultural tables, but they are given in the revenue report. Wheat forms the most important produce in Oudh, as in the North-West Provinces. I take it to represent the whole produce. In the revenue report ending 30th September, 1868, the average produce per acre is given at 892 lbs.—say 900 lbs. Now, in Oudh, irrigated land is nearly within 10 per cent. of unirrigated land. I shall give the above produce per acre for both, as the table also gives this as the average of all land. The year 1867-8 was somewhat below an average good season, and the prices, therefore, higher than they would be for an average good season year. I take them, however, as they are. The average for wheat, first quality, is given at Rs. 1-9-7 per maund of 80 lbs., and for second quality Rs. 1-8-4—the average will be about Rs. 1-9. As a small correction for the prices being of an inferior season, the average being on the usual wrong principle, and the second quality being the largest quantity, I shall deduct only 10 per cent. The total cultivated area is 12,486 square miles, or 7,991,040 acres. The total produce, at 900 lbs. of wheat per acre, will be 7,191,936,000 lbs.; and the total value, at the rate of Rs. 1-9 per maund of 80 lbs., will be Rs. 14,04,67,500. This, less 10 per cent., will be Rs. 12,64,20,750, or say £13,000,000, for a population of 9,500,000.

SUMMARY.

Provinces.	Value of the Produce of Cultivated Land.	Population.	Produce per head.
	£		Rs.
Central Provinces	16,000,000	9,000,000	18
Punjab	36,000,000	17,500,000	21
North-West Provinces	40,000,000	30,000,000	14
Bengal	96,000,000	67,000,000	15
Madras	36,000,000	26,500,000	14
Bombay	40,000,000	11,000,000	36
Oudh	13,000,000	9,500,000	14
Total	277,000,000	170,500,000	

Such is the produce of India for a good season year, in which any second crops will be fully included. I have not taken the produce of grazing-land, or straw, or kurby, though the cattle required for cultivation and stock need not only all these grazing-lands, but also a portion of the produce of the cultivated land, such as some grains, fodder, and other produce. From the above total of £277,000,000 it is necessary to deduct for seed for next year, say, only 6 per cent., that is, allowing sixteen-fold for produce of the land. The balance will be about £260,000,000 as the produce of cultivation, during a good season, for human use and consumption for a year. If the Government of India would calculate this production correctly, it would find the total a good deal under the above figures.

Other Items of India's Wealth.

I have next to add for annual produce of stock for consumption, annual value of manufacturing industry, net opium revenue, cost of production of salt, coals, and mines, and profits of foreign commerce.

Salt, opium, coal, and profits of commerce will be about £17,000,000. For annual price of manufacturing industry or stock, I have not come across full particulars. The manufacturing industry in the Punjab—where there are some valuable industries, such as shawls, silks, etc., to the total estimated value of the "annual out-turns of all works"—is put down as about £3,774,000. From this we deduct the value of the raw produce; and if I allow this value to be doubled by all the manufactures, I shall be making a good allowance. Say, then, that the value of the industry is about £2,000,000, including the price of wool; the manufactures of other parts of India are not quite as valuable. Therefore, for the population of all British India, which is about ten times that of the Punjab, if I take £15,000,000 for the value of manufacturing industry, I shall not be far from the mark. The total for Central Provinces for 1870-1 for all manufactures is about £1,850,000. There are no very valuable industries; allow, therefore, £850,000 for the value of the industry for a population of 9,000,000. In this proportion, the total value for India will be about, say, £17,000,000. For the annual produce of stock, and fish for human consumption, as milk or meat, I can hardly get sufficient data to work upon. I hope Government will give the particulars more fully, so that the annual production of stock for consumption, either as milk or meat, may be known. I set it down as £15,000,000 as a guess only.

All this will make up a total of about £307,000,000. I add for any contingencies another £30,000,000, making at the utmost £340,000,000 for a population of 170,000,000, or 40s. a head for an average *good season*. I have no doubt that, if the Statistical Department worked out the whole correctly and fully, they would find the total less. Again, when further allowance is made for bad seasons, I cannot help thinking that the result will be nearer 30s. than 40s. a head. One thing is evident—that I am not guilty of any under-estimate of produce.

Income per Head.

Adding this additional £63,000,000 in proportion of population, that is to say 7s. 5d. per head, the total production per head of each province will be as follows:—Central Provinces, 43s. 5d.; Punjab, 49s. 5d.; N. W. Provinces, 35s. 5d.; Bengal, 37s. 5d.; Madras, 35s. 5d.; Bombay, 79s. 5d.; Oudh, 35s. 5d.—Average, 40s.

Necessary Consumption.

I now consider what is necessary for the bare wants of a human being, to keep him in ordinary good health and decency.

I have calculated production chiefly for the year 1867-8. I shall take the same year for ascertaining the necessary consumption.

Surgeon S. B. Partridge, Government Medical Inspector of Emigrants, in a statement dated Calcutta, 26th March, 1870,[1] proposes the following as a scale of diet to supply the necessary ingredients of nourishment for the emigrant coolies during their voyage, living in a state of quietude:—

Rice Diet for One Man.	ozs.	For Flour Diet	ozs.
Rice	20·0	Flour	16·0
Dhal	6·0	Dhal	4·0
Preserved Mutton	2·5	Preserved Mutton	2·5
Vegetables	4·27	Vegetables	4·27
Ghee	1·0	Ghee	1·5
Mustard Oil	0·5	Mustard Oil	0·5
Salt	1·0	Salt	1·0
Total	35·27	Total	29·77

[1] The *Indian Economist* of 15th October, 1870, Statistical Reporter, page 45.

The administration report of Bengal for 1870-1 gives in appendix 11 D_2, the following "scale of provision for ships carrying Indian emigrants to British and foreign colonies west of the Cape of Good Hope."

"*Daily Allowance to each statute Adult [Children above two and under ten years of age to receive half rations.]*"

Class.	Articles.	oz.	drs.	Remarks.
Grain	Rice	20	0	
	Flour	16	0	
	Dhal, for rice-eaters	6	0	(Four kinds of dhals make up this quantity.)
	Dhal, for flour-eaters	4	0	
Oil	Ghee, for rice-eaters	1	0	Half an ounce extra allowance of ghee to each adult for every day that dried fish is supplied.
	Ghee, for flour-eaters	1	8	
	Mustard Oil	0	8	
Meats, &c.	Preserved Mutton	2	8	In lieu of preserved mutton to be supplied at scale rate, dried fish for 2 to 3 weeks. Fresh mutton (sheep) 1 week.
Vegetables	1 oz. pumpkins or yams, 2 oz. potatoes, 2 oz. onions	5	0	In lieu of fresh potatoes, a sufficient quantity of preserved potatoes to allow 2 oz. twice a week to each adult, or about 5 weeks' supply at scale rate.
Curry Stuff, &c.	Garlic	0	0½	
	Mustard Seed	0	0½	
	Chillies	0	0½	
	Black Pepper	0	1½	
	Coriander Seed	0	2	
	Turmeric	0	4	
	Tamarind	0	8	
	Salt	0	8	
Narcotic	Prepared tobacco	0	7	
	Leaf	0	3	
	Firewood	2	0	Or in lieu of firewood, its equivalent in coal for half the quantity.

Besides the above there is an allowance for dry provision to be used at the discretion of the surgeon, for medical comforts, medicine, instruments, and appliances for hospital and dispensary. Again, for confirmed opium-eaters or *ganja*-smokers, the surgeon superintendent is to see a proper quantity supplied. Surgeon Partridge's scale is absolutely necessary to supply the necessary ingredients of nitrogen and carbon; not the slightest luxury—no sugar or tea, or any little enjoyment of life, but simple animal subsistence of coolies living in a state of quietude. I have worked out below the cost of living according to Surgeon Partridge's scale for the year 1867-8 at Ahmedabad prices. The scale in the Bengal administration report provides curry-stuff and narcotics in addition, which I have not calculated in this table, though it can hardly be said that they are not necessaries to those poor people.

Cost of necessary living at Ahmedabad prices, on 30th January, 1868, as given in the "Bombay Government Gazette."

Rice, second sort, 20 ozs. per day, or 37½ lbs. per month, at 15 lbs. per rupee . . .	Rs.	2	8	0
Dhal 6 oz. per day, or 11¼ lbs. per month, at 20 lbs.[1] per rupee	,,	0	9	0
Preserved mutton 2·50 oz. per day, or 4 lbs. 11 oz. per month, at 6½ lbs.[2] per rupee .	,,	0	11	7
Vegetable 4.27 oz. per day, or 8 lbs. per month, at 20 lbs.[3] per rupee . . .	,,	0	6	5
Ghee 1 oz. per day, or 1 lb. 14 oz. per month, at 2 lbs. 1 oz. per rupee	,,	0	11	0
Mustard oil 0·5 oz. per day, or 1 lb. 8 oz. per month, at 6 lbs.[4] per rupee	,,	0	4	0
Salt 1 oz. per day, or 1 lb. 14 oz. per month, at 38 lbs.[5] per rupee	,,	0	0	10
Per Month . .	Rs.	5	2	10

The annual cost of living, or subsistence only, at Ahmedabad prices, is thus Rs. 62-2.

Cost of Subsistence.

The following is an estimate of the lowest absolute scale of necessaries of a common agricultural labourer in the Bombay Presidency annually, by Mr. Kazee Shahabudin:—

Food—

1½ lbs. Rice per day, at Rs. 2 to Rs. 2-8 per maund of 40 lbs., say	Rs.	28	8
Salt, including waste, about 1 oz. a day .	,,	1	0
¼ lb. Dhal	,,	9	0
Vegetables	,,	0	0
Food-oil.	,,	5	0
Condiments, chillies, &c.	,,	0	0
Tobacco	,,	5	0
	Rs.	48	8

[1] There are three kinds of dhal: Oorud, Moong, and Toor. I take an average.

[2] I don't find price of preserved mutton. I have taken of mutton.

[3] No price is given for vegetables. I take it the same as dhal.

[4] No price of mustard oil is given. I have taken for teel, which is the cheapest among the four kinds of oil given in the table.

[5] This is the price of common sea salt, which would require to be taken more than a ¼ oz. to make up for the ¼ oz. of good salt required. Also there is some wastage or loss.

Clothing—

3 Dhotees a year	Rs.	3 0
1 pair champal (shoes)	,,	0 12
½ a turban	,,	1 8
1 Bundee (jacket)	,,	1 0
2 Kamlees (blankets)	,,	1 8
1 Rumal (handkerchief)	,,	0 2
1 Rain-protector	,,	0 4
	Rs.	8 2

The dress of the female of the house—

1½ Saree (dress)	Rs.	3 12
1 Cholee (short jacket)	,,	0 12
Oil for head	,,	1 8
Bangrees (glass bangles)	,,	0 6
¼ Champal (shoes)	,,	0 4
Extras	,,	1 0
	Rs.	7 10

The old members of the family will require as much.

Lodging—

Hut (labour taken as his own)	Rs.	25 0
Hut repairs (bamboos, &c.), per annum	,,	4 0
Oil for lamp, per day	,,	0 0⅛
Barber per month	,,	0 1
Domestic utensils per annum	,,	0 12

Say altogether Rs. 12 to Rs. 15 for the family.

Subsistence per Head.

Taking one-quarter less, for reasons stated further on, to calculate the cost per head of family, the result will be—

Food	Rs. 36	Without any provision for social and religious wants, letting alone luxuries, and anything to spare for bad seasons.
Clothing	,, 6	
Lodging	,, 3	
	Rs. 45	

The report of the Bombay Price Commission gives the following particulars of the wants of the lowest servants of Government (pages 85. 86), supplied from the Poona District :—

Articles.	Quantities per month.	Cost per month in 1863.		Remarks.
	Seers.	Rs.	a.	
Rice	12	1	8	It will be observed that simple living and clothing are here exhibited, and nothing is taken into account for support of dependent members of family, servants, religious and other domestic expenses.
Bajri	12	1	4	
Toor Dhal, &c.	4	0	12	
Ghee	0¾	0	10	
Vegetables	...	0	6	
Oil	1¼	0	6	
Firewood	...	0	8	
Salt	1	0	1	
Mussala	...	0	2	
Chillies	0½	0	2	
Milk	4	0	8	
Betelnut-leaves	...	0	8	
	Rs.	6	11	

Clothing—

	Cost per Month.		
Turbans	Rs.	0	8
Dhotee	,,	0	10
Puncha	,,	0	2
Rumal	,,	0	0½
Coats	,,	0	3
Waistcoat	,,	0	2
Shoes	,,	0	1½
Total	Rs.	1	11
Grand Total	Rs.	8	6 per month.

For Poona the above scale is calculated to cost Rs. 6-11 per month, or Rs. 80-4 per annum, at the high prices of 1863, while my estimate, according to Surgeon Partridge's scale for 1867-8, is Rs. 5-2-10 per month, or Rs. 62-2 per annum—nearly 24 per cent. less, as prices have gone lower. For clothing, the estimate for 1863 is Rs. 1-11 per month, or Rs. 20-8 per annum, while Mr. Shahabudin's estimate is only Rs. 8-2 in 1868. Even allowing for fall in price Mr. Shahabudin's estimate is lower, and calculated on a very low scale for an agricultural labourer in the poorest districts, while that of 1863 is for the lowest class of Government servants. Upon the whole, therefore, the estimate given for 1867-8, as for the bare necessaries of a common agricultural labourer, is evidently under the mark.

Lately I found the following in the "Statement of the Moral and Material Progress of India" for 1871-2:—"The best account of the Bombay peasantry is still probably that by Mr. Coats, written fifty years ago. The clothes of a man then cost about 12s. and the furniture of his house about £2."—(Parliamentary Return No. 172 of 28th April, 1873.)

I have not been able to work out the details of cost of living in other parts of India. For the present I give the following approximate comparison for 1867-8 :—

Jails.

Provinces.	Cost of Living.			Cost of Clothing.			Total.		
	Rs.	a.	p.	Rs.	a.	p.	Rs.	a.	p.
Central Provinces	25	8	0	5	8	0	31	0	0
Punjab	23	6	0	3	13	0	27	3	0
North-West Provinces	18	8	0	3	5	0	21	13	0
Bengal[1]	28	3	0	3	8	0	31	11	0
Madras	[2]49	2	7	3	15	9	53	2	4
Bombay	41	13	0	5	10	0	47	7	0
Oudh	....			....			....		

PROPORTION OF CHILDREN TO ADULTS.

Now, the Bengal Census Report of 1872, page 109 of the appendix, gives the percentage of population according to age as follows :—

Males.		Females.		
Not exceeding 12 Years.	Above 12 Years.	Not exceeding 12 Years.	Above 12 Years.	
18·8	31·3	15·7	34·2	The Census of the N.W. Provinces gives nearly the same result. Above 12 years, adults, 64·4 per cent.; under 12, 35·6 per cent. (See Administration Report for 1871—72, page 55; Census Report, vol. 1, page 31.)

[1] Administration Report of Jails for 1871, page 39 of Appendix.

[2] This appears to be a very large expenditure. Besides, the average is taken on the wrong principle, without taking the number of the prisoners in each district into account. The correct average will be above Rs. 50.

The total adults, that is, above 12 years, are 65·5 per cent., and infants or children under 12 years, 34·5 per cent., which gives the proportion of two adults to each child, or one child to every three persons.

Production Compared with Cost of Living.

From taking the cost of adults per head to be a, and cost of the mass per head to be x, and supposing that, out of 34 per cent. of children under 12, only 17 per cent. cost anything, say one-half of the adult (though the Bengal provision is half for children from two to ten years), while the other 17 cost nothing at all, the problem will be—

$$66a + 17\tfrac{a}{2} + 17 \times 0 = 100x$$
$$x = \frac{74\frac{1}{2}a}{100}, \text{ or say } \frac{75a}{100} \text{ or } \tfrac{3}{4}a;$$

i.e., the cost outside jail, or for the whole mass per head, will be about three-fourths of inside the jail, allowing the jail for adults only. Thus, taking the cost of three persons in the jail, or of three adults to four persons outside, or of the mass, it comes to this :—

Production per Head.			Three-fourths of Jail Cost of Living, or Cost per head outside Jail.
Central Provinces	Rs. $21\frac{3}{4}$	or say Rs. 22	Rs. 23
Punjab	„ $24\frac{3}{4}$	„ „ 25	„ 20
North-West Provinces	„ $17\frac{3}{4}$	„ „ 18	„ 16
Madras	„ $17\frac{3}{4}$	„ „ 18	„ 41
Bengal	„ $18\frac{3}{4}$	„ „ 19	„ 23-12
Bombay	„ $39\frac{3}{4}$	„ „ 40	„ 35
Oudh	„ $17\frac{3}{4}$	„ „ 18	

It will be seen, from a comparison of the above figures, that, even for such food and clothing as a criminal obtains, there is hardly enough of production even in a good season, leaving alone all little luxuries, all social and religious wants, all expenses of occasions of joy and sorrow, and any provision for bad season. It must, moreover, be borne in mind that every poor labourer does not get the full share of the average production. The high and middle classes get a much larger share, the poor classes much less, while the lowest cost of living is generally above the average share.

Such appears to be the condition of the masses of India. They do not get enough to provide the bare necessaries of life.

On the subject of necessary consumption, I shall be very glad if some members of this Association, or others who possess or can ascertain the necessary information, will supply it, as I have not been able to make such minute and extended enquiries myself as I could wish.

Deficit of Imports Compared with the Exports of India.

The total imports and exports of the United Kingdom for the years 1858 to 1870 are—

Imports	£3,608,216,242 (including Bullion).
Exports	£2,875,027,301 „ „

This shows an *excess of imports* over exports of £733,188,941, *i.e.*, the imports are above 25 per cent. greater than the exports.

This excess is to be increased to the extent of about £125,000,000, the balance of loans to India included in the exports, less interest on these loans included in imports of about £60,000,000, and by such further amounts as may be made up by balances of loans and interests with foreign parts. As England is the greatest lending country in the world, the ultimate result of excess of commercial imports over commercial exports will most probably be above, rather than under, £733,000,000 or 25 per cent. of exports. At all events, it will not be less than 15 per cent.

For British North America, the total imports and exports, including bullion, for the years 1854 to 1868, are—

Imports	£200,257,620
Exports	£154,900,367

This shows an excess of imports over exports of £45,357,253, *i.e.*, the imports are about 29 per cent. more than the exports, subject to a modification of the extent to which it has received from, or given loan to, foreign parts. As far as I can see, it is a borrower, and the excess to that extent will be lesser.

For Australia, the total imports and exports, including bullion, for the years 1854 to 1868, are—

Imports	£443,407,019
Exports	£384,503,081

The excess of imports over exports is therefore £58,903,938, *i.e.*, the imports are 15 per cent. more than the exports, subject to modification, as in the case of British North America, for its foreign debt. These figures show that the normal condition of the foreign commerce of any country is generally such that for its exports there is always a return in imports equal to the exports, *plus* profits. On an average, commercial profits may be taken at 20 per cent. Indian merchants generally insure by sailing vessels 25 per cent. more, and by steamers 15 per cent., for profits, as by steamers the same capital may be turned over oftener. If I take general commercial profits as 15 per cent., I shall be quite under the mark.

Now we must see what the case is with India. The exports of India for the years 1835 to 1872 being about £1,120,000,000, the imports, with an addition of 15 per cent. to exports for profits (of about £168,000,000), should be about £1,288,000,000. Besides this, India has incurred to foreign parts a debt of about £50,000,000 for the public debt, and about £100,000,000 for railways, during the same period.

The Drain to England.

Now, on the other hand, in return for the exports, *plus* profits, of £1,288,000,000, and £150,000,000 of the loans, India has actually imported, during the last 38 years, from 1835 to 1872 (not, as would be the case in a normal condition, £1,430,000,000, but) only about £943,000,000, leaving a balance of about £500,000,000, which England has kept back as its benefit, chiefly arising from the political position it holds over India. This is without including any interest at all. Towards this drain, the net opium revenue contributed by China amounts to about £141,000,000. The balance of about £360,000,000 is derived from India's own produce and profits of commerce. The profits of commerce are, say, about £168,000,000. Allowing them the *whole opium revenue* and the *whole profits of commerce* as having gone towards the drain, there is still a deficiency of nearly £200,000,000, which must have gone out of the produce of the country. Deducting from this £200,000,000 the interest on the railway loans remitted to England, the balance still sent from the very produce of the country is about £144,000,000. Strictly speaking, the whole £200,000,000 should be considered as a drain from the very produce of the country, because it is the exhaustion caused by the drain that disables us from building our railroads, etc., from our own means. If we did not suffer the exhaustion we do, and even then if we found it to our benefit to borrow from England, the case would be one of a healthy natural business, and the interest then remitted would have nothing to be deplored in it, as in the case of other countries, which, being young, or with undeveloped resources, and without much means of their own, borrow from others, and increase their own wealth thereby, as Australia, Canada, the United States, or any other native-ruled country that so borrows. However, as matters stand at present, we are thankful for the railway loan, for in reality that, though as a loan (with the profits during the American War), has revived us a little. But we are sinking fast again.

Increase of the Drain.

Allowing for the railway interest as a mere matter of business, and analysing the deficit of imports, or drain to England, as only about £453,000,000, the following is the yearly average for every five years :—

Years.	Yearly Average. £
1835 to 1839	5,347,000
1840 ,, 1844	5,930,000
1845 ,, 1849	7,760,000
1850 ,, 1854	7,458,000
1855 ,, 1859	7,730,000
1860 ,, 1864	17,300,000
1865 ,, 1869	24,600,000
1870 ,, 1872	27,400,000

Now, can it be shown by anybody that the production during these 38 years has been such as to leave the same amount per head every year, and surplus besides, to make up the above £200,000,000 taken away from the produce of the country, in *addition* to opium revenue and profits of commerce? In that case it will be that India is no better off now, but is only in the same condition as in 1834. If it can be shown that the production of the country has been such as to be the same per head during all these years, and a surplus greater than £200,000,000 besides, then will it be that any material benefit has been derived by India to the extent of such excess of surplus over £200,000,000. It must, however, be remembered that, in the years about 1834, the condition of the people had already gone down very low by the effects of the previous deficits, as will be seen further on from the official opinions I have given there.

The benefit to England by its connection with India must not be measured by the £500,000,000 only during the last 38 years. Besides this the industries of England receive large additional support for supplying all European stores which Government need, and all those articles which Europeans want in India from their habits and customs, not from mere choice, as may be the case with natives. All the produce of the country, thus exported from sheer necessity, would otherwise have brought returns suitable to native wants, or would have remained in the country, in either case, to the benefit of the produce or industry of India. Be it clearly borne in mind that all this additional benefit to English industries is entirely independent of, and in addition to, the *actual deficit* between the export, *plus* profits and imports. Everything I allude to is already included in the imports. It is so much additional capital drawn away, whether India will or no, from the industry of India to the benefit of English industry. There is, again, the further legitimate benefit to England of the profits of English firms there carrying on commerce with India, the profits of the shipping trade, and insurance. The only pity—and a very great one too—is that the commerce between England and India is not so large as it should and can be, the present *total* exports of India to all the outside world being only about 5s. a head, while the exports of the United Kingdom are about £6 10s. a head, of British North America about £3 a head, and of Australia about £19 a head, including gold (and exclusive of gold, about £11 a head). Again, what are imports into India from the United Kingdom, including treasure, Government stores of every kind, railway and other stores, articles for European consumption, and everything for native consumption and use? Only less than 3s. a head, as below:—

Total Imports, including Treasure, into India from the United Kingdom.

1868 . . .	£31,629,315	Say £32,000,000, on an average, for a population of about 225,000,000, or less than 3s. a head.
1869 . . .	35,309,973	
1870 . . .	30,357,055	
1871 . . .	28,826,264	

(Parliamentary Return [c. 587] of 1872, page 16—Trade and Navigation Returns of the United Kingdom.)

Small Amount of Imports from England.

What a vast field there is for English commerce in India! Only £1 a head will be equal to nearly the whole present exports of the United Kingdom to all parts of the world. There is one further circumstance against British-Indian subjects, which will show the actual drain from the produce of the country of more than £200,000,000 as borne by British India. The exports from India do not all belong to British India; a portion belongs to the Native States. These States naturally get back their imports equal to their exports, *plus* profits—less only the tribute they pay to British India, of only about £720,000 altogether per annum, of which even a portion is spent in their own States. No account can I take here of the further loss to India (by famines) of life and property, which is aggravated by the political exhaustion. It is complained that England is at the mercy of India for its loan of some £200,000,000, but let it be borne in mind that, within the next few years, that sum will have been drawn by England, while India will continue to have its debt over its head.

The figures of the deficit previous to 1834 I cannot get. I hope the India Office will prepare a table similar to this for this previous period, in order that it may be ascertained how India had fared materially under British rule altogether.

The effect of the deficit is not equally felt by the different presidencies. Bengal suffers less than the others on account of its permanent settlement. I do not mean that as any objection to such settlement, but I state it merely as a fact.

India's Tribute.

The Court of Directors, in the year 1858, deliberately put forth before the Parliament and public of England the statement (Parliamentary Return No. 75 of 1858) that "the great excess of exports above imports is being regularly liquidated in silver." Now, is it not India's misfortune that not one man in the India House pointed out how utterly incorrect, misleading, and mischievous this statement was?

Now, Mr. Laing makes the following statement before the present Finance Committee:—"*Question 7660 of 2nd Report.*—Would it not be correct to state that the difference between the value of the exports from India, and the imports into India, which now amount, I think, to the sum of about

£20,000,000 represents the tribute which India annually pays to England? *Answer.*—No, I think not; I should not call it a tribute when there is a balance of trade of that sort between the two countries. There are many other countries which are in the same condition of exporting considerably more than they import from one particular country, and the balance of trade is adjusted either by other payments which have to be made, or by transactions through third countries, or finally by remittance of bullion."

First of all, the question was not about India's commerce with any particular country, but about *all* its exports and imports. And next, taking his answer as it is, it is altogether incorrect and inapplicable to India, as must be evident from the facts I have already laid before you.

Next comes Mr. Maclean. He is reported to have said before this Committee something to the effect that, if we compare India, for instance, with the United States, which can hardly be called a country that is being drained of its natural wealth, we will find that the excess of exports over imports in the United States is very much greater than the corresponding excess in India. Now, let us see what the facts are. I have prepared a table, and have taken the figures from the year 1795—the earliest I could get. From the totals I have excluded the years 1802-6, 1808-14, 1818-20, because the imports for them are not given, and the years 1863-6 for reasons well known (the American War). The result till 1869 (I cannot get later authentic figures) is not, as Mr. Maclean says, that "the excess of exports over imports in the United States is very much greater than the corresponding excess in India," but that the excess of *imports* over exports is about $493,000,000 till 1847, and £43,000,000 from 1848-69, excepting the years I have mentioned above; and if all the necessary modifications from various other circumstances be made, the excess of the imports will be found necessarily much greater. In fact, the United States are no exception to the ordinary laws of political economy, in a country where the rule is a native, and not a foreign one. I have made up my tables from Parliamentary Returns.

The deficit of £500,000,000 in imports, does not, as I have already explained, show the whole drain; for the English stores, whether Government or private, are all already *included in the imports*, nor is any interest calculated. With interest, the drain from India would amount to a very high figure.

The Elements of the Drain.

This drain consists of two elements—first, that arising from the remittances by European officials of their savings, and for their expenditure in England for their various wants both there and in India; from pensions and salaries paid in England; and from Government expenditure in England and India. And the second, that arising from similar remittances by non-official Europeans. As the drain prevents India from making any capital, the British by bringing back the capital which they have drained from India itself, secure almost a monopoly of all trade and important industries, and thereby further exploit and drain India, the source of the evil being the official drain.

Official Opinion on the Drain.

We may draw our own inferences about the effects of the drain, but I give you below official opinions on the subject, from early times to the present day, for each Presidency.

Bengal.

1787. Sir John Shore's Opinion.

Sir John Shore, in 1787, says, in his famous minute (appendix to 5th report, Parliamentary Return No. 377 of 1812):—

"129. Secondly, it is a certain fact that the zemindars are almost universally poor . . . Justice and humanity calls for this declaration.

"130. . . . . I do not, however, attribute this fact to the extortions of our Government, but to the causes which I shall hereafter point out, and which will be found sufficient to account for the effect. I am by no means convinced that the reverse would have taken place if the measure of our exactions had been more moderate.

"131. Thirdly, the Company are merchants, as well as sovereigns of the country. In the former capacity they engross its trade, whilst in the latter they appropriate the revenues. The remittances to Europe of revenues are made in the commodities of the country which are purchased by them.

"132. Whatever allowance we may make for the increased industry of the subjects of the State, owing to the enhanced demand for the produce of it (supposing the demand to be enhanced), there is reason to conclude that the benefits are more than counterbalanced by evils inseparable from the system of a remote foreign dominion. . . .

"135. Every information, from the time of Bernier to the acquisition of the Dewani, shows the internal trade of the country, as carried on between Bengal and the upper parts of Hindustan, the Gulf of Moro, the Persian Gulf, and the Malabar Coast, to have been very considerable. Returns of specie and goods were made through these channels by that of the foreign European companies, and in gold direct for opium from the eastward.

"136. But from the year 1765 the reverse has taken place. The Company's trade produces no equivalent returns, specie is rarely imported by the foreign companies, or brought into Bengal from other parts of Hindustan in any considerable quantities.

"141. If we were to suppose the internal trade of Hindustan again revived, the export of the production of the country by the company must still prevent those returns which trade formerly poured in. This is an evil inseparable from a European government.

Page 194.—"A large proportion of the rents of the country are paid into the Company's treasury, and the manufactures are applied to remit to England the surplus which remains after discharging the claims on this Government, *and to augment the commerce and revenue of Great Britain.*"

1790. Lord Cornwallis' Opinion.

Lord Cornwallis' minute on land settlements, dated 10th February, 1790, says:—"The consequence of the heavy drain of wealth from the above causes (viz., large annual investment to Europe, assistance to the treasury of Calcutta, and to supply wants of other presidencies), with the addition of that which has been occasioned by the remittances of private fortunes, have been for many years past, and are now, severely felt, by the great diminution of the current specie, and by the languor which has thereby been thrown upon the cultivation and the general commerce of the country."

1816. Mr. Montgomery Martin's Opinion.

The East India Company, on finding the provinces of Bengal and Behar continuously deteriorating, caused a long and minute survey of the condition of the people. This survey extended over nine years, from 1807 to 1816. The reports, however, lay buried in the archives of the India House till Mr. Montgomery Martin brought them to light. He sums up the result of these official minute researches in the following remarkable words (vol. I, page 11):—"It is impossible to avoid remarking two facts as peculiarly striking—first, the richness of the country surveyed; and second, the poverty of its inhabitants."

Before proceeding further, I must first say that the drain to which these great men have referred was much less than at present. I give the figures in Mr. Martin's words (page xii):—"The annual drain of £3,000,000 on British India has amounted in 30 years, at 12 per cent. (the usual Indian rate) compound interest, to the enormous sum of £723,900,000 sterling. . . . . So constant and accumulating a drain, even in England, would soon impoverish her. How severe then must be its effects on India, where the wage of a labourer is from twopence to threepence a day?"

In volume III, page 4, etc., alluding to the nine years' survey, Mr. Martin says that the obscurity to which such a survey was consigned was to be deplored, "and can only be accounted for by supposing that it was deemed impolitic to publish to the world so painful a picture of human poverty, debasement, and wretchedness"; and Mr. Martin draws many other painful conclusions.

1837. Mr. F. J. Shore's Opinion.

Coming down to later times, Mr. Frederick John Shore, of the Bengal Civil Service, has left us the following account of the condition of the people in 1837 (vol. II, page 28):—"But the halcyon days of India are over; she has been drained of a large proportion of the wealth she once possessed, and her energies have been cramped by a sordid system of misrule to which the interests of millions have been sacrificed for the benefit of the few." . . . . "The gradual impoverishment of the people and country, under the mode of rule established by the British Government, has hastened their (old merchant princes') fall."

"The grinding extortion of the English Government has effected the impoverishment of the country and people to an extent almost unparalleled."

For the manner in which the cotton industry of India was destroyed, see note at page 37 of the same volume. The chapter ends in these words (vol. II, pp. 515-6): "But because the Indians are in the present day so far behind us in arts and sciences, we are not justified in concluding that they are not capable of improvement were circumstances favourable to them. Complaints are made that whatever is to be done, an appeal is made to Government—a road, a school, a charitable institution—everything must be done by Government! How can it be otherwise? In England, where so much wealth is possessed by the community, diffused over all classes, and where there are local authorities to superintend them, the greatest improvements are planned and executed by private individuals; but in India, where the Government grasps at everything and leaves the people only a bare subsistence, having destroyed almost every local authority which formerly existed, and where the interests, that is, the immediate interests, of the rulers are very different from those of the governed, the people have a right to expect that some small part of what is taken from them shall be expended on their benefit." In his concluding remarks (vol. ii, page 516), Mr. Shore says:—"More than 17 years have elapsed since I first landed in this country; but on my arrival, and during my residence of about a year in Calcutta, I well recollect the quiet, comfortable, and settled conviction, which in those days existed in the minds of the English population, of the blessings conferred on the natives of India by the establishment of the English rule. Our superiority to the native Governments which we have supplanted; the excellent system for the administration of justice which we had introduced; our moderation; our anxiety to benefit the people—in short, our virtues of every description—were descanted on as so many established truths, which it was heresy to controvert. Occasionally I remember to have heard some hints and assertions of a contrary nature from some one who had spent many years in the interior of the country; but the storm which was immediately raised and thundered on the head of the unfortunate individual who should presume to question the established creed was almost sufficient to appal the boldest.

"Like most other young men who had no opportunities of judging for themselves, it was but natural that I should imbibe the same notions; to which may be added the idea of universal depravity of the people, which was derived from the same source."

After stating how his transfer to a remote district brought him into intimate contact with natives, how he found them disaffected towards British rule, and how this conviction in spite of himself was irresistible, he says:—"This being the case, an attempt to discover the reasons for such sentiments on the part of the native population was the natural result. Well-founded complaints of oppression and extortion, on the part of both Government and individuals, were innumerable. The question then was, why, with all our high professions, were not such evils redressed? This, however, I was assured, was impossible under the existing system; and I was thus gradually led to an inquiry into the principles and practice of the British-Indian administration. Proceeding in this, I soon found myself at no loss to understand the feelings of the people both towards our Government and to ourselves. It would have been astonishing indeed had it been otherwise. The fundamental principle of the English had been to make the whole Indian nation subservient, in every possible way, to the interests and benefits of themselves. They have been taxed to the utmost limit; every successive province, as it has fallen into our possession, has been made a field for higher exaction; and it has always been our boast how greatly we have raised the revenue above that which the native rulers were able to extort. The Indians have been excluded from every honour, dignity, or office which the lowest Englishman could be prevailed upon to accept. . . . . . The summary is that the British Indian Government has been practically one of the most extortionate and oppressive that ever existed in India—one under which injustice has been and may be committed both by the Government and big individuals, provided the latter be rich, to an almost unlimited extent, and under which redress from injury is almost unattainable; the consequence of which is that we are abhorred by the people, who would hail with joy and instantly join the standard of any Power whom they thought strong enough to occasion our downfall. That this is correct regarding a Government conducted on the principles which have hitherto actuated us is too lamentably true; but had the welfare of the people been our object, a very different course would have been adopted, and very different results would have followed; for, again and again I repeat it, there is nothing in the circumstance itself, of our being foreigners of different colour and faith, that should occasion the people to hate us. We may thank ourselves for having made their feelings towards us what they are."

In vol. 1, page 162, Mr. Shore says:—The ruin of the upper classes (like the exclusion of the people from a share in the government) was a necessary consequence of the establishment of the British power; but had we acted on a more liberal plan, we should have fixed our authority on a much more solid foundation."

1875. Col. Marriot's Opinion.

Colonel Marriot, at the East India Association meeting in July last, referring to Bengal, said:—"But he had no doubt that he accurately quoted the words of the present Lieut.-Governor of Bengal in saying that the mass of the population is probably poorer, and in a lower social position, than any in India."

The "Material and Moral Progress" for 1871-2 (page 100), says that "the Calcutta missionary conference had dwelt on the miserable and abject condition of the Bengal ryots, and there is evidence that they suffer many things, and are often in want of absolute necessaries."

Bombay.

1836. Mr. Saville Marriot's Opinion.

Mr. Saville Marriot, "one of the Commissioners of Revenue in the Deccan," and afterwards a Member of Council, says in 1836, in his letter to Sir R. Grant:—"You will readily conceive that my opinions are the result rather of practical experience than deduction drawn from scientific views. . . .

"For many years past, I have, in common with many others, painfully witnessed their decline (the people's); and more especially that part of the community which has emphatically been styled the 'sinews of the State'—the peasantry of India. It is not a single, but a combination of causes, which has produced this result. Some of these are, and have been from the beginning, obvious to those who have watched with attention the development of the principles of our rule in relation to such as have been superseded, become blended with our system, or are opposed to it in practical effect. Others are less apparent, and some complex; whilst another class of the decline may possibly be involved in obscurity.

"It is a startling but too notorious a fact, that, though loaded with a vastly greater absolute amount of taxation, and harassed by various severe acts of tyranny and oppression, yet the country was in a state of prosperity under the native rule when compared with that into which it has fallen under the avowedly mild sway of British administration. Though, in stating the subject, I have used the expression 'a vastly greater absolute amount of taxation,' yet I would beg to be understood as being fully aware those terms must be treated in a qualified sense, since it is manifest that, relatively reviewed, a smaller numerical amount of taxation may, with reference to the means of payment, be, in point of fact, more burdensome than a much larger one where the resources are more adequate to the object. But, in the particular case in point, it is, I believe, ability which has diminished; and that, too, to many grades below the proportionate fall in the pecuniary amount of fiscal demand. To the pecuniary injurious result are also to be added the many unfavourable circumstances inseparable for a time from a foreign rule. In elucidation of the position *that this country is verging to the lowest ebb of pauperism*, I would adduce a fact pregnant with considerations of the most serious importance, namely, that of late years a large portion of the public revenue has been paid by encroachment upon the capital of the country, small though that capital is in itself. I allude to the property of the peasantry, which consists of personal ornaments of the precious metals and jewels, convertible, as occasions require, to profitable purposes, and accommodations in agricultural pursuit, most frequently in the shape of pawn, till the object has been attained. I feel certain that an examination would establish *that a considerable share of this and other property, even to cattle and household utensils*, has been for ever alienated from its proprietors to make good the public revenue. In addition to *this lamentable evidence of poverty* is another of equal force, to be seen in all parts of the country, in the numerous individuals of the above class of the community wandering about for the employment of hirelings, which they are glad to obtain even for the most scanty pittance. In short, *almost everything forces the conviction that we have before us a narrowing progress to utter pauperism*."[1]

Mr. Marriot in another place (page 11), says:—"Most of the evils of our rule in India arise directly from, or may be traced to, the heavy tribute which that country pays to England."

And with regard to this tribute, he quotes the Chairman of a Court of Proprietors held on the 28th February, 1845, as follows:—"India paid to the mother-country, in the shape of home charges, what must be considered the annual tribute of £3,000,000 sterling; and daily poured into the lap of the mother-country a continual stream of wealth in the shape of private fortunes." To this should be added all earnings of Europeans, except what they spent in India for Indian supplies; which would show that there is something far beyond even private fortunes which is continuously poured into the lap of England.

Mr. Marriot goes on to say:—"It will be difficult to satisfy the mind that any country could bear such a drain upon its resources without sustaining very serious injury. And the writer entertains the fullest conviction that investigation would effectually establish the truth of the proposition as applicable to India. He has himself most painfully witnessed it in those parts of the country with which he was connected, and he has every reason to believe tnat the same evil exists, with but slight modification, throughout our Eastern Empire."

Again says Mr. Marriot (page 17):—"A different state of things exists in the present day on that point; and, though the people still, and gratefully so, acknowledge the benefits they have derived from the suppression of open violence, yet they emphatically and unanswerably refer their increasing penury as evidencing the existence of a canker-worm that is working their destruction. The sketch which I have given shows a distressing state of things; but lamentable as it may appear, I would pledge myself to establish the facts advanced, and that the representation is not overdrawn."

[1] Mr. Marriot's pamphlet, republished in 1857, page 13. The italics are mine.

1848. Mr. Giberne's Opinion.

Mr. Robert Knight says:—"Mr. Giberne, after an absence of fourteen years from Guzerat, returned to it, as judge, in 1840. 'Everywhere'—he told the Commons' Committee on Cotton Cultivation in 1848—'he marked deterioration,' and 'I did not see so many of the more wealthy classes of the natives. The aristocracy, when we first had the country, used to have their gay carts, horses, and attendants, and a great deal of finery about them, and there seems to be an absence of all that. . . . The ryots all complain that *they had had money once, but they had none now*.'"

1868. Mr. Robert Knight's Opinion.

In a private letter, dated 1849, "written by a gentleman high in the Company's service," and quoted in a pamphlet in 1851, the decay of Guzerat is thus described:—"Many of the best families in the province, who were rich and well-to-do when we came into Guzerat in 1807, have now scarcely clothes to their backs. . . . Our demands in money on the talookdars are more than three times what they originally paid, without one single advantage gained on their parts. Parties from whom they have been compelled to borrow at ruinous rates of interest enforced their demands by attachment of their lands and villages; thus they sink deeper and deeper in debt, without the chance of extricating themselves. What, then, must become of their rising family?"[1]

1838. Lieut. Nash's Opinion.

Lieutenant A. Nash, after giving a table of the prices of grain from 1809 to 1838 in Indapore (Bombay Government Selections, No. 107, New Series, page 118), says:—"The table is chiefly interesting in showing the gradual diminution in the price of corn from the days of the Peishwas to our own. By comparing the prices at the commencement with those at the end of the table, and then reading the list over, this circumstance will become apparent." I give this table in my notes on prices.

[1] Mr. Robert Knight's paper read before the East India Association, 3rd March, 1868.

MADRAS.

1854. MR. J. B. NORTON'S OPINION.

Mr. John Bruce Norton, in his letter to Mr. Robert Lowe in 1854, quotes the words of Mr. Bourdillon—"one of the ablest revenue officers in the Madras Civil Service, and a Member of the Commission on Public Works"—about the majority of the ryots:—*Page* 21.—"Now, it may certainly be said of almost the whole of the ryots, paying even the highest of these sums, and even of many holding to a much larger amount, that they are always in poverty and generally in debt." *Page* 22.—"A ryot of this class, of course, lives from hand to mouth. He rarely sees money. . . . His dwelling is a hut of mud walls and thatched roof—far ruder, smaller, and more dilapidated than those of the better classes of ryots above spoken of, and still more destitute, if possible, of anything that can be called furniture. His food, and that of his family, is partly thin porridge made of the meal of grain boiled in water, and partly boiled rice, with a little condiment; and generally the only vessels for cooking and eating from, are of the coarsest earthenware, much inferior in grain to a good tile or brick in England, and unglazed. Brass vessels, though not wholly unknown among this class, are rare."

About the labourer he says:—"As respects food, houses, and clothing, they are in a worse condition than the class of poor ryots above spoken of. It appears from the foregoing details that the condition of the agricultural labourer in this country is very poor. . . . In fact, almost the whole of his earnings must necessarily be consumed in a spare allowance of coarse and unvaried food, and a bare sufficiency of clothing. The wretched hut he lives in can hardly be valued at all. As to anything in the way of education or mental culture, he is utterly destitute of it."

1869. SIR GEORGE CAMPBELL'S OPINION.

Such is the testimony in the year 1854. Now let us come down to so late a time as 1869. Mr. (now Sir George) Campbell, in his paper on tenure of land in India, published by the Cobden Club, quotes from an official authority a report made so late as 1869 about the Madras Presidency, as follows :—" The bulk of the people are paupers. They can just pay their cesses in a good year, and fail altogether when the season is bad. Remissions have to be made, perhaps every third year, in most districts. There is a bad year in some one district, or group of districts, every year."

Again, the Parliamentary Report of the Moral and Material Progress of India for 1868-9, page 71, says—" Prices in Madras have been falling continuously."

PUNJAB.

The administration report for 1855-6 (Government of India Selections, No. 18, 1856) gives the following table :—

Average Prices.

For Ten Years up to 1850—51.	Wheat, Rs. 2 per maund of 82 lb.	Indian Corn, Rs. $1\frac{11}{16}$ per maund.
1851-2 . . .	Rs. 1 per maund.	Rs. $0\frac{14}{16}$ per maund.
1852-3 . . .	,, $1\frac{3}{16}$,,	,, $1\frac{1}{16}$,,
1853-4 . . .	,, $1\frac{3}{16}$,,	,, $1\frac{2}{16}$,,
1854-5 . . .	,, 1 ,,	,, $0\frac{13}{16}$,,
1855-6 . . .	,, $1\frac{1}{16}$,,	,, $0\frac{14}{16}$,,

With the usual effects of the introduction of a foreign rule, and the seasons happening to be good, the result was a fall in prices to nearly half during the five years after the annexation. The political portion of the causes of this depression is well described in a subsequent report, and how a change in that political portion produced a favourable reaction in the province.

1858. SIR J. LAWRENCE'S OPINION.

The administration report of 1856-8 (Parliamentary Return No. 212 of 1859, page 16), " prepared under the direction of Sir J. Lawrence, K.C.B., Chief Commissioner of Punjab, by R. Temple, Secretary to Chief Commissioner, Punjab," says :—" In former reports it was explained how the circumstance of so much money going out of the Punjab contributed to depress the agriculturist. The native regular army was Hindustani ; to them was a large share of the Punjab revenues disbursed, of which a part only they spent on the spot, and a part was remitted to their homes. Thus it was that, year after year, lakhs and lakhs were drained from the Punjab, and enriched Oudh. But within the last year, the native army being Punjabi, all such sums have been paid to them, and have been spent at home. Again, many thousands of Punjabi soldiers are serving abroad. These men not only remit their savings, but also have sent quantities of prize property and plunder, the spoils of Hindustan, to their native villages. The effect of all this is already perceptible in an increase of agricultural capital, a freer circulation of money, and a fresh impetus to cultivation."

This is just the cause which, in a far more aggravated form and on a far larger scale, operates on the whole of British India in its relations with England. Millions are drained to England; and till the reversing cause of the retaining and return of wealth in some way comes into operation, the evils of the drain cannot be remedied. And what is the condition of the labourer now?

1868. Punjab Government's Report.

Here is the Punjab Governments' own answer in the administration report for 1867-8 (page 88). After stating the rates of unskilled labour as ranging from two annas (three-pence) to five annas (seven and a half pence) per diem, and alluding to a considerable rise in rates in places affected by the railway and other public works, where labour in any shape commands higher remuneration than formerly, the report says:—"It may be doubted whether the position of the unskilled labouring classes has materially improved."

N.-W. Provinces.

1862. Col. Baird Smith's Opinion.

Colonel Baird Smith's report on the famines of the North-West Provinces (Parliamentary Return No. 29 of 1862), referring to the famine of 1837, says:—*Page* 57.—"From the time of our earliest acquisition of any part of these up to 1833, our fiscal system, notwithstanding some improvements on the native method which were gradually introduced, had been thoroughly bad." *Page* 59—"Speaking in general terms, therefore, native society in the N.-W. Provinces had to face the calamity in 1837, debilitated by a fiscal system that was oppressive and depressing in its influence. . . . In India we all know very well that when the agricultural class is weak, the weakness of all other sections of the community is the inevitable consequence."

1872. Mr. Halsey's Opinion.

I have not come across Mr. Halsey's report on the assessment of Cawnpore, but I take an extract from one given in the *Bombay Gazette* Summary of 21st June, 1872, page 12:—"I assert that the abject poverty of the average cultivator of this district is beyond the belief of any one who has not seen it. He is simply a slave to the soil, to the zemindar, to the usurer, and to Government. . . . . I regret to say that, with these few exceptions, the normal state of between three-fourths and four-fifths of the cultivators of this district is as I have above shown. It may appear to many to be exaggerated, and from the nature of the case, it is of course impossible to produce figures in support of it; nevertheless, it is the result of my personal observations, and I feel confident the result of the whole discussion will be to prove I have not overstated the truth."

The figures I have given of the total produce of the North-West Provinces prove by fact what Mr. Halsey gives as his observations. Hardly 27s. per head—say even 30s.—cannot but produce the result he sees.

Central Provinces.

1873. Mr. W. G. Pedder's Opinion.

Here is the latest testimony about the people. Mr. W. G. Pedder says[1]:—"Who [the people], if an almost universal consensus of opinion may be relied on, are rapidly going from bad to worse under our rule, is a most serious question, and one well deserving the attention of Government.

India.

Lords Lawrence and Mayo.

Lastly, to sum up the whole, here is Sir John Lawrence (Lord Lawrence) testifying so late as 1864 about all India:—"India is, on the whole, a very poor country; the mass of the population enjoy only a scanty subsistence." And Lord

[1] *Times of India* Summary of 6th June, 1873.

Mayo, on the 3rd March, 1871, says, in his speech in the Legislative Council:—"I admit the comparative poverty of this country, as compared with many other countries of the same magnitude and importance, and I am convinced of the impolicy and injustice of imposing burdens upon this people which may be called either crushing or oppressive."

"Mr. Grant Duff, in an able speech which he delivered the other day in the House of Commons, the report of which arrived by last mail, stated, with truth, that the position of our finance was wholly different from that of England. 'In England,' he stated, 'you have a comparatively wealthy population. The income of the United Kingdom has, I believe, been guessed at £800,000,000 per annum; the income of British India has been guessed at £300,000,000 per annum. That gives well on to £30 per annum as the income of every person in the United Kingdom, and only £2 per annum as the income of every person in British India.'

"I believe that Mr. Grant Duff had good grounds for the statement he made, and I wish to say, with reference to it, that we are perfectly cognisant of the relative poverty of this country as compared with European States."

So here is a clear admission by high authorities of what I had urged in my paper on the "Wants and Means of India," and what I now urge, that India's production was only about 40s. a head.

And now in the year 1873, before the Finance Committee, Lord Lawrence repeats his conviction that the mass of the people of India are so miserably poor that they have barely the means of subsistence. It is as much as a man can do to feed his family or half feed them, let alone spending money on what may be called luxuries or conveniences. Mr. Grant Duff asked Mr. Lawson so late as in May, 1870, in the House of Commons, whether he meant to "grind an already poor population to the very dust."

Condition of England under a Similar Drain.

The following picture about England itself under similar circumstances, may, I hope, enable the British people to realise our condition. The parallel is remarkable, and the picture in certain portions life-like of the present state of India. Draper's "Intellectual Development of Europe," 5th edition, *Page* 365.—"In fact, through the operation of the

Crusades, all Europe was tributary to the Pope (Innocent III.) . . . . A steady drain of money from every realm. Fifty years after the time of which we are speaking, Robert Grostale, the Bishop of Lincoln, and friend of Roger Bacon, caused to be ascertained the amount received by foreign ecclesiastics in England. He found it to be thrice the income of the king himself. This was on the occasion of Innocent IV. demanding provision to be made for three hundred additional Italian clergy by the Church of England; and that one of his nephews —a mere boy—should have a stall in Lincoln Cathedral." *Page* 397.—" In England—for ages a mine of wealth to Rome —the tendency of things was shown by such facts as the remonstrances of the Commons with the Crown on the appointment of ecclesiastics to all the great offices, and the allegations made by the 'Good Parliament' as to the amount of money drawn by Rome from the kingdom. They asserted that it was five times as much as the taxes levied by the king, and that the Pope's revenue from England was greater than the revenue of any Prince in Christendom." *Page* 434.— " It is manifest by legal enactments early in the fourteenth century. . . . By the Parliamentary bill of 1376, setting forth that the tax paid in England to the Pope for ecclesiastical dignities is fourfold as much as that coming to the king from the whole realm ; that alien clergy, who have never seen, nor cared to see, their flocks, convey away the treasure of the country." *Page* 477.—" The inferior, unreflecting orders were in all directions exasperated by its importunate unceasing exactions of money. In England, for instance, though less advanced intellectually than the Southern nations, the commencement of the Reformation is perhaps justly referred as far back as the reign of Edward III., who, under the suggestion of Wickliffe, refused to do homage to the Pope; but a series of weaker princes succeeding, it was not until Henry VII. that the movement could be continued. In that country, the immediately existing causes were, no doubt, of a material kind, such as the alleged avarice and impurity of the clergy, the immense amount of money taken from the realm, the intrusion of foreign ecclesiastics." *Page* 478.— " As all the world had been drained of money by the Senate and Cæsars for the support of republican or imperial power, so there was a need of like supply for the use of the pontiffs. The collection of funds had often given rise to contentions between the ecclesiastical and temporal authorities, and in some of the more sturdy countries had been resolutely resisted."

The result of this drain from England to Italy was the condition of the people as pictured at pages 494-5, than which nothing could be more painful. Mr. Draper says:—"For many of the facts I have now to mention, the reader will find authorities in the works of Lord Macaulay, and Mr. Froude on English History. My own reading in other directions satisfies me that the picture here offered represents the actual condition of things. . . .

"There were forests extending over great districts; fens forty or fifty miles in length, reeking with miasma and fever, though round the walls of the abbeys there might be beautiful gardens, green lawns, shady walks, and many murmuring streams. . . . The peasant's cabin was made of reeds or sticks, plastered over with mud. His fire was chimneyless—often it was made of peat. In the objects and manner of his existence he was but a step above the industrious beaver who was building his dam in the adjacent stream. . . . Vermin in abundance in the clothing and beds. The common food was peas, vetches, fern-roots, and even the bark of trees. . . . The population, sparse as it was, was perpetually thinned by pestilence and want. Nor was the state of the townsman better than that of the rustic; his bed was a bag of straw, with a fair round log for his pillow. . . . It was a melancholy social condition when nothing intervened between reed cabins in the fen, the miserable wigwams of villages, and the conspicuous walls of the castle and the monastery. . . . Rural life had but little improved since the time of Cæsar; in its physical aspect it was altogether neglected. . . .

"England, at the close of the age of faith, had for long been a chief pecuniary tributary to Italy, the source from which large revenues have been drawn, the fruitful field in which herds of Italian ecclesiastics had been pastured. . . . At the beginning of the sixteenth century, the island was far more backward, intellectually and politically, than is commonly supposed."

We see then, to what condition the people of England were reduced under the Italian drain. India cannot but share the same fate under similar causes, unless England, as she sincerely means to do, adopts the necessary precautions and remedies to prevent such results.

Drain through Investment of English Capital.

Before I close the subject of the drain and its consequences, I direct your attention to a few facts connected with the subject of railways, and such other useful public works. You are well aware that I strongly desire these works, but I cannot shut my eyes to the following facts :—

America, for instance, requires money to build a railway, takes a loan and builds it—and everybody knows it is immensely benefited. I need not read to you a chapter on political economy why it is so. I need only say every man employed in the construction of that railway is an American; every farthing, therefore, that is spent out of the loan remains in the country. In the working of the railway every man is an American; every farthing taken out of the produce of the country for its conveyance remains in the country; so, whatever impetus is given to the production of the country, and increase made in it, is fully enjoyed by the country, paying out of such increase in its capital and production the interest of the loan, and in time the loan itself. Under such ordinary economic circumstances, a country derives great benefit from the help of loans from other countries. In India, in the construction of the railroad, a large amount of the loan goes towards the payment of Europeans, a portion of which, as I have explained before, goes out of the country. Then, again, in the working of the railway, the same drawback, leaving therefore hardly any benefit at all to India itself, and the whole interest of the loan must also go out of the country. So our condition is a very anomalous one—like that of a child to which a fond parent gives a sweet, but to which, in its exhausted condition, the very sweet acts like poison, and, as a *foreign substance*, by irritating the weak stomach makes it throw out more, and causes greater exhaustion. In India's present condition the very sweets of every other nation appear to act on it as poison. With this continuous and ever increasing drain by innumerable channels, as our normal condition at present, the most well-intentioned acts of Government become disadvantageous. Sir Richard Temple clearly understands this phenomenon, as I have already shown. But, somehow or other, he seems to have now forgotten what he so clearly pointed out a score of years ago. Many a time, in discussing with English friends the question of the material drain generally, and the above remarks on railways, irrigation works, etc., I found it a very difficult task to convince. Fortunately, a great authority enunciates the fundamental principles very clearly and convincingly, and I give them below, hoping that an authority like that of the late Mr. Mill, will, on economic principles especially, command attention.

John Stuart Mill's Dicta.

I give a few short extracts from Mill's "Political Economy," chapter V. :—

"Industry is limited by capital."

"To employ industry on the land is to apply capital to the land."

"Industry cannot be employed to any greater extent than there is capital to invest."

"There can be no more industry than is supplied by materials to work up, and food to eat. Yet in regard to a fact so evident, it was long continued to be believed that laws and governments, without creating capital, could create industry."

"While, on the one hand, industry is limited by capital, so on the other every increase of capital gives, or is capable of giving, additional employment to industry, and this without assignable limit."

"A second fundamental theorem respecting capital relates to the source from which it is derived. It is the result of saving. All capital, and especially all addition to capital, are the result of saving."

"What supports and employs productive labour is the capital expended in setting it to work, and not the demand of purchasers for the produce of the labour when completed. Demand for commodities is not demand for labour."

"The demand for commodities determines in what particular branch of production the labour and capital shall be employed. It determines the *direction* of labour, but not the more or less of the labour itself, or of the maintenance or payment of the labour. These depend on the amount of the capital, or other funds directly devoted to the sustenance and remuneration of labour."

"This theorem—that to purchase produce is not to employ labour: that the demand for labour is constituted by the wages which precede the production, and not by the demand which may exist for the commodities resulting from the production—is a proposition which greatly needs all the illustration it can receive. It is to common apprehension a paradox.

Their Application to India.

These principles applied to the particular case of India, amount to this:—Poor India has not even to support its absolute want, even were the whole production employed in supporting labour. But as this is not the case—as there must be some portion of the produce consumed unproductively in luxuries—the share for the support of labour for reproduction becomes still more scanty; saving, and therefore addition to capital, being altogether out of the question. Moreover, not only is there no saving at the present rate of production, but there is actual continuous yearly abstraction from this scanty production. The result is an additional evil consequence in the capability of labour deteriorating continuously, for "industry is limited by capital"—so the candle burns at both ends—capital going on diminishing on the one hand, and labour thereby becoming less capable, on the other, to reproduce as much as before. The last theorem of Mill is a clear answer to those who say that, because the railways open up a market for the commodities, the produce of the country *must* increase. I need only repeat the "demand for commodities is not demand for labour," and that "industry cannot be employed to any greater extent than there is capital to invest."

If these principles are fairly borne in mind, and the element of the drain from India fairly considered, the gradual impoverishment of India, under the existing system of administration, will cease to appear a paradox.

THE MORAL DRAIN.

Beyond the positions of deputy-collectors or extra-commissioners, or similar subordinate positions in the Engineering, Medical, and all other services (with a very few somewhat better exceptions), all experience and knowledge of statesmanship, of administration or legislation, of high scientific or learned professions, are drained away to England when the persons possessing them give up their service and retire to England.

Sir T. Munro's Opinion.

The result, in Sir T. Munro's words, is this:—"The consequence of the conquest of India by British arms would be, in place of raising, to debase the whole people."—(Life of Sir T. Munro, page 466, quoted in Mr. Torrens' "Empire in Asia.") For every European employed beyond absolute necessity, each native capable of filling the same position is displaced in his own country. All the talent and nobility of intellect and soul, which nature gives to every country, is to India a lost treasure. There is, thus, a triple evil—loss of wealth, wisdom, and work to India — under the present system of administration. Whether the power of education which the British rulers are raising with the glorious object of raising the people of India, and which is day by day increasing, shall be a bulwark or weakness hereafter to the British rule, is a question of great importance. As matters stand at present, in the words of Sir Bartle Frere:—"And now, wherever I go, I find the best exponents of the policy of the English Government, and the most able coadjutors in adjusting that policy to the peculiarities of the natives of India, among the ranks of the educated natives." Of the future who can say? It lies in the hands of our rulers whether this power they are raising shall continue to be their "coadjutor," or become their opponent. The merit or fault will be entirely their own.

Sir J. Malcolm's Opinion.

Sir J. Malcolm says:—"We are not warranted by the History of India, nor indeed by that of any other nation in the world, in reckoning upon the possibility of preserving an Empire of such a magnitude by a system which excludes, as ours does, the natives from every station of high rank and honourable ambition. Least of all would such a system be compatible with the plans now in progress for spreading instruction. . . . If we do not use the knowledge which we impart, it will be employed against us. . . . We find in all communities, bold, able and ambitious individuals who exercise an influence and power over the class to which they belong, and these must continue enemies to a Government, however just and humane in its general principles, under which they are neither trusted nor employed. . . . High and aspiring men can find no spot beyond the limits of our authorities, and such must either be systematically watched and repressed as enemies of our power, or cherished and encouraged as the instruments of its exercise; there is no medium. In the first case, the more decidedly we proceed to our object, the better for our safety; but I should, I confess, have little confidence in the success of such a proceeding. As one head of the hydra was lopped off, another would arise; and as well might we strive to stem the stream of the Ganges, as to depress to the level of our ordinary rule the energies and hopes which must continually arise in so vast and various a population as that of India."[1]

There can be but one conclusion to the present state of affairs—either the people will become debased, as Munro thinks; or dead to all true wisdom, experience, honour, and ambition to serve one's country; or use their knowledge of it against the very hand that gives it. As Sir John Malcolm observes—"If these plans [of spreading instruction] are not associated with the creation of duties that will employ the minds which we enlighten, we shall only prepare elements that will hasten the destruction of our Empire. The moral evil to us does not thus stand alone. It carries with it its Nemesis, the seeds of the destruction of the Empire itself."

PRESSURE OF TAXATION.

In Lord Mayo's speech of the 3rd March, 1871 (*Times of India* Summary of 8th April, 1871), he endeavours to refute the assertion that Indian taxation is "crushing." His Lordship on this point has made several assumptions which require examination. I shall therefore first consider whether the conclusion drawn is legitimate, and whether all necessary elements of comparison have been taken into account.

LORD MAYO'S DENIAL.

I have already shown that the production of India is hardly 40s. a head, and that Lord Mayo has adopted that estimate

[1] Malcolm's "Government of India," page 174.

as being based on good reasons by Mr. Grant Duff. After admitting this fact, Lord Mayo compares the taxation of India with that of some other countries. In doing this, he deducts as land-revenue (whether rightly or wrongly will be seen hereafter) the opium, tributes, and other small receipts from Indian taxation, and then compares the balance with the taxation of other countries. I do not know whether he has made similar deductions from the taxation of the latter. The result of his comparison would appear to be that, while India pays only 1s. 10d. per head of taxation per annum, Turkey pays 7s. 9d., Russia 12s. 2d., Spain 18s. 5d., Austria 19s. 7d., and Italy 17s. per head per annum. The conclusion drawn is that the taxation of India is not "crushing." What idea his lordship attaches to the word "crushing" I cannot say, but he seems to forget the very first premise that the total production of the country is admitted to be 40s. per head. Now, this amount is hardly enough for the bare necessaries of life, much less can it supply any comforts, or provide any reserve for bad times; so that living from hand to mouth, and that on "scanty subsistence" (in the words of Lord Lawrence), the very touch of famine carries away hundreds of thousands. Is not this in itself as "crushing" to any people as it can possibly be? And yet out of this wretched income they have to pay taxation!

His Lordship has, moreover, left out a very important element from account. He is well aware that whatever revenue is raised by other countries—for instance, the £70,000,000 by England—the whole of it returns back to the people, and remains *in* the country; and, therefore, the *national capital, upon which* the production of a country depends, does not suffer diminution; while with India, as I have already shown, the case is quite different. Out of its poor production of 40s. a head, some £25,000,000 go clean out of the country, thereby diminishing its capital and labour for reproduction every year, and rendering the taxation more and more crushing.

A Fair Comparison with Other Nations.

I shall now consider what would have been the fairest way of making the comparison of taxation. Every nation has a certain amount of income from various sources, such as production of cultivation, minerals, farming, manufactures, profits of trade, &c. From such total income all its wants are to be supplied. A fair comparison as to the incidence of taxation will be to see the proportion of the amount which the Government of the country takes for its administration, public debts, &c., to the total income. You may call this amount taxation, revenue, or anything you like; and Government may take it in any shape or way whatsoever. It is so much taken from the income of the country for the purposes of Government. In the case of India, whether Government takes this amount as land-tax or opium revenue, or in whatever other form, does not matter, the fact remains that out of the total income of the country, Government raises so much revenue for its purposes which otherwise would have remained with the people.

Taking, therefore, this fair test of the incidence of taxation, the result will be that England raises £70,000,000 out of the national income of some £800,000,000, that is about 8 per cent., or about £2 10s. per head from an income of about £30 per head; whereas the Indian Government raises £50,000,000 out of the national income of £340,000,000, that is, about 15 per cent., or 6s. per head out of an income of 40s. per head.

Had his lordship stated the national income and population of the countries with which he has made the comparison, we would have then seen what the percentage of their revenue to their income was, and from how much income per head the people have to pay their 7s. to 19s. 7d. per head of taxation, as quoted by his lordship.

Further, if, in consequence of a constant drain from India from its poor production, the income of the country continues to diminish, the percentage of taxation to income will be still greater, even though the amount of taxation may not increase. But, as we know the tendency of taxation in India has, during several years, been to go on increasing every year, the pressure will generally become more and more oppressive and crushing, unless our rulers, by proper means, restore India to at least a healthy, if not a wealthy, condition. It must, moreover, be particularly borne in mind that, while a ton may not be any burden to an elephant, a few pounds will crush a child; that the English nation may, from its average income of £30 a head, be able to pay £2 10s. per head, while, to the Indian nation, 6s. out of 40s. may be quite unbearable and crushing. The capacity to bear a burden with ease, or to be crushed by it, is not to be measured by the percentage of taxation, but by the abundance, or otherwise, of the means or income to pay it from. From abundance you may give a large percentage with ease; from sufficiency, the same burden may just be bearable, or some diminution may make it so; but from insufficiency, any burden is so much privation.

But as matters stand, poor India has to pay not the same percentage of taxation to its income as in England, but nearly double; *i.e.*, while England pays only about 8½ per cent. of its national income for the wants of its Government, India has to pay some 15 per cent. of its income for the same purpose; though here that income per head of population is some thirteenth part of that of England, and insufficient in itself for even its ordinary wants, leaving alone the extraordinary political necessity to pay a foreign country for its rule.

Every single ounce of rice, therefore, taken from the "scanty subsistence" of the masses of India, is to them so much starvation, so much more crushing.

Lord Mayo calls the light taxation of the country, which he calculates at 1s. 10d. a head, as a happy state of affairs. But that, in so lightly-taxed a country, to get a 6d. more per head without oppression should tax the highest statesmanship and intelligence without success, is in itself a clear demonstration that there must be something very rotten in the state of India, and that the pressure of taxation must have already arrived short of the proverbial last straw that breaks the camel's back.

The United Kingdom pay a total revenue of about £2 10s. per head. India's whole production is hardly £2 a head. It pays a total revenue (less net opium) of hardly 5s. a head, and is unable to pay a shilling more. Why so? Short of only representation, India is governed on the same principles and system as the United Kingdom, and why such extraordinarily different results? Why should one prosper and the other perish, though similarly governed?

Not True Free Trade.

I take this opportunity of saying a few words about the recent telegram that Lord Salisbury had instructed the Indian Government to abolish the duties on cottons, as the matter is closely connected with the subject of my paper. The real object, says to-day's *Times of India*, is to "nip in the bud" the rising factories in India—the ostensible reason assigned is free trade. Now, I do not want to say anything about the real selfish objects of the Manchesterians, or what the political necessities of a Conservative Government may be under Manchester pressure. I give credit to the Secretary of State for honesty of purpose, and take the reason itself that is given on this question—viz., free trade. I like free trade, but after what I have said to night, you will easily see that free trade between England and India in a matter like this is something like a race between a starving, exhausting invalid, and a strong man with a horse to ride on. Free trade between countries which have equal command over their own resources is one thing, but even then the Colonies snapped their fingers at all such talk. But what can India do? Before powerful English interests, India must and does go to the wall. Young colonies, says Mill, may need protection. India needs it in a far larger degree, independent of the needs of revenue, which alone have compelled the retention of the present duties. Let India have its present drain brought within reasonable limits, and India will be quite prepared for any free trade. With a pressure of taxation nearly double in proportion to that of England, from an income of one-fifteenth, and an exhaustive drain besides, we are asked to compete with England in free trade? I pray our great statesmen to pause and consider these circumstances.

PRICES.

We hear much about the general enormous rise of prices, and conclusions drawn therefrom that India is prosperous. My figures about the total production of the country are alone enough to show that there is no such thing as that India is a prosperous country. It does not produce enough for mere existence even, and the equilibrium is kept up by scanty subsistence, by gradual deterioration of physique, and destruction. No examination, therefore, of the import of bullion, or of rise of prices and wages, is necessary to prove the insufficiency of production for the maintenance of the whole population. When we have such direct positive proof of the poverty of the country, it should be useless to resort to, or depend upon, any indirect evidence or conclusions. But as there appears to me much misapprehension and hasty conclusion from a superficial examination of the phenomena of prices, wages, and bullion, I deem it necessary to say something upon these subjects. I shall consider each subject separately. High prices may occur from one of the three following causes :—

1st.—From a natural healthy development of foreign commerce, which brings to the country fair profits upon the exports of the country; or, in other words, the imports exceed the exports by a fair percentage of profits, and thus add to the wealth and capital of the country.

2nd.—From a quantity of money thrown into the country, not as the natural profits of foreign commerce, but for some special purpose independent of commercial profits, such as the railway and other loans of India expended in certain parts where the works are carried on, and where, therefore, a large collection of labour takes place requiring food that is not produced there; and on account of bad or imperfect communications occasioning a local and temporary rise in prices.

3rd.—From scarcity of food or other necessaries, either on account of bad season or bad communications, or both; in other words, either there is not enough of food produced, or the plenty of one district cannot supply the deficiency of another, or both.

Causes of High Prices.

We may now see how each of these causes has operated. As to the first cause, it is clear that so far from India adding any profits to its wealth from foreign commerce, not only does an amount equal to the whole profits of foreign commerce, including the whole of the opium revenue, go elsewhere, but even from the very produce of the country some £7,000,000 more annually. This shows, then, that there is no increase of capital or wealth in the country, and consequently no such general rise in prices as to indicate any increase of prosperity. From want of proper communications, produce in provinces near the seaports is exported to foreign countries, not because the foreign countries give better prices than can be obtained in this country, but because, if not exported, the produce would simply perish. For instance, Bengal and Madras export rice at any reasonable prospect of profits, even though in some of the interior parts there may be scarcity, or even famine, as in the case of the North-West Provinces, Orissa, and Rajpootana.

The first cause, therefore, is not at all operative in India in raising prices; on the contrary, the constant drain diminishes capital, and thereby gradually and continuously diminishes the capability of the country even to keep up its absolutely necessary production. Besides the necessity of seeking foreign commerce on account of bad communications, there is a portion of the exports which is simply compulsory—I mean that portion which goes to England to pay for the political drain. So far, therefore, the alleged increase of prices in India does not arise from any natural addition to its wealth by means of a healthy and profitable foreign commerce. Then, the next thing to be examined is whether the different kinds of produce exported from British India are so exported because foreign countries offer more profitable markets for them, that is to say, offer greater prices than can be obtained in the country itself; thus indicating that, though prices have risen in the country itself, still higher prices are got from foreign countries. Suppose we find that Indian produce has been selling in foreign countries at about the same prices for the last fifteen years, what will be the inevitable conclusion? Either that, in the country itself, there is no great rise of prices, or that the people of India are such fools that, though there is an "enormous" rise in prices in their own country, they send their produce thousands of miles away—to get what? Not *higher* prices than can be got in the country itself, but sometimes much less! We may take the principal articles of export from India. The exceptional and temporary rise in the price of cotton, and its temporary effect on some other produce, was owing to the American War; but that is gradually coming down to its former level, and when America once makes up its four or five million bales, India will have a hard struggle. The opening of the Suez Canal has been a great good fortune, or Indian cotton would in all likelihood have been driven out of the English market particularly, and perhaps from European markets also.

Fluctuation in Price of Cotton.

The following table will show how near the prices are

returning to their old level before the American War (Parliamentary Return [c. 145] of 1870):—

Average price per cwt.	£	s.	d.	Average price per cwt.	£	s.	d.	Average price per cwt.	£	s.	d.	Average price per cwt.	£	s.	d.
1857...	2	8	8	1858...	2	10	7	1859...	2	5	10	[1]1860..	1	17	0
1861...	2	17	5	1862...	6	5	9	1863...	8	18	11	1864...	8	9	9
1865...	6	5	7	1866...	4	12	0	1867...	3	2	10	1868...	3	12	8
1869...	4	5	8	1870...	3	5	6								

So far the rise in cotton is going; but great as this rise has been, it has hardly reached the prices of former years, as will be seen hereafter. Leaving the exceptional prices of cotton during the cotton famine out of consideration, let us examine the most important articles of export; and if we find that these articles have fetched about the same price for nearly fifteen years past, there could not have been any normal general rise in the country itself of which the exporters could take advantage, and thereby prefer earning more profits by selling in the country itself, than getting less by exporting to foreign parts.

PRICE OF COFFEE.

Take *Coffee*.—The average prices in the United Kingdom (Parliamentary Return [c. 145] of 1870) are per cwt.:—

Years.	£	s.	d.	Years.	£	s.	d.	Years.	£	s.	d.
1855 . .	3	3	0	1860 . .	3	18	2	1865 . .	3	16	2
1856 . .	3	11	8	1861 . .	3	16	2	1866 . .	3	16	4
1857 . .	3	15	3	1862 . .	3	18	8	1867 . .	3	19	1
1858 . .	3	11	7	1863 . .	4	0	6	1868 . .	3	6	1
1859 . .	3	13	6	1864 . .	3	9	8	1869 . .	3	7	11
								1870 . .	3	6	6
Average .	3	11	0	Average .	3	16	7	Average .	3	12	0

This does not show any rise.

PRICE OF INDIGO.

Take *Indigo*:—

Years.	Average price per cwt. £	s.	d.	Years.	Average price per cwt. £	s.	d.	Years.	Average price per cwt. £	s.	d.
1855 . .	27	8	0	1860 . .	33	13	11	1865 . .	31	7	2
1856 . .	30	11	4	1861 . .	37	8	7	1866 . .	31	5	1
1857 . .	33	1	0	1862 . .	36	11	3	1867 . .	35	17	6
1858 . .	35	18	0	1863 . .	28	4	7	1868 . .	40	4	2
1859 . .	31	8	9	1864 . .	30	10	0	1869 . .	38	2	6
								1870 . .	35	4	8

[1] This year there was a large American crop.

The average of first five years, 1855-59, is £31 13s. 5d., of 1860-64, £33 5s. 8d., of 1865-70, £35 6s. 10d.—making a rise of 12 per cent. over the first five years. Now, this is an article in which India may be said to have a sort of monopoly, and yet there is virtually no rise from any increased demand. The average of the last six years is raised by the year 1868, but the quantity imported into the United Kingdom was in that year 2,000 cwts. less than in the previous year, and the scarcity gave a temporary high price.

Price of Rice.

Now take *Rice*.—This is the most important article; rise or fall in its price requires careful consideration. It is the alleged rise of price in this article which is held up as proving the prosperity of the country.

The average price of rice in the United Kingdom, after paying all charges and profits from India to arrival in England, is per cwt.:—

Years.	*s.*	*d.*	Years.	*s.*	*d.*	Years.	*s.*	*d.*	Years.	*s.*	*d.*
1855 .	14	6	1859 .	10	9	1863 .	11	11	1867 .	14	3
1856 .	10	6	1860 .	13	0	1864 .	11	2	1868 .	12	2
1857 .	11	3	1861 .	12	8	1865 .	12	4	1869 .	10	8
1858 .	8	10	1862 .	11	10	1866 .	13	1	1870 .	10	11

Averages of five years, 1855-59, 11s. 2d.; 1860-64, 12s. 1½d.; 1865-70, 12s. 3d.

This does not show that there is any material rise any more than the varying wants of the country and the average fluctuations of all ordinary articles of commerce, taking also into consideration the effect of the American War during some of these years. Such are the prices paid in England for Indian rice during the past fifteen years, and yet India had three or four famines, and in the famine districts food could not be got to save life at any price. If the United Kingdom got Indian rice at the above steady prices, how could there have been any real natural "enormous" rise of prices in India proving its prosperity? This simple fact is enough to show conclusively that, if the United Kingdom could get its thousands of tons of Indian rice at such steady prices during the past fifteen years, there is no such thing as an enormous general healthy rise of prices throughout the country. Whatever partial local and temporary rise there has been in certain localities has arisen, as will be seen hereafter, from partial local and temporary causes, and not from any increase of prosperity.

PRICE OF SILK.

Take *Silk*.—The prices of silk are as follows :—

Years.	Price per lb. s.	d.	Years.	Price per lb. s.	d.	Years.	Price per lb. s.	d.
1855 . .	12	9	1860 . .	20	2	1865 . .	23	6
1856 . .	18	10	1861 . .	16	10	1866 . .	22	0
1857 . .	19	8	1862 . .	18	8	1867 . .	21	2
1858 . .	17	8	1863 . .	18	8	1868 . .	23	8
1859 . .	19	1	1864 . .	18	5	1869 . .	23	0
						1870 . .	22	4
Average .	17	7	Average .	18	7	Average .	22	7⅓

This shows an apparent rise of 28 per cent. over the first five years, but the quantities imported in the years 1867, 1868, and 1869 were very small, being in 1867, 2,469 lbs., in 1868, 32,103 lbs., in 1869, 17,845 lbs. Whereas in 1865 it is 183,224 lbs., in 1866, 123,561 lbs., and in 1870, 123,600 lbs. There is then a rise in the price of this article, only a scarcity rise. Besides, its fate hangs upon the China market, and its produce in India yet is too small to have any important effect on general prices in ordinary economic conditions, much less when all such little or large profit is not retained by the country at all. The total quantity of waste as well as raw silk exported from India to all foreign parts is about £1,500,000 worth.

PRICE OF SUGAR.

Sugar.—There are three or four qualities of sugar imported into the United Kingdom from India. I give below the price of middling as a fair representative of the bulk :—

Years.	Price per cwt. £	s.	d.	Years.	Price per cwt. £	s.	d.	Years.	Price per cwt. £	s.	d.	Years.	Price per cwt. £	s.	d.
1855 .	1	9	8	1859 . .	1	7	9	1863	1	6	5	1867 . .	1	3	3
1856 . .	1	12	6	1860 . .	1	7	1	1864 .	1	5	11	1868 . .	1	3	6
1857 . .	1	17	6	1861 . .	1	8	5	1865 . .	1	3	6	1869 . .	1	7	2
1858 . .	1	10	3	1862 . .	1	6	9	1866 . .	1	3	4	1870 . .	1	5	7

The averages are from 1855-59, £1 11s. 6d., 1860-64, £1 6s. 11d., and 1865-70, £1 4s. 5d. There is, then, an actual decline, and it cannot, therefore, be expected that there was a rise in India notwithstanding.

PRICE OF LINSEED.

Linseed.—Average prices as follows per quarter :—

Years.	£	s.	d.	Years.	£	s.	d.	Years.	£	s.	d.
1855 . .	3	11	6	1860 . .	2	12	9	1865 . .	3	0	5
1856 . .	2	18	0	1861 . .	2	15	10	1866 . .	3	8	11
1857 . .	3	2	0	1862 . .	3	4	7	1867 . .	3	6	9
1858 . .	2	15	1	1863 . .	3	4	7	1868 . .	3	1	8
1859 . .	2	9	9	1864 . .	2	19	7	1869 . .	2	18	9
								1870 . .	2	19	7
Average	2	19	3	Average	2	19	6	Average	3	2	8

This shows a rise of about 5 per cent., which is nothing when allowance is made for the temporary effect of the American War from 1861, and the prices have latterly gone down again to the level of the average, 1855-59.

PRICE OF RAPESEED.

Rapeseed per quarter :—

Years.	£	s.	d.	Years.	£	s.	d.	Years.	£	s.	d.	Years.	£	s.	d.
1855..	3	9	8	1859..	2	4	8	1863	2	19	6	1867..	2	12	6
1856..	2	18	6	1860..	2	16	11	1864..	2	16	11	1868..	2	11	4
1857..	3	1	0	1861..	2	19	6	1865..	3	5	7	1869..	2	18	11
1858..	2	13	4	1862..	3	7	4	1866..	2	17	11	1870..	3	4	11

This also shows the temporary effect of the American War, and hardly any rise, the averages being—1855-59, £2 17s. 5d.; 1860-64, £3 : and 1865-70, £2 18s. 6d.

PRICE OF WOOL.

Wool.—Average price per lb. :—

Years.	d.	Years.	d.	Years.	d.	Years.	d.
1855 . .	$8\frac{1}{4}$	1859 . .	$7\frac{3}{4}$	1863 . .	$11\frac{5}{8}$	1867 . .	$7\frac{7}{8}$
1856 . .	9	1860 . .	$8\frac{1}{4}$	1864 . .	$11\frac{1}{2}$	1868 . .	$7\frac{5}{8}$
1857 . .	$8\frac{3}{4}$	1861 . .	$7\frac{3}{4}$	1865 . .	$11\frac{3}{8}$	1869 . .	$7\frac{1}{2}$
1858 . .	$6\frac{3}{4}$	1862 . .	10	1866 . .	$9\frac{15}{16}$	1870 . .	$7\frac{7}{16}$

The temporary effect of the American War is clearly to be seen in the above prices, and latterly they are getting down again to their old level.

PRICE OF INDIAN TEA.

Indian Tea.—Average price per lb. :—

Years.	s.	d.	Years.	s.	d.	Years.	s.	d.	Years.	s.	d.
1856 .	2	$4\frac{3}{4}$	1860 .	1	9	1864 .	2	3	1868 .	1	$\frac{11}{16}$
1857 .	2	$1\frac{1}{4}$	1861 .	1	$9\frac{1}{8}$	1865 .	2	$3\frac{1}{4}$	1869 .	1	$8\frac{7}{8}$
1858 .	2	0	1862 .	1	9	1866 .	1	$11\frac{1}{16}$	1870 .	1	9
1859 .	2	0	1863 .	1	$11\frac{7}{8}$	1867 .	1	$9\frac{1}{2}$			

Here again is a decline.

Causes of Local Rise in Prices.

I have given above the most important articles of export, and it cannot be concluded from the above figures that prices have increased in India to any material extent, much less "enormously." The necessary causes for a healthy rise do not exist; the effect, therefore, is only a dream. On the contrary, the causes to diminish capital and labour are unceasingly at work, and the consequence can only be increased poverty instead of prosperity.

Cause No. 2, stated by me at the commencement of this paper, will partly account for such rise as has actually taken place in some parts of India, and has misled many persons to the conclusion of a general rise and increased prosperity.

During the last twenty years, something like £82,000,000 (Railway Report, 1869) have been sent to India for railway works, out of which some £26,000,000 are spent in England for stores, etc., and about £55,000,000 remitted to India to be spent here. This amount has been spent in certain parts, with the effect of raising prices there in two ways. Large numbers of labourers are collected in such places, and to a great extent agricultural labour is diminished in their neighbourhood, the want of good communication preventing other parts from supplying the demand.

The result is, that less food is produced and more mouths to feed, and, with the labourers well paid, a temporary and local rise of prices is the inevitable consequence. On looking over the maps, and examining the prices given in the tables of Administration Reports, it will be easily seen that, in every Presidency in good seasons, the localities of high prices have been those only where there have been large public works going on. For instance, in the Central Provinces in the year 1867-8, when there was an average good season, the districts in which the price of rice was highest were—Hoshungabad, Rs. 5 per maund; Baitool, Rs. 4 per maund; Nursingpore, Rs. 3-12 per maund; Jubbulpore, Rs. 3-12 per maund; Nagpore, Rs. 3-8 per maund; and Saugur, Rs. 3-9 per maund. While the lowest prices were—Raipore and Belaspore, Re. 1 per maund; Sumbulpore, Rs. 1-2; Balaghaut, Rs. 2; Bhandara, Rs. 2; Chindwara, Rs. 1-8. Now, the places having the highest prices are almost all those along, or in the neighbourhood of, railway lines, or carrying on some public works; and those with the lowest prices are away from the lines, etc. In 1868-69, the range of prices is about the same, though higher on account of bad season, Hoshungabad being Rs. 8 and Raipore Rs. 2; and through the season being unequal in different parts, there is some corresponding divergence from the preceding year.

Take the *Madras Presidency*.—The districts with highest prices in 1867-68 are:—

Cuddapah .	Rs. 492 per garce[1]	Coimbatoor .	Rs. 474 per garce
Madura . .	,, 477 ,,	Bellary . .	,, 469 ,,

The districts with the lowest prices are:—

Vizagapatam	Rs. 203 per garce	Ganjam . .	Rs. 232 per garce
Godavery .	,, 222 ,,	South Canara	,, 308 ,,

Almost all the high-price districts are on the railway line, or have some public works. The districts of the lowest prices are away from the line. In the Godavery district I do not know how far irrigation has helped to produce abundance.

Take the *Punjab* for June, 1868-9.—The report gives prices for the following districts only:—

Delhi	Wheat 26 seers	or	52	lbs.	per	Re. 1
Umballa . . .	,,	,,	48	,,		,,
Sealkote . . .	,,	,,	38	,,		,,
Lahore	,,	,,	34	,,		,,
Multan	,,	,,	34	,,		,,
Peshawur . . .	,,	,,	30	,,		,,

Now, the first three are those where railways are finished, the last three are those where new lines are being constructed.

In the *North-West Provinces*.—For the month of June, 1868 (I have taken this month in which there was no scarcity; the months after, prices gradually rose to famine prices):—

Meerut	27 seers	8 chittacks or	55	lbs.	per	Re. 1
Saharunpore . .	25 ,,	14 ,,	50	,,	nearly	,,
Bareilly . . .	25 ,,		50	,,		,,
Moradabad . . }						
Muttra . . . . }	24 ,,		48	,,	,,	,,
Agra . . . . }						
Cawnpore . . .	22 ,,		44	,,	,,	,,
Benares . . .	18 ,,	4 ,,	36½	,,	,,	,,
Allababad . . .	17 ,,		34	,,	,,	,,
Mirzapore . .	17 ,,		34	,,	,,	,,
Ajmere . . .	16 ,,		32	,,	,,	,,

[1] Garce = 9,256 lbs. (Parliamentary Return 362 of 1853).

The East Indian Railway being finished, the irrigation works now going on are beginning to tell; the Agra Canal raising prices at Agra and Muttra.

Cawnpore and the places mentioned after it have had railway works in progress about them. In these Provinces, besides railways, there is public works expenditure from Imperial funds close upon a crore of rupees during 1868-69, greater part of which is spent in places where prices are high.

In the *Bombay Presidency*.—What with cotton money lately poured in, and perhaps not quite re-drained yet, and large railway works going on for some time past, prices are comparatively higher than in all the other parts of India, but most so only where railway works and cotton combined, such as all such places on the Bombay, Baroda, and Central India line as Surat, Broach, Kaira, Ahmedabad, etc., or on the G.I.P. line, either northward or southward. Belgaum and Dharwar, not being on a line, have not high prices.

All the very high prices in the Bombay Presidency in the year 1863 (the year of the enquiry of the Price Commission) are things of the past. For instance, in the Report of the Commission, the prices given for the town of Belgaum for November, 1863, are (page 32):—

Seers (of 80 tolas or 2 lbs.) per Rupee.

	14th Nov. Seers.	21st Nov. Seers.
Coarse Rice	8	6
Bajri	10	7
Jowari	9½	7

Contrast these with the prices in 1867-68:—

	Nov. 1867. Seers.	Nov. 1868. Seers.
2nd Sort Rice	14·40	13·9
Bajri	24	26
Jowari	28	35

In *Bengal*.—All places which are cheapest in 1868 are distant from the rail lines—Tipperah, Purneah, Cuttack, Puri, Dacca, Maunbhum. Even in some places where the railway line has passed, the prices are not so high—as they are, I think, rice-producing districts—such as Rajmahal and Bankurah. As in other parts of India, it will be found that in Bengal also prices rose for a time where railway and other public works were building. These facts show that railway capital, and money for other public works, raised prices temporarily in certain localities.

I must not be misunderstood, however. I do not mean to complain of any such temporary effect produced during the prosecution of such public works as railways, roads, canals, or irrigation-works, or any work of reproduction or saving. My object is only to show that the statement often made, that India is prosperous and happy because prices have risen, is a conclusion not warranted by actual facts: and that any partial, local, or temporary rise in prices is attributable to the temporary and local expenditure of railway and other loans, or of Imperial and local funds on public works.

Normal Decrease in Prices under British Rule.

So far I have shown that any rise that has taken place has been only local and temporary, as long as railways or public works were building there. I shall now show more directly how, in every Province as it came under British rule, prices went down, as the natural consequence of the drain setting in under the new system, and that there has not been a general rise of prices.

Take *Madras*.—Return 362 of 1853 gives "the average price per cwt. of Munghi, 2nd sort, in the month of January, 1813," as 7s. 6½d. to 9s. 8d., and Bengal table-rice 14s. 0½d. After his, Madras kept sinking, till, in 1852, there is 3s. to 3s. 6¾d. per cwt., and the Board of Revenue felt it necessary to inquire into "the general decline of prices, and to find out any general measures of relief" to meet falling prices.—(Madras Selections, No. XXXI. of 1856, page 1.) This selection gives prices from almost all districts of Madras, and the general result is that there is a continuous fall in prices (excepting scarcity years) from the commencement of the century to 1852, the year of the reports. Then further on, what are the prices now in the first half of March, 1873?

Rice, 1st sort.		
Present fortnight ...	Seers 12·4	or lbs. 27·28
Past ,, ...	,, 12·4	
Rice, Common.		
Present fortnight ...	Seers 15·6	or lbs. 34·32
Past ,, ...	,, 13·9	,, 30·8

So that best sort is about 8s. 2½d. per cwt.; common sort 6s. 6½d. to 7s. 4d. per cwt. (*Indian Gazette*, 5th April, 1873). 1 seer = 2·2 lbs.

This is the only number of the *Indian Gazette* I have come

across. Again, the average price of Madras rice for the year 1868 in the United Kingdom, after paying for freight, insurance, commission, profits, and all other charges from Madras to arrival in that country, was 9s. 8d. per cwt. (Trade Returns, 1868), while the price for January, 1813, given above, is 8s. 2¾d. in Madras itself. Or, let us take the export price in the ports of the Madras Presidency. The export price of cargo rice in the ports of the Madras Presidency, according to the price currents of the Madras Chamber of Commerce, in the year 1867, is put down uniformly in the price tables at Rs. 6 per bag of 164 lbs., or two Indian maunds; but in the remarks in which precise quotations are given, the price ranges from Rs. 3-15 to Rs. 6-2. Rs. 6, though a higher price than the average for a bag of 164 lbs., is equal to 8s. 2d. per cwt.; and even this price, though not higher than that of 1813, was owing to bad season and short crop; and certainly prices consequent upon bad seasons are not an indication of prosperity. In the year 1868, the season being average good, the price quoted for cargo rice is Rs. 3-15 per bag. Now and then, in the remarks, higher prices are quoted, but Rs. 4 will be quite an approximate average. Rs. 4 per bag is nearly 5s. 6d. per cwt. During 1869, the same Rs. 3-15 is the general quotation; but the season of 1869 not being good, prices went up in 1870 to Rs. 5-8, with an average of about Rs. 5, or about 6s. 10d. per cwt. Thus, then, there is no material rise in price in the Madras Presidency compared with the commencement of this century. The subsequent fall made the poor people wretched. Government inquired and reduced the assessment, which, with the expenditure on railways, &c., gave some little relief. But the depression is not yet got over. On the contrary, the Material and Moral Progress (Report for 1869, Parliamentary Return [c. 213 of 1870], page 71) tells us that "prices in Madras have been falling continuously," and my impression is that they so still continue.

Bengal.—The Parliamentary Return 362 of 1853 gives the prices at Calcutta from 1792 only (and that is stated to be a year of famine), when there was already about that period much depression by the action of the Company's rule. I cannot get in this return earlier prices of the time of the native rule to make a fair comparison. For 1813 the prices given in the then depressed condition are from 2s. 8¾d. to

3s. 7d. A comparison with this depression of the present prices is, of course, not fair. In 1832, Patna rice is quoted at 7s. 5¾d. per cwt., and Patchery at 7s. 1¾d. Now, the best sort of rice of Patna in the first half of March, 1873, is quoted 21·50 seers, or 43 lbs. per rupee, or about 5s. 1½d. per cwt. In 1852 the above return quotes Patna at 5s. 4½d. per cwt. Colonel Baird Smith, in his famine report (Parliamentary Return 29 of 1962, page 55) quotes as follows the ordinary prices of grain, etc., "from an official statement prepared from authentic documents by the Fiscal of Chinsura," at that station between the years 1770 and 1813 (as given in "Gleanings in Science," vol. I, page 369, 1829)—rice best sort 28 seers per rupee, coarse sort 40 seers per rupee. The same statement gives prices for the year 1803 also for ordinary rice at 40 seers per rupee (page 56). And in the *Bengal Government Gazette* for the year 1867-68, it will be found that, in some places in Bengal, the ordinary price of cheapest sort of rice is even then between 40 and 50 seers per rupee (this seer being 2 lbs.) So we have the same story as Madras. Bengal first sank, and helped by a permanent settlement, by the railway loan, cotton, etc., again got over the depression to a certain extent.

Bombay.—The same return, 362 of 1853, gives the average price of rice between the highest and lowest prices of the year 1812-13, as 15s. 4½d. per cwt. This price goes on declining to about 3s. 5d. to 7s. 6¾d. in 1852, and what is it now in the first half of March of 1873 (*Indian Gazette*, 5th April, 1873, page 448) after all favourable circumstances of railways and other public works, some of them still going on, cotton-wealth, etc.?

Rice, best sort.

	Seers.			
Present fortnight . . .	7·4	= 16·28 lbs.	less than	14s. per cwt.
Previous " . . .	6·8	= 15 "	"	15s. "
Rice, Common	10	= 22 "	"	10s. "

The average between the highest and lowest prices will be about 12s. 6d. per cwt., when in 1812-13 this is 15s. 4½d.

In the report of the Indapore re-settlement (Bombay Selections, CVII., new series, pages 118 and 71), the price of jowari is given from 1809 to 1865-66:—

	Years.	Pucca seers per Rupee.		Years.	Pucca seers per Rupee.		Years.	Pucca seers per Rupee.
Feb.	1809	24	Feb.	1819	17	Feb.	1829	80
,,	1810	24	,,	1820	19½	,,	1830	46
,,	1811	22	March	1821	32	May	1831	40
,,	1812	25½	,,	1822	32	Feb.	1832	60
,,	1813	27	,,	1823	32	,,	1833	23
March	1814	28	April	1824	36¾	,,	1834	46
Feb.	1815	33½	,,	1825	12½	,,	1835	48
,,	1816	26	Feb.	1826	44	,,	1836	38
April	1817	48½	,,	1827	64	,,	1337	66
Feb.	1818	24	,,	1828	32			

After giving these prices, Lieutenant A. Nash remarks:— "This table is chiefly interesting as showing the gradual diminution in the price of corn from the days of the Peishwas to our own. By comparing the prices at the commencement with those at the end of the table, and then reading the list over, this circumstance will become very apparent."

About the year 1836-37, when prices had gone down very low, the Survey Settlement commenced, and the prices subsequently are given for Indapore as follows:—

Years.	Seers per Rupee.	Years.	Seers per Rupee.	Years.	Seers per Rupee.
1836-37	43	1846-47	15	1856-57	32
1837-38	36	1847-48	48	1857-58	39
1838-39	67	1848-49	72	1858-59	32
1839-40	44	1849-50	72	1859-60	39
1840-41	64	1850-51	38	1860-61	33
1841-42	56	1851-52	40	1861-62	27
1842-43	68	1852-53	56	1862-63	16
1843-44	72	1853-54	56	1863-64	13
1844-45	60	1854-55	29	1864-65	16
1845-46	36	1855-56	32	1865-66	18

Now, from the year of the Mutiny, followed by the cotton famine, the times were exceptional, so that the prices in 1856, or about that period, can only be considered normal, and that is about 32 seers, while in 1809-13 about 25 seers. Now, in 1867-68 the average from November, 1867, to September, 1868, for Ahmednuggar (*Bombay Government Gazette* price list) is about 24½ seers.

Thus, then, it is the old story. From the time of the Peishwa, prices kept going down under the British rule till, with the aid of railway loans, cotton windfall, etc., they have laboured up again, with a tendency to relapse.

I take the following figures from the Price Commission Report of Bombay (Finance Committee's Report of 1871, page 617). I take jowari as the chief grain of the Presidency:—

Tolas per Rupee.

Years.	Poona.	Belgaum.	Ahmedabad.	Years.	Poona.	Belgaum.	Ahmedabad.
1824	1,892	2,480	2,560	1827	3,268	2,800	3,600
1825	1,548	2,600	1,840	1828	2,752	2,640	4,000
1826	3,040	2,200	3,240	1829	3,440	4,200	4,800

Instead of quoting here the whole table, which is already published in the first Report of the Finance Committee, page 617, I take six years, from 1850 to 1855 :—

Tolas per Rupee.

Years.	Poona.	Belgaum.	Ahmedabad.	Years.	Poona.	Belgaum.	Ahmedabad.
1850	3,056	4,240	3,520	1853	4,128	3,200	2,800
1851	3,440	4,560	4,320	1854	2,504	3,040	3,400
1852	3,440	3,280	2,800	1855	2,432	2,540	4,520

Even taking the rough average without consideration of quantities in each year, the latter six years are lower than the former. It is only about and after 1857 that prices rose under exceptional and temporary circumstances—the Mutiny and the American War, aided by the expenditure on railways, etc. After the American War, prices have commenced falling. Contrast the prices in 1863 with those of 1867-68 for the same places—Poona, Belgaum, and Ahmedabad (I take the rough averages from the monthly prices given in the *Bombay Government Gazette* for 1867-68) :—

Tolas per Rupee.

Year.	Poona.	Belgaum.	Ahmedabad.	Years.	Poona.	Belgaum.	Ahmedabad.
1863	1,120	720	880	1867-68	1,786	2,633	1,180

For 1868 and 1869. This year, except in the southern part of the Southern Division, was a bad season, and the Bombay Administration Report says that the distress in two districts, Poona and Ahmednuggar, became "so great that it became necessary to afford relief to the labouring poor by undertaking works of public utility." In the Northern Division, in Ahmedabad, Kaira, and the Punch Mahals, "the scanty rains of June and July were followed by severe floods in August, which were succeeded by drought. In Khandeish there was an entire failure of the later rains in some talookas." In some talookas, with no rain, "there were no crops to watch, and no harvest to reap." In Khandeish, also, relief works had become necessary, as the effects of scarcity were heightened by immigration from Rajpootana. Such was the generally unfavourable character of the season, and yet the rough average of retail prices from the *Bombay Government Gazette* is as follows for the same three places :—

Tolas of Jowari per Rupee.

Nov. to Oct.	Poona.	Belgaum.	Ahmedabad.
1868-69	1,227	2,100	930

(lower than those of 1863).

I may just say a word here about the Price Commission Report of Bombay of 1864 to which I have referred above, and from which Sir Bartle Frere has made up his statement, embodied in the first report of the Finance Committee, that all the tables given in it, as averages either of a number of years or of a number of places, are worthless for any correct and practical conclusions with regard to the actual change in prices or the actual condition of the people. Because, in these averages, as is generally done, no regard, I think, is had for the different quantities of produce in different years or different places. This remark applies, as I have already said before, to all averages taken on the wrong principle of adding up prices and dividing by the number of the prices.

Take *Cotton.*—I cannot get a list of prices in India, but the prices in Liverpool may be taken as a sufficient index of the changes in India. Dr. J. Forbes Royle, in his "Culture and Commerce of Cotton in India" (1851), gives before the title-page a diagram of the prices and quantity of American and Indian cotton imported into the United Kingdom from the year 1806 to 1848. The price of Indian cotton in Liverpool in 1806 is 16¼d., in 1807 15¼d. In 1808 it went up to 20d., and then declined, till in 1811 it touched 12d. It rose again, till in 1814 it went up to 21d. It had subsequently various fluctuations, till in 1832 it just touched 4½d., but again continued to be above, till 1840, with an average above 6d. It subsequently continued at a low average of about 4d., and would have remained so to this day, or perhaps gone out of the English market altogether, as was very nearly the case in 1860, but for the American War which sent it up. Now, looking at the figures given above, it will be seen that, now that the temporary impulse of the American War is over, cotton is fast sinking again, and we can no longer expect to see again that high curve of the first quarter of the present century ranging from 7d. to 21d. The Suez Canal opening direct communication with European ports, has only saved the Indian cotton trade from perishing altogether. The Administration Report of 1871-72 gives a distressing picture of the season over nearly the whole of the Presidency, and of the inability of the people to stand it; and are the prices of such years to be glad about, and to be taken in averages of rise?

The Central Provinces.—In the Central Provinces the average price of rice, as I have pointed out before, for the year 1867-68—a year of average good season—is Rs. 1-8 per maund of 80 lbs., not a high price certainly; and if these be an "enormous" rise in former prices, what wretched prices must they have been before? I have not materials for comparison with prices before the British rule.

Of the *North-West Provinces* I have not come across sufficient materials to make a fair comparison, but from what data I have, I feel that the conclusion about these Provinces will be similar to those of other parts of India.

As an imperfect indication, I may refer to the table given in Colonel Baird Smith's report of prices in 1860, and those of 1868-69 given in the Administration Report. Both years have nearly the same common features—in 1860, in July and August, scarcity prices; in 1868-69, latter part of the year, of scarcity. On a comparison, the prices of 1868-69 are, if anything, something lower on the whole, except at Allahabad and Cawnpore, where railway works are in progress. I give this comparison on opposite page.

Prices of fine Wheat at the undermentioned places.
SEERS PER RUPEE.

At the end of		Saharunpore.	Meerut.	Allyghur.	Cawnpore.	Allahabad.	Muttra.	Agra.
May,	1860.	26-13	22-8	19	25	24-1	21-12	17-8
	1868.	25-14	27		23	18		23
June,	1860.	25-12	20	18	23	22-8	19	18
	1868.	25-14	27-8		22	17	24	24
July,	1860.	(missing)						
	1868.	23-11	26-8		21	17-8	24	23
August,	1860.	11-12	11-8	12-4	18	21-4	9-12	10
	1868.	18-4	22		17	15	18	19-8
September,	1860.	13-2	11-8	10-8	17	20	9	9-12
	1868.	11-13	11-4		16	15	16-2	14
October,	1860.	9-9	9-8	11-4	17	18-12	10-12	11
	1868.	12-15	17-12					

This really does not show any enormous rise during the nine years which of all others are supposed to have raised prices most.

Take the *Punjab*.—The prices of wheat in Lahore are (Report of Punjab, 1850-51, page 74) as follows:—

Years.	lbs. per Rupee.	Years.	lbs. per Rupee.
1844 . . .	45	1848 . . .	54
1845 . . .	46	1849 . . .	38
1846 . . .	39½	1850 . . .	43½
1847 . . .	46		

Mr. John (now Lord) Lawrence repeats, in his report of 1855-56 (page 28), that, for ten years up to 1850-51, wheat was Rs. 2 per maund of 82 lbs., *i.e.*, during the native rule, ten years previous to annexation, the price was 41 lbs. per rupee. Now, the Administration Report for 1855-56 (Government of India Selection No. XVIII, of 1856) gives the following table:—

AVERAGE PRICES.

For 10 Years up to 1850-51.	Wheat Rs. 2 per maund of 82 lbs.
1851-52	Rs. 1 per maund.
1852-53	,, $1\frac{3}{16}$,,
1853-54	,, $1\frac{3}{16}$,,
1854-55	,, 1 ,,
1855-56	,, $1\frac{1}{16}$,,

This table shows how prices fell after the annexation. Assessments were revised and lowered, railway and other public works created demand for labour, and another additional very important element operated, which, in the words of Sir R. Temple, is this:—"But within the last year, the Native Army being Punjabi, all such sums have been paid to them and have been spent at home. Again, many thousands of Punjabi soldiers are serving abroad. These men not only remit their savings, but also have sent quantities of prize, property, and plunder, the spoils of Hindustan, to their native villages. The effect of all these is already perceptible in an increase of agricultural capital, a freer circulation of money, and a fresh impetus to cultivation."

Now, the prices after all such favourable circumstances, even as late as 1867-68, are about the same as they were in 1844-47—about 34 to 46 lbs. per rupee. In 1868-69 the prices are higher on account of bad season.

I trust I have made it clear that the so-called rise in prices is only a pulling up from the depth they had sunk into under the natural economic effect of British rule, by the temporary help of the railway and other loans, and by the windfall of the high cotton prices for a short period—so that India got back a little of its lost blood, though the greater portion of it is borrowed.

Higher Prices due to Scarcity.

But, among the causes of the occasional rise in prices, and whose effects are indiscriminately mixed up in the averages, there is one which no person who gives the slightest consideration to it will regard as a matter for congratulation. Besides the public works expenditure causing high prices locally, the additional cause to which I allude is scarcity and bad season. Such rise will not certainly be regarded by anybody as a sign of prosperity, but calculation of averages often includes these scarcity prices, and their results and conclusions are mischievous, in leading to wrong practical action. For instance, take the Central Provinces. The average price of rice for all the districts is Rs. 1-8 per maund for 1867-68, while in 1868-69 it is Rs. 4-4-9 per maund, and this is entirely owing to a bad season. But there are writers who do not, or would not, see the bad season. They see only the high prices, and clamour prosperity and for increased assessments.

In the North-West Provinces the price of wheat is given, say, in Saharunpore, above 50 lbs. per rupee in June, 1868, and in December, 1868, it rises to as much as 20 lbs. per rupee. I give a few more figures from the Report of 1868-69 :—

	April, 1868.		Sept., 1868.	
	seers.	chittacks.	seers.	chittacks.
Meerut . .	26	0	11	4
Moradabad . .	26	10	13	7
Bareilly . .	25	10	15	5
Muttra . .	24	0	16	2
Agra . . .	23	0	14	0

So are these places more prosperous in September than in April, when they are, in fact, suffering from near famine prices?

Again, for 1871-2 (Administration Report for 1871-72, pages 1 and 2), both the *kharif* (autumn crop) and *rabi* (spring crop) had been short, and the consequence was rise in prices. Is such rise a healthy sign of prosperity?

In Madras the price of cargo rice is, all throughout, in

1868-69, about Rs. 3-15 per bag, and by the end of July, 1870, it goes up to Rs. 5-10 owing to bad season.

HIGHER PRICES DUE TO FAMINE.

The comparitive high prices of 1865 to 1867 were owing to bad season; 1867-68, a good season, brought them down. Bad season again, and a rise and continuous fall since 1870. Return No. 335 of 1867 on the Orissa famine gives a list of prices rising many times, in the time of various famines; and are these prices of prosperity? Leaving extreme cases of past famine alone, let us take present times.

Punjab.—The Administration Report for 1868-69 says (page 101)—" Appendix III. EI shows that food was cheaper in June, 1868, than during the preceding year, but in January, 1869, prices had risen to famine rates in consequence of the drought that prevailed during the intervening months. In January, 1869, wheat was selling at Delhi at 11¼ seers (22½ lbs.) per rupee, and in the other districts specified in the return as follows :—

Umballa . .	9¼ seers.	Multan . .	11¼ seers.
Lahore . .	9¾ ,,	Peshawur .	14 6/16 ,,
Sealkote . .	10¾ ,,		

Now, the prices in the above places in January and June, 1868, were :—

	January.	June.		January.	June.
Delhi . .	25 seers.	26 seers.	Sealkote .	16 seers.	19 seers.
Umballa .	20½ ,,	24 ,,	Multan .	13¾ ,,	17 ,,
Lahore .	17 ,,	18 ,,	Peshawur	15 ,,	20½ ,,

So the prices are more than doubled in January, 1869. And this unfortunate state continues, after a little relief.

Here is the summary of the table in the Report for 1869-70 (page 95) :—

	1st June, 1868.	1st January, 1869.	1st June, 1869.	1st January, 1870.	
Delhi . .	26 seers.	11¼ seers.	15 seers.	9 seers.	Prices in seers of 2 lbs. per rupee.
Umballa .	24 ,,	9¼ ,,	13¼ ,,	9 ,,	
Lahore . .	18 ,,	9¾ ,,	13½ ,,	9½ ,,	
Sealkote .	19 ,,	10¾ ,,	13¼ ,,	10½ ,,	
Multan . .	17 ,,	11¼ ,,	12½ ,,	9¾ ,,	
Peshawur .	20½ ,,	14 6/16 ,,	17⅞ ,,	17⅞ ,,	

To sum up—the course of prices during the last two years has been, if anything, downward, except in places of drought or famine, or new public works; and all my remarks based upon 1867-68-69 will, I think, derive greater force from the statistics of the past two years.

I trust I have proved that there has been no general healthy rise of prices in any part of India from the time of its acquisition by the British. On the contrary, there has been continuous depression, till the railway loans, etc., and cotton money revived it a little, and that even temporarily and locally, from its extreme previous illness. And that very often the so-called high prices are the result of misfortune, of scarcity, rather than of increased prosperity.

It will tax the ability of Indian statesmen much, and will require a great change in the policy of the British rule, before India will see prosperity, or even rise above its absolute wants.

WAGES.

It is alleged that there is great rise in wages, and that therefore India is increasing in prosperity. Almost all remarks applied to prices will do for this. The rise is only when railway and other works are going on, and is only local and temporary. In other parts there is no material alteration.

In Bengal.

With regard to *Bengal*, there is the same difficulty as in the case of prices—that I cannot get earlier wages than 1790-91, which were depressed times. I find for the year 1830-31 the daily wages of a cooly was on zemindari estates two annas in the Collectorates of Dinagepore, Bakergunge, Dacca, 24-Purgunnahs, Murshedabad, in the Purgunnahs of Calcutta, Barughati (Return No. 362 of 1853).

Now, in the year 1866-67, the daily wage of unskilled labour in several districts of Bengal, where even public works were going on, were as follows:—

	a.	p.
1st Division Grand Trunk-road Division	2	6
2nd ,, ,, ,,	2	0
Patna Branch Road Division	2	0
Barrakar Division	2	2
Tirhoot ,,	1	6
Behar Road ,,	2	0
Barrackpore ,,	2	8
Purneah ,,	2	6
Bhagulpore ,,	2	6

		a.	p.
Behrampore ,,	. . . .	2	6
Dinapore ,,	. . . .	1	6
Ramghur ,,	. . . . 2 to	1	6
24-Pergunnahs	. . . .	2	6
Chittagong Division	. . . .	2	6
Burdwan ,,	. . . .	2	6
	. . . .	1	6

In some divisions it is as high as four annas, but the general rate is as above, and it is the rates paid by the Public Works Department. So the general average rate of a cooly on the zemindari estates, I think, cannot be much above two annas a day—just what it was 40 years ago. I have obtained the above figures from the Public Works Department through a friend in Calcutta.

IN BOMBAY.

Bombay.—Sir Bartle Frere has given a table from the Price Commission Report of 1864 of Bombay, of the monthly wages of a cooly or common labourer (Finance Committee, first Report, page 616). On examining this table (which I do not repeat here), it will be seen that there is hardly a rise in wages worth mentioning between the average of 1824-29 and 1850-59, the intervening period having some depression. It is after 1859, as in the case of prices and from same causes (Mutiny, railways, and cotton), wages rose suddenly. But that they are falling again will be evident from what is passing in Bombay itself, as the centre of the greatest activity, and as where large public works are still going on, one would hardly expect a fall. I obtained the following figures from one of the Executive Engineers' office for wages paid by the Public Works Department. The following rates were current during the last six years in Bombay (the letter is dated 11th June, 1872):—

Years.	Wages of Biggari per diem.		Wages of Women.		Wages of Boys.	
	a.	p.	a.	p.	a.	p.
1867-68 . . .	6	0	4	0	3	0
1868-69 . : .	6	0	4	0	3	0
1869-70 . . .	5	0	3	6	2	4
1870-71 . . .	5	0	3	0	2	4
1871-72 . . .	5	0	3	0	2	4

This is a fall from 1863, when in Bombay the maximum was Rs. 13-8 per month, and minimum Rs. 7-12 per month, or 7 annas and $2\frac{1}{2}$ pies per diem, and 4 annas and $1\frac{2}{3}$ pies per diem respectively. Now, had large public buildings not been building in Bombay, these wages would have gone much lower than given in the tables above. I am not aware how the wages are during 1872 and 1873, but my impression is that they are lower, and will be again down, after the present buildings are finished, to the old levels shown in the table to which I have already referred (page 616 of Finance Committee's first Report).

In Punjab.

In *Punjab* the highest rate in 1867-68 is 5 annas and 4 annas per day, chiefly in those parts where public works are going on, such as Sealkote, Multan, Lahore, etc. But even in these the lowest and in most of the other districts the rate generally is 2 annas. The average given of wages of unskilled labour in the Report for 1868-69 is—

Highest, 3 annas 3 pies, or $4\frac{7}{8}$d.
Lowest, 2 annas 5 pies, or $3\frac{5}{8}$d.

This average is taken without any reference to the number of persons earning the different wages. Were this element considered, the average would come down to the old famous 3d. a day. There is the further element—to consider how many days of the year are the different wages earned! However, even with regard to any high rate, that is, in some districts, the Punjab Government says what is applicable to other parts of India under similar circumstances. The Administration Report for 1867-68 (page 83) says:—"The rates of unskilled labour range from 2 annas (3d) to 5 annas ($7\frac{1}{2}$d.) per diem. There has been a considerable rise in rates in places affected by the railway and other public works, and labour in any shape commands higher remuneration than formerly; but as prices of the necessaries of life have risen in even a higher ratio, owing chiefly to the increase of facility of export, it may be doubted whether the position of the unskilled labouring classes has materially improved." Leaving the cause to be what it may, this is apparent, that higher wages in some places have not done much good to the poor labourer. The general rate of wages is, however, about 2 annas.

In the Central Provinces.

In the *Central Provinces* (excepting those parts where railway works have been going on), in Raipore, Belaspore,

Sumbulpore, Balaghat, Bhundara and Chindwara, the rate of wages for unskilled labour is generally 2 annas only, both for the years 1867-68 and 1868-69. On the other hand, where railway works are going on and the price of food is high, wages are also high—as in Hoshungabad, 3 annas; Baitool, 4 annas; Nursingpore, 3 annas; Jubbulpore, 5 annas; Nagpore, 3 annas, etc. Thus, only locally and temporarily are there high wages in some parts. The general rate of wages is not improved. Even with all such high wages for a few, the average all over the Provinces in 1868-69, as well as in 1870-71, is put down as 3 annas, or 4½d.; but if the number of those earning the different wages, and the number of days when such wages are earned, were considered, as well as the temporary effect of the buildings of public works, we shall again come to our old friend 3d. per day, or perhaps less. Except, therefore, all over India where railway or public works have congested labour temporarily, without good facility of communication of bringing food, the general rate of wages is scarcely above 2 annas a day. The notion of a general rise of wages, and of the vastly improved condition of the labourer is a delusion. Here is the latest summary of wages on the highest authority (Material and Moral Progress of India for 1871-72, pages 100, 101). In Punjab, wages are 6d. to 2d. a day for unskilled labour. In Oudh 1½d. for unskilled labour a day. In Central Provinces, unskilled labour is 3d. to 1½d. per day. In the Bombay Presidency unskilled labour is 6d. to 3d. a day. The rates of other Provinces are not given. It must be remembered that the lower figure is the rate earned by the majority; and are these present rates of 1½d. to 3d. an enormous rise on the former ones?

BULLION.

It is often alleged that India has imported large quantities of bullion, and is very much enriched thereby. Let us see what the facts are!

First of all, India has not got its imports of silver as so much profits on its exports, or making up so much deficit of imports against exports and profits. As far as exports go, I have already shown that the imports (including all bullion) are short of exports *plus* profits, to the extent of not only the whole profits, but the whole opium revenue, and a good deal from the produce itself besides. The import of bullion has been chiefly from commercial and financial necessities, as will be seen further on, except during the few years of the American War, when some portion was sent in because the people could not suddenly create a large demand for English goods in payment of profits. The total balance of the imports and exports of bullion from the year 1801 to 1863, according to Parliamentary Return 133 of 1864, is £234,353,686; and from 1864 to 1869, according to Return c. 184 of 1870, is £101,123,448 (which includes, mark! the years of the great cotton windfall, and large remittances for railway loans), making altogether £335,477,134 from 1801 to 1869. The British rulers introduced universally the system of collecting all revenue in money instead of in kind. This circumstance produced a demand for coin. The foreign trade of the country having increased (though without any benefit to India), increased the demand for coin. The coinage of India from 1801 to 1869, according to the same returns, amounts to £265,652,749, exclusive of coinage in Madras for the years 1801 to 1807, and for Bombay for the years 1821-22, 1824-1831, and 1833 (particulars of which are not given), leaving a balance of about £70,000,000 of bullion for all other wants of the country. It may be said that some of the coinage must have been re-melted. This cannot be to a large extent, as specie is 2 per cent. cheaper than coin, as the mint charge is 2 per cent. for coining. Mr. Harrison, in reply to question 3993 of the Finance Committee, confirms this—that the coinage "is burdened with a charge of 2 per cent., which is a clear loss to all persons wishing to use it for any other purpose than that of coin."

Then there is the wear and tear to consider. The wear and tear of shillings and sixpences given by the Return (24 of 1817) is 28 per cent. on shillings, and 47 per cent. on sixpences. The period of the wear is not given in the return. In India, this wear, from the necessity of moving large quantity of coin for Government purposes, and a much rougher and more widespread use of the coin by the people generally, the percentage per annum must be a large one indeed.

Mr. Harrison again says on the subject—"*Question* 3992.—But do you, then, think that a million fresh coinage a year is sufficient to supply the wants of India? *Mr. Harrison.*—More than sufficient, I suppose, to supply the waste of coin or metal." This, I cannot help thinking, is under the mark, but it shows that nearly a million a year must be imported for simply making up waste of coin or metal.

The coinage of India as per return is, from 1801 to 1869, about £266,000,000 (not including the coinage in Native States). Deducting only £66,000,000 for wastage for the sixty-nine years, there should be in circulation £200,000,000. Taking the wide extent of the country (equal to all Europe, except Russia, it is said), this amount for revenue, commercial, and social purposes is not an extravagant one. Strike off even £50,000,000 for re-melting, though at the loss of 2 per cent. value; I take the coin as only £150,000,000. Deducting this amount and wastage of £66,000,000—or say even £50,000,000 only (to be under the mark)—making a total of £200,000,000, there will remain for all other social and industrial wants, besides coinage, about £135,000,000. This, distributed over a population of above 200,000,000, hardly gives 13s. 6d. per head, that is to say, during altogether sixty-nine years, India imported only 13s. 6d. per head of bullion for all its various purposes, except coin. What an insignificant sum!! Take even the whole import altogether of £335,000,000 during the long period of sixty-nine years, and what is it? Simply about 33s. 6d. per head for all possible purposes, and without making any allowance for wear and tear. Just see what the United Kingdom has retained for its purposes. I cannot get any returns of imports of silver and gold before 1858. I take only, then, 1858 to 1869 (both inclusive). The total imports are £322,628,000, and the total exports £268,319,000, leaving a balance of about £54,300,000. Deducting about £10,000,000 for the excess of the quantity in the Bank of England at the end of 1869 over 1857, there remain about £44,000,000 for the social and trade use of the country, allowing equal amounts for coin in 1858 and 1869. This, therefore, is about 30s. a head retained by the United Kingdom within a period of twelve years, independent of its circulating coin, while India retained only 33s. 6d. a head during a period of sixty-nine years for *all* its purposes. Much is said about the hoarding by the Natives, but how little is the share for each to hoard, and what amounts are in a shape hoardings, in all plate, jewellery, watches, etc., the people use in England! I do not suppose that any Englishman would say that the natives of India ought to have no taste and no ornaments or articles of use, and must only live like animals; but, after all, how little there is for each, if every one had his share to hoard or to use. The fact is, that, far from hoarding, millions who are living on "scanty subsistence" do not know what it is to have a silver piece in their possession. It cannot be otherwise. To talk of oriental wealth now, as far as British India is concerned, is only a figure of speech, a dream! When we talk of all the silver having a purchasing power, we forget how minutely and widely a large portion of it must be distributed in India to be of any use for national purposes. The notion that the import of silver has made India rich is another strange delusion! There is one important circumstance which is not borne in mind. The silver imported is *not* for making up the balance of exports and profits over imports, or for what is called balance of trade. Far from it, as I have already explained. It is imported as a simple necessity, but it therefore no more makes India richer because so much *silver* is imported. If I give out £20 worth of goods to anybody, and in return get £5 in other goods and £5 in silver, and yet if by so doing, though I have received only £10 worth in all for the £20 I have parted with, I am richer by £5 because I have received £5 in silver, then my richness will be very unenviable indeed. The phenomenon in fact has a delusive effect. Besides not giving due consideration to the above circumstances, the bewilderment of many people at what are called enormous imports of silver in India is like that of a child which, because it can itself be satisfied with a small piece of bread, wonders at a big man eating up a whole loaf, though that loaf may be but a very "scanty subsistence" for the poor big man.

The little England can have £1 a head out of £30,000,000, the big India must have £200,000,000 to give this share per head to its population. Yet this 33s. 6d. per head in sixty-nine years appears to the bewildered Englishman something enormously larger than 30s. a head in twelve years they themselves have got, and that as a portion of the profits of trade—while India has it for sheer necessity, and at the highest price, as silver is its last destination, and paying that price by the actual produce of the country, not from any profits of trade, thereby diminishing to that extent its own means of subsistence.

Export of Bullion.

There is one more point to be borne in mind. How much did the East India Company first drain away from India, before it, as a matter of necessity, began to re-import bullion for its wants? What are the statistics of the imports and exports of bullion before 1801?

Where can we find an account of the fortunes which the Company's servants made, by foul means or fair, in spite of their masters' orders, and which they may have taken over to their country in various ways independently of the custom-house, with themselves in their own boxes?

Sir John Shore (afterwards Lord Teynmouth) says in his minute of 1787 (Report of Select Committee of 1812, appendix, page 183) in reference to Bengal:—

"137. The exports of specie from the country for the last twenty-five years have been great, and particularly during the last ten of that period. It is well understood, although the remittances to China are by the Government, provided by bills, that specie to a large amount has been exported to answer them. . . . Silver bullion is also remitted by individuals to Europe; the amount cannot be calculated, but must, since the Company's accession to the Dewany, have been very considerable.

"140. Upon the whole, I have no hesitation in concluding that, since the Company's acquisition of the Dewany, the current specie of the country has been *greatly diminished* in quantity; that the old channels of importation by which the drains were formerly replenished are now in a great measure closed; and that the necessity of supplying China, Madras, and Bombay with money, as well as the exportation of it by the Europeans to England, will continue still further to exhaust the country of its silver. . . .

"142. It is obvious to any observation that the specie of the country is much diminished; and I consider this as a radical evil."

In a quotation I have given before, Lord Cornwallis mentions "the great diminution of the current specie," in pointing out the result of the drain.

Such was the exhaustion of British territory in India of

its specie before it began to re-import. The East India Company and their servants carried away *via* China or direct to England, the former the surplus of revenue, the latter their savings and their bribes, in specie. The country was exhausted, and was compelled to re-import specie for its absolute wants, and it is from the time of such re-importations after exhaustion that we have the return of bullion from the year 1801, and which, after all, is only 34s. a head for all possible wants, commercial, social, religious, revenue, industrial, trade, railway and other public works, or any other, in a period of sixty-nine years. And having no specie left to pay for the heavy English drain, it began to pay in its produce and manufactures, diminishing thereby the share of its children year by year, and their capacity for production. Be it remembered also that this import of specie includes all imported for building railways, and which is a debt on the country to be repaid. This debt to the end of 1869 was some £82,000,000.

As far as I could, I have now placed before you a series of facts and figures directly bearing upon the question of the poverty of India. I now place before you a few further notes as to the moral effect which the chief causes of the poverty of India has produced on our British rulers.

NON-FULFILMENT OF SOLEMN PROMISES.

"We have not fulfilled our duty, or the promises and engagements which we have made," are the words of the highest Indian authority, His Grace the Duke of Argyll. The evil which is the cause of the excessive drain from India, and its consequent poverty, and which consists in the excessive employment of Europeans in every possible way, leads the British Government into the false and immoral position and policy of not fulfilling "their duty, or the promises and engagements made by them." I shall now illustrate this phase of the condition of the Natives in some of the various departments of the State. Here is a bold and solemn promise made forty years ago. Parliament enacted in 1833 (Chapter LXXXV, Section LXXXVII.)—"And be it enacted that no Native of the said territories, nor any natural-born subject of His Majesty resident therein, shall, by reason only of his religion, place of birth, descent, colour, or any of them, be disabled from holding any place, office, or employment under the said Company."

Macaulay on Employment of Native Indians.

At the enactment of this clause, Mr. Macaulay, on July 10, 1833, in defending the East India Company's Charter Bill on behalf of Government, said as follows—on this part of the Bill, in words worthy of an English gentleman :—

"There is, however, one part of the Bill on which, after what has recently passed elsewhere, I feel myself irresistibly impelled to say a few words. I allude to that wise, that benevolent, that noble clause which enacts that no native of our Indian Empire shall, by reason of his colour, his descent, or his religion, be incapable of holding office. At the risk of being called by that nickname which is regarded as the most opprobrious of all nicknames by men of selfish hearts and contracted minds—at the risk of being called a philosopher—I must say that, to the last day of my life, I shall be proud of having been one of those who assisted in the framing of the Bill which contains that clause. We are told that the time can never come when the natives of India can be admitted to high civil and military office. We are told that this is the condition on which we hold our power. We are told that we are bound to confer on our subjects—every benefit which they are capable of enjoying?—No. Which it is in our power to confer on them?—No. But which we can confer on them without hazard to our own dominion. Against that proposition I solemnly protest, as inconsistent alike with sound policy and sound morality.

"I am far, very far, from wishing to proceed hastily in this delicate matter. I feel that, for the good of India itself, the admission of Natives to high offices must be effected by slow degrees. But that when the fulness of time is come, when the interest of India requires the change, we ought to refuse to make that change lest we should endanger our own power—this is a doctrine which I cannot think of without indignation. Governments, like men, may buy existence too dear.

"*Propter vitam vivendi perdere causas* is a despicable policy either in individuals or in States. In the present case, such a policy would be not only despicable but absurd. The mere extent of empire is not necessarily an advantage. To many Governments it has been cumbersome, to some it has been fatal. It will be allowed by every statesman of our time that the prosperity of a community is made up of the prosperity of those who compose the community, and that it is the most childish ambition to covet dominion which adds to no man's comfort or security. To the great trading nation, to the great manufacturing nation, no progress which any portion of the human race can make in knowledge, in taste for the conveniences of life, or in the wealth by which those conveniences are produced, can be matter of indifference. It is scarcely possible to calculate the benefits which we might derive from the diffusion of European civilisation among the vast population of the East. It would be on the most selfish view of the case far better for us that the people of India were well-governed and independent of us, than ill-governed and subject to us—that they were ruled by their own kings, but wearing our broadcloth and working with our cutlery, than that they were performing their *salaams* to English collectors and English magistrates, but were too ignorant to value, or too poor to buy, English manufactures. To trade with civilised men is infinitely more profitable than to govern savages. That would, indeed, be a doting wisdom which, in order that India might remain a dependency, would make it a useless and costly dependency—which would keep a hundred millions of men from being our customers in order that they might continue to be our slaves. It was, as Bernier tells us, the practice of the miserable tyrants whom he found in India, when they dreaded the capacity and spirit of some distinguished subject, and yet could not venture to murder him, to administer to him a daily dose of the *pousta*—a preparation of opium, the effect of which was in a few months to destroy all the bodily and mental powers of the wretch who was drugged with it, and to turn him into a helpless idiot. That detestable artifice, more horrible than assassination itself, was worthy of those who employed it. It is no model for the English nation. We shall never consent to administer the *pousta* to a whole community, to stupify and paralyse a great people whom God has committed to our charge, for the wretched purpose of rendering them more amenable to our control. What is that power worth which is founded on vice, on ignorance, and on misery—which we can hold only by violating the most sacred duties which, as governors, we owe to the governed—which, as a people blessed with far more than an ordinary measure of political liberty, and of intellectual light, we owe to a race debased by three thousand years of despotism and priest-craft? We are free, we are civilised to little purpose, if we grudge to any portion of the human race an equal measure of freedom and civilisation. Are we to keep the people of India ignorant in order that we may keep them submissive? or do we think that we can give them knowledge without awaking ambition, or do we mean to awaken ambition, and to provide it with no legitimate vent? Who will answer any of these questions in the affirmative? Yet one of them must be answered in the affirmative by every person who maintains that we ought permanently to exclude the Natives from high office. I have no fears. The path of duty is plain before us; and it is also the path of wisdom, of national prosperity, of national honour.

"The destinies of our Indian Empire are covered with thick darkness. It is difficult to form any conjectures as to the fate reserved for a State which resembles no other in history, and which forms by itself a separate class of political phenomena; the laws which regulate its growth and its decay are still unknown to us. It may be that the public mind of India may expand under our system, till it has outgrown the system; that, by good government, we may educate our subjects into a capacity for better government, that, having become instructed in European knowledge, they may in some future age demand European institutions. Whether such a day will ever come I know not. But never will I attempt to avert or to retard it. Whenever it comes, it will be the proudest day in English History. To have found a great people sunk in the lowest depths of slavery and superstition, to have so ruled them as to have made them desirous and capable of all the privileges of citizens, would indeed be a title to glory all our own. The sceptre may pass away from us. Unforeseen accidents may derange our most profound schemes of policy. Victory may be inconstant to our arms. But there are triumphs which are followed by no reverses. There is an empire exempt from all natural causes of decay. Those triumphs are the pacific triumphs of reason over barbarism; that empire is the imperishable empire of our arts and our morals, our literature and our laws."

I should not add one word of any other speeches, though others also had spoken at the time, and with general approbation, of the sentiments expressed; I would only say, that had these pledges and policy been faithfully followed, now, after forty years, great blessing would have been the result both to England and India. Once more I appeal to the British to revive the memory of those noble sentiments, follow the "plain path of duty that is before you." That unfortunate plea—unfortunate both for England and India—of political danger was fully considered and deliberately cast aside by the statesmen who enacted "that wise, that benevolent, that noble clause," as unworthy of the British nation, and they as deliberately adopted the policy of plain duty and true glory.

In such language and with such noble declaration was this clause proclaimed to the world. I have made a copy of all the speeches delivered in Parliament on this subject since 1830; but as I cannot insert them all here, I content myself with one of the early ones which I have read to you, and the latest delivered by the highest Indian authority which I give further on.

Again, in 1858, our Gracious Majesty, in solemn, honest, and distinct terms, gave the following pledge in her gracious proclamation:—"We hold ourselves bound to the Natives of our Indian territories by the same obligations of duty which bind us to all our other subjects, and these obligations, by the blessing of Almighty God, we shall faithfully and conscientiously fulfil. It is our further will that, so far as may be, our subjects, of whatever race or creed, be freely and impartially admitted to offices in our service, the duties of which they may be qualified, by their education, ability, and integrity, duly to discharge." Such were the great solemn pledges given by the Queen and Parliament.

The Duke of Argyll's Promises.

We may now see what the present (1873) highest authority, His Grace the Secretary of State for India, says as to the due fulfilment of these pledges, when the East India Association were making efforts in respect of the admission of natives in the Covenanted Civil Service.

The following is the correspondence between the East India Association and Mr. Grant Duff in 1873, giving His

Grace's speech, and a brief account of the events from 1867 to 1873 :—

EAST INDIA ASSOCIATION,
20, *Great George Street, Westminster*,
London, September, 1873.

To M. E. GRANT DUFF, Esq., M.P.,
Under-Secretary of State for India, India Office.

SIR,—By the direction of the Council of the East India Association, I have to request you to submit this letter for the kind consideration of His Grace the Secretary of State for India.

On the 21st August, 1867, this Association applied to Sir Stafford Northcote, the then Secretary of State for India, asking that the competitive examination for a portion of the appointments to the Indian Civil Service should be held in India, under such rules and arrangements as he might think proper, and expressing an opinion that, after the selection had been made in India by the first Examination, it was essential that the selected candidates should be required to come to England to pass their further examinations with the selected candidates for this country.

Sir Stafford Northcote soon after introduced a clause in the Bill he submitted to Parliament, entitled "The Governor-General of India Bill."

The enactment of this Bill continued in abeyance, until, under the auspices of His Grace the present Secretary of State, it became law on the 25th March, 1870, as "East India (Laws and Regulations) Act." Moving the second reading of the Bill on the 11th March, 1869, His Grace, in commenting upon Clause 6, in a candid and generous manner made an unreserved acknowledgment of past failures of promises, non-fulfilment of duty, and held out hopes of the future complete fulfilment to an adequate extent, as follows :—

"I now come to a clause—the 6th—which is one of very great importance, involving some modification in our practice, and in the principles of our legislation as regards the Civil Service in India. Its object is to set free the hands of the Governor-General, under such restrictions and regulations as may be agreed to by the Government at home, to select, for the Covenanted Service of India, Natives of that country, although they may not have gone through the competitive examination in this country. It may be asked how far this provision is consistent with the measures adopted by Parliament for securing efficiency in that service; but there is a previous and, in my opinion, a much more important question which I trust will be considered—how far this provision is essential to enable us to perform our duties and fulfil our pledges and professions towards the people of India? . . .

"With regard, however, to the employment of Natives in the government of their country, in the Covenanted Service, formerly of the Company and now of the Crown, I must say that we have not fulfilled our duty, or the promises and engagements which we have made.

"In the Act of 1833 this declaration was solemnly put forth by the Parliament of England:—'And be it enacted that no Native of the said territories, nor any natural-born subject of His Majesty resident therein, shall, by reason only of his religion, place of birth, descent, colour, or any of them, be disabled from holding any place, office, or employment under the said Company.'

"Now, I well remember that in the debates in this House in 1853, when the renewal of the charter was under the consideration of Lord Aberdeen's Government, my late noble friend Lord Monteagle complained, and I think with great force, that, while professing to open every office of profit and employment under the Company or the Crown to the Natives of India, we practically excluded them by laying down regulations as to fitness which we knew Natives could never fulfil. If the only door of admission to the Civil Service of India is a competivive examination carried on in London, what chance or what possibility is there of Natives of India acquiring that fair share in the administration of their own country which their education and abilities would enable them to fulfil, and therefore entitle them to possess? I have always felt that the regulations laid down for the competitive examination rendered nugatory the declaration of the Act of 1833; and so strongly has this been felt of late years by the Government of India, that various suggestions have been made to remedy the evil. One of the very last—which, however, has not yet been finally sanctioned at home, and respecting which I must say there are serious doubts—has been suggested by Sir John Lawrence, who is now about to approach our shores, and who is certainly one of the most distinguished men who have ever wielded the destinies of our Indian Empire. The palliative which he proposes is that nine scholarships—nine scholarships for a government of upwards of 180,000,000 of people!—should be annually at the disposal of certain Natives, selected partly by competition, and partly with reference to their social rank and position, and that these nine scholars should be sent home with a salary of £200 a year each to compete with the whole force of the British population seeking admission through the competitive examinations. Now, in the first place, I would point out the utter inadequacy of the scheme to the ends of the case. To speak of nine scholarships distributed over the whole of India as any fulfilment of our pledges or obligations to the Natives would be a farce. I will not go into details of the scheme, as they are still under consideration; but I think it is by no means expedient to lay down as a principle that it is wholly useless to require Natives seeking employment in our Civil Service to see something of English society and manners. It is true that, in the new schools and colleges, they pass most distinguished examinations, and, as far as books can teach them, are familiar with the history and constitution of this country; but there are some offices with regard to which it would be a most important, if not an essential, qualification that the young men appointed to them should have seen something of the actual working of the English constitution, and should have been impressed by its working, as any one must be who resides for any time in this great political society. Under any new regulations which may be made under this clause, it will, therefore, be expedient to provide that Natives appointed to certain places shall have some personal knowledge of the working of English institutions. I would, however, by no means make this a general condition, for there are many places in the Covenanted Service of India for which Natives are perfectly competent, without the necessity of visiting this country; and I believe that by competitive examinations conducted at Calcutta, or even by pure selection, it will be quite possible for the Indian Government to secure able, excellent, and efficient administrators."

The clause thus introduced, in a manner worthy of an English generous-minded nobleman, and passed into law, is as follows:—

"6. Whereas it is expedient that additional facilities should be given for the employment of Natives of India, of proved merit and ability, in the Civil Service of Her Majesty in India, be it enacted that nothing in the 'Act for the Government of India,' twenty-one and twenty-two Victoria, chapter one hundred and six, or in the 'Act to confirm certain appointments in India, and to amend the law concerning the Civil Service there,' twenty-four and twenty-five Victoria, chapter fifty-four, or in any other Act of Parliament, or other law now in force in India, shall restrain the authorities in India, by whom appointments are or may be made to offices, places, and employments in the Civil Service of Her Majesty in India, from appointing any Native of India to any such office, place, or employment, although such Native shall not have been admitted to the said Civil Service of India in manner in section thirty-two of the first-mentioned Act provided, but subject to such rules as may be from time to time prescribed by the Governor-General in Council, and sanctioned by the Secretary of State in Council, with the concurrence of a majority of members present; and that, for the purpose of this Act, the words 'Natives of India' shall include any person born and domiciled within the dominions of Her Majesty in India, of parents habitually resident in India, and not established there for temporary purposes only; and that it shall be lawful for the Governor-General in Council to define and limit from time to time the qualification of Natives of India thus expressed; provided that every resolution made by him for such purpose shall be subject to the sanction of the Secretary of State in Council, and shall not have force until it has been laid for thirty days before both Houses of Parliament."

It is now more than three years since this clause has been passed, but the Council regret to find that no steps have apparently yet been taken by His Excellency the Viceroy to frame the rules required by it, so that the Natives may obtain the due fulfilment of the liberal promise made by His Grace.

The Natives complain that, had the enactment referred to the interests of the English community, no such long and unreasonable delay would have taken place, but effect would have been given to the Act as quickly as possible; and they further express a fear that this promise may also be a dead-letter.

The Council, however, fully hope that further loss of time will not be allowed to take place in promulgating the rules required by the Act. The Natives, after the noble and generous language used by His Grace, naturally expect that they will not be again doomed to disappointment, and most anxiously look forward to the promulgation of the rules—to give them, in some systematic manner, "that fair share in the administration of their own country which their education and abilities would enable them to fulfil, and therefore entitle them to possess," not only as a political justice, but also as a national necessity, for the advancement of the material and moral condition of the country.

I remain, Sir,

Your obedient Servant,

W. C. PALMER, Capt.

Acting Honorary Secretary of the East India Association.

INDIA OFFICE, LONDON,

10th October, 1873.

SIR,—I am directed by the Secretary of State for India in Council to acknowledge the receipt of your letter of the 2nd October, relative to the provisions of the 33rd Victoria cap. 3., section 6; and to inform you that the subject is understood to be under the consideration of the Government of India, the attention of which has been twice called to it.

2. The Duke of Argyll in Council will send a copy of your letter to the Government of India, and again request·the early attention of that authority to that subject.

I am, Sir,

Your obedient Servant,

(Sd.) M. E. GRANT DUFF.

The Acting Honorary Secretary, East India Association.

Such is the candid confession of non-performance of duty and non-fulfilment of solemn pledges for thirty-six years, and the renewed pledge to make amends for past failures and provide adequate admission for the future for a fair share in the administration of our own country. The inadequacy clearly shown by the ridicule of nine scholarships for 180,000,000 souls, and the proposal to adopt means "for the abolition of the monopoly of Europeans." When was this confession and this new pledge made? It was to pass the 6th clause of Act 33 Vic., cap. 3. The clause was passed on 25th March, 1870, one year after the above speech was made, and nearly three years after it was first proposed. Next March (1874) it will be four years since this clause has been passed. Twice did Sir C. Wingfield ask questions in the House of Commons, and no satisfactory reply was given. At last the East India Association addressed the letter which I have read to you to the India Office, and from the reply you have seen how slow our Indian authorities had been, so as to draw three reminders from the Secretary of State.

With regard to the remark in the letter as to the complaint of the Natives that, "had the enactment referred to the interests of the English community, no such long and unreasonable delay would have taken place," I need simply point to the fact of the manner in which the Coopers Hill College was proposed and carried out in spite of all difficulties.

Suspension of the Nine Scholarships.

Now about the scholarships to which His Grace alluded in his speech. These scholarships had nothing to do with the provision for affording facilities to Natives to enter the Covenanted Service. They were something for a quite different purpose. The following correspondence of the East India Association of 3rd March, 1870, with Mr. Grant Duff, gives briefly the real state of the case :—

East India Association,
20, *Great George Street*,
Westminster, S.W., *3rd March*, 1870.

Sir,—I am directed by the Council of the East India Association to request you to submit, for the kind consideration of His Grace the Duke of Argyll, the following resolutions passed at a large meeting of the Bombay Branch of the East India Association.

Resolutions.

That the Managing Committee, Bombay Branch, be requested to bring to the notice of the head body in London, the recent suspension of the Government of India scholarships, and at the same time to lay before it the following representations on the subject :—

1. That the Bombay Branch has learnt with great regret that the Government scholarships, lately established to enable Indian youths to proceed to England for educational purposes, are not to be awarded this year.

2. That the Bombay Branch are aware that the Right Hon. the Secretary of State for India considers these scholarships as quite an inadequate provision for a government of 180,000,000 souls, and they look forward with hopeful confidence to the day when His Grace will unfold before the British Legislature a measure suggested by his long experience and study of Indian affairs, elaborated and matured by the generous and large-minded sympathy and interest which he has always evinced towards the Natives of India, and worthy at once of his own high name and intellect, and those of the country which has entrusted him with his present high post.

3. That, while thus far from being unmindful of the good intentions which have most probably prompted the suspension of these scholarships, the Bombay Branch feel bound to submit that, even as a temporary and inadequate measure, these scholarships were calculated to do an amount of good which the preparation of a larger and more comprehensive scheme did not by any means in the meantime render it imperative to forego.

4. That the suddenness of the suspension of these scholarships has given it a sort of retrospective effect with regard to those youths who framed their course of study in the expectation of obtaining the benefits of the notifications issued by the several Indian Governments in respect of these scholarships, thus entailing great disappointment on particular individuals.

5. That the East India Association will have the kindness to carry the above representations to the Right Hon. the Secretary of State for India, in the manner it may deem most proper and effective.

In submitting these resolutions, the Council respectfully urge that the object of the proposer, the late lamented Sir H. Edwards, of this prayer for scholarships in the memorial presented the 21st August, 1867, to the late Secretary of State, Sir S. Northcote, was "to aid the Natives not merely to enable them to compete for the Civil Service, but to return in various professions to India, so that by degrees they might form an enlightened and unprejudiced class, exercising a great and beneficial influence on Native society, and constituting a link between the masses of the people and the rulers." It is evident that Lord Lawrence, the then Governor-General of India, also understood and declared the objects of these scholarships to be as above; for, in the resolution No. 360, the object is stated to be "of encouraging Natives of India to resort more freely to England for the purpose of perfecting their education, and of studying the various learned professions, or for the civil and other services in this country;" and also, in another part of the same resolution, it is declared to be "not only to afford to the students facilities for obtaining a University degree, and for passing the competitive examinations for admission into the Indian Civil Service, but also to enable them to pursue the study of Law, Medicine, or Civil Engineering, and otherwise prepare themselves for the exercise of a liberal profession."

The Council, therefore, venture to submit that, considering the important objects pointed out by Sir H. E. Edwards, it is very desirable that the scholarships be continued.

The Council are glad to find, from your speech in the House of Commons, that the question of these scholarships has not yet been settled, and they therefore trust that His Grace will accede to the request so urgently made in the above resolutions.

The Council have every reason to believe that the Natives of the other Presidencies also share similar feelings, and confidently leave the matter in the hands of His Grace.

I have the honour to be,
Your obedient Servant,
DADABHAI NAOROJI,
Hon. Secretary.

MOUNTSTUART E. GRANT DUFF, Esq., M.P.,
Under-Secretary of State for India.

INDIA OFFICE, *March* 18, 1870.

SIR,—I am directed by the Secretary of State for India in Council to acknowledge the receipt of your letter of the 3rd instant, on the subject of the Government of India scholarships.

In reply, I am instructed to inform you that the Secretary of State in Council has very fully considered the whole subject, and does not deem it expedient to proceed further with the scheme of scholarships.

You are aware that a Bill is now before Parliament which will enable the Government to give to the Natives of India more extensive and important employment in the public service.

I am, Sir, Your obedient Servant,

HERMAN MERIVALE.

It is now (1873) nearly four years, and this "employment" is still under consideration; but the scholarships which had nothing to do with this matter, after being proclaimed to the world in the *Indian Gazette*, and after a brief life of one year, are gone. I next examine how far the great pledges of 1833 and 1858 have been carried out in the uncovenanted and other services.

THE UNCOVENANTED SERVICE.

Sir S. Northcote, in his despatch of 8th February, 1868, wrote to the Indian Government:—"The Legislature has determined that the more important and responsible appointments in those provinces shall be administered exclusively by those who are now admitted to the public service solely by competition, but there is a large class of appointments in the regulation, as well as in the non-regulation provinces, some of them scarcely less honourable and lucrative than those reserved by law for the Covenanted Civil Service, to which the Natives of India have certainly a preferential claim, but which, as you seem to admit, have up to this time been too exclusively conferred upon Europeans. These persons, however competent, not having entered the service by the prescribed channel, can have no claim upon the patronage of the Government—none, at least, that ought to be allowed to override the inherent rights of the Natives of the country; and therefore, while all due consideration should be shown to well-deserving incumbents, both as regards their present position and their promotion, there can be no valid reason why the class of appointments which they now hold should not be filled, in future, by Natives of ability and high character." Now, is this done? I have not been able to get a complete return of the higher Uncovenanted Servants. I shall use what I have got. The Government of India, in their dispatch in the Financial Department, to the Secretary of State for India, No. 227, dated 4th October, 1870, gives two tables; the first headed—"Abstract of Appendix A referred to in the 6th paragraph of the above dispatch, being a statement of the number of offices in India which were filled in 1869 by Uncovenanted Servants, but *which might have been filled by Covenanted Servants or Military Officers*." Now, this list gives of such Uncovenanted Servants 1,302 Europeans and 221 Natives.

I am sorry I cannot get a return of the salaries of these 1,302 European Uncovenanted Servants; but, with regard to Natives, the second table of the same dispatch shows that out of these 221

Only 1	gets a	salary of Rs.	1,500 to 1,600	per month,
1	,,	,,	1,200 to 1,300	,,
1	,,	,,	1,100 to 1,200	,,
11	,,	,,	1,000 to 1,100	,,
5	,,	,,	800 to 900	,,
14	,,	,,	700 to 800	,,
47	,,	,,	600 to 700	,,
60	,,	,,	500 to 600	,,
125	,,	,,	400 to 500	,,
265				

"One Native Judge of the Bengal High Court at Rs.4,160-10-8 per mensem."

Out of the last 125 there must be about 44 which the Government of India did not think fit for the Covenanted Servants or Military Officers. And it must also be borne in mind that the 1,302 do not include all those Uncovenanted appointments which are filled by military officers already. If we can get a return of all Uncovenanted appointments from Rs.400 upwards, we shall then see how "the inherent right" possessors, the children of the soil, have fared, even in the Uncovenanted Service, before and since the dispatch.

If anything, the tendency and language of the Indian Government is such, in the very correspondence from which I have given the table, that even the small number of Natives may be squeezed out. All appointments that are worth anything are to pass to the Covenanted Servants and the military officers, and to the rest the Natives are welcome! Here and there, perhaps, a few better crumbs will be thrown to them. I sincerely hope I may prove a false prophet. An annual return is necessary to show whether Sir S. Northcote's dispatch has not been also one more dead-letter.

The Engineering Service.

When Coopers Hill Engineering College was in contemplation, some correspondence passed between me and His Grace the Secretary of State. In this I gave detailed particulars of the cases of Messrs. Daji Nilkunt, Lallubhoy Kheshowlal, Chambas Appa, Gungadhur Venaek, and Bomanji Sorabji. Now, the first four had duly qualified themselves, and were entitled to be promoted to the Engineering Department as far back as 1861, and the fifth in 1867, and yet they never got admission into the Engineering Department as far as I was then (1873) aware, though a large number of appointments had been made during the period. I said, in connection with this part of my letter, that such treatment and bitter disappointments produced much mischief, that the Public Works Department rules were a mere farce, etc., etc., and requested enquiry. This His Grace promised to do, but I do not know what has been done. But Mr. Grant Duff, in his speech on 3rd March, 1871, in Parliament, said: "Then we are told that we were asking too much money, that the Engineering College would be merely a college for the rich. We replied that we asked £150 a year for three years, in return for which we gave to those young men who passed through the college £420 in their very first year of service. It is said, too, that we are excluding the Natives from competing. So far from this being the case, young Englishmen are obliged to pay for being educated for the Public Works Department, while young Natives of India are actually paid for allowing themselves to be educated for that service, and the scholarships available for that purpose are not taken up." Now, somehow or other, it did not please Mr. G. Duff to tell the whole truth. He omitted the most essential part of the whole story. He did not tell the honourable members that what he said about the encouragement with regard to the English youths, only a minute before, did not at all exist with regard to the Natives. He did not tell that, in return for any Natives who duly qualify themselves in India, we do not give £420 in their very first year of service, or allow them fair and equal promotion with the English. The Native, on the contrary, has every possible discouragement thrown in his way, as will be seen subsequently. And, lastly, in his peroration, what great things done by the "we" of the India Office, Mr. Duff points out: "We claim to have done, first, an imperative duty to India in getting for her the trained engineering ability which she wanted." From whom, gentlemen? Not from her own children, but from *English* youths, as if India was simply a howling desert and had no people in it at all, or was peopled by mere savages and had no national wants. But after this clever way of benefitting India, Mr. Duff proceeds to point out what the "we" have done for England: "We have created a new profession. We have widened the area of competition. We have offered a first-rate education cheaper than a third-rate education can now be got. We have done service even to those institutions which growl most at us. . . . . We have done service to practical men. . . . . Lastly, we have done good service to English scientific education." It would appear as if India and Indians existed only to give England the above advantages. Now, here is His Grace giving the first intimation of his intention for establishing a college on 28th July, 1870, before the House of Lords. And on what ground does he recommend it? Among others, the following:—"It would afford an opening to young men in THIS country, which they would, he thought, be anxious to seize, because it would enable them to secure a very considerable position almost immediately on their arrival in India, where they would start with a salary of about £400 a year, and rise in their profession by selection and ability. They would be entirely at the disposal of the Governor-General of India, and they would have the prospect of retiring with a pension larger than in former times." It would appear that while saying this, His Grace altogether forgets that, besides these "anxious" young gentlemen of England, there were India's own children also, who had the first claim to be provided for in their own country, if India's good were the real policy of England; and that there were solemn pledges to be fulfilled, and the national wants of India to be considered. Why did it not occur to him that similar provision should be made for the Natives?

The case of the five Natives referred to before is enough

to show how the code and rules were a mere farce. But this is not all. The following will show how even when a positive pledge for one appointment was given in Bombay, in addition to the rules of the code already referred to—how even that was trifled with, and how only under strong protest of the Principal of the College and the Director of Public Instruction that it is restored this year (1873). In 1869, Sir Seymour Fitzgerald, at the Convocation, exhorted the students to emulate their forefathers in their engineering skill, etc. I immediately complained, in a letter to the *Times of India*, of the uselessness of such exhortations, when every care was taken that the Natives shall *not* get into the service. Soon after, it was some consolation to find a little encouragement held out, and the first Licentiate of Engineering every year was guaranteed an Assistant Engineership, and the first year Government became liberal and gave three instead of one. But the fates again pursue us, and that guarantee of *one* Assistant Engineership soon virtually vanished. Let the authorities themselves speak on this subject.

In the report of 1869-70, the Director of Public Instruction said (page 65)—"In the University Examination three candidates passed the examination for the degree of L. C. E. The best of these received the appointment in the Engineering Branch of the Public Works Department, which Government guarantees yearly. Eight such appointments are guaranteed to the Thomason College at Roorkee, where the first Department on 1st April, 1870, contained 31 students, while the University Department of the Poona College contained 38 on the same date. But the Poona College has no cause to complain of want of encouragement, as Government has since been pleased to appoint the remaining two Licentiates also to be Assistant Engineers. All the graduates of the year have thus been admitted to a high position in the public service, and I hope that they will justify the liberality of Government." So far so good. But the effort of liberality soon passed off; and we have a different tale the very next year, which is the very second year after the guarantee.

The Principal of the Poona College says (Report 1870-71, para. 8, Public Instruction Report, page 365)—"The three students who obtained the degree of L. C. E. in 1869 have all been provided with appointments by Government. Up to the present, however, the first student at the L. C. E.

examination in 1870 has not been appointed, though it is now more than six months since he passed. This delay on the part of the Public Works Department in conferring an appointment guaranteed by Government, will, I fear, affect injuriously our next year's attendance."

Upon this the Director of Public Instruction says: "In 1870 two students of the University class passed the examination for the degree of Licentiate, and eight passed the first examination in Civil Engineering. The great attraction to the University department of the College is the appointment in the Engineering branch of the Public Works Department, guaranteed by Government yearly to the student who passed the L. C. E. examination with highest marks. This guarantee has failed on this occasion" (the usual fate of everything promised to Natives), "as neither of the Licentiates of 1870 has yet received an appointment. For whatever reason the Public Works Department delays to fulfil its engagement, it is much to be regretted that any doubt should be thrown on the stability of the Government's support."

Such is the struggle for the guarantee of *one* appointment —I repeat, *one single appointment*—to the Natives of the Bombay Presidency, and the following is the way in which Government gets out of its guarantee, and replies to the just complaint for the precious great boon: "The complaint made in para. 657, the Report for 1870-71, that Government had withdrawn the Engineering appointment promised to the graduate in C. E. who shall pass with the highest marks, appears to be without sufficient foundation. All that Government has done is to limit the bestowal of this appointment to those who pass in the first class, while three appointments in the upper subordinate establishments (of the Public Works Department) are reserved for those who pass the final examination of the College. This would seem at present sufficient encouragement to the pupils of the institution, and the confinement of the highest prize to those who pass in the first class will probably act as a stimulus to increased exertion on the part of candidates for degrees."

We may now see what the Principal of the College says on this. (Extract from Report of Principal of Poona Engineering College, 1871-72, Director of Public Instruction's Report, page 500.) The Principal says: "Government have, however, I regret to say, during the past year withdrawn the guarantee of one appointment annually to the first student in order of merit at the L.C.E. examination, and have ordered that in future, to gain the single appointment, *a first-class degree* is to be considered necessary. This condition practically removes the guarantee altogether; for, with the present high standard laid down for the University test, it will not be possible for a student to obtain 66⅔ per cent. more frequently than once perhaps in five or six years. I have proposed that 50 per cent., which is the standard for a first-class B.A., be also adopted as the standard for the first-class degree in Civil Engineering. . . . The offer of an appointment to the student who obtains a first-class degree only, is, as I have already said, equivalent to a withdrawal of the guarantee altogether. The University calendar shows that a first-class at the B.A. examination has only been gained by 11 students out of 129 who have been admitted to the degree, and I do not suppose that any larger proportion will obtain a first-class at the Engineering examination. In what condition, then, do the graduates in Civil Engineering at present stand? One man, Abraham Samuel Nagarkar, who passed the L.C.E. examination in 1870, was offered *a third grade overseership* at Rs. 60 per mensem—a post which he could have obtained by simply passing successfully the final examination of the second department of the College. The case of another Licentiate, Mr. Narayen Babaji Joshi, is a still harder one. This youth passed the final examination of the second department of this College (taking second place) in October, 1867. He subsequently served as an overseer in the Public Works Department for two years, during which time he conducted himself to the entire satisfaction of his superiors. He resigned his appointment, and joined the University class in this College in November, 1869; and now that he has obtained the University degree, for which he has sacrificed a permanent appointment, he is without any employment, and is obliged to hold a post in the College on Rs. 50 per mensem—a much lower salary than he had when he was an overseer in the Public Works Department two and a half years ago. . . . But *the Engineering graduates have absolutely no future* to look forward to, and it cannot be expected that candidates will be found to go up for the University degree if there be absolutely no likelihood of subsequent employment. At present almost all the engineering employment in the country is in the hands of Government. The work of the old Railway Companies in this Presidency is completed, and the new railways are being undertaken under Government supervision. Except in the Presidency towns, there is little scope for private engineering enterprise, and if Government does not come to the assistance of the College and its University graduates, the University degree will, three or four years hence, be entirely unsought for, and the University department of the College will be numbered among the things of the past." I understand from Mr. Nowroji Furdoonji's evidence that Government has yielded, and re-guaranteed one appointment as before. Such is the story of the grand guarantee of one appointment in our Presidency. Now with regard to promotions.

In 1847, after a regular course of three years under Professor Pole, nine Natives passed a severe examination, and were admitted into the Public Works Department, but, to their great disappointment, not in the Engineering department. The little batch gradually dispersed—some leaving the service, seeing poor prospects before them. After a long eleven years, three of them had the good fortune of being admitted in the Engineering department in 1858, but one only now continues in the service. What is Mr. Kahandas's position later on? In the list of 1st October, 1868, I find him an Executive Engineer of the third class, while the following is the position of others in the same list, for reasons I do not know:—Three Executive Engineers of the 2nd Grade whose date of appointment in the Department is 1859, and of one in 1860. Of the five Executive Engineers of the 3rd Grade above Mr. Kahandas, the date of appointment of three is 1860, of one is 1862, and of another 1864. How Mr. Kahandas is placed at present relatively with others I have not yet ascertained. Mr. Naservanji Chandabhoy, after all sorts of praises, is much less fortunate, and leaves the service, as he calls it, in disgust. Now we may see how our neighbours are faring.

Madras.

The following is the cry from Madras. In the Report on Public Instruction for the year 1870-71, at page 242, Captain Rogers, the Acting Principal of the Civil Engineering College, says: "In the case of Natives, it is evidently the difficulty of obtaining employment, after completing the course, which deters them from entering the institution." The Director of Public Instruction, Mr. E. B. Powell, says (page 21): "It is to be remarked with regret that, owing to the absence of encouragement, the first department exists rather in name than in reality. It is clearly most important that educated Natives of the country should be led to take up Civil Engineering as a profession; but in the present state of things, when almost all works are executed by Government, Hindus of the higher classes cannot be expected to study Civil Engineering without having a fair prospect of being employed in the superior grades of the Public Works Department."

ROORKEE ENGINEERING COLLEGE.

In its first institution in 1848, the Natives were not admitted in the upper subordinate class at all—till the year 1862. In the Engineering Department I work out from the College Calendar of 1871-72 the Natives passed and their present appointment, as follows:—

	Year.	Names of Natives passed.	Their present Appointments.
1.	1851	Ameerkhan	—
2.	1852	Huree Charan	—
3.	,,	Kanyalal	Exc. Engr. 2nd Grade.
4.	1853	Nilmoner Mitra	—
5.	1854	Azmutoollah	—
6.	1855	Rampursad	—
7.	,,	Madhosadan Chatterji	Asst. Engr. 1st Grade.
8.	1858	Soondarlal	—
9.	1859	Narandas	—
10.	,,	Ghasuram	—
11.	,,	Sheoprasad	—
12.	1860	Khetternath Chatterji	Asst. Engr. 1st Grade.
13.	1862	Isser Chandar Sircar	,, ,, ,,
14.	,,	Beharilal	,, ,, ,,
15.	1870	Rhadhilal	Engineer Apprentice.
16.	,,	Bujputroy	,, ,,
17.	1871	Bhajat Sing	—
18.	,,	Sher Nath	—

Out of the total number of 112 that passed from 1851 to 1870 there are 16 Natives, and seven only have appointments at present. Why the others have not I am not able to ascertain. About the first Bengalee that passed, the *Hindoo Patriot* says he was so ill-treated that he resigned Government service in disgust, and alludes to another having done the same. From the falling-off from the year 1862 to 1870, I infer that there was no encouragement to Natives. Out of the 96 Europeans passed during the same time, 10 only have "no present appointments" put after their name, and two are with their regiments. Again, Kanyalal, who passed in 1852, is an Executive Engineer of the 2nd Grade, while one European who passed a year after, two Europeans who passed two years after, and three Europeans who passed three years after, are Executive Engineers 1st Grade; and two passed two years after, one passed three years after, one passed five years after, and one passed six years after, are also Executive Engineers 2nd Grade; and these lucky persons have superseded some European seniors also. Madhosadan Chatterji, passed in 1855, is now an Assistant Engineer of the 1st Grade, while two Europeans passed a year after him are *Executive Engineers* of 1st Grade, one passed two years after him is in "Survey Department" (and I cannot say whether this is higher or not), one passed three years after is an Executive Engineer of the 2nd Grade; and of those passed four years after him, two are Executive Engineers of 3rd Grade, one Executive Engineer of 4th Grade, and one Deputy Conservator of Forests (I do not know whether this is higher); and two Assistant Engineers of the 1st Grade, *i.e.*, in the same footing with him; of those passed five years after, one is Executive Engineer of 3rd Grade, two Executive Engineers of 4th Grade, and one Assistant Engineer of 1st Grade; of those passed six years after, one is Executive Engineer 3rd Grade, and one Executive Engineer 4th Grade; of those passed seven years after, two are Executive Engineers 4th Grade, one Assistant Superintendent 1st Grade Revenue Survey, and one Assistant Engineer 1st Grade; of those passed eight years after, one is Executive Engineer 4th Grade, and one Assistant Superintendent 1st Grade Survey Department; of those passed nine years after, four are Executive Engineers of 4th Grade, one is Assistant Superintendent 1st Grade Survey Department, and two are Assistant Engineers 1st Grade; of those passed ten years after, one is Executive Engineer 4th Grade, one Deputy Assistant Superintendent (?) Revenue Survey, and one Assistant Engineer of 1st Grade; of those passed 11 years after, one is Assistant Engineer 1st Grade; of those passed 12 years after, one is Executive Engineer 4th Grade, one is Assistant Engineer 1st Grade, and one is Deputy Conservator of Forests. As to the Natives, the above-mentioned one passed in 1855, one passed in 1860, and two in 1862—are all only Assistant Engineers of the 1st Grade, so that the very few who have been fortunate enough to get appointments are all at a stand at the 1st Grade of Assistant Engineers, except one who is Executive Engineer of the 2nd Grade. What may be the reason of such unequal treatment? And yet Mr. Grant Duff coolly tells Parliament "that the scholarships available for that purpose are not taken up," as if these scholarships for two or three years were the end and aim of their life-career. The upper subordinate department was entirely closed to Natives till 1862; the lower subordinate was only open to them. Under such circumstances, is it any wonder that the Natives do not go in for the higher Engineering Department? I cannot do better than let the Principal of the College himself speak to show how he struggles to get a guarantee for the Natives which he thinks will not commit Government to more than one or two appointments annually, and what he thinks of the fitness of Natives and their first claims (Principal Lang's Report for 1870-71, College Calendar for 1871-72, page 269): "Nor can I hope to see many Natives join it, although I consider that they have perhaps the first claims upon the College, and should be more encouraged to enter the higher grades of the Public Works Department. . . . A sub-overseer as turned out of this College is in many particulars a more highly-trained subordinate, after his two years' curriculum, than the overseer who leaves after one session in the College; and I am by no means prepared to assent that he is not, on 35 rupees a month, quite as useful a man in most cases as the European overseer on Rs. 100. . . . But few, however, comparatively of the higher or wealthier families have furnished candidates for the superior grades of the Engineering profession. . . . That the Natives of this country under favourable conditions are capable of excellence both as architects and builders, the beauty and solidity of many of the historical monuments of the country fully testify; and that they could compete with European skill in the choice and composition of building materials, may be proved by comparing an old terrace-roof at Delhi or Lahore with an Allahabad gun-shed, or many a recent barrack."

After referring to the encouragement given to one Native, the Principal proceeds: "But I consider that yet more encouragement should be given. I do not think that the Natives have yet made sufficient way in the profession to feel confidence in themselves, or to command the confidence of the public. Such we may hope to see effected ere long, but the time has not yet come for State aid and encouragement to be withdrawn; and it is with this view that I have urged that, for the *present*, Government should guarantee appointments to all passed Native students in the Engineering classes, whether they stand amongst the first eight on the lists at the final examinations or not, especially as such a guarantee would commit them to but very few—one or two—appointments annually. When the guarantee did commit Government to a larger number of appointments it would be time to withdraw it; its object would have been gained, the stream would have set in in the required direction, and might be expected to flow on.

"18. Although this proposition has not yet received the approval of the Government of India, I hope that it may be found possible to sanction it, as such a guarantee, published in the calendar and circulars of the College, will be a thoroughly satisfactory assurance to a candidate or student that it rests only with himself to command an entrance into the Public Works Department."

Such is the struggle, and such are the reasons which Mr. Duff might have told Parliament why the scholarships were not taken up.

Bengal.

Bengal appears to have been liberal about 1867-68, but, with the usual misfortune of Natives, seems to be falling off. The Administration Report of 1871-2 speaks in somewhat hopeful language, but we must wait and see. I give the extracts from the reports of the College since 1867-68 to explain what I mean (Educational Report of 1867-68, p. 522, Presidency College): "The six Licentiates of 1867-68 have received appointments in the grade of Assistant Engineers in the Public Works Department on probation." I understand all the six to be Natives.

(1868-69, page 437): "Three out of the four final students of the Session of 1867-68 went up to the University examination for a license, and two were passed—one in the first class, and one in the second." (Page 438): "The two Licentiates were awarded scholarships. . . . But after being attached for a short time to some of the works in progress in Calcutta, they applied for and obtained appointments as Engineer apprentices in the Public Works Department." Why they applied for the apprenticeship, and did not get the Assistant Engineership, I cannot ascertain. It looks as if this were the first step towards the cessation of former liberality, for we see afterwards as follows (Report 1869-70, page 302)—"There were eight students in the final class of the Session who went up to the University examination. One was a B.C.E., and he passed in the second class. The other seven went in for the license, and four passed in the second." Whether these have obtained appointments I cannot say; there is complete silence on this matter—as if this were the second step towards the discouragement. We do not read even of the apprenticeship now. (Report 1870-71, page 305): "Nine of the students in the third year class went up to the University examination for a license, and three were passed, one being placed in the first class, and two in the second." I could not find out whether appointments were given to these—the report is again silent. The following is the hopeful, but unfortunately not very clear, language of His Honour the Lieutenant-Governor (Bengal Administration Report, 1871-72, page 237): "Students who obtain a Licentiate's certificate are, after a short probation, eligible for the grade of Assistant Engineer." Now, what this expression "eligible" means, it is difficult to say. Were not the five men of Bombay, about whom I have already spoken, eligible to be Assistant Engineers? And there they were with the precious eligibility, and that only, in their possession for years, and I do not know whether this eligibility of some of the previous Bengal successful Licentiates has ripened into appointment.

"The several branches of the Public Works Department have hitherto been able to provide employment for all, or nearly all, the students who pass the several Civil Engineering examinations, and adopt Engineering as a profession." The word "nearly" is again a very suspicious one. That the subordinates may be all employed is a necessity—for Europeans cannot be got for inferior work, but if the word "nearly" is applied to the Licentiates, then we have the same story as in the other Presidencies. In 1872, seven have passed the Licentiate and one the degree of Bachelor.

It would be very interesting and gratifying to know whether these eight have obtained appointments as Assistant Engineers, or will get them. Altogether, I think some forty-five passed the Licentiate since 1861—a return of how these men have fared in their appointments and promotion will be a welcome one. The following sentence is an encouraging one, and makes me think that Bengal has not been so unjust as the other Presidencies:—"Some Bengalees who graduated in the Civil Engineering College have already obtained lucrative and responsible posts in the Engineering Departments of Government, and a few years' experience will show whether Bengalees are, or are not, unsuited for, and whether the best Bengalee students will continue to keep aloof from, the profession of Civil Engineering." Are these appointments like those of the passed Natives of Roorkee, to a certain point and no further ; or have the Natives fared, and will they fare, equally with the Europeans in their promotion ? The only pity is that the word "some" commences this sentence instead of *all*, unless it means all who have graduated, or who liked to enter Government service. We shall have not only to know whether the Bengalee is or is not unsuited, etc., but also what treatment he receives at the hands of the P. W. Department in his future career. Unless both these matters are taken together, the conclusion about suitability or otherwise will be simply absurd and worthless.

THE NATIVE MEDICAL SERVICE.

In this also the Natives are put at a great disadvantage in having to go to England to find admission. But apart from this, the treatment in India is as follows. I give below a statement of the difference between the treatment of the European and Native divisions.

SUB-ASSISTANT SURGEONS.

SUB-ASSISTANT SURGEONS.	APOTHECARY CLASS.
(1) *Preliminary Education*—	(1) *Preliminary Education*—
Individuals, Natives of Bombay, who ultimately wish to become sub-assistant surgeons, must enter the Medical College by first producing the University certificate of having passed the Matriculation or First Examina-	The members of the apothecary class enter the service as hospital apprentices, and candidates who enter the service pass a most elementary examination, consisting of reading an ordinary school-book, some knowledge of

tion in Arts. When admitted, they have to pay an entrance fee of Rs. 25, and a monthly fee of Rs. 5 throughout the College course of five years.

explaining sentences, dictation, and arithmetic as far as Rule of Three and fractions. A candicate satisfying the examiners on these points is admitted into the Medical Service as a hospital apprentice, and draws from Rs. 16 to Rs. 20 a month, with an additional allowance of Rs. 10 for rations or batta. It will thus be seen that the members of the apothecary class enter the Medical Service in the first place, and this gives them the privilege of acquiring a *free* medical education at the Medical College, that is, *without any cost*, and while in the receipt of Government pay.

COURSE OF STUDY.

(2) A *full* and *thorough* college course on the following subjects:—Anatomy, physiology, chemistry, materia medica, comparative anatomy, pharmacy, medicine, surgery, medical jurisprudence, midwifery, opthalmic surgery, hygiene, practical chemistry, practical toxicology, dissections, hospital practice, and surgical operations. This course extends over *five* long years—in so thorough and complete a manner as to be equal, and in some cases superior to the College courses given in Great Britain. These constitute the *students' classes*. They are composed of students from the Hindoo, Parsee, Mussalman, and Portuguese communities.

(2) Hospital apprentices, after enlisting into the Medical Service, serve at some regimental hospital for two years, during which time they are transferred to Sir Jamsetji Jijibhoy Hospital, and, whilst serving there as medical apprentices, draw Government pay; they are also admitted into the College as medical apprentices to acquire medical knowledge. These apprentices then are made to attend the same lectures which are given to the students proper to whose classes they are attached, but the standard of their acquirements and final examinations is altogether different; it is greatly inferior to that of the students proper. The apprentices are called upon to attend the College for *three* years only.

(3) At the end of three years the students proper have to pass what is called the First L. M. Examination at the University of Bombay. At the end of the fifth year, the second or final L. M. Examination has to be passed, and, if successful, the students receive the degree of L. M. Before the Bombay University came into existence there were

(3) At the end of the three years they are examined by the College Professors in the College itself, and if they pass *their* standard of examination, they are made "passed hospital apprentices." They now leave the College to serve again at some regimental hospital and draw Rs. 50 a month.

N.B.—In the last two paras. it

two corresponding examinations, then called A and B Examinations, and at the end of five years' course the successful students received the diplomas and were called G. G. M. C. It is from these successful students that the sub-assistant surgeons were made, but within the last two years they are also made (very unjustly) from the apothecary and hospital assistant classes, as will be seen further on, on very different and comparatively trifling examinations.

(4) There are three classes of sub-assistant surgeons, as under:—

	Pay.	Allowance.	Total.
3rd Class Sub-Assistant Surgeon during the first 7 years' service .	Rs. 100	Rs. 100	Rs. 200
2nd Class Sub-Assistant Surgeon between 7 and 14 years' service	,, 150	,, 150	,, 300
1st Class Sub-Assistant Surgeon after 14 years' service till the end of his service	,, 200	,, 150	,, 350

(5) A sub-assistant surgeon cannot become an honorary assistant surgeon. During the course of the last 23 years, during which the class of sub-assistant surgeons is in existence, no

is stated that the apprentices attend the same class-lectures for three years as the students proper. This arrangement is adopted in the College as the Professors cannot give separate course to the students and to the apprentices. But the amount of knowledge required at the final examination of the apprentices at the end of three years is much smaller than the knowledge required at the final examination of the students proper at the end of five years.

(4) The "passed hospital apprentices" then go on with their regimental duties, and are promoted in the following order, till they reach the grade of senior apothecary:—

	Rs.
Passed Hospital Apprentice	50
Assistant Apothecary under 5 years	75
Assistant Apothecary after 5 years	100
Apothecary under 5 years .	150
Apothecary after 5 years .	200
Senior Apothecary	400

Education of the Apothecaries.

Soon after the opening of the G. M. College, Government ordered that the members of the apothecary class should receive medical education in the College. They then attended the same lectures as are given to the students' classes for *three* years, at the end of which period they are examined. The standard of the examination is the same easy one which is now adopted for the apprentices, also at the end of three years' course. These examinations are taken at the College, not by the Bombay University.

(5) The members of the apothecary class can be made honorary assistant surgeons. An honorary assistant surgeon, or an assistant apothecary, or apothecary, draws Rs. 450 a month

medical charge ever given to him has brought him more pay than Rs. 350 a month.

if placed in temporary medical charge of a Native regiment.

(6) No provision of this sort for sub-assistant surgeon.

(6) When an honorary assistant surgeon, or an apothecary, or an assistant apothecary, is allowed to retain medical charge of a Native corps for upwards of five years, his salary is increased to Rs. 600 a month.

(7) The following is the Financial Resolution No. 2,295 of April, 1867:—

"Governor-General of India in Council is pleased to lay down the following revised scale of consolidated salaries for uncovenanted medical officers, other than sub-assistant surgeons, when in medical charge of civil stations." From this it is clear that sub-assistant surgeons are particularly debarred from receiving the advantages of this Financial Resolution; they cannot become uncovenanted medical officers.

(7) Honorary assistant surgeons and other members of the apothecary class, when employed in independent medical charge of civil stations, will receive pay according to the scale laid down in Financial Department's Notification No. 2,295, dated the 25th April, 1867, namely—

	Rs.
Under 5 years' service in independent civil charge	350
From 5 to 10 years	450
From 10 to 15 years	550
Above 15 years	700

(8) The following two sub-assistant surgeons hold medical charge of the stations opposite their names, with their pay:—

	Rs.
Burjorjee Ardesir, Savuntvaree	350
Abdool Rahim Hakim, Bassadore	200

These are the only two sub-assistant surgeons who hold charge of civil stations. There are now 34 sub-assistant surgeons on the Bombay Medical Establishment; not one of them receives more than Rs. 350 a month; 34 sub-assistant surgeons receive pay as follows:—

		Monthly Rs.
8 Sub-Assistants	each	350
9 ,,	,,	300
12 ,,	,,	200
5 ,,	,,	100

(8) The following apothecaries are in medical charge of the stations placed opposite to their names, with their pay:—

	Rs.
B. Burn, Nassick	700
A. Pollard, Dapoolee	450
D. Munday, Vingorla	350
E. H. Cook, Shewan	350
J. Leahy, Sukkur	450
L. George, Gogo	480
J. Sinclair, Kolapore	450
J. Anderson, House-Surgeon to J. J. Hospital	450
W. Conway, Sada Political Agency	350
W. Waite, Khandeish Bheel Corps	450
T. MacGuire, Honorary Assistant Surgeon	450

And there are others also, but they are omitted here, as their salaries cannot be made out just now.

Rank or Position.

(9) The rank of sub-assistant surgeons is that of "*Native com-*

(9) Apothecaries generally are *warrant medical officers* (Rule 8 of

missioned officers of the army," whose designations and pay are as follows:—

	Monthly.
Subadar	Rs. 100
Jemadar	,, 35
Havildar	,, 16

Sub-assistant surgeons must remain sub-assistant surgeons all their lifetime, with such low rank as Native commissioned officers, whose education is next to nothing. It is also understood that when in civil employ (which is not often the case) the sub-assistant surgeons hold the relative ranks of mamlatdars, deputy collectors, and subordinate judges. Their relative ranks were mentioned in the first set of rules published some 24 years ago. They are omitted in the rules of "Sub-Assistant Surgeons and Charitable Dispensaries," published by Government under date 25th March, 1861. Rule 8 says: "In official intercourse it is the wish of Government that sub-assistant surgeons should be treated with the same degree of respect which is paid to Native commissioned officers of the army, etc." What this "etc." means I do not know.

1st July, 1868)—5 apothecaries now hold the rank of *honorary assistant surgeon*, or that of lieutenant; junior assistant apothecaries can reach the rank of sub-assistant surgeons by a College study of two years, and the same privilege is allowed to hospital assistants. This is being done within the last two years. Now, contrast the rules for the sub-assistant surgeons with those of the apothecary class, so very different and favourable in every respect for the favoured class.

These rules can be seen in the supplement to the *Indian Medical Gazette* of 1st July, 1868. They are too long for insertion here.

PROMOTION.

SUB-ASSISTANT SURGEONS.

(10) For the students who form the College classes proper.

For the graduates of the Grant Medical College there was first an entrance examination in the College. Then the A examination (medical) at the end of three years' College course, and a final examination at the end of five years' course. After the opening of the Bombay University the Entrance Examination is the present Matriculation Examination. Then, at the end of the third year, there is the First L. M. Examination taken at the

ASSISTANT APOTHECARIES AND APOTHECARIES.

(10) The only examinations which the members of the apothecary class are required to undergo are two—namely, one (of English knowledge) on the apprentices entering the Medi cal Service, that is, the same as mentioned in par. 1 under the head of "Preliminary Education;" the second is the medical examination, which is taken at the end of three years' College course, as mentioned in par. 3 and N.B. There are no more examinations than these two, although the apothecary may

University, and at the end of the fifth year there is the Second L. M. Examination.

After this the student becomes a sub-assistant surgeon, and is admitted into the 3rd class. After seven years' service he is *again examined* in the College, and, if successful, is promoted to the 2nd class of sub-assistant surgeon. Then, at the end of 14 years' service, he is *examined again*, and, if successful, is promoted to the 1st class of sub-assistant surgeon. After this there is no promotion till the sub-assistant surgeon is either pensioned or dies.

(11) Thus for the graduates or licentiates becoming sub-assistant surgeons, and during 30 years' service, there are *five* examinations—one Entrance, and four Medical, viz. :—

1st.—The First Entrance or the Matriculation Examination on entering the College.

2nd.—First L. M. Examination.

3rd.—Second L. M. Examination.

Then, after joining the Medical Service as sub-assistant surgeon—

4th.—First promotion examination at the end of 7 years' service.

5th.—Second promotion examination at the end of 14 years' service.

N.B.—The last two examinations are taken with a view to find out whether the sub-assistant surgeon has kept up to the advances made by the Medical Service.

serve the State for full 30 years, and although he may rise from the rank of apprentice (Rs. 16 pay) to that of uncovenanted medical officer on Rs. 700 monthly.

(11) During 30 years' service there are only two examinations—one in English, the entrance examination ; and the other the medical, at the end of three years' course—and the man may rise up to Rs. 700 per month. For further encouragement, Rule 46 of the Rules of 1868 provides for the further advancement of the junior members of the apothecary class, when well recommended, to rise to the position of sub-assistant surgeon, and allowed after 5 years' service to attend the Medical College for a period not exceeding two years, to qualify themselves for the grade of sub-assistant surgeon. Now, the rule does not state whether after these two years' study the person has to pass any such examination as the 2nd L. M. before he is appointed to the post. But I think it is merely a much simpler examination at the College—and not the University examination of 2nd L. M., or anything like it. N.B.—An assistant apothecary is promoted to the grade of full apothecary, and this again to that of senior apothecary, and the latter again to that of uncovenanted medical officer or honorary assistant surgeon *without any examination whatever*.

(12) Sub-assistant surgeons are pensioned agreeably to the rules of the Uncovenanted Service generally. Widows of this service are refused any pension. This subject is brought forward to show how well the apothecaries are cared for.

(12) Special provisions are made for the apothecary class for retiring, invalid, and wound pensions, as from paras. 22 to 26 of General Order No. 550 of 1868. Para. 27 provides pensions to the *widows* of the apothecary class.

What can be a better test of the comparative merits of these two classes of servants than the following, and how different is their treatment in spite of all professions of equality of all British subjects, without reference to colour or creed!—

GRADUATES AND L. MS.

During the last sixteen years the following graduates of G. M. College and licentiates of medicine of the University of Bombay have passed the examination of assistant surgeon in England, without a single failure, and they are all now in the Medical Service. Many more would prove their competence but for the unfair disadvantage at which they are placed in having to go to England at much expense and inconvenience.

G. G. M. C. I.—Rustomji Byramji, M.D. He passed in 1856; so he is now full surgeon. He is now serving at Jacobabad.

L. M. 2.—Atmaram S. Jayaker, assistant surgeon, passed in 1867, acting civil surgeon at Muscat.

L. M. 3.—A. J. Howell, assistant surgeon, passed in 1869.

L. M. 4.—Ruttonlal Girdhurlal, M.D., an assistant surgeon, passed in 1872. He is now serving in the Bengal Presidency. Although he was a candidate from Bombay, he preferred to go to the Bengal Presidency.

Besides all these—

G. G. M. C.—Dr. Muncherji Byramji Cohola, M.D., should be mentioned. This gentleman is now in the Bombay Medical Service as an uncovenanted medical officer and superinten-

APOTHECARIES.

This class of subordinate medical servants are in existence fully for half-a-century at least. Their number has always been large, and they are now 105 in all.

Not a single apothecary or assistant apothecary has up to this day ventured to appear for the examination of an assistant surgeon.

It is true that five apothecaries now hold the *honorary* rank of assistant surgeon, but this honorary rank is only given to them in India by the Indian Government in consequence of that strange order of the Government of India No. 550 of 1868.

Before the publication of this order the two most senior apothecaries used to be made honorary sub-assistant surgeons, beyond which grade they could not aspire. Nowadays the same senior apothecaries laugh at the idea of being called sub-assistant surgeons, as Government could accord them the higher rank of honorary assistant surgeon. The attainment of this rank does not involve the idea of any examination whatever. All promotions take place in this class of servants by length of service only.

dent of vaccination, Northern Division. He had gone to England to pass for an assistant surgeon, but unfortunately for him he had gone there soon after the Indian Mutiny, when all Natives of India were prohibited admission into the Indian Medical Service, and therefore he had to return disappointed to Bombay without the examination. He, however, passed a successful examination in England for M.D.

Even an honorary assistant surgeonship is not accorded to the sub-assistant surgeon, no matter what his merits.

This comparison shows how Natives, far better educated, are put very much inferior in rank, position, and emoluments to Europeans very much inferior in acquirements. The class of Natives from which alone some have gone over and successfully passed the examination in England is put below a class of Europeans from which not one has even ventured, as far as I can ascertain, to stand the ordeal of the same examination.

Telegraph and Forest Services.

In the Telegraph and Forest service it is the same; Natives are virtually debarred by being required to go to England to enter the higher departments, as far as I am aware. So here we are after forty years, as if the great enactment, of which great statesmen were proud, had never taken place, and all pledges, even such as that of Her most Gracious Majesty, were idle words.

Now I conclude my notes on the Poverty of India. As I told you before, these notes were written more than two to three years ago. It remains to be seen what modification should be made in these views by the light of the events of the subsequent years. For the present the inevitable conclusion is that there is a heavy and exhausting annual drain, both material and moral, from India caused by the excessive employment of Europeans; and to remedy this unnatural and serious evil, such employment needs to be limited to some reasonable extent, so that India may be able to retain to itself some portion of the profits of its trade, and, by thus increasing its capital and prosperity, may be strengthened and confirmed in its loyalty and gratitude to the British nation. I hoped to be able to speak more definitely on this point, but though it is now nearly three years since Sir D. Wedderburn moved for a return of the number, salaries, allowances, etc., of all Europeans and Natives employed in all the departments of the State drawing a salary of above Rs. 100, it is not forthcoming yet.

I expected that such a return would enable us to consider more carefully the extent and remedy of the serious evil I am complaining of. I would have closed my paper here, but as I have seen what appears to be a confirmation of the remedy I ask for, of the necessity of clipping European service, from a most unexpected quarter, I desire to say a few more words. The quarter I mean is the *Bombay Gazette*, or Mr. Maclean. If I understand him rightly, we do not appear to be far from each other, except what difference may arise from his interpretation of his own words. In his paper of 23rd March last, in commenting upon the causes of "the debased rupee," he considers home remittances to have some effect in that direction. And he proposes the remedy. I give his own words. He says—"To decrease these (home remittances) by clipping establishments, or rather re-framing them on an economical basis *by never employing other than Natives of this country*,[1] except where good policy and public convenience demand it, and if possible by establishing some check on the extravagant follies of the Secretary of State, should be the task of the Indian Government." This is just what I ask now, and what I asked before the Select Committee. Not only that the Native services will be economical in themselves, but that, even if they were as highly paid as the European services were at present, the economical result to India will be pure gain, as all such payments will continue and remain as the wealth and capital of the country. The only thing to be ascertained is, what Mr. Maclean's ideas are as to the extent of the employment of Europeans that "good policy and public convenience may demand."

The demoralising effect upon our rulers of this fundamental and serious evil shows itself in various ways, besides the most prominent one of the open non-performance of engage-

[1] The italics are mine.

ments, etc., which I have already pointed out. Take, for instance, the revenue legislation for the Presidency of Bombay. This legislation, instead of maintaining the height of English justice, in which it commenced in the earlier Regulations of 1827, and in which English prestige took its foundation, gradually degenerated into a legalised Asiatic despotism, till the new Revenue Jurisdiction Bill crowned the edifice, and by which the Collector, who was hitherto the "king," now becomes the emperor, and whose will generally will be the law of "the land."

The drain of India's wealth on the one hand, and the exigencies of the State expenditure increasing daily on the other, set all the ordinary laws of political economy and justice at naught, and lead the rulers to all sorts of ingenious and oppressive devices to make the two ends meet, and to descend more and more every day to the principles of Asiatic despotism, so contrary to English grain and genius. Owing to this one unnatural policy of the British rule of ignoring India's interests, and making it the drudge for the benefit of England, the whole rule moves in a wrong, unnatural, and suicidal groove.

As much as our rulers swerve from "the path of duty that is plain before them," so much do they depart from "the path of wisdom, of national prosperity and of national honour."

Nature's laws cannot be trifled with, and so long as they are immutable, every violation of them carries with it its own Nemesis as sure as night follows day.

MR. DADABHAI NAOROJI'S REPLY TO CRITICISMS ON "THE POVERTY OF INDIA."

I begin with Mr. Maclean. His remarks consist of violent declamation and criticism proper. With the former I have nothing to do.

He has very much misunderstood my papers. As a first instance:—when he asks me to deduct the exports of India (less the exports from Native States) from my estimate of the production of India, he does not see that my estimate is for the *total production* in India, and that what is exported is not to be deducted therefrom. Besides, my estimate is for British India, and is not affected in any way by the exports from the Native States.

As a second instance—he asks me to add £15,000,000 for Cotton manufactures. My estimate of production *includes* all *raw* Cotton of British India. The only thing to be added (which is already included in my estimate) is the additional value the raw Cotton acquires by the application of industry in its conversion into cloth. Coal and foreign stores that are used in the mills are paid for from and are therefore *included* in the production I have estimated. The only additional value is that of the labour employed. But even if we allowed the *whole* additional value acquired by raw cotton in its conversion into cloth, what will it be? Mr. Maclean's Guide to Bombay (1875) gives the number of the then working spindles (which is much later than the time of my notes) as about six lacs in the whole of the Bombay Presidency. Taking 5 ozs. per day per spindle, and 340 working days in the year, the total quantity of raw cotton consumed will be about 81,300 Candies, which, at Rs. 150 per Candy amounts to about £1,220,000. The price of cloth is generally about double the price of raw cotton, as I have ascertained from the details of two or three mills of Bombay, so that the whole addition caused by the mills to the value of raw cotton is only nearly 1¼ millions, say 1½ millions sterling to leave a wide margin. Then, again, there are about the time of my notes, yarn imports into India worth about £2,500,000 per annum. This, of course, is paid for from the production of the country. The value added to it is its conversion into cloth. Now the cost of weaving is about 25 per cent. of the value of yarn, so that the value thus added is about £600,000, say a million to include any contingency, making the total value to be added to the raw production of about £2,500,000. If deduction is made for coal and foreign stores, this amount will be much lessened. Again we know that hand spinning is much broken down, and there can be but a little quantity of cloth woven out of hand-spun yarn in India. Giving even £500,000 more for that industry, the outside total of addition to the raw produce would come to, as a high estimate, £3,000,000 instead of the £15,000,000 which Mr. Maclean asks me to add without giving a single figure for his data. Let him give any reasonable data, and I shall gladly modify my figures so far. As a third instance of his misunderstanding my paper—when he asks me to take £5,000,000 for gold and silver ornaments made in this country, he forgets that gold and silver are not produced in this country. All bullion is *imported* and is paid for from the produce of India. It, therefore, can add nothing to my estimate of production. The only addition is the industry employed on it to convert it into ornaments. This industry for the ordinary Native ornaments will be amply covered by taking on an average an eighth of the value of the metal, which will give about £625,000, or, say, three quarters of a million sterling, or even a million, while Mr. Maclean wants me to take £5,000,000.

As a fourth instance:—while Mr. Maclean tells me erroneously to add £15,000,000 and £5,000,000 when there should be hardly one fifth of these amounts, he does not see that I have actually allowed in my paper for all manufacturing industrial value to be added to that of raw produce as £17,000,000. And further for any omissions £30,000,000 more (*Supra* pp. 24-5).

These four instances, I think, would be enough to show the character of Mr. Maclean's criticism, and I pass over several other similar and other mistakes and mis-statements. I come to what is considered as his most pointed and most powerful argument, but which, in reality, is all moonshine. After contradicting flatly in my paper his assertion that the exports of the United States were in excess of imports, I had said that I had no reliable figures for the years after 1869. To this he replies: "Here they are," and he gives them as follows. I quote his own words.

"Mr. Dadabhai says he cannot get 'authentic figures' of American trade for a later year than 1869—Here they are for him:—

Imports.	Merchandise and bullion. £	Exports.	Merchandise and bullion. £
1869 . . .	87,627,917	1869 . . .	99,330,735
1870 . . .	97,779,351	1870 . . .	117,534,993
1871 . . .	112,552,770	1871 . . .	138,084,908
1872 . . .	117,250,899	1872 . . .	128,337,183
1873 . . .	132,709,295	1873 . . .	142,240,730
1874 . . .	119,172,249	1874 . . .	130,582,689
	£667,085,481		£756,111,238

"The excess of exports over imports for the six years is, therefore, 89 millions sterling, giving a yearly average of nearly 15 millions against only 11½ for India. The explanation of the deficit in imports in the case of the United States is, of course, similar to that which accounts for so much of the Indian deficit. The United States form a favourite field for investment of English Capital, the interest of which is paid by America in the form of exports of produce. Yet we never heard an American citizen complain that his country was being drained of its wealth for the benefit of foreigners. He is only anxious to borrow as much English Capital as he can, knowing that invested in reproductive works, it will repay him a hundred-fold the paltry rate of interest he has to send abroad."

To these remarks of Mr. Maclean I reply that he is as utterly wrong *now* as he was *before*. When he first made the mistake which I have pointed out in my paper there was some excuse for him—that he was misled by what was supposed to be a book made up from authoritative statements—but after I flatly contradicted him once, it was his duty to ascertain whether my contradiction was correct, and if so not to follow the same blind guide again. He did nothing of the kind, and his conduct now was quite inexcusable in dealing recklessly with such important matters. He has taken his figures from the "Statesman's Year Book." This book has made curious mistakes. It has *included* bullion in the figures for exports of "Merchandise," and *again* given bullion separately; and it has *not* converted the "*currency*" value of exports of "domestic produce" from the Atlantic ports, into *gold.* These two and some such other mistakes render this book's figures for the years taken by Mr. Maclean utterly wrong. I give the following illustration of these mistakes in the figures for the year ending 30th June, 1871.

The correct official[1] figures are:—

RE-EXPORTS.
(gold value.)

Merchandise.	Gold and Silver.	Total.
$14,421,270	$14,038,629	$28,459,899

EXPORTS.

Merchandise.		Specie and bullion. Gold Value.		Total.
from Atlantic ports.	from Pacific Ports.	from Atlantic Ports.	from Pacific Ports.	*Mixed Value.*
Currency Value.	Gold Value.			
$	$	$	$	$
464,300,771	13,712,624	76,187,027	8,318,229	562,518,651
equal to gold Value.		Total		equal to Gold Value.
$				$
414,826,393	13,712,624	84,505,256		513,044,273

TOTAL EXPORTS.

Domestic exports. (Gold Value.)	Re-exports. (Gold Value.)	Total. (Gold Value.)
$	$	$
513,044,273	28,459,899	541,504,172

Now instead of the above correct official figure of $541,504,172 as the *total* exports from the United States (including bullion), the Statesman's book makes "Merchandise" $590,978,550 and bullion $98,441,989, which I find to be made up as follows:—It takes from the official returns *total mixed* value of domestic Exports, $562,518,651 and then adds to it the *total* re-exports $28,459,899, and makes the addition of the two figures as the total for "Merchandise"—viz., $590,978,550. It will now be seen by a comparison of

[1] Monthly Reports on the Commerce and Navigation of the United States. By the Chief of the Bureau of Statistics for the year ending 30th June, 1871, page 386.

these figures with the official ones, that the "Currency" value of the domestic Exports from the Atlantic ports is *not* converted into gold, and that though in the two official totals of $562,518,651 and $28,459,899, bullion is *already included*, the total of these in the Statesman's book is given for "Merchandise" alone and a further statement is given for bullion as $98,441,989, made up nearly of $84,505,256 of domestic exports, and $14,038,629 of re-exports.

Mr. Maclean takes the total $590,978,550 of "Merchandise" (which *already includes* bullion) and bullion *over again*, $98,543,885, and makes the exports $689,420,539 or £138,084,908. It will thus be seen that Mr. Maclean's figure for 1871 contains bullion to the extent of $98,543,885, or £19,889,198 taken *twice*, and the "*currency*" value of domestic produce exported from the Atlantic ports, is *not* converted into gold value, making a further error of $49,474,378; or the total error in Mr. Maclean's figure for exports for 1871 alone is $98,543,885 + $49,474,378 = $148,018,263, or nearly £31,000,000 sterling @ 50d. per $.

I take 50d. per $ as the Parliamentary Returns for foreign States No. XII. has taken this rate of Exchange.

Mr. Maclean has given the figures for six years. I am not able to verify the figures for 1874, so I give a comparison of the *official correct* figures and Mr. Maclean's figures for the years ending June, 1869 to 1873.

The Statesman's book's wrong figures.

Years ending June.	Imports.		Exports.	
	Merchandise.	Bullion.	Merchandise.	Bullion.
	$	$	$	$
1869 . .	417,506,379	19,807,876	439,134,529	57,138,380
1870 . .	462,377,587	26,419,179	529,519,302	58,155,666
1871 . .	541,493,774	21,270,024	590,978,550	98,441,989
1872 . .	572,510,304	13,743,689	561,808,381	79,877,534
1873 . .	642,030,539	21,480,937	626,595,077	84,608,574
	2,635,918,583	102,721,705	2,748,035,839	378,222,143
Add . .	102,721,705		378,222,143	
Total . .	2,738,640,288	Imports.	3,126,257,982	Total Exports.
			2,738,640,288	Deduct Imports.
			387,617,694	Excess of *Exports*.

Official correct figures.[1]

Years ending June.	Imports. Including bullion, gold value.	Exports. Including bullion, gold value. Domestic.	Foreign.	Total.
	$	$	$	$
1869	437,314,255	318,082,663	25,173,414	
1870	462,377,587	420,500,275	30,427,159	
1871	541,493,708	512,802,267	28,459,899	
1872	640,338,706	501,285,371	22,769,749	
1873	663,617,147	578,938,985	28,149,511	
Total Imports .	2,745,141,403	2,331,609,561	134,979,732	2,466,589,293
Deduct Exports .	2,466,589,293			
Excess of *Imports*	278,552,110			

Mr. Maclean's total error for the five years 1869 to 1873 is therefore $278,552,110 + 387,617,694 = $666,169,804 = £138,785,000 @ 50d. per $; or $133,233,961 = £27,757,000 per annum.

In making, however, a comparison between the trade returns of India and the United States, there is one important matter to be considered, and which, when taken into account, as it ought to be, the Imports of the United States will be some 16 per cent. more than they are above shown to be. In India the exports are declared at the value at the ports of export. It is the same with the United States. The imports in India are declared at the "*wholesale cash price* less trade discount"[2] at the *Port of Import*, which means the value at the foreign port of export, plus freight, insurance, and other charges to the Indian port of import, and also plus 10 per cent. for profits. This is the principle on which the imports are declared in the Custom Houses in India, when the tariff value is not already fixed, or the market price not agreed upon by the importer and the Custom House. But in the case of the United States the declared value[3] of im-

[1] Monthly Reports on Commerce and Navigation of the United States. By Edward Young, Ph.D., Chief of the Bureau of Statistics for the year ending 30th June, 1874, page 177.

[2] Customs Act (6) of 1863, Section 180; also enquiry at the Customs House gave 10 per cent. to be added on the Importer's Invoice, or 20 per cent. on the Manufacturer's Invoice.

[3] Annual Report of Commerce and Navigation, 1873, says, page 3, "Import entries: sworn specie values at foreign places of export."

ports is only the value declared at the *foreign port* from which the Merchandise was *exported*, which means, *without* adding the cost of freight, insurance, and other charges and 10% profits. Now Mr. Edward Young, the "Chief of the Bureau of Statistics, Treasury Department" of the United States calculates 6%[1] as representing the freight from foreign ports to America.

This 6% for freight (without taking the further additional charges for insurance, commission, &c., into account) together with the 10% as calculated in India for declaration for Imports, makes it necessary to add 16% to the Imports of the United States before the actual excess of imports of the United States on the principle adopted in India can be ascertained and compared with that of India. In that case the actual excess of imports over exports in the United States will be $717,774,734 = £149,536,403[2] for the five years 1869 to 1873, or $143,554,947 = £29,907,280 per annum. Thus the correct result about the United States (on the principle of the Indian Custom House) is that, instead of there being an excess of *exports* of 15 millions sterling per annum, there is actually an excess of *imports* of *double* that amount, or nearly 30 millions sterling, thus making a difference between Mr. Maclean's and the correct figures of nearly 45 millions sterling per annum.

Now after all Mr. Maclean's recklessness what does he come to? He clearly admits my most important statements. He says:—

"It has been estimated that the amount of the annual earnings of Englishmen connected with India, which are thus transmitted home, cannot be less than £20,000,000,

[1] Monthly reports for the year ending 30th June, 1874, page 352: "The value of the imports of merchandise as presented in the first table being those at the ports of shipment, it will be proper to add thereto the amount of freights to the several ports of the United States. . . . It is believed that 6 per cent. on the total value of imports is an estimate of approximate accuracy."

[2]

Total imports..	$2,745,141,403
Add 16 p.c.....	439,222,624
	3,184,364,027
Deduct exports..	2,466,589,293

Excess of imports $717,774,734 at 50d. for 5 years = £149,536,403
Average per annum, $143,554,947 at 50d. = £29,907,280.

and we should be inclined to place it at a *very much higher figure*.[1]

Again :—" To decrease these (home remittances) by clipping establishments or, rather, reframing on an economical basis by *never employing other than Natives of this country*,[1] except when good policy and public convenience demand it, and if possible by establishing some check on the extravagant follies of the Secretary of State, should be the task of the Indian Government."

This is just what I say, that there is an enormous transfer of the wealth of this country to England, and the remedy is the employment of Natives only, beyond the exigencies of the British rule. But for this single circumstance, his remarks about the United States would apply to India perfectly well, *viz* :—" He (the American) is only anxious to borrow as much English capital as he can, knowing that invested in reproductive works it will repay him a hundred-fold the paltry rate of interest he has to send abroad."

The Indian will do *just the same*, but Mr. Maclean, blinded by his blind patriotism, does not see that this is just the difficulty; that while the American derives *the full benefit* of what he borrows, the Indian borrowing with one hand, has to give the money away to England with the other hand in these "home remittances" of Englishmen and "home charges," getting for himself the *burden* only of the debt. The very idea of comparing the circumstances and condition of the United States and India as being similar is simply absurd, for which another reason will be given further on. When Mr. Maclean has digested the figures I have given above there will be time enough to discuss whether even if the United States exported more than it imported for any particular period or periods, there will be anything at all similar to India's case. The fact is there is no such similarity except the interest paid on loans for reproductive works.

Next Mr. Shapoorjee says I have discarded official figures and substituted my own. I have done nothing of the kind. I have requested him to point out, but he has not done so. Mr. Shapoorjee says India is in the same boat with the United States. From the remarks I have already made, it may be seen that no weight can be given to this statement. In sup-

[1] Italics are mine.

port of his assertion he says the United States have foreign debts of about £1,625 millions. I requested him to show m any official or sufficiently reliable authority for these figures, and he shows me none.

From what I have already shown about the imperfections of even such a book as the "Statesman's Year Book," and the reckless reliance of Mr. Maclean upon it, I cannot but be careful in accepting such off-hand assertions of Mr. Shapoorjee. He is kind enough to advise me to adhere to official figures, and I need simply request him to do the same himself. Like Mr. Maclean, Mr. Shapoorjee also does not read my paper carefully; or he would not have said a word about America's public debt. He would have seen that I have excluded from my total of imports and exports those very years in which the United States contracted nearly the whole of its public debt (1863 to 1866). Again, Mr. Shapoorjee tells us that the Railways of the United States "could not have cost less than £20,000 a mile," while the Railway Manual for 1873-4, which Mr. Shapoorjee has kindly lent me, gives the average cost at $55,116, and Mr. Maclean's guide, the Statesman's Book, gives $50,000 a mile. This is about £10,000 to £11,000, or nearly half of Mr. Shapoorjee's figure; and thus nearly half of his "£850 millions if not more" of foreign Capital for Railways disappears. Now I give one more reason why Mr. Shapoorjee's figure of 1,625 millions sterling as the present foreign debts of the United States cannot be accepted. Mr. Edward Young, whom I have already mentioned, the highest official and authority on the treasury statistics of the United States, calculates and gives (in his official "Monthly Reports on the Commerce and Navigation of the United States for the year ending June 30th, 1874, page 352) his own personal and unofficial estimate of the "Aggregate foreign debts" of the United States. He says: "Although there were no national securities held abroad at the commencement of our late war, yet some of the bonds of the commonwealth of Pennsylvania, and, probably, of Massachusetts and other States, as well as railroad shares and securities, were owned in Europe. In the absence of accurate data on the subject, it is believed that fifty millions is an ample estimate for these *ante bellum* securities. With this addition, our aggregate foreign debt amounts to nearly TWELVE HUNDRED MILLION DOLLARS." Such is Mr. Young's estimate of the aggregate debts, "national, State, Municipal and Corporation—held in foreign countries"—*i.e.*, $1,200,000,000, when Mr. Shapoorjee asks us to take the figure nearly seven times larger—£1,625,000,000 equal to $7,800,000,000. Mr. Shapoorjee will, I trust, therefore excuse me for not accepting his figures and his conclusions based thereon. Again, Mr. Shapoorjee has been good enough to give me an extract from the *Westminster Review* of January, 1876. This extract gives (in 1875) the national production of the United Kingdom as £28 per head of population; of the United States as £25 per head, and of Russia as £7-10 per head, France £22, Austria £18, and Italy £15; while India hardly produces £2 a head. The simple fact, then, that the United States is the second richest country in the world, and its people have *all* their revenues and resources at *their own* command and for *their own* benefit only, is enough to shew that it is simply absurd and idle to compare it, in its circumstances and condition, as being in the same boat with the half-starving and ever-draining India. Mr. Shapoorjee's and Mr. Maclean's wonder that the Americans are not lachrymal is a great wonder in itself. When the Americans are subjected to a "home remittance" to a foreign country of some "very much higher figure" than twenty millions sterling a year, and "Home charges," and when a large number of foreigners engross all official and important positions to their own exclusion, causing thereby such heavy drain, *then* will be the proper time to make a comparison between America and India.

Mr. Shapoorjee's comparison with Russia and other European States is equally unreasonable. In spite of the inferior administration of Russia and the great Military expenditure, its national income is nearly four times as much as that of India, and that of the other European States is much larger still; and they have no "home remittances and charges" to remit, which India has to do from its wretched income of hardly £2 per head per annum.

Mr. Schrottky misunderstands me when he thinks that in the present discussion about the *Material Condition* of India I mention the necessity of the employment of Natives as anything more than the only remedy by which the capital of the country can be saved to itself to enable the agricultural as well as all other industries to get the necessary life-blood for their maintenance and progress. If it be possible that every European coming to India would make it his home, so that the item of the "home remittance and charges" is nearly eliminated, it would not matter at all, so far as the present question of the material prosperity of the country is concerned, whether the European or the Native is in office. The only remedy is that either the European must, like the Mahomadan conquerors, become Natives and *remain in* the country, or remain *out* of office beyond the exigency of the British rule, and for which British interests Britain must pay its share. If not, then it is idle to hope that India can rise in material prosperity, or be anything else but a wretched drudge for England's benefit. On the other hand a natural and just policy will make India with its teeming population one of the, if not the best customer for England and the best field for England's enterprise, and its agriculture will derive all the aid which Mr. Schrottky could desire in the goodness of his heart. Under the present unnatural policy England takes from India's scanty; under a natural and just policy, it will gain from India's *plenty*, and Manchester may have its free trade to its heart's utmost content.

To Mr. Trant I have to say only this, that mere assertions are not worth much and that all his political economy may be all right, in a Native-governed country, but when he takes the element of the "home remittances and charges" into account, he will not differ much from me.

In reply to Mr. Collet's remarks, I have to request him to take several elements into account which he appears to have forgotten.

1. To add 15 per cent.[1] profits to exports (during the

[1] For the following countries the profits, or excess of imports over exports, are as under, subject to modification for foreign debts or loans.

The United Kingdom . .	25 per cent.	(1858 to 1870)
Australia	15 ,,	(1858 to 1868)
British North America . .	29 ,,	(,, ,,)

[*Supra*, pp. 32-33.]

United States	18 per cent.	(1869 to 1873)

as under:—

Imports	$2,745,141,403
Add 6 per cent. freight (leaving other charges—commission insurance, etc., alone)	164,708,484
	$2,909,849,887
Deduct exports	2,466,589,293
Excess of imports, or profits—say 18 per cent. above exports .	$443,260,594

American War the percentage of profits on the exported produce was very much larger).

2. To deduct from imports nearly £140,000,000 of foreign debt (public and railway) incurred during the eighteen years he has taken.

3. To remember that the profits of opium as well as of all India's commerce are as much India's property and resources as the profits in coal, iron, and all other exported produce and manufactures of England are England's property and resources, though all such profits are derived from foreign nations, and that all the profits of opium and general commerce of India are included in my total production of India.

4. To remember that notwithstanding that opium and the profits of commerce are legitimate property and resources of India, that even after deducting these amounts, or that in addition to these amounts being sent away to England, there is the further amount of about £200,000,000 in principal alone gone to England during the thirty-eight years I have taken; and that Mr. Collet has not pointed out any mistake in my calculations.

For his eighteen years also, if he will take the items he has forgotten, his result will not differ from mine.

For 1858 to 1875 his figures for exports are		£910,995,000
Add 15 per cent. profits		136,649,250
Total proceeds of exports		1,047,644,250
His imports are	£764,310,000	
Deduct loans imported, about	140,000,000	
Actual commercial imports (including Government stores)		624,310,000
Excess of proceeds of exports		423,334,250
Deduct railway interest		51,133,987
Transfer to England from India's resources (excluding interest in railway loans)		372,200,263
This transfer is equal to the whole of the opium revenue	£108,156,107	
The whole of profits on exports	136,649,250	
And furthermore from India's resources	127,394,906	

Or nearly £130,000,000 in addition to the railway interest. The actual transfer is even larger than this, as will be seen further on.

Mark, then, during Mr. Collet's eighteen years *all* opium

revenue, *all* profits of commerce and guaranteed interest on railways are transferred to England, and £130,000,000 besides, making a total in principal alone of £424,000,000, or £372,000,000 excluding railway interest. Moreover it must be remembered that during the American War great profits were made, and this having to be added to the exports is so much more transferred to England.

Thus as Mr. Collet's figures are imperfect I need not trouble the meeting with any comments on the confusion into which he has fallen on account thereof. I have taken his own figures and shown what they lead to as the best way of pointing out his mistake. He seems to have also a somewhat confused notion of a balance sheet. But this is not the time or place for me to go into that matter.

Thanks to my critics, they have led me into a closer examination of some points, and I find the case of India worse than what I have already made out. I have to modify some of my figures[1] which I now do.

I have shown that the imports into India (*including* bullion) from 1835 to 1872 are £943,000,000. Now in making out a nation's balance sheet with foreign countries, the balance of profit should be taken between the price of exports at the port of export, and the price of imports, as *laid down* or costing at the port of import, and not the *market* price at the place of import, which includes the profit on the import obtained in the importing country itself.

I may illustrate thus. I laid out Rs. 1,000 in cotton and sent it to England. There it realised proceeds, say, Rs. 1,150. This may be remitted to me in silver, so that when the transaction is completed, I receive in my hands Rs. 1,150 in the place of Rs. 1,000 which I had first laid out, so that the country has added Rs. 150 thereby to its capital. But suppose instead of getting silver I imported, say, 10 bales of piece goods which laid down in Bombay for Rs. 1,150. The gain to the country so far, is the same in both cases—an addition of Rs. 150. But any gain to me *after* that, in the sale of these piece goods in India itself, is *no* gain to India. Suppose I sold these goods for Rs. 1,300. That simply means that I had these goods and another person had Rs. 1,300, and we simply exchanged. The country has no addition

[1] (*Supra*, p. 33.)

made to its already existing property. It is the same, viz., the 10 bales of piece goods and Rs. 1,300; only they have changed hands. Bearing this in mind, and also that the declared value of imports into India is not the *laying down* price but the market[1] price, which means the *laying down* price plus 10 per cent. profit, it is necessary for ascertaining the *real* profits from the *foreign commerce* of India to deduct 10 per cent. from the declared value of imports (merchandise). Doing this, the total imports from 1835 to 1872 should be taken £943,000,000 minus £62,000,000,[2] which will be equal to £881,000,000. In that case the real deficit of imports under what the imports ought to have been (£1,438,000,000) will be £557,000,000 in place of the nearly £500,000,000 I have given in my paper.

The figure of the amount, after deducting opium and profits of commerce, will be £248,000,000, instead of nearly £200,000,000; or the total transfer of wealth to England in addition to the railway interest (£40,000,000) will be £517,000,000 instead of £453,000,000 given in my paper, and the yearly average of every five years of this amount of £517,000,000 will be proportionately larger, about 13 per cent.:—

Averages will be about

1835—1839 . .	£6,000,000	1855—1859 . .	£8,700,000
1840—1844 . .	6,600,000	[3]1860—1864 . .	19,000,000
1845—1849 . .	8,700,000	1865—1869 . .	27,500,000
1850—1854 . .	8,400,000	1870—1872 . .	31,000,000

This average during the American War would be much increased if the whole profits on the exported produce of the time could be ascertained.

In preparing this reply I have had to work out all the figures hurriedly, but I hope they will be found correct.

I have not seen the late Administration Reports, but I trust they give fuller details than the previous ones with which I had to deal, and, if so, more precise results could be attained as to the actual annual production of the country, which is the most important point to be settled to give us an

[1] See the second note at page 131.

[2] Imports-merchandise, 1834-5 to 1872, £618,000,000, 10 per cent. of which is nearly £62,000,000.

[3] I could not find the amount of enfaced paper given for every year before 1860. I have therefore taken the whole amount in 1860, which increases the average for 1860-64 and correspondingly diminishes the average of the previous years, but not to a large extent.

accurate knowledge of the actual poverty or otherwise of this country.

Since I wrote the above I purchased a copy of the latest Administration Report of Bengal (1874-5) to see if I can at present give some more definite statistics about production than I have already done in my paper. Fancy my disappointment when I read Sir R. Temple saying :—

"Again the survey embraced only the exterior boundaries of each village or parish, and afforded no details of cultivation and waste, culturable or unculturable."

To the latter part of Mr. Collet's paper I have simply to reply—any amount of mere assertion or assumption can do no good. The question is a simple matter of facts and science. Is there so much cultivated land or not; is there so much produce or not; and are such and such the prices or not? And then common arithmetic gives you certain results. No amount of indirect reasoning or assumption can falsify facts and arithmetic and make 2 and 2 equal 5. So far as the official statistics are imperfect, it is the duty of the Government to give to the public full details. We know the national production of other countries, and there is no reason why the Indian Government should not be able to give us such most important similar information. That will be the best and surest guide and test of the actual condition of the people of India, and our rulers will see their way clearly to the most proper and effectual remedies. I have not the least doubt in my mind about the conscience of England and Englishmen, that if they once clearly see the evil, they will *not shrink* to apply the proper remedies. My estimate of 40s. a head has been accepted and argued upon by an Under-Secretary of State (Mr. G. Duff), and a Viceroy (Lord Mayo), and another Viceroy (Lord Lawrence) has told us that the mass of the people are half fed. It is not the question of the ordinary proportion of the poor in every country. Mr. Grant Duff in his reply to Mr. Lawson asked whether the "already poor population of India" was to be ground down "to the very dust" by the removal of the opium duty. So the margin between the present condition of India and of being ground down "to the very dust" is only the opium revenue. This is prosperity with a vengeance. I would not take up more of your time. Mr. Collet's remarks about the United States are already disposed of in the reply to Mr. Maclean. I have been lately reading the expression "balance in favour of India." The writers evidently suppose that what they call the balance of trade in favour of India was something that India had to receive sometime or other. They do not seem to understand that of all the *deficit* of import under the proceeds of export, not a single pie *in cash or goods* is to be received by India. That similarly, that of all the *excess* of imports in all the other parts of the British Empire to the extent of 15 to 25 per cent. over exports, or 18 per cent. in the United States, not a single farthing has to be paid to any country. It is in fact the profit of their exports, and the deficit of India, is so much transfer of its wealth to England. If I sent £100 worth of goods and get back only £80 worth, with no chance of getting the remaining £20, as well as the profits of my venture, *in cash or goods*, and then to call this "balance in my favour" is ndeed a very unenviable condition. On this subject I can only request attention to my papers instead of detaining you any longer.

Mr. Dadabhai concluded by saying that he was very much obliged to the meeting extending so much indulgence to him, and at the same time to many gentlemen who had come forward for discussion. When they first met in that hall, their fear was that they would have none to oppose as there would be none to criticise the paper. But he was much and very agreeably surprised that he had been criticised by many, and he was sure that this would bring out the real truth, and he hoped that from this day hence Mr. Maclean and his party would leave the United States alone and exert their influence to make India something like the United States. (Hear, hear, and cheers.)

The Remedy.

When I wrote these notes in 1873, or read them in 1876, I little dreamt that they would so soon obtain such terrible confirmation as the present deplorable famines have given them.

The chief cause of India's poverty, misery, and all material evils, is the exhaustion of its previous wealth, the continuously increasing exhausting and weakening drain from its annual production by the very excessive expenditure on the European portion of all its services, and the burden of a large amount a year to be paid to *foreign* countries for interest on the public debt, which is chiefly caused by the British rule.

The obvious remedy is to allow India to keep what it produces, and to help it as much as it lies in the power of the British nation to reduce her burden of the interest on the public debt; with a reasonable provision for the means absolutely necessary for the maintenance of the British rule. And for such means Britain must pay its proper share for its own interests.

For this purpose it is necessary on the one hand *to limit, within a certain amount*, the total of *every* kind of expenditure (pay, pensions, and every possible kind of allowance) for the *European* portion of *all* the services both in England and India, directly or indirectly connected with or under the control of Government (including, therefore, guaranteed railways or other works, manufactures, local funds, &c.), and to guarantee the public debt; and, on the other hand, for the important political object of maintaining the British rule, to reserve by law, for *Europeans alone*, such places of power of control only as may be absolutely necessary for the purpose, with a fair proportion of the Army, within the limited amount of expenditure for the European portion of all the services. These European services being as much for the benefit and interests of Britain as for those of India, Britain must pay her proper share for their expenditure.

Under some judicious arrangement of the kind I propose, the people of India, being allowed to keep most of what they produce, will rise in material prosperity under what is, upon the whole, a good system of administration, blessing the hand that gave such prosperity, and *increasing the benefit to the English people also manifold*, by the extensive commercial relations that must necessarily be then developed between England and India; and all fears of any danger to the British rule will be dispelled, both from the gratitude, loyalty, and *self-interest* of the people of India, and from the possession of important posts of power and a fair portion of commissions in the Army. Then will Macaulay's words be verified to the *glory of England*, as also to her *benefit*:—

"We shall never consent to administer the *pousta* to a whole community, to stupefy and paralyse a great people whom God has committed to our charge," and we shall not "keep a hundred millions (now two hundred and fifty millions) of men from being our customers, in order that they might continue to be our slaves."

THE CONDITION OF INDIA.

CORRESPONDENCE BETWEEN THE SECRETARY OF STATE FOR INDIA AND DADABHAI NAOROJI.

Journal of the East India Association, January, 1883.

PREFATORY NOTE.

IN reprinting the following documents as an extra number of the *Journal* the Council of the Association desire to point out that, while the author's (Mr. Dadabhai Naoroji) statements and conclusions must be taken on his personal responsibility, the facts set forth and the arguments advanced are entitled to most careful consideration alike by statisticians, economists, and politicians. Readers will readily perceive the nature of each paper or table, and its place in the whole review here presented of the great question of what is really the Condition of the People of India. Substantially, the series consists of—(*a*) Mr. Dadabhai's elaborate analysis and summary of statistics of production in use of the large province of India—the Punjab; (*b*) three memoranda, the first of which, being in full rejoinder to a reply on the Punjab paper, issued with the authority of the India Office, relates to the economic and industrial condition of India as a whole. Of the others, No. 2 treats of the "Moral Poverty of India," deepened, as the author seeks to show, by the people of the country being so largely excluded from the higher walks of administrative work and responsibility. This essay is well worthy of close examination by any thoughtful politician into whose hands these papers may fall. The No. 3 Memorandum offers searching criticism on certain of the conclusions recorded by the Famine Commissioners of 1880, more especially those relating to the actual incidence of taxation, and the very grave difficulties caused by the inevitable withdrawal of India's resources consequent on its being a dependency. Mr. Dadabhai's arguments under this head are put forward with all the earnestness of a sincere patriot, but in such form that both skilled economists and practical politicians are bound to take account of them. The Council believe that it will be for the true advantage, both of England and India—of the ruling and dependent country—that these essays, by a Native of India, should be widely disseminated and dispassionately examined.

The Council would wish to take this opportunity of expressing their high estimation of the ability, zeal, and labour which Mr. Dadabhai Naoroji has devoted to the composition of his valuable and important treatise.

EDWARD B. EASTWICK,

December 16th, 1882. *Chairman of Council.*

32, Great St. Helens, London.
24th May, 1880.

TO THE RIGHT HON. THE MARQUIS OF HARTINGTON, THE SECRETARY OF STATE FOR INDIA, INDIA OFFICE.

MY LORD,—I beg to submit a series of tables, working out in detail the total production of the Punjab for the year 1876-7.

My objects in troubling your Lordship are as follows:—

In 1876 I read some papers on the "Poverty of India" before the Bombay Branch of the East India Association. These papers are published in the *Journals* of the Association, and I send herewith a copy (Vol. IX, pages 236 and 352; Vol. X, pages 83 and 133). At pages 237-9 I have explained how the mode of taking the averages adopted in the various Administration Reports of India was quite wrong. When preparing my papers on the "Poverty of India" I had not sufficient time to work out all the averages for all the provinces in detail. I have now worked out in detail the averages of all the production tables of the Administration Report of the Punjab for 1876-7. I request now that the different Governments in India may be directed to supply their tables of production as fully as are prescribed by the Statistical Committee of Calcutta, that the averages may be correctly taken, as I have done in the enclosed tables, and that, in addition to the tables prescribed, may also be given a summary of the total agricultural production, like the one given at page 166 of my tables, a summary of the whole production (agricultural, manufactures, and mines), like that at page 168, and a table of the absolute necessaries of life for an agricultural labourer, like that at pages 171, 172.

It is only when such complete information is furnished by the Indian authorities that any true conception can be formed of the actual material condition of India from year to year, and our British rulers can only then clearly see, and grapple with effectually, the important problem of the material condition of India, and the best means of improving it.

I have also to solicit your Lordship to submit my tables to the Statistical Department of the India Office, and to direct it to oblige me by pointing out any mistakes of facts or figures there may be in them.

In troubling your Lordship with these requests, I have no other object than to help, as far as my humble opportunities go, to arrive at the real truth of the actual material condition of India; for it is only natural that without the knowledge of the whole truth on this most important subject, all efforts, however well and benevolently intentioned, must generally result in disappointment and failures.

I also earnestly desire and solicit that your Lordship will kindly take into your consideration the representations I have urged in my papers on the "Poverty of India."

I remain, my Lord,
Your Lordship's most obedient Servant,
DADABHAI NAOROJI.

ADMINISTRATION REPORT OF PUNJAB, 1876-7.

Page 77.—"Upon the whole, the character of the weather during the year 1876-7 was favourable for agriculture."

I have taken one seer, equal to 2·057 lbs., from the compilation entitled "Prices of Food Grains throughout India, 1861-76," compiled in the Financial Department of the Government of India, Calcutta, 1878.

The prices I have adopted are the average of the prices given in the report for 1st January, 1876, 1st June, 1876, and 1st January, 1877; the last being the latest price that is given in the Report.

For all such particulars or figures as are *not* given in the Report, I have consulted a Punjab farmer, and adopted such information as he has given me.

There are some figures in the Report which are evidently mistakes, and are much in excess of probability; but I have not altered them; though by retaining them as given in the Report, the quantity and value of some of the articles become much higher than what they must most probably really be.

Excepting such mistakes, the farmer thinks the tables of the Report give a fair representation of the produce of Punjab, the averages being worked out in the right way they should be, and not as they are given in the Report, worked on a wrong principle.

RICE.

Districts.	Acres.	Per Acre.	Total Quantity.	Price per Re. 1.	Total Value.
		lbs.	lbs.	lbs.	Rs.
1 Delhi . . .	27,900	920	25,668,000	13·71	18,72,210
2 Gurgaon . .	1,591	720	1,145,520	19·2	59,662
3 Karnál . . .	53,113	1,152	61,186,176	21·94	27,88,795
4 Hissar . . .	10,506	745	7,826,970	23·31	3,35,777
5 Rohtak . . .	5,326	670	3,568,420	25·37	1,40,655
6 Sirsa	8,285	869	7,199,665	21·94	3,28,152
7 Umballa . .	117,941	880	103,788,080	19·88	52,20,728
8 Ludhiána . .	3,963	1,096	4,343,448	16·45	2,64,039
9 Simla . . .	1,875	620	1,162,500	18·51	62,804
10 Jullundar . .	9,192	1,085	9,973,320	16·45	6,06,281
11 Hoshiarpur .	28,835	752	21,683,920	17·82	12,16,830
12 Kángra . . .	147,766	415	61,322,890	29·48	20,80,152
13 Amritsar . .	20,128	974	19,604,672	18·51	10,59,139
14 Gurdáspur . .	81,583	755	61,595,165	15·77	39,05,844
15 Siálkot . . .	74,100	1,029	76,248,900	30·85	24,71,601
16 Lahore . . .	22,415	861	19,299,315	30·17	6,39,685
17 Gujránwála .	9,925	759	7,533,075	19·88	3,78,927
18 Firozepore . .	6,543	795	5,201,685	20·91	2,48,765
19 Ráwalpindi .	1,093	970	1,060,210	12·34	85,916
20 Jhelum . . .	233	943	219,719	11·65	18,860
21 Gujrát . . .	6,969	586	4,083,834	17·82	2,29,171
22 Shahpur . .	990	790	782,100	22·63	34,560
23 Mooltan . .	9,800	750	7,350,000	13·71	5,36,105
24 Jhang . . .	127	281	35,687	13·71	2,603
25 Montgomery .	7,870	1,145	9,011,150	13·71	6,57,268
26 Mazaffargarh .	10,178	852	8,671,656	16·45	5,27,152
27 D. I. Khan . .	1,366	196	267,736	12·85	20,835
28 D. G. Khan .	14,001	513	7,182,513	18·	3,99,028
29 Bannu . . .	125	880	110,000	12·85	8,560
30 Peshávar . .	10,325	894	9,230,550	13·45	6,86,286
31 Hazára . . .	12,274	1,152	14,139,648	28·8	4,90,960
32 Kohát . . .	2,361	1,507	3,558,027	14·83	2,39,920
Total . .	708,699	Average 796	564,054,551	Average 20·42	2,76,17,270

I take produce of rice as 25-fold, and deduct 4 per cent. for seed. The quantity will then become 541,492,369 lbs., and value Rs. 2,65,12,580. Again, the price of rice given in the Report is for "first sort" only. The medium or second sort forms the bulk, and there is a lower sort still. The second sort is generally about 75 per cent. of the first sort. I take upon the whole 85 per cent. The value, then, for the whole bulk will be Rs. 2,25,35,693.

WHEAT.

Districts.	Acres.	Per Acre.	Total Quantity.	Price per Re. 1.	Total Value.
		lbs.	lbs.	lbs.	Rs.
1 Delhi . . .	159,900	913	145,988,700	53·82	27,12,536
2 Gurgaon . .	132,425	856	113,355,800	49·37	22,96,046
3 Karnál . . .	113,110	1,319	149,192,090	48·68	30,64,751
4 Hissar . . .	39,048	548	21,398,304	48·34	4,42,662
5 Rohtak . . .	99,428	732	72,781,296	49·37	14,74,200
6 Sirsa . . .	56,310	255	14,359,050	49·02	2,92,922
7 Umballa . .	296,322	1,000	296,322,000	51·25	57,81,892
8 Ludhiána . .	137,012	1,013	138,793,156	51·08	27,17,172
9 Simla . . .	3,610	550	1,985,500	38·39	51,719
10 Jullundar . .	269,010	1,339	360,204,390	49·37	72,96,017
11 Hoshiarpur .	349,863	692	242,105,196	48·68	49,73,401
12 Kángra . .	144,170	460	66,318,200	37·02	17,91,415
13 Amritsar . .	263,265	1,038	273,269,070	52·11	52,44,081
14 Gurdáspur . .	325,529	856	278,652,824	50·74	54,91,778
15 Siálkot . . .	197,000	910	179,270,000	49·02	36,57,078
16 Lahore . . .	368,000	557	204,976,000	50·39	40,67,791
17 Gujránwála .	203,745	793	161,569,785	50·74	31,84,268
18 Firozepore .	241,180	736	177,508,480	58·97	30,10,148
19 Ráwalpindi .	424,135	776	329,128,760	68·9	47,76,905
20 Jhelum . .	480,273	933	448,094,709	64·45	69,52,594
21 Gujrát . . .	268,316	736	197,360,576	57·42	34,37,139
22 Shahpur .	199,325	790	157,466,750	58·62	26,86,229
23 Mooltan .	186,040	655	121,856,200	41·83	29,13,129
24 Jhang . . .	161,169	674	108,627,906	49·37	22,00,281
25 Montgomery .	263,494	1,252	329,894,488	53·48	61,68,558
26 Mazaffargarh .	201,363	1,248	251,301,024	43·88	57,27,006
27 D. I. Khan .	176,055	777	136,794,735	69·42	19,70,537
28 D. G. Khan .	156,594	765	119,794,410	44·57	26,87,781
29 Bannu . .	262,728	523	137,406,744	88·28	15,56,487
30 Peshávar . .	232,975	600	139,785,000	57·47	24,32,312
31 Hazára . . .	100,570	993	99,866,010	58·97	16,93,505
32 Kohát . . .	97,533	816	79,586,928	70·89	11,22,682
Total . .	6,609,497	Average 840·4	5,555,014,081	Average 53·48	10,38,75,022

I take produce of wheat 25-fold, and deduct 4 per cent. for seed. The quantity will be 5,332,813,517 lbs., and value will be Rs. 9,97,20,021. The price given in the Report is for first sort only. The second sort forms the bulk, and is generally about 12 per cent. lower in price. I take only 8 per cent. lower for the whole bulk.

The value of the whole will then be Rs. 9,17,42,419.

MAKAI (INDIAN CORN).

Districts.	Acres.	Per Acre.	Total Quantity.	Price per Re. 1.	Total Value.
		lbs.	lbs.	lbs.	Rs.
1 Delhi . . .	13,900	1,500	20,850,000	72·	2,89,583
2 Gurgaon . .	1,344	..	2,016,000	75·42	26,730
3 Karnál .	6,215	,,	9,322,500	67·19	1,38,748
4 Hissar . .	89	,,	133,500	51·42	2,596
5 Rohtak .	73	,,	[2]109,500	..	..
6 Sirsa . . .	466	,,	[2]699,000	..	..
7 Umballa . .	100,736	,,	151,104,000	62·4	24,21,538
8 Ludhiána .	62,802	,,	94,203,000	66·51	14,16,373
9 Simla . . .	1,282	,,	1,923,000	45·94	41,859
[1]10 Jullundar	86,392	[1]1,544	133,389,248	63·08	21,14,604
11 Hoshiarpur .	105,651	1,500	158,476,500	55·54	28,53,375
12 Kángra . .	65,093	,,	97,639,500	39·77	24,55,104
[1]13 Amritsar . .	44,426	[1]1,412	62,729,512	65·14	9,62,995
14 Gurdáspur .	49,977	1,500	74,965,500	53·48	14,01,748
15 Siálkot . .	33,000	,,	49,500,000	58·28	8,49,450
16 Lahore . .	34,150	,,	51,225,000	65·82	7,78,258
17 Gujránwála .	16,535	,,	24,802,500	61·02	4,06,465
18 Firozepore .	42,428	,,	63,642,000	81·59	7,80,022
19 Ráwalpindi .	66,392	,,	99,588,000	94·62	10,52,504
20 Jhelum . .	2,423	,,	3,634,500	64·45	56,392
21 Gujrát . .	16,507	,,	24,760,500	68·57	3,61,098
22 Shahpur . .	884	,,	1,326,000	63·08	21,020
23 Mooltan . .	142	,,	213,000	50·05	4,255
24 Jhang . . .	2,317	,,	3,475,500	65·82	52,803
25 Montgomery.	2,512	,,	3,768,000	49·37	76,321
26 Mazaffargarh	..	..	..	..	..
27 D. I. Khan .	17	1,500	25,500	90·85	280
28 D. G. Khan .	30	,,	[2]45,000	..	..
29 Bannu . .	37,069	,,	55,603,500	124·27	4,47,441
30 Peshávar. .	80,542	,,	120,813,000	84·42	14,31,094
31 Hazára . .	198,025	,,	297,037,500	95·09	31,23,751
32 Kohát . .	12,920	,,	19,380,000	97·92	1,97,916
	[1]130,818	Average 1,499·17	196,118,760	Average 68·4	2,37,64,323
	953,521	1,500·	1,430,281,500	[2]add for 853,500 lbs.	12,478
Total .	1,084,339		1,626,400,260		2,37,76,801

[1] In the Report crop per acre is given for two districts only, marked[1]. The average for these two—viz., 1499·17—say 1,500 lbs., is applied to all other districts by me.

[2] No price is given in the Report for the three districts marked[2]. The average of the others—viz., 68·4 lbs.—is applied to these.

For Makai I take 50-fold, and therefore deduct 2 per cent. for seed. The total quantity will then be 1,593,872,255 lbs., and value will be Rs. 2,33,01,265.

JOW (BARLEY).

Districts.	Acres.	Per Acre.	Total Quantity.	Price per Re. 1.	Total Value.
		lbs.	lbs.	lbs.	Rs.
1 Delhi	61,290	503	30,828,870	73·02	4,22,197
2 Gurgaon	197,145	,,	99,163,935	69·94	14,17,842
3 Karnál	29,856	,,	15,017,568	72·68	2,06,625
4 Hissar	30,312	,,	15,246,936	83·65	1,82,270
5 Rohtak	42,353	,,	21,303,559	75·42	2,82,465
6 Sirsa	101,408	,,	51,008,224	108·33	4,70,859
7 Umballa	35,787	,,	18,000,861	72·	2,50,011
8 Ludhiána	106,202	,,	53,419,606	86·39	6,18,354
9 Simla	3,134	,,	1,576,402	50·74	31,068
10 Jullundar	25,211	[1]856	21,580,616	75·42	2,86,139
11 Hoshiarpur	21,602	503	10,865,806	76·79	1,41,500
12 Kángra	56,831	[1]250	14,207,750	52·11	2,72,649
13 Amritsar	36,509	503	18,364,027	84·34	2,17,738
14 Gurdáspur	123,635	,,	62,188,405	63·08	9,85,865
15 Siálkot	122,000	,,	61,366,000	83·65	7,33,604
16 Lahore	57,181	,,	28,762,043	82·96	3,46,697
17 Gujránwála	64,082	,,	32,233,246	88·45	3,64,423
18 Firozepore	195,298	,,	98,234,894	100·1	9,81,367
19 Ráwalpindi	43,383	,,	21,821,649	77·48	2,81,642
20 Jhelum	17,879	,,	8,993,137	76·11	1,18,159
21 Gujrát	67,094	,,	33,748,282	82·28	4,10,163
22 Shahpur	15,657	,,	7,875,471	78·16	1,00,760
23 Mooltan	11,832	[1]800	9,465,600	59·65	1,58,685
24 Jhang	6,083	503	3,059,749	74·74	40,938
25 Montgomery	21,802	,,	10,966,406	69·94	1,56,797
26 Mazaffargarh	10,987	[1]679	7,460,173	60·34	1,23,635
27 D. I. Khan	19,203	503	9,659,109	94·28	1,02,451
28 D. G. Khan	5,925	,,	2,980,275	60·42	49,325
29 Bannu	26,282	,,	13,219,846	133·7	98,876
30 Peshâwar	238,161	,,	119,794,983	104·30	11,48,561
31 Hazára	70,079	,,	35,249,737	102·98	3,42,296
32 Kohát	10,014	,,	5,037,042	109·28	46,092
Total	1,874,217		942,700,207	Average 82·76	1,13,90,053

[1] Crop per acre is given for only these four districts, the average of which for 104,861 acres is 503 lbs., and this average is applied to all the other districts for 1,769,356 acres.

For barley I take 16-fold. Deducting for seed $\frac{1}{16}$, the total quantity will be 883,781,444 lbs., and the value will be Rs. 1,06,78,175.

GRAM.

Districts.	Acres.	Per Acre.	Total Quantity.	Price per Re. 1.	Total Value.
		lbs.	lbs.	lbs.	Rs.
1 Delhi . . .	57,500	645	37,087,500	72·	5,15,104
2 Gurgaon . .	101,184	[1]620	62,734,080	71·65	8,75,562
3 Karnál . . .	119,935	[1]680	81,555,800	72·34	11,27,395
4 Hissar . . .	76,534	645	49,364,430	80·22	6,15,363
5 Rohtak . . .	119,240	[1]790	94,199,600	78·16	12,05,214
6 Sirsa . . .	37,762	645	24,356,490	102·85	2,36,815
7 Umballa . .	175,094	,,	112,935,630	76·11	14,83,847
8 Ludhiána . .	171,984	,,	110,929,680	77·82	14,25,464
9 Simla . . .	5	,,	3,225	51·08	63
10 Jullundar . .	65,158	[1]1,233	80,339,814	73·37	10,94,995
11 Hoshiarpur .	46,324	645	29,878,980	61·02	4,89,658
12 Kángra . . .	370,802	[1]290	107,532,580	51·08	21,05,179
13 Amritsar . .	103,350	[1]1,394	144,069,900	84·	17,15,117
14 Gurdáspur .	31,347	645	20,218,815	73·37	2,75,573
15 Siálkot . .	21,500	,,	13,867,500	74·05	1,87,272
16 Lahore . . .	171,216	,,	110,434,320	89·82	12,29,507
17 Gujránwála .	31,682	,,	20,434,890	83·65	2,44,290
18 Firozepore .	255,898	,,	165,054,210	96·68	17,07,221
19 Ráwalpindi .	38,263	,,	24,679,635	76·79	3,21,391
20 Jhelum . . .	34,115	,,	22,004,175	65·14	3,37,798
21 Gujrát . . .	34,728	,,	22,399,560	68·	3,08,194
22 Shahpur . .	23,817	,,	15,361,965	74·05	2,07,453
23 Mooltan . .	8,404	,,	5,420,580	57·25	94,682
24 Jhang . . .	12,026	,,	7,756,770	73·37	1,05,721
25 Montgomery .	81,616	,,	52,642,320	77·48	6,79,431
26 Mazaffargarh .	12,679	[1]1,942	24,622,618	55·54	4,43,331
27 D. I. Khan .	11,922	645	7,689,690	95·13	80,833
28 D. G. Khan .	1,961	,,	1,264,845	47·74	26,494
29 Bannu . . .	53,037	[1]286	15,168,582	106·28	1,42,722
30 Peshawar . .	947	645	610,815	44·05	13,866
31 Hazára . . .	222	,,	143,190	61·71	2,320
32 Kohát . . .	1,984	,,	1,279,680	70·36	18,187
Total . .	2,272,236	Average 645	1,466,041,869	Average 75·89	1,93,16,062

[1] Crop per acre is given for these districts only. The average from them is applied to others—viz., 645 lbs.

I take gram 30-fold. Deducting for seed accordingly, the total quantity will be 1,417,173,807 lbs., and the value will be Rs. 1,86,72,194.

INFERIOR GRAIN (as noted below).[1]

Districts.	Acres.	Per Acre.	Total Quantity.	Price per Re. 1.	Total Value.
		lbs.	lbs.	lbs.	Rs.
1 Delhi . . .	114,677	522	59,816,394	66·85	8,95,458
2 Gurgaon . .	404,175	447	180,666,225	66·	27,37,367
3 Karnál . . .	196,787	521	102,526,027	64·79	15,82,436
4 Hissar . .	1,256,158	393	493,670,094	76·79	64,28,833
5 Rohtak . . .	441,437	412	181,872,044	64·79	28,07,100
6 Sirsa . .	680,225	118	80,266,550	104·39	7,68,910
7 Umballa	195,893	680	133,207,240	66·16	20,13,410
8 Ludhiána . .	214,111	1,355	290,120,405	68·91	42,10,135
9 Simla . . .	3,406	520	1,771,120	40·11	44,156
10 Jullundar . .	165,767	395	65,477,965	62·05	10,55,245
11 Hoshiarpur .	111,933	685	76,674,105	58·41	13,12,687
12 Kángra . . .	30,366	362	[2]10,992,492	..	..
13 Amritsar . .	71,937	590	42,442,830	67·88	6,25,262
14 Gurdáspur. .	154,306	648	99,990,288	48·	20,83,131
15 Siálkot . . .	94,070	745	70,082,150	65·14	10,75,869
16 Lahore . .	141,579	374	52,950,546	69·94	7,57,085
17 Gujránwála .	123,515	449	55,458,235	64·45	8,60,484
18 Firozepore. .	477,728	608	290,458,624	82·11	35,37,433
19 Ráwalpindi .	287,941	554	159,519,314	92·91	17,16,923
20 Jhelum . . .	209,379	722	151,171,638	70·28	21,50,990
21 Gujrát . . .	239,640	632	151,452,480	80·91	18,71,863
22 Shahpur	68,819	1,100	75,700,900	66·16	11,44,209
23 Moolton . .	98,847	468	46,260,396	51·08	9,05,646
24 Jhang . . .	55,474	218	12,093,332	60·17	2,00,986
25 Montgomery	63,883	686	43,823,738	55·54	7,89,048
26 Mazaffargarh .	76,969	693	53,339,517	49·37	10,80,403
27 D. I. Khan .	43,618	485	21,154,730	89·13	2,37,346
28 D. G. Khan .	178,113	640	113,992,320	54·17	21,04,344
29 Bannu . . .	105,488	536	56,541,568	111·42	5,07,463
30 Peshâwar . .	107,183	550	58,950,650	59·48	9,91,100
31 Hazára . . .	52,074	960	49,991,040	74·05	6,75,098
32 Kohât . . .	69,465	770	53,488,050	112·28	4,76,380
		Average		Average	
Total . .	6,534,963	510·5	3,335,968,007	69·78	4,76,46,800
				Add	1,57,530
					4,78,04,330

Seed required per Acre.		for Acres.
[1] Joár, per acre 40 lbs.	×	2,221,535
Bájrá . . 16 ,,	×	2,339,796
Kangni . . 8 ,,	×	58,434
Chína . . . 16 ,,	×	74,842
Moth . . 24 ,,	×	982,208
Matter . . . 20 ,,	×	106,865
Másh . . . 16 ,,	×	213,465
Múng . . 16 ,,	×	263,324
Masúr . . . 32 ,,	×	187,544
Arhar . . 16 ,,	×	86,950
		6,534,963

The total of the products of these —168,694,604 divided by the total 6,534,963 of acres, will give an average of 26 lbs. per acre of seed for a crop of average 510 lbs.—say 20-fold. Deducting, then, 5 per cent. for seed, the total quantity will be 3,169,169,607 lbs., and total value will be Rs. 4,54,14,114.

[2] The price for this is not given.

It should be noted that the prices of jowár, bájrá, másh, múng, and arhar are nearly the same generally, but of the remaining five kinds of grain—viz., moth, kangni, chiná, matter, masúr—the prices are generally nearly 25 per cent. lower. The prices I have used in the table are as given in the Report for jowár and bájrá only, though the acreage of the lower priced grains is 1,409,893 acres out of 6,534,963 acres, or above 20 per cent. If the allowance for the lower price of the five kinds of grain mentioned above were made, the value will evidently be much lower than I have given above. It requires also be noted that out of the inferior grains a portion goes for the feed of animals in about the following proportions:—

Grain.	Proportion for Human Use.	Proportion for Animal Use.
Bájrá	$\frac{1}{2}$	$\frac{1}{2}$
Jowár	$\frac{1}{3}$	$\frac{2}{3}$
Moth	$\frac{1}{4}$	$\frac{3}{4}$
Másh	$\frac{2}{3}$	$\frac{1}{3}$
Also Jow	$\frac{1}{4}$	$\frac{3}{4}$
Gram	$\frac{1}{2}$	$\frac{1}{2}$

So that out of the total acreage of grains of all the above kinds, viz.:—

Gram	2,272,236 × $\frac{1}{2}$	= 6,000,512 acres, are for animal use, or nearly three-fifths of the total acres, 9,903,457.
Bájrá	2,339,796 × $\frac{1}{2}$	
Jowár	2,221,535 × $\frac{2}{3}$	
Jow	1,874,217 × $\frac{3}{4}$	
Moth	982,208 × $\frac{3}{4}$	
Másh	213,465 × $\frac{1}{3}$	
	9,903,457	

And out of the whole acreage of *all* kinds of grain—*i.e.*, 19,083,971 acres—about 30 per cent. is used for producing food for animals.

POPPY (OPIUM).

Districts.	Acres.	Per Acre.	Total Quantity.	
		lbs.	lbs.	
7 Umballa . .	3,620	18	65,160	
8 Ludhiâna. .	69	..	..	
9 Simla . . .	244	3	732	
10 Jullundar. .	578	..	..	
11 Hoshiarpur .	163	..	..	
12 Kângra . .	1,539	3	4,617	
13 Amritsar . .	877	19	16,663	
14 Gurdâspur .	278	..	..	
15 Siâlkot . .	140	..	..	
16 Lahore . .	770	5	3,850	
17 Gujrânwâla .	147	10	1,470	
18 Firozepore .	263	..	..	
19 Râwalpindi .	53	15	795	
20 Jhelum . .	81	14	1,134	
21 Gujrât . .	336	15	5,040	
22 Shahpur . .	2,182	10	21,820	
23 Mooltan . .	25	6	150	
24 Jhang . . .	27	10	270	
25 Montgomery.	94	9	846	
26 Mazaffargarh	40	11	440	
27 D. I. Khan .	23	8	184	
28 D. G. Khan .	535	20	10,700	
29 Bannu . .	15	..	..	
30 Peshâwar .	67	3	201	
31 Hazâra . .	182	9	1,638	
Total . .	12,348	Average 12·51	135,710 for 10,842 acres. add 18,840 ,, 1,506 ,, 154,550 ,, 12,348 ..	for which no crop per acre is given, at 12·51 average.

Government pays Rs. 5 per seer, or Rs. 2½ per lb. to the producer. The total value will therefore be Rs. 3,86,375.

The additional value at which Government sells opium is a part of the national income, as it is chiefly paid by a foreign country as profit of trade, and therefore (as I have done in my "Poverty of India") the net opium revenue will have to be added to the total production of the country. The particular provinces only from which this revenue is derived —viz., Bengal, Bombay, and other opium-producing places— cannot be credited with this income. It belongs to the whole nation, as every place is not quite free to cultivate opium.

TOBACCO.

Districts.	Acres.	Per Acre.	Total Quantity.	Price per Re. 1.	Total Value.
		lbs.	lbs.	lbs.	Rs.
1 Delhi . . .	7,472	888	6,635,136	5·14	12,90,882
2 Gurgaon . .	2,424	600	1,454,400	14·4	1,01,000
3 Karnál. . .	917	525	481,425	16·45	29,266
4 Hissar . .	2,812	582	1,636,584	16·45	99,488
5 Rohtak . .	1,851	514	951,414	16·45	57,836
6 Sirsa . . .	381	850	323,850	14·4	23,489
7 Umballa . .	4,661	560	2,610,160	12·34	2,11,520
8 Ludhiána. .	1,550	925	1,433,750	27·25	52,614
[1]9 Simla . . .	5	846	4,230	9·6	440
10 Jullundar . .	2,793	1,561	4,359,873	24·68	1,76,656
11 Hoshiarpur .	3,782	1,733	6,554,206	19·88	3,29,688
12 Kángra . .	776	532	412,832	12·34	33,454
13 Amritsar . .	2,169	984	2,134,296	18·51	1,15,305
14 Gurdáspur .	3,973	1,040	4,131,920	16·45	2,51,180
15 Siálkot . . .	5,785	917	5,304,845	16·45	3,22,483
16 Lahore . .	3,460	461	1,595,060	16·45	96,964
17 Gujránwála .	3,259	669	2,180,271	17·14	1,27,203
18 Firozepore .	5,879	651	3,827,229	13·03	2,93,724
19 Ráwalpindi .	1,380	1,080	1,490,400	16·45	90,601
20 Jhelum . .	622	792	492,624	17·83	27,628
21 Gujrát . . .	2,389	593	1,416,677	12·34	1,14,803
22 Shahpur . .	838	1,700	1,424,600	12·34	1,15,445
23 Mooltan . .	1,839	656	1,206,384	6·51	1,85,312
24 Jhang . . .	1,173	820	961,860	12·34	77,946
25 Montgomery.	851	1,042	886,742	16·46	53,872
26 Mazaffargarh	978	780	762,840	15·09	50,552
27 D. I. Khan .	2,029	615	1,247,835	12·68	98,409
28 D. G. Khan .	783	740	579,420	7·28	79,590
29 Bannu . . .	452	870	393,240	20·6	19,089
30 Peshávar .	1,250	880	1,100,000	21·85	50,343
31 Hazára . .	27	480	12,960	17·83	726
[1]32 Kohát . . .	3,307	846	2,797,722	10·97	2,55,033
		Average		Average	
Total . .	71,867	846	60,804,785	12·58	48,32,541

[1] The produce per acre for these is not given in the Report. I have applied the average of the other districts—viz., 846 lbs.—to these.

No deduction is made for nursery or seed. The average of 12·58 lbs. per rupee is rather a high price. It is considered 12 seers or 24 lbs. per rupee would be nearer the average. I have, as above, kept the Report's price though it is considered so high.

Turmeric.

Neither produce per acre nor price is given in the Report. I take 10 maunds for green, which gives 2 maunds dry or 164 lbs. dry per acre. The price is taken at, say, 10 lbs. per Re. 1.

4,130 acres × 164 lbs. = 677,320 lbs.; at 10 lbs. per Re. = Rs. 67,732.

Coriander Seed.

As above, neither produce per acre nor price is given in the Report. I take as follows:—

6,934 acres × 330 lbs. dry per acre = 2,288,220 lbs. at 16 lbs. per Re. = Rs. 1,43,014.

Ginger.

As above.

286 acres × 205 lbs. per acre (dry) = 58,630 lbs.; at 7 lbs. per Re. = Rs. 8,376.

Chillies.

Produce per acre given for four districts only, viz.:—

	Acres		Lbs.	
No. 2 acres	774	× 600 lbs. =	464,400	lbs.
13	611	× 410 ,, =	250,510	,,
18	3,604	× 924 ,, =	3,330,096	,,
30	77	× 640 ,, =	49,280	,,
		Average		
Total..	5,066	808 ,,	4,094,286	,,
Add for	18,452	at ,, ,,	14,909,216	,,
	23,518		19,003,502	,,

The average of 808 lbs. is applied to the rest. The total quantity then is 19,003,502 lbs. of green crop. Dry quantity will be one fifth, or 3,800,700 lbs., and at 8 lbs. per Re. the value will be Rs. 4,75,100.

Other Kinds of Drugs and Spices.

These are chiefly ajmá, bádián, jeree, and sowá. Neither produce per acre nor price is given in the Report. I take as follows:—

Acres 35,074 at 330 lbs. per acre = 11,574,420 lbs.; at average of 14 lbs. per Re. = Rs. 8,26,744.

Oil Seeds.

	Districts.	Acres.	Per Acre.	Total Quantity.
			lbs.	lbs.
1	Delhi	10,260	293	3,006,180
2	Gurgaon	11,506	237	2,726,922
3	Karnál	13,018	500	6,509,000
4	Hissar	21,582	242	5,222,844
5	Rohtak	12,304	297	3,654,288
6	Sirsa	79,160	80[1]	6,332,800
7	Umballa	27,229	560	15,248,240
8	Ludhiána	11,172	668	7,462,896
9	Simla	...	...	...
10	Jullundar	11,392	715	8,145,280
11	Hoshiarpur	25,911	310	8,032,410
12	Kángra	18,442	352	6,491,584
13	Amritsar	35,996	582	20,949,672
14	Gurdáspur	24,923	408	10,168,584
15	Siálkot	23,806	777	18,497,262
16	Lahore	81,894	260	21,292,440
17	Gujránwála	17,952	307	5,511,264
18	Firozepore	70,315	601	42,259,315
19	Ráwalpindi	69,294	311	21,550,434
20	Jhelum	60,169	481	28,941,289
21	Gujrát	50,375	291	14,659,125
22	Shahpur	4,712	750	3,534,000
23	Mooltan	9,541	462	4,407,942
24	Jhang	3,473	252	875,196
25	Montgomery	29,076	477	13,869,252
26	Mazaffargarh	24,453	288	7,042,464
27	D. I. Khan	17,660	464	8,194,240
28	D. G. Khan	20,473	492	10,072,716
29	Bannu	4,004	136	544,544
30	Peshâwar	30,244	460	13,912,240
31	Hazára	21,005	533	11,195,665
32	Kohát	5,348	251	1,342,348
	Total	846,689	Average 392	331,652,436

[1] This evidently is some mistake. It may be 280.

Districts, 32; total acres, 846,689; average per acre, 392 lbs.; total quantity, 331,652,436 lbs.

The price of these seeds is not given in the Report. I take as follows: Linseed and sarso, Rs. 3 per maund, or 27 lbs. per Re. 1; til seed, Rs. 4 per maund, or 20 lbs. per Re. 1; taramira, Rs. 2½ per maund, or 32 lbs. per Re. 1.

The quantity of these seeds is about in proportion of 55 per cent. of linseed and sarso, 15 per cent. of til, 30 per cent. of taramira. The price then will be—

55 per cent. × 27 lbs. = 1,485
15 " × 20 " = 300
30 " × 32 " = 960
} Average, 27·45 lbs. per Re. 1.

Taking 27 lbs. per Re. 1, the total value will be Rs. 1,22,83,423.

Linseed . . 6 lbs. for seed per acre	× 55 per cent.		Average 7·15 lbs. per acre.
Sarso . . 8 „ „ „			
Til . . . 6 „ „ „	× 15 „		
Taramira . 8 „ „ „	× 30 „		

Taking 7 lbs. of seed required per acre for produce of 392 lbs. gives 56-fold. Deducting 56th part, the total quantity will become 325,730,071 lbs., and total value will become Rs. 1,20,64,076.

COTTON.

Districts.	Acres.	Per Acre.	Total Quantity.	Price per Re. 1.	Total Value.
		lbs.	lbs.	lbs.	Rs.
1 Delhi . . .	24,565	186	4,569,090	6·51	7,01,857
2 Gurgaon . .	47,855	164	7,848,220	6·51	12,05,563
3 Karnál . . .	21,510	140	3,011,400	6·43	4,68,336
4 Hissar . . .	20,323	87	1,768,101	6·17	2,86,564
5 Rohtak . . .	49,073	70	3,435,110	7·2	4,77,098
6 Sirsa . . .	77	64	4,928	6·17	798
7 Umballa . .	27,332	72	1,967,904	6·34	3,10,395
8 Ludhiána . .	11,488	85	976,480	6·34	1,54,019
9 Simla . . .	...	...	...	...	...
10 Jullundar . .	26,093	122	3,183,346	5·14	6,19,328
11 Hoshiarpur .	24,420	136	3,321,120	5·49	6,04,940
12 Kángra . . .	6,733	22	148,126	5·14	28,818
13 Amritsar . .	23,597	64	1,510,208	5·65	2,67,293
14 Gurdáspur .	37,474	50	1,873,700	5·14	3,64,533
15 Siálkot . . .	11,425	65	742,625	5·65	1,31,438
16 Lahore . .	25,305	138	3,492,090	5·49	6,36,082
17 Gujránwála .	33,376	129	4,305,504	5·49	7,84,244
18 Firozepore .	9,680	158	1,529,440	6·17	2,47,883
19 Ráwalpindi .	33,745	128	4,319,360	4·46	9,68,466
20 Jhelum . . .	25,557	122	3,117,954	5·27	5,91,642
21 Gujrát . . .	24,716	43	1,062,788	4·63	2,29,543
22 Shahpur . .	26,029	50	1,301,450	5·49	2,37,058
23 Mooltan . .	16,550	82	1,357,100	5·65	2,40,194
24 Jhang . . .	16,881	87	1,468,647	5·27	2,78,680
25 Montgomery .	15,838	149	2,359,862	5·31	4,44,418
26 Mazaffargarh	29,632	124	3,674,368	6·	6,12,394
27 D. I. Khan .	11,175	115	1,285,125	6·	2,14,187
28 D. G. Khan .	29,739	84	2,498,076	5·7	4,38,259
29 Bannu . . .	7,544	73	550,712	5·36	1,02,744
30 Peshâwar . .	16,468	105	1,729,140	5·23	3,30,619
31 Hazára . .	8,280	100	828,000	4·11	2,01,460
32 Kohát . . .	6,396	121	773,916	4·41	1,75,491
Total . .	668,876	Average 105	70,013,890	Average 5·66	1,23,54,344

[1] The produce per acre for this is not given in the Report. The average of the others (652 acres) is applied to this.

The average of 105 lbs. per acre is evidently too high; 80 lbs. will be nearer the mark. If so, the above quantity and value are nearly 36¼ per cent. above the right quantity and value.

Very probably some of the figures of produce per acre are for uncleaned or seed cotton. The report uses the word "cotton" only in the column of produce per acre, while in the column for prices it uses the words "cotton (cleaned)."

HEMP.

Districts.	Acres.	Per Acre.	Total Quantity.
		lbs.	lbs.
1 Delhi	2,100	[1] 1,158	2,431,800
2 Gurgaon	516	116	59,856
3 Karnál	1,085	450	488,250
4 Hissar	2,788	153	426,564
5 Rohtak	16,146	465	7,507,890
7 Umballa	1,619	220	356,180
8 Ludhiána	1,637	305	499,285
10 Jullundar	3,655	398	1,454,690
11 Hoshiarpur	6,424	192	1,233,408
12 Kángra	5,263	312	1,642,056
13 Amritsar	1,002	444	444,888
14 Gurdáspur	1,622	352	570,944
15 Siálkot	3,205	177	567,285
16 Lahore	537	306	164,322
17 Gujránwála	355	406	144,130
18 Firozepore	1,649	218	359,482
19 Ráwalpindi	417	120	50,040
20 Jhelum	203	360	73,080
21 Gujrát	971	286	277,706
22 Shahpur	2	250	500
25 Montgomery	[2] 25	366	9,150
30 Peshâwar	39	240	9,360
Total	51,260	Average. 366	18,770,866

[1] This is apparently a mistake. The figure is too high.

[2] The crop per acre for this district not being given in the Report, I have given it the average, 366.

In the Report the figures of crop per acre are given under the heading "Fibres." In the columns per "acres cultivated," cotton and hemp are given under the heading of "Fibres;" and as produce per acre of cotton is given separately, the produce per acre under the heading "Fibres" applies to hemp. The prices are not given in the Report. I take ordinarily prepared fibre as 20 lbs. per rupee. The value of 18,770,866 lbs. at 20 lbs. per rupee will be Rs. 9,38,543.

KASSAMBA (SAFFLOWER).

Neither produce per acre nor price is given in the Report. I take 40 lbs. per acre of dry prepared stuff, and price 2½ lbs. per Re 1.

Acres, 24,708 × 40 lbs. = 988,320; at 2½ lbs. per Re. 1 gives Rs. 3,95,328.

INDIGO.

Districts.	Acres.	Per Acre.	Total Quantity.
		lbs.	lbs.
1 Delhi	100	30	3,000
2 Gurgaon	56	100	5,600
3 Kárnal	588	30	17,640
4 Hissar	[1] 785	...	...
5 Rohtak	[1] 1,526	...	...
7 Umballa	1,798	62	111,476
8 Ludhiána	2,647	33	87,351
10 Jullundar	754	41	30,914
11 Hoshiarpur	1,162	44	51,128
18 Firozepore	26	24	624
21 Gujrát	47	101	4,747
23 Mooltan	75,364	26	1,959,464
24 Jhang	2	29	58
25 Montgomery	8	20	160
26 Mazaffargarh	20,603	50	1,030,150
28 D. G. Kahn	23,999	29	695,971
Total	129,465	Average. 31·44	3,998,283
			[1] add 72,658
			4,070,941

[1] For these (2,311 acres) produce per acre is taken of the average for the others—viz., 31·44.

The price is not given in the Report. I take Annas 12 per lb., which will give the total value to be Rs. 30,53,205.

VEGETABLES.

Districts.	Acres.	Per Acre.	Total Quantity.	Price per Re. 1.	Total Value.
		lbs.	lbs.	lbs.	Rs.
1 Delhi	11,700	4,753	55,610,100	43·88	12,67,322
2 Gurgaon	[1]9,387	[1]6,000	56,322,000	28·8	19,55,625
3 Kárnal	846	4,753	4,021,038	39·77	1,01,107
4 Hissar	3,485	,,	16,564,205	28·8	5,75,146
5 Rohtak	920	,,	4,372,760	35·65	1,22,658
6 Sirsa	677	,,	3,217,781	27·43	1,17,308
7 Umballa	3,495	,,	16,611,735	35·65	4,65,967
8 Ludhiána	7,560	,,	35,932,680	30·17	11,91,006
9 Simla	7	,,	33,271	60·34	551
10 Jullundar	7,731	,,	36,745,443	27·43	13,39,607
11 Hoshiarpur	3,586	,,	17,044,258	32·91	5,17,905
12 Kángra	6,551	,,	31,136,903	49·37	6,30,684
13 Amritsar	15,175	,,	72,126,775	36·34	19,84,776
14 Gurdáspur	6,790	,,	32,272,870	27·43	11,76,553
15 Siálkot	3,000	,,	14,259,000	32·91	4,33,272
16 Lahore	5,746	,,	27,310,738	24·68	11,06,593
17 Gujránwála	56,988	,,	270,863,964	39·77	68,10,761
18 Firozepore	[1]4,274	[1]2,015	8,612,110	32·91	2,61,686
19 Ráwalpindi	4,660	4,753	22,148,980	40·45	5,47,564
20 Jhelum	3,709	,,	17,628,877	31·54	5,58,937
21 Gujrát	21,904	,,	104,109,712	28·8	36,14,920
22 Shahpur	11,072	,,	52,625,216	..	..
23 Mooltan	29,239	,,	138,972,967	26·74	51,97,194
24 Jhang	23,203	,,	110,283,859	20·57	53,61,393
25 Montgomery	1,423	,,	6,763,519	27·43	2,46,574
26 Mazaffargarh	3,095	,,	14,710,535	21·25	6,92,260
27 D. I. Khan	803	,,	3,816,659	33·42	1,14,202
28 D. G. Khan	794	,,	3,773,882	20·57	1,83,465
29 Bannu	4,152	,,	19,734,456	45·25	4,36,120
30 Peshâwar	3,631	,,	17,258,143	32·05	5,38,475
31 Hazára	598	,,	2,842,294	45·25	62,813
32 Kohát	599	,,	2,847,047	31·45	90,526
Total	256,800	Average 4,753	1,220,573,777	Average 30·98	3,77,02,970 for 1,167,948,561 lbs.

[1] Produce per acre is given for vegetables for these two districts only, and the average of these—viz., 4,753—is applied to all others.

The prices I have taken above are given in the Report for potato only, and the average comes to, say, 31 lbs. per Re. 1. This is a high average price. The average price of potato will be nearer 60 than 31 lbs. I take, however, the average of 31 lbs.

Now out of the vegetables grown, about one-eighth only will be potato, and seven-eighths other kind of general vegetables. This will give, out of 1,220,573,777 lbs., seven-eighths of general vegetables = 1,068,002,055 lbs.

The price of vegetables is not given in the Report. It may be taken as 1½ maunds per Re. 1 or 124 lbs., say 100 lbs. per Re. 1, which will give the total value of vegetables to be about Rs. 1,06,80,020.

Again, the average of 4,753 lbs. is of vegetables, but

potato will be only about 30 maunds or 2,460 lbs. per acre; and as potato will be about one-eighth of the acreage planted with vegetables, or about 32,100 acres, the total quantity of potato will be 32,100 × 2,460 = 78,966,000 lbs. This, at the price of 31 lbs. per Re. 1, will give Rs. 25,47,290. I make no deduction for seed potato, or seed for vegetables.

TEA.

The produce per acre is given for one district only; but the Report, at page 78, takes the general average to be the same —viz., 96 lbs. The price is not given. I take 3 lbs. per Re. 1.

Total acres, 8,884 × 96 lbs. 852,864 lbs.; at 3 lbs. per Re. 1 will give Rs. 2,84,288.

SUGAR.

Districts.	Acres.	Per Acre.	Total Quantity.	1st sort. Price per Re. 1.	Total Value.
		lbs.	lbs.	lbs.	Rs.
1 Delhi	34,881	[1,2]1,500	52,321,500	5·49	95,30,328
2 Gurgaon	1,125	646	726,750	6·68	1,08,795
3 Kárnal	14,309	,,	9,243,614	7·03	13,14,881
4 Hissar	34	,,	[3]21,964	..	..
5 Rohtak	33,324	,,	21,527,304	8·14	26,44,631
6 Sirsa	6	[1]389	2,334	6·34	368
7 Umballa	25,540	[1]280	7,151,200	5·83	12,26,620
8 Ludhiána	14,400	[1]661	9,518,400	6·86	13,87,521
9 Simla	..	..	..	..	..
10 Jullundar	43,963	[1]531	23,344,353	6·51	35,85,922
11 Hoshiarpur	42,015	[1]597	25,082,955	6·51	38,52,988
12 Kángra	8,139	[1]494	4,020,666	6·43	6,25,297
13 Amritsar	36,579	646	23,630,034	7·11	33,23,492
14 Gurdáspur	41,375	[1]360	14,895,000	5·65	26,36,283
15 Siálkot	29,009	646	18,739,814	6·51	28,78,619
16 Lahore	2,527	,,	1,632,442	5·65	2,88,927
17 Gujránwála	26,625	,,	17,199,750	7·2	25,27,743
18 Firozepore	1,916	[1]410	785,560	6·	1,30,926
19 Ráwalpindi	2,381	646	1,538,126	6·34	2,42,606
20 Jhelum	414	,,	267,444	5·83	45,873
21 Gujrát	7,221	[1]660	4,765,860	6·51	7,32,082
22 Shahpur	1,312	646	[3]847,552	..	..
23 Mooltan	3,726	,,	2,406,996	6·17	3,90,112
24 Jhang	260	[1]261	67,860	5·91	11,482
25 Montgomery	113	646	72,998	6·17	11,831
26 Mazaffargarh	4,355	,,	2,813,330	5·83	4,82,560
27 D. I. Khan	88	,,	56,848	5·65	10,061
28 D. G. Khan	55	,,	35,530	5·23	6,793
29 Bannu	5,443	,,	3,516,178	5·36	6,56,003
30 Peshâwar	9,914	,,	6,404,444	6·08	10,53,362
31 Hazára	561	,,	362,406	5·49	66,022
32 Kohát	20	,,	12,920	5·74	2,250
Total	391,630	Average 646	253,012,132	Average 6·34	3,97,74,378 for 252,142,616 lbs., excluding the two quantities marked [3].

[1] For these districts only is the produce per acre given in the Report. I have applied the average of these to others.

[2] This is evidently a mistake. Though other districts, such as

The average price, as obtained on the basis of the prices given in the Report, is for "first sort," or what is called "misri." But there are different qualities of sugar—viz., gól, red sugar, ordinary second sort sugar, and best or first sort sugar. Taking the price of first sort as averaging 6 lbs. per rupee, the prices of the other kinds are :—

Gól	24 lbs. per rupee	Of these the first two form nearly two-thirds, and the last two form one-third of the whole quantity.
Red Sugar . . .	16 ,, ,,	
Ordinary Second	7 ,, ,,	
First sort . . .	6 ,, ,,	

Taking in this ratio, we get

Two-thirds at 20 lbs. = $13\frac{1}{3}$ }
One-third ,, $6\frac{1}{2}$,, = $2\frac{1}{6}$ } or $15\frac{1}{2}$, or say 15 lbs. per rupee.

The whole quantity, being 253,012,132 lbs., will, at 15 lbs. per rupee, give the total value Rs. 1,68,67,475.

For seed, to deduct cane equal to 40 lbs. of sugar per acre. This gives 16-fold, and taking the higher average of 646 lbs., I deduct, say, 6 per cent.

The whole quantity is then 237,831,405 lbs., and the whole value is then Rs. 1,58,55,427.

If, as I have pointed out above, the average of Delhi were taken at 500 lbs. instead of 1,500 lbs., which would make the average produce of the whole of Punjab 487 lbs. instead of 646 lbs., the above quantity and value will prove some 30 per cent. higher than they should be.

It may be noted here that the Report itself makes the average 449 lbs. only, on the fallacious principle of simply adding up and dividing by the number of districts; while, when properly calculated, the figure should be 646 instead of 449. This is an instance of how misleading and incorrect the averages are as they are generally calculated in the Administration Reports.

Ludhiána, are better than Delhi, and while 661 lbs. is considered a fair average for Ludhiána, 1,500 for Delhi cannot be correct. It is more likely 500 than 1,500. If 500 be adopted, the average will become 487 instead of 646 lbs. And it is also considered that an average of about 489 lbs. will be near the mark. I have allowed the figure 1,500 to remain, though this increases the average above 487 lbs. nearly 32 per cent.

PUNJAB, 1876-7.

SUMMARY OF PRODUCE OF ALL DISTRICTS.

Produce.	Acres.	Total Quantity	Average per Acre.	Total Value.	Average Price per Re. 1.
		lbs.	lbs.	Rs.	lbs.
Rice	708,699	541,492,369	796	2,25,35,693	20·42
Wheat	6,609,497	5,332,813,517	840·4	9,17,42,419	53·48
Makai (Indian Corn)	1,084,339	1,593,872,255	1,500	2,33,01,265	68·4
Jow (Barley)	1,874,217	883,781,444	503	1,06,78,175	82·76
Gram	2,272,236	1,417,173,807	645	1,86,72,194	75·89
Inferior Grains	6,534,963	3,169,169,607	510·5	4,54,14,114	69·78
Poppy (Opium)	12,348	154,550	12·51	3,86,375	·4 { Rs. 2½ per lb. paid by Govt.
Tobacco	71,867	60,804,785	846	48,32,541	12·58
Turmeric	4,130	677,320	164 (dry)	67,732	10
Coriander Seed	6,934	2,288,220	330 "	1,43,014	16
Ginger	286	58,630	205 "	8,376	7
Chillies	23,518	3,800,700 (dry)	{ 808 (green) 161·6 (dry) }	4,75,100	8
Other kinds of drugs and spices	35,074	11,574,420	330	8,26,744	14
Oil Seeds	846,689	325,730,071	392	1,20,64,076	27
Cotton	668,876	70,013,890	105	1,23,54,344	5·66
Hemp	51,260	18,770,866	366	9,38,543	20
Kassamba (Safflower)	24,708	988,320	40 (dry)	3,95,328	2·5
Indigo	129,465	4,070,941	31·44	30,53,205	1⅓
Vegetables	256,800	{ 1,068,002,055	4,753	1,06,80,020	100 Green Vegetables
		78,966,000	2,460	25,47,290	31 Potato
Tea	8,884	852,864	96	2,84,288	3
Sugar	391,630	237,831,405	646	1,58,55,427	15 { Average of four qualities
Total	21,616,420			27,72,56,263	

PUNJAB, 1876–7.

MANUFACTURES.

Goods.	Value given in the Report.	Deduct for raw Material already calculated and included in the Produce, or imported and paid from Produce.		Balance representing Labour.
	Rs.		Rs.	Rs.
Silks	19,62,049	Say half for material (imported)	9,81,024	9,81,024
Cottons	1,75,05,556	„ 40 per cent. „ „	70.02,222	1,05,03,334
Wool	9,42,329			9,42,329
Fibres	6,41,578	„ 20 „ „ „	1,28,315	5,13,263
Paper	1,58,565	„ 25 „ „ „	39,641	1,18,924
Wood	67,28,686			67,28,686
Iron	43,26,132	„ One-third „ „	14,42,044	28,84,088
Brass and Copper	6,38,573	„ 40 per cent. „ „	2,55,429	3,83,144
Building	43,22,867			43,22,867
Leather	63,21,802			63,21,802
Gold and Silver Lace	56,27,054	„ Two-thirds „ „	37,51,370	18,75,685
Dyeing	7,38,926	„ Materials not stated		7,38,926
Oil	12,45,966	„ Two-thirds, or say one-half Material	6,22,983	6,22,983
Shawls	8,96,507	„ One-twelfth Material imported	74,709	8,21,798
Other Manufactures	30,81,205	Not Described		30,81,205
		Total		4,08,40,058

MINES.

There is no clear statement of the value of the produce of mines given in this report. The chief article is salt. The Report does not give any account of the cost of salt.

Parl. Return No. 176 of 1878 gives (page 30) "the quantity manufactured, excavated, or purchased" during the year (1876-7) as 1,795,956 maunds. In the statistics published by the Government of India (1875) at Calcutta, Part III, page 79, it is said: "Since 4th July, 1870, one anna per maund has "been charged as the cost price of the salt, in addition to the duty." At this rate the above production of salt—viz., 1,795,956 maunds—will cost Rs. 1,12,247. Duty is paid from the produce of the country.

For other minerals I can get no estimate. I roughly, and as a very outside estimate, put down the *whole* product of mines at Rs. 3 lakhs.

STOCK.

I am unable to make any estimate of the annual addition to stock during the year. All that portion, however, which is used for agricultural or manufacturing purposes need not be estimated, as its labour, like that of the agriculturist and the manufacturer himself, is included in the agricultural or manufacturing produce. The portion of the annual produce or addition, which is used for other than agricultural and manufacturing purposes, such as carriage and food and milk, needs to be added to the production of the year. Though I cannot estimate this, still it will not matter much, for, as I have shown in the table for inferior grains, a certain portion of them goes in the feed of animals, and as this portion supplies the feed of the *whole* stock that requires grain and not merely that of the *annual* addition, the non-estimate of that portion of the *annual* addition to the stock which is used for carriage and for food may be more than covered by the value of the grain used for animals. Moreover, as I also give a margin upon the total estimate for any omission, any such item will be fully provided for.

SUMMARY OF THE TOTAL PRODUCTION OF PUNJAB, 1876-7.

	Value.
Agricultural Produce	Rs. 27,72,56,263
Manufactures	4,08,40,058
Mines	3,00,000
	Rs. 31,83,96,321

In order to meet any omissions (fish, etc.), I allow a further margin of above 3½ crores of rupees, making, say, the whole produce of Punjab 35⅓ crores of rupees, or at 2s. per rupee = £35,330,000, which for a population of 17,600,000 gives £2 per head per annum at the outside for the year 1876-7.

The approximate estimate I had made out for the year 1867-8 in my paper on the "Poverty of India" was 49s. 5d., showing that either my calculation for the year 1867-8 was too high, or the production of the Province has diminished in value. The truth most likely is between both.

At all events, unless any error of importance is pointed out, it seems clearly established that the value of the production of one of the best provinces in India is Rs. 20 per head per annum at the outside.

FOOD PRODUCE, 1876-7.

GRAIN.

	Total Quantity. lbs.
Rice	541,492,369
Wheat	5,332,813,517
Makai (Indian Corn)	1,593,872,255
Jow (Barley)	883,781,444
Gram	1,417,173,807
Inferior Grains	3,169,169,607
Total	12,938,302,999

Quantity Raised for Animals.			About		
Gram	1,417,173,807	lbs.	× ½ =		708,586,903
Jow	883,781,444	,,	× ¾ =		662,836,083
Jowár	2,221,535	acres	× ⅔ =	1,481,023	(lbs. per acre less seed (510—26.))
Bájra	2,339,796	,,	× ½ =	1,169,898	
Moth	982,208	,,	× ¾ =	736,656	
Másh	213,465	,,	× ⅓ =	71,155	
Total				3,458,732 × 484 =	1,674,026,288
				Total	3,045,449,274

Balance remaining for human use . . 9,892,853,725

Or 562 lbs. per annum, or 1 lb. 8·65 oz. per day per head for a population of 17,600,000.

Even taking the *whole* quantity of grain as for human use, and thus not allowing any portion at all for animals (which would, of course, not be right to do), the quantity per annum will be 735 lbs., or 2 lbs. per day per head.

In the value I have calculated for grain I have taken the *whole* grain—*i.e.*, including the portion for animals.

VEGETABLES.

General Vegetables.

Total quantity, 1,068,002,055 lbs., gives 60·7 lbs. per annum, or 2·66 oz. per day per head.

POTATO.

Total quantity, 78,966,000 lbs., gives 4·48 lbs. per annum, or 2 oz. per day per head.

LAND REVENUE OF THE PRINCIPAL PROVINCES OF INDIA FOR 1875-6.[1]

	Revenue.	Population.	Revenue per head.		
	Rs.		Rs.	a.	p.
Bengal	3,77,65,067	60,502,897	0	10	0
Punjab	2,00,15,260	17,611,498	1	2	2
N.-West Provinces . .	4,24,57,444	30,781,204	1	6	0¾
Madras	4,54,50,128	31,672,613	1	6	11
Bombay (including Sind)	3,69,43,563	16,302,173	2	4	3

[1] I have taken 1875-6, for, on account of the famines in the Bombay and Madras Presidencies in the year 1876-7, a comparison for the year 1876-7 will be an unfair one.

PUNJAB, 1876-7.

Cost of Absolute Necessaries of Life of an Agricultural Labourer.

Food.—*Man.*

Items.	Quantity per day.	Quantity for 1 Year.	Price for Re. 1.	Cost for 1 Year.	Remarks.
	Seers.	Seers.	Seers.	Rs. As.	
Flour . . .	1	365	25	14 9	The price in the Report is 20 seers for first sort; I have taken 25 per cent. lower price for lower quality.
Rice	$\frac{1}{4}$	91	13	7 0	The price in the Report is 10 seers for first sort; I take 30 per cent. lower price for inferior quality.
Dal	$\frac{1}{8}$	45	18	2 8	The price in the Report is 16 seers; I take it 12 per cent. lower.
Salt	1 oz.	11	$9\frac{1}{4}$	1 3	The price of the Report, which is Government sale price.
Ghee. . . .	1 "	11	3	3 11	The price in the Report is less than 2 seers. In taking 3 seers, I lower it above 50 per cent., or rather to the price of oil. The quantity, 1 oz., is also rather low for a Punjabee.
Condiment .	2 pies worth	...	...	3 13	These are regarded as under the mark.
Tobacco . .	$1\frac{1}{2}$ " "	...	...	2 14	
Vegetables .	1 " "	...	...	1 8	
			Total .	37 2	Without any meat, sugar, milk, or any drink, or any kind of luxury whatever.

Woman.

All the above items will be nearly the same, except tobacco. Deducting tobacco, it will be Rs. 34-2 as.; say Rs. 32.

Two more Members in a Family.

One young person, say, between 12 and 18, say Rs. 26, though there will not be so much difference.
One " " under 12, say " 0, though this cannot be the case generally.

PUNJAB, 1876-7.

COST OF ABSOLUTE NECESSARIES OF LIFE OF AN AGRICULTURAL LABOURER.—*Continued.*

CLOTHING FOR ONE YEAR.

Man.	Rs.	a.	Woman.	Rs.	a.	Remarks.
2 Dhotees	1	0	2 Pajamas . .	1	0	No holiday clothing, nor for occasions of joy and sorrow are reckoned.
2 Pairs Shoes	1	0	1 Gagra . . .	2	0	
1 Turban	1	0	2 Chadars . .	1	8	
2 Bandis for warm and cold weather . . .	1	8	4 Cholees . .	1	0	
2 Kamlees	4	0	Bangles . .	0	8	
1 Small piece of cloth for Langootee, etc.	0	4	2 Pairs Shoes .	0	8	
1 Chadar	0	12	Hair-dressing	0	3	
2 Pajama	0	12				
Total .	10	4		6	11	

For one young person, say, Rs. 6; for the second, say, nothing.

FAMILY EXPENSES IN COMMON.

	Rs.	a.		
Cottage, Rs. 60; say . . .	4	0	for one year.	Calculated on the lowest scale, without any furniture, such as cots or mats, or stools or anything.
Repairs	3	0	,,	
Cooking and other utensils .	3	8	,,	
Firewood, ¼ anna per day .	5	11	,,	
Lamp Oil, 1 oz. per day, at 3 seers per Re 1	3	12	,,	
	19	15		

TAKING FOUR IN THE FAMILY.

	Food.	Clothing.		Family Expenses.		Total.
	Rs.	Rs.	a.	Rs.	a.	
Man	37	10	4			
Woman	32	6	11			
Youth (12 to 18) .	26	6	0			
Child (under 12) .	0	0	0			
	95	22	15	19	15	137-14—say, Rs. 136

Which will be Rs. 34 per head per annum in a family of four, against the production of Rs. 20 per annum at the outside.

No wedding, birth, and funeral expenses calculated, nor medical, educational, social, and religious wants, but simply the absolute necessaries for existence in ordinary health, at the lowest scale of cost and quantity.

The prices this year are the lowest during ten years.

The Report says (page 83): "Salt and tobacco show a rise in price." This is a mistake into which the writer is led by the mistake of the clerk in taking his totals and division by the number of districts. The figures in Table 45 (page clxxvii), in the line of the "general average" of tobacco, viz., 4-5 and 5-7, are wrong; and so also in the line of salt, 7 and 7-5 are wrong. I do not mean these figures are wrong on account of the fallacious principle of the Report in taking averages, but in taking the average according to the Report's own method—*i.e.*, of adding up the columns and dividing by the number of districts.

It is requested that any further communication on this subject may be addressed to— The Under-Secretary of State for India, India Office, London, S.W.	India Office, S.W. *9th August*, 1880.

SIR,—I am directed by the Secretary of State for India to acknowledge the receipt of your letter of the 24th May, enclosing a table of statistics relating to the value of the production of the Punjab for the year 1876-77.

In reply, I am to thank you for your communication, but with reference to your request that the several Governments in India may be directed to supply similar statistics of production, I am to remark that as regards the important province of Bengal, means do not exist of supplying the information you desire; whilst as regards those Provinces for which such information does already exist, it appears very questionable whether the results given, owing to the absence of any sufficient machinery for their preparation, can be relied upon as trustworthy. Your letter and its enclosure have, however, been sent out to the Government of India.

I enclose herewith for your information copy of a memorandum upon your letter, and also copies of statistics similar to those compiled by yourself, which have been recently prepared in this Office.

I am, Sir, your obedient Servant,

LOUIS MALLET.

Mr. Dadabhai Naoroji.

[ENCLOSURE.]

Memorandum on a Letter from MR. DADABHAI NAOROJI, *dated 24th May*, 1880.

In this letter Mr. Dadabhai Naoroji requests that the several Governments in India may be instructed to furnish statistical information regarding the agricultural, mining and manufacturing produce of their respective administrations, and that a summary may also be given, similar to one which he has prepared for the Punjab, and which he submits with his letter, in order that "a true conception may be formed of the actual material condition of India from year to year." He also asks that his tables may be submitted to the Statistical Department of the India Office, and that any mistakes of facts or figures may be pointed out to him.

In January, 1879, I made calculations for the greater part of India similar to those made by Mr. Dadabhai Naoroji for the Punjab; copies of these are attached.[1] I do not, however, put much faith in the accuracy of the figures from which these calculations are made. The agricultural statistics of India, as they are published, can hardly be very reliable, as they are based upon averages, each average referring to a very large area, in which there may be, and probably are, many variations of conditions and circumstances; whilst in parts, such as the large and wealthy Presidency of Bengal, no statistics of agricultural produce are available.

In examining Mr. Dadabhai Naoroji's paper, it appears that in his calculations he has omitted to make any allowance for the value of straw, and he has made no attempt to estimate the value of the increase of agricultural stock, but he has added an arbitrary sum for the latter and for other omitted items.

Having, however, arrived at some figures supposed to represent the value of the produce of a certain district, the question arises as to how these figures should be applied in order to show the comparative prosperity or otherwise of the people in that district. Mr. Dadabhai has adopted the principle of equally apportioning the value of agricultural produce and manufactures, as ascertained by him from the statistics available, amongst the whole population, without distinguishing how many are agriculturists, how many

[1] I have not inserted these tables, as those concerning Punjab are nearly similar to mine.

mechanics, and how many belong to other trades and professions, or possess property, and whose incomes, therefore, are derived directly neither from agriculture nor from manufactures. Thus he omits all reference to railway wealth, Government stock, house property, profits of trade, salaries, pensions, non-agricultural wages, professional incomes, and returns to investments, and all other sources from which a man who does not grow food himself may obtain the means of purchasing it.

From the Census Report of 1871 it appears that, out of a total population of 17,611,498 under British administration in the Punjab, 9,689,650 are returned as agriculturists, 1,776,786 male adults, equivalent to about 4,500,000 population, as engaged in industrial occupations; thus leaving a population of nearly 3,500,000 directly dependent neither upon agriculture, manufactures, nor mining, and who must therefore derive their means of subsistence from other sources.

Mr. Dadabhai makes out the total value of the agricultural produce of the Punjab to be Rs. 27,69,71,976,[1] and that from manufactures and mines Rs. 4,11,40,058. To this he adds, to meet any omissions, a further margin of 3½ crores, making the whole produce of the Punjab 35¼ crores of rupees, "which, for a population of 17,600,000, gives Rs. 20 per head per annum at the outside for the year 1876-7," to which year the figures he has taken refer. At pages 171, 172 of his tables he shows that the cost of absolute necessaries of life of an agricultural labourer is Rs. 34 per annum, but he omits to explain how, under these circumstances, the people of the Punjab managed to live, and leaves the reader to draw his own conclusions how, with only Rs. 20 per annum, he can provide for an expenditure of Rs. 34.

Adopting Mr. Dadabhai's figures, with regard to which I will take no exception, I think it may be shown, by another process of reasoning than that which he adopts, that they point to the Punjab agriculturist being in a good condition of prosperity rather than the reverse. First, I think it must be admitted that the agricultural produce belongs in the first instance to the man who grows it. From it he and his family will first provide themselves with food, and the remainder he will sell, either for money to enable him to pay his assessment,

[1] There was an error in my table; this amount should be Rs. 27,72,56,263.—D. N.

etc., or in barter for clothing and other necessaries, whilst a part will go to pay wages for labourers and others dependent upon him.

Now, if these premises be admitted, it may be shown that, allowing three-fourths of a seer (1½ lb.) of grain per head per day, according to the calculations given by Mr. A. P. Macdonnel in his "Food Grain Supply and Famine Relief in Behar and Bengal" (p. 8), or, say, 550 lbs. per annum per head of agricultural population, and allowing 6½ per cent. of the gross produce for seed, an equal quantity for cattle-feed, and 2 per cent. for waste, or together 15 per cent., the value of the surplus agricultural produce is sufficient to yield Rs. 24 per head per annum for other requirements, and Rs. 22 per head after deduction of the land revenue demand, or, say, £8 16s. per annum per family of four persons.

The other population of the Punjab (omitting Native States) numbers 7,921,848, for whom the remaining food grain grown, after allowing for the food of agriculturists, cattle, seed, waste, etc., amounting to 5,401,151,059 lbs., is sufficient to provide them with an average rate of over 600 lbs. per head per annum. To supply them with 550 lbs. per head per annum would take 4,357,016,400 lbs., leaving a surplus of 1,044,134,659 lbs., or over 450,000 tons, for export. The food grain grown in the Punjab is, therefore, apart from other food supplies, more than sufficient to feed the whole population, and it is well known that considerable quantities of wheat are exported thence.

The numbers engaged in manufactures in the Punjab I have stated to be about 4,500,000. The net value of manufactures, after deducting the value of raw material, is given by Mr. Dadabhai as only Rs. 4,08,40,058, or about Rs. 9 per head per annum of the population engaged therein. This, I think, sufficiently shows that there must be some error in the value given. F. C. DANVERS.

India Office, 28th June, 1880.

32, Great St. Helens, London,
12th August, 1880.

SIR LOUIS MALLET, *the Under-Secretary of State for India, India Office, London, S.W.*

SIR,—I have received your letter of the 9th inst., and I tender my sincere thanks to his Lordship the Secretary of

State for India for the kind attention he has given to my letter of the 24th May last, and for forwarding it to the Government of India.

The necessity for having correct information about the material condition of India is so very great, both to rulers and the subjects, that I venture to say that any reasonable and well-directed expenditure for this object would be productive of great good; and that, therefore, the Government of India may be requested to improve the existing machinery as much as it may be needed to obtain from the different Governments the tables of production and consumption with as much approximate accuracy as possible. The tables, even so far as are at present supplied, are useful, and I cannot think that it would be difficult for the different Governments to improve the existing arrangements, so as to get sufficiently approximate results for the guidance of the legislation and administration of the country with the greatest practical good, and without the commission of such mistakes as are unavoidably made in the ignorance of the actual state and wants of the country.

For Bengal, also, I hope some means may be devised to obtain such information.

It does not remain for me now, with the evidence of your present letter and its enclosures before me, to impress upon the India Office the great importance of these statistics; for I find that when I commenced working at these tables, about the beginning of last year, the India Office had already got these very tables prepared for their use, and I cannot but express my gladness to find such to be the case.

I am sorry I am not at present well able to give such attention to the enclosures of your letter as I desire, as I am not in good health and am under medical treatment.

I remain,
Your obedient Servant,
DADABHAI NAOROJI.

32, Great St. Helens, London.
13th September, 1880.

SIR LOUIS MALLET, *the Under-Secretary of State for India, India Office, London, S.W.*

SIR,—In continuation of my letter of the 12th ult., I now beg to submit, for the consideration of his Lordship the

Secretary of State for India, the accompanying memorandum on Mr. Danver's two papers of 4th January, 1879, and 28th June, 1880, and I hope his Lordship will give it the same kind attention that was shown to my former letter.

I request that copy of this letter and memo. be sent to the Indian Government, as I think that views similar to those of Mr. Danvers more or less prevail in India also.

I shall esteem it a great favour if it is pointed out to me that I am mistaken in any of my views now put forth. My only desire is to find out the truth, and that India may receive and enjoy the blessings and benefits which the British nation is really capable of bestowing on her, if once British statesmen give their usual conscientious attention to her concerns.

I remain, Sir,

Your obedient Servant,

DADABHAI NAOROJI.

Memorandum on MR. DANVERS' *Papers of 28th June*, 1880, *and 4th January*, 1879.

Mr. Danvers says: "In examining Mr. Dadabhai Naoroji's paper, it appears that in his calculations he has omitted to make any allowance for the value of straw, and he has made no attempt to estimate the value of the increase of agricultural stock, but he has added an arbitrary sum for the latter and for other omitted items."

I have omitted not only straw, but also grass, cotton seed, and any fodder or other food for animals which I have not taken in my tables; and further, I should also omit all that portion of the inferior grains which I have shown in my table at page 155 of this book, of about 30 per cent. of the whole acreage of grains, and which is grown for the food of animals.

The reason is this; the principle to be considered is—first, either the whole *gross* annual production of the country may be taken (including straw, grass, etc., etc.), and from this *gross* production, before apportioning it per head of human population, a deduction should be made for the portion required for all the stock, which, in the case of the Punjab, is above 7,000,000 large cattle and near 4,000,000 sheep and goats; or, second, all straw, grass, and every production raised for animal food should be left out of calculation, and only the rest of the production which is and can be turned to human use should be apportioned among the human population.

Mr. Danvers may adopt either of the above two methods, whichever he may consider would give most correctly the actual production for human use. It would not be correct to include the produce raised for animal use, and then not to make the necessary deduction for such use. I would put this matter in another form.

Suppose on the 1st of January, 1880, we have in India a certain amount of material wealth in all its various forms, and we take complete stock of it; that during the year following the country works in all its varieties of ways, consumes for all its various human, animal, and instrumental wants from the store existing on the 1st January, 1880; and that after the end of the year, on 1st January, 1881, we gather together or take stock of every possible kind of material production (agricultural, mineral, and manufacturing, and addition from profits of foreign trade) during the year. This production during the year will have to meet all the wants of the next year. If this production prove less than what would be wanted for the next year, then there would be a deficiency, and either the original wealth or capital of the country will have to be drawn upon, or the people will be so much less supplied with their wants in some shape or other; in either way showing a diminution of prosperity, both as property and capacity. If, on the other hand, the whole material production of the year prove more than what would be necessary for the next year for all ordinary or usual wants, then a surplus would accrue, and so far, in some permanent form, add to the capital of the country and increase its prosperity.

I request, therefore, that Mr. Danvers may be asked to work out the total production and wants of India for, say, the last dozen years on correct principles of calculation, from such materials as are already available at the India Office, supplementing such information as may be deficient by asking from India and from experienced retired officials who are now in this country. Such tables will show what the actual material condition of the country is, and whether it is increasing or diminishing in prosperity. Unless such information is obtained, the Government of the country will be blind and in the dark, and cannot but result in misery to India, and discredit to the rulers, their best intentions notwithstanding. It is hopeless to expect intelligent government without the aid of such important information annually.

I am glad Mr. Danvers has made an estimate of the annual increase of agricultural stock in his paper of 4th January, 1879, and as I have to say something upon this paper further on, I do not say anything here upon the subject of stock.

Mr. Danvers says: "Mr. Dadabhai has adopted the principle of equally apportioning the value of agricultural produce and manufactures, as ascertained by him from the statistics available, amongst the whole population, without distinguishing how many are agriculturists, how many mechanics, and how many belong to other trades or professions, or possess property, and whose incomes, therefore, are derived directly neither from agriculture nor from manufactures. Thus he omits all reference to railway wealth, Government stock, house property, profits of trade, salaries, pensions, non-agricultural wages, professional incomes, and returns to investments, and all other sources from which a man who does not grow food himself may obtain the means of purchasing it.

"From the Census Report of 1871, it appears that, out of a total population of 17, 611,498 under British administration in the Punjab, 9,689,650 are returned as agriculturists, 1,776,786 adult males, equivalent to about 4,500,000 of population, as engaged in industrial occupations; thus leaving a population of nearly 3,500,000 directly dependent neither upon agriculture, manufactures, nor mining, and who must, therefore, derive their means of subsistence from other sources."

I take each of the items :—

1st, "Railway Wealth." I am not sure what Mr. Danvers means by "railway wealth." In his paper of 4th January, 1879, he regards railways as "enhancing the value of food grains, and adding, *pro tanto*, to the wealth of the districts through which they run." If he means in the above extract by "railway wealth" something different, then that needs to be explained. In the meantime, I adopt the interpretation as I make out with the aid of his paper of 4th January, 1879.

Suppose 100 maunds of wheat exist in the Punjab, and its cost to the producer, say, is Rs. 100—suppose that this wheat is carried by railway to Bombay, and its value at Bombay is Rs. 125; does Mr. Danvers mean that this circumstance has *added* Rs. 25, or anything at all, to the existing wealth of India?

If so then no such thing has happened. The 100 maunds of wheat existed in the Punjab, and the Rs. 125 existed in Bombay, before the wheat was moved an inch. After the movement, the only result has been change of hands. The wheat has gone to Bombay, and the Rs. 125 are distributed between the owner at Punjab, who receives Rs. 100, and the railway owners and workers, and the merchant who carried through the transaction, who between them divide the Rs. 25. By the mere fact of the removal of the wheat from the Punjab to Bombay not a single grain of wheat nor a single pie of money is *added* to what already existed in India before the wheat was touched. Such "railway wealth" does not exist. If the mere movement of produce can *add* to the existing wealth, India can become rich in no time. All it would have to do is to go on moving its produce continually all over India, all the year round, and under the magic wheels of the train wealth will go on springing till the land will not suffice to hold it. But there is no royal (even railway) road to material wealth. It must be produced from the materials of the earth till the great discovery is made of converting motion into matter. I should not be misunderstood. I am not discussing here the benefits of railways, whatever they are to any country or to India. To show that the people of India are not deriving the usual benefits of railways I give hereafter a short separate section. Here it is enough for me to state that railways are, in a way, an indirect means of increasing the material production of any country, but that, whatever that "means" is, its result is fully and completely included in the estimate of the actual annual production of the country, and that there is nothing more to be *added* to such actual material production of the year.

2nd, "Government Stock." Suppose I hold a lakh of rupees of Government 4 per cent. rupee paper. It does not from itself produce or create or make to grow out any money or food or any kind of material wealth for me. It simply means that Government will give me Rs. 4,000 every year, and that, not by creating anything by any divine power, but from the revenue of the country; and this revenue can be got from only the actual material production of the year. So in reality my income of Rs. 4,000 from "Government Stock" is nothing more or less than a share out of the production of the country, and is, therefore, fully and completely included therein. No addition has to be made from "Government Stock" to the actual material production of the year. No such addition exists at all.

3rd, "House Property." Suppose I have taken a house at a yearly rental of Rs. 1,000. The house does not grow or create the rent by the mere fact of my occupying it. I have to pay this amount out of my income of Rs. 4,000 from Government Stock, and so the house-owner receives through me and the Government his share out of the production of the country. The discussion of the other items further on will show that, be my income from any of the various sources Mr. Danvers suggests, it is ultimately and solely derived from, and is included in, the yearly production of the country, and the owners of "house property" simply take their share, like everybody else, from this same store.

4th, "Profits of Trade." I take, first, foreign trade. Mr. Danvers is quite right that the foreign trade of a country adds to its annual income or production.[1] But, unfortunately, the case with India is quite otherwise. The present system of British administration not only sweeps away to England the whole profits of the foreign trade, but also drains away a portion of the annual production itself of the country. So that, instead of India making *any* addition from its "profits of foreign trade" to its yearly production, a deduction has to be made from such production in estimating the actual quantity that ultimately remains for the use of the people of India. A portion of the actual production, through the channel of foreign trade, goes clean out of the country to England, without an atom of material return. The manner in which the foreign trade of India becomes the channel through which India's present greatest misfortune and evil operate, I treat further on in a separate section, to avoid confusion. It is enough for me to say here that, as matters actually stand, instead of there being, as should be, any addition from foreign trade to the annual production of India, there is actually a diminution, or drain of it clean out of the country to England, to the extent of some £18,000,000

[1] Taking the aggregate wealth of the world, foreign trade even adds nothing. It simply then becomes internal trade, and is mere change of hands, as explained further on.

a year, together with, and over and above, all its "profits of trade." I grieve, therefore, that I have nothing to *add* from "profits of trade," as Mr. Danvers suggests, but much to *subtract*.

I take next the internal trade. Resuming the illustration of the 100 maunds of wheat at Punjab, say a merchant buys at Rs. 100 and sends it to Bombay, where he gets Rs. 125. The result simply is that the wheat is still the same 100 maunds, and the Rs. 125 that existed in Bombay are still Rs. 125, but that out of Rs. 25 the merchant receives his "profit of trade," and the railway its charges for carrying. Not a single atom of money or wheat is added to the existing wealth of the country by this internal trade; only a different distribution has taken place. I should not be misunderstood. I am not discussing here the usefulness of internal trade, whatever it is; I am only pointing out that any increase in the material income of the country by the mere transactions of the internal trade is a thing that does not exist, and that whatever benefits and "profits of trade" there are from internal trade, are fully and completely included in the ultimate result of the actual material production of the year.

5th, "Salaries and Pensions." These will be official and non-official. Official salaries and pensions are paid by Government from revenue, and this revenue is derived from the production of the country; and so from that same store are all such salaries and pensions derived. For non-official salaries or pensions the phenomenon is just the same. I pay my clerks or servants either from my profits of trade, or interest of Government Stock, or from rent of my house property, or from any of the sources which Mr. Danvers may suggest, but one and all of these incomes are drawn from the same store—the annual material production of the country. All salaries and pensions are thus fully and completely included in the estimate of the production.

But this is not all. In these salaries and pensions, etc., do we come to the very source of India's chief misfortune and evil, which, as I have already said, works through the medium of the foreign trade. It is the salaries and pensions, and all other expenditure incident to the excessive European agency, both in England and India, which is India's chief curse, in the shape of its causing the exhausting drain which is destroying India. In the ordinary and normal circumstances of a country, when all the salaries, pensions, etc., are earned by the people themselves, and remain in the country itself to fructify in the people's own pockets, there is no such thing as an addition to the annual production of the country from "salaries and pensions." But as far as India is concerned the case is much worse. All salaries and pensions, etc., paid to Europeans in England and India, beyond the absolute necessity of the maintenance or supervision of British rule, are actually, first, a direct deprivation of the natural provision for similar classes of the people of the country, and, second, a drain from the property and capacity of the country at large. So, unfortunately, is there nothing to be *added*, as Mr. Danvers asks, from "salaries and pensions," but much to be *subtracted* that is either spent in England or remitted to England from the resources of India, and for which not a particle returns, and what is enjoyed in India itself by the Europeans.

Mr. Danvers may kindly consider his own salary. It is derived from the production of India. It is brought to England, and not a farthing out of it returns to India. Even if it returned it would be no *addition* to the wealth of India; but as it does not return, it is so much actual *diminution* from the means of the subsistence of the people. I should not be misunderstood. That for a good long time a reasonable amount of payment for British rule is necessary for the regeneration of India is true, and no thinking Native of India denies this. It is the evil of excessive payment that India has to complain of. But what I have to point out here is that salaries and pensions, even to the Natives themselves, are no addition to the wealth, and much less are those which are not paid to the people of the country. The increase supposed by Mr. Danvers does not exist. There is, on the contrary, much diminution.

6th, "Non-Agricultural Wages." A person employed by a farmer, say as a labourer, upon building his house, is paid from the farmer's agricultural income. A person employed by a merchant, a householder, a stockholder, a pensioner, or a salaried man, or on a railway, is paid from their income, which, as I have explained, is derived from the only great store—the annual material production of the country. In short, every labourer—mental or physical—has his share for his subsistence, through various channels, from the only one fountain-head—the annual material production of the country. There is no source outside the production (including any addition to it from profits of foreign trade) from which any individual derives his means of subsistence.

7th, "Professional Incomes." I consult a doctor, or a solicitor. The mere act of my consulting these professional gentlemen does not enable me to create money to pay them. I must pay them from my income as an agriculturist, or a miner, or a manufacturer, or a stockholder, or a householder, etc.; and my such income is all and solely derived from the material production of the country.

I need not now go any further into a repetition of the same argument with regard to—

8th, "Returns to investments and all other sources from which a man who does not grow food himself may obtain the means of purchasing it"; or leaving a population "directly dependent neither upon agriculture, manufactures, nor mining, and who must therefore derive their means of subsistence from other sources."

There *do not exist* any such "other sources," except profits of foreign trade. But, unfortunately for India, instead of foreign trade bringing any profits, it is actually the channel by which, in addition to all such profits, a portion of the production itself is also swept away. So India exhibits the strange phenomenon that her people cannot get any benefit from profits of foreign trade, and cannot enjoy for their subsistence even their own production, fully or adequately. The result of all the different influences—forces, labour, knowledge, land, climate, railways, or all other kinds of public works, good government, justice, security of property, law, order—and all the above eight and other so-called sources of income, is *fully and completely* comprised in the *ultimate resultant* of all of them—viz., the actual material income of the year. Its increase or decrease every year is, in fact, *the* test of the ultimate and full result of all the above direct and indirect means of the production of a country. If the material income of the year does not suffice for all the wants of the whole people for the year, the existing "capital" wealth of the country is drawn upon, and, so far, the capital and the capacity for annual production are diminished.

I submit, therefore, that Mr. Danvers' argument of the "other sources" has to be laid aside.

Mr. Danvers says: "Mr. Dadabhai makes out the total value of the agricultural produce of the Punjab to be Rs. 27,72,56,263, and that from manufactures and mines, Rs. 4,11,40,058. To this he adds, to meet any omissions, a further margin of 3½ crores, making the whole produce of the Punjab 35¼ crores of rupees, 'which, for a population of 17,600,000, gives Rs. 20 per head per annum at the outside for the year 1876-7,' to which year the figures he has taken refer. At page 172 of his tables he shows that the cost of absolute necessaries of life of an agricultural labourer is Rs. 34 per annum, but he omits to explain how, under these circumstances, the people of the Punjab managed to live, and leaves the reader to draw his own conclusions how, with only Rs. 20 per annum, he can provide for an expenditure of Rs. 34."

Why, that is the very question I want Government to answer: How can they expect people to manage to live, under such circumstances, without continuously sinking into poverty? The first real question is, Are these facts or not? If not, then what are the actual facts of the "means and wants" of the people of India? If they are, then the question is for Mr. Danvers and Government to answer, how people can manage to live. The answer to the question is, however, obvious—viz., that as the balance of income every year available for the use of the people of India does not suffice for the wants of the year, the capital-wealth of the country is being drawn upon, and the country goes on becoming poorer and poorer, and more and more weakened in its capacity of production; and that the American War, for a little while, gave, and the various loans give, a show of prosperity, to end in greater burdens and greater destruction by famines.

These facts of the insufficiency of the means for the wants go to prove the late Lord Lawrence's statements, made in 1864, as Viceroy, and, in 1873, before the Finance Committee. In 1864 he said that India was, on the whole, a very poor country, and the mass of the people enjoyed only a scanty subsistence; and, in 1873, he repeated that the mass of the people of India were so miserably poor that they had barely the means of subsistence; that it was as much as a man could do to feed his family, or half feed them, let alone spending money on what might be called luxuries or conveniences. Such, then, is the manner in which the people of India manage to live: scanty subsistence, and dying away by millions at the very touch of drought. In the case of the Punjab, as the latest British possession, and least drained, and from other circumstances noted below,[1] the people have had, as yet, better resources, in their "capital"-wealth, to draw upon; but taking India as a whole, Lord Lawrence's words are most deplorably but too true.

I need not discuss Mr. Danvers' paper of 28th June, 1880, any further. The fallacy of "other sources" besides agriculture, mines, manufactures, and foreign trade, pervades his whole argument; and in the latter part of the paper two different matters are mixed up, a little misapprehension has taken place as to my meaning, and some part is irrelevant.

The whole question now before us is simply this:—

First, what the whole actual, material, annual income of India is, as the ultimate balance of all sources and influences; that is available for the use of the *whole people of India*.

Secondly, what the absolutely necessary wants and the usual wants of all classes of the people are; and

Thirdly, whether the income of India is equal to, less, or more than such wants.

[1] The Punjab is favoured by nature and by circumstances. By nature, inasmuch as it is one of the most fertile parts of India. It is "Punj-aub:" the land of the five waters, and it has both natural and artificial irrigation. It is favoured by circumstances, inasmuch as that (excepting Bengal, in its special fortunate circumstances of the permanent settlement) Punjab pays the least land revenue—viz, the Punjab pays Re. 1-2-2 per head per annum, the North-West Provinces pay Re. 1-6, Madras Re. 1-7, and Bombay Rs. 2-4-3 (see my tables page 170). I have taken these figures for 1875-6; those for 1876-7 would be unfair and abnormal, on account of the Bombay and Madras Famines. Further, the Punjab has been further favoured by other circumstances in the following way:—

The Administration Report of 1856-8 says: "In former Reports it was explained how the circumstance of so much money going out of the Punjab contributed to depress the agriculturists. The Native regular army was Hindustani; to them was a large share of the Punjab revenue disbursed, of which a part only was spent on the spot, and a part was remitted to their home. Thus it was that year after year, lakhs and lakhs were drained from the Punjab and enriched Oudh. But within last year, the Native army being Punjabi, all such sums have been paid to them, and have been spent at home. Again, many thousands of Punjabi soldiers are serving abroad; these men not only remit their savings, but have also sent a quantity of prize property and plunder—the spoils of Hindustan—to their Native villages. The effect of all this is already perceptible in an increase of agricultural capital, a freer circulation of money, and a fresh impetus to cultivation."

It will be seen that the Punjab has more capital to draw upon, and has some addition to its resources at the expense of the other provinces, to make up for some of its deficiency of production.

By carefully ascertaining these facts every year, shall we ever be able to know truly whether India is progressing in prosperity, or sinking in poverty, or is in a stationary condition? This is the whole problem, and it must be boldly faced and clearly answered if the mission of Britain is the good of India, as I firmly believe it to be.

As to the question, how and by whom, directly or indirectly, the income is actually produced, and how and by whom, and through what channels, this income is distributed among the whole people, that is an entirely different matter, and, though important in itself and involving much legislation, is quite separate from the first and fundamental question of the whole total of the means and wants of India.

I may explain the misapprehension to which I alluded above. In my tables for consumption, in taking "the cost of absolute necessaries of life of an agricultural labourer," I meant him as merely representing the lowest class of labourers of all kinds, so as to show the lowest absolutely necessary wants of the people.

I am under the impression that there is a Statistical Committee at Calcutta, which has existed for the past twenty years, and I hope it will adopt means to give complete tables of the wants and means of India.

As I am requesting his Lordship the Secretary of State for India that Mr. Danvers be asked to work out the wants and means of the people of India during the last twelve years, and that the Government of India may adopt means to perfect the machinery for getting complete information for the future, I submit a few remarks on Mr. Danvers' tables of January 4, 1879, so kindly sent to me. As I have my Punjab tables only for comparison, I examine Mr. Danvers' Punjab tables only.

In his table of quantities of all the inferior grains Mr. Danvers has taken the crop per acre of only some of the grains whose average is 510 lbs. per acre. But the produce of makai and gram, which are included by Mr. Danvers in the inferior grains, is larger, and the result is a large error. The acreage of makai is 1,084,339 acres, and the average produce per acre is 1,500 lbs., so that this produce is under-estimated to the extent of taking only about one-third of the actual quantity. The average produce of gram is 645 lbs. per acre, and the acreage is 2,272,236 acres. On this large acreage there is nearly 26 per cent. of under-estimate. The result of the whole error in the table of inferior grains is that the total quantity is taken by Mr. Danvers as 6,504,880,162 lbs., when it actually is 7,371,110,343 lbs., or above 866,200,000 lbs. more.

In the prices of inferior grains it is necessary to make proper allowance for the lower prices of such grains as moth, kangni, chíná, matar, and masur, which are nearly 25 per cent. lower than the other grains—jowár, bájrá, másh, múng, and arhar. This makes an over-estimate of £240,000. The prices for makai, jow, and gram are given in the Report, and separate estimates should, therefore, be made of the values of these grains, to obtain all possible approximation to truth and accuracy.

The total under-estimate by Mr. Danvers is £1,300,000 in the value of inferior grains.

In "other crops" the value assumed by Mr. Danvers is nearly one-fourth of what I make by taking every item separately—*i.e.*, I make Rs. 19,16,294 against Mr. Danvers' Rs. 4,73,200.

In the following articles Mr. Danvers has adopted the average given in the Report, which, as pointed out by me on previous occasions, is taken on the fallacious principle of adding up the produce per acre of the districts and dividing by the number of districts, without any reference to the quantity of acreage of each district.

Produce.	Incorrect Average.	Correct Average.	Error. Correct Average.	
			More per cent.	Less per cent.
Vegetables . . .	4,008	4,753	18½	..
Sugar[1]	449	646	44	..
Cotton[1]	102	105	3	..
Tobacco	825	846	2½	..
Fibres	322	366	13¾	..
Indigo	47	31	..	33
Opium	10	12·5	25	..

[1] As to some probable errors in these two articles in the Report, I have already given my views in my tables.

In the case of indigo, cotton, tobacco, and hemp, the error has not been large, as the incorrect average is adopted by Mr. Danvers for a few districts only. I notice such differences as 2½ and 3 per cent. also, because, in dealing with figures of hundreds and thousands of millions, these percentages, singly as well as collectively, seriously disturb the accuracy of results. It is very necessary to avoid, as much as possible, all *avoidable* errors, large or small, so that then reliance can be placed upon the results.

The Report gives the price of first sort sugar only, but which, applied to the whole quantity of all kinds, makes the value of nearly two-thirds of the whole quantity quite two and a half times greater than it actually is; the over-estimate comes to nearly £1,800,000.

The price of indigo as ascertained by me (Rs. 60 per maund), is nearly 20 per cent. higher than that assumed by Mr. Danvers (Rs. 50 per maund).

Mr. Danvers has taken a seer=2 lbs., when in reality it is nearly 6 per cent. of a pound larger, which becomes a serious error in the large amounts to be dealt with.

Mr. Danvers has adopted the prices of 1st January, 1877, only, instead of taking an average of the prices of the four periods given in the Report to represent the whole year.

In his remarks at page 16, Mr. Danvers makes no allowance for seed, which is an important item. He includes straw, all inferior grains, and cotton seed, and yet makes no allowance at all for the feed of animals (some 7,000,000 large cattle, and near 4,000,000 sheep and goats) before apportioning the produce per human head. Grass being not taken makes some allowance for animals so far.

I cannot say on what grounds (page 16) 4 per cent. is assumed for annual increase of large cattle, and 15 per cent. of sheep and goats. I have not got the Report for 1878-9, when the next quinquennial enumeration of stock must have been made, but on comparing the numbers of the last two enumerations of 1868-9 and 1873-4, the result is as follows:—

	1868-9.	1873-4.	Increase.	Decrease.	Per Cent.
Cows, Bullocks, and Buffaloes[1] . .	6,797,561	6,570,212	..	227,349	$3\frac{1}{3}$
Horses .	96,226	84,639	..	11,507	12
Ponies. . .	51,302	51,395	93	..	
Donkeys	257,615	288,118	30,503	..	11·8
Camels .	148,582	165,567	16,985	..	11·4
Total . .	7,351,286—	7,159,931	=	191,355	
Sheep and Goats . . .	3,803,819	3,849,842	46,023	..	$1\frac{1}{4}$

[1] In the report of 1868-9 the heading is only "Cows and Bullocks,'

From this comparison it appears that in the important items of cows, bullocks, and buffaloes, instead of any increase, there is actually a decrease of 227,349, or 3⅛ per cent., during the five years. In horses, also, there is a decrease of about 2½ per cent. every year, instead of 4 per cent. increase. In ponies the increase is hardly ⅛ per cent. in five years, in donkeys about 11 per cent., and in camels about 11 per cent. in all the five years, or about 2¼ per cent. per year, instead of 4 per cent. In sheep and goats the increase is hardly 1¼ per cent. in five years, instead of 15 per cent. per year. For cows and bullocks, and sheep and goats, there is one allowance to be made—viz., for what are killed for food. To make out the increase in cows, etc., of 4 per cent. every year, nearly 4¾ per cent. must have been killed every year for food, and for sheep and goats the percentage of killed should be nearly 14¾ per cent. per annum. Is it so?

Mr. Danvers has assumed ghi produced in the Punjab to be four times as much as imported (52,303 maunds) into it, and he thus makes the quantity produced to be 209,212 maunds. Now the value of the imported ghi is also given in the Report as Rs. 9,64,028, which taken four times would be £385,611. But Mr. Danvers has overlooked this actual price, and adopted the fallacious average of the table of prices in the Report, which makes the price 1s. 12c. per rupee. At this incorrect price the value will be £478,198, or nearly 25 per cent. more than the actual value given in the Report. But not only has there been this incorrect increase thus made, but, by some arithmetical mistake, the value put down by Mr. Danvers is above three times as much as even this increased amount—*i.e.*, instead of £478,198, Mr. Danvers has put down £1,501,096. If this be not merely an arithmetical mistake, it requires explanation.

Mr. Danvers has taken the import of ghi from "foreign trade" only, and has overlooked a further quantity of import, "inter-provincially," of 16,312 maunds, of the value of £34,741, which, taken four times, would be £138,964, making up the total value of the assumed produce of ghi in the Punjab to be £385,611 + £138,964 = £524,575.

while in 1876-7, it is given as "Cows, Bullocks, and Buffaloes." Now if buffaloes are not included in 1868-9, the diminution in cattle will be very much larger. Most probably buffaloes are included in 1868-9 figures. But this must be ascertained. It is a serious matter.

Working upon Mr. Danvers' own assumption, and what information I have been at present able to obtain, it appears that the assumption of four times the import, or £525,000, will be an under-estimate by a good deal. I am not at present able to test the accuracy of Mr. Danvers' assumption of the produce of milk, nor of the information I am using below, but I give it just as I have it, to illustrate the principle. I adopt Mr. Danvers' assumption of 10 per cent. of the whole cattle to be milch-animals. The number then will be 657,000. Of these, cows may be taken, I am told by a Punjabi, as 75 per cent., and buffaloes 25 per cent. This will give 164,250 buffaloes and 492,750 cows. Each buffalo may be taken, on an average, as giving six seers of milk per day for six months in the year, and each cow about three seers. The quantity of milk will then be—

164,250 × 6 seers × 180 days = 177,390,000 seers.
492,750 × 3 seers × 180 days = 266,085,000 seers.

Total ... ... 443,475,000 seers.

Mr. Danvers assumes for milk used in the province to be about Rs. 10 per annum from each of the 10 per cent. of the cattle, and, taking the price of milk to be 16 seers per rupee, the quantity of milk used would be 657,000 × 160 = 105,120,000 seers. This deducted from the above total produce of milk will give (443,475,000—105,120,000) 338,355,000 seers as converted into ghi. The produce of ghi is about $\frac{1}{8}$th to $\frac{1}{16}$th of milk, according to quality. Assuming $\frac{1}{12}$th as the average, the total quantity of ghi will be about 28,196,250 seers = 704,906 maunds, or, allowing a little for wastage, say 700,000 maunds, which, at the import price (Rs. 13,11,445 for 68,615 maunds) of Rs. 19 per maund, will give about £1,339,300, or nearly 2$\frac{2}{3}$ times as much as Mr. Danvers has assumed. I have endeavoured in a hurry to get this information as well as I could, but it can be obtained correctly by the officials on the spot. My object at present is simply to show, that calculated on Mr. Danvers' assumption of milch-cattle and milk used, how much ghi should be produced in the country, if the information I have used be correct.

For hides and skins the export only is taken into account, but a quantity must be consumed in the province itself, which requires to be added.

The value assumed, Rs. 100 per horse, is rather too high. Rs. 60 or Rs. 70, I am told, would be fairer; so also for ponies, Rs. 25 to Rs. 30 instead of Rs. 35; and camels, Rs. 60 or Rs. 70 or Rs. 75 instead of Rs. 100. For sheep, etc., Re. 1½ instead of Re. 1 would be fairer.

But, as I have said above, officials in India can give all this information correctly for every year, and I do not see any reason why this should not be done. I urgently repeat my request that the wants and means of the last twelve or fifteen years may be ordered by his Lordship the Secretary of State to be carefully worked out, as far as practicable, and that future Reports should be required to give complete information.

Railways.

I may take railways to represent public works. The benefits generally derived from railways are these: they distribute the produce of the country from parts where it is produced, or is in abundance, to the parts where it is wanted, so that no part of the produce is wasted, which otherwise would be the case if no facility of communication existed. In thus utilising the whole produce of the country, the railway becomes directly a saving agent, and indirectly thereby helps in increasing the production of the country.

It brings the produce to the ports at the least possible cost for exportation and commercial competition for foreign trade, and thus indirectly helps in obtaining the profits of foreign trade, which are an increase to the annual income of a country.

Every country in building railways, even by borrowed capital, derives the benefit of a large portion of such borrowed capital, as the capital of the country, which indirectly helps in increasing the production of the country. Excepting interest paid for such borrowed capital to the foreign lending country, the rest of the whole income remains *in the country.*

But the result of *all* the above benefits from railways is ultimately realised and comprised in the actual annual income of the country.

The misfortune of India is that she does not derive the above benefits, as every other country does.

You build a railway in England, and, say, its gross income is a million. All the employés, from the chairman down to the common labourer, *are Englishmen.* Every farthing that is spent from the gross income is so much returned to Englishmen, as direct maintenance to so many people *of England*, and to England at large, as a part of its general wealth. Whether the shareholders get their 5 per cent., or 10 per cent., or 1 per cent., or 0 per cent., or even lose, it matters not at all to the whole country. Every farthing of the income of the million is fully and solely enjoyed by *the people of the country*, excepting only (if you borrowed a portion of the capital from foreign parts) the interest you may pay for such loan. But such interest forms a small portion of the whole income, and every country with good railways can very well afford to pay. All the benefits of railways are thus obtained and enjoyed by *the people of the country.*

Take the case of the United States. India and the States are both borrowers for their railways (the latter only partially), and they both pay interest to the lending countries. They both buy, say, their rails, machinery, etc., from England, the States buying only a portion. So far, they are under somewhat similar circumstances; but here the parallel ends. In the United States every cent. of the income of the railway (excepting the interest on the foreign loan) is the income of *the people of the country*—is a direct maintenance for the people employed on it, and an indirect property of the whole country, and remaining *in* it.

In India the case is quite different. First, for the directors, home establishments, Government superintendence, and what not, in England, a portion of the income must go from India; then a large European staff of employés (excepting only for inferior and lowest places or work left for Natives) must eat up and take away another large portion of the income; and to the rest the people of the country are welcome, with the result that, out of their production which they give to the railways, only a *portion* returns to them, and *not the whole*, as in all other countries (except interest on foreign loan), and the diminution lessens, so far, the capacity of production every year. Such expenditure, both in England and India, is so much direct deprivation of the natural maintenance of as many people of India of similar classes, and a loss to the general wealth and means of the people at large. Thus the whole burden of the debt is placed on the shoulders of the people of India, while the benefit is largely enjoyed and carried away by the people of England; and yet Englishmen raise up their hands in wonder why India should not be happy, pleased, and thankful! Some years ago I asked Mr. J. Danvers to make a return, in his annual Railway Report, of the salaries and every other kind of disbursement on Europeans, both in England and India. If I remember rightly (I cannot just now lay my hands on the correspondence), he was kind enough to promise he would try. But I do not know that this information has been given. Let us have this information, and we shall then know why India does *not* derive the usual benefits from railways; how many Europeans displace as many Natives of the same class, and deprive them of their natural means of subsistence (some 3,600 in India, and all those in England), and what portion of the income the people of India do not see or enjoy a pie of.

Instead, therefore, of there being any "railway wealth" to be added to the annual production or income of India, it will be seen that there is much to be deducted therefrom to ascertain what *really* remains for the use of its own people; for the income of railways is simply a portion or share of the production of the country, and what is eaten up and taken away by Europeans is so much taken away from the means of the people.

It is no wonder at all that the United States have their 70,000 or more miles of railways, when India, under the *British Government*, with all its wonderful resources, with all that good government can do, and the whole British wealth to back, has hardly one-tenth of the length, and that even with no benefit to the people of the country. In short, the fact of the matter is that, as India is treated at present, all the new departments, opened in the name of civilisation, advancement, progress, and what not, simply resolve themselves into so much new provision for so many more Europeans, and so much new burden on exhausting India. We do pray to our British rulers, let us have railways and all other kinds of beneficial public works by all means, but let *us* have their natural benefits, or talk not to a starving man of the pleasures of a fine dinner. We should be happy to, and thankfully, pay for such European supervision and guidance as may be absolutely necessary for successful work; but do not in Heaven's and Honesty's names, talk to us of benefits which *we do not* receive, but have, on the contrary, to pay for from our own. If *we* are allowed to derive the usual benefits of railways and other public works, under such government as the British—of law, order, and justice—we would not only borrow £200,000,000, but £2,000,000,000, and pay the interest with as many thanks, with benefit both to ourselves and to England, as India would then be her best and largest commercial customer.

The real important question, therefore, in relation to public works is, not how to stop them, but how to let *the people of the country* have their full benefits. One of the most important parts of England's great work in India is to develop these public works, but to the *people's* benefit, and not to their detriment—*not that they should slave, and others eat.*

Foreign Trade.

Resuming our illustration of the 100 maunds of wheat from the Punjab, arriving at Bombay, costing to the Bombay merchant Rs. 125, we suppose that this merchant exports it to England. In ordinary course and natural conditions of trade, suppose the Bombay merchant, after two or three months, gets his net proceeds of Rs. 150 either in silver or as a bale of piece-goods, which could be sold at Bombay for Rs. 150. The result, then, of this "foreign trade" is that, before the wheat left Bombay, there were 100 maunds of wheat costing Rs. 125 at the time of export, and *after* the operation, India has either Rs. 150, or a bale of cotton goods worth Rs. 150. There is thus a clear "profit of trade" of Rs. 25, or, in other words, an addition of Rs. 25 worth, either in silver or goods, to the annual income or production of the country. This, in ordinary commercial language, would be: India exported value Rs. 125 in the shape of wheat, and imported value Rs. 150 in the shape of silver or merchandise, or both, making a trade profit of Rs. 25.

Under ordinary natural circumstances such is the result of foreign trade to every country. I shall take the instance of the United Kingdom, and we may see what its ordinary foreign trade profits have been during a few past years—say from 1871 to 1878.

PROFITS OF FOREIGN TRADE OF THE UNITED KINGDOM.

Imports.				Exports.					
Years.	Merchandise.	Treasure. (Gold and Silver.)	Total.	Years.	Merchandise.	Treasure. (Gold and Silver.)	Total.	Foreign Trade Profits.	Per Cent.
	£	£	£		£	£	£	£	
1871	331,015,480	38,140,827	369,156,307	1871	283,574,700	33,760,671	317,335,371	51,820,936	
1872	354,693,624	29,608,012	384,301,636	1872	314,588,834	30,335,861	344,924,695	39,376,941	
1873	371,287,372	33,599,231	404,886,603	1873	311,004,765	28,899,285	339,904,050	64,982,553	
1874	370,082,701	30,379,188	400,461,889	1874	297,650,464	22,853,593	320,504,057	79,957,832	
1875	373,939,577	33,264,789	407,204,366	1875	281,612,323	27,628,042	309,240,365	97,964,001	
1876	375,154,703	37,054,244	412,208,947	1876	256,776,602	29,464,082	286,240,684	125,968,263	
1877	394,419,682	37,152,799	431,572,481	1877	252,346,020	39,798,119	292,144,139	139,428,342	
1878	368,770,742	32,422,955	401,193,697	1878	245,483,858	26,686,546	272,170,404	129,023,293	
	Grand Total . .		3,210,985,926		Grand Total . .		2,482,463,765	728,522,161	= 29·34

The result of the above table is, that during the eight years the United Kingdom has received as trade profits 29·34 per cent. This result requires the following further consideration. It includes the results of all money-trade or loans to and from foreign countries. Suppose England has lent £100,000,000 to foreign countries; that forms a part of exports. Suppose it has received in interest, say, £5,000,000; that forms a part of the imports, and unless any portion of the principal of the loan is returned, the whole or balance (if a portion is paid) of the loan remains outstanding, and is so much more to be added to the above figure of trade profits. Again, there is the political profit from India of some £27,000,000 a year (as shown further on). That forms a part of the import, and has to be deducted from the figure of trade profits. England contributes to the expenses of the colonies. This is a part of its exports. Thus the formula will be:—

£728,522,161 + outstanding balance of loans of the eight years — the political drain from India to England (£216,000,000) + contributions to the colonies = the actual profits of all commercial and monetary transactions with the world; or, in other words = the actual profits of the foreign trade of the eight years.

Now the figure £728,522,161 is 29·34 per cent. The political drain of India forms nearly 9 per cent. out of this. There remains above 20 per cent. + the amounts of balance of loans and contributions to the colonies, as the actual rate of profits of the foreign trade of the United Kingdom.

I may fairly adopt this rate, of at least 20 per cent., for the profits of the foreign trade of India; but to be quite under the mark, I adopt only 15 per cent.

Now we may see what actually happens to India, taking the same period of 1871-8.

The actual Exports (excluding Government Stores and Treasure): Merchandise and Gold and Silver =	£485,186,749
Take Profits only 15 per cent. . . . . . . =	72,778,012
The Imports as they *ought to be*	£557,964,761
Actual Imports (excluding Government Stores and Treasure): Merchandise and Gold and Silver .	342,312,799
Deficit in Imports, or what is drained to England . (*i.e.*, nearly £27,000,000 a year.)	215,651,962
Again taking actual Exports	485,186,749
And also actual Imports	342,312,799
Abstraction from the *very produce* of the country (besides the whole profit) is = ...	£142,875,950

in eight years, or nearly £18,000,000 a year, or 29·4 per cent.

Thus, with all the advantages of good government, law, order, justice, etc., railways, and every other influence of a civilised rule, the actual result is that not only does India *not* get a *single farthing* of the 15 or 20 per cent., or whatever it be, of the profits of her foreign trade, but actually has a further amount of nearly 30 per cent. of her exports kept away from her. This is not all. There is, moreover, the halter round her neck of the accumulated railway debt of nearly £100,000,000 held in England (from which her people have not derived the usual benefits), about £60,000,000 of public debt (out of £134,000,000—mostly owing to wars) held in England, and £5,000,000 spent in England on account of State public works. And yet Englishmen wonder why India is poor, and her finances inelastic! Good heavens! when will this bleeding to death end?

Keeping as much as possible on the right side, we find some £18,000,000 from the production itself swept away from India, besides all her profits, and besides what Europeans enjoy in India itself, to the so much exclusion and deprivation of her own people. But this item of £18,000,000 would be found much under the mark. For instance, all duty-articles imported into India are, I believe, valued at 10 per cent. more than their laying-down value. If so, roughly taken, the customs revenue, being £2,500,000, represents roughly a duty at 5 per cent. on £50,000,000; and to make up this £50,000,000, with 10 per cent. extra, requires an addition to the actual value of imports of about £5,000,000. If so, then there will be this much above £18,000,000 taken away from the actual production of India, besides the whole trade profits, maintenance of Europeans in India, debts, etc.

The real abstraction from the very *produce* of the country is, most likely, much above £20,000,000 a year, and the whole loss above £30,000,000 a year, besides what is enjoyed in India itself by Europeans.

Under such circumstances it is no wonder at all that famine and finance should become great difficulties, and that finance has been the grave of several reputations, and shall continue to be so till the discovery is made of making two and two equal to five, if the present unnatural treatment of India is to continue.

Far, therefore, from there being anything to be added to the annual income of India, as Mr. Danvers thinks, from the "profits of trade," there is the deplorable fact of much to be deducted in the case of India; and the consequences of such abstraction, in impoverishment and destruction by famines, etc., lay mostly at the door of the present unnatural policy of the British administration. Let our rulers realize this fact intelligently, and face it boldly, in a way worthy of the British moral courage and character, and the whole scene will be entirely changed—from deplorable poverty to prosperity, from the wail of woe to joy and blessing. Our misfortune is that the great statesmen of this country have not the necessary time to see into Indian matters, and things are allowed to drift blindly, or England would never become, as she unwittingly is at present, the destroyer of india. Her conscience is sound.

It is natural that in all discussions on finance, curtailment of expenditure and economy are, at first blush, recommended—to cut the coat according to cloth. But, unfortunately, no one asks the question why the cloth is short; why, under such rule as that of the English, India should not do well, if not quite as well as these islands, but should be only able to pay the wretched revenue of some 6s. a head, and that even after "wringing out the last farthing."

No doubt vigilance for economy will always be a necessity in the best of States (not excepting England, as debates in Parliament testify) as long as the world lasts. But the real question, the most important question of all questions, at present is, not how to get £60,000,000 or £100,000,000, for the matter of that, if that be necessary, but how *to return to the people* what is raised from them.

There is no reason whatever why India, with all her vast resources, the patient industry of the people, and the guidance and supervision of British high officials, should not be able to pay two or three times her present wretched revenue, say £100,000,000 or £150,000,000, for efficient administration by her own people, under British supervision, and for the development of her unbounded material resources. Is it not unsatisfactory, or even humiliating, that British statesmen should have to confess that they have hopelessly to depend for about a sixth of the net revenue on supplying opium to another vast human race; and to ask despairingly what they were to do to get this amount of revenue from India itself. Then again, nearly as much more income has to be raised by an oppressive and heavy tax on salt; so that between a third and fourth of the net revenue has to be derived—a part by pinching and starving the poor millions of India in one of the absolute necessaries of life, and the other part by poisoning and demoralising the millions of China. Surely, that a great people like the English, with their statesmanship of the highest order, and with all their genuine desire to do good to and advance mankind, should not be able to get the necessary revenues from India, from her own healthy and natural prosperity, is a strange phenomenon in this advanced age.

Only restore India to her *natural* economical conditions. If, as in England, the revenue raised from the people *returned to the people*—if the income of railways and other public works taken from the people, returned to the people, to fructify in their pockets, then would there be no need for anxiety for finance or famines, or for pinching in salt, or poisoning with opium, millions of the human race. India would then pay with ease £100,000,000 or £200,000,000 of revenue, and would not be the worse for it. It would be far better also, which would then be the case, that India should be able to purchase £1 or £2 worth a head of British manufactures, and become England's best and largest customer, instead of the wretched one she is at present.

I repeat, therefore, with every earnestness, that the most important question of the day is, how to stop the bleeding drain from India. The merit or good of every remedy will depend upon and be tested by its efficacy in stopping this deplorable drain, without impairing the wants of the administration, or checking India's natural progress towards prosperity.

There is a deep conviction among educated and thoughtful Natives that if there is any one nation more than another on the face of the earth that would on no account knowingly do a wrong to, or enslave, degrade, or impoverish a people, and who, on feeling the conviction of any injury having been unintentionally done by them, would at once, and at all reasonable sacrifice, repair the injury without shrinking, that nation is the British nation. This conviction keeps the thinking Natives staunch in their loyalty to the British rule. They know that a real regeneration, civilisation, and advancement of India materially, morally, and politically, depends upon a long continuance of the British rule. The peculiarly happy combination of high civilisation, intense love of liberty, and nobility of soul in the British, cannot but lead them to the desire of the glory of raising a vast nation, instead of trampling upon them. This noble desire has found expression from some of their best men.

The English people have a task before them in India for which there is no parallel in the history of the world. There has not been a nation who, as conquerors, have, like the English, considered the good of the conquered as a duty, or felt it as their great desire; and the Natives of India may, with the evil of the present drain stopped, and a representative voice in their legislation, hopefully look forward to a future under the British rule which will eclipse their greatest and most glorious days.

May the light of Heaven guide our rulers!

DADABHAI NAOROJI.

32, Great St. Helens, London,
13th September, 1880.

India Office, S.W.,
15th October, 1880.

SIR,—I am directed to acknowledge the receipt of your letter of the 13th September, which, together with its enclosure, has been duly laid before the Secretary of State for India.

I am, Sir, your obedient Servant,

Mr. Dadabhai Naoroji. LOUIS MALLET.

32, Great St. Helens, London,
16th November, 1880.

SIR LOUIS MALLET, *the Under-Secretary of State for India, India Office, London, S.W.*

SIR,—Thanking you for your letter of the 15th ultimo, informing me that my letter of 13th September, with enclosure, had been duly laid before his Lordship the Secretary of State for India, and hoping that the same kind attention will be given to it as to my previous letter, and that if I am wrong in any of my views I would be corrected, I beg to submit for his Lordship's kind and generous consideration the accompanying Memorandum No. 2, on the "Moral Poverty of India, and Native Thoughts on the British Indian Policy."

I am, Sir, your obedient Servant,

DADABHAI NAOROJI.

16th November, 1880.

MEMORANDUM No. 2.

The Moral Poverty of India and Native Thoughts on the Present British Indian Policy.

In my last paper I confined myself to meeting Mr. Danvers' line of argument on the question of the material destruction and impoverishment of India by the present British Indian policy. I endeavoured to show that this impoverishment and destruction of India was mainly caused by the unnatural treatment it received at the hands of its British rulers, in the way of subjecting it to a large variety of expenditure upon a crushing foreign agency both in India and England, whereby the children of the country were displaced and deprived of their natural rights and means of subsistence in their own country; that, by what was being taken and consumed in India itself, and by what was being continuously taken away by such agency clean out of the country, an exhaustion of the very life-blood of the country was unceasingly going on; that not till this disastrous drain was duly checked, and not till the people of India were restored to their natural rights in their own country, was there any hope for the material amelioration of India.

In this memorandum I desire to submit for the kind and generous consideration of his Lordship the Secretary of State for India that, from the same cause of the deplorable drain, besides the material exhaustion of India, the moral loss to her is no less sad and lamentable.

With the material wealth go also the wisdom and experience of the country. Europeans occupy almost all the higher places in every department of Government directly or indirectly under its control. While *in* India they acquire India's money, experience, and wisdom; and when they go, they carry both away with them, leaving India so much poorer in material and moral wealth. Thus India is left without, and cannot have those elders in wisdom and experience who in every country are the natural guides of the rising generations in their national and social conduct, and of the destinies of their country; and a sad, sad loss this is!

Every European is isolated from the people around him. He is not their mental, moral, or social leader or companion. For any mental or moral influence or guidance or sympathy with the people he might just as well be living in the moon. The people know not him, and he knows not, nor cares for, the people. Some honourable exceptions do, now and then, make an effort to do some good if they can, but in the very nature of things these efforts are always feeble, exotic, and of little permanent effect. These men are not always in the place, and their works die away when they go.

The Europeans are not the natural leaders of the people. They do not belong to the people; they cannot enter their thoughts and feelings; they cannot join or sympathise with their joys or griefs. On the contrary, every day the estrangement is increasing. Europeans deliberately and openly widen it more and more. There may be very few social institutions started by Europeans in which Natives, however fit and desirous to join, are not deliberately and insultingly excluded. The Europeans are, and make themselves, strangers in every way. All they effectually do is to eat the substance of India, material and moral, while living there, and when they go, they carry away all they have acquired, and their pensions and future usefulness besides.

This most deplorable moral loss to India needs most serious consideration, as much in its political as in its national aspect. Nationally disastrous as it is, it carries politically with it its own Nemesis. Without the guidance of elderly wisdom and experience of their own natural leaders, the education which the rising generations are now receiving is naturally leading them (or call it misleading them if you will) into directions which bode no good to the rulers, and which, instead of being the strength of the rulers, as it ought to be and can be, will turn out to be their great weakness. The fault will be of the rulers themselves for such a result. The power that is now being raised by the spread of education, though yet slow and small, is one that in time must, for weal or woe, exercise great influence; in fact, it has already begun to do so. However strangely the English rulers, forgetting their English manliness and moral courage, may, like the ostrich, shut their eyes, by gagging acts or otherwise, to the good or bad influences they are raising around them, this good or evil is rising nevertheless. The thousands that are being sent out by the universities every year find themselves in a most anomalous position. There is no place for them n their mother-land. They may beg in the streets or break stones on the roads for ought the rulers seem to care for their natural rights, position and duties in their own country. They may perish or do what they like or can, but scores of Europeans must go from this country to take up what belongs to them, and that in spite of every profession, for years and years past and up to the present day, of English statesmen, that they must govern India for India's good, by solemn Acts and declarations of Parliament, and, above all, by the words of the august Sovereign herself. For all practical purposes all these high promises have been hitherto almost wholly the purest romance, the reality being quite different.

The educated find themselves simply so many dummies, ornamented with the tinsel of school education, and then their whole end and aim of life is ended. What must be the inevitable consequence? A wild spirited horse, without curb or reins, will run away wild, and kill and trample upon every one that comes in his way. A misdirected force will hit anywhere, and destroy anything. The power that the rulers are, so far to their credit, raising will, as a Nemesis, recoil against themselves, if, with this blessing of education, they do not do their whole duty to the country which trusts to their righteousness, and thus turn this good power to their own side. The Nemesis is as clear from the present violence to nature, as disease and death arise from uncleanliness and rottenness. The voice of the power of the rising education is, no doubt, feeble at present. Like the infant, the present dissatisfaction is only crying at the pains it is suffering. Its notions have not taken any form or shape or course yet, but it is growing. Heaven only knows what it will grow to! He who runs may see that if the present material and moral destruction of India continues, a great convulsion must inevitably arise, by which either India will be more and more crushed under the iron heel of despotism and destruction, or may succeed in shattering the destroying hand and power. Far, far is it from my earnest prayer and hope that such should be the result of the British rule. In this rule there is every element to produce immeasurable good, both to India and England, and no thinking Native of India would wish harm to it, with all the hopes that are yet built upon the righteousness and conscience of the British statesman and nation.

The whole duty and responsibility of bringing about this desired consummation lies upon the head and in the hands of the Indian authorities *in England*. It is no use screening themselves behind the fiction and excuse that the Viceroys and authorities in India are difficult to be got to do what they ought, or that they would do all that may be necessary. They neither can nor will do this. They cannot go against Acts of Parliament on the one hand, and, on the other, the pressure of European interests, and of European selfishness and guidance, is so heavy in India, that the Viceroys in their first years are quite helpless, and get committed to certain courses; and if, in time, any of them, happening to have sufficient strength of character and confidence in their own judgment, are likely to take matters in their own hands, and, with any moral courage, to resist interests hostile or antagonistic to the good of the people, the end of their time begins to come near, their zeal and interest begin to flag, and soon they go away, leaving India to roll up Sisyphus's stone again with a new Viceroy. It is the highest Indian authority here, the Secretary of State for India, upon whom the responsibility wholly rests. He alone has the power, as a member of and with the weight of the British Cabinet, to guide the Parliament to acts worthy of the English character, conscience, and nation. The glory or disgrace of the British in India is in his hands. He has to make Parliament lay down, by clear legislation, how India *shall* be governed for "*India's good*," or it is hopeless for us to look forward for any relief from our present material and moral destruction, and for future elevation.

Englishmen sometimes indulge the notion that England is secure in the division and disunion among the various races and nationalities of India. But even in this new forces are working their way. Those Englishmen who sleep such foolish sleep of security know very little of what is going on. The kind of education that is being received by thousands of all classes and creeds is throwing them all in a similar mould; a sympathy of sentiment, ideas, and aspirations is growing amongst them; and, more particularly, a political union and sympathy is the first fruit of the new awakening, as all feel alike their deprivation and the degradation and destruction of their country. All differences of race and religion, and rivalry, are gradually sinking before this common cause. This beginning, no doubt, is at present insignificant; but it is surely and steadily progressing. Hindus, Mahomedans, and Parsees are alike asking whether the English rule is to be a blessing or a curse. Politics now engross their attention more and more. This is no longer a secret, or a state of things not quite open to those of our rulers who would see. It may be seen that there is scarcely any union among the different nationalities and races in any shape or ways of life, except only in political associations. In these associations they go hand in hand, with all the fervour and sympathy of a common cause. I would here touch upon a few incidents, little though they are, showing how nature is working in its own quiet way.

Dr. Birdwood has brought to the notice of the English public certain songs now being spread among the people of Western India against the destruction of Indian industry and arts. We may laugh at this as a futile attempt to shut out English machine-made cheaper goods against hand-made dearer ones. But little do we think what this movement is likely to grow into, and what new phases it may take in time. The songs are at present directed against English wares, but they are also a natural and effective preparation against other English things when the time comes, if the English in their blindness allow such times to come. The songs are full of loyalty, and I have not the remotest doubt in the sincerity of that loyalty. But if the present downward course of India continue, if the mass of the people at last begin to despair of any amelioration, and if educated youths, without the wisdom and experience of the world, become their leaders, it will be but a *very, very* short step from loyalty to disloyalty, to turn the course of indignation from English wares to English rule. The songs will remain the same; one word of curse for the rule will supply the spark.

Here is another little incident with its own significance. The London Indian Society, a political body of many of the Native residents of London, had a dinner the other day, and they invited guests. The three guests were, one Hindu, one

Mahomedan, and one Parsee. The society itself is a body representing nearly all the principal classes of India. It is small, and may be laughed at as uninfluential, and can do nothing. But it shows how a sympathy of political common cause is bringing the different classes together, and how, in time, such small seeds may grow into large trees. Every member of this little body is carrying back with him ideas which, as seeds, may produce crops, sweet or bitter, according to the cultivation they may receive at our rulers' hands.

I turn to one bright incident on the other side. True to their English nature and character, there are some Englishmen who try to turn the current of Native thought towards an appreciation of English intentions, and to direct English thought towards a better understanding of England's duty to India. The East India Association is doing this beneficent work, more especially by the fair and English character of its course of bringing about free and full discussion upon every topic and from every point of view, so that, by a sifting of the full expression of different views, truth may be elicited. Though yet little appreciated by the English public, the English members of this Association are fulfilling the duty of patriotism to their own country and of benefaction towards India. How far their good efforts will succeed is yet to be seen. But they at least do one thing. These Englishmen, as well as public writers like Fawcett, Hyndman, Perry, Caird, Knight, Bell, Wilson, Wood, and others, vindicate to India the English character, and show that when Englishmen as a body will *understand* their duty and responsibility, the Natives of India may fairly expect a conduct of which theirs is a sample—a desire, indeed, to act rightly by India. The example and earnestness of these Englishmen, though yet small their number, keep India's hope alive—that England will produce a statesman who will have the moral courage and firmness to face the Indian problem, and do what the world should expect from England's conscience, and from England's mission to humanity.

I have thus touched upon a few incidents only to illustrate the various influences that are at work. Whether the result of all these forces and influences will be good or bad remains, as I have said, in the hands of the Secretary of State for India.

In my last paper I said the thinking Natives were as yet

staunch in their loyalty to the British rule, as they were yet fully hopeful of the future from the general character and history of the English people. They believe that when the conscience of the English nation is awakened, it will not be long before India receives full and thorough redress for all she has been suffering. While thus hopeful of the future, it is desirable that our rulers should know and consider what, as to the past, is passing in many a thinking Native mind.

They are as grateful as any people can be for whatever real good of peace and order and education has been done for them, but they also ask what good, upon the whole, England has done to India. It is sadly poor, and increasing in poverty, both material and moral. They consider and bewail the unnatural treatment India has been receiving.

They dwell upon the strange contrast between the words and deeds of the English rulers; how often deliberate and solemn promises are made and broken. I need not here instance again what I have at some length shown in my papers on the Poverty of India[1] under the heading of "Non-Fulfilment of Solemn Promises."[2]

I would refer here to one or two characteristic instances only. The conception for an Engineering College in London was no sooner formed than it became an accomplished fact; and Mr. Grant Duff, then Under-Secretary of State, in his place in Parliament, proclaimed what great boons "we" were conferring on the English people, but quite oblivious at whose sacrifices. It was an English interest, and the thing was done as quick as it was thought of. On the other hand, a clause for Native interests, proposed in 1867, took three years to pass, and in such a form as to be simply ineffectual. I asked Sir Stafford Northcote, at the time of the proposal, to make it some way imperative, but without effect. Again, after being passed after three years, it remained a dead letter for seven years more, and might have remained so till Doomsday for aught any of the Indian authorities cared. But, thanks to the persevering exertions of one of England's true sons, Sir Erskine Perry, some steps were at last taken to frame the rules that were required, and it is now, in the

[1] In this book, pp. 90-125.

[2] The Duke of Argyll, as Secretary of State for India, said in his speech of 11th March, 1869, with regard to the employment of Natives in the Covenanted Service: "I must say that we have not fulfilled our duty, or the promises and engagements which we have made."

midst of a great deal of fine writing, making some, though very slow, progress. For such, even as it is, we are thankful; but greater efforts are necessary to stem the torrent of the drain. Turning to the Uncovenanted Service, Sir Stafford Northcote's despatch of 8th February, 1868, declared that Europeans should not be allowed in this service to override "the inherent rights of the Natives of the country." Now, in what spirit was this despatch treated till very lately? Was it not simply, or is it not even now, almost a dead letter?

In the matter of the load of the public debt of India, it is mainly due to the wars of the English conquests in India, and English wars abroad in the name of India. Not a farthing has been spent by England for its British Indian Empire. The burden of all England's wars in Asia has been thrown on India's shoulders. In the Abyssinian War, India narrowly and lightly escaped; and in the present Afghan War, her escape from whatever portion she may be saved is not less narrow. Though such is the character of nearly the whole of the public debt (excluding for public works), being caused by the actions by which England has become the mistress of a great Empire, and thereby the first nation in the world, she would not move her little finger to give India any such help as is within her power, without even any material sacrifice to herself—viz., that of guaranteeing this public debt, so that India may derive some little relief from reduced interest.

When English interests are concerned, their accomplishment is often a foregone conclusion. But India's interests always require long and anxious thought—thought that seldom begins, and when it does begin, seldom ends in any thorough good result. It is useless to conceal that the old pure and simple faith in the honour and word of the English rulers is much shaken, and were it not for the faith in the conscience of the statesmen and people in *this* country, any hope of good by an alteration of the present British Indian policy would be given up.

The English rulers boast, and justly so, that they have introduced education and Western civilisation into India; but, on the other hand, they act as if no such thing had taken place, and as if all this boast was pure moonshine. Either they have educated, or have not. If they deserve the boast, it is a strange self-condemnation that after half a century or more of such efforts, they have not yet prepared a sufficient number of men fit for the service of their own country. Take even the Educational Department itself. We are made B.A.'s and M.A.'s and M.D.'s, etc., with the strange result that we are not yet considered fit to teach our countrymen. We must yet have forced upon us even in this department, as in every other, every European that can be squeezed in. To keep up the sympathy and connexion with the current of European thought, an English head may be appropriately and beneficially retained in a few of the most important institutions; but as matters are at present, all boast of education is exhibited as so much sham and delusion.

In the case of former foreign conquests, the invaders either retired with their plunder and booty, or became the rulers of the country. When they only plundered and went back, they made, no doubt, great wounds: but India, with her industry, revived and healed the wounds. When the invaders became the rulers of the country, they settled down *in* it, and whatever was the condition of their rule, according to the character of the sovereign of the day, there was at least no material or moral drain in the country.[1] Whatever the country produced remained in the country; whatever wisdom and experience was acquired in her services remained among her own people. With the English the case is peculiar. There are the great wounds of the first wars in the burden of the public debt, and those wounds are kept perpetually open and widening, by draining away the life-blood in a continuous stream. The former rulers were like butchers hacking here and there, but the English with their scientific scalpel cut to the very heart, and yet, lo! there is no wound to be seen, and soon the plaster of the high talk of civilisation, progress, and what not, covers up the wound! The English rulers

[1] Sir Stafford Northcote, in his speech in Parliament on 24th May, 1867, said:—"Nothing could be more wonderful than our Empire in India, but we ought to consider on what conditions we held it, and how our predecessors held it. The greatness of the Mogul Empire depended upon the liberal policy that was pursued by men like Akbar availing themselves of Hindu talent and assistance, and identifying themselves as far as possible with the people of the country. He thought that they ought to take a lesson from such a circumstance, and if they were to do their duty towards India, they could only discharge that duty by obtaining the assistance and counsel of all who were great and good in that country. It would be absurd in them to say that there was not a large fund of statesmanship and ability in the Indian character."—*Times*, of 25th May, 1867.

stand sentinel at the front door of India, challenging the whole world, that they do and shall protect India against all comers, and themselves carry away by a back-door the very treasure they stand sentinel to protect.

In short, had England deliberately intended to devise the best means of taking away India's wealth in a quiet continuous drain, without scandalising the world, she could not have hit upon a more effectual plan than the present lines of policy. A Viceroy tells us the people of India enjoy but scanty subsistence; and this is the outcome of the British rule.

No doubt the exertions of individual Europeans at the time of famines may be worthy of admiration; the efforts of Government and the aid of the contributions of the British people to save life, deserve every gratitude. But how strange it is that the British rulers do not see that after all they themselves are the main cause of the destruction that ensues from droughts; that is the drain of India's wealth by *them* that lays at their own door the dreadful results of misery, starvation, and deaths of millions; England does not know famines, be the harvest however bad or scanty. She has the means of buying her food from the whole world. India is being unceasingly deprived of these means, and when famine comes the starving have to be taxed so much more to save the dying.

England's conduct in India is in strange contrast with her conduct with almost any other country. Owing to the false groove in which she is moving, she does violence to her own best instincts. She sympathises with and helps every nationality that struggles for a constitutional representative government. On the one hand, she is the parent of, and maintains, the highest constitutionalism; and, on the other, she exercises a clear and, though thoughtlessly, a despoiling despotism in India, under a pseudo-constitutionalism, in the shape of the farce of the present Legislative Councils.

Of all countries in the world, if any one has the greatest claim on England's consideration, to receive the boons of a constitutional representative government at her hands, and to have her people governed as England governs her own, that country is India, her most sacred trust and charge. But England, though she does everything she can for other countries, fights shy of, and makes some excuse or other to avoid, giving to the people of India their fair share in the legislation of their country. Now I do not mean to say that India can suddenly have a full-blown Parliament, and of such wide-spread representation as England enjoys. But has England made any honest efforts to gradually introduce a true representation of the people, excepting some solitary exceptions of partial municipal representation? I need not dwell upon the present farce of the nomination system for the Legislative Councils, and of the dummies that are sometimes nominated. I submit that a small beginning can be well made now. I would take the Bombay Presidency as an instance. Suppose the present Legislative Council is extended to twenty-one members, thirteen of these to be nominated from officials and non-officials by the Government, and eight to be elected by the principal towns of the Presidency. This will give Government a clear majority of five, and the representative element, the minority, cannot do any harm, or hamper Government; in England the majority determines the Government. In India this cannot be the case at present, and so the majority must follow the Government. It would be, when something is extremely outrageous, that the minority would, by force of argument and truth, draw towards it the Government majority; and even in any such rare instance, all that will happen will be that Government will be prevented from doing any such outrageous things. In short, in such an arrangement, Government will remain all-powerful, as it must for a long time to come; while there will be also independent persons, actually representing the people, to speak the sentiments of the people; thereby giving Government the most important help, and relieving them from much responsibility, anxiety, and mistakes. The representative element in the minority will be gradually trained in constitutional government. They will have no inducement to run wild with prospects of power; they will have to maintain the reasons of their existence, and will, therefore, be actuated by caution and good sense. They can do no harm, but a vast amount of good, both to the Government and the governed. The people will have the satisfaction that their rulers were doing their duty, and endeavouring to raise them to their own civilisation.

There are in the Bombay Presidency the following towns of more than 50,000 population. Bombay having by far the largest, and with its importance as the capital of the Presidency, may be properly allowed three representatives.

The towns are—

[1]Bombay.		Poona.		Ahmedabad.		Surat.		Kurrachi.		Sholapore.
644,405	..	118,886	..	116,873	..	107,149	..	53,536	..	53,403

Thus, Bombay having three, the Gujerati division of the Presidency will be represented by Ahmedabad and Surat, the Maratha portion by Poona and Sholapore, and Sind by Kurrachi, making altogether eight members, which will be a fair, though a small, representation to begin with. Government may with advantage adopt a larger number; all I desire and insist is, that there must be a fair *representative* element in the Councils. As to the qualifications of electors and candidates for election, Government is quite competent to fix upon some, as they did in the case of the Bombay Corporation, and such qualifications may from time to time be modified as experience may suggest. With this modification in the present Legislative Council, a great step will have been taken towards one of the greatest boons which India asks and expects at England's hands. Without some such element of the people's voice in all the Legislative Councils, it is impossible for Englishmen, more and more estranged and isolated as they are becoming, to be able to legislate for India in the true spirit and feeling of her wants.

After having a glorious history of heroic struggles for constitutional government, England is now rearing up a body of Englishmen in India, trained up and accustomed to despotism, with all the feelings of impatience, pride, and high-handedness of the despot becoming gradually ingrained in them, and with the additional training of the dissimulation of constitutionalism. Is it possible that such habits and training of despotism, with which Indian officials return from India, should not, in the course of time, influence the English character and institutions? The English in India, instead of raising India, are hitherto themselves descending and degenerating to the lower level of Asiatic despotism. Is this a Nemesis that will in fulness of time show to them what fruit their conduct in India produced? It is extraordinary how nature may revenge itself for the present unnatural course of England in India, if England, not yet much tainted by this

[1] "Statistical Abstract of British India, 1879," page 21.

demoralisation, does not, in good time, check this new leaven that is gradually fermenting among her people.

There is the opium trade. What a spectacle it is to the world! In England no statesman dares to propose that opium may be allowed to be sold in public houses at the corners of every street, in the same way as beer or spirits. On the contrary, Parliament, as representing the whole nation, distinctly enacts that "opium and all preparations of opium or of 'poppies,' as 'poison,' be sold by certified chemists only, and every box, bottle, vessel, wrapper, or cover in which such poison is contained, be distinctly labelled with the name of the article and the word 'poison,' and with the name and address of the seller of the poison." And yet, at the other end of the world, this Christian, highly civilised, and humane England forces a "heathen" and "barbarous" Power to take this "poison," and tempts a vast human race to use it, and to degenerate and demoralise themselves with this "poison"! And why? Because India cannot fill up the remorseless drain; so China must be dragged in to make it up, even though it be by being "poisoned." It is wonderful how England reconciles this to her conscience. This opium trade is a sin on England's head, and a curse on India for her share in being the instrument. This may sound strange as coming from any Natives of India, as it is generally represented as if India it was that benefited by the opium trade. The fact simply is that, as Mr. Duff said, India is nearly ground down to dust, and the opium trade of China fills up England's drain. India derives not a particle of benefit. All India's profits of trade, and several millions from her very produce (scanty as it is, and becoming more and more so), and with these all the profit of opium, go the same way of the drain—to England. Only India shares the curse of the Chinese race. Had this cursed opium trade not existed, India's miseries would have much sooner come to the surface, and relief and redress would have come to her long ago; but this trade has prolonged the agonies of India.

In association with this trade is the stigma of the Salt-tax upon the British name. What a humiliating confession to say that, after the length of the British rule, the people are in such a wretched plight that they have nothing that Government can tax, and that Government must, therefore, tax an absolute necessary of life to an inordinate extent! The slight flash of prosperity during the American War showed how the people of India would enjoy and spend when they have anything to enjoy and spend; and now, can anything be a greater condemnation of the results of British lines of policy than that the people have nothing to spend and enjoy, and pay tax on, but that they must be pinched and starved in a necessary of life?

The English are, and justly and gloriously, the greatest champions of liberty of speech. What a falling off must have taken place in their character when, after granting this boon to India, they should have even thought of withdrawing it! This act, together with that of disarming the people, is a clear confession by the rulers to the world that they have no hold as yet upon the affection and loyalty of the people, though in the same breath they make every profession of their belief in the loyalty of the people. Now, which is the truth? And are gagging and disarming the outcome of a long benign rule?

Why do the English allow themselves to be so perpetually scared by the fears of Russian or any other foreign invasion? If the people of India be satisfied, if their hearts and hands be with England, she may defy a dozen Russias. On the other hand, do British statesmen think that, however sharp and pointed their bayonets, and however long-flying their bullets, they may not find the two hundred millions of the people of India her political Himalaya to be pierced through, when the present political union among the different peoples is more strengthened and consolidated?

There is the stock argument of over-population. They talk, and so far truly, of the increase by British peace, but they quite forget the destruction by the British drain. They talk of the pitiless operations of economic laws, but somehow they forgot that there is no such thing in India as the natural operation of economic laws. It is not the pitiless operations of economic laws, but it is the thoughtless and pitiless action of the British policy; it is the pitiless eating of India's substance in India, and the further pitiless drain to England; in short, it is the pitiless *perversion* of economic laws by the sad bleeding to which India is subjected, that is destroying India. Why blame poor Nature when the fault lies at your own door? Let natural and economic laws have their full and fair play, and India will become another England, with manifold greater benefit to England herself than at present.

As long as the English do not allow the country to produce what it can produce, as long as the people are not allowed to enjoy what they can produce, as long as the English are the very party on their trial, they have no right, and are not competent, to give an opinion whether the country is over-populated or not. In fact, it is absurd to talk of over-population—*i.e.*, the country's incapability, by its food or other produce, to supply the means of support to its people—if the country is unceasingly and forcibly deprived of its means or capital. Let the country keep what it produces, for only then can any right judgment be formed whether it is over-populated or not. Let England first hold hands off India's wealth, and then there will be disinterestedness in, and respect for, her judgment. The present cant of the excuse of over-population is adding a distressful insult to agonising injury. To talk of over-population at present is just as reasonable as to cut off a man's hands, and then to taunt him that he was not able to maintain himself or move his hands.

When persons talk of the operation of economic laws they forget the very first and fundamental principles. Says Mr. Mill: "Industry is limited by capital." "To employ industry on the land is to apply capital to the land." "Industry cannot be employed to any greater extent than there is capital to invest." "There can be no more industry than is supplied by materials to work up, and food to eat; yet in regard to a fact so evident, it was long continued to be believed that laws and Governments, without creating capital, could create industry." And while Englishmen are sweeping away this very capital, they raise up their hands and wonder why India cannot have industry.

The English are themselves the head and front of the offending, and yet they talk of over-population, and every mortal irrelevant thing but the right cause—viz., their own drain of the material and moral wealth of the country.

The present form of relations between the paramount Power and the Princes of India is un-English and iniquitous. Fancy a people, the greatest champions of fair-play and justice, having a system of political agency by which, as the Princes say, they are stabbed in the dark; the Political Agents making secret reports, and the Government often acting thereon, without a fair enquiry or explanation from the Princes. The Princes, therefore, are always in a state of alarm as to what may befall them unawares. If the British authorities deliberately wished to adopt a method by which the Princes should always remain alarmed and irritated, they could not have hit upon a more effective one than what exists. If these Princes can feel assured that their treaty rights will be always honourably and faithfully observed, that there will be no constant nibbling at their powers, that it is not the ulterior policy of the British to pull them down gradually to the position of mere nobles of the country, as the Princes at present suspect and fear, and if a more just and fair mode of political agency be adopted, I have not the least hesitation in saying that, as much from self-interest alone as from any other motive, these Princes will prove the greatest bulwark and help to perpetuate British supremacy in India. It stands to reason and common-sense that the Native Princes clearly understand their interest, that by a power like the British only, with all the confidence it may command by its fairness as well as strength, can they be saved from each other and even from themselves. Relieved of any fear from the paramount Power, they will the more readily listen to counsels of reform which they much need. The English can then exercise their salutary influence in advising and helping them to root out the old corrupt *régimes*, and in making them and their courtiers to understand that power was not self-aggrandizement, but responsibility for the good of the people. I say, from personal conversation with some of the Princes, that they thoroughly understand their interest under the protection of the present paramount Power.

It is useless for the British to compare themselves with the past Native rulers. If the British do not show themselves to be vastly superior in proportion to their superior enlightenment and civilisation, if India does not prosper and progress under them far more largely, there will be no justification for their existence in India. The thoughtless past drain we may consider as our misfortune, but a similar future will, in plain English, be deliberate plunder and destruction.

I do not repeat here several other views which I have already expressed in my last memorandum.

I have thus given a general sketch of what is passing in

many Natives' minds on several subjects. It is useless and absurd to remind us constantly that once the British fiat brought order out of chaos, and to make that an everlasting excuse for subsequent shortcomings and the material and moral impoverishment of the country. The Natives of the present day have not seen that chaos, and do not feel it; and though they understand it, and very thankful they are for the order brought, they see the present drain, distress and destruction, and they feel it and bewail it.

By all means let Englishmen be proud of the past. We accord them every credit for the order and law they brought about, and are deeply thankful to them; but let them now face the present, let them clearly realise, and manfully acknowledge, the many shortcomings of omission and commission by which, with the best of intentions, they have reduced India to material and moral wretchedness; and let them, in a way worthy of their name and history, repair the injury they have inflicted. It is fully in their power to make their rule a blessing to India, and a benefit and a glory to England, by allowing India her own administration, under their superior controlling and guiding hand; or, in their own oft-repeated professions and words, "by governing India for India's good."

May the God of all nations lead the English to a right sense of their duty to India is my humble and earnest prayer.

DADABHAI NAOROJI.

32, Great St. Helens, London,
4th January, 1881.

SIR LOUIS MALLET, *the Under-Secretary of State for India, India Office, London, S.W.*

SIR,—I beg to request you to submit the accompanying Memorandum, No. 3, on some of the statements in the "Report of the Indian Famine Commission, 1880," to his Lordship the Secretary of State for India, and I hope his Lordship will give his kind and generous consideration to it.

I remain, Sir, your obedient Servant,

DADABHAI NAOROJI.

No. 3.

MEMORANDUM ON A FEW STATEMENTS IN THE REPORT OF THE INDIAN FAMINE COMMISSION, 1880.

Part II, Chapter I, Section 7, treats of Incidence of Taxation. I submit that the section is fallacious, gives an erroneous notion of the true state of the matter, and is misleading. We shall see what the reality is.

The income of a country consists of two parts :

1. The internal total annual material production of the country (agricultural, manufactures, mines, and fisheries).
2. The external annual profits of foreign trade.

There is no other source or income beyond these two, excepting in the case of British India, the tributes and contributions of Native States, of about £700,000.

The incidence of taxation of any country means that a certain amount or portion is taken out of this income for purposes of Government. Call this portion revenue, tax, rent, service, contributions, blessing, curse, or by any name from A to Z in the English vocabulary ; the fact simply is, that the country has to give a certain proportion out of its income for purposes of Government. Every farthing that the country has thus to contribute for Government has to be produced or earned from fo eign trade, or, in other words, has to be given from the annual income. No portion of it is rained down from heaven, or produced by some magic by the Government of the country. The £24,000,000 which the Commissioners call "other than taxation" do not come down from the heavens, nor are to be obtained from any other source than the annual income of the country, just the same as what they call taxation proper. And so also, what the Commissioners call "rent," with regard to the revenue derived from land.

Whatever plans, wise or unwise, a Government adopt of distributing the incidence of the revenue among different classes of people ; from whatever and how many soever different sources Government may obtain its revenue ; by whatever hundred-and-one names may these different items of revenue be called—the sum total of the whole matter is, that out of the annual income of the country a certain portion is raised for the purposes of Government, and the real incidence of this revenue in any country is the proportion it bears to the actual annual income of the country, call the different modes of raising this revenue what you like.

Now England raises at present for purposes of government about £83,000,000. The income of the United Kingdom is well-nigh £1,000,000,000[1] a year. The proportion, therefore, of the revenue of £83,000,000, or even £84,000,000, is about 8⅓ per cent. out of the annual income.

Now India's income, as I have first roughly shown in 1870, in my paper on the "Wants and Means of India,"[2] and subsequently in my paper on the "Poverty of India,"[3] is hardly £340,000,000 per annum. This statement has not been refuted by anybody. On the contrary, Mr. Grant Duff, though cautiously, admitted in his speech in 1871, in these words: "The income of British India has been guessed at £300,000,000 per annum." And Lord Mayo quoted Mr. Grant Duff's speech soon after, without any contradiction, but rather with approval. If the fact be otherwise, let Government give the correct fact every year. Out of this income of £300,000,000 the revenue raised in India for purposes of government is £65,000,000, or very near 22 per cent.

Thus, then, the actual heaviness of the weight of revenue on India is quite two and a half times as much as that on England. This is the simple fact, that out of the grand income of £1,000,000,000 of only 34,000,000 of population, England raises for the purposes of government only 8⅓ per cent.; while out of the poor wretched income of £300,000,000 of a population of nearly 200,000,000, two and a half times more, or nearly 22 per cent., are raised in India for the same purpose; and yet people coolly and cruelly write that India is lightly taxed. It must be further realised what this disproportionate pressure upon a most prosperous and wealthy community like that of England, and the most wretched and

[1] The "Westminster Review" of January, 1876, gives the national production for 1875 of the United Kingdom as £28 per head of population. I do not know whether profits of trade are included in this amount. Mr. Grant Duff, in 1871, took £800,000,000, or, roundly, £30 per head of population. The population is above 34,000,000, which, at £28, gives £952,000,000.

[2] "Journal of the East India Association," Vol. IV., page 283.

[3] In this book, pp. 25 and 51.

poverty and famine-stricken people of India, means. To the one it is not a flea-bite, to the other it is starvation and death of millions under her present unnatural treatment. For this is not all; a far deeper and worse depth lies behind.

Let me, then, once more repeat, that out of the grand income of £1,000,000,000 a year, England gives only 8½ per cent. for Government purposes, while out of the wretched poverty of India, of an income of £300,000,000, she gives 22 per cent. for purposes of government. Now comes the worst evil of the whole, to which English writers, with few exceptions, always shut their eyes.

Of the £83,000,000 of revenue which is raised in England, every farthing returns, in some shape or other, to the people themselves. In fact, England pays with one hand and receives back with the other. And such is the case in every country on the face of the earth, and so it must be; but poor India is doomed otherwise. Out of the £65,000,000 taken from her wretched income, some £30,000,000 or £40,000,000 are never returned to the people, but are eaten up in the country, and taken away out of the country, by those who are not the people of the country—by England, in short. I pass over this mournful topic here, as I have to refer to it again further on.

I may be taken to task that I am making a very definite statement when I talk of "some £30,000,000 or £40,000,000" as being eaten up and taken away by England. The fault is not mine, but that of Government. In 1873, Sir David Wedderburn moved for a return of the number, salaries, etc., of all the Services. The return was ordered in July, 1873. It is now over seven years, but has not been made. Again, in 1879, Mr. Bright moved for returns (salaries, etc., 19th June, 1879), and Sir David Wedderburn moved for returns (East India Services, 20th and 23rd June, 1879, and East India Services, 24th June, 1879). These returns have not yet been made. I hope they are being prepared. When these returns are made, we shall know definitely and clearly what the amount is that, out of the revenue of £65,000,000, does not at all return to the people of India, but is eaten up in, and carried away from, India every year by England. Such returns ought to be made every year. Once it is made, the work of succeeding years will be only the alterations or revision for the year; or revised estimates every two or three years even will do. To Government itself a return like this will be particularly useful. They will then act with clear light instead of groping in darkness as at present, and, though actuated with the best of intentions, still inflicting upon India untold misfortunes and miseries. And it will then see how India, of all other countries in the world, is subjected to a most unnatural and destructive treatment.

The next sections, viii. and ix., on trade and railways, are pervaded with the same fallacies as those of Mr. Danvers' Memo. of 28th June, 1880, and to which I replied in my letter of 13th September, 1880. I, therefore, do not go over the same ground here again. I need only refer to one statement, the last sentence of paragraph four of section viii. :—

"As to the other half of the excess which is due to the cost of English administration, there can hardly be room for doubt that it is to the advantage of India to pay the sum really necessary to secure its peaceful government, without which no progress would be possible; and so long as this condition is not violated, it does not seem material whether a part of the charge has to be met in England or not."

A statement more wrong in its premises and conclusion can hardly be met with. Let us see.

By "the other half of the excess" is meant £8,000,000.

The Commissioners tell the public that India pays £8,000,000 for securing peaceful government. This is the fiction; what are the facts?

England, of *all* nations on the face of the earth, enjoys the utmost security of life and property of every kind, from a strong and peaceful government. For this England "*pays*" £83,000,000 a year.

In the same manner India "pays" not £8,000,000, but £65,000,000 for the same purpose, and should be able and willing to "*pay*" twice or thrice £65,000,000 under natural circumstances, similar to those of England.

Thus England "pays" £83,000,000, and India "pays" £65,000,000 for purposes of peaceful government. But here the parallel ends, and English writers, with very few exceptions, fight shy of going beyond this point, and misstate the matter as is done in the above extract. Let us see what is beyond.

Of the £83,000,000 which England "pays" for security of

life and property, or peaceful government, every farthing returns to the people themselves. It is not even a flea-bite or any bite to the people of England that they "*pay*" £83,000,000 for peaceful government. They simply give with one hand and receive back with the other. The country and the people enjoy the *full benefit* of every farthing they either produce in the country or earn with foreign trade.

But with India the *fact* is quite otherwise. Out of the £65,000,000 which she "*pays*," like England, for peaceful government, £30,000,000 or £40,000,000 do *not* return to the people of the country. These £30,000,000 or £40,000,000 are eaten up in the country and carried away from the country by a foreign people. The people of India are thus deprived of this enormous amount year after year, and are, as a natural consequence, weakened more and more every year in their capacity for production; or, in plain words, India is being simply destroyed.

The *romance* is that there is security of life and property in India; the reality is that there is no such thing.

There is security of life and property in one sense or way —*i.e.*, the people are secure from any violence from each other or from Native despots. So far there is real security of life and property, and for which India never denies her gratitude. But from England's own grasp there is no security of property at all, and, as a consequence, no security for life. India's property is not secure. What is secure, and well secure, is that England is perfectly safe and secure, and does so with perfect security, to carry away from India, and to eat up in India, her property at the present rate of some £30,000,000 or £40,000,000 a year.

The reality, therefore, is that the policy of English rule, as it is (not as it can and should be), is an everlasting, unceasing, and every day increasing foreign invasion, utterly, though gradually, destroying the country. I venture to submit that every right-minded Englishman, calmly and seriously considering the problem of the present condition and treatment of India by England, will come to this conclusion.

The old invaders came with the avowed purpose of plundering the wealth of the country. They plundered and went away, or conquered and became the Natives of the country. But the great misfortune of India is that England did *not* mean or wish, or come with the intention of plundering, and yet events have taken a course which has made England the worst foreign invader she has had the misfortune to have. India does not get a moment to breathe or revive. "More Europeans," "More Europeans," is the eternal cry; and this very Report itself of the Commission is not free from it.

The present position of England in India has, moreover, produced another most deplorable evil from which the worst of old foreign invasions was free; that with the deprivation of the vital material blood of the country, to the extent of £30,000,000 or £40,000,000 a year, the whole higher "wisdom" of the country is also carried away.

I therefore venture to submit that India *does not* enjoy security of her property and life, and also, moreover, of "knowledge" or "wisdom." To millions in India life is simply "half-feeding," or starvation, or famines and disease.

View the Indian problem from any point you like, you come back again and again to this central fact, that England takes from India every year £30,000,000 or £40,000,000 worth of her property, with all the lamentable consequences from such a loss, and with a continuous diminution of the capacity of India for production, together with the moral loss of all higher wisdom.

India would be quite able and willing to "pay," as every other country or as England "pays," for peaceful government; but no country on the face of the earth can stand the deprivation of property that India is subjected to without being crushed to death.

Suppose England were subjected to such a condition at the hand of some foreign Power; would she not, to a man, clamour, that far better would they fly at each other's throat, have strifes in streets of civil wars, or fights in fields for foreign wars, with all the chances of fame or fortune on survival, than submit to the inglorious miserable deaths from poverty and famines, with wretchedness and disease in case of survival? I have no hesitation in appealing to any Englishman to say which of the two deaths he would prefer, and I shall not have to wait long for the reply.

What is property worth to India which she can only call her own in name, but not in reality, and which her own children cannot enjoy? What is life worth to her, that must perish by millions at the very touch of drought or distress, or can have only a half-starving existence?

The confusion and fallacy in the extract I have given above, therefore, consists in this. It is not that India pays for peaceful government some £8,000,000; she pays for it £65,000,000, just as England pays £84,000,000. But there is one feature peculiar to India—she needs British wise and beneficent guidance and supervision. British aid of this kind can, under any circumstances, be but from outside the Indian family—*i.e.*, foreign. This aid must be reasonably paid for by India. Now, if the whole foreign agency of European men and materials required under the direct and indirect control of Government, both in India and England, in every shape or form, be clearly laid down, to be confined within the limit of a fixed "foreign list" of, say, £5,000,000, or even say £8,000,000, though very much, which the Commissioners ask India to pay, India could very probably pay without being so destroyed as at present. But the present thoughtless and merciless exhaustion of some £30,000,000 or £40,000,000, or may be even much more, is crushing, cruel, and destructive.

In fact, leaving the past alone as a misfortune, the continuance of the present drain will be, in plain English, nothing less than plunder of an unceasing foreign invasion, and not a reasonable price for a beneficent rule, as the Commissioners wrongly and thoughtlessly endeavour to persuade the public.

The great misfortune of India is, that the temptation or tendency towards selfishness and self-aggrandisement of their own countrymen is too great and blinding for Englishmen (with few exceptions) connected with India to see that power is a sacred trust and responsibility for the good of the people. We have this profession to any amount, but unless and till the conscience of England, and of English honest thinkers and statesmen, is awakened, the performance will remain poor, or *nil*, as at present.

Lord Ripon said, "India needs rest." Truer words could not be spoken. Yes, she needs rest; rest from the present unceasing and ever-increasing foreign invasion, from whose unceasing blows she has not a moment allowed to breathe.

I said before that even this Famine Report was not free from the same clamour, "More Europeans, more Europeans!" Whenever any question of reform arises, the only remedy that suggests itself to English officials' minds is, "Apply more European leaches, apply more European leeches!"

The Commission suggests the institution of an Agricultural Department, and a very important suggestion it is. But they soon forget that it is *for India* this is required, that it is at India's expense it has to be done, that it is from India's wretched income that this expenditure has to be provided, and that India cannot afford to have more blood sucked out of her for more Europeans, while depriving so much her own children; in short, that Native agency, under a good English head or two, would be the most natural and proper agency for the purpose. No; prostrate as India is and for which very reason the Commission was appointed to suggest a remedy, they can only say, "More Europeans," as if no such thing as a people existed in India.

Were any Englishman to make such a proposal for England, that French or German youths be instructed at England's expense, and that such youths make up the different public departments, he would be at once scouted and laughed at. And yet these Commissioners thoughtlessly and seriously suggest and rĕcommend to aggravate the very evil for which they were expected to suggest a remedy.

I appeal most earnestly to his Lordship the Secretary of State for India, that, though the department suggested by the Commissioners is very important, his Lordship will not adopt the mode which the Commissioners have suggested with good intentions, but with thoughtlessness about the rights and needs of India; that, with the exception of some thoroughly qualified necessary Europeans at the head, the whole agency ought to be Native, on the lines described by the Commissioners. There can be no lack of Natives of the kind required, or it would be a very poor compliment indeed to the educational exertions of the English rulers during the past half-century.

A new danger is now threatening India. Hitherto India's wealth *above* the surface of the land has been draining away to England; now the wealth *under* the surface of the land will also be taken away, and India lies prostrate and unable to help herself. England has taken away her capital. That same capital will be brought to take away all such mineral wealth of the country as requires the application of large capital and expensive machinery. With the exception of the employment of the lower class of bodily and mental labourers, the larger portion of the produce will, in several shapes, be eaten up and carried away by the Europeans, first as servants, and next in profits and dividends; and poor India will have to thank her stars that she will get some crumbs in the lower employments of her children. And great will be the sounding of trumpets of the wealth found in India, and the blessings conferred on India, just as we have sickeningly dinned into our ears, day after day, about railways, foreign trade, etc.

Now, this may sound very strange, that, knowing full well the benefits of foreign capital to any country, I should complain of its going to India. There is, under present circumstances, one great difference in the modes in which English capital goes to every other country and India. To every other country English capitalists *lend*, and there is an end of their connexion with the matter. The *people* of the country use and enjoy the benefit of the capital in every way, and pay to the capitalists their interest or dividend, and, as some capitalists know to their cost, not even that. But with India the case is quite different. English capitalists do not merely lend, but with their capital they themselves invade the country. The produce of the capital is mostly eaten up by their own countrymen, and, after that, they carry away the rest in the shape of profits and dividends. The people themselves of the country *do not* derive the same benefit which is derived by every other country from English capital. The guaranteed railways not only ate up everything in this manner, but compelled India to make up the guaranteed interest also from her produce. The remedy then was adopted of making State railways. Now, under the peculiar circumstances of India's present prostration, State works, would be, no doubt, the best means of securing to India the benefits of English capital. But the misfortune is that the same canker eats into the State works also—the same eating up of the substance by European employés. The plan by which India can be really benefitted would be that all kinds of public works or mines, or all works that require capital, be undertaken by the State, with English capital and *Native* agency, with so many thoroughly competent Europeans at the head as may be absolutely necessary.

Supposing that there was even extravagance or loss,

Government making up any deficiency in the interest of the loans from general revenue, will not matter much, though there is no reason why, with proper care, a Native agency cannot be formed good enough for efficient and economic working. Anyhow, in such a case the people of India will then really derive the benefit of English capital, as every other country does, with the certainty of English capitalists getting their interest from the Government, who have complete control over the revenues of India, and can, without fail, provide for the interest.

For some time, therefore, and till India, by a change in the present destructive policy of heavy European agency, has revived, and is able to help herself in a free field, it is necessary that all great undertakings which India herself is unable to carry out, for developing the resources of the country, should be undertaken by the State, but carried out chiefly by Native agency, and by preparing Natives for the purpose. Then will India recover her blood from every direction. India sorely needs the aid of English capital; but it is English *capital* that she needs, and not the English invasion to come also and eat up both capital and produce.

As things are taking their course at present with regard to the gold mines, should they prove successful great will be the trumpeting of India's increased wealth; whilst, in reality, it will all be carried away by England.

In the United States the people of the country enjoy all the benefits of their mines and public works with English capital, and pay to England her fair interest; and in cases of failure of the schemes, while the people have enjoyed the benefit of the capital, sometimes both capital and interest are gone. The schemes fail, and the lenders of capital may lament, but the people have enjoyed the capital and the produce as far as they went.

I have no doubt that, in laying my views plainly before the Secretary of State, my motives or sentiments towards the British rule will not be misunderstood. I believe that the result of the British rule *can be* a blessing to India and a glory to England—a result worthy of the foremost and most humane nation on the face of the earth. I desire that this should take place, and I therefore lay my humble views before our rulers without shrinking. It is no pleasure to me to dwell incessantly on the wretched, heart-rending, blood-boiling condition of India; none will rejoice more than myself if my views are proved to be mistaken. The sum total of all is, that without any such intention or wish, and with every desire for the good of India, England has in reality been the most disastrous and destructive foreign invader of India, and, under present lines, unceasingly and every day increasingly continues to be so. This unfortunate *fact* is to be boldly faced by *England;* and I am sanguine that if once England realises this position she will recoil from it, and vindicate to the world her great mission of humanity and civilisation among mankind. I am writing to English *gentlemen*, and I have no fear but that they will receive my sincere utterances with the generosity and love of justice of English gentlemen.

In concluding these remarks I feel bound to say that, as far as I can judge from Mr. Caird's separate paper on the "Condition of India," he appears to have realised the abnormal economical condition of India: and I cannot but feel the true English manliness and moral courage he has displayed, that, though he went out an avowed defender of the Indian Government, he spoke out his convictions, and what he saw within his opportunities. India needs the help of such manly, conscientious, true-hearted English gentlemen to study and probe her forlorn condition, and India may then fairly hope for ample redress ere long at England's hands and conscience.

DADABHAI NAOROJI.

32, Great St. Helens, London.
January 4th, 1881.

India Office, S.W., *16th February*, 1881.

SIR,—I am directed by the Secretary of State for India in Council to acknowledge your letters of the 16th November and 4th January last, with accompaniments.

I am, Sir, your obedient Servant,

T. L. SECCOMBE.

Mr. Dadabhai Naoroji.

SIR M. E. GRANT DUFF'S
VIEWS ABOUT INDIA.

Contemporary Review, August, 1887.

I.

I offer some observations on Sir Grant Duff's reply to Mr. Samuel Smith, M.P., in this "Review." I do so not with the object of defending Mr. Smith. He is well able to take care of himself. But of the subjects with which Sir Grant Duff has dealt, there are some of the most vital importance to India, and I desire to discuss them.

I have never felt more disappointed and grieved with any writings by an Englishman than with the two articles by Sir Grant Duff—a gentleman who has occupied the high positions of Under-Secretary of State for India and Governor of Madras. Whether I look to the superficiality and levity of his treatment of questions of serious and melancholy importance to India, or to the literary smartness of offhand reply which he so often employs in the place of argument, or to the mere sensational assertions which he puts forward as proofs, I cannot but feel that both the manner and matter of the two articles are, in many parts, unworthy of a gentleman of Sir Grant Duff's position and expected knowledge. But what is particularly more regrettable is his attitude towards the educated classes, and the sneers he has levelled against higher education itself. If there is one thing more than another for which the Indian people are peculiarly and deeply grateful to the British nation, and which is one of the chief reasons of their attachment and loyalty to British rule, it is the blessing of education which Britain has bestowed on India. Britain has every reason to be proud of, and to be satisfied with, the results, for it is the educated classes who realise and appreciate most the beneficence and good intentions of the British nation; and by the increasing influence which they are now undoubtedly exercising over the people, they are the powerful chain by which India is becoming more and more firmly linked with Britain. This education has produced its natural effects, in promoting civilisation and independence of character—a result of which a true Briton should not be ashamed and should regard as his peculiar glory. But it would appear that this independence of character and the free criticism passed by the educated classes on Sir Grant Duff's acts have ruffled his composure. He has allowed his feelings to get the better of his judgment. I shall have to say a few words on this subject hereafter.

Sir Grant Duff asks the English tourists, who go to India "for the purpose of enlightening their countrymen when they come home"—"Is it too much to ask that these last should take the pains to arrive at an accurate knowledge of facts before they give their conclusions to the world?" May I ask the same question of Sir Grant Duff himself? Is it too much to ask him, who has occupied high and responsible positions, that he, as far more bound to do so, should take the pains to arrive at an accurate knowledge of facts before he gives his conclusions to the world? Careless or mistaken utterances of men of his position, by misleading the British public, do immeasurable harm, both to England and India.

Of the few matters which I intend to discuss there is one —the most important—upon which all other questions hinge. The correct solution of this fundamental problem will help all other Indian problems to settle themselves under the ordinary current discussions of every day. Before proceeding, however, with this fundamental question, it is necessary to make one or two preliminary remarks to clear away some misapprehensions which often confuse and complicate the discussion of Indian subjects.

There are three parties concerned—(1) The British nation (2) those authorities to whom the Government of India is entrusted by the British nation, and (3) the Natives of British India.

Now, I have no complaint whatever against the British nation or British rule. On the contrary, we have every reason to be thankful that of all the nations in the world it has been our good fortune to be placed under the British nation—a nation noble and great in its instincts; among the most advanced, if not the most advanced, in civilization; foremost in the advancement of humanity in all its varied wants and circumstances; the source and fountainhead of true liberty and of political progress in the world; in short, a nation in which all that is just, generous and truly free is most happily combined.

The British nation has done its part nobly, has laid down,

and pledged itself before God and the world to, a policy of justice and generosity towards India, in which nothing is left to be desired. That policy is complete and worthy of its great and glorious past and present. No, we Indians have no complaint against the British nation or British rule. We have everything from them to be grateful for. It is against its servants, to whom it has entrusted our destinies, that we have something of which to complain. Or rather, it is against the system which has been adopted by its servants, and which subverts the avowed and pledged policy of the British nation, that we complain, and against which I appeal to the British people.

Reverting to the few important matters which I desire to discuss, the first great question is—What is Britain's policy towards India? Sir Grant Duff says: "Of two things one: either we mean to stay in India and make the best of the country—directly for its own advantage, indirectly for that of ourselves and of mankind at large, or we do not." Again, he says: "The problem is how best to manage for its interest, our own interest, and the interest of the world. . . ." Now, if anybody ought to know, Sir Grant Duff ought, that this very problem, exactly as he puts it and for the purposes he mentions, has been completely and exhaustively debated, decided upon, and the decision pledged in the most deliberate manner, in an Act of Parliament more than fifty years ago, and again most solemnly and sacredly pledged more than twenty-five years ago. Sir Grant Duff either forgets or ignores these great events. Let us see, then, what this policy is. At a time when the Indians were in their educational and political infancy, when they did not and could not understand what their political condition then was or was to be in the future, when they had not uttered, as far as I know, any complaints, nor demanded any rights or any definite policy towards themselves, the British nation of their own accord and pleasure, merely from their own sense of their duty towards the millions of India and to the world, deliberately declared before the world what their policy should be towards the people of India. Nor did the British people do this in any ignorance or want of forethought or without the consideration of all possible consequences of their action. Never was there a debate in both Houses of Parliament more complete and clear, more exhaustive, more deliberately looked at from all points of view, and more calculated for the development of statesmanlike policy and practical good sense. The most crucial point of view—that of political danger or of even the possible loss of India to Britain—was faced with true English manliness; and the British nation, through their Parliament, then settled, adopted, and proclaimed to the world what their policy was to be—viz., the policy of justice and of the advancement of humanity.

I can give here only a very few extracts from that famous debate of more than half a century ago—a debate reflecting the highest glory on the British name.

Sir Robert Peel said :—

"Sure I am at least that we must approach the consideration of it with a deep feeling, with a strong sense of the responsibility we shall incur, with a strong sense of the moral obligation which imposes it upon us as a duty to promote the improvement of the country and the welfare and well-being of its inhabitants, so far as we can consistently with the safety and security of our dominion and the obligations by which we may be bound. . . . ."

The Marquis of Lansdowne, in the House of Lords, said :—

"But he should be taking a very narrow view of this question, and one utterly inadequate to the great importance of the subject, which involved in it the happiness or misery of one hundred millions of human beings, were he not to call the attention of their Lordships to the bearing which this question and to the influence which this arrangement must exercise upon the future destinies of that vast mass of people. He was sure that their Lordships would feel, as he indeed felt, that their only justification before God and Providence for the great and unprecedented dominion which they exercised in India was in the happiness which they communicated to the subjects under their rule, and in proving to the world at large, and to the inhabitants of Hindoostan, that the inheritance of Akbar (the wisest and most beneficent of Mahomedan princes) had not fallen into unworthy or degenerate hands. . . . ." His Lordship, after announcing the policy intended to be adopted, concluded : "He was confident that the strength of the Government would be increased by the happiness of the people over whom it presided, and by the attachment of those nations to it."

Lord Macaulay's speech is worthy of him, and of the great nation to which he belonged. I have every temptation to quote the whole of it, but space forbids. He calls the proposed policy "that wise, that benevolent, that noble clause," and he adds :—

"I must say that, to the last day of my life, I shall be proud of having been one of those who assisted in the framing of the Bill which contains that clause . . . . Governments, like men, may buy existence too dear. 'Propter vitam vivendi perdere causas' is a despicable policy either in individuals or States. In the present case such a policy would be not only despicable but absurd. . . . . To the great trading nation, to the great manufacturing nation, no progress which any portion of the human race can make in knowledge, in taste for the conveniences of life, or in the wealth by which those conveniences are produced, can be matter of indifference. . . . . To trade with civilised men is infinitely more profitable than to govern savages. That would indeed be a doting wisdom, which, in order that India might remain a dependency, would make it a useless and costly dependency—which would keep a hundred millions of men from being our customers in order that they might continue to be our slaves. It was, as Bernier tells us, the practice of the miserable tyrants whom he found in India, when they dreaded the capacity and spirit of some distinguished subject, and yet could not venture to murder him, to administer to him a daily dose of the pousta, a preparation of opium, the effect of which was in a few months to destroy all the bodily and mental powers of the wretch who was drugged with it, and to turn him into a helpless idiot. That detestable artifice, more horrible than assassination itself, was worthy of those who employed it. It is no model for the English nation. We shall never consent to administer the pousta to a whole community, to stupify and paralyse a great people whom God has committed to our charge, for the wretched purpose of rendering them more amenable to our control. . . . . I have no fears. The path of duty is plain before us; and it is also the path of wisdom, of national prosperity, of national honour. . . . . To have found a great people sunk in the lowest depths of misery and superstition, to have so ruled them as to have made them desirous and capable of all the priviliges of citizens, would indeed be a title to glory—all our own. The sceptre may pass away from us. Unforeseen accidents may derange our most profound schemes of policy. Victory may be inconstant to our arms. But there are triumphs which are followed by no reverses. There is an empire exempt from all natural causes of decay. Those triumphs are the pacific triumphs of reason over barbarism; that empire is the imperishable empire of our arts and our morals, our literature and our law."

Now what was it that was so deliberately decided upon—that which was to promote the welfare and well-being of the millions of India, involve their happiness or misery, and influence their future destiny; that which was to be the only justification before God and Providence for the dominion over India; that which was to increase the strength of the Government and secure the attachment of the nation to it; and that which was wise, benevolent and noble, most profitable to English trade and manufacture, the plain path of duty, wisdom, national prosperty and national honour, and calculated to raise a people sunk in the lowest depths of misery and superstition to prosperity and civilisation? It was this "noble" clause in the Act of 1833, worthy of the British character for justice, generosity and humanity: "That no Native of the said territories, nor any natural-born subject of his Majesty resident therein, shall, by reason only of his religion, place of birth, descent, or any of them, be disabled from holding any place, office or employment under the said Company."

I now ask the first question. Is this deliberately declared policy honestly promised, and is it intended by the British nation to be honestly and honourably fulfilled; or is it a lie and a delusion, meant only to deceive India and the world? This is the first clear issue.

It must be remembered, as I have already said, that this wise and noble pledge was given at a time when the Indians had not asked for it. It was of Britain's own will and accord, of her own sense of duty towards a great people whom Providence had entrusted to her care, that she deliberated and gave the pledge. The pledge was given with grace and unasked, and was therefore the more valuable and more to Britain's credit and renown. But the authorities to whom the performance of this pledge was entrusted by the British nation did not do their duty, and left the pledge a dead letter. Then came a time of trouble, and Britain triumphed over the Mutiny. But what did she do in that moment of triumph? Did she retract the old, great and noble pledge? Did she say, "You have proved unworthy of it, and I withdraw it." No! True to her instincts of justice, she once more and still more emphatically and solemnly proclaimed to the world the same pledge, even in greater completeness and in every form. By the mouth of our great Sovereign did she once more give her pledge, calling God to witness and seal it and bestow His blessing thereon; and this did the gracious proclamation of 1858 proclaim to the world:—

"We hold ourselves bound to the Natives of our Indian territory by the same obligations of duty which bind us to all our other subjects; and those obligations, by the blessing of Almighty God, we shall faithfully and conscientiously fulfil.

"And it is our further will that, so far as may be, our subjects, of whatever race or creed, be freely and impartially admitted to offices in our service, the duties of which they may be qualified by their education, ability, and integrity duly to discharge.

"In their prosperity will be our strength, in their contentment our security, and in their gratitude our best reward. And may the

God of all power grant to us and to those in authority under us strength to carry out these our wishes for the good of our people."

Can pledges more sacred, more clear, and more binding before God and man be given?

I ask this second question. Are these pledges honest promises of the British Sovereign and nation, to be faithfully and conscientiously fulfilled, or are they only so many lies and delusions? I can and do expect but one reply: that these sacred promises were made honestly, and meant to be honestly and honourably fulfilled. The whole Indian problem hangs upon these great pledges, upon which the blessings and help of God are invoked. It would be an insult and an injustice to the British nation, quite unpardonable in me—with my personal knowledge of the British people for more than thirty years—if I for a moment entertained the shadow of a doubt with regard to the honesty of these pledges.

The third question is—Whether these pledges have been faithfully and conscientiously fulfilled. The whole position of India is this: If these solemn pledges be faithfully and conscientiously fulfilled, India will have nothing more to desire. Had these pledges been fulfilled, what a different tale of congratulation should we have had to tell to-day of the prosperity and advancement of India and of great benefits to and blessings upon England. But it is useless to mourn over the past. The future is still before us.

I appeal to the British nation that these sacred and solemn promises should be hereafter faithfully and conscientiously fulfilled. This will satisfy all our wants. This will realize all the various consequences, benefits and blessings which the statesmen of 1833 have foretold, to England's eternal glory, and to the benefit of England, India and the world. The non-fulfilment of these pledges has been tried for half a century, and poverty and degradation are still the lot of India. Let us have, I appeal, for half a century the conscientious fulfilment of these pledges, and no man can hesitate to foretell, as the great statesmen of 1833 foretold, that India will rise in prosperity and civilization, that "the strength of the Government would be increased by the happiness of the people over whom it presided, and by the attachment of those nations to it." As long as fair trial is not given to these pledges it is idle, and adding insult to injury, to decide anything or to seek any excuses against us and against the fulfilment of the pledges.

If this appeal is granted, if the British nation says that its honest promises must be honestly fulfilled, every other Indian question will find its natural and easy solution. If, on the other hand, this appeal shall go in vain—which I can never believe will be the case—the present unnatural system of the non-fulfilment of the great policy of 1833 and 1858 will be an obstacle and a complete prevention of the right and just solution of any other Indian question whatever. From the seed of injustice no fruit of justice can ever be produced. Thistles will never yield grapes.

I now come to the second important question—the present material condition of India as the natural result of the non-fulfilment of the great pledges. Mr. Samuel Smith had remarked that there was among the well-educated Natives "a widespread belief that India is getting poorer and less happy," and he has subsequently expressed his own impressions: "The first and deepest impression made upon me by this second visit to India is a heightened sense of the poverty of the country." Now, to such a serious matter, what is Sir Grant Duff's reply? First, a sneer at the educated classes and at higher education itself. Next, he gives a long extract from an address of the local reception committee of the town of Bezwada, in which, says the address, by means of an anicut, "at one stroke the mouths of a hungry and dying people have been filled with bread, and the coffers of the Government with money." Now, can levity and unkindness go any further? This is the reply that a great functionary gives to Mr. Smith's serious charge about the poverty of India. What can the glowing, long extract from the address of the committee of Bezwada mean, if Sir Grant Duff did not thereby intend to lead the British public into the belief that, because the small town of Bezwada had acknowledged a good thing done for it, therefore in *all* India all was happy and prospering? However, Sir Grant Duff could not help reverting, after a while, to the subject a little more seriously, and admitting that "there is in many parts of India frightful poverty." What, then, becomes of the glowing extract from the Bezwada address, and how was that a reply to Mr. Smith's charge? However, even after making the admission of the "frightful poverty in many parts of India," he disposes off-hand of the grave matter—remarking that other people in other countries are also poor, as if that were a justification of "the frightful poverty in many parts of India," under a rule like that of the British, and conducted by a service the most highly praised and the most highly paid in the world. Sir Grant Duff, with a cruel levity, only asks two or three questions, without any proof of his assumptions and without any attention to the circumstances of the comparisons, and at once falls foul of the educated classes, as if thereby he gave a complete reply to the complaint about the poverty. Now, these are the three questions he puts :—"The question worth answering is: Do the Indian masses obtain, one year with another, a larger or smaller amount of material well-being than the peasantry of Western Europe?" And he answers himself: "Speaking of the huge province of Madras, which I, of course, know best—and I have visited every district in it—I think they do. . . ." They "do" what? Do they obtain a larger or smaller amount? His second question is: "But is there not the same, and even worse, in our own country?" And lastly, he brings down his clincher thus:—"As to our system 'draining the country of its wealth,' if that be the case, how is it visibly increasing in wealth?" And he gives no proof of that increased wealth. Thus, then, does Sir Grant Duff settle the most serious questions connected with India. First, a sneer at educated men and higher education, then the frivolous argument about the town of Bezwada, and afterwards three off-hand questions and assertions without any proof. In this way does a former Under-Secretary of State for India, and only lately a ruler of thirty millions of people, inform and instruct the British public on the most burning Indian questions. We may now, however, see what Sir Grant Duff's above three questions mean, and what they are worth, and how wrong and baseless his assertions are.

Fortunately, *Mr.* Grant Duff has already replied to *Sir* Grant Duff. We are treated by Sir Grant Duff to a long extract from his Budget speech of 1873. He might have as well favoured us, to better purpose, with an extract or two from some of his other speeches. In 1870 Mr. Grant Duff asks Sir Wilfrid Lawson a remarkable question during the debate on Opium. He asks: "Would it be tolerable that to enforce a view of morality which was not theirs, which had never indeed been accepted by any large portion of the human race, we should grind an already poor population to the very dust with new taxation?" Can a more complete reply be given to Sir Grant's present questions than this reply of Mr. Grant Duff: that the only margin that saves "an already poor population" *from being ground to the very dust* is the few millions that are obtained by poisoning a foreign country (China).

Again *Mr.* Grant Duff supplies another complete reply to *Sir* Grant Duff's questions. In his Budget speech of 1871, he thus depicts the poverty of India as compared with the condition of England—"one of the countries of Western Europe" and the "our own country" of his questions. Just at that time I had, in a rough way, shown that the whole production or income of British India was about Rs. 20 (40s.) per head per annum. Of this Mr. Grant Duff made the following use in 1871. He said: "The position of the Indian financier is altogether different from that of the English one. Here you have a comparatively wealthy population. The income of the United Kingdom has, I believe, been guessed at £800,000,000 per annum. The income of British India has been guessed at £300,000,000 per annum. That gives well on to £30 per annum as the income of every person of the United Kingdom, and only £2 per annum as the income of every person in British India. Even our comparative wealth will be looked back upon by future ages as a state of semi-barbarism. But what are we to say of the state of India? How many generations must pass away before that country has arrived at even the comparative wealth of this?"

But now Sir Grant Duff ignores his own utterances as to how utterly different the cases of England and India are. Mr. Grant Duff's speech having been received in India, Lord Mayo thus commented upon it and confirmed it:—

"I admit the comparative poverty of this country, as compared with many other countries of the same magnitude and importance, and I am convinced of the impolicy and injustice of imposing burdens upon this people which may be called either crushing or oppressive. Mr. Grant Duff in an able speech which he delivered the other day in the House of Commons, the report of which arrived by the last mail, stated with truth that the position of our finance was wholly different from that of England. 'In England,' he stated, 'you have comparatively a wealthy population. The income of the United Kingdom has, I believe, been guessed at

£800,000,000 per annum; the income of British India has been guessed at £300,000,000 per annum: that goes well on to £30 per annum as the income of every person in the United Kingdom, and only £2 per annum as the income of every person in British India.' I believe that Mr. Grant Duff had good grounds for the statement he made, and I wish to say, with reference to it, that we are perfectly cognisant of the relative poverty of this country as compared with European States."

Here, again, is another answer to Sir Grant Duff's questions, by the late Finance Minister of India. Major (Sir) E. Baring, in proof of his assertion of "the extreme poverty of the mass of the people" of British India, makes a comparison not only with "the Western countries of Europe" but with "the poorest country in Europe." After stating that the income of India was not more than Rs. 27 per head, he said, in his Budget speech of 1882: "In England, the average income per head of population was £33 per head; in France it was £23; in Turkey, which was the poorest country in Europe, it was £4 per head."

It will be seen, then, that *Mr.* Grant Duff and a higher authority than *Sir* Grant Duff have already fully answered Sir Grant Duff's questions. The only thing now remaining is whether Sir Grant Duff will undertake to prove that the income of British India has now become equal to that of the Western countries of Europe; and if so, let him give us his facts and figures to prove such a statement—not mere allusions to the prosperity of some small towns like Bezwada, or even to that of the Presidency towns, but a complete estimate of the income of *all* British India, so as to compare it with that of England, France, or "Western countries of Europe."

I may say here a word or two about "the huge province of Madras, which," says Sir Grant, "I, of course, know best, and I have visited every district in it." We may see now whether he has visited with his eyes open or shut. I shall be glad if Sir Grant Duff will give us figures to show that Madras to-day produces as much as the Western countries of Europe.

Sir George Campbell, in his paper on tenure of land in India, says, from an official Report of 1869, about the Madras Presidency, that "the bulk of the people are paupers." I have just received an extract from a friend in India. Mr. W. R. Robertson, Agricultural Reporter to the Government of Madras, says of the agricultural labourer :—

"His condition is a disgrace to any country calling itself civilised. In the best seasons the gross income of himself and his family does not exceed 3d. per day throughout the year, and in a bad season their circumstances are most deplorable. . . . . I have seen something of Ireland, in which the condition of affairs bears some resemblance to those of this country, but the condition of the agricultural population of Ireland is vastly superior to the condition of the similar classes in this country."

There cannot be any doubt about the correctness of these views; for, as a matter of fact, as I have worked out the figures in my paper on "The Poverty of India," the income of the Madras Presidency in 1868-69 was only about Rs. 18 per head per annum.

Such is the Madras Presidency, which Sir Grant Duff has visited with his eyes apparently shut.

I shall now give a few statements about the "extreme poverty" of British India, by persons whose authority would be admitted by Sir Grant Duff as far superior to his own. In 1864 Sir John (afterwards Lord) Lawrence, then Viceroy, said: "India is on the whole a very poor country; the mass of the population enjoy only a scanty subsistence." And again, in 1873, he repeated his opinion before the Finance Committee that the mass of the people were so miserably poor that they had barely the means of subsistence. It was as much as a man could do to feed his family, or half-feed them, let alone spending money on what might be called luxuries or conveniences. In 1881 Dr. (Sir W.) Hunter, the best official defender of the British Indian Administration, told the British public that 40,000,000 of the people of British India "go through life on insufficient food." This is an official admission, but I have no moral doubt that, if full enquiries were made, twice forty millions or more would be found "going through life on insufficient food;" and what wonder that the very touch of famine should destroy hundreds of thousands or millions. Coming down at once to the latest times, Sir E. Baring said, in his finance speech in 1882:—

"It has been calculated that the average income per head of population in India is not more than Rs. 27 a year; and, though I am not prepared to pledge myself to the absolute accuracy of a calculation of this sort, it is sufficiently accurate to justify the conclusion that the tax-paying community is *exceedingly poor*. To derive any very large increase of revenue from so poor a population as this is obviously impossible, and if it were possible would be unjustifiable."

Again, in the course of the debate he repeated the statement about the income being Rs. 27 per head per annum, and said in connexion with salt revenue: "But he thought it was quite sufficient to show the *extreme poverty of the mass of the people*." Then, after stating the income of some of the European countries, as I have stated them before, he proceeded: "He would ask honourable members to think what Rs. 27 per annum was to support a person, and then he would ask whether a few annas was nothing to such poor people." I asked Sir E. Baring to give me his calculations to check with mine, but he declined. But it does not matter much, as even "not more than Rs. 27" is *extreme poverty of the mass of the people*. Later still the present Finance Minister, in his speech on the Income Tax, in January 1886, described the mass of the people as "men whose income at the best is barely sufficient to afford them the sustenance necessary to support life, living, as they do, upon the barest necessaries of life."

Now, what are we to think of an English gentleman who has occupied the high and important positions of an Under-Secretary of State for India and Governor of the thirty millions of Madras, and who professes to feel deep interest in the people of India, treating such grave matters as their "extreme poverty" and "scanty subsistence" with light-heartedness like this, and coolly telling them and the British public that the people of Bezwada were gloriously prosperous, and that there, "at one stroke, the mouths of a hungry and dying people have been filled with bread and the coffers of the Government with money!"

I shall now give a few facts and figures in connexion with the condition of India, and with some of the other questions dealt with by Sir Grant Duff. First, with regard to the poverty to which Mr. Samuel Smith referred. Sir Grant Duff may rest assured that I shall be only too thankful to him for any correction of my figures by him or for any better information. I have no other object than the truth.

In my paper on "The Poverty of India" I have worked out from official figures that the total income of British India is only Rs. 20 (40s., or, at present exchange, nearer 30s.) per head per annum. It must be remembered that the mass of the people cannot get this average of Rs. 20, as the upper classes have a larger share than the average; also that this Rs. 20 per head includes the income or produce of foreign planters or producers, in which the interest of the Natives does not go further than being mostly common labourers at competitive wages. All the profits of such produce are enjoyed by, and carried away from the country by, the foreigners. Subsequently, in my correspondence with the Secretary of State for India in 1880, I placed before his lordship, in detailed calculations based upon official returns, the income of the most favoured province of the Punjab and the cost of absolute necessaries of life there for a common agricultural labourer. The income is, at the outside, Rs. 20 per head per annum, and the cost of living Rs. 34. No wonder then that forty or eighty millions or more people of British India should "go through life on insufficient food." My calculations, both in "The Poverty of India" and "The Condition of India" (the correspondence with the Secretary of State), have not yet been shown by anybody to be wrong or requiring correction. I shall be glad and thankful if Sir Grant Duff would give us his calculations and show us that the income of British India is anything like that of the Western countries of Europe.

I give a statement of the income of the different countries from Mulhall's "Dictionary of Statistics":—

Countries.	Gross earnings per inhabitant.	Countries	Gross earnings per inhabitant.
England	£41	Belgium	£22.1
Scotland	32	Holland	26
Ireland	16	Denmark	23·2
United Kingdom	35·2	Sweden and Norway	16·2
France	25·7	Switzerland	16
Germany	18·7	Greece	11·8
Russia	9·9	Europe	18
Austria	16·3	United States	27·2
Italy	12	Canada	26·9
Spain	13·8	Australia	43·4
Portugal	13·6		

The table is not official. In his "Progress of the World" (1880), Mulhall gives—Scandinavia, £17; South America, £6; India, £2. What is then poor India's whole income per head? Not even as much as the United Kingdom pays to its revenue only per head. The United Kingdom pays to revenue nearly 50s. per head, when wretched India's whole income is 40s. per head, or rather, at the present exchange, nearer 30s. than 40s. Is this a result for an Englishman to boast about or to be satisfied with, after a century of British administration? The income of British India only a third of that of even the countries of South America! Every other part of the British Empire is flourishing except wretched India.

Sir Grant Duff knows well that any poverty in the countries of Western Europe is not from want of wealth or income, but from unequal distribution. But British India has her whole production or income itself most wretched. There is no wealth, and therefore the question of its right distribution, or of any comparison with the countries of Western Europe or with England is very far off indeed. Certainly a gentleman like Sir Grant Duff ought to understand the immense difference between the character of the conditions of the poor masses of British India and of the poor of Western Europe; the one starving from scantiness, the other having plenty, but suffering from some defect in its distribution. Let the British Indian Administration fulfil its sacred pledges and allow plenty to be produced in British India, and then will be the the proper time and occasion to compare the phenomena of the conditions of Western Europe and British India. The question at present is, why, under the management of the most highly paid services in the world, India cannot produce as much even as the worst governed countries of Europe. I do not mean to blame the individuals of the Indian services. It is the policy, the perversion of the pledges, that is at the bottom of our misfortunes. Let the Government of India only give us every year properly made up statistical tables of the whole production or the income of the country, and we shall then know truly how India fares year after year, and we shall then see how the present system of administration is an obstacle to any material advancement of India. Let us have actual facts about the real income of India, instead of careless opinions like those in Sir Grant Duff's two articles.

Instead of asking us to go so far as Western Europe to compare conditions so utterly different from each other, Sir Grant Duff might have looked nearer home, and studied somewhat of the neighbouring Native States, to institute some fair comparison under a certain similarity of circumstances. This point I shall have to refer to in the next article, when dealing with a cognate subject. Sir Grant Duff says: "I maintain that no country on the face of the earth is governed so cheaply in proportion to its size, to its population and to the difficulties of government." Surely Sir Grant Duff knows better than this. Surely he knows that the pressure of a burden depends upon the capacity to bear it: that an elephant may carry tons with ease, while a child would be crushed by a hundredweight. Surely he knows the very first axiom of taxation—that it should be in proportion to the means of the taxpayer. Mulhall very properly says in his Dictionary: "The real incidence of all taxation is better shown by comparison with the people's earnings." Let us see facts. Let us see whether the incidence in British India is not *heavier than that of England itself*. The gross revenue of the United Kingdom in 1886 is £89,581,301; the population in 1886 is given as 36,707,418. The revenue per head will be 48s. 9d. The gross revenue of British India in 1885 is (in £1 = ten rupees) £70,690,000, and population in 1881, 198,790,000—say roundly, in 1885, 200,000,000. The revenue of the United Kingdom does not include railway or irrigation earnings; I deduct, therefore, these from the British Indian revenue. Deducting from £70,690,000, railway earnings £11,898,000, and irrigation and navigation earnings £1,676,000, the balance of gross revenue is £57,116,000, which taken for 200,000,000, gives 5s. 8½d.—say 5s. 8d.—per head. Now the United Kingdom pays 48s. 9d. per head from an income of £35·2 per head, which makes the incidence or pressure of 6·92 per cent. of the income. British India pays 5s. 8d. out of an income of 40s., which makes the incidence or pressure of 14·3 per cent. of the income. Thus, while the United Kingdom pays for its gross revenue only 6·92 per cent. out of its rich income of £35·2 per head, British India pays out of its scantiness and starvation a gross revenue of 14·3 per cent. of its income; so that, wretchedly weak and poor as British India is, the pressure upon it is more than doubly heavier than that on the enormously wealthy United Kingdom; and yet Sir Grant Duff says that no country on the face of the earth is governed so cheaply as British India, and misleads the British public about its true and deplorable condition. But what is worse, and what is British India's chief difficulty, is this: In England, all that is paid by the people for revenue returns back to them, is enjoyed by them, and fructifies in their own pockets; while in India, what the people pay as revenue does not all return to them, or is enjoyed by them, or fructifies in their pockets. A large portion is enjoyed by others, and carried away clean out of the country. This is what makes British India's economic position unnatural.

I give below the incidence of a few more countries:—Percentage of expenditure to income: Germany, 10·7; France, 13·23; Belgium, 9·5; Holland, 9·61; Russia, 10·1; Denmark, 5·17; United States, 3·9; Canada, 5·0; Australia, 16·2. But in all these cases, whatever is spent returns back to the people, whether the percentage is large or small.

The Budget Estimate of 1887-88 is nearly £77,500,000, so the percentage of incidence will increase still higher. Sir Grant Duff's object in this assertion is to justify the character and prove the success of the present British Indian policy. It will be hereafter seen that this very argument of his is one of the best proofs of the failure of this policy and of the administration based upon it. Sir Grant Duff says: "Mr. Smith proceeds to admit that India has absorbed some £350,000,000 sterling of silver and gold in the last forty years, but makes the very odd remark that, although English writers consider this a great proof of wealth, it is not so regarded in India." To this, what is Sir Grant Duff's reply? Of the same kind as usual: mere careless assertions, and a fling at the misrepresentation about the educated classes. He says:—

> "It may suit A or B not to regard two and two as making four, but arithmetic is true, nevertheless; and there is the bullion, though doubtless one of the greatest boons that could be conferred upon India would be to get the vast dormant hoards of gold and silver which are buried in the ground or worn on the person brought into circulation. Can that, however, be hoped for as long as the very people whom Mr. Smith treats as exponents of Native opinion do their utmost to excite hostility against the British Government?"

To avoid confusion I pass over for the present without notice the last assertion. It will be seen further on what different testimony even the highest Indian authorities give upon this subject. With regard to the other remarks, it is clear that Sir Grant Duff has not taken the pains to know what the Natives say, and what the actual state of the matter is, with regard to these economic conditions. The best thing I can do to avoid useless controversy is to give in my second article a series of facts and official figures, instead of making bare assertions of opinion without any proofs, as Sir Grant Duff says. These economic questions are of far greater and more serious importance, both to England and India, than Sir Grant Duff and others of his views dream of. These facts and figures will show that British India has not received such amounts of gold and silver as is generally supposed, or as are more than barely adequate to its ordinary wants. The phenomenon of the import of bullion into British India is very much misapprehended, as will be shown in my second article; and Sir Grant Duff's assertions are misleading, as such meagre, vague, and off-hand assertions always are. By the present policy British India is prevented from acquiring any capital of its own, owing to the constant drain from its wretched income, and is on the verge of being ground down to dust. Such foreign capital as circulates in British India carries away its own profits *out* of British India, leaving the masses of its people as poor as ever, and largely going through life on insufficient food.

November, 1887.

II.

I shall now consider the important questions of trade, bullion, population, drain, etc., to which Sir Grant Duff has referred. As promised in my first article, I shall at once proceed to give official facts and figures, which will enable the public to judge for themselves.

I begin with the question of the trade of British India. What is the true trade of British India? The trade returns of British India, as published in Blue-books, both in England and India, are misleading to those who do not study them with certain necessary information to guide them. What are given as trade returns of British India are not such really, as I explain below. The exports of the produce of a country form the basis of its trade. It is in return for such exports, together with ordinary commercial profits, that the country receives its imports. I shall first analyse the so-called exports of British India. A large portion of them, together with their profits, never return to British India in any shape, either of merchandise or treasure; though in every true trade all exports with their profits ought so to return. The present exports of British India consist of—

1. The exports of produce belonging to the Native States.

2. The exports of produce belonging to the territories beyond the land frontiers.

3. The exports of the produce belonging to European or other foreign planters or manufacturers, the profits of which are enjoyed in and carried away out of the country by these foreigners, and do not belong to or become a portion of the capital of the people of British India. The only interest the people have in these exports is that they are the labourers, by whose labour, at poor wages, the resources of their own country are to be brought out for the profit of the foreigners, such profit not to remain in the country.

4. Remittances for "home charges," including interest on public debt held in England, and loss in exchange, and

excluding interest on debt which is incurred for railways and other productive works.

5. Remittances for interest on foreign debt incurred for railways and other productive public works. What in this case the lenders get as interest is all right; there is nothing to complain of in that. In other countries, beyond the interest to be paid to the lenders, the rest of the whole benefit of such loans remains to the people of the country. This, however, is not the case with British India.

6. Private remittances of Europeans and other foreigners to their own countries for their families, and on account of their savings and profits. These remittances, together with item four, and what the foreigners enjoy in the country itself, are so much deprivation of the people, and cause the exhausting annual drain out of the very poor produce or income of British India. This is India's chief evil.

7. The remainder are the only *true* trade exports of the produce belonging to the people of British India.

Let us now examine the actual figures of the so-called exports of British India, say for 1885. For easier understanding I give the figures in sterling, taking the conventional £1 = Rs. 10. The amount of merchandise exported is £83,200,528. This, however, consists of not only domestic produce and manufactures of all India, but also foreign merchandise re-exported. I do not include treasure in these exports, for the simple reason that the gold or silver is not produced in India, but is simply a re-exportation out of what is imported from foreign parts. I take all my figures from the statistical abstracts published among Parliamentary returns, except when I mention any other source. I take, then, exports of merchandise to be £83,200,528. We must first know how much of this belongs to the Native States. The official trade returns give us no information on this important point, as they should. I shall therefore make a rough estimate for the present. The population of all India is nearly 254,000,000, out of which that of the Native States is 55,000,000, or about 21·5 per cent.; or say, roundly, one-fifth. But the proportion of their exports will, I think, be found to be larger than one-fifth. All the opium exported from Bombay comes from the Native States. A large portion of the cotton exported from Bombay comes from the Native States. According to Hunter's "Imperial Indian Gazetteer,' one-sixth of such cotton comes from Kathiawad alone. To be on the safe side, I take the total of exports of the Native States to be one-fifth only—*i.e.*, £16,600,000. Next, the export of merchandise from the frontier countries is about £5,300,000. I may roughly take only one-quarter of this as exported out of India. That will be £1,300,000.

The exports of coffee, indigo, jute manufactures, silk, tea, etc., which are mostly those belonging to foreign planters and manufacturers, amount to about £11,500,000. I cannot say how much of this belongs to Native planters, and not to foreigners. I may take these exports as £10,000,000.

Remittances made for "home charges" (excluding interest on railway and productive works loans), including interest on public debt and loss in exchange, come to about £11,500,000.

Remittances for interest on foreign loans for railways and other public works are about £4,827,000. I cannot say how much interest on the capital of State railways and other productive works is paid in England as part of the interest paid on "debt" (£2,612,000). If I take debt as £162,000,000, and capital laid out on productive works £74,000,000, the proportion of interest on £74,000,000 out of £2,612,000 will be about £1,189,000. If so, then the total amount of interest on *all* railways and public works will be about £6,000,000, leaving all other home charges, including exchange and interest on public debt, as £11,500,000, as I have assumed above.

Private remittances of Europeans and other foreigners for their families, and of savings and profits, and for importing merchandise suitable for their consumption, may be roughly estimated at £10,000,000, though I think it is much more.

The account, then, of the *true* trade exports of British India stands thus:—

Total exports of all India and Frontier States		£83,200,000
Native States	£16,600,000	
Frontier Territory	1,300,000	
European planters	10,000,000	
Home charges	11,500,000	
Interest on all railways and public works loans	6,000,000	
Private remittances	10,000,000	
		55,400,000
The true trade exports of the people of British India		£27,800,000

Or say, roundly, £30,000,000 for a population of nearly

200,000,000, giving 3s. per head per annum. If proper information could be obtained, I believe this amount would turn out to be nearer £20,000,000 than £30,000,000 for the *true* trade exports of the people of British India. To be on the safe side, I keep to £30,000,000. It must be remembered that this item includes all the re-exports of foreign merchandise, which have to be deducted to get at the true exports of domestic produce.

Is this a satisfactory result of a century of management by British administrators? Let us compare this result with the trade exports of other parts of the British Empire. As I have no information about the foreign debt of those parts, for the interest of which they may have to export some of their produce, I make allowance for their *whole* public debt as so much foreign debt. This, of course is a too large allowance. I take interest at 5 per cent., and deduct the amount from the exports. I am, therefore, evidently under-estimating the exports of the other parts of the British Empire. As the exports of British India include re-exports of foreign merchandise, I have taken the exports of all other countries, in a similar way, for a fair comparison. No deduction for any payment of interest on foreign debt is made for the United Kingdom, as it is more a lender than a borrower. I cannot give here the whole calculation, but only the results, and they are these:—

Countries.	True trade exports per head (1885). s. d.	Countries.	True trade exports per head (1885). s. d.
The United Kingdom . .	149 4	Cape of Good Hope (exclusive of diamonds) . . .	35 5
Australia (including bullion and specie which it produces)	271 0	North American Colonies .	70 5
Natal	28 8	West India Islands . .	75 4
		British India only . .	3 0

Let us next take some of the foreign countries, and see how wretched British India's trade is when compared with even them. For a few of the foreign countries I can get particulars of their public debt, but not of that portion of it which is foreign debt. I have taken the amount of the *whole* public debt, and allowed 5 per cent. interest on it, to be deducted from the exports, as if it were all foreign debt. In this way I have under-estimated the true trade exports. These countries I mark with an asterisk; those marked † include bullion. For these I cannot get separate returns for merchandise only. In the case of the United States the figure is really a great under-estimate, as I take its foreign debt as equal in amount to its whole public debt, and also as I take interest at 5 per cent. I cannot get particulars of the foreign debts, if they have any, of other countries, and some allowance will have to be made for that. But in all these cases the amount of exports is so large, as compared with the paltry figure of British India, that the contrast remains most striking:—

Countries.	Exports per head. *s.*	*d.*	Countries.	Exports per head. *s.*	*d.*
*Russian Empire	12	0	Austro-Hungarian Empire	47	0
*Norway	61	7	†Roumania	27	0
Sweden	61	6	†Greece	39	9
*Denmark	97	5	Egypt	38	9
German Empire	107	2	*United States	55	6
Holland	348	1	†Mexico	20	1
*Belgium	375	2	†Chili	149	0
*France	68	7	†Argentine Republic	90	8
†Portugal	33	9	†Uruguay	198	2
Spain	36	5	Japan	3	8
*Italy	17	9	British India	3	0

Even Japan, only so lately opened up, is exporting more than British India.

After seeing how poor the *true trade* exports are of the people of British India from the point of view of British India's interests, let us next examine the matter from the point of view of *England's* interest. What benefit has England's trade derived, after possessing and administering British India for more than a hundred years, under a most expensive administration, with complete despotic control over it, the people having no voice and no control of any kind. Has British India so improved as to become an important customer for British goods? There was no protection, no heavy duties to hamper British imports, as in other parts of the British Empire itself, or in foreign countries. And yet we find that British India is by far the most wretched customer for British produce or manufactures. Here are the facts:—The total of the exports of British produce from the United Kingdom to India is, for the year 1885, £29,300,000. As I have explained before about exports from India, that they are not all from British India, so also these exports from the United Kingdom to India are not all for British India, though they enter India by British Indian ports. These British exports have to be distributed among—(1) Native States; (2) frontier territories; (3) consumption of Europeans; (4) railway and Government stores; and (5) the remainder for the Natives of British India. Let Government give us correct information about these particulars, and then we shall be able to know how insignificant is the commercial benefit England derives from her dominion over British India. I shall not be surprised if it is found that the real share of the people of British India in the British exports is not half of the £29,300,000 imported into India. It must be remembered that whatever is received by the Native States and the frontier territories is in *full* return, with the ordinary profits of 15 per cent., for their exports to the United Kingdom. Their case is not like that of British India. They have no such exhausting drain as that of British India, beyond paying the small tribute of about £700,000. If I take £15,000,000 as British produce received for the consumption of the Native subjects of British India, I think I am on the safe side. What is this amount for a population of 200,000,000? Only 1s. 6d. per head. Take it even at 2s. per head if you like, or even £25,000,000, which will be only 2s. 6d. per head. What a wretched result *for four-fifths of the whole British Empire!* The population of British India is 200,000,000, and that of the rest of the British Empire outside India, including the United Kingdom, about 52,000,000.

I now compare the exports of British produce to British India with those to other parts of the British Empire and to other foreign countries. I give the results only:—

BRITISH EMPIRE.

Exports of British Produce per Head for 1885.

To Countries.	s.	d.	To Countries.	s.	d.
British India . 1*s*. 6*d*. or	2	6	Ceylon	3	10
North American Colonies .	30	8	Mauritius	14	2
West Indian Islands and Guiana	37	10	Cape of Good Hope and Natal	45	8
British Honduras . . .	66	7	West African Settlements .	57	3
Australasia	155	8	Possessions on the Gold Coast	13	10
Straits Settlements . .	86	10			

Some deductions may have to be made from these figures.

What a sad story is this! If British India took only £1 per head, England would export to British India alone as much as she exports at present to the *whole* world (£213,000,000). What an amount of work would this give to British industries and produce! Will the British merchants and manufacturers open their eyes? Will the British working men understand how enormous their loss is from the present policy, which involves besides a charge of dishonourable violation of sacred promises that clings to the British name? If India prospered and consumed British produce largely, what a gain would it be to England and to the whole world also! Here, then, will be Sir Grant Duff's "India's interest, England's interest, and the world's interest" to his hearts content, if he will with a true and earnest heart labour to achieve this threefold interest in the right way.

Let us next take other foreign countries, with most or all of which England, I think, has no free trade, and see how British India stands the comparison even with them :—

EXPORTS OF BRITISH PRODUCE PER HEAD.

To Countries.	s.	d.	To Countries.	s.	d.
British India	2	6	Russia (perhaps partly supplied through intermediate countries)	0	11⅓
Germany	7	3	Greece	10	1
France	7	11	*Turkey in Europe	16	8
Sweden and Norway	10	8	*Turkey in Asia	3	10
Denmark and Iceland	19	4	Egypt	10	2
Holland (this may be supplying some portion of Central Europe	44	3	United States	8	9
Belgium (do. do.)	28	3	*Central America	4	7
Portugal	8	0	*Brazil	10	5
Spain	3	9	Uruguay	54	0
Italy (perhaps partly supplied by intermediate countries)	4	9	Argentine Republic	31	8
Austrian territory (ditto)	0	8	Chili	12	4
			Japan	1	1

* Whitaker's Almanac.

Japan, so lately opened, has commenced taking 1s. 1d. worth per head. These figures tell their own eloquent tale. Is it too much to expect that, with complete free trade and British management, and all "development of resources," the prosperity of British India ought to be such as to consume of British produce even £1 a head, and that it would be so if British India were allowed to grow freely under natural economic conditions?

In the first article I referred to the capacity of British India for taxation. Over and over again have British Indian financiers lamented that British India cannot bear additional taxation without oppressiveness. Well, now what is the extent of this taxation which is already so crushing that any addition to it would "grind British India to dust"? It is, as I have shown in the first article, after squeezing and squeezing as much as possible, only 5s. 8d. per head per annum, and according to the present budget a little more—say 6s. Let us see what the capacity for taxation of other parts of the British Empire and of other foreign countries is, and even of those Native States of India where anything like improved government on the British Indian system is introduced. I give results only:—

BRITISH EMPIRE.

Gross Revenue per Head per Annum.

Countries.	s.	d.	Countries.	s.	d.
British India	6	0	Natal	29	10
United Kingdom	48	9	Cape of Good Hope	53	1
Ceylon	8	6	North American Colonies	31	7
Mauritius	40	5	West India Islands	23	1
Australia	139	8	British Guiana	32	2

FOREIGN COUNTRIES.

Gross Revenue per Head per Annum.

Countries.	s.	d.	Countries.	s.	d.
Russia in Europe	24	5	Austro-Hungary	40	6
Norway	23	6	Italy	39	10
Sweden	19	8	Greece	37	7
Denmark	26	11	Servia	16	3
German Empire	13	6	Bulgaria	12	3
Prussia	41	2	Roumania	20	3
Saxony	22	8	Egypt (proper)	30	11
Grand Duchy of Oldenburgh	18	6	United States (different States have their separate revenue besides)	26	10
Saxe-Coburg and Gotha	17	0			
Bavaria	44	9			
Wurtemburg	27	8	Mexico	15	3
Grand Duchy of Baden	27	2	Brazil	26	1
Grand Duchy of Hesse	21	8	Guatemala	24	0
Alsace-Lorraine	24	8	Nicaragua	18	9
Holland	47	1	Salvador	29	8
Belgium	45	7	Orange Free State	36	9
France	73	6	Persia	8	7
Portugal	31	6	Republic of Peru	18	2
Spain	41	10	All territory directly under Turkey	13	3
Switzerland	12	2			

N.B.—Some of the above figures are worked out of Whitaker's Almanac, 1886.

It will be seen that British India's capacity for paying taxation is very poor indeed compared to that of any other country of any consequence. Of the above figures I cannot say which may be oppressive to the people. I give this as a fact, that these people pay so much for being governed. But it must be further borne in mind that every farthing of what these people pay returns back to them, which is not the case with British India. Can it be said of any of these countries that one-fifth or one-third of its people goes through life on insufficient food from sheer poverty of only 40s. income, and not from imperfect distribution?

I shall next take the case of some of the Native States of India. I have taken some where during the minorities of the Princes English officials have administered the State, and put them into order and good government. The capacity for taxation which I give below is not the result of any oppressive taxation, but of the natural developments by improved government, and of the increasing prosperity of the people. I give instances in the Bombay Presidency that I know, and of which I have been able to get some particulars.

GROSS REVENUE PER HEAD (£1 = Rs. 10).

	s.	d.		s.	d.
Baroda	12	3	Gondal	18	0
Cutch	7	11	Morbi	17	2
Bhavnagar	12	6	Wadhwan	18	10

These States have no debts. Baroda, Bhavnagar, and Gondal have built and are extending their own railways, and all have built and are building their own public works from revenue, and have good balances. Baroda has a balance in hand of £2,100,000, equal to eighteen months' revenue; Cutch has £140,000, equal to eight months' revenue; Bhavnagar has £560,000, equal to two years' revenue; and Gondal has £150,000, equal to fifteen months' revenue. I give only one or two short extracts from official statements. Sir W. Hunter, in his "Imperial Gazetteer," says about Bhavnagar in connexion with Kathiawad: "Bhavnagar has taken the lead in the material development of her resources, and is the first State in India which constructed a railway at her own expense and risk." I may say that Gondal did the same in conjunction with Bhavnagar, and Baroda had done that long before. In handing over the rule of Gondal to the Prince on the completion of his minority, Major Nutt, the British Administrator, and in charge of the State at the time, says with just pride and pleasure, in reference to the increase of revenue from £80,000 in 1870 to £120,000 in 1884: "One point of special interest in this matter is, that the increase in revenue has not occasioned any hardship to Gondal subjects.

On the contrary, never were the people generally—high and low, rich and poor—in a greater state of social prosperity than they are now." The Bombay Government has considered this "highly satisfactory."

At the installation of the present Chief of Bhavnagar, Mr. Peile, the Political Agent, describes the State as being then "with flourishing finances and much good work in progress. Of financial matters I need say little; you have no debts, and your treasury is full." When will British Indian financiers be able to speak with the same pride, pleasure, and satisfaction? "No debt, full treasury, good work in progress, increase of revenue, with increase of social prosperity, for high and low, rich and poor." Will this ever be in British India under the present policy? No.

There are some other States in Kathiawad in which higher taxation per head than that of British India is paid by the people, though I do not know that it is said that there is oppressive taxation there. I may instance Junagadh as 11s. per head, with £500,000 balance in hand, equal to fifteen months' revenue; and Nawanagar as 16s. 3d. per head, and gradually paying off some debt. I have no doubt that Native States will go on rapidly increasing in prosperity as their system of government goes on improving. I know from my own personal knowledge as Prime Minister of Baroda for one year that that State has a very promising future indeed. There are several other Native States in India in which the gross revenue per head is higher than that of British India. All the remaining first and second class Kathiawar States are from 8s. to 13s. per head; Gwalior, 7s. 8d.; Indore, 13s. 5d.; Bhurtpore, 8s. 8d.; Dholepur, 8s. 10d.; Tonk, 7s.; Kotah, 11s. 4d.; Jallawar, 8s. 10d. Only just now Sindia lends £3,500,000 to the British Government; Holkar, I think, has lent £1,000,000 for the Indore railway.

There cannot be much oppression in these States, as the Political Agents' vigilance and superintendence, and the fear of the displeasure of Government, are expected to prevent it.

Then Sir Grant Duff maintains that no country on the face of the earth is governed so cheaply as British India. In the first place, this is a fiction, as the heaviness of burden on poverty-stricken British India is more than double than that on the enormously rich England; and secondly, Sir Grant Duff's object is to show that this cheapness is a proof of the success of the present British Indian policy. But, on the contrary, the facts and figures I have given above about British India's wretched income and capacity for-taxation, its insignificant trade, and the very paltry commercial benefit to England, are conclusive proofs of anything but success in improving the prosperity of the people. Moreover, for the so-called cheapness, it is no thanks or credit to Government. It is not of choice that Government takes only 6s. per head. On the contrary, it is always longing, ever moaning, and using every possible shift to squeeze out more taxation if it can. By all means make British India capable of paying even 20s. per head (if not 50s. per head, like England) for revenue, without oppression and misery; or make its income £20 per head, if not £41, like that of England; and then fairly claim credit for having raised to some material extent the prosperity of British India. Let us have such *results*, instead of tall talk and self-complacent assertions. Had Government given us year after year correct information about the actual income and condition of the people of British India, Britain would then have known the deplorable results of the neglect of, and disobedience to, her deliberate and sacred mandates.

Again, Sir Grant Duff's boast of the cheapness of government is wrong, even in the misleading sense in which he maintains it. He tries to show that because British India pays only 6s. per head, it is therefore the most cheaply governed country on the face of the earth—*i.e.*, no other country pays a less amount per head. But even in this he is not quite accurate. He would have found this out had he only looked about in India itself, and he would have saved himself the surprise which he expresses at Mr. Smith being startled when he (Mr. Smith) was told that taxation was lighter in Native States than in British India. As a matter of fact, there *are* some Native States in which the revenue per head is lighter than in British India. Whether that is a desirable state of affairs or not is another question; but when he twits Mr. Smith he should have ascertained whether what Mr. Smith was told was at all correct or not. There *are* some of the Native States where the gross revenue is very nearly as low as or even less than 6s. per head: Hyderabad, 6s. 4d.; Patiala, 6s. 4d; Travancore, 5s. 8d.; Kolhapur, 5s. 6d.; Mysore, 4s. 10d.; Dungapore 2s.;

Marwar, 4s. 10d.; Serohi, 2s. 3d.; Jeypore, 4s. 3d.; Banswara, 3s. 8d.; and Kishengarh, 4s. 10d. Travancore is known as a well-governed country. £15,000 of its revenue is interest on British Indian Government securities, and it holds a balance in hand in Government securities and otherwise of £564,000—equal to nearly eleven months' revenue. Jeypore has the reputation of being a well-governed State. There are similarly even some foreign countries outside India which are as "cheaply governed" as British India: United States of Columbia, 5s. 10d.; Republic of Bolivia, 5s. 11d.

Sir Grant Duff refers to the absorption of gold and silver and to hoarding. What are the facts about British India? In my "Poverty of India" I have treated the subject at some length. The total amount (after deducting the exports from imports) retained by India during a period of eighty-four years (1801 to 1884), including the exceptionally large imports during the American war, is £455,761,385. This is for *all* India. The population at present is 254,000,000. I may take the average of eighty-four years roughly—say 200,000,000. This gives 45s. 6d. per head for the whole eighty-four years, or 6½d. per head per annum. Even if I took the average population as 180,000,000, the amount per head for the eighty-four years would be 50s. or 7d. per head per annum. Of the United Kingdom I cannot get returns before 1858. The total amount of treasure retained by the United Kingdom (after deducting export from imports) is, for twenty-seven years from 1858 to 1884, £86,194,937. Taking an average of 31,000,000 of population for twenty-seven years, the amount retained for these twenty-seven years is 55s. 7d. per head, or very nearly 2s. 1d. per head per annum; while in India for more than three times the same period the amount is only 45s. 6d. per head, or 6½d. per head per annum. France has retained from 1861 to 1880 (Mulhall's Dictionary) £208,000,000; and taking the population—say 37,000,000—that gives 112s. per head in twenty years, 5s. 7d. per head per annum.

Sir Grant Duff ought to consider that the large amount of bullion is to be distributed over a vast country and a vast population, nearly equal to five-sixths of the population of the whole of Europe; and when the whole population is considered, what a wretched amount is this of gold and silver—viz., 6½d. per head per annum—received for all possible wants! India does not produce any gold or silver. To compare it with Europe—Europe retained in ten years, 1871-1880 (Mulhall, "Progress of the World," 1880), £327,000,000 for an average population of about 300,000,000 or 21s. 10d. per head, or 2s. 2d. per head per annum. India during the same ten years retained £65,774,252 for an average population of, say, 245,000,000; so that the whole amount retained for the ten years is about 5s. 4d., or only 6½d. per head per annum, against 21s. 10d. and 2s. 2d. respectively of Europe. This means that India retained only one-fourth of what Europe retained per head per annum during these ten years. It must be further remembered that there is no such vast system of cheques, clearing-houses, etc., in India, as plays so important a part in England and other countries of Europe. Wretched as the provision of 6½d. per head per annum is for *all* wants —political, social, commercial, etc.—there is something far worse behind for British India. All the gold and silver that I have shown above as retained by India is not for British India only, but for the Native States, the frontier territories, and the European population; and then the remainder is for the Native population of British India. We must have official information about these four divisions before we can form a correct estimate of what British India retains. The Native States, as I have said before, have no foreign drain except the small amount of tribute of about £700,000. Some frontier territories receive something instead of paying any tribute. These States therefore receive back for the exports of their merchandise, and for the ordinary trade profits on such exports, full returns in imports of merchandise and treasure, and this treasure taken away by the Native States and frontier territories forms not a small portion of what is imported into India. It must also be considered how much metal is necessary every year for waste of coin and metal, and for the wants of circulating currency. When Government can give us all such information, it will be found that precious little remains for British India beyond what it is compelled to import for its absolute wants. I hope England does not mean to say that Englishmen or Englishwomen may sport as much as they like in ornaments or personal trinkets or jewellery; but that the wretch of a Native of British India, their fellow-subject, has no business or right to put a few shillings' worth of trinkets on his wife or daughter's person; or that Natives must simply live the lives of brutes, subsist on their "scanty subsistence," and thank their stars that they have that much.

I will now try to give some indication of what bullion British India actually retains. Mr. Harrison gave his evidence before the Parliamentary Committee of 1871-74 that about £1,000,000 of fresh coinage was more than sufficient to supply the waste of coin or metal. Is it too much to assume that in the very widespread and minute distribution, over a vast surface and a vast population, of small trinkets or ornaments of silver, and their rough use, another million may be required to supply waste and loss? If only a pennyworth per head per annum be so wanted, it would make a million sterling. Next, how much goes to the Native States and the frontier territories? Here are a few significant official figures as an indication: The "Report of the external land trade and railway-borne trade of the Bombay Presidency for 1884-85" (p.2), says of Rajputana and Central India—"13. The imports from the external blocks being greater than the exports to them, the balance of trade due by the Presidency to the other provinces amounts to Rs. 12,01,05,912, as appears from the above table and the following." I take the Native States from the table referred to.

EXCESS OF IMPORTS IN BOMBAY PRESIDENCY.

From Rajputana and Central India . . .	Rs. 5,55,46,753
,, Berar	1,48,91,355
,, Hyderabad	8,67,688
Total . .	Rs. 7,13,05,796

Or £7,130,579. This means that these Native States have exported so much more merchandise than they have imported. Thereupon the Report remarks thus:—"The greatest balance is in favour of Rajputana and Central India, caused by the import of opium from that block. Next to it is that of the Central Provinces. It is presumed that these balances are paid back *mainly in cash*" (the *italics* are mine). This, then, is the way the treasure goes; and poor British India gets all the abuse—insult added to injury. Its candle burns not only at both ends, but at all parts. The excessive foreign agency eats up in India and drains away out of India a portion of its wretched income, thereby weakening and exhausting it every year drop by drop, though not very perceptibly, and lessening its productive power or capability. It has poor capital, and cannot increase it much. Foreign capital does nearly all the work, and carries away all the profit. Foreign capitalists from Europe and from Native States make profits from the resources of British India, and take away those profits to their own countries. The share that the mass of the Natives of British India have is to drudge and slave on scanty subsistence for these foreign capitalists; not as slaves in America did, on the resources of the country and land belonging to the masters themselves, but on the resources of their own country, for the benefit of the foreign capitalists. I may illustrate this a little. Bombay is considered a wealthy place, and has a large capital circulating in it, to carry on all its wants as a great port. Whose capital is this? Mostly that of foreigners. The capital of the European exchange banks and European merchants is mostly foreign and most of the Native capital is also foreign—*i.e.*, that of the Native bankers and merchants from the Native States. Nearly £6,000,000 of the capital working in Bombay belongs to Native bankers from the Native States. Besides, a large portion of the wealthy merchants, though more or less settled in Bombay, are from Native States. Of course I do not mean to say anything against these capitalists from Europe or Native States. They are quite free and welcome to come and do what they can. They do some good. But what I mean is, that British India cannot and does not make any capital, and must and does lose the profit of its resources to others. If British India were left to its own free development it would be quite able to supply all its own wants, would not remain handicapped, and would have a free field in competition with the foreign capitalists, with benefit to all concerned. The official admission of the amount of the drain goes as far as £20,000,000 per annum; but really it will be found to be much larger (excluding interest on railway and public works loans):—add to this drain out of the country what is eaten and enjoyed in the country itself by others than the Natives of the country, to the deprivation by so much of these Natives, and some idea can be formed of the actual and continuous depletion. Now, take only £20,000,000 per annum to be the extent of the drain, or even £10,000,000 per annum; this amount, for the last thirty years only, would have sufficed to build all the present and great many more railways and other public works. There is another way in which I may illustrate the burning of the candle at all parts. First of all, British India's own wealth is carried away out of it, and then that wealth is brought back to it in the shape of loans, and for these loans British India must find so much more for interest; the whole thing moving in a most vicious and provoking circle. Will nothing but a catastrophe cure this? Even of the railway, etc., loans the people do not derive the full benefit. I cannot go into details about this here. I refer to my correspondence with the Secretary of State for India.[1] Nor can I go here into the calculations about the drain. I can only refer to my papers on "The Poverty of India" and "Condition of India."[2] Let Sir Grant Duff kindly show me where I am wrong in those papers, and I shall be thankful; or he will see that no country in the world, not even England excepted, can stand such a drain without destruction. Even in those days when the drain was understood to be only £3,000,000 per annum, Mr. Montgomery Martin wrote in these significant and distressing words:[3]—

> "The annual drain of £3,000,000 on British India has amounted in thirty years, at 12 per cent. (the usual Indian rate) compound interest, to the enormous sum of £723,900,000 sterling. . . . So constant and accumulating a drain, even in England, would soon impoverish her. How severe, then, must be its effects on India, where the wage of a labourer is from twopence to threepence a day! Were the hundred millions of British subjects in India converted into a *consuming* population, what a market would be presented for British capital, skill, and industry!"

What, then, must be the condition now, when the drain is getting perhaps ten times larger, and a large amount besides is eaten up in the country itself by others than the people? Even an ocean would be dried up if a portion of its evaporation did not always return to it as rain or river. If interest were added to the drain, what an enormous loss would it be!

In the darkness of the past we see now a ray of light and hope when the highest Indian authority begins to perceive not only the material disaster, but even the serious "political danger" from the present state of affairs. I only hope and pray that Britain will see matters mended before disaster comes. Instead of shutting his eyes like an ostrich, as some persons do, the Secretary of State for India only last year, in

[1] *Supra*, pp. 193-196.
[2] *Supra*, pp. 33, 196-199.
[3] "Eastern India, 1838," vol. i, p. xii.

his despatch of 26th January, 1886, to the Treasury, makes this remarkable admission about the consequences of the present "character of the government," of the foreign rule of Britain over India :—

> "The position of India in relation to taxation and the sources of the public revenues is very peculiar, not merely from the habits of the people and their strong aversion to change, which is more specially exhibited to new forms of taxation, but likewise *from the character of the government*, which is in the hands of foreigners, who hold all the principal administrative offices, and form so large a part of the Army. The impatience of new taxation, which would have to be borne wholly as a consequence of the foreign rule imposed on the country, and virtually to meet additions to charges arising outside of the country, would constitute a political danger the real magnitude of which, it is to be feared, is not at all appreciated by persons who have no knowledge of or concern in the government of India, but which those responsible for that government have long regarded as of the most serious order." [The italics are mine.]

This gives some hope. If, after the faithful adoption of the policy of 1833 and 1858, our material condition does not improve, and all the fears expressed in the above extract do not vanish, the fault will not be Britain's, and she will at least be relieved from the charge of dishonour to her word. But I have not the shadow of a doubt, as the statesmen of 1833 and the proclamation of 1858 had no doubt, that the result will be a blessing both to England and India.

A second ray of hope is this. Many Englishmen in England are taking active interest in the matter. Mr. Bright, Mr. Fawcett, Sir C. Trevelyan, and others have done good in the past. Others are earnestly working now—Mr. Slagg, Mr. Wilson, Mr. Digby, Mr. S. Smith, Mr. Hyndman, and several others. A further ray of hope is in an increasing number of members of Parliament interesting themselves in Indian matters, such as Dr. Hunter, Mr. S. Smith, Dr. Clark, Mr. Cremer, Sir J. Phear, Sir W. Plowden, and many others; and we cannot but feel thankful to all who have taken and are taking interest in our lot. All unfortunately, however, labour under the disadvantage of want of full information from Government, and the difficulty of realising the feelings and views of the Natives. But still they have done much good. I must also admit here that some Anglo-Indians begin to realise the position. We owe much to men like Sir W. Wedderburn, Sir G. Birdwood, Major Bell, Mr. Ilbert, Mr. Cotton, and others of that stamp, for their active sympathy with us. Mr. Bright hit the blot as far back as 1853 in his speech of the 3rd of January: "I must say that it is my belief that if a country be found possessing a most fertile soil and capable of bearing every variety of production, and that notwithstanding the people are in a state of extreme destitution and suffering, the chances are that there is some fundamental error in the government of the country." It is not necessary to go far to seek for this fundamental error. It is the perversion of the policy of 1833, which in the more widened and complete form of 1858 is virtually still a dead letter.

Much is said about poor Natives wasting money in marriages, etc. I hope it is not meant that these poor wretches have no right to any social privileges or enjoyments, and that their business is only to live and die like brutes. But the fact of the matter is, that this is one of those fallacies that die hard. Let us see what truth the Deccan Riots Commission brings to light. The Report of that Commission says (page 19, par. 54): "The results of the Commission's enquiries show that undue prominence has been given to the expenditure on marriage and other festivals as a cause of the ryots' indebtedness. The expenditure on such occasions may undoubtedly be called extravagant when compared with the ryots' means; but the occasions occur seldom, and probably in a course of years the total sum spent this way by any ryot is not larger than a *man in his position is justified in spending on social and domestic pleasures*." (The italics are mine.) And what is the amount the poor ryot spends on the marriage of his son! Rs. 50 to 75 (£5 to £7 10s.) say the Commissioners.

Sir Grant Duff says: "We have stopped war, we are stopping famine. How are the ever-increasing multitudes to be fed?" Is not Sir Grant Duff a little hasty in saying, "We are stopping famine." What you are doing is to starve the living to save the dying. Make the people themselves able to meet famine without misery and deaths, and then claim credit that you are stopping famine. However, the true answer to the question, "How are the ever-increasing multitudes to be fed?" is a very simple one, if gentlemen like Sir Grant Duff will ever have the patience to study the subject. The statesmen of 1833 and of 1858 have in the clearest and most emphatic way answered this question.

They knew and said clearly upon what the welfare and well-being of the hundreds of millions depended. They laid down unequivocally what would make British India not only able to feed the increasing multitudes, but prosperous and the best customer of England; and Mr. Grant Duff's following kind question of 1871 will be fully answered: "But what are we to say about the state of India? How many generations must pass away before that country has arrived at even the comparative wealth of this (England)?" This benevolent desire of Mr. Grant Duff would be accomplished in no long time. This question of population, of "the ever-increasing multitudes," requires further examination. Macaulay, in his review of Southey's "Colloquies on Society," says:—

> "When this island was thinly peopled, it was barbarous; there was little capital, and that little was insecure. It is now the richest and the most highly civilised spot in the world, but the population is dense. . . . But when we compare our own condition with that of our ancestors, we think it clear that the advantages arising from the progress of civilisation have far more than counterbalanced the disadvantages arising from the progress of population. While our numbers have increased tenfold, our wealth has increased hundredfold. . . . If we were to prophesy that in the year 1930 a population of fifty millions, better fed, clad, and lodged than the English of our time, will cover these islands, . . . many people would think us insane. We prophesy nothing; but this we say, if any person had told the Parliament which met in perplexity and terror after the crash in 1720, that in 1830 the wealth of England would surpass all their wildest dreams, . . . that for one man of ten thousand pounds then living there would be five men of fifty thousand pounds, . . . our ancestors would have given as much credit to the prediction as they gave to 'Gulliver's Travels.'"

I claim no prophecy, but the statesmen of 1833 have prophesied, and the Proclamation of 1858 has prophesied. Do what they have said, and their prophecies shall be fulfilled.

Now let us see a few more facts. Because a country increases in population it does not necessarily follow that it must become poorer; nor because a country is densely populated that therefore it must be poor. Says Macaulay: "England is a hundredfold more wealthy while it is tenfold denser." The following figures speak for themselves:—

Countries.	Inhabitants per sq. mile about 1880.	Income per inhabitant (Mulhall's Dictionary of Statistics, 1886).
Belgium	487	£22·1
England	478 (1886)	41 (1882)
Holland	315	26
Italy	257	12

Countries.	Inhabitants per sq. mile about 1880.	Income per inhabitant (Mulhall's Dictionary of Statistics, 1886).
British India	229	2
Germany	217	18·7
Austria	191	16·3
France	184	25·7
Switzerland	184	16
Ireland	153 (1886)	16 (1882)
Denmark	132	23·2
Scotland	128 (1886)	32 (1882)
Portugal	126	13·6
Turkey	120 (Mulhall)	4 (Sir E. Baring)
Spain	85	13·8
Greece	69	11·8
Russia in Europe	41	9·9
Sweden	27	16·2
Norway	15	

The densest Province of British India is Bengal (443). Thus here are countries denser and thinner than British India, but *every one* of them has a far better income than British India. Belgium, denser than the densest Presidency of British India, is eleven times more wealthy; England as dense, is twenty times more wealthy. Here are some very thinly populated countries: Mexico, 13 per square mile; Venezuela, 4·7; Chili, 8·8; Peru, 18·6; Argentine Republic, 2·6; Uruguay, 7·8; and several others. Are they therefore so much richer than England or Belgium? Here is Ireland, at your door. About its people the Duke of Argyll only a few weeks ago (22nd of April last), in the House of Lords, said: "Do not tell me that the Irish labourer is incapable of labour, or energy, or exertion. Place him in favourable circumstances, and there is no better workman than the Irishman. I have myself employed large gangs of Irishmen, and I never saw any navvies work better; and besides that, they were kind and courteous men." The population of Ireland is less than one-third as dense as that of England; and yet how is it that the income of England is £41 and that of Ireland only £16 per inhabitant, and that the mass of the people do not enjoy the benefit of even that much income, and are admittedly wretchedly poor?

British India's resources are officially admitted to be enormous, and with an industrious and law-abiding people, as Sir George Birdwood testifies, it will be quite able to produce a large income, become as rich as any other country, and easily provide for an increasing population and increasing taxation, if left free scope.

Lastly, a word about the educated classes, upon whose devoted heads Sir Grant Duff has poured down all his vials of wrath. Here are some fine amenities of an English gentleman of high position: "Professional malcontents; busy, pushing talkers; ingeniously wrong; the pert scribblers of the Native Press; the intriguers; pushing pettifoggers, chatterboxes; disaffected cliques; the *crassa ignorantia;* little coteries of intriguers; silly and dishonest talk of Indian grumblers; politicising sophists threaten to be a perfect curse to India," etc.

I leave these flowers of rhetoric alone. Not satisfied even with this much, he has forgotten himself altogether, and groundlessly charged the educated classes—"who do their utmost to excite hostility against the British Government," "who do their utmost to excite factitious disloyalty." I repel this charge with only two short extracts. I need not waste many words.

The following, from the highest authority, is ample, clear, and conclusive. The Government of India, in their despatch of the 8th of June, 1880, to the Secretary of State for India, bear this emphatic testimony: "To the minds of at least the educated among the people of India—and the number is rapidly increasing—any idea of the subversion of British power is abhorrent, from the consciousness that it must result in the wildest anarchy and confusion." Secondly, on the auspicious day of the Jubilee demonstration the Viceroy of India, in his Jubilee speech, says:—

> "Wide and broad indeed are the new fields in which the Government of India is called upon to labour—but no longer, as of aforetime, need it labour alone. Within the period we are reviewing education has done its work, and we are surrounded on all sides by Native gentlemen of great attainments and intelligence, from whose hearty, loyal and honest co-operation we may hope to derive the greatest benefit. In fact, to an administration so peculiarly situated as ours their advice, assistance, and solidarity are essential to the successful exercise of its functions. Nor do I regard with any other feelings than those of approval and goodwill their natural ambition to be more extensively associated with their English rulers in the administration of their own domestic affairs."

Look upon this picture and upon that!

Two Indian National Congresses have been held during the past two years—the second great one, at Calcutta, having 430 delegates present from all parts of India, and of all classes of the people; and what is it that both these Congresses have asked? It is virtually and simply the "conscientious fulfilment" of the pledges of 1833 and 1858. They are the pivot upon which all Indian problems turn. If India is to be retained to Britain, it will be by men who insist upon being just, and upon the righteous fulfilment of the proclamation of 1858. Any one can judge of this from the kind of ovations given to Lord Ripon and Sir W. Wedderburn on their retirement.

Here, again, our gracious Empress in the year of her auspicious Jubilee once more proclaims to the world and assures us, in her response to the Bombay Jubilee Address last June, "It had always been, and will always be, her earnest desire to maintain unswervingly the principles laid down in the proclamation published on her assumption of the direct control of the government of India." We ask no more.

SPEECHES
IN THE
HOUSE OF COMMONS.

EAST INDIA REVENUE ACCOUNT.

AMENDMENT FOR A FULL AND INDEPENDENT PARLIAMENTARY ENQUIRY.

August 14th, 1894.

Mr. Naoroji (Finsbury, Central) said he undertook now to second this Resolution, and before going into the subject of the different parts of which it consisted he would say a few preliminary words. The Government of India distinctly admitted and knew very well that the educated people of India were thoroughly loyal. The hon. Member for Kingston (Sir R. Temple) had stated that the state of the country and of the people often invited or demanded criticism on the part of the Natives. It was in every way desirable that their sentiments and opinions should be made known to the ruling classes, and such outspoken frankness should never be mistaken for disloyalty or disaffection. Nothing was nearer to his (Mr. Naoroji's) mind than to make the fullest acknowledgment of all the good that had been done by the connexion of the British people with India. They had no complaint against the British people and Parliament. They had from them everything they could desire. It was against the system adopted by the British Indian authorities in the last century and maintained up till now, though much modified, that they protested. The first point in the Motion was the condition of the people of India. In order to understand fully the present condition of the people of India, it was necessary to have a sort of sketch of the past, and he would give it as briefly as possible. In the last century the Administration was everything that should not be desired. He would give a few extracts from letters of the Court of Directors and the Bengal Government. In one of the letters the Directors said (8th of February, 1764):—

"Your deliberations on the inland trade have laid open to us a scene of most cruel oppression; the poor of the country, who used always to deal in salt, beetlenut, and tobacco, are now deprived of their daily bread by the trade of the Europeans."

Lord Clive wrote (17th of April, 1765):—

"The confusion we behold, what does it arise from?—rapacity and luxury, the unwarrantable desire of many to acquire in an instant what only a few can or ought to possess."

Another letter of Lord Clive to the Court of Directors said (30th of September, 1765):—

"It is no wonder that the lust of riches should readily embrace the proffered means of its gratification, or that the instruments of your power should avail themselves of their authority and proceed even to extortion in those cases where simple corruption could not keep pace with their rapacity. Examples of this sort set by superiors could not fail of being followed in a proportionate degree by inferiors; the evil was contagious, and spread among the civil and military down to the writer, the ensign, and the free merchant."

He would read one more extract from a letter of the Court of Directors (17th of May, 1766):—

"We must add that we think the vast fortunes acquired in the inland trade have been obtained by a scene of the most tyrannic and oppressive conduct that ever was known in any age or country."

Macaulay had summed up:—

"A war of Bengalees against Englishmen was like a war of sheep against wolves, of men against demons. . . . The business of a servant of the Company was simply to wring out of the Natives a hundred or two hundred thousand pounds as speedily as possible."

Such was the character of the Government and the Administration in the last century; when all this was disclosed by the Committee of 1772 of course a change was made, and a change for the better. He would now give the opinion of Anglo-Indian and English statesmen, and the House would observe that he did not say a single word as to what the Indians themselves said. He put his case before the House in the words of Anglo-Indian and English statesmen alone; some of them had expressed great indignation with usual British feeling against wrong-doing, others had expressed themselves much more moderately. Sir John Shore was the first person who gave a clear prophetic forecast of the character of this system and its effects as early as 1787. He then said (Ret. 377 of 1812):—

"Whatever allowance we may make for the increased industry of the subjects of the State, owing to the enhanced demand for the produce of it (supposing the demand to be enhanced), there is reason to conclude that the benefits are more than counterbalanced by evils inseparable from the system of a remote foreign dominion."

The words were true to the present day. In 1790 Lord

Cornwallis said, in a Minute, that the heavy drain of wealth by the Company, with the addition of remittances of private fortunes, was severely felt in the languor thrown upon the cultivation and commerce of the country. In 1823 Sir Thomas Munro pointed out that were Britain subjugated by a foreign Power, and the people excluded from the government of their country, all their knowledge and all their literature, sacred and profane, would not save them from becoming in a generation or two a low-minded, deceitful, and dishonest race. Ludlow, in his *British India*, said :—

> "As respects the general condition of the country, let us first recollect what Sir Thomas Munro wrote years ago, 'that even if we could be secured against every internal commotion and could retain the country quietly in subjection, he doubted much if the condition of the people would be better than under the Native Princes'; that the inhabitants of the British Provinces were 'certainly the most abject race in India'; that the consequences of the conquest of India by the British arms would be in place of raising to debase the whole people."

Macaulay, in introducing the clause of our equality with all British subjects, our first Charter of our emancipation in the Bill of 1833, said in his famous and statesmanlike speech :—

> "That would, indeed, be a doting wisdom which, in order that India may remain a dependency . . . . which would keep a hundred millions of men from being our customers in order that they might continue to be our slaves."

And, to illustrate the character of the existing system, he said :—

> "It was, as Bernier tells us, the practice of the miserable tyrants whom he found in India, when they dreaded the capacity and spirit of some distinguished subject, and yet could not venture to murder him, to administer to him a daily dose of the pousta, a preparation of opium, the effect of which was in a few months to destroy all the bodily and mental powers of the wretch who was drugged with it, and to turn him into a helpless idiot. This detestable artifice, more horrible than assassination itself, was worthy of those who employed it. It is no model for the English nation. We shall never consent to administer the pousta to a whole community—to stupify and paralyse a great people whom God has committed to our charge—for the wretched purpose of rendering them more amenable to our control."

In a speech (19th of February, 1844) he said :—

> "Of all forms of tyranny I believe that the worst is that of a nation over a nation."

Lord Lansdowne, in introducing the same clause of the Bill of 1833 into the House of Lords, pointed out that he should be taking a very narrow view of this question, and one utterly inadequate to the great importance of the subject, which involved in it the happiness or misery of 100,000,000 of human beings, were he not to call the attention of their Lordships to the bearing which this question, and to the influence which this arrangement must exercise upon the future destinies of that vast mass of people. With such high sense of statesmanship and responsibility did Lord Lansdowne of 1833 break our chains. The Indian authorities, however, never allowed those broken chains to fall from our body, and the grandson—the Lord Lansdowne of 1893—now rivetted back those chains upon us. Look upon this picture and upon that! And the Indians were now just the same British slaves, instead of British subjects, as they were before their emancipation in 1833. Mr. Montgomery Martin, after examining the records of a survey of the condition of the people of some Provinces of Bengal or Behar, which had been made for nine years from 1807–16, concluded:—

"It is impossible to avoid remarking two facts as peculiarly striking: First, the richness of the country surveyed; and, second, the poverty of its inhabitants."

He gave the reason for these striking facts. He said:—

"The annual drain of £3,000,000 on British India has amounted in 30 years at 12 per cent. (the usual Indian rate) compound interest to the enormous sum of £723,900,000 sterling. So constant and accumulating a drain, even in England, would soon impoverish her. How severe, then, must be its effects in India where the wage of a labourer is from 2d. to 3d. a day."

The drain at present was seven times, if not ten times, as much. Mr. Frederick Shore, of the Bengal Civil Service, said, in 1837:—

"But the halcyon days of India are over. She has been drained of a large proportion of the wealth she once possessed, and her energies have been cramped by a sordid system of misrule to which the interests of millions have been sacrificed for the benefit of the few. The fundamental principle of the English had been to make the whole Indian nation subservient in every possible way to the interests and benefits of themselves."

And he summarised thus:—

"The summary was that the British Indian Government had been practically one of the most extortionate and oppressive that ever existed in India. Some acknowledged this, and observed that it was the unavoidable result of a foreign yoke. That this was correct regarding a Government conducted on the principles which had hitherto actuated us was too lamentably true, but, had the welfare of the people been our object, a very different course would have been adopted, and very different results would have followed. For again and again I repeat that there was nothing in the circumstance itself of our being foreigners of different colour and faith that should occasion the people to hate us. We might thank ourselves for having made their feelings towards us what they were. Had we acted on a more liberal plan we should have fixed our authority on a much more solid foundation."

After giving some more similar authorities, Sir R. Temple and others, the hon. gentleman proceeded: Mr. Bright, speaking in the House of Commons in 1858, said :—

"We must in future have India governed, not for a handful of Englishmen, not for that Civil Service whose praises are so constantly sounded in this House. You may govern India, if you like, for the good of England, but the good of England must come through the channels of the good of India. There are but two modes of gaining anything by our connexion with India—the one is by plundering the people of India, and the other by trading with them. I prefer to do it by trading with them. But in order that England may become rich by trading with India, India itself must become rich."

Sir George Wingate, with his intimate acquaintance with the condition of the people of India, as the introducer of the Bombay land survey system, pointed out, with reference to the economic effects upon the condition of India, that taxes spent in the country from which they were raised were totally different in their effect from taxes raised in one country and spent in another. In the former case the taxes collected from the population were again returned to the industrial classes; but the case was wholly different when taxes were not spent in the country from which they were raised, as they constituted an absolute loss and extinction of the whole amount withdrawn from the taxed country; and he said, further, that such was the nature of the tribute the British had so long exacted from India—and that with this explanation some faint conception may be formed of the cruel, crushing effect of the tribute upon India—that this tribute, whether weighed in the scales of Justice or viewed in the light of the British interests, would be found to be at variance with humanity, with common sense, and with the received maxim of economical science. Mr. Fawcett quoted Lord Metcalf (5th May, 1868), that the bane of the British-Indian system was, that the advantages were reaped by one class and the work was done by another. This havoc was going on increasing up to the present day. Lord Salisbury, in a Minute [Ret. c. 3086-1 of 1881], pointed out that the injury was exaggerated in the case of India, where so much of the revenue was exported without a direct equivalent—that as India must be bled, the lancet should be directed to the parts where the blood was congested or at least sufficient, not to the rural districts which were already feeble from the want of blood. This bleeding of India must cease. Lord Hartington (the Duke of Devonshire) declared (23rd Aug., 1883) that India was insufficiently governed, and that if it was to be better governed, that could only be done by the employment of the best and most intelligent of the Natives in the Service; and he further advised that it was not wise to drive the people to think that their only hope lay in getting rid of their English rulers. Lastly, with regard to the present condition of India, and even serious danger to British power, a remarkable confirmation was given, after a hundred years, to Sir John Shore's prophecy of 1787, by the Secretary of State for India in 1886. A letter of the India Office to the Treasury said (Ret. c. 4868 of 1886):—

"The position of India in relation to taxation and the sources of the public revenue is very peculiar, not merely from the habits of the people and their strong aversion to change, which is more specially exhibited to new forms of taxation, but likewise from the character of the government, which is in the hands of foreigners, who hold the principal administrative offices and form so large a part of the Army. The impatience of the new taxation, which will have to be borne wholly as a consequence of the foreign rule imposed on the country and virtually to meet additions to charges arising outside of the country, would constitute a political danger, the real magnitude of which, it is to be feared, is not at all appreciated by persons who have no knowledge of or concern in the government of India, but which those responsible for that government have long regarded as of the most serious order."

To sum up—as to the material condition of India—the main features in the last century were gross corruption and oppression by the Europeans; in the present century, high salaries and the heavy weight of the European services—their economic condition. Therefore, there was no such thing as the finances of India. No financier ever could make a real healthy finance of India, unless he could make two and two equal to six. The most essential condition was wanting. Taxes must be administered by and disbursed to those who paid. That did not exist. From the taxes raised every year a large portion was eaten up and carried away from the country by others than the people of British India. The finances of that country were simply inexplicable, and could not be carried out; if the extracts he had read meant anything, they meant that the present evil system of a foreign domination was destroying them, and was fraught with political danger of the most serious order to British power itself. It had been clearly pointed out that India was extremely poor. What advantage had been derived by India during the past 100 years under the administration of the most highly-praised and most highly-paid officials in the world? If there was any condemnation of the existing system, it was in the result that the country was poorer than any country in the world. He could adduce a number of facts and figures of the practical effect of the present system of administration, but there was not the time now. The very fact of the wail of the Finance Ministers of this decade was a complete condemnation. He was quite sure that the right hon. gentleman the Secretary of State for India was truly desirous to know the truth, but he could not know that clearly unless certain information was placed before the House. He would suggest, if the right hon. gentleman allowed, a certain number of Returns which would give the regular production of the country year by year, and the absolute necessaries of a common labourer to live in working health. In connexion with the trade test there was one fallacy which he must explain. They were told in Statistical Returns that India had an enormous trade of nearly £196,000,000, imports and exports together. If he sent goods worth £100 out of this country to some other country, he expected there was £100 of it returned to him with some addition of profit. That was the natural condition of every trade. In the Colonies and in European countries there was an excess of imports over exports. In the United Kingdom for the past 10 years—1883 to 1892—the excess had been 32 per cent., in Norway it was 42 per cent., Sweden 24 per cent., Denmark 40 per cent., Holland 22 per cent., France 20 per cent., Switzerland 28 per cent., Spain 9 per cent., Belgium 7 per cent., and so on. Anyone with common sense would, of course, admit that if a quantity of goods worth a certain amount of money were sent out, an additional profit was expected in return; if not, there could not be any commerce;

but a man who only received in return 90 of the 100 sent out would soon go into the Bankruptcy Court. Taking India's profits to be only 10 per cent. instead of 32 per cent., like those of the United Kingdom, and after making all deductions for remittances for interest on public works loans, India had received back Rs. 170,000,000 worth of imports less than what she exported annually. On the average of 10 years (1883 to 1892) their excesses of exports every year, with compound interest, would amount to enormous sums lost by her. Could any country in the world, England not excepted, stand such a drain without destruction? They were often told they ought to be thankful, and they were thankful, for the loans made to them for public works; but if they were left to themselves to enjoy what they produced with a reasonable price for British rule, if they had to develop their own resources, they would not require any such loans with the interest to be paid on them, which added to the drain on the country. Those loans were only a fraction of what was taken away from the country. India had lost thousands of millions in principal and interest, and was asked to be thankful for the loan of a couple of hundreds of millions. The bulk of the British Indian subjects were like hewers of wood and drawers of water to the British and foreign Indian capitalists. The seeming prosperity of British India was entirely owing to the amount of foreign capital. In Bombay alone, which was considered to be a rich place, there were at least £10,000,000 of capital circulating belonging to foreign Europeans and Indians from Native States. If all such foreign capital were separated there would be very little wealth in British India. He could not go further into these figures, because he must have an occasion on which he could go more fully into them. If only the right hon. gentleman the Secretary of State for India would give them the Returns which were necessary to understand more correctly and completely the real condition of India, they would all be the better for it. There was another thing that was very serious. The whole misfortune at the bottom, which made the people of British India the poorest in the world, was the pressure to be forced to pay, roughly speaking, 200,000,000 rupees annually for European foreign services. Till this evil of foreign domination, foretold by Sir John Shore, was reduced to reasonable dimensions, there was no hope, and no true and healthy finance for India. This canker was destructive to India and suicidal to the British. The British people would not stand a single day the evil if the Front Benches here—all the principal military and civil posts and a large portion of the Army—were to be occupied by some foreigners on even the plea of giving service. When an English official had acquired experience in the Service of twenty or thirty years, all that was entirely lost to India when he left the country, and it was a most serious loss, although he did not blame him for leaving the shore. They were left at a certain low level. They could not rise; they could not develop their capacity for higher government, because they had no opportunity; the result was, of course, that their faculties must be stunted. Lastly, every European displaced an Indian who should fill that post. In short, the evil of the foreign rule involved the triple loss of wealth, wisdom, and work. No wonder at India's material and moral poverty! The next point was the wants of the Indians. He did not think it would require very long discussion to ascertain their wants. They could be summed up in a few words. They wanted British honour, good faith, righteousness, and justice. They should then get everything that was good for themselves, and it would benefit the rulers themselves, but unfortunately that had not been their fortune. Here they had an admission of the manner in which their best interests were treated. Lord Lytton, in a confidential Minute, said:—

> "No sooner was the Act passed than the Government began to devise means for practically evading the fulfilment of it. . . . We all know that these claims and expectations never can or will be fulfilled. We have had to choose between prohibiting them and cheating them, and we have chosen the least straightforward course."

He would not believe that the Sovereign and the Parliament who gave these pledges of justice and honour intended to cheat. It was the Indian Executive who had abused their trust. That Act of 1833 was a dead letter up to the present day. Lord Lytton said:—

> "Since I am writing confidentially, I do not hesitate to say that both the Governments of England and of India appear to me up to the present moment unable to answer satisfactorily the charge of having taken every means in their power of breaking to the heart the words of promise they had uttered to the ear."

What they wanted was that what Lord Salisbury called

"bleeding" should have an end. That would restore them to prosperity, and England might derive ten times more benefit by trading with a prosperous people than she was doing now. They were destroying the bird that could give them ten golden eggs with a blessing upon them. The hon. member for Kingston, in his "India in 1880," said:—

> "Many Native statesmen have been produced of whom the Indian nation may justly be proud, and among whom may be mentioned Salar Jung of Hyderabad, Dinkar Rao of Gwalior, Madhao Rao of Baroda, Kirparam of Jammu, Pundit Manphal of Alwar, Faiz Ali Khan of Kotah, Madhao Rao Barvi of Kolahpur, and Purnia of Mysore."

Mountstuart Elphinstone said, before the Committee of 1833:—

> "The first object, therefore, is to break down the separation between the classes and raise the Natives by education and public trust to a level with their present rulers."

He addressed the Conservative Party. It was this Party who had given the just Proclamation of 1858—their greater Charter—in these words:—

> "We hold ourselves bound to the Natives of our Indian territories by the same obligations of duty which bind us to all our other subjects, and those obligations, by the blessing of Almighty God, we shall faithfully and conscientiously fulfil."

It was again the Conservative Party that, on the assumption of the Imperial title by our Sovereign, proclaimed again the equality of the Natives, whatever their race or creed, with their English fellow-subjects, and that their claim was founded on the highest justice. At the Jubilee, under the Conservative Government again, the Empress of India gave to her Indian subjects the gracious assurance and pledge that—

> "It had always been and always will be her earnest desire to maintain unswervingly the principles laid down in the Proclamation published on her assumption of the direct control of the Government of India."

He (Mr. Naoroji) earnestly appealed to this Party not to give the lie to these noble assurances, and not to show to the world that it was all hypocrisy and national bad faith. The Indians would still continue to put their faith in the English people, and ask again and again to have justice done. He appealed to the right hon. gentleman the Secretary of State for India, and to the Government, and the Liberal Party, who gave them their first emancipation. They felt deeply grateful for the promises made, but would ask that these words be now converted into loyal, faithful deeds, as Englishmen for their honour are bound to do. Some weeks ago the right hon. gentleman the member for Midlothian wrote a letter to Sir John Cowan in which he stated that the past sixty years had been years of emancipation. Many emancipations had taken place in these years; the Irish, the Jews, the slaves, all received emancipation in that wave of humanity which passed over this country, and which made this country the most brilliant and civilised of the countries of the world. In those days of emancipation, and in the very year in which the right hon. gentleman began his political career, the people of India also had their emancipation at the hands of the Liberal Party. It was the Liberal Party that passed the Act of 1833 and made the magnificent promises explained both by Macaulay and Lansdowne. He would ask the right hon. gentleman the member for Midlothian to say whether, after the Liberal Party having given this emancipation at the commencement of his political career, he would at the end of it, while giving emancipation to 3,000,000 of Irishmen, only further enslave the 300,000,000 of India? The decision relating to the simultaneous examinations meant rivetting back upon them every chain broken by the act of emancipation. The right hon. gentleman in 1893, in connexion with the Irish question, after alluding to the arguments of fear and force, said:—

> "I hope we shall never again have occasion to fall back upon that miserable argument. It is better to do justice for terror than not to do it at all; but we are in a condition neither of terror nor apprehension; but in a calm and thankful state. We ask the House to accept this Bill, and I make that appeal on the grounds of honour and of duty."

Might he, then, appeal in these days when every educated man in India was thoroughly loyal, when there was loyalty in every class of the people of India, and ask was it not time for England to do justice to India on the same grounds of "honour and duty"? The right hon. Member also said:—

> "There can be no more melancholy, and in the last result no more degrading spectacle upon earth than the spectacle of oppression, or of wrong in whatever form, inflicted by the deliberate act of a nation upon another nation, especially by the deliberate act of such a country as Great Britain upon such a country as Ireland."

This applied to India with a force ten times greater. And he appealed for the nobler spectacle of which the right hon. gentleman subsequently spoke. He said :—

> "But, on the other hand, there can be no nobler spectacle than that which we think is now dawning upon us, the spectacle of a nation deliberately set on the removal of injustice, deliberately determined to break—not through terror, not in haste, but under the sole influence of duty and honour—determined to break with whatever remains still existing of an evil tradition, and determined in that way at once to pay a debt of justice, and to consult by a bold, wise, and good act, its own interests and its own honour."

These noble words applied with tenfold necessity to Britain's duty to India. It would be in the interest of England to remove the injustice under which India suffered more than it would be in the interest even of India itself. He would repeat the prayer to the right hon. gentleman the member for Midlothian, that he would not allow his glorious career to end with the enthralment of 300,000,000 of the human race whose destinies are entrusted to this great country, and from which they expect nothing but justice and righteousness. The right hon. gentleman the Secretary of State for India the other day made a memorable speech at Wolverhampton. Among other things, he uttered these noble words :—

> "New and pressing problems were coming up with which the Liberal Party would have to deal. These problems were the moral and material conditions of the people, for both went very much together. They were the problems that the statesmen of the future would have to solve. Mr. Bright once said that the true glory of a nation was not in ships and colonies and commerce, but in the happiness of its homes, and that no Government and no Party deserved the confidence of the British electorate which did not give a foremost place in its legislation and administration to those measures which would promote the comfort, health, prosperity, well-being, and the well-doing of the masses of the people."

He would appeal to the right hon. gentleman the Secretary for India that in that spirit he should study the Indian problem. Here in England they had to deal with only 38,000,000 of people, and if the right hon. gentleman would once understand the Indian problem and do them the justice for which they had been waiting for sixty years, he would be one of the greatest benefactors of the human race. He appealed also to the present Prime Minister with confidence, because he had had an opportunity of knowing that the Prime Minister thoroughly understood the Indian problem. Few Englishmen so clearly understood that problem or the effect of the drain on the resources of India. He saw clearly also how far India was to be made a blessing to itself and to England. Would he begin his promising career as Prime Minister by enslaving 300,000,000 of British subjects? He appealed to him to consider. He could assure the right hon. gentleman the Secretary of State for India that the feeling in India among the educated classes was nearing despair. It was a very bad seed that was being sown in connexion with this matter if some scheme was not adopted, with reasonable modifications, to give some effect to the Resolution for simultaneous examinations as was promised a few months ago. The Under-Secretary for India assured them in the last Indian Budget Debate that neither he nor the Secretary of State for India had any disposition of thwarting or defeating that Resolution. Indians then felt assured on the point, and their joy was great. But what must be their despair and disappointment when such statements are put before the House of Commons and the country as were to be found in this dark Blue Book. It was enough to break anybody's heart. It would have broken his but for the strong faith he had in the justice of the British people and the one bright ray to be found even in that Return itself, which had strengthened him to continue his appeal as long as he should live. That ray has come from the Madras Government. They had pointed out that they felt bound to do something. They also pointed out the difficulties in the way, but these difficulties were not insurmountable. About the want of true living representation of the people he would not now say anything. Every Englishman understood its importance. The next point in the Motion was the ability to bear existing burdens. Indians were often told by men in authority that India was the lightest taxed country in the world. The United Kingdom paid £2 10s. per head for the purposes of the State. They paid only 5s. or 6s. per head, and, therefore, the conclusion was drawn that the Indians were the most lightly-taxed people on earth. But if these gentlemen would only take the trouble of looking a little deeper they would see how the matter stood. England paid £2 10s. per head from an income of something like £35 per head, and their capacity, therefore, to pay £2 10s. was sufficiently large. Then, again, this £2 10s. returned to them—every farthing of it—in some form or another. The proportion they paid to the State in the shape of Revenues was, therefore, something like only 7 or 8 per cent. India paid 5s. or 6s. out of their wretched incomes of £2, or 20 rupees, as he calculated, or 27 rupees, as calculated by Lord Cromer. But even taking the latter figure, it would not make any great difference. The three rupees was far more burdensome compared with the wretched capacity of the people of India to bear taxation than the £2 10s. which England paid. At the rate of production of Rs. 20 per head India paid 14 per cent. of her income for purposes of revenue—nearly twice as heavy as the incidence of the United Kingdom. Even at the rate of production of Rs. 27 per head the Indian burden was 11 per cent. Then, again, take the test of the Income Tax. In the United Kingdom 1d. in the Income Tax gave some £2,500,000; but in India, with ten times the population, 1d. only gave about Rx. 300,000, with an exemption of only Rx. 50 instead of £150 as in this country. In the last 100 years the wealth of England had increased by leaps and bounds, while India, governed by the same Englishmen, was the same poor nation that it was all through the century that had elapsed, and India at the present moment was the most extremely poor country in the world, and would be poor to the end of the chapter if the present system of foreign domination continued. He did not say that the Natives should attain to the highest positions of control and power. Let there be Europeans in the highest positions, such as the Viceroy, the Governors, the Commander-in-Chief of the Forces, and the higher military officers, and such others as might be reasonably considered to be required to hold the controlling powers. The controlling power of Englishmen in India was wanted as much for the benefit of India as for the benefit of England. The next point in the Motion was, what were the sources of Indian Revenue? The chief sources of the Revenue were just what was mainly obtained from the cultivators of the soil. Here in this country the landlords—the wealthiest people — paid from land only 2 or 3 per cent. of the Revenues, but in India land was made to contribute something like Rx. 27,000,000 of the total Revenue of about Rx. 67,000,000. Then the Salt Tax, the most cruel Revenue imposed in any civilised country, provided Rx. 8,600,000, and that with the opium formed the bulk of the Revenue of India, which was drawn from the wretchedness of the people and by poisoning the Chinese. It mattered not what the State received was called—tax, rent, revenue, or by any other name they liked—the simple fact of the matter was, that out of a certain annual national production the State took a certain portion. Now it would not also matter much about the portion taken by the State if that portion, as in this country, returned to the people themselves, from whom it was raised. But the misfortune and the evil was that much of this portion did not return to the people, and that the whole system of Revenue and the economic condition of the people became unnatural and oppressive, with danger to the rulers. In this country the people drank nearly £4 per head, while in India they could not produce altogether more than half that amount per head. Was the system under which such a wretched condition prevailed not a matter for careful consideration? So long as the system went on, so long must the people go on living wretched lives. There was a constant draining away of India's resources, and she could never, therefore, be a prosperous country. Not only that, but in time India must perish, and with it might perish the British Empire. If India was prosperous, England would be prosperous ten times more than she was at present by reason of the trade she could carry on with India. England at present exported some £300,000,000 worth of British produce, yet to India she hardly exported produce to the value of 2s. 6d. per head. If India were prosperous enough to buy even £1 worth per head of English goods she would be able to send to India as much as she now sent to the whole world. Would it not, then, be a far greater benefit to England if India were prosperous than to keep her as she was? The next point in the Motion was the reduction of expenditure. The very first thing should be to cancel that immoral and cruel "compensation" without any legal claim even. That was not the occasion to discuss its selfishness and utter disregard of the wretchedness of the millions of the people. But as if this injustice were not enough, other bad features were added to it, if my information be correct. The compensation was only for remittances to this country. But instead of this, every European and Eurasian, whether he had to make any family remittances or not, was to have a certain addition to his salary. That was not all. The iniquity of making race distinctions was again adopted in this also; Europeans and

Eurasians, whether remittances had to be made or not, were to receive compensation ; but an Indian, who had actually to make remittances for the education of his sons, could have no consideration. But he (Mr. Naoroji) deprecated the whole thing altogether—to take from the wretched to give to the better-off. This compensation should be cancelled as the first step in reduction. As the Chancellor of the Exchequer said the other day in his splendid speech at his magnificent ovation by the Liberal Members, in speaking of the land-owners, the burden was always shifted on to other shoulders, and always on those least able to pay. This was exactly the principle of Anglo-Indian authorities. If it was really intended to retrench with regard to expenditure in India, why not begin with the salary list ? The Viceroy surely could get his bread and butter with £20,000 a year instead of £25,000. The Governors could surely have bread and cheese for £6,000 or £8,000 instead of £10,000, and so on down till the end of the salary list was reached at Rs. 200 a month. This would afford a much-needed relief, because India could not really afford to pay. Sir William Hunter had rightly said that if we were to govern the Indian people efficiently and cheaply we must govern them by means of themselves, and pay for the administration at the market rates of Native labour; that the good work of security and law had assumed such dimensions under the Queen's government of India that it could no longer be carried on or even supervised by imported labour from England, except at a cost which India could sustain, and he had prophesied that 40 years hereafter they would have had an Indian Ireland multiplied fifty-fold on their hands. The Service must change from that which was dear, and at the same time unsatisfactory, to one which would require less money and which would at the same time be fruitful to the people themselves. Next, three Secretaries of State and two Viceroys the other day in the House of Lords condemned in the strongest terms the charge that was made by the War Office for troops in India. But it seemed that one Secretary for India (Lord Kimberley) trembled to approach the War Minister, because each new discussion resulted in additional charges and additional burdens. He also truly said that the authorities here, not having to pay from their own pockets, readily made proposals of charges which were unjust and unnecessary, to make things agreeable. The consequence was that charges were imposed which were unjust and cruel. In fact, whatever could have the name of India attached to it, India was forced to pay for it. That was not the justice which he expected from the English. With reference to these military charges, the burden now thrown upon India on account of British troops was excessive, and he thought every impartial judgment would assent to that proposition, considering the relative material wealth of the two countries and their joint obligations and benefits. All that they could do was to appeal to the British Government for an impartial consideration of the relative financial capacity of the two countries, and for a generous consideration to be shown by the wealthiest nation in the world to a dependency so comparatively poor and so little advanced as India. He believed that if any Committee were appointed to enquire, with the honest purpose of finding out how to make India prosperous and at the same time to confer as much if not more benefit to England, they could very easily find out the way, and would be able to suggest what should be done. Now, with regard to the financial relations between India and England, it was declared over and over again that this European Army and all European servants were for the special purpose of maintaining the power of the British Empire. Were they, therefore, not for some benefit to England? Were they only for the service of India, for their benefit and for their protection? Was it right that they did avowedly use machinery more for their own purposes than for the purposes of India, and yet make India pay altogether? Was it right, if India's prosperity was, as Lord Roberts said, so indissolubly bound up with their own, and if the greatness and prosperity of the United Kingdom depended upon the retention of India, that they should pay nothing for it, and that they should extract from it every farthing they possibly could? They appealed to their sense of justice in this matter. They were not asking for this as any favour or concession. They based their appeal on the ground of simple justice. Here was a machinery by which both England and India benefited, and it was only common justice that both should share the cost of it. If this expenditure on the European Army and the European Civil Services, which was really the cause of their misery, was for the benefit of both, it was only right that they, as honourable men, should take a share. Their prayer was for an impartial and comprehensive enquiry so that the whole matter might be gone into, and that the question of principles and policy which, after all, was one for their statesmen to decide, should be properly dealt with. They knew that during the rule of the East India Company an enquiry was made every 20 years into the affairs of India. This was no reflection upon the Government; it was simply to see that the East India Company did their duty. There was such an enquiry in 1853, and he thought it was time, after 40 years had elapsed since the assumption of British rule by the Queen, that there should be some regular, independent enquiry like that which used to take place in former days, so that the people and Parliament of this country might see that the Indian authorities were doing their duty. The result of the irresponsibility of the present British Administration was that the expenditure went on unchecked. He admitted fully that expenditure must go on increasing if India was to progress in her civilisation; but if they allowed her to prosper, India would be able not only to pay her £60,000,000 out of the 300,000,000 of population, but she would be able to pay twice, three times, and four times as much. It was not that they did not want to expend as much as was necessary. Their simple complaint was that the present system did not allow India to become prosperous, and so enable her to supply the necessary revenue. As to the character of the enquiry, it should be full and impartial. The right hon. member for Midlothian said on one occasion not long ago, when the question of the Opium Trade was under discussion in that House:—

> "I must make the admission that I do not think that in this matter we ought to be guided exclusively, perhaps even principally, by those who may consider themselves experts. It is a very sad thing to say, but unquestionably it happens not infrequently in human affairs that those who might, from their position, know the most and the best, yet, from their prejudices and prepossessions, know the least and the worst. I certainly for my part do not propose to abide finally and decisively by official opinion."

And the right hon. gentleman went on to say that what the House wanted, in his opinion, was "independent but responsible opinion," in order to enable him to proceed safely to a decision on the subject which was to be considered. He was asking by this Resolution nothing more than what the right hon. gentleman the member for Midlothian had said was actually necessary for the Opium Commission. How much more necessary it was when they meant to overhaul and examine all the various departments of administration, and the affairs of 300,000,000 of people, all in a state of transition in civilisation—complicated especially by this evil of foreign rule! What was wanted was an independent enquiry by which the rulers and the ruled might come to some fair and honourable understanding with each other which would keep them together in good faith and good heart. He could only repeat the appeal he had made, in the words of the Queen herself, when her Majesty in her great Indian Proclamation said :—

> "In their prosperity will be our strength, in their contentment our security, and in their gratitude our best reward!"

And then she prayed :—

> "And may the God of all power grant to us and to those in authority under us strength to carry out these our wishes for the good of our people!"

He said Amen to that. He appealed once more to the House and to the British people to look into the whole problem of Indian relations with England. There was no reason whatever why there should not be a thorough good understanding between the two countries, a thorough good will on the part of Britain, and a thorough loyalty on the part of India, with blessings to both, if the principles and policy laid down from time to time by the British people and by the British Parliament were loyally, faithfully, and worthily, as the English character ought to lead them to expect, observed by the Government of that country.

Amendment proposed, to leave out from the word "That," to the end of the Question, in order to add the words—

> "In the opinion of this House, a full and independent Parliamentary enquiry should take place into the condition and wants of the Indian people, and their ability to bear their existing financial burdens; the nature of the revenue system and the possibility of reductions in the expenditure; also the financial relations between India and the United Kingdom, and generally the system of Government in India."—(*Mr. S. Smith.*)

AMENDMENT TO THE ADDRESS.

February 12th, 1895.

Mr. Naoroji (Finsbury, Central) moved an Amendment to add the following to the Address :—

"And we humbly pray that Your Majesty will be graciously pleased to direct Your Majesty's Ministers to so adjust the financial relations between the United Kingdom and British India, with regard to all the expenditure incurred in the employment of Europeans in the British-Indian Services, Civil and Military, in this Country and in India, that some fair and adequate portion of such expenditure should be borne by the British Exchequer in proportion to the pecuniary and political benefits accruing to the United Kingdom from Your Gracious Majesty's sway over India; and that the British Treasury should sustain a fair and equitable portion of all expenditure incurred on all military and political operations beyond the boundaries of India in which both Indian and British interests are jointly concerned."

Having expressed his regret that generally it was not the practice to mention India and to indicate any concern for its interests in the Queen's Speech, he said he was ready to acknowledge with gratitude the advantage which had ensued to the people of India from British rule. He had no desire to minimise those benefits: at the same time, he did not appeal to that House or to the British nation for any form of charity to India, however poverty-stricken she is. He based the claims of India on grounds of justice alone. The question was not at all one of a Party character, and therefore he addressed what he had to say to the English people as a whole. He was often supposed to complain about the European officials personally. It was not so. It was the system which made the officials what they were, that he complained about. They were the creatures of circumstances. They could only move in the one-sided groove in which they were placed by the evil system. Further, his remarks applied to British India and not to the Native States. It had been sometimes said that he resorted to agitation in bringing forward the claims of India, but on that point he would only quote a few words from Macaulay, who said in one of his speeches—

> "I hold that we have owed to agitation a long series of beneficent reforms which could have been effected in no other way. . . . The truth is that agitation is inseparable from popular Government. . . . Would the slave trade ever have been abolished without an agitation? Would slavery ever have been abolished without agitation?"

He would add that their slavery would not be abolished without agitation and it was well that it should be abolished by peaceful agitation, rather than by revolution caused by despair. He next proposed to consider the respective benefits to Britain and India from their connexion. From the annual production of India the Government took about 700,000,000 rupees for the expenditure of the State. The first result of this cost was law and order, the greatest blessing that any rule could confer, and Indians fully appreciated this benefit of safety from violence to life, limb, and property. Admitting this benefit to India, was it not equally or even more vital benefit to the British in India, and more particularly to the British rule itself? Did not the very existence of every European resident in India depend upon this law and order, and so also of the British power itself? The Hindus (and the Mahomedans also, the bulk of whom are Hindus by race) were, by their nature, in their very blood, by the inheritance of social and religious institutions of some thousands of years, peaceful and law-abiding. Their division into the four great divisions was the foundation of their peaceful nature. One class was devoted to learning. Peace was an absolute necessity to them. The fighting and ruling and protecting business was left to the small second class. The third and the largest class—the industrial, the agricultural, the trading, and others—depended upon peace and order for their work, and the fourth serving class were submissive and law-abiding. The virtue of law-abiding was a peculiarly and religiously binding duty upon the Hindus, and to it does Britain owe much of its present peaceful rule over India. It will be Britain's own fault if this character is changed. It was sometimes said that England conquered India with the sword, and would hold it by the sword; but he did not believe this was the sentiment of the British people generally. He could not better emphasise this than in the words of their present great Indian General. Lord Roberts had said that :—

"However efficient and well-equipped the Army of India might be—were it indeed absolute perfection, and were its numbers considerably more than at present—our greatest strength must ever rest on the firm base of a united and contented people."

That was the spirit in which he spoke. At present India shared far less benefits than justice demanded. Hundreds of millions of rupees were drawn from, and taken out of, the country for the payment of European officials of all kinds, without any material equivalent being received for it ; capital was thus withdrawn, and the Natives prevented from accumulating it ; and under the existing system a large part of the resources and industries of the country was thrown into the hands of British and other capitalists. The 300,000,000 or so of rupees which the India Office draws every year at present is so much British benefit in a variety of ways. British India was indeed British India, and not India's India. He next examined the material or pecuniary benefit derived by Britain and India. Out of about 700,000,000 rupees raised annually from the annual production of the country, nearly 200,000,000 rupees were appropriated in pay, pensions, and allowances to Europeans in this country and in India. This compulsorily obtained benefit to Britain crippled the resources of British Indians, who could never make any capital and must drag on a poverty-stricken life. Hundreds and thousands of millions of wealth passed in principal and interest thereon from India to Britain. Thousands of Europeans found a career and livelihood in India, to the exclusion of the children of the soil, who thus lost both their bread and their brains thereby. Not only that. This crippled condition naturally threw nearly all the requirements of India more or less into British hands, which, under the patronage and protection of the British officials, monopolised nearly everything. British India was, next to officials, more or less for British professionals, traders, capitalists, planters, shipowners, railway holders, and so on, the bulk of the Indians having only to serve for poor income or wages that they earned. In a way a great mass of the Indians were worse off than the slaves of the Southern States. The slaves being property were taken care of by their masters. Indians may die off by millions by want and it is nobody's concern. The slaves worked on their masters' land and resources, and the masters took the profits. Indians have to work on their own land and resources, and hand the profits to the foreign masters. He offered a simple test. Supposing that by some vicissitudes of fortune, which he hoped and prayed would never occur, Britain was conquered by a foreign people. This was no impossible assumption in this world. When Cæsar landed in this country no one could have dreamt that the savages he met here would in time be the masters of the greatest Empire in the world, and that the same Rome and Italy, then the masters of the world, would in turn become a geographical name only. Well, suppose this House was cleared of Englishmen and filled with foreigners, or perhaps shut up altogether, all power and plans in their hands, eating and carrying away much of the wealth of this country year after year, in short, Britain reduced to the present condition and system of government of India, would the Britons submit to it a single day if they could help it? So law-abiding as they are, will not all their law-abiding vanish? No! The Briton will not submit; as he says, "Britons will never be slaves," and may they sing so for ever. Now, he asked whether, though they would never be slaves, was it their mission to make others slaves? No; the British people's instincts are averse to that. Their mission is and ought to be to raise others to their own level. And it was that faith in the instinctive love of justice in the British heart and conscience that keeps the Indian so loyal and hopeful. There was no doubt an immense material benefit to England accruing from the administration of India, but there was no corresponding benefit to the Indian people under the present evil system. For the sake of argument merely, he would assume that the material benefit was equal to the inhabitants of India as well as to the British people, and even on that assumption he contended that the British people were bound for the benefit they derived to take their share of the cost of producing that benefit. The position had been correctly described by Lord Salisbury, who said :—

"The injury is exaggerated in the case of India, where so much of the Revenue is exported without a direct equivalent. As India must be bled, the lancet should be directed to the parts where the blood is congested, or at least sufficient, not to those already feeble for the want of it."

That was correct as far as the present British system in India was concerned, and "India must be bled." The result of this was that their Finance Ministers were obliged to lament and complain, year after year, of the extreme poverty of India, which did not enable them to bring its finances into a properly sound condition. The subject of the poverty of India embraced many aspects in its cause and effects. But this was not the occasion on which such a vast subject could be dealt with adequately. It was the natural and inevitable result of the evil of foreign dominion as it exists in the present system, as predicted by Sir John Shore, above a hundred years ago. In order to give an idea of the position of India as compared with that of England he would point only to one aspect. The Secretary of State for India in his speech last year, on going into Committee on the Indian Budget, made a very important statement. He said:—

"Now as to the Revenue, I think the figures are very instructive. Whereas in England the taxation is £2 11s. 8d. per head, in Scotland, £2 8s. 1d. per head, and in Ireland, £1 12s. 5d. per head, the Budget which I shall present to-morrow will show that the taxation per head in India is something like 2s. 6d., or one-twentieth the taxation of the United Kingdom, and one-thirteenth that of Ireland."

The Member for Flintshire (Mr. S. Smith) then asked, "Does he exclude the Land Revenue?" And the right hon. gentleman replied:—

"Yes. So far as the taxation of India is concerned, taking the rupee at 1s. 1d., it is 2s. 6d. per head."

The exclusion of Land Revenue was unfair, but this was not the time to discuss that point fully. The Land Revenue did not rain from heaven. It formed part and parcel of the annual wealth from which the State Revenue is taken in a variety of different names—call it tax, rent, excise, duty, stamps, income-tax, and so on. It simply meant that so much was taken from the annual production for the purposes of Government. The figures taken by the right hon. gentleman for the English taxation is also the gross Revenue, and similarly must this Indian Revenue be taken, except Railway and Navigation Revenue. That statement of the right hon. gentleman, if it meant anything, meant that the incidence of taxation in India was exceedingly light compared with the incidence of taxation in England. It was the usual official fiction that the incidence of taxation in India was small as compared with that of this country. But when they considered the incidence of taxation they must consider not simply the amount paid in such taxation, but what it was compared with the capacity of the person who paid it. An elephant might with ease carry a great weight, whilst a quarter ounce, or a grain of wheat, might be sufficient to crush an ant. Taking the capacity of the two countries, the annual product or income of England was admitted to be something like £35 per head. If there was a taxation of £2 10s. as compared with that it was easy to see that the incidence or heaviness was only about 7 per cent. of the annual wealth. If, on the other hand, they took the production of India at the high official estimate of 27 rupees per head—though he maintained it was only 20 rupees—even then the percentage, or incidence of taxation, was about 10 or 11 per cent., or at 20 rupees the incidence was nearly 14 per cent., *i.e.*, nearly double what it was in England. To say, therefore, that India was lightly taxed was altogether a fiction. The fact was, as he stated, that the pressure of taxation in India, according to its means of paying, was nearly double that of wealthy England, and far more oppressive, as exacted from poverty. That was not all. The case for India was worse, and that was the fundamental evil of the present system. In the United Kingdom, if about £100,000,000 are raised as revenue, every farthing returns to the people themselves. But in British India, out of about Rs. 700,000,000 about Rs. 200,000,000 are paid to foreigners —besides all the other British benefits obtained from the wretched produce of Rs. 20 per head. Even an ocean, if it lost some water every day which never returned to it, would be dried up in time. Under similar conditions wealthy England even would be soon reduced to poverty. He hoped it would be felt by hon. members that India, in that condition, could derive very little benefit from British administration. He spoke in agony, not in indignation, both for the sake of the land of his career, and for the land of his birth, and he said that if a system of righteousness were introduced into India instead of the present evil system, both England and India would be blessed, the profit and benefit to England itself would be ten times greater than it now was, and the Indian people would then regard their government by this country as a blessing, instead of being inclined to contemn it. England, with India contented, justly treated, and prosperous, may defy half-a-dozen Russias, and may drive back Russia to the very gates of St. Petersburg. The Indian will then fight as a patriot for his own hearth and home. Punjab alone will be able to provide a powerful army. Assuming again, for purpose of argument, that their benefit in India was equal to the British benefit, then he said that the British must share the cost of the expenditure which produced these results, and for which both partners profited equally. But in his amendment he did not ask that even half of the whole cost should be borne by the British people, but only for that part of the expenditure which was incurred on Europeans, and that entirely for the sake of British rule. If it was not for the necessity of maintaining British rule there would be no need to drain India in the manner in which it was now drained by the crushing European Services. Lord Roberts, speaking in London, May, 1893, said:—

> "I rejoice to learn that you recognise how indissolubly the prosperity of the United Kingdom is bound up with the retention of that vast Eastern Empire."

But if the interests of England and India were indissolubly bound up, it was only just and proper that both should pay for the cost of the benefits they derived in equal and proper proportions. Lord Kimberley, in a speech at the Mansion House, in 1893, said:—

> "We are resolutely determined to maintain our supremacy over our Indian Empire . . . . that" (among other things) "supremacy rests upon the maintenance of our European Civil Service. . . . . We rest also upon our magnificent European force which we maintain in that country."

The European Civil Services and European residents, he contended, were the weakest part in the maintenance of their rule in India. Whenever any unfortunate troubles did arise, as in 1857, the European Civil Service, and Europeans generally, were their greatest difficulty. They must be saved, they were in the midst of the greatest danger, and in such circumstances they became their greatest weakness. The loyal Indians saved many lives. To suppose that their Civil Service, or the British people, could have any other safety than that which arose from the satisfaction of India, was to deceive themselves. Whatever might be the strength of their military force, their true security in the maintenance of their rule in India depended entirely on the satisfaction of the people. Brute force may make an empire, but brute force would not maintain it; it was moral force and justice and righteousness alone that would maintain it. If he asked that the whole expenditure incurred on Europeans should be defrayed from the British Treasury he should not be far wrong, but, for the sake of argument, he was prepared to admit that the benefit derived from the employment of Europeans was shared equally by Europeans and Natives. He therefore asked that at least half of the expenditure incurred on Europeans here and in India should be paid from the British Exchequer. Indians were sometimes threatened that if they raised the question of financial relations, something would have to be said about the navy. Apart from a fair share for the vessels stationed in India, why should England ask India to defray any other portion of the cost of the navy? The very sense of justice had probably prevented any such demand being made. The fame, gain, and glory of the navy was all England's own. There was not a single Indian employed in the navy. It was said the navy was necessary to protect the Indian commerce. There was not a single ship sailing from or to India which belonged to India. The whole of the shipping was British, and not only that, but the whole cargo while floating was entirely at the risk of British money. There was not an ounce exported from India on which British money did not lie through Indian banks. In the same way, when goods were exported from England, British money was upon them. The whole floating shipping and goods was first British risk. Lastly, there is every inch of the British navy required for the protection of these blessed islands. Every Budget, from either Party, emphasises this fact, that the first line of defence for the protection of the United Kingdom alone, demands a navy equal to that of any two European Powers. He had asked for several returns from the Secretary of State. If the right hon. géntleman would give those returns, the House would be able to judge of the real material condition of India; until those returns were presented, they would not be in a position to understand exactly the real condition of India under the present system. He would pass over all the small injustices, in charging every possible thing to India, which they would not dare to do with the Colonies. India Office buildings, Engineering College building, charge for recruiting, while the soldiers form part and parcel of the army here; the system of short service occasioning transport expenses, and so on, and so on. While attending the meeting upon the Armenian atrocities, he could not help admiring the noble efforts that the English always made for the protection of the suffering and oppressed. It is one of the noblest traits in the English character. Might he appeal to the same British people, who were easily moved to generosity and compassion when there was open violence, to consider the cause why in India hundreds of thousands of people were frequently carried away through famine and drought, and that millions constantly lived on starvation fare? Why was it that after a hundred years of administration by the most highly paid officials, the people of India were not able to pay one-twentieth part of the taxation which the United Kingdom paid, or even one-thirteenth which poor Ireland paid? Were the English satisfied with such a result? Is it creditable to them? While England's wealth had increased, India's had decreased. The value of the whole production of India was not £2 per head per annum, or, taking into account the present rate of exchange, it was only 20s. The people here spent about £4 per head in drink alone, while India's whole production is only a pound or two per head. Such should not be the result of a system which was expected to be beneficent. He appealed to the people of this country to ask and consider this question. If there were famine here food would be poured in from the whole world. Why not so in India? Why the wretched result that the bulk of the people had no means to pay for food? Britain has saved India from personal violence. Would it not also save millions from want and ravages of famine owing to their extreme poverty caused by the evil which Sir J. Shore predicted. The late Mr. Bright told his Manchester friends that there were two ways of benefiting themselves, the one was by plunder, and the other was by trade, and he preferred the latter mode. At present, England's trade with India was a miserable thing. The British produce sent to all India was about worth 2s. per head per annum. If, however, India were prosperous, and able to buy, England would have no need to complain of duties and the want of markets. In India there was a market of 300 millions of civilised people. If the wants of those people were provided for, with complete free trade in her own hands and control, England would be able to eliminate altogether the word "unemployed" from her dictionary: in fact, she would not be able to supply all that India would want. The other day the Chancellor of the Exchequer said that where injustice and wrong prevailed, as it did prevail in Armenia, a Liberal Government was called upon to obtain the co-operation of European powers in order to repress the wrong. Might he appeal to the right hon. gentleman to give an earnest and generous consideration to India? The right hon. gentleman the member for Midlothian made a very grand speech on his birthday upon the Armenian question. He appealed to that right hon. gentleman, and to all those of the same mind, to consider and find out the fundamental causes which make the destitution of forty or fifty millions—a figure of official admission—and destruction of hundreds of thousands by famine, possible, though British India's resources are admitted on all sides to be vast. In the present amendment his object was to have that justice of a fair share in expenditure to be taken by Britain in proportion to her benefits. He asked for no subsidy, but only for common justice. By a certain amount of expenditure they derived certain benefits; they were partners, therefore let them share equally the benefits and the costs. His amendment also had reference to expenditure outside the boundaries of India. He maintained that if England undertook operations in Burmah, Afghanistan, and in other places beyond the borders of India for the protection of British rule, she was bound by justice to defray at least half the cost. The benefit of these operations was for both Britain and India. The principle was admitted in the case of the last Afghan war, which was certainly not a very necessary war, but the Liberal Government defrayed a portion of the expenditure. That India should be required to pay the cost of all the small wars and aggressions beyond her boundaries, or political subsidies, was not worthy of the British people, when these were all as much, or more necessary, for their own benefit and rule as for the benefit of India. He hoped he was not appealing to deaf ears. He knew that when any appeal was made on the basis of justice, righteousness, and honour, the English people responded to it, and with the perfect faith in the English character he believed his appeal would not be in vain. The short of the whole matter was, whether the people of British India were British citizens or British helots. If the former, as he firmly believed to be the desire of the British people, then let them have their birthright of British rights as well as British responsibilities. Let them be treated with justice, that the cost of the benefits to both should be shared by both. The unseemly squabble that was now taking place on the question of Import Duties between the Lancashire manufacturers on the one hand and the British Indian Government on the other illustrated the helpless condition of the people of India. This was the real position. The Indian Government arbitrarily imposed a burden of a million or so a year on the ill-fed Indians as a heartless compensation to the well-fed officials, and have gone on adding to expenditure upon Europeans. They want money, and they adopt Lord Salisbury's advice to bleed where there is blood left, and also by means of Import Duties tax the subjects of the Native States. The Lancashire gentlemen object and want to apply the lancet to other parts that would not interfere with their interests—and thus the quarrel between them. However that is decided, the Indians are to be bled. He did not complain of the selfishness of the Lancashire people. By all means be selfish, but be intelligently selfish. Remember what Mr. Bright said—Your good can only come through India's good. Help India to be prosperous, and you will help your prosperity. Macaulay truly said:—

> "It would be a doting wisdom which would keep a hundred millions (now more than two hundred millions) of men from being our customers in order that they might continue to be our slaves."

They had no voice as to the expenditure of a single farthing in the administration of Indian affairs. The British Indian Government could do what they liked. There was, of course, an Indian Council; but when a Budget was proposed it had to be accepted. The representatives of the Council could make a few speeches, but there the matter ended. The people of India now turned to the people of Great Britain, and, relying on the justice of their claim, asked that they should contribute their fair share in proportion to any benefits which this country might derive from the possession of India.

ROYAL COMMISSION
ON THE
ADMINISTRATION OF EXPENDITURE IN INDIA.

1895.

The following ten statements which were placed before the Royal Commission on "Indian Expenditure and Apportionment of Charge," are published here in their original form, with slight revision, though in the Report of the Commission they are curtailed in deference to the wishes of the President and majority of the Commission.

I.

National Liberal Club, London,
17th October, 1895.

DEAR LORD WELBY,—I beg to place before you and other Members of the Commission a few notes about the scope and importance of its work.

The Reference consists of two parts. The first is: "To enquire into the Administration and Management of the Military and Civil Expenditure incurred under the authority of the Secretary of State for India in Council, or of the Government of India."

This enquiry requires to ascertain whether the present system of the Administration and Management of Expenditure, both here and in India, secures sufficiency and efficiency of services, and all other satisfactory results, at an economical and affordable cost; whether there is any peculiar inherent defect, or what Mr. Bright called "fundamental error"[1] in this system; and the necessity or otherwise of every expenditure.

I shall deal with these items as briefly as possible, simply as suggestively and not exhaustively:—

"SUFFICIENCY."—The Duke of Devonshire (then, 1883, Lord Hartington) as Secretary of State for India has said[2]: "There can in my opinion be very little doubt that India is insufficiently governed."

Sir William Hunter has said[3]: "The constant demand for improvement in the general executive will require an increasing amount of administrative labour."

"EFFICIENCY."—It stands to reason that when a country is "insufficiently governed," it cannot be efficiently governed, however competent each servant, high and low, may be. The Duke of Devonshire assumes as much in the words, "if the country is to be better governed." So does Sir William

[1] Speech in House of Commons, 3/6/1853
[2] *Ib.*, 23/8/83.
[3] "England's Work in India," p. 131, 1880.

Hunter: "If we are to govern the Indian people efficiently and cheaply." These words will be found in the fuller extracts given further on.

"ECONOMICAL AND AFFORDABLE COST."—The Duke of Devonshire has said[1]: "The Government of India cannot afford to spend more than they do on the administration of the country, and if the country is to be better governed, that can only be done by the employment of the best and most intelligent of the Natives in the Service."

Sir William Hunter, after referring to the good work done by the Company, of the external and internal protection, has said[2]: "But the good work thus commenced has assumed such dimensions under the Queen's Government of India that it can no longer be carried on, or even supervised by imported labour from England except at a cost which India cannot sustain," . . . . "forty years hereafter we should have had an Indian Ireland multiplied fifty-fold on our hands. The condition of things in India compels the Government to enter on these problems. Their solution and the constant demand for improvement in the general executive, will require an increasing amount of administrative labour. India cannot afford to pay for that labour at the English rates, which are the highest in the world for official service. But she can afford to pay for it at her own Native rates, which are perhaps the lowest in the world for such employment." "You cannot work with imported labour as cheaply as you can with Native labour, and I regard the more extended employment of the Natives not only as an act of justice but as a financial necessity." "The appointment of a few Natives annually to the Covenanted Civil Service will not solve the problem. . . . . If we are to govern the Indian people efficiently and cheaply, we must govern them by means of themselves, and pay for the Administration at the market rates of Native labour."[3]

"ANY INHERENT DEFECT."—Mr. Bright said[4]:—"I must say that it is my belief that if a country be found possessing a most fertile soil and capable of bearing every variety of production, and that notwithstanding the people are in a

[1] House of Commons, 23/8/1883.
[2] "England's Work in India," p. 130.
[3] "England's Work in India," pp. 118-19.
[4] House of Commons, 3/6/1853.

state of extreme destitution and suffering, the chances are there is some fundamental error in the government of that country."

I take an instance: Suppose a European servant draws a salary of Rs. 1,000 a month. He uses a portion of this for all his wants, of living, comfort, etc., etc. All this consumption by him is at the deprivation of an Indian who would and could, under right and natural circumstances, occupy that position and enjoy that provision. This is the first partial loss to India, as, at least, the services enjoyed by the Europeans are rendered by Indians as they would have rendered to any Indian occupying the position. But whatever the European sends to England for his various wants, and whatever savings and pension he ultimately, on his retirement, carries away with him, is a complete drain out of the country, crippling her whole material condition and her capacity to meet all her wants—a dead loss of wealth together with the loss of work and wisdom—*i.e.*, the accumulated experience of his service. Besides, all State expenditure in this country is a dead loss to India.

This peculiar inherent evil or fundamental error in the present British Indian administration and management of expenditure and its consequences have been foretold more than a hundred years ago by Sir John Shore (1787): "Whatever allowance we make for the increased industry of the subjects of the State, owing to the enhanced demand for the produce of it (supposing the demand to be enhanced), there is reason to conclude that the benefits are more than counterbalanced by evils inseparable from the system of a remote foreign dominion."[1] And it is significantly remarkable that the same inherent evil in the present system of administration and management of expenditure has been, after nearly a hundred years, confirmed by a Secretary of State for India. Lord Randolph Churchill has said in a letter to the Treasury (1886)[2]: "The position of India in relation to taxation and the sources of public revenue is very peculiar, not merely from the habits of the people and their strong aversion to change, which is more specially exhibited to new forms of taxation, but likewise from the character of the government, which is in the hands of foreigners who hold

[1] Parliamentary Return 377 of 1812. Minute, para. 132.
[2] Par. Return [c. 4868], 1886.

all the principal administrative offices and form so large a part of the Army. The impatience of the new taxation which will have to be borne wholly as a consequence of the foreign rule imposed on the country, and virtually to meet additions to charges arising outside of the country, would constitute a political danger the real magnitude of which it is to be feared is not at all appreciated by persons who have no knowledge of or concern in the government of India, but which those responsible for that government have long regarded as of the most serious order."

Lord Salisbury, as Secretary of State for India, put the same inherent evil in this manner: "The injury is exaggerated in the case of India, where so much of the revenue is exported without a direct equivalent." And he indicates the character of the present system of the administration and management of expenditure as being that "India must be bled."[1] I need not say more upon this aspect of the inherent evil of the present system of expenditure.

"THE NECESSITY OR OTHERWISE" of any expenditure is a necessary preliminary for its proper administration and management, so as to secure all I have indicated above. You incidentally instanced at the last meeting that all expenditure for the collection of revenue will have to be considered —and so, in fact, every expenditure in both countries will have its administration, management and necessity, to be considered.

The second part of the Reference is "The apportionment of charge between the Governments of the United Kingdom and of India for purposes in which both are interested."

What we shall have to do is, first to ascertain all the purposes in which both countries are interested by examining every charge in them, and how far each of them is respectively interested therein.

In my opinion there are some charges in which the United Kingdom is almost wholly or wholly interested. But any such cases will be dealt with as they arise.

After ascertaining such purposes and the extent of the interest of each country the next thing to do would be to ascertain the comparative capacity of each country, so as to

[1] Par. Return [c. 3086-1], 1881, p. 144. Minute, 29/4/75.

fix the right apportionment according to such extent of interest and such capacity.

I shall just state here what has been already admitted to be the comparative capacity by high authorities. Lord Cromer (then Major Baring), as the Finance Minister of India, has said in his speech on the Budget (1882): "In England the average income per head of population was £33; in France it was £23; in Turkey, which was the poorest country in Europe, it was £4 per head." I may add here that Mulhall gives for Russia above £9 per head. About India Lord Cromer says: "It has been calculated that the average income per head of population in India is not more than Rs.27 a year; and though I am not prepared to pledge myself to the absolute accuracy of a calculation of this sort, it is sufficiently accurate to justify the conclusion that the taxpaying community is exceedingly poor. To derive any very large increase of revenue from so poor a population as this is obviously impossible, and, if it were possible, would be unjustifiable." "But he thought it was quite sufficient to show the extreme poverty of the mass of the people." I think the principles of the calculation for India and the other countries are somewhat different; but that, if necessary, would be considered at the right time. For such large purposes with which the Commission has to deal these figures might be considered enough for guidance. I then asked Lord Cromer to give me the details of his calculations, as my calculations, which, I think, were the very first of their kind for India, had made out only Rs.20 per head per annum. Though Rs.27 or Rs.20 can make but very small difference in the conclusion of "extreme poverty of the mass of the people," still to those "extremely poor" people whose average is so small, and even that average cannot be available to every individual of them, the difference of so much as Rs.7, or nearly 33 per cent., is a matter of much concern. Lord Cromer himself says: "He would ask honourable members to think what Rs.27 per annum was to support a person, and then he would ask whether a few annas was nothing to such poor people."

Unfortunately, Lord Cromer refused to give me his calculations. These calculations were, I am informed, prepared by Sir David Barbour, and the results embodied in a Note. I think the Commission ought to have this Note and details of calculations, and also similar calculations, say for the last five years or longer, to the latest day practicable. This will enable the Commission to form a definite opinion of the comparative capacity, as well as of any progress or otherwise in the condition of the people, and the average annual production of the country.

The only one other authority on the point of capacity which I would now give is that of Sir Henry Fowler as Secretary of State for India. He said[1]: "Now as to the revenue, I think the figures are very instructive. Whereas in England the taxation is £2 11s. 8d. per head; in Scotland, £2 8s. 1d. per head; and in Ireland £1 12s. 5d. per head; the Budget which I shall present to-morrow will show that the taxation per head in India is something like 2s. 6d., or one-twentieth the taxation of the United Kingdom and one-thirteenth of that of Ireland." And that this very small capacity of 2s. 6d. per head is most burdensome and oppressive is admitted on all hands, and the authorities are at their wits' ends what to do to squeeze out more. So far back as 1870[2] Mr. Gladstone admitted about India as a country, "too much burdened," and in 1893,[3] he said: "The expenditure of India and especially the Military expenditure is alarming."

Sir David Barbour said[4]: "The financial position of the Government of India at the present moment is such as to give cause for apprehension." "The prospects of the future are disheartening."[5]

Lord Lansdowne, as Viceroy, said[6]: "We should be driven to lay before the Council so discouraging an account of our Finances, and to add the admission, that, for the present, it is beyond our power to describe the means by which we can hope to extricate ourselves from the difficulties and embarrassments which surround us." "My hon. friend is, I am afraid, but too well justified in regarding our position with grave apprehension." "We have to consider not so much the years which are past and gone as those which are immediately ahead of us, and if we look forward to these,

[1] Budget Debate, 15/8/94.
[2] Hansard, vol. 201, p. 521, 10/5/1870.
[3] Hansard, vol. 14, p. 622, 30/6/1893.
[4] Par. Return 207, of 1893. Financial Statement, 23/3/93.
[5] *Ib.*, para. 28.
[6] Par. Return 207, of 1893. Financial Statement, 23/3/93.

there can be no doubt that we have cause for serious alarm."[1]

Many such confessions can be quoted. And now when India is groaning under such intolerable heavy expenditure, and for the relief of which, indeed, this very Royal Commission has come into existence, the utmost that can be squeezed out of it to meet such expenditure is 2s. 6d. per head. Thus by the statement of Sir H. Fowler as Secretary of State for India, the relative capacity of poor India at the utmost pressure is only one-twentieth of the capacity of the prosperous and wealthy United Kingdom. But there is still something worse. When the actual pressure of both taxations as compared with the respective means of the two countries is considered, it will be found that the pressure of taxation on "extremely poor" India is much more heavy and oppressive than that on the most wealthy country of England.

Even admitting for the present the overestimate of Lord Cromer of Rs. 27 income, and the underestimate of Sir H. Fowler about 2s. 6d. revenue raised, the pressure of percentage of the Indian Revenue, as compared with India's means of paying, is even then slightly higher than that of the United Kingdom. But if my estimates of means and revenue be found correct, the Indian pressure or percentage will be found to be fifty or more per cent. heavier than that on the United Kingdom.

You have noticed a similar fallacy of regarding a smaller amount to be necessarily a lighter tax in the Irish Royal Commission.

"2613.[2] You went on to make rather a striking comparison between the weight of taxation in Ireland and Great Britain, and I think you took the years 1841 to 1881. In answer to Mr. Sexton, taking it head by head, the incidence of taxation was comparatively very light I may say in 1841, and very heavy comparatively in 1881?—Yes.

"2614. I would ask you does not that want some qualification. If you take alone without qualification the incidence of taxation upon people, leaving out of view entirely the fact whether the people have become in the interval poorer or richer, will you not get to a wrong conclusion? Let me give

[1] Par. Return 207, of 1893, p. 110. Financial Statement, 23/3/93.
[2] Par. Return [c.7720-1], 1895. Lord Welby.

you an instance of what I mean. I will take such a place as the Colony of Victoria. Before the gold discoveries you had there a small, sparse, squatting population, probably very little administered, and paying very few taxes. Probably in such a case you would find out that the incidence of taxation at that time was extremely small?—Yes.

"2615. But take it thirty or forty years later when there was a greater population, and what I am now dwelling upon, an improvement in wealth, you would find out that the incidence of taxation was very much heavier per head; for instance, perhaps 5s. per head at first, and perhaps £2 in the second; but it would be wrong to draw the conclusion from that fact that the individuals were relatively more heavily taxed at the later period than the first. Would it not?"

Similarly it would be wrong to draw the conclusion that the individuals of England were more heavily taxed than those of India, because the average of the former was £2 11s. 8d. and that of the latter was 2s. 6d. An elephant may carry a ton with ease, but an ant will be crushed by a quarter ounce.

Not only is India more heavily taxed than England to supply its expenditure, but there is another additional destructive circumstance against India. The whole British taxation of £2 11s. 8d. per head returns entirely to the *people themselves* from whom it is raised. But the 2s. 6d. so oppressively obtained out of the poverty-stricken Indians does not all return to them. No wonder that with such a destructive and unnatural system of "the administration and management of expenditure" millions perish by famine, and scores of millions, or—as Lord Lawrence said (1864)—"the mass of the people, enjoy only a scanty subsistence." Again in 1873, before the Select Committee of the House of Commons, Lord Lawrence said: "The mass of the people of India are so miserably poor that they have barely the means of subsistence. It is as much as a man can do to feed his family or half-feed them, let alone spending money on what may be called luxuries or conveniences." I was present when this evidence was given, and I then noted down these words. I think they are omitted from the published report, I do not know why and by whom. In considering therefore the administration and management of expenditure and the apportionment of charge for common purposes, all such circumstances are most vital elements, the importance of the attention to which cannot be over-estimated.

The *Times* of 2nd July last, in its article on "Indian Affairs," estimates the extent and importance of the work of the Commission as follows: "Great Britain is anxious to deal fairly with India. If it should appear that India has been saddled with charges which the British taxpayer should have borne, the British taxpayer will not hesitate to do his duty. At present we are in the unsatisfactory position which allows of injurious aspersions being made on the justice and good faith of the British nation, without having the means of knowing whether the accusations are true or false. Those accusations have been brought forward in the House of Lords, in the House of Commons, and in a hundred newspapers, pamphlets and memorials in India. Individual experts of equal authority take opposite sides in regard to them. Any curtailment of the scope of the Royal Commission's enquiry which might debar reasonable men from coming to a conclusion on these questions would be viewed with disappointment in England and with deep dissatisfaction throughout India."

Now what are the "accusations" and "injurious aspersions" on the justice and good faith of the British nation? Here are some statements by high authorities as to the objects and results of the present system of the administration and management of expenditure of British Indian revenues.

Macaulay pointed out: "That would indeed be a doting wisdom, which, in order that India might remain a dependency, would make it a useless and costly dependency—which would keep a hundred millions of men from being our customers in order that they might continue to be our slaves."[1]

Lord Salisbury says: "India must be bled."[2]

Mr. Bright said: "The cultivators of the soil, the great body of the population of India, are in a condition of great impoverishment, of great dejection, and of great suffering."[3]

"We must in future have India governed, not for a handful of Englishmen, not for that Civil Service whose praises are so constantly sounded in this House. You may

[1] Hansard, vol. 19. p. 533. 10/7/1833.
[2] Par. Return [c. 3086-1], 1881.
[3] House of Commons, 14/6/1858.

govern India, if you like, for the good of England, but the good of England must come through the channels of the good of India. There are but two modes of gaining anything by our connexion with India. The one is by plundering the people of India, and the other by trading with them. I prefer to do it by trading with them. But in order that England may become rich by trading with India, India itself must become rich."[1]

Now as long as the present system is what Mr. Bright characterises by implication as that of plundering, India cannot become rich.

"I say that a Government put over 250,000,000 of people, which has levied taxes till it can levy no more, which spends all that it can levy, and which has borrowed £100,000,000 more than all that it can levy—I say a Government like that has some fatal defect, which, at some not distant time, must bring disaster and humiliation to the Government and to the people on whose behalf it rules."[2]

Mr. Fawcett said: "Lord Metcalf had well said that the bane of our system was that the advantages were reaped by one class and the work was done by another."[3]

Sir George Wingate[4] says with regard to the present system of expenditure: "Taxes spent in the country from which they are raised are totally different in their effect from taxes raised in one country and spent in another. In the former case the taxes collected from the population . . . . are again returned to the industrious classes. . . . But the case is wholly different when the taxes are not spent in the country from which they are raised. . . . They constitute . . . . an absolute loss and extinction of the whole amount withdrawn from the taxed country . . . . might as well be thrown into the sea. . . . Such is the nature of the tribute we have so long exacted from India. . . . From this explanation some faint conception may be formed of the cruel, crushing effect of the tribute upon India." "The Indian tribute, whether weighed in the scales of justice, or viewed in the light of our own interest, will be found to be

[1] House of Commons, 24/6/1858.
[2] Speech in the Manchester Town Hall, 11/12/1877.
[3] Hansard, vol. 191, p. 1841, 5/5/1868.
[4] "A Few Words on our Financial Relations with India." (London, Richardson Bros., 1859.)

at variance with humanity, with common-sense, and with the received maxims of economic science."

Lord Lawrence, Lord Cromer, Sir Auckland Colvin and others declare the extreme poverty of British India, and that after a hundred years of the administration of expenditure by the most highly-praised and most highly-paid service in the world—by administrators drawn from the same class which serves in England.

Sir John Shore, as already stated, predicted a hundred years ago that under the present system the benefits are more than counterbalanced by its evils.

A Committee of five members[1] of the Council of the Secretary of State for India said, in 1860, that the British Government was exposed to the charge of keeping promise to the ear and breaking it to the hope; and Lord Lytton[2] said, in 1878, the same, with greater emphasis, in a Minute which it is desirable the Commission should have.

Lord Lytton said[3]: "The Act of Parliament is so undefined, and indefinite obligations on the part of the Government of India towards its Native subjects are so obviously dangerous, that no sooner was the Act passed than the Government began to devise means for practically evading the fulfilment of it. Under the terms of the Act, which are studied and laid to heart by that increasing class of educated Natives whose development the Government encourages without being able to satisfy the aspirations of its existing members, every such Native, if once admitted to Government employment in posts previously reserved to the covenanted service, is entitled to expect and claim appointment in the fair course of promotion to the highest post in that service. We all know that these claims and expectations never can or will be fulfilled. We have had to choose between prohibiting them and cheating them, and we have chosen the least straightforward course. The application to Natives of the competitive examination system—as conducted in England—and the recent reduction in the age at which candidates can compete are all so many deliberate and transparent subter-

[1] Sir J. P. Willoughby, Mr. Mangles, Mr. Arbuthnot, Mr. MacNaughton, Sir E. Perry.

[2] Report of the first Indian National Congress, p. 30.

[3] I believe this to be in a Minute 30/5/1878 (?) to which the Government of India's Despatch of 2/5/1878 refers. Par. Return [c. 2376, 1870, p. 15].

fuges for stultifying the Act, and reducing it to a dead letter. Since I am writing confidentially, I do not hesitate to say that both the Governments of England and of India appear to me, up to the present moment, unable to answer satisfactorily the charge of having taken every means in their power of breaking to the heart the words of promise they had uttered to the ear."

The Duke of Argyll said[1]: "I must say that we have not fulfilled our duty or the promises and engagements which we have made."

When Lord Northbrook pleaded[2] (1883) the Act of Parliament of 1833, the Court of Directors' explanatory despatch and the great and solemn Proclamation of 1858, Lord Salisbury in reply said: "My lords, I do not see what is the use of all this political hypocrisy."[3]

The Act for which Macaulay said: "I must say that to the last day of my life I shall be proud of having been one of those who assisted in the framing of the Bill which contains that clause;" the clause which he called "that wise, that benevolent, that noble clause;" and which Lord Lansdowne supported in a noble speech as involving "the happiness or misery of 100,000,000 of human beings," and as "confident that the strength of the Government would be increased;" and the great and most solemn proclamation of the Sovereign on behalf of the British nation are, according to Lord Salisbury, "political hypocrisy!" Can there be a more serious and injurious aspersion on the justice and good faith of the British nation?

The Duke of Devonshire pointed out that it would not be wise to tell a patriotic Native that the Indians shall never have any chance "except by their getting rid in the first instance of their European rulers."[4]

From the beginning of British connexion with India up to the present day India has been made to pay for every possible kind of expenditure for the acquisition and maintenance of British rule, and Britain has never contributed her fair share (except a small portion on few rare occasions, such as the last Afghan War) for all the great benefits it has

[1] Speech in House of Lords, 11/3/1869.
[2] Hansard, vol. 277, p. 1792, 9/4/1883.
[3] *Ib.*, p. 1798.
[4] House of Commons, 23/8/1883.

always derived from all such expenditure and "bleeding" or "slaving" of India. And so this is a part of the important mission of this Commission, to justly apportion charge for purposes in which both countries are interested.

Such are some of the "accusations" and "injurious aspersions being made on the justice and good faith of the British nation," while truly "Great Britain is anxious to deal fairly with India." Justly does the *Times* conclude that "any curtailment of the scope of the Royal Commission's enquiry which might debar reasonable men from coming to a conclusion on these questions would be viewed with disappointment in England and with deep dissatisfaction throughout India."

The *Times* is further justified when Sir Henry Fowler himself complained of "a very strong indictment of the British government of India" having been "brought before the House and the country."[1] And it is this indictment which has led to the enquiry.

On the 10th of this month the *Times*, in a leader on the conduct of the Transvaal with regard to trade and franchise, ends in these words: "A man may suffer the restriction of his liberty with patience for the advancement of his material prosperity. He may sacrifice material prosperity for the sake of a liberty which he holds more valuable. When his public rights and his private interests are alike attacked the restraining influences on which the peace of civilised societies depends are dangerously weakened."

So, when the Indian finds that the present administration and management of expenditure sacrifice his material prosperity, that he has no voice in the administration and management of the expenditure of his country, and that every burden is put upon his head alone—when thus both "his public rights and private interests are alike attacked the restraining influences on which the peace of civilised societies depends are dangerously weakened."

Sir Louis Mallet ends his Minute of 3rd February, 1875, on Indian Land Revenue with words which deserve attention as particularly applicable to the administration, management, and necessity of Indian expenditure.[2] He says: "By a perpetual interference with the operation of laws which our

[1] House of Commons, 15/8/1894.
[2] Par. Return [c. 3086-1], 1881, p. 135.

own rule in India has set in motion, and which I venture to think are essential to success—by a constant habit of palliating symptoms instead of grappling with disease—may we not be leaving to those who come after a task so aggravated by our neglect or timidity that what is difficult for us may be impossible for them ?"

I understand that every witness that comes before the Commission will not be considered as of any party, or to support this or that side, but as a witness of the Commission coming for the simple object of helping the Commission in finding out the actual whole truth of every question under consideration.

I shall esteem it a favour if, at the next meeting, you will be so good as to place this letter before the Commission. I may mention that I am sending a copy to every member of the Commission, in order that they may be made acquainted beforehand with its contents.

Yours truly,

DADABHAI NAOROJI.

II.

National Liberal Club,

4th December, 1895.

DEAR LORD WELBY,—Referring to the first part of the reference to our Commission, it is necessary to know—as one of the most important tests—the Results of the present system of the Administration and Management of Expenditure in the Moral and Material Condition of India. With this view Parliament itself enacted (1858) (21 and 22 Vic., Cap. 106, Sec. LIII.) to lay before it "a Statement prepared from detailed reports from each Presidency and district in India in such form as shall best exhibit the moral and material progress and condition of India in each such Presidency."

On some aspects of this branch of the Enquiry, viz., Results, I beg to place before you and the Commission my correspondence with the Secretary of State for India (see *supra* pp. 145-230). In my first letter to the Secretary of State for India, at (*supra*) page 147, I have referred to, and forwarded with it, some papers read by me in 1876 (see *supra* pp. 1-142).

At (*supra*) page 173, the reply of the Secretary of State for India refers to an enclosure in it of statistics. These statistics are not printed in the enclosed book. I therefore send herewith the only copy I have.

I shall feel much obliged by your kindly placing this letter and the enclosures before the Commission at the next meeting. In the meantime I shall send a copy of this letter and the book to every member of the Commission.

Yours truly,

DADABHAI NAOROJI.

III.

National Liberal Club,
London, S.W.

9th January, 1896.

DEAR LORD WELBY,—I now submit to the Commission a further representation upon the most important test of the present "Administration and Management of Expenditure," viz., its results.

Kindly oblige me by laying it before the Commission at the next meeting. I shall send a copy of it to every member of the Commission. As the reference to the Commission embraces a number of most vital questions—vital both to England and India—I am obliged to submit my representation in parts. When I have finished I shall be willing, if the Commission think it necessary, to appear as a witness to be cross-examined upon my representations. If the Commission think that I should be examined on each of my representations separately, I shall be willing to be so examined.

In the Act of 1858 (sec. LIII) Parliament provided that among other information for its guidance the Indian authorities should lay before it every year "A Statement prepared from detailed Reports from each Presidency and District in India, in such form as shall best exhibit the Moral and Material Progress and Condition of India in each such Presidency." Thereupon such Reports were ordered by the Government of India to be prepared by the Government of each Presidency.

As a beginning the Reports were naturally imperfect in details. In 1862 the Government of India observed: "There is a mass of statistics in the Administration Reports of the various Local Governments . . . . but they are not compiled on any uniform plan . . . . so as to show the statistics of the Empire" (Fin. Con., June, '62). The Statistical Committee, which the Government of India had organised for the purpose, prepared certain Forms of Tables, and after receiving reports on those forms from the different governments made a Report to the Government of India, with revised Forms of Tables (Office Memorandum, Financial Department, No. 1,043, dated 28/2/66). The members of this Committee were Mr. A. Grote, president, and Messrs. G. Campbell, D. Cowie, and G. Smith.

I confine myself in this statement to the tables concerning only the material condition of India, or what are called "Production and Distribution."

The following are the tables prescribed :—

PRODUCTION AND DISTRIBUTION.

FORM D.—AGRICULTURE.

Under a former Section provision is made for information regarding soils so far as nature is concerned, and we have now to do with what the soil produces, and with all that is necessary to till the soil, all of which is embraced under the heads—Crop, Stock, Rent, and Production.

CROPS CULTIVATED IN ACRES, ACTUAL OR APPROXIMATE.—1.

Name of District	Rice	Wheat	Other Food Grains	Oil Seeds	Sugar	Cotton	Opium	Indigo	Fibres	Tobacco	Tea	Coffee	Vegetables, &c., &c.
Total													

STOCK.—2.

District	Cows and Buffaloes	Horses	Ponies	Donkeys	Sheep and Goats	Pigs	Carts	Ploughs	Boats
Total									

RATES OF RENT AND PRODUCE.—3.

District	Average Rent per Acre for Land suited for									
	Rice	Wheat	Inferior Grains	Indigo	Cotton	Opium	Oil Seeds	Fibres	Sugar	Tobacco
General Average										

Average Produce of Land per Acre in lbs.

District	Rice	Wheat	Inferior Food Grains	Indigo	Cotton	Opium	Oil Seeds	Fibres	Sugar	Tobacco	Tea	Coffee, &c., &c.
General Average												

FORM E.

Price of Produce and Labour at the end of the year.

PRODUCE.—1.

Price of Produce per maund of 80 lbs.

District	Rice	Wheat	Linseed	Jute	Cotton	Sugar	Salt	&c., &c.
General Average								

Prices—*continued.*				LABOUR.—2.						
				Wages per diem.						
Plough Bullocks each	Sheep each	Fish per seer	Iron per maund, &c., &c.	District	Skilled	Unskilled	Cart per day	Camel per day	Donkeys per score per day	Boat per ditto
				General average						

NOTE.—The general character of the staple of the district should be stated as "Cotton, Indigenous," "Cotton, New Orleans," "Sugar, Raw," "Sugar, Refined," "Salt, Rock," "Salt, Samber Lake," and so on.

FORM F.

MINES AND QUARRIES.

Where Situated	Mineral Produced	Number of Mines	Annual Produce	Remarks

FORM G.—MANUFACTURES.

	Class of Manufactures.								
	Silk	Cotton	Wool	Other Fibres	Paper	Wood	Iron	Brass and Copper	Building, &c., &c.
Number of Mills and Manufactories									
Private Looms or Small Works									
Number of Workmen in Large Works: Female									
Number of Workmen in Large Works: Male									
Number of Workmen in Small Works or Independent Artizans									
Number of European Superintendents in Large Works									
Value of block in ditto									
Estimated Annual Outturn of all Works									
Total									

It will be seen from these tables that they are sufficient for calculating the total "production" of any province, with such additions for sundry other produce as may be necessary, with sufficient approximacy to accuracy, to supply the information which Parliament wants to know about the progress or deterioration of the material condition of India.

Sir David Barbour said, in reply to a question put by Sir James Peile:—

"2283. It does not by any means follow that people are starving because they are poor?—Not in the least. You must recollect that the cost of the necessaries of life is very much less in India than it is in England."

Now the question is, whether, even with this "very much less cost" of the necessaries and wants of life, these necessaries and wants of life even to an absolute amount, few as they are, are supplied by the "production of the year." Sir D. Barbour and others that speak on this point have not given any proof that even these cheap and few wants are supplied, with also a fair reserve for bad seasons. It is inexplicable why the Statistical Committee failed to prescribe the tables for the necessary consumption—or, as the heading of Form D. called "Distribution"—if they really meant to give Parliament such full information as to enable it to judge whether "the mass of the people," as Lord Lawrence said, "lived on scanty subsistence" or not. The Statistical Committee has thus missed to ask this other necessary information, viz., the wants of a common labourer to keep himself and his family in ordinary, healthy working condition—in food, clothing, shelter, and other necessary ordinary social wants. It is by the comparison of what is *produced* and what is *needed* by the people even for the absolute necessaries of life (leave alone any luxuries) that anything like a fair idea of the condition of the people can be formed. In my first letter to the Secretary of State for India, of 24th May, 1880, I have worked out as an illustration all the necessary tables both for "production" and "distribution," *i.e.*, absolute necessaries of life of a common labourer in Punjab.

If the demands of Parliament are to be loyally supplied (which, unfortunately, is almost invariably not the attitude of Indian authorities in matters concerning the welfare of the Indians and honour of the British name depending thereon) there is no reason whatever why the information required is not fully furnished by every province. They have all the necessary materials for these tables, and they can easily supply the tables both for "production" and "distribution" or necessary consumption, at the prices of the year of all necessary wants. Then the Statistical Department ought to work up the average per head per annum for the whole of India of both "production" and "distribution." Unless such information is supplied, it is idle and useless to endeavour to persuade the Commission that the material condition of the people of British India is improving. It was said in the letter of the Secretary of State for India to me of 9th August, 1880, that in Bengal means did not exist of supplying the information I desired. Now that may have been the case in 1880, but it is not so now; and I cannot understand why the Bengal Government does not give the tables of production at all in its Administration Report. The only table, and that the most important one, for which it was said they had not the means, and which was not given in the Administration Report, is given in detail in the "Statistical Abstract of British India for 1893-4" (Parl. Ret. [C. 7,887] 1895), pp. 141-2.

No. 73.—Crops Under Cultivation in 1893-4 (p. 141).
Administration—Bengal.

ACRES.

Rice.	Wheat.	Other Food Grains (including Pulses).	Other Food Crops.	Sugar Cane.	Coffee.
38,200,300	1,620,200	11,636,000	3,130,900	1,083,400	......

ACRES—*continued*.

Tea.	Cotton.	Jute.	Other Fibres.	Oil Seeds.	Indigo.
110,800	201,280	2,228,200	207,100	3,253,000	614,200

ACRES—*continued.*

Tobacco.	Cinchona.	Miscellaneous.	Total area under crops.	Deduct area cropped more than once.	Actual Area on which crops were grown.
730,500	2,900	424,900	64,444,200	10,456,900	53,987,300

Then, at page 142, there is also given total area under crops—of area under irrigation—64,444,200 acres. Certainly, if they can know the total area, they can ascertain the average of some of the principal crops. Then as to the crops per acre of some of the principal produce, they can have no difficulty in ascertaining, and the prices are all regularly published of principal articles of food. There can be no difficulty in obtaining the prices of all principal produce. The whole matter is too important to be so lightly treated. The extreme importance of this information can be seen from the fact that Parliament has demanded it by an Act, and that Sir Henry Fowler himself made a special and earnest challenge about the condition of the people. He said in his speech on 15th August, 1894, when he promised the Select Committee :—

"The question I wish to consider is whether that Government, with all its machinery as now existing in India, has or has not promoted the general prosperity of the people in its charge; and whether India is better or worse off by being a Province of the British Crown."

And this is the question to which an answer has to be given by this Commission—whether the present administration and management of the Military and Civil Expenditure incurred in both countries, "has or has not," as one of its results, "promoted the general prosperity of the people" of British India. Or is, or is not, the result of this administration and management of expenditure "scanty subsistence" for the mass of the people as admitted by Lord Lawrence, and "extreme poverty" as stated by Lord Cromer, Sir Auckland Colvin, and Sir David Barbour among the latest Finance Ministers—a poverty compared with which even the most oppressed and misgoverned Russia is prosperity itself, the income of which is given by Mulhall as above £9 per head per annum, when Lord Cromer gives the income of British

India as "not more than Rs. 27 per head per annum," and I calculate it as not more than Rs. 20 per head per annum. Even this wretched income, insufficient as it is, is not all enjoyed by the people, but a portion never returns to them, thereby continuously though gradually diminishing their individual capacity for production. Surely there cannot be a more important issue before the Commission as to the results of the administration and management of expenditure, as much or even more for the sake of Britain itself than for that of India.

Before proceeding further on the subject of these statistics it is important to consider the matter of the few wants of the Indian in an important aspect. Is the few wants a reason that the people should not prosper, should not have better human wants and better human enjoyments? Is that a reason that they ought not to produce as much wealth as the British are producing here? Once the Britons were wandering in the forests of this country, and their wants were few; had they remained so for ever what would Britain have been to-day? Has not British wealth grown a hundred times, as Macaulay has said? And is it not a great condemnation of the present British administration of Indian expenditure that the people of India cannot make any wealth—worse than that, they must die off by millions, and be underfed by scores of millions, produce a wretched produce, and of that even somebody else must deprive them of a portion!

The British first take away their means, incapacitate them from producing more, compel them to reduce their wants to the wretched means that are left to them, and then turn round upon them and, adding insult to injury, tell them: "See, you have few wants; you must remain poor and of few wants. Have your pound of rice—or, more generously, we would allow you two pounds of rice—scanty clothing and shelter. It is we who must have and would have great human wants and human enjoyments, and you must slave and drudge for us like mere animals, as our beasts of burden." Is it that the mass of the Indians have no right or business to have any advancement in civilisation, in life and life's enjoyments, physical, moral, mental and social? Must they always live to the brute's level—must have no social expenses—is that all extravagance, stupidity, want of intelligence, and what not? Is it seriously held, in the words of

Lord Salisbury: "They (the Natives of India) know perfectly well that they are governed by a superior race" (*Hansard*, vol. 277, 9/4/83, page 1,798), and that that superior race should be the masters, and the Indians the slaves and beasts of burden? Why the British-Indian authorities and Anglo-Indians generally (of course with honourable and wise exceptions) do every mortal thing to disillusion the Indians of the idea of any superiority by open violation and dishonour of the most solemn pledges, by subtle bleeding of the country, and by obstructing at every point any step desired by the British people for the welfare of the Indians. I do hope, as I do believe, that both the conscience and the aspiration of the British people, their mission and charge, which it is often said Providence has placed in their hands, are to *raise* the Indians to their own level of civilisation and prosperity, and not to degrade themselves to the lowness of Oriental despotism and the Indians to mere helots.

I may here again point out some defects in these statistics so as to make them as accurate as they can possibly be made, in supplying the Commission with the necessary information. It is surprising that Indian highly-paid civilians should not understand the simple arithmetic of averages; and that they should not correct the mistake even after the Secretary of State for India forwarded my letter pointing out the mistake.

The mistake is this. Supposing the price of rice in one district is R. 1 per maund, and in another district Rs. 3 per maund, then the average is taken by simply adding 3 and 1 and dividing by 2, making it to be Rs. 2 per maund, forgetting altogether to take into account the quantities sold at Rs. 3 and R. 1 respectively. Supposing the quantity sold at R. 1 per maund is 1,000,000 maunds and that sold at Rs. 3 is only 50,000 maunds, then the correct average will be :—

	Maunds.		Rs.		Rs.
	1,000,000	×	1	=	1,000,000
	50,000	×	3	=	150,000
Total . .	1,050,000				1,150,000

which will give Rs. 1 1 an. 6 pies per maund, instead of the incorrect Rs. 2 per maund, as is made out by simply adding 1 and 3 and dividing by 2.

In my "Poverty of India" I have given an actual illustration (*supra* pp. 3-4). The average price of rice in the

Administration Report of the Central Provinces for 1867-8 was made out to be, by the wrong method, Rs. 2 12 an. 7 pies, while the correct price was only Rs. 1 8 an. Also the correct average of produce was actually 759 lbs. per acre, when it was incorrectly made out to be 579 lbs. per acre. Certainly there is no excuse for such arithmetical mistakes in information required by Parliament for the most important purpose of ascertaining the result of the British Administration of the expenditure of a vast country.

In the same way averages are taken of wages without considering how many earn the different wages of 1½, 2, 3 or more annas per day and for how many days in the year.

In the Irish Commission you yourself and the Chairman have noticed this fallacy.

Witness, Dr. T. W. Grimshaw.

Question 2925. (Lord Welby): Do you take a mean price?—I take a mean price between highest and lowest.

2926. (Chairman): An arithmetical mean price without reference to the quantities?—Yes.

2927. (Lord Welby): For instance, supposing for nine months there had been a low price, and the remaining three a high price, the mean would hardly represent a real mean, would it?—You are correct in a certain sense. . . . .

Trade.—Totals are taken of both imports and exports together and any increase in these totals is pointed out as proof of a flourishing trade and increasing benefit when in reality it is no such thing, but quite the reverse altogether. I shall explain what I mean.

Suppose a merchant sends out goods to a foreign country which have cost him £1,000. He naturally expects to get back the £1,000 and some profit, say 15 per cent.; *i.e.*, he expects to receive back £1,150. This will be all right; and suppose he sends out more, say £2,000 worth, the next year and gets back his £2,300, then it is really an increasing and profitable trade. But suppose a merchant sent out goods worth £1,000 and gets back £800 instead of £1,150 or anything above £1,000; and again the second year he sent £2,000 worth and got back £1,600. To say that such a trade is a flourishing or profitable trade is simply absurd. To say that because the total of the exports and imports of the first year was £1,800, and the total of the exports and imports in the second year was £3,600, that therefore it was a cause for rejoicing, when in reality it is simply a straight way to bankruptcy with a loss of £200 the first year, and £400 the second year (leaving alone profits), and so on. Such is the condition of British India. Instead of getting back its exports with some profit, it does not get back even equal to the exports themselves, but a great deal less every year. Why then, it may be asked, does India not go into bankruptcy as any merchant would inevitably go? And the reason is very simple. The ordinary merchant has no power to put his hand in other persons' pockets, and make up his losses. But the despotic Government of India, on the one hand, goes on inflicting on India unceasing losses and drain by its unnatural administration and management of expenditure, and, on the other hand, has the power of putting its hands unhindered into the pockets of the poor taxpayer and make its account square.

While the real and principal cause of the sufferings and poverty of India is the deprivation and drain of its resources by foreigners by the present system of expenditure, the Anglo-Indians generally, instead of manfully looking this evil in the face, ignore it, and endeavour to find all sorts of other excuses. It is very necessary that the Commission should have the opportunity of fairly considering those excuses. Now, one way I can deal with them would be for myself to lay them down as I understand them; or, which is far better, I should deal with them as they are actually put forth by some high Anglo-Indian official. As I am in a position to do so, I adopt the second course. A high official of the position of an Under-Secretary of State for India and Governor of Madras, Sir Grant Duff, has already focussed all the official reasons in two papers he contributed to the *Contemporary Review*, and I have answered them in the same *Review* in 1887. I cannot therefore do better than to embody my reply here, omitting from it all personal remarks or others irrelevant to the present purpose. In connexion with my reply, I may explain here that it is because I have taken in it £1 = Rs. 10 that the incidence of taxation is set down as 6s. per head per annum, while Sir H. Fowler's estimate is only 2s. 6d. per head at the present depressed exchange and excluding land revenue. Sir H. Fowler excludes land revenue from the incidence as if land revenue, by being called "rent," rained from heaven, and was not raised as much from the production of the country as any other part of the revenue. The fact of the matter is that in British India as in every other country, a certain portion of the production of the country is taken by the State, under a variety of names—land tax or rent, salt revenue, excise, opium, stamps, customs, assessed taxes, post office surplus, law and justice surplus, etc., etc. In some shape or other so much is taken from the production, and which forms the incidence of taxation. The evil which India suffers from is not in what is raised or taken from the "production" and what India, under natural administration, would be able to give two or three times over, but it is in the manner in which that revenue is spent under the present unnatural administration and management of expenditure whereby there is an unceasing "bleeding" of the country.

My reply to Sir Grant Duff was made in 1887. This brings some of the figures to a later date than my correspondence with the Secretary of State for India. Single-handed I have not the time to work out figures to date, but I shall add afterwards some figures which I have already worked out for later than 1887. I give below my reply to Sir Grant Duff as I have already indicated above.

All the subjects treated in the following extracts are the direct consequences of the present system of "the administration and management of expenditure in both countries." It is from this point of view that I give these extracts. (See my reply, in August and November, 1887, to Sir Grant Duff, *supra*, pp. 231-272.)

I give below some of the latest figures I already have to compare the results of the administration of expenditure in India with those of other parts of the British Empire.

TEN YEARS (1883-1892).

Countries.	Imports (including Gold and Silver). £	Exports (including Gold and Silver). £	Excess of Imports over Exports. £	Percentage of Trade Profits
United Kingdom . . . (Par. Ret. [C.7,143] 1893.)	4,247,954,247	3,203,603,246	1,044,351,001	32
Australasia	643,462,379	582,264,839	61,197,540	10·5[1]
North American Colonies	254,963,473	205,063,294	49,900,179	24·4
Straits Settlements . . (Par. Ret. [C.7,144] 1893.)	204,613,643	181,781,667	22,831,976	12·5

[1] Australasia is a large gold and silver exporting country. Profits on this are a very small percentage. The profits on other produce or merchandise will be larger than 10·5 per cent., and it should also be borne in

CAPE OF GOOD HOPE AND NATAL. I cannot give figures, as the gold brought into the Colonies from Transvaal is not included in the imports; while exports include gold and silver.

NATAL. In this also goods in transit are not included in imports, although included in exports.

BRITISH INDIA. Far from any excess of imports or trade profits, there is, as will be seen further on, actually a large deficit in imports (Rx. 774,099,570) from the actual exports (Rx. 944,279,318). Deficit from its own produce (Rx.170,179,748)—18 per cent.

INDIA.

Particulars of the Trade of India and the losses of the Indian people of British India; or, The Drain.

TEN YEARS (1883-1892). (Return [C. 7,193,] 1893.)

India's total Exports, including Treasure.	
Rx. 944,279,318	
,, 188,855,863	Add, as in other countries, say 20 per cent. excess of imports or profits (U.K. is 32 per cent.).
Rx. 1,133,135,181	or the amount which the imports should be. But
,, 774,099,570	only are the actual imports.
Rx. 359,035,611	is the loss of India for which it has not received back a single farthing either in Merchandise or treasure.

Now the question is what has become of this Rx.359,000,000 which India *ought* to have received but has not received.

This amount includes the payment of interest on railway and other public works loans.

Owing to our impoverishment, our utter helplessness, subjection to a despotism without any voice in the administration of our expenditure, our inability to make any capital, and, therefore, forced to submit to be exploited by foreign capital, every farthing of the above amount is a loss and a drain to British India. We have no choice; the whole position is compulsory upon us. It is no simple matter of

mind that Australasia, like India, is a borrowing country, and a portion of its exports, like that of India, goes for the payment of interest on foreign loans. Still, it not only pays all that interest from the profits of trade, but secures for itself also a balance of 10·5 per cent. profits, while India must not only lose all its profits of trade but also Rx. 170,000,000 of its own produce. Were India not "bleeding" politically it would also be in a similar condition of paying for its loans and securing something for itself out of the trade profits.

business to us. It is all simply the result of the despotic administration of expenditure of our resources.

Still, however, let us consider these loans as a matter of business, and see what deduction we should make from the above amount.

The loans for public works during the ten years (Par. Ret. [c. 7193] 1893, p. 298) are:—Rx. 34,350,000 (this is taken as Rs. 10 = £1—p. 130), or £34,350,000. This amount is received by India, and forms a part of its imports.

The interest paid during the ten years in England is £57,700,000. This amount, being paid by India, forms a part of its exports. The account, then, will stand thus:—

India received or imported as loans £34,350,000 in the ten years. India paid or exported as interest £57,700,000, leaving an excess of exports as a business balance £23,350,000, or, say, at average 1s. 4d. per rupee, Rx. 37,360,000.

This export made by India in settlement of public works loans interest account may be deducted from the above unaccounted amount of Rx. 359,000,000, leaving a balance of Rx. 321,640,000 still unreceived by India.

The next item to be considered is public debt (other than for public works). This debt is not a business debt in any possible way. It is simply the political burden put upon India by force for the very acquisition and maintenance of the British rule. It is entirely owing to the evil administration of expenditure in putting every burden on India. Make an allowance for even this forced tribute.

The public debt of India (excluding public works) incurred during the ten years is £16,000,000 (p. 298), of which, say, £8,000,000 has interest to be paid in London. (I do not know how much is raised in India and how much in England. I think I asked the India Office for this, but it is difficult to get definite information from it.) The interest paid in London during the ten years is £28,600,000. This forms part of the exports of India. The £8,000,000 of the debt incurred during the ten years form part of the imports of India, leaving a balance of, say, £21,000,000. On public debt account to be further deducted from the last balance of unaccounted loss of Rx. 321,640,000, taking £21,000,000 at 1s. 4d. per rupee will give about Rx. 33,000,000, which, deducted from Rx. 321,640,000, will still leave the unaccounted loss or drain of Rx. 288,000,000. I repeat that as far as the economic effect on India of the despotic administration and management of expenditure under the British rule is concerned, the whole amount of Rx. 359,000,000 is a drain from the wretched resources of India.

But to avoid controversy, allowing for all public debt (political and commercial), there is still a clear loss or drain of Rx. 288,000,000 in ten years, with a debt of £210,000,000 hanging round her neck besides.

Rx. 288,000,000 is made up of Rx. 170,000,000 from the very blood or produce of the country itself, and Rx. 118,000,000 from the profits of trade.

It must be also remembered that freight, insurance, and other charges after shipment are not calculated in the exports from India, every farthing of which is taken by England. When these items are added to the exports the actual loss to British India will be much larger than the above calculations. I may also explain that the item of stores is accounted for in the above calculations. The exports include payment for these stores, and imports include the stores. The whole of the above loss and burden of debt has to be borne by only the Indian taxpayers of *British India.* The Native States and their capitalists, bankers, merchants, or manufacturers, and the European capitalists, merchants, bankers, or manufacturers get back their full profits.

In the above calculation I have taken 20 per cent. as what ought to be the excess of imports under natural circumstances, just as the excess of the United Kingdom is 32 per cent. But suppose I take even 15 per cent. instead of 20 per cent., then the excess of imports would be, say, Rx. 311,000,000 instead of nearly Rx. 359,000,000. From this Rx. 311,000,000, deduct, as above, Rx. 37,000,000 for public works account and Rx. 33,000,000 for political public debt account, there will still be a loss or drain of Rx. 241,000,000 in ten years.

Strictly considered in India's helpless condition, there has been a drain of its wealth to the extent of Rx. 360,000,000 in the ten years.

But, as I have said, to avoid all futile controversy, after allowing fully for all debt, there is still a drain of Rx. 241,000,000 or Rx. 24,000,000 a year during the ten years.

But it must be also remembered that besides the whole of the above drain, either Rx. 359,000,000, or Rx. 241,000,000, there is also the further loss of all that is consumed in India itself by foreigners so far, to the deprivation and exclusion of the children of British India.

Now let it be once more understood that there can be no objection to any capitalist, or banker, or merchant, or manufacturer going to India on his own account and making any profits there, *if we are also left free to do our best in fair competition*, but as long as we are impoverished and made utterly helpless in our economic condition by the forced and unnatural present system of the administration and management of expenditure, the whole profits of foreigners (European or Indian) is British India's irreparable loss.

The moral, therefore, of this phenomenon is that Sir John Shore's prediction of 1787, about the evil effect of foreign domination by the adoption of the present system of the administration and management of expenditure, is amply and deplorably fulfilled. Truly has Macaulay said: "The heaviest of all yokes is the yoke of the stranger." It cannot be otherwise under the existing administration and management of expenditure. What an enormous sum, almost beyond calculation, would British India's loss amount to in the present century (leaving alone the last century of unparalleled corruption, plunder, and oppression by Europeans) when calculated with compound interest! A tremendously "cruel and crushing" and destructive tribute indeed!

With regard to the allegation that the fall in exchange has stimulated exports from India, here are a few figures which tell their own tale :—

Exports in 1870-1	Rx. 64,690,000
" " 1890-1	Rx. 102,340,000

or an increase of about 60 per cent. This is the increase in the 20 years of the fall of exchange.

Now take 1850, exports	£18,700,000
" " 1870, "	£64,690,000

i.e., an increase of nearly 3½ times. Was this increase owing to fall in Exchange? There was then no such fall in exchange. And what good was this increase to India? As shown above, in ten years only she has been drained to the extent indicated, besides what is eaten in the country by those who are not her children. The increase in trade, excepting that of Native and Frontier States, is not natural and economic for the benefit of the people of *British* India. It is mostly only the form in which the increasing crushing tribute and the trade-profits and wants of foreigners are provided by the poor people of British India, the masses of whom live on scanty subsistence, and are ill-fed, ill-clothed, and ill-habited hewers of wood and drawers of water for them.

But there is another most important consideration still remaining.

While British India is thus crushed by a heavy tribute which is exacted by the upper classes and which must end in disaster, do the British industrial people, or the great mass, derive such benefit as they ought to derive, with far greater benefit to England itself, besides benefitting India?

Here is this wretched result so far as the producers of British and Irish produce are concerned, or the British trade with India is concerned.

In 1893 all British and Irish produce exported to all India is only £28,800,000 for a population of 285,000,000, or 2s. per head per annum. But a large portion of this goes to the Native States and frontier territories. British Indian subjects themselves (221,000,000) will be found to take hardly a shilling or fifteen pence worth per head per annum. And this is all that the British people export to British India. If British India were more righteously treated and allowed to prosper, British produce will be exported to British India as much or a great deal more than what the British people are exporting to the whole world. A word to our Lancashire friends. If they would open their eyes to their true interests, and give up squabbling about these wretched cotton duties, they would see that a market of 220,000,000 people of British India, besides the 64,000,000 of the Native States, will require and take (if you take your hand off their throat), more than Lancashire will be able to supply. Look at the wretched Lancashire trade with the poverty-stricken British Indians:—

In 1892-3 India imported yarn £ 2,683,850 }
Manufactures £22,942,015 } = £25,625,865

for a population of 285,000,000, or about 1s. 9d. per head per annum. But if you deduct Native States and Frontier States, it will possibly be 1s. per head for British India. Why should it not be even £1 or more per head if British India be not "bled"? And Lancashire may have £250,000,000 or more of trade instead of the wretched £25,000,000. Will

Lancashire ever open its eyes, and help both itself and India to be prosperous?

ARGUMENT OF POPULATION.

Increase from 1881 to 1891:—

	Increase.	Population per Square Mile.
England and Wales	11·6 per cent.	. 500
British India	9·7 ,,	. 230

In 1801 the population of England and Wales (Mulhall's Dictionary, p. 444) was 8,893,000, say 9,000,000.

In 1884 the population was 27,000,000 (Parl. Ret. [c. 7,143], 1893), or three times as much as in 1801.

The income of England and Wales (Mul., p. 320) in 1800 was £230,000,000.

In 1884, while the population increased to 27,000,000, or three times that of 1801, the income increased to £976,000,000 (Mul., p. 321), or nearly 4¼ times that of 1800.

The population of England and Wales (Mul., p. 444) in 1672 was 5,500,000. The income in 1664 (Mul., p. 320) was £42,000,000.

In 1884 (Mul., p. 321), population 27,000,000, increased five times; income £976,000,000, increased more than twenty-three times.

As comparison with earlier times Macaulay said (*supra*, p. 269): "While our numbers have increased tenfold, our wealth has increased hundredfold."

These facts do not show that increase of population has made England poorer. On the contrary, Macaulay truly says "that the advantages arising from the progress of civilisation have far more than counterbalanced the disadvantages arising from the progress of population."

Why, then, under the administration of the "greatest" and most highly-paid service in the world, derived from the same stock as the administrators of this country, and, as Mr. Bright says, "whose praises are so constantly sounded in this House," is India, after a long period, at present the most "extremely poor" country in the world? And yet how can the result be otherwise under the existing administration and management of expenditure, based upon the evil principle that "India must be bled"? The fault is not of the officials. It is the evil and outrageous system of expenditure, which cannot but produce such pernicious and deplorable results, which, if not remedied in time, must inevitably bring about a retribution the extent and disaster of which can hardly be conceived. Officials over and over again tell us that the resources of India are boundless. All the resources of civilisation have been at their command, and here is this wretched and ignominious result—that while England has gone on increasing in wealth at a greater progress than in population, India at this moment is far poorer than even the misgoverned and oppressed Russia, and poorer even than Turkey in its annual production, as Lord Cromer pointed out in 1882.

I think I need not say anything more upon the first part of our Reference. If I am required to be cross-examined on the representations which I have submitted, I shall then say whatever more may be necessary for me to say.

I have shown, by high authorities and by facts and figures, one result of the existing system of "The administration and management of the Military and Civil Expenditure incurred under the authority of the Secretary of State for India in Council, or of the Government of India"—viz., the most deplorable evil of the extreme poverty of the mass of the people of British India—suicidal and dishonourable to British name and rule, and destructive and degrading to the people of British India, with a "helot system" of administration instead of that of British citizenship.

The following remarks in a leader of the *Times* of 16th December, 1895, in connexion with the Transvaal, is, short of compulsory service, applicable with ten times more force to the British rule of British India. The *Times* says:—

"The time is past even in South Africa when a helot system of administration organised for the exclusive advantage of a privileged minority can long resist the force of enlightened public opinion. If President Kruger really possesses any of those statesmanlike qualities which are sometimes ascribed to him, he will hasten to accept the loyal co-operation of these *Ouitlanders*, who have already done so much and who are anxious to do more for the prosperity and progress of the South African Republic."

I would apply this to British India. The time is past in British India when a "helot system of administration," organised for the exclusive advantage of a privileged minority, and existing to the great dishonour of the British name for a century and a half, can long resist the force of enlightened public opinion, and the dissatisfaction of the people themselves. If the British statesmen of the present day possess those statesmanlike qualities which the statesmen of 1833 showed about India—to "be just and fear not," which the great Proclamation of 1858 proclaimed to the world, and which Sir H. Fowler so lately (3/9/'95) described as having "the courage of keeping our word"—they will hasten to accept the loyal co-operation of the people of India, with whose blood mainly, and with whose money entirely, has the British Indian Empire been both built up and maintained; from whom Britain has drawn thousands of millions, or untold wealth calculated with interest; who for British righteousness would return the most devoted and patriotic loyalty for their own sake, and whose prosperity and progress, as Lord Roberts said, being indissolubly bound up with those of Britain, would result in largely increasing the prosperity of the British people themselves, in the stability of the British rule and in the redemption of the honour and good name of Britain from the dishonour of many broken pledges. The deplorable evil result of the present "administration and management of expenditure," in violation of solemn pledges, is so subtle, so artistic, so unobservably "bleeding," to use Lord Salisbury's word, so plausibly masked with the face of beneficence, and being unaccompanied with any open compulsion or violence to person or property which the world can see and be horrified with, that, as the poet says :—

> "Those lofty souls have telescopic eyes,
> That see the smallest speck of distant pain,
> While at their feet a world of agony,
> Unseen, unheard, unheeded, writhes in vain."
>
> —*Great Thoughts*, 31/8/'95.

Even a paper like the *Pioneer* of Allahabad (21/9/'95) which cannot be accused of being opposed to Anglo-Indian views, recognises that India "has also perhaps to undergo the often subtle disadvantages of foreign rule." Yes, it is these "*subtle* disadvantages of foreign rule" which need to be grappled with and removed, if the connexion between India and England is to be a blessing to both, instead of a curse. This is the great and noble task for our Commission. For, indeed, it would be wise to ponder whether and how far Lord Salisbury's—a statesman's—words at the last Lord Mayor's dinner, apply to British India. He said :—

"That above all treaties and above all combinations of external powers, 'the nature of things' if you please, or 'the providence of

God,' if you please to put it so, has determined that persistent and constant misgovernment must lead the government which follows it to its doom; and while I readily admit that it is quite possible for the Sultan of Turkey, if he will, to govern all his subjects in justice and in peace, he is not exempt more than any other potentate from the law that injustice will bring the highest on earth to ruin."

The administration of expenditure should be based on this principle, as Sir Louis Mallet (c. 3086—1) 1881, p. 142, has said :—

"If India is to be maintained and rendered a permanent portion of the British Empire, this must be accomplished in some other way than by placing our future reliance on the empirical arts of despotism" and not on those low motives of making India as simply an exploiting ground for our "boys" as Sir C. Crossthwaite desired when he had the candour of expressing the motive of British action when speaking about Siam at the Society of Arts (vol. 39—19/2/'92—p. 286). All that gentleman cared for was this. "The real question was who was to get the trade with them and how we could make the most of them, so as to find fresh markets for our goods and *also employment for those superfluous articles of the present day, our boys*" (the italics are mine), as if the whole world was created simply for supplying markets to the one people, and employment to their boys. Still, however, you can have ten times more trade than you have at present with India, far more than you have at present with the whole world, if you act on lines of righteousness, and cast off the second mean motive to enslave other people to give employment to your "boys," which certainly is not the motive of the British people. The short of the whole matter is, that under the present evil and unrighteous administration of Indian expenditure, the romance is the beneficence of the British rule, the reality is the "bleeding" of the British rule. Under a righteous "administration of expenditure," the reality will be the blessing and benefit both to Britain and India, and far more trade between them than we can form any conception of at present.

Yours truly,

DADABHAI NAOROJI.

IV.

National Liberal Club,
London, S.W.

15th February, 1896.

DEAR LORD WELBY,—I now request your favour of laying before the Commission this letter of my views on the second part of the Reference, viz., "The apportionment of charge between the Governments of the United Kingdom and of India for purposes in which both are interested."

The word England, or Britain, is always used by me as embracing the United Kingdom.

I do not know whether there is any portion of the Indian charge (either in this country or in India) in which Britain is not interested. The one chief object of the whole expenditure of government is to govern India in a way to secure internal law and order and external protection. Now in both internal law and order and external protection, the interests of Britain are as great or rather greater than those of India. That India is protected from lawlessness and disorder is unquestionably a great boon and benefit to it. But orderly or disorderly India shall always remain and exist where it is, and will shape its own destiny somehow, well or badly. But without law and order British rule will not be able to keep its existence in India. British rule in India is not even like Russian rule in Russia. However bad and oppressive the latter may be, whatever revolution or Nihilism there may occur, whatever civil wars or secret disasters may take place, the Russians and their Rulers remain all the same in Russia; only that power changes from one hand into another, or from one form into another. Only a few days ago (18th January, 1896) the Russian Tsar, styling himself "Emperor and Autocrat of all the Russias," issued a Manifesto for his coronation as follows:—

"By the grace of God we, Nicholas II, Emperor and Autocrat of all the Russias, etc., make known to all our faithful subjects that, with the help of the Almighty, we have resolved to place upon ourselves the Crown, in May next, in the Ancient Capital of Moscow, after the example of the pious Monarchs our forefathers, and to receive the Holy Sacrament according to established usage; uniting with us in this Act our most beloved consort the Empress Alexandra Feodorovna.

"We call upon all our loyal subjects on the forthcoming solemn day of Coronation to share in our joy and to join us in offering up fervent prayers to the Giver of all good that He may pour out upon us the gifts of the Holy Spirit, that He may strengthen our Empire, and direct us to the footsteps of our parent of imperishable memory, whose life and labours for the welfare of our beloved fatherland will always remain a bright example.

"Given at St. Petersburg, this first day of January in the year of Our Lord 1896, and the second year of our reign.

"NICHOLAS."

—The *Times*, 20th January, 1896.

Now, blood is thicker than water. Notwithstanding all the autocratic oppression that the Russian people may have suffered for all past time, every soul will rise to the call, and rejoice in the joy of the occasion. And, whether the present system of government and power endures or vanishes, the Russian rule—whatever form it takes—will always be Russian, and for the Russians.

Take England itself. It beheaded one king, banished another, turned out its Parliament at the point of the bayonet, had civil wars of various durations, and disasters. Whatever was the change, it was English rule for Englishmen. But the British in India is quite a different thing. They are aliens, and any disaster to them there has entirely a different result. In the very first paper that was read before the East India Association of London (2/5/1867) I said:—

"No prophet is required to foretell the ultimate result of a struggle between a discontented two hundred millions and a hundred thousand foreign bayonets. A drop of water is insignificant, but an avalanche may somtimes carry everything before it. The race is not always to the swift. A disaffected nation may fail a hundred times, and may rise again; but one or two reverses to a foreigner cannot but be fatal. Every failure of the Natives, adding more burdens, will make them the more impatient to throw off the foreign yoke."

Can the British Sovereign call upon the Indians as she can call upon the British people, or as the Russian Tsar can call upon the Russians, to share in her joy? Yes, on one condition. The people of India must feel that, though the English Sovereign and people are not kindred in birth and blood, they are kindred in sympathetic spirit, and just in dealing; that, though they are the stepmother, they treat the step-children with all the affection of a mother—that the British rule is their own rule. The affection of the Indian people is the only solid foundation upon which an alien rule can stand firm and durable, or it may some day vanish like a dream.

To Britain all the law and order is the very breath of its nostrils in India. With law and order alone can it live in India. Let there arise disorder and violence to-morrow, and what will become of the small number of Europeans, official and non-official, without even any direct battles or military struggle?

If a thoroughly intelligent view of the position of Britain in India is taken the interests of Britain are equally vital, if not far more vital, in the maintenance of good and satisfactory government, and of law and order, than those of India; and, in a just view, all the charge or cost in both countries of such good government and law and order in India should be apportioned between the two countries, according to the importance of respective interests and to the proportion of the means or capacity of each partner in the benefit.

Certainly no fair and just-minded Englishman would say that Britain should have all the gain, glory, and every possible benefit of wealth, wisdom, and work of a mighty Empire, and the price or cost of it should be all burdened on the shoulders of India.

The correct judgment upon our second part of the reference will depend upon the fundamental principle upon which the British Administration ought to stand.

1. Is British rule for the good of both India and Britain, and a rule of justice and righteousness? or,

2. Is the British rule solely for the benefit of Britain at the destruction of India—or, in other words, the ordinary rule of foreign despotism, "the heaviest of all yokes, the yoke of the stranger" (Macaulay)?

The first is the avowed and deliberate desire and solemn promise and pledge of the British people. The second is the performance by the servants of the British nation—the Indian authorities—in the system of the administration adopted and relentlessly pursued by them.

The present British-Indian system of administration would not take long to degenerate and run into the Russian system and troubles, but for the check and drag of the British public wish, opinion, and voice.

Now, my whole argument in this representation will be based on the first principle—viz., the good of both India and England and justice and righteousness. I would, therefore, dispose of the second in a brief manner—that the second (England's benefit and India's destruction) is not the desire of the British people.

It has been the faith of my life, and it is my faith still, that the British people will do justice to India.

But, however, as unfortunately the system based on the second principle—the system which Lord Salisbury has described as of "bleeding" and "hypocrisy"—exists, it is desirable to remember the wise words of Lord Salisbury himself, uttered not long ago when he said (Lord Mayor's dinner on 9th November last): "'The nature of things' if you please, or 'the providence of God' if you please to put it so, has determined that persistent and constant misgovernment must lead the government which follows it to its doom . . . . that injustice will bring the highest on earth to ruin." The Duke of Devonshire has pointed out that the result of the present system would be to make the Indians to come to the conclusion that the Iudians shall never have any chance "except by their getting rid in the first instance of their European rulers."

The question is, do the British people desire such a system, to exercise only the right of brute force for their sole benefit? I for one, and I can say without any hesitation that all the educated and thinking Indians do not believe so. It is their deep faith and conviction that the conscience of tbe British people towards India is sound, and that if they once fully understood the true position they would sweep away the whole present unrighteous system. The very fact that this Commission is appointed for the first time for such a purpose, viz., to deal out fairly between the two countries an "apportionment of charge for purposes in which both are interested" is sufficient to show the awakening consciousness and desire to do justice and to share fairly the costs as well as the benefits. If further public indication was at all needed the *Times*, as I have quoted in my first representation, has put it very clearly: "Great Britain is anxious to deal fairly with India. If it should appear that India has been saddled with charges which the British taxpayer should have borne the British taxpayer will not hesitate to do his duty." I would not, therefore, pursue any further the assumption of the second principle of selfishness and despotism, but continue to base my remarks upon the basis of the first principle of the desire and determination of the British people for justice and righteousness towards India.

I have stated above that the whole cost of administration is vital to the very existence of the British rule in India, and largely essential to the prosperity of the British people. Lord Roberts, with other thoughtful statesmen, has correctly stated the true relation of the two countries more than once. Addressing the London Chamber of Commerce he said: "I rejoice to learn that you recognise how indissolubly the prosperity of the United Kingdom is bound up with the retention of that vast Eastern Empire" (*Times*, 25/5/93). And again, at Glasgow, he said "that the retention of our Eastern Empire is essential to the greatness and prosperity of the United Kingdom" (*Times*, 29/7/93). And further he also clearly points out upon what such an essential retention ultimately depends. Does it depend upon tyranny, injustice, bleeding hypocrisy, "plundering," upon imposing the relations of master and slave upon large, well equipped and efficient armies; on the unreliable props of brute force? No. He says, "But however efficient and well equipped the army of India may be, were it indeed absolute perfection, and were its numbers considerably more than they are at present, our greatest strength must ever rest on the firm base of a united and contented India." Sir William Harcourt said in his speech (House of Commons, 3/9/95), "As long as you have the people of India your friends, satisfied with the justice and policy of your rule, your Empire then will be safe."

Professor Wordsworth has said (*Bombay Gazette*, 3/3/83): "One of the greatest Englishmen of the last generation said that if ever we lost our Indian Empire we should lose it like every other we had lost, or were about to lose, by alienating the affections of the people."

Am I not then justified in asking that it is right and just, in order to acquire and preserve the affections of the people, that the cost of that administration which is essential to your "greatness" and your "prosperity," by which your prosperity is indissolubly bound up with that of India, and upon the secureness and law and order of which depends your very existence in India and as a great Empire, should be fairly shared by the United Kingdom?

Leaving this fair claim to the calm and fair consideration of this Commission and to the sense of justice of the British people, I take a less strict view of the duty of England. It is said that India should make all such payments as she would make for her government and her internal and external protection even if there were no British rule and only its own Native rule. Now suppose this is admitted, what is the position? Certainly in that case there will be no employment of Europeans. The present forced, inordinate, and arbitrary employment of Europeans in both the civil and military services in both countries is avowedly entirely and solely owing to British rule and *for British purposes and British interests*—to maintain British supremacy. If there were no British rule there would be no Europeans employed by the Native rulers. India accordingly may pay for every Indian employed, but justice demands that the expenditure on Europeans in both countries required for the sole interests of British rule and for British purposes should be paid by the British exchequer. I am not going to discuss here whether even British rule itself needs all the present civil and military European agency. On the contrary, the civil element is their greatest weakness, and will be swept away in the time of trouble from discontent and disaffection; and the military element, without being either efficient or sufficient in such crises, is simply destructive to India, and leading to the very disaster which is intended to be averted or prevented by it. Be this as it may, this much is clear: that the whole European agency, both civil and military, in England and in India is distinctly avowed and admitted to be for the interests of England, *i.e.*, to protect and maintain her supremacy in India against internal or external dangers. Lord Kimberley has put this matter beyond all doubt or controversy, that the European services are emphatically for the purpose of maintaining British supremacy. He says (dinner to Lord Roberts by the Lord Mayor—*Times*, 13th June, 1893):—

"There is one point upon which I imagine, whatever may be

our party politics in this country, we are all united; that we are resolutely determined to maintain our supremacy over our Indian Empire. That I conceive is a matter about which we have only one opinion, and let me tell you that that supremacy rests upon three distinct bases. One of those bases, and a very important one, is the loyalty and good-will of the Native Princes and population over whom we rule. Next, and not less important, is the maintenance of our European Civil Service, upon which rests the foundation of our administration in India. . . . Last, not because it is the least, but because I wish to give it the greatest prominence, we rest also upon the magnificent European force which we maintain in that country, and the splendid army of Native auxiliaries by which that force is supported. . . . Let us firmly and calmly maintain our position in that country; let us be thoroughly armed as to our frontier defences, and then I believe we may trust to the old vigour of the people of this country, come what may, to support our supremacy in that great Empire."

Now this is significant: while Lord Kimberley talks all these grand things, of resolute determination, etc., etc., to maintain British supremacy, and for all British purposes, he does not tell at whose cost. Is it at British cost, as it is for British purposes, or even any portion of that cost? He has not told the British public openly that it is for every farthing at the cost of the Indians, who are thus treated as mere slaves—all the gain, glory and Empire "ours," and all the burden for the Indian helots! Then, as I have already said, the second and third bases—the European civil and military services—are illusory, are only a burden and destruction to India, without being at all a sufficient security in the time of any internal and external trouble, and that especially the civil service is suicidal to the supremacy, and will be the greatest weakness. Then it may also be noticed in passing that Lord Kimberley gives no indication of the navy having anything important to do with, or make any demand on, India.

However, be all this as it may, one thing is made clear by Lord Kimberley, that, as far as Britain is concerned, the only motive which actuates her in the matter of the second and third bases—the European civil and military services—is her own supremacy, and nothing else; that there can be no difference of opinion in Britain why European services in both countries are forced upon India, viz., solely and entirely for British purposes and British interests, for "the resolute determination to maintain *our* supremacy."

I would be, therefore, asking nothing unreasonable, under the Reference to this Commission, that what is entirely for

British purposes must in justice be paid for by the British people, and the Indian people should not be asked to pay anything. I, however, still more modify this position. Notwithstanding that the European services, in their present extent and constitution, are India's greatest evil and cause of all its economic miseries and destruction, and the very badge of the slavery of a foreign domination and tyranny, that India may consider itself under a reasonable arrangement to be indirectly benefited by a certain extent of European agency, and that for such reasonable arrangement India may pay some fair share of the cost of such agency employed in India. As to all the State charges incurred in this country for such agency, it must be remembered that, in addition to their being entirely for British purposes, they are all, every farthing, earned by Europeans, and spent, every farthing, in this country. It is a charge forced upon India by sheer tyranny, without any voice or consent of India. No such charge is made upon the Colonies. The Colonial Office building and establishment is all a charge upon the British Exchequer. All charges, therefore, incurred in this country for the India Office and its establishment, and similar ones for State purposes, should under any circumstances be paid from the British Exchequer.

I shall put, briefly, this moderately just "apportionment of charge" in this way:—

India and England should pay all salaries which are to be paid to their own people, within their own limits, respectively —*i.e.*, England should pay for all Englishmen employed in England, and India should pay for all Indians employed in India; and as to those of one country who are employed in the other country—*i.e.*, Englishmen employed in India, and Indians employed in England—let there be some fair and reasonable apportionment between the two countries—taking, as much as possible, into consideration their respective benefits and capacity of means.

As to pensions, a reasonable salary being paid during service in India, no pensions to follow; so that, when Europeans retire from India, there should be no charge on England for pensions, the employees having made their own arrangements for their future from their salaries.

By this arrangement India will not only pay all that it would pay for a government by itself, supposing the English were not there, but also a share in the cost in India for what England regards as absolutely necessary for her own purpose of maintaining her Empire in India.

I may say a few words with regard to the navy. On no ground whatever of justice can India be fairly charged any share for the navy, except so far as it falls within the principle stated above, of actual service in Indian harbours.

1. The whole navy as it exists, and as it is intended to be enlarged, is every inch of it required for the protection and safety of this country itself—even if Britain had no Empire—for its own safety—for its very existence.

2. Every farthing spent on the navy is entirely earned by Englishmen; not the slightest share goes to India, in its gain, or glory, or employment, or in any way.

3. In the time of war between England and any European Powers, or the United States, the navy will not be able to protect British commerce itself.

4. There is no such thing, or very insignificant, as Indian foreign commerce or Indians' risk in what is called British Indian foreign commerce. The whole of what is called British Indian foreign trade is entirely first British risk and British capital. Every inch of the shipping or cargo on the seas is British risk of British East India banks, British marine insurance companies, and British merchants and shipowners and manufacturers. Any person who has any knowledge of how the whole of what is called British Indian foreign trade is carried on will easily understand what I mean.

5. No European Power will go to attack India from the sea, leaving the British navy free to pursue it.

6. Suppose there was no English navy to pursue, Lord Roberts' united and contented, and therefore patriotic, India will give such an irresistible Indian force at the command of Britain as to give a warm reception to the invader, and drive him back into the sea if he ever succeeded in landing at all.

With regard to the absolute necessity to the United Kingdom itself for its *own safety* of the whole navy as it exists and is intended to be increased, there is but one universal opinion, without any distinction of parties. It will be easy to quote expressions from every prominent politician. It is, in fact, the great subject of the day for which there is perfect unanimity. I would content myself, however, with a few words of the highest authority in the realm under the Sovereign, the Prime Minister, and also of the Chancellor of the Exchequer. Lord Salisbury said in his Brighton speech :—

"But dealing with such money as you possess . . . . that the first claim is the naval defence of England. I am glad that you welcome that sentiment. . . . . It is our business to be quite sure of the safety of this island home of ours whose inaccessibility is the source of our greatness, that no improvement of foreign fleets, and no combination of foreign alliances, should be able for a moment to threaten our safety at home. . . . . We must make ourselves safe at sea whatever happens. . . . . But after all, safety—safety from a foreign foe—comes first before every other earthly blessing, and we must take care in our responsibility to the many interests that depend upon us, in our responsibility to the generations that are to succeed us, we must take care that no neglect of ours shall suffer that safety to be compromised."

Sir M. Hicks-Beach, the Chancellor of the Exchequer, so late as 28th January last (the *Times*, 29/1/96), said emphatically and in a fighting mood: "We must be prepared. We must never lose the supremacy of the sea. Other nations had not got it, and could afford to do without it: but supremacy of the sea was vital to our very existence."

With such necessity for England's own safety, whether she had India or not, any burden to be placed on India can only be done on the principle of the right of might over our helplessness, and by treating India as a helotdom, and not in justice and fairness. Yes; let India have complete share in the *whole* Imperial system, including the Government of this country, and then talk of asking her to contribute to Imperial expenses. Then will be the time to consider any such question as it is being considered in relations with Ireland, which enjoys, short of Home Rule, which is vital to it, free and full share in the whole Imperial gain and glory—in the navy, army, and civil services of the Empire. Let all arrangements exist in India as they exist here for entrance into all the Imperial Services here and elsewhere, and it will be time and justice to talk of India's share in Imperial responsibilities. Certainly not on the unrighteous and tyrannical principle of all gain and glory, employment, etc., for England, and share of cost on India, without any share in such gain, glory, employment, etc.

As to the bugbear of Russian invasion. If India is in a contented state with England, India will not only give an account of Russia, but will supply an army, in the most patriotic spirit, large enough to send Russia back to St. Petersburg. India will then fight for herself in fighting for Britain. In satisfied India Britain has an inexhaustible and irresistible store of fighting power, enough and more to fight Britain's battles all over the world, as it has been doing. Lord Beaconsfield saw this and showed it by bringing Indian troops to Malta. Only *pay honestly* for what you take, and not dishonourably or tyrannically throw burdens upon India for your own purposes and interests. *With* India Britain is great and invincible; without India Britain will be a small Power. Make India feel satisfaction, patriotism, and prosperity under your supremacy and you may sleep securely against the world. But with discontented India, whatever her own fate may be—may be subjected by Russia or may repel Russia—England can or will have no safe position in India. Of course, as I have said before, I am arguing on the assumption that justice is to be dealt out by this Commission to both countries on the basis of the might of right. If that is not to be the case, and right of might is to be the deciding principle, if the eternal moral force is not to be the power, but the ephemeral brute force is to be the predominant partner, then of course I have no argument. All argument, then, will be idle breath at present till nature in time, as it always does, vindicates and revenges itself, and unrighteousness meets with its doom.

Our Commission has a great, holy, and patriotic task before it. I hope it will perform it, and tell the British people the redress that is justly due to India. The very first and immediate justice that should be done by England is the abolition of the Exchange Compensation—which is neither legal nor moral—or pay it herself; inasmuch as every farthing paid will be received by English people and in England. It is a heartless, arbitrary, and cruel exaction from the poverty of India, worse than Shylocky—not only the pound of flesh of the bond, but also the ounce of blood. As to the general question of apportionment, I have stated the principle above.

Now another important question in connexion with "apportionment of charge" has to be considered, viz., of any expenses incurred outside the limits of India of 1858.

I shall take as an illustration the case of North-West frontier wars. Every war, large or small, that is carried on beyond the frontiers of 1858 is distinctly and clearly mainly for Britain's Imperial and European purposes. It is solely to keep her own power in India. If it were not for the maintenance of her own power in India and her position in Europe she would not care a straw whether the Russians or any other power invaded India or took it. The whole expenditure is for Imperial and European purposes. On 11th February, 1880, Mr. Fawcett moved the following Amendment to the Address in reply to the Queen's Speech (*Hansard*, vol. 250, p. 453):—

"But humbly desire to express our regret that in view of the declarations that have been made by your Majesty's ministers that the war in Afghanistan was undertaken for Imperial purposes, no assurance has been given that the cost incurred in consequence of the renewal of hostilities in that country will not be wholly defrayed out of the revenues of India."

Mr. Fawcett then said (*Hansard*, vol. 250, p. 454):—

"And, fourthly, the most important question, as far as he was able to judge, of who was to pay the expenses of the war. . . . . It seemed to be quite clear that the expenses of the war should not be borne by India, and he wished to explain that so far as India was concerned this was not to be regarded as a matter of generosity but of justice and legality. . . . . The matter must be decided on grounds of strict justice and legality. . . . . (P. 457) It was a remarkable thing that every speech made in that House or out of it by ministers or their supporters on the subject showed that the war was a great Imperial enterprise, those who opposed the war having always been taunted as being "parochial" politicians who could not appreciate the magnitude and importance of great Imperial enterprises. . . . . (P. 458) He would refer to the speeches of the Viceroy of India, the Prime Minister, and the Secretary of State for Foreign Affairs upon the subject. . . . . In December, 1878, the noble earl[1] warned the peers that they must extend their range of vision, and told them that they were not to suppose that this was a war which simply concerned some small cantonments at Dakka and Jellalabad, but one undertaken to maintain the influence and character not of India, but of England in Europe. Now were they going to make India pay the entire bill for maintaining the influence and character of England in Europe? . . . . His lordship[2] treated the war as indissolubly connected with the Eastern question. . . . . Therefore it seemed to him (Mr. Fawcett) that it was absolutely impossible for the Government, unless they were prepared to cast to the winds their declarations, to come down to the House and regard the war as an Indian one. . . . . All he desired was a declaration of principle, and he would be perfectly satisfied if some one representing the Government would get up and say that they had always considered this war as an Imperial

[1] The Prime Minister.
[2] The Marquis of Salisbury.

one, for the expenses of which England and India were jointly liable."

Afterwards Mr. Fawcett said (p. 477) :—

"He was entirely satisfied with the assurance which had been given on the part of the Government that the House should have an opportunity of discussing the question before the Budget was introduced, and would therefore beg leave to withdraw his amendment."

In the House of Lords, Lord Beaconsfield emphasised the objects to be for British Imperial purposes (25/2/80—*Hansard*, vol. 250, p. 1,094) :—

"That the real question at issue was whether England should possess the gates of her own great Empire in India. . . . . We resolved that the time has come when this country should acquire the complete command and possession of the gates of the Indian Empire. Let me at least believe that the Peers of England are still determined to uphold not only the Empire but the honour of this country."

So it is clear that the object of all the frontier wars, large or small, was that "*England* should possess the gates of *her own* great Empire," that "*this country* should acquire the complete command and possession of the gates of the Indian Empire," and uphold not only the Empire, but also "the honour of this country." Can anything be more clear than the Imperial character of the frontier wars?

Mr. Fawcett, again, on 12/3/80, moved (*Hansard*, vol. 251, p. 922) :—

"That in view of the declarations which have been officially made that the Afghan war was undertaken in the joint interests of England and India, this House is of opinion that it is unjust to defray out of the revenues of India the whole of the expenditure incurred in the renewal of hostilities with Afghanistan."

Speaking to this motion, Mr. Fawcett, after referring to the past declarations of the Prime Minister, the Secretary of State for Foreign Affairs, and the Chancellor of the Exchequer, quoted from the speech of the Viceroy soon after his arrival (p. 923) :—

"I came to India, and just before leaving England for India I had frequent interviews with Lord Salisbury, the then Indian Secretary, and I came out specially instructed to treat the Indian frontier question as an indivisible part of a great Imperial question mainly depending for its solution upon the general policy of her Majesty's Government. . . ."

And further on Mr. Fawcett said (p. 926) :—

"What was our policy towards self-governed Colonies and towards India not self-governed? In the self-governed Colony of the Cape we had a war for which we were not responsible. Who was to pay for it? It would cost the English people something like £5,000,000. In India there was a war for which the Indian people were not responsible—a war which grew out of our own policy and actions in Europe—and we are going to make the Indian people, who were not self-governed and were not represented, pay every sixpence of the cost."

And so Lord Salisbury, as Secretary of State for India, and the Viceroy had cleared up the whole position—"to treat the Indian frontier question as an indivisible part of a great Imperial question, mainly depending for its solution upon the general policy of her Majesty's Government," and the Indian people having no voice or choice in it.

Mr. Gladstone, following Mr. Fawcett, said (p. 930):—

"It appears to me that, to make such a statement as that the judgment of the Viceroy is a sufficient expression of that of the people of India, is an expression of paradox really surprising, and such as is rarely heard among us. . . . (P. 932) In my opinion my hon. friend the member for Hackney has made good his case. . . . Still, I think it fair and right to say that, in my opinion, my hon. friend the member for Hackney has completely made good his case. His case, as I understand it, has not received one shred of answer. . . . (P. 933) In the speech of the Prime Minister, the speech of Lord Salisbury, and the speech of the Viceroy of India, and, I think my hon. friend said, in a speech by the Chancellor of the Exchequer, this Afghan war has been distinctively recognised as partaking of the character of an Imperial war. . . . But I think not merely a small sum like that, but what my right hon. friend the Chancellor of the Exchequer would call a solid and substantial sum, ought to be borne by this country, at the very least. . . . (P. 935) As regards the substance of the motion, I cordially embrace the doctrine of my hon. friend the member for Hackney. There is not a constituency in the country before which I would not be prepared to stand, if it were the poorest and most distressed in the land, if it were composed of a body of men to all of whom every addition of a farthing for taxes was a sensible burden, and before them I would be glad to stand and plead that, when we have made in India a war which our own Government have described as in part an Imperial war, we ought not for a moment to shrink from the responsibility of assuming at least a portion of the cost of that war, in correspondence with that declaration, instead of making use of the law and argument of force, which is the only law and the only argument which we possess or apply to place the whole of this burden on the shoulders of the people of India."

The upshot of the whole was that England contributed £5,000,000 out of £21,000,000 spent on this war, when one would have naturally expected a "far more solid and substantial" sum from rich England, whose interest was double, both Imperial and European. But the extent of that contribution is not the present question with me. It is the principle that "the Indian frontier question is one indivisible part of a great Imperial question, mainly depending for its solution upon the general policy of her Majesty's Government," and that, therefore, a fair apportionment must be made of all the charge or cost of all frontier wars, according to the extent of the interest and of the means of each country.

Coming down to later times, the action of Mr. Gladstone on 27th April, 1885, to come to the House of Commons to ask for £11,000,000—and the House accepting his proposal—on the occasion of the Penjdeh incident, is again a most significant proof of the Imperial character of these frontier wars. He said (*Hansard*, vol. 297, p. 859):—

"I have heard with great satisfaction the assurance of hon. gentlemen opposite that they are disposed to forward in every way the grant of funds to us to be used as we best think for the maintenance of what I have upon former occasions described as a National and Imperial policy. Certainly, an adequate sense of our obligations to our Indian Empire has never yet been claimed by any party in this country as its exclusive inheritance. In my opinion he will be guilty of a moral offence and gross political folly who should endeavour to claim on behalf of his own party any superiority in that respect over those to whom he is habitually opposed. It is an Imperial policy in which we are engaged."

Lastly, last year (15/8/95) the present leader of the House of Commons (Mr. Balfour) in his speech referred to "a serious blow to *our* prestige;" "that there are two and *only two* great powers they (the tribesmen) have to consider," "*to us*, and *to us* alone, must they look as a suzerain power." "To depend upon the British throne." (The italics are mine.) So it is all "ours" and "us" for all gain and glory and Imperial possessions, and European position—except that India must be forced to pay the bill. Is this the sense and conscience of *English justice* to make India pay the whole cost of the Chitral war or any frontier war?

Though the real and principal guiding motive for the British Government for these frontier wars is only Imperial and European for "its resolute determination" of keeping its possession of India and position in Europe, still India does not want to ignore its indirect and incidental benefit of being saved from falling into Russia's hands, coupled with the hope that when British conscience is fully informed and aroused to a true sense of the great evils of the present system of administration, these evils will be removed. India, therefore, accepts that these frontier wars, as far as they may be absolutely necessary, involves Indian interests also, and would be willing to pay a fair share according to her means.

India, therefore, demands and looks to the present Commission hopefully to apportion a fair division for the cost of all frontier wars in which India and England have and had purposes of common interest. This whole argument will apply to all wars, on *all* the frontiers of India—East, West, North, or South. With reference to all wars outside *all* the frontiers of India and in which India has no interest, Britain should honestly pay India fully for all the services of men or materials which she has taken and may take from India—not, as in the Abyssinian War, shirk any portion. Sir Henry Fowler, in his speech in the House of Commons (22/7/93), said:—"I say on behalf of the English people, they want to deal with Ireland, not shabbily but generously." I believe that the English people wish to deal with India also justly and generously. But do their servants, the Indian authorities, act in that way? Has not India greater claims than even Ireland on the justice and the generosity of the English people? Inasmuch as the Irish people have the voice of their own direct representatives in Parliament on their own and Imperial affairs, while India is helpless and entirely at the mercy of England, with no direct vote of her own, not only in Parliament, but even in the Legislative Councils in India, on any expenditure out of her own revenues. Ireland not only has such voice, but has a free and complete share in all the gain and glory of the British Empire. An Irishman can occupy any place in the United Kingdom or India. Can an Indian occupy any such position, even in his own country, let alone in the United Kingdom? Not only that, but that these authorities not only do not act justly or generously, but they treat India even "shabbily."

Let us take an illustration or two. What is it if not shabby to throw the expenses of Prince Nassarulla's visit upon the Indian people! There is the Mutiny of 1857. The causes were the mistakes and mismanagement of your own authorities; the people had not only no share in it, but actually were ready at your call to rise and support you. Punjab sent forth its best blood, and your supremacy was triumphantly maintained, and what was the reward of the people? You inflicted upon the people the whole payment to the last farthing of the cost of that deplorable event, of your own servants' making. Not only then was India unjustly treated, but even "shabbily." Let Lord Northbrook speak: House of Lords (15/5/93—*Debates*, vol. xii, p. 874):—

"The whole of the ordinary expenses in the Abyssinian expedition were paid by India.[1] Only the extraordinary expenses being paid by the Home Government, the argument used being that India would have to pay her troops in the ordinary way, and she ought not to seek to make a profit out of the affair. But how did the Home Government treat the Indian Government when troops were sent out during the Mutiny? Did they say, 'we don't want to make any profit out of this'? Not a bit of it. Every single man sent out was paid for by India during the whole time, though only temporary use was made of them, including the cost of their drilling and training as recruits until they were sent out."

Can anything be more "shabby," not to use a stronger word. Here you send troops for your own very existence. The people help you as best they can, and you not only not pay even any portion of the expenditure but reward the people for their loyalty with the infliction of not only the whole expense and additional burdens but even as shabbily as Lord Northbrook discloses. Is this the way by dealing unjustly and shabbily with the people that you teach them and expect them to stand by you in the time of trouble! And still more, since then, you have in a marked way been treating the people with distrust, and inflicting upon them unnecessarily and selfishly a larger and more expensive army to be paid for as wholly and as shabbily as the army of the Mutiny—viz., including the cost or a portion of the cost of their drilling and training as recruits until they are sent out, though all the troops are in this country and they form an integral part of the British Army. And the whole expenditure of the frontier wars including Chitral is imposed upon the Indian people, though avowedly incurred for Imperial aud European purposes, excepting that for very shame, a fourth of the cost of the last Afghan War was paid from the British Exchequer, thanks to Mr. Fawcett. In fact the whole European army is an integral part of the British Army, India being considered and treated as a fine training ground for the British Army, at any expense, for English gain, glory, and prestige, and as a hunting ground for "our boys," and as a

[1] With it India had nothing to do, and yet Britain did not pay all expenses.

point of protection for British Imperial and European position, leaving the Indians the helotry or the proud privilege of paying for everything to the last farthing, without having the slightest voice in the matter! The worst of the whole thing is that having other and helpless people's money to spend, without any check from the British taxpayer, there is no check to any unnecessary and extravagant expenditure.

Now even all these unjust inflictions for the Mutiny, and all past tyranny were considered somewhat, if not fully, compensated by that great, noble, and sacred with invocation of Almighty God, Proclamation of 1858, by which it was proclaimed to India and to the world that the Indian subjects were raised to an equality with the British subjects in their citizenship and British rights. And is that solemn pledge kept? Not a bit of it. On the contrary all such pledges are pronounced by Lord Salisbury as "hypocrisy," by Lord Lytton as "cheating" by "deliberate and transparent subterfuges," and "by breaking to the heart the word of promise they had uttered to the ear," by a Committee of the Council of the India Office itself as "keeping promise to the ear and breaking it to the hope," and by the Duke of Argyll as "we have not fulfilled our promises."

Can it be expected that by such methods of financial injustice and violation of pledges can be acquired the affection of the people upon which mainly and ultimately depends, as many a statesman has said, the stability of the British supremacy?

At Glasgow on November 14, 1895, Mr. Balfour said: "You all remember that the British Army—and in the British Army I include those Native soldiers, fellow subjects of ours, who on that day did great work for the Empire of which they are all citizens."—This is the romance. Had Mr. Balfour spoken the reality, he would have said: "Include those Native soldiers, the drudges of ours, who on that day did great work for the Empire of which they are kept-down subjects." For does not Mr. Balfour know that, far from being treated as "fellow subjects" and "citizens of the Empire," the Indians have not only to shed their blood for the Empire, but even *to pay every farthing* of the cost of these wars for "our Empire" and "our European position," that no pledges however solemn and binding to treat Indians as "fellow subjects" or British citizens have been faithfully kept either in letter or spirit, that however much these Indians may be brave and shed their blood for Imperial purposes or be made to pay "cruel and crushing tribute" they are not allowed any vote in the Imperial Parliament or a vote in the Indian Legislative Councils on their own financial expenditure, that their employment in the officering of the Army, beyond a few inferior positions of Subadar Major or Jamadar Major, etc., is not at all allowed, that they are distrusted and disarmed—are not allowed to become volunteers—that every possible obstacle is thrown and "subterfuge" resorted to against the advancement of the Indians in the higher positions of all the Civil Services, and that the simple justice of allowing Indians an equality to be simultaneously examined in their own country, for *Indian* services, decided by Act and resolution of Parliament and solemnly pledged by the great Proclamation, is resisted by every device and subterfuge possible unworthy of the English character. Is it not a mockery and an insult to call the Indians "fellow subjects and citizens of the Empire" when in reality they are treated as under-heel subjects?

Here are Rs. 128,574,590, or nearly Rs. 129,000,000, spent from April, 1882, to March, 1891 (Parl. Return, 91 of 1895), beyond "the West and North-west frontiers of India," after the disastrous expenditure of £21,000,000 in the last Afghan War (of which only a quarter was paid by the British Exchequer). Every pie of this nearly Rs. 129,000,000 is exacted out of the poverty-stricken Indians, and all for distinctly avowed Imperial and European British purposes. I do not know whether the Rs. 129,000,000 includes the ordinary pay of all the soldiers and officers employed in the Frontier Service, or whether it is only the extraordinary military expenditure that is included. If the ordinary pay is not included, then the amount will be larger than Rs. 129,000,000. And these are "our fellow subjects" and "our Imperial citizens"! To shed blood for Imperial purposes and to pay the whole cost also!

Lord George Hamilton said at Chiswick (*Times*, 22/1/96): "He hoped that the result of the present Government's tenure of office would be to make the British Empire not merely a figure of speech, but a living reality." Now is not this as much romance as that of Mr. Balfour's, instead of being a "living reality"? All the questions I have asked for

Mr. Balfour's expressions apply as forcibly to the words of the present Secretary of State of India, who ought to know the real despotically subjected position of the people of British India, forming two-thirds of the Empire. Yes, the British Empire can be made a "living reality" of union and devoted attachment, but not under the present system of British Indian administration. It can be, when in that system, justice, generosity, fair apportionment of charges, and honour, and "courage of keeping the word" shall prevail over injustice, helotdom, and dishonour of open violation of the most solemn words of honour.

Now Mr. Chamberlain, at Birmingham (*Times*, 27/1/96), said in reference to the African Republic :—

> "Now, I have never denied that there is just cause for discontent in the Transvaal Republic. The majority of the population there pay nine-tenths of the taxation, and have no share whatever in the government of the country. That is an anomaly which does not exist in any other civilised community, and it is an anomaly which wise and prudent statesmanship would remove. I believe it can be removed without danger to the independence of the Republic, and I believe until it is removed you have no permanent guarantee against future internal disturbances."

Do not these words apply with ten times force to the case of India, and is not that wise and prudent statesmanship which is preached here required to be practised in connexion with the greatest part of the British Empire? I venture to use Mr. Chamberlain's words :—

> "I believe (the anomaly) can be removed without danger to the stability of the British power, or, rather, with devoted and patriotic attachment to the British connexion; and I believe that until it is removed you have no permanent guarantee against future internal disturbances."

The *Times* (1/2/96) in a leader on Lord Salisbury's speech before the Nonconformist Unionist Association, in a sentence about the Outlanders, expresses what is peculiarly applicable to the present position of India. It says :—

> "The Outlanders in the Transvaal—not a minority, but a large majority—are deprived of all share of political power and of the most elementary privileges of citizenship, because the dominant class, differing from them in race and feeling, as Lord Salisbury says, 'have the government and have the rifles.'"

The Indians must provide every farthing for the supremacy of the minority of "the dominant class," and should not have the slightest voice in the spending of that every farthing, and find every solemn pledge given for equality of British citizenship flagrantly broken to the heart in letter and in spirit. And why? Is it because, as Lord Salisbury says, "they have the Government and have the rifles;" or as Mr. Gladstone said about India itself, "the law and argument of force, which is the only law and argument which we possess or apply." This Commission has the duty, at least so far as a fair apportionment of charge is concerned, to redress this great wrong.

Do the British Indian authorities really think that the Indians are only like African savages, or mere children, that, even after thousands of years of civilisation, when the Britons were only barbarians; after the education they have received at the blessed British hands, producing, as Lord Dufferin said, "Native gentlemen of great attainments and intelligence" (Jubilee speech); they do not see and understand these deplorable circumstances of their true position of degradation and economic destruction? Or do these authorities not care, even if the Indians did understand, as long as they can mislead the British people into the belief that all is right and beneficent in British India, when it is really not the case?

But the faith of the Indians in the conscience of the British people is unbounded and unshakeable, and the little incidents of bright spots keep up that faith, such as the justice of not burdening the Indian people with the cost of the Opium Commission, and—even though inadequate and partial—the payment of one-fourth of the cost of the last Afghan War. It is these acts of justice that consolidate the British rule and tend towards its stability.

I believe now, as I have always believed, that the English people wish and want to deal with India justly and generously. When I say that I believe in the British character of fair play and justice, it is not a sentiment of to-day or yesterday. In the very first political speech of my life, made as far back as 1853, at the formation of the Bombay Association, on the occasion of the Parliamentary Enquiry on Indian Affairs for the renewal of the Company's Charter, I said:—

"When we see that our Government is often ready to assist us in everything calculated to benefit us, we had better, than merely complain and grumble, point out in a becoming manner what our real wants are. . . . . If an Association like this be always in readiness to ascertain by strict enquiries the probably good or bad effects of any proposed measure, and whenever necessary to memorialise Government on behalf of the people with respect to them, our kind Government will not refuse to listen to such memorials."

And under that belief the Bombay Association, the British Indian Association of Bengal, and the Madras Association, memorialised the then Select Committee on Indian affairs—for redress of grievances.

Now, after not very short of nearly half a century of hopes and disappointments, these are still my sentiments to-day—that with correct and full knowledge the British people and Parliament will do what is right and just.

I may here take the opportunity of making a remark or two about the wide extent of the scope of the enquiry of this Commission in the first part of the Reference.

Lord Cranborne, soon after having been Secretary of State for India, said (24/5/67) in reference to the powers of the Council of the Secretary of State for India :—

> "It possesses by Act of Parliament an absolute and conclusive veto upon the Acts of the Government of India with reference to nine-tenths, I might almost say ninety-nine hundredths, of the questions that arise with respect to that Government. Parliament has provided that the Council may veto any despatch which directs the appropriation of public money. Everyone knows that almost every question connected with Government raises in some way or other the question of expenditure."

The first part of the Reference to this Commission thus embraces "almost every question connected with Government." "Ninety-nine hundredths of the questions that arise with respect to that Government."

This view is fully confirmed by the enquiry by the Select Committee of 1871-4. The Reference to it was "to enquire into the Finance and Financial Administration of India," and our first reference is fully of the same scope and character. Now what was the extent of the subjects of the enquiry made by that Committee? The index of the proceedings of the four years (1871-4) has a table of contents headed : "Alphabetical and Classified List of the principal headings in the following Index, with the pages at which they will be found." And what is the number of these headings? It is about 420. In fact, there is hardly a subject of Government which is not enquired into.

Yours truly,

DADABHAI NAOROJI.

V.

National Liberal Club,
London, S.W.,

21st March, 1896.

DEAR LORD WELBY,—I have to request you kindly to put before the Commission this further representation from me on the subjects of our enquiry. This will be my last letter, unless some phase of the enquiry needed any further explanation from me.

Looking at the first part of the enquiry from every point of view, with regard to the administration and management of expenditure, we come back again and again to the view expressed by the Duke of Devonshire and Sir William Hunter and others. The Duke of Devonshire has said: "If the country is to be better governed, that can only be done by the employment of the best and most intelligent of the Natives in the Service." Sir William Hunter has said: "But the good work thus commenced has assumed such dimensions under the Queen's Government of India that it can no longer be carried on or even supervised by imported labour from England except at a cost which India cannot sustain. . . . If we are to govern the Indian people efficiently and cheaply, we must govern them by means of themselves, and pay for the administration at the market rates of Native labour."

From all I have said in my previous representations it must have been seen that the real evil and misery of the people of British India does not arise from the *amount* of expenditure. India is capable, under natural circumstances, of providing twice, three times or more the expenditure, as the improvement of the country may need, in attaining all necessary progress. The evil really is in the way in which that expenditure is administered and managed, with the effect of a large portion of that expenditure not returning to the people from whom it is raised—in short, as Lord Salisbury has correctly described as the process of "bleeding." No country in the world (England not excepted) can stand such bleeding. To stop this bleeding is the problem of the day—bleeding both moral and material. You may devise the most perfect plan or scheme of government, not only humanly but divinely perfect—you may have the foreign officials, the very angels themselves—but it will be no earthly good to the people as long as the bleeding management of expenditure continues the same. On the contrary, the evil will increase by the very perfection of such plan or scheme for improvements and progress. For as improvements and progress are understood to mean, at present, it is more and more bleeding by introducing more and more the foreign bleeding agency.

The real problem before the Commission is not how to nibble at the expenditure and suggest some poor reductions here and there, to be put aside in a short time, as is always done, but how to stop the material and moral bleeding, and leaving British India a freedom of development and progress in prosperity which her extraordinary natural resources are capable of, and to treat her justly in her financial relations with Britain by apportioning fairly the charge on purposes in which both are interested. Or, to put the problem in its double important bearings, in the words of an eminent statesman, "which should at once afford a guarantee for the good government of the people, and for the security of British rights and interests" (Lord Iddesleigh), as will be seen further on. I am glad to put before the Commission that this problem has been not merely enunciated, but that, with the courage of their convictions, two eminent statesmen have actually carried it out practically, and have done that with remarkable success. I am the more glad to bring forward this case before the Commission, as it also enables me to adduce an episode in the British Indian administration on the conduct of the Indian authorities in both countries and other Anglo-Indian officials, which reflects great credit upon all concerned in it—and as my information goes, and as it also appears from the records, that her Majesty personally has not a little share in this praise, and in evoking a hearty Indian gratitude and loyalty to herself. This episode also clearly indicates or points to the way as to what the true natural relations should be between Britain and India, with the result of the welfare and prosperity of both, and the security and stability of British supremacy.

In my previous letters I have confined myself to the evil results—suicidal to Britain and destructive to India—of the present unnatural system of the administration and management of expenditure and the injustice of the financial relations between the two countries, loudly calling for a just apportionment of charge for purposes in which both are interested.

Without dwelling any further on this melancholy aspect, I shall at once proceed to the case to which I have alluded above, and in connexion with which there have been true statesmanlike and noble declarations made as to the right relations between Britain and India as they ought to exist. This case is in every way a bright chapter in the history of British India. The especially remarkable feature of this case is that notwithstanding the vehement and determined opposition to it from all Indian authorities for some thirty-six years, after this wise, natural, and righteous course was decided upon by her Majesty and the Secretary of State for India of the time, all the authorities, both here and in India, carried it out in the most loyal, earnest, and scrupulous manner and solicitude worthy of the British name and character—in striking contrast with the general conduct of these authorities, by which they have almost always frustrated and made dead letters of Acts and resolutions of Parliament and royal proclamations and most solemn pledges on behalf of the British people by all sorts of un-English "subterfuges," "cheating devices" (Lytton), "hypocrisy" (Salisbury), "non-fulfilment of pledges" (Duke of Argyll, Lytton, and others), etc., in matters of the advancement and elevation of the Indian people to material and moral prosperity, and to real British rights and citizenship. Had they fortunately shown the same loyalty and true sense of their trust to these Acts and resolutions of Parliament, to the solemn proclamations and pledges, as have been shown in the case I am referring to, what a different, prosperous, and grateful India would it have been to-day, blessing the name of Britain, and both to its glory and gain. It is not too late yet. It will be a pity if it ever becomes too late to prevent disaster.

On 22nd January, 1867, Lord Salisbury (then Lord

Cranborne and Secretary of State for India) said (*Hansard*, vol. 185, p. 839) :—

"But there are other considerations, and I think the hon. gentleman (Sir Henry Rawlinson) stated them very fairly and eloquently. I do not myself see our way at present to employing very largely the Natives of India in the regions under our immediate control. *But it would be a great evil if the result of our dominion was that the Natives of India who were capable of government should be absolutely and hopelessly excluded from such a career.* The great advantage of the existence of Native States is that they afford an outlet for statesmanlike capacity such as has been alluded to. I need not dwell upon the consideration to which the hon. gentleman so eloquently referred, but I think *that the existence of a well-governed Native State is a real benefit, not only to the stability of our rule,* but because, more than anything, it raises the self-respect of the Natives and forms an ideal to which the popular feelings aspire. . . . . Whatever treaties or engagements may be entered into, I hope that I shall not be looked upon by gentlemen of the Liberal party as very revolutionary if I say *that the welfare of the people of India must override them all.* I quite admit the temptations which a paramount power has to interpret that axiom rather for its own advantage than its own honour. There is no doubt of the existence of that temptation, but that does not diminish the truth of the maxim." [The italics are mine.]

On 24th May, 1867, Lord Iddesleigh (then Sir Stafford Northcote and Secretary of State for India) said (*Hansard*, vol. 187, p. 1068) :—

"He believed that the change in education in India, and the fact that the Natives now saw what their system of government was and is, had told most beneficially on that country. He had, therefore, confidence that we might establish a state of things in Mysore which would have a happy effect on the administration of the country. What had taken place in other parts of India? Travancore forty years ago was in as bad a state as Mysore, yet its administration under British influence had so greatly improved that Travancore was now something like a model Native State. *Our Indian policy should be founded on a broad basis. There might be difficulties; but what we had to aim at was to establish a system of Native States which might maintain themselves in a satisfactory relation.* Keeping the virtues of Native States, and getting rid, as far as possible, of their disadvantages. We must look to the great *natural* advantages which the government of a Native State must *necessarily* have. Under the English system there were advantages which would probably never be under Native Administration—regularity, love of law and order and justice."

Had Lord Iddesleigh lived he would have with pleasure seen that the advantages he refers to are being attained in the Native States; and in Mysore itself, as well as in several other States, they have been largely already attained. And under the eye of the British Government there is progress everywhere.. Lord Iddesleigh proceeds :—

"But Native Administration had the advantage in *sympathy between the governors and the governed*. Governors were able to appreciate and understand the prejudices and wishes of the governed; especially in the case of Hindu States, the religious feelings of the people were enlisted in favour of their governors instead of being roused against us.[1] He had been told by gentlemen from India that nothing impressed them more than walking the streets of some Indian town, they looked up at the houses on each side and asked themselves, 'what do we really know of these people—of their modes of thought, their feelings, their prejudices—and at what great disadvantage, in consequence, do we administer the government.' The English Government must necessarily labour under great disadvantages,[2] and *we should endeavour as far as possible to develop the system of Native government to bring out Native talent and statesmanship, and to enlist in the cause of government all that was great and good in them*. Nothing could be more wonderful than our Empire in India; but we ought to consider on what conditions we hold it and how our predecessors held it. The greatness of the Mogul Empire depended on the liberal policy that was pursued by men like the great Emperor Akbar and his successors availing themselves of Hindu talent and assistance, and identifying themselves as far as possible with the people of the country. They ought to take a lesson from such circumstances. *If they were to do their duty towards India they could only discharge that duty by obtaining assistance and counsel of all who are great and good in that country*. It would be absurd in them to say that there was not a large fund of statesmanship and ability in the Indian character. They really must not be too proud. They were always ready to speak of the English government as so infinitely superior to anything in the way of Indian government. But if the Natives of India were disposed to be equally critical, it would be possible for them to find out weak places in the harness of the English administration. The system in India was one of great complexity. It was a system of checks and counter checks, and very often great abuses failed to be controlled from want of a proper knowledge of and sympathy with the Natives." [The italics are mine.]

On the same day Lord Salisbury, supporting Lord Iddesleigh, said (*Hansard*, vol. 187, p. 1073):—

"*The general concurrence of opinion of those who know India best is that a number of well-governed small Native States are in the highest degree advantageous to the development of the political and moral condition of the people of India*. The hon. gentleman (Mr. Laing) arguing in the strong official line seems to take the view that everything is right in British territory and everything dark in Native territory. Though he can cite the case of Oudh, I venture to doubt if it could be established as a general view of India as it exists at present. If Oudh is to be quoted against Native government, the

[1] The same can be said about the Muhammadans and other people.

[2] The greatest of them is the economic evil which Lord Salisbury has truly called the bleeding of the country.

Report of the Orissa Famine, which will be presented in a few days, will be found to be another and far more terrible instance to be quoted against English rule. *The British Government has never been guilty of the violence and illegality of Native Sovereigns. But it has faults of its own, which, though they are far more guiltless in intention, are more terrible in effect.* Its tendency to routine; its listless heavy heedlessness, sometimes the result of its elaborate organisation; a fear of responsibility, an extreme centralisation—all these results, traceable to causes for which no man is culpable, *produce an amount of inefficiency which, when reinforced by natural causes and circumstances, creates a terrible amount of misery.* All these things must be taken into consideration when you compare our elaborate and artificial system of government with the more rough and ready system of India. In cases of emergency, unless you have men of peculiar character on the spot, the simple form of oriental government will produce effects more satisfactory than the more elaborate system of English rule. I am not by this denying that our mission in India is to reduce to order, to civilise and develop the Native Governments we find there.[1] But I demur to that wholesale condemnation of a system of government which will be utterly intolerable on our own soil, but which has grown up amongst the people subjected to it. It has a fitness and congeniality for them impossible for us adequately to realise, but which compensate them to an enormous degree for the material evils which its rudeness in a great many cases produces. I may mention as an instance what was told me by Sir George Clerk, a distinguished member of the Council of India, respecting the Province of Kathiawar, in which the English and Native Governments are very much intermixed. There are no broad lines of frontier there, and a man can easily leap over the hedge from the Native into the English jurisdiction. Sir George Clerk told me that the Natives having little to carry with them were continually in the habit of migrating from the English into the Native jurisdiction, but that he never heard of an instance of a Native leaving his own to go into the English jurisdiction. This may be very bad taste on the part of the Natives; but you have to consider what promotes their happiness, suits their tastes, and tends to their moral development in their own way. If you intend to develop their moral nature only after an Anglo-Saxon type, you will make a conspicuous and disastrous defeat." [The italics are mine.]

In the above extract Lord Salisbury says that the inefficiency reinforced by natural causes and circumstances creates a terrible amount of misery. These natural causes and circumstances which create the terrible amount of misery are pointed out by Lord Salisbury himself, as Secretary of State for India, in a Minute (29/4/75). He says "the injury is exaggerated in the case of India, where so much of the revenue is exported without a direct equivalent." And that

[1] This is being actually done. Every effort is being made to bring the administration of the Native States to the level of the organisation of the British system which is not a little to the credit of the British Government.

under these causes and circumstances, the result is that "India must be bled," so that he truly shows that though under the British rule there is no personal violence, the present system of the administration of expenditure cannot but create and does "*create a terrible amount of misery.*"

Further, the crude and defective system of administration under the old system of Native rule is all changed and cannot apply to the present administration in British India. Any alteration that may be deemed necessary to be made for remedying this "terrible amount of misery" would not involve in British India any alteration at all in the existing developed plan or system of the organisation of the administration.

Now the moral of the above extracts from the speeches of Lords Salisbury and Iddesleigh is clear. Under the present system of administration of government and expenditure and unjust financial relations, in the very nature of things, there is a perpetual and inevitable result of terrible misery, of slavery (Macaulay), absolute hopelessness of higher life or career, despair, self-abasement, without any self-respect (Salisbury), extreme destitution and suffering (Bright), extreme poverty (Lawrence, Cromer, Barbour, Colvin), degradation (Monroe), etc., etc. And as a consequence of such deplorable results, an inherent and inevitable "danger of the most serious order" (Lord R. Churchill) to the stability of British supremacy. British rule under such circumstances can only continue to be a foreign crushing tyranny, leading the people to yearn (the Duke of Devonshire) to get rid of their European rulers, etc., etc.

On the other hand (Salisbury) "the existence of a well-governed Native State is a real benefit, not only to the stability of the British rule, but more than anything it raises the self-respect of the Natives and forms an ideal to which the popular feeling aspires." And "that a number of well-governed small Native States are in the highest degree advantageous to the development of the political and moral" (I may add, the material) "condition of the people of India." Lord Iddesleigh says on the same lines: "What we had to aim at was to establish a system of Native States which might maintain themselves in a satisfactory relation." And what is of far more importance, he actually inaugurated the great experiment, by which he proposed to solve the great problem, "which should at once afford a guarantee for the good government of the people and for the security of British rights and interests," and to which I desire to draw the attention of the Commission. In short, the lesson of the extracts is that the British Indian administration as it exists at present is positively and seriously dangerous to the British supremacy, and of terrible misery to the people; while a system of Native States will raise the people, and at the same time firmly secure the stability of the British supremacy and largely conduce to the prosperity of both countries—Britain and India.

Now comes the great merit—which will always be remembered by Indians with deep gratitude—of these two Statesmen (Salisbury and Iddesleigh). They did not rest satisfied with mere declaration of fine and great sentiments and then sleep over them, as has been done on many an occasion to the misfortune of poor India. No, they then showed that they had the courage of their convictions and had confidence in the true statesmanship of their views. In this good work her Majesty took a warm interest and encouraged them to carry it out. The result was the memorable—and ever to be remembered with gratitude—despatch of 16th April, 1867, of Lord Iddesleigh, for the restoration of Mysore to the Native rule, notwithstanding thirty-six years of determined opposition of the authorities to that step (Parl. Ret. 239, 30/4/'67).

And now I come to the episode to which I have referred above, and about which I write with great gratification and gratitude, of the conduct of all the authorities in both countries and of all the Anglo-Indian officials who had any share in this good work, backed as I have said already, by the good-hearted and influential interest and support of her Majesty herself. They may have made some errors of judgment, but there was universally perfect sincerity and loyalty to the trust. Among those concerned (and whose names it is a pleasure to me to give) were, as Secretaries of State for India, Lord Iddesleigh, the Duke of Argyll, Lord Salisbury, Viscount Cranbrook, and the Duke of Devonshire (from 1867 till 1881, when the late Mahárájá was invested with power); as Viceroys, Lord Lawrence, Lord Mayo, Lord Northbrook, Lord Lytton, and Lord Ripon; and lastly, the Chief Commissioners and other officials of Mysore. The chief merit in the conduct of all concerned was this. Lord Iddesleigh laid down in his despatch of 16th of April, 1867 :—

> "Without entering upon any minute examination of the terms of the Treaties of 1799, her Majesty's Government recognise, in the policy which dictated that settlement, a desire to provide for the maintenance of an Indian dynasty on the throne of Mysore, *upon terms which should at once afford a guarantee for the good government of the people and for the security of British rights and interests.* Her Majesty is animated by the same desire, and shares the views to which I have referred. . . . . Her Majesty desires to maintain that family on the throne in the person of his Highness's adopted son. . . . . It is therefore the intention of her Majesty that the young Prince should have the advantage of an education suitable to his rank and position and calculated to prepare him for the duties of administration." [The italics are mine.]

This being once settled, though against all previous opposition, and necessitating the withdrawal of Europeans from the Services, all the authorities and officials concerned, to their honour and praise, instead of putting any obstacles in the way, or trying to frustrate the above intentions, discharged their trust most loyally, and with every earnestness and care and solicitude to carry the work to success. The Blue-books on Mysore from the despatch of 16th April, 1867, to the installation of the late Mahárájá in 1881, is a bright chapter in the history of British India, both in the justice, righteousness, and statesmanship of the decision, and the loyalty and extreme care of every detail in carrying out that decision—with success and satisfactory results in both objects set forth in the despatch, viz., "*the good government of the people, and the security of British rights and interests.*"

I wish the India Office would make a return on Mysore relations and affairs up to date, in continuation of Ret. No. 1 of 1881 (c. 3026), to show how the good and creditable work has been continued up to the present time. I think I need not enter here into any details of this good work from 1867 to 1881 of the British officials : the Blue-books tell all that. Of the work of the late Mahárájá from 1881 till his death at the end of 1894, it would be enough for me to give a very brief statement from the last Address of the Dewan to the Representative Assembly held at Mysore on 1st October, 1895, on the results of the late Mahárájá's administration during nearly fourteen years of his reign, as nearly as possible in the Dewan's words. The Mahárájá was invested with power on 25th March, 1881. Just previous to it, the State had encountered a most disastrous famine by which a fifth of the population had been swept away, and the State had run into a debt of 80 lakhs of rupees to the British Government. The cash balance had become reduced to a figure insufficient for the ordinary requirements of the administration. Every source of revenue was at its lowest, and the severe retrenchments which followed had left every department of State in an enfeebled condition. Such was the beginning. It began with liabilities exceeding the assets by 30¾ lakhs, and with an annual income less than the annual expenditure by 1¼ lakhs. Comparing 1880-1 with 1894-5, the annual revenue rose from 103 to 180½ lakhs, or 75·24 per cent., and after spending on a large and liberal scale on all works and purposes of public utility, the nett assets amounted to over 176 lakhs in 1894-5, in lieu of the nett liability of 30¾ lakhs with which his Highness's reign began in 1881.

	Rs.
In 1881 the balance of State funds was ...	24,07,438
Capital outlay on State Railways	25,19,198
Against a liability to the British Government of	80,00,000

Leaving a balance of liability of Rs. 30¾ lakhs.

On 30th June, 1895:

ASSETS—		
(1) Balance of State Funds		1,27,23,615
(2) Investment on account of Railway Loan Repayment Fund		27,81,500
(3) Capital outlay on Mysore-Harihar Railway		1,48,03,306
(4) Capital outlay on other Railways ...		41,33,390
(5) Unexpended portion of Capital borrowed for Mysore-Harihar Railway (with British Government) ...		15,79,495
		3,60,21,306
LIABILITIES—		
(1) Local Railway Loan ...	Rs. 20,00,000	
(2) English Railway Loan ...	1,63,82,801	
		1,83,82,801
Net Assets		Rs. 1,76,38,505
ADD OTHER ASSETS—		
Capital outlay on original Irrigation Works	Rs. 99,08,935	

Besides the above expenditure from current revenue, there is the subsidy to the British Government of about Rs. 25,00,000 a year, or a total of about Rs. 3,70,00,000 in the fifteen years from 1880-1 to 1894-5, and the Mahárájá's civil list of about Rs. 1,80,00,000, during the fifteen years also paid from the current revenue. And all this together with increase in expenditure in every department. Under the circumstances above described, the administration at the start of his Highness's reign was necessarily very highly centralised. The Dewan, or the Executive Administrative head, had the direct control, without the intervention of departmental heads of all the principal departments, such as the Land Revenue, Forests, Excise, Mining, Police, Education, Mujroyi, Legislative. As the finances improved, and as department after department was put into good working order and showed signs of expansion, separate heads of departments were appointed, for Forests and Police in 1885, for Excise in 1889, for Mujroyi in 1891, and for Mining in 1894. His Highness was able to resolve upon the appointment of a separate Land Revenue Commissioner only in the latter part of 1894. Improvements were made in other departments—Local and Municipal Funds, Legislation, Education, etc. There are no wails which unfortunately the Finance Ministers of British India are obliged to raise, year after year, of fall in Exchange, over-burdening taxation, etc., etc.

And all the above good results are side by side with an increase of population of 18·34 per cent. in the ten years from 1881 to 1891, and there is reason to believe that during the last four years the ratio of increase was even higher. During the fourteen years the rate of mortality is estimated to have declined 6·7 per mille.

But there is still the most important and satisfactory feature to come, viz., that all this financial prosperity was secured not by resort to new taxation in any form or shape. In the very nature of things the present system of administration and management of Indian expenditure in British India cannot ever produce such results, even though a Gladstone undertook the work. Such is the result of good administration in a Native State at the very beginning. What splendid prospect is in store for the future if, as heretofore, it is allowed to develop itself to the level of the British system with its own Native Services, and not bled as poor British India is.

Lord Iddesleigh is dead (though his name will never be forgotten in India, and how he would have rejoiced!), but well may her Majesty, Lord Salisbury, and all others concerned in it, and the British people, be proud of this brilliant result of a righteous and statesmanlike act, and may feel secure of the sincere and solid loyalty, gratitude, and attachment of the rulers and people of Mysore to the British supremacy.

Here, then, is the whole problem of the right and natural administration of expenditure, etc., and stability of British supremacy was solved, and that most successfully, by Lords Salisbury and Iddesleigh. It is now clear, by actual facts and operation, that the present system of expenditure, in all aspects of the administration of British India, is full of evil to the people and danger to British supremacy, while, on the other hand, "a number of well-governed Native States," under the active control and supremacy of Britain, will be full of benefit and blessing both to Britain and India and a firm foundation for British supremacy. And all this prophecy of Lords Salisbury and Iddesleigh has been triumphantly fulfilled. Lord Iddesleigh set to himself the problem "which should at once afford a guarantee for the good government of the people and for the security of British rights and interests," and most successfully solved it.

The obvious conclusion is that the only natural and satisfactory relations between an alien supremacy and the people of India can be established on this basis alone. There are these obvious advantages in these relations:—

The British supremacy becomes perfectly secure and founded upon the gratitude and affection of the people, who, though under such supremacy, would feel as being under their own rulers and as being guided and protected by a mighty supreme power.

Every State thus formed, from the very nature of its desire for self-preservation, will cling to the supreme power as its best security against disturbance by any other State.

The division in a number of States becomes a natural and potent power for good in favour of the stability of the British supremacy. There will be no temptation to any one State to discard that supremacy, while, on the other hand, the supreme Government, having complete control and power over the whole government of each State, will leave no chance for any to go astray. Every instinct of self-interest and self-preservation, f gratitude, of high aspirations, and of all the best parts of human nature, will naturally be on the side and in favour of British supremacy which gave birth to these States. There will be an emulation among them to vie with each other in governing in the best way possible, under the eye and control of the supreme Government on their actions, leaving no chance for misgovernment. Each will desire to produce the best Administration Report every year. In short, this natural system has all the elements of consolidation of British power, of loyalty, and stability, and of prosperity of both countries. On the other hand, under the present system, all human nature and instincts are against you, and must inevitably end in disintegration, rebellion, and disaster. No grapes from thistles! Evil will have its nemesis. I hope and pray that this Commission will rise to the height of its mission, and accomplish it to the glory of this country and the prosperity of both.

I must not be misunderstood. When I use the words "Native States," I do not for a moment mean that these new States are to revert to the *old* system of government of Native rule. Not at all. The system of all departments that exists at present, the whole mode of government, must not only remain as it is, but must go on improving till it reaches as nearly as possible the level of the more complete mode of British government that exists in this country. The change to be made is, that these States are to be governed by Native agency, on the same lines as at present, by employing, as the Duke of Devonshire says, "the best and most intelligent of the Natives," or as Lord Iddesleigh says, "all that was great and good in them."

One question naturally presents itself. Are new dynastic Indian rajahs to be created for these new States? That is a question that men like Lord Salisbury himself and the Indian authorities are best able to answer. There may be difficulties in dynastic succession. If so, the best mode of the headship under some suitable title of these States may be by appointment by Government, and aided by a representative council. This mode has certain evident advantages, viz., questions of dynastic succession may be avoided, Government will be free to secure the best man for the post, and Government will then have complete control over the States, especially with an English Resident, as in all Native States at present. If thought necessary, this control may be made still more close by having at the beginning for some time an English joint administrator instead of a Resident.

Sir Charles Dilke has, in one of his letters to me, said :—

> "I also agree as to reduction of Europeans (so far as the non-military people go). Indeed, *I* agree *without* limit, and would substitute for our direct rule a military protectorate of Native States, as I have often said."

In another letter to me, which is published in the September number of INDIA, in 1893, Sir Charles dwells upon the same subject at some length, proposing to follow up the case of Mysore and to divide India into a number of Native States.

With regard to the financial relations between Britain and India, whether for military or civil charges, I have already expressed my views in my last representation. I would not, therefore, make any further remarks here.

Once this natural and righteous system of government by Native States is adopted, so as to make the administration of expenditure fully productive of good results to both countries, I may with every confidence hope that the authorities, as in the case of Mysore, will loyally and scrupulously do their best to carry out the plan to success by establishing in India every necessary machinery for preparation, examinations, and tests of character and fitness of the Indians "to (as Lord Iddesleigh says) develop the system of Native government, to bring out Native talent and statesmanship, and to enlist in the cause of government all that was great and good in them."

The prevention and cure of the evils of the present material and moral bleeding, arising from the existing system of the administration and management of expenditure, from unjust financial relations between the two countries, and for the redemption of the honour of this country from the dishonour of the violation of the most solemn and binding pledges, are absolutely necessary, if India is to be well governed, if British supremacy is to be made thoroughly stable, and if both countries are to be made prosperous by a market for trade of nearly 300,000,000 of civilised and prosperous people.

I do not here consider any other plan of Government to secure effectively the double object laid down by Lord Iddesleigh, because I think the plan proposed and carried out by him is the most natural and the best, and most secure for the continuance of British supremacy.

I also do not enter into any details, as all possible difficulties of details, and the means by which they were overcome, are all recorded in the Mysore Blue-books.

I submit to the Commission that unless the patriotism and prosperity of the people of India are drawn to the side of British supremacy, no plan or mode of government, under the existing system of expenditure, will be of any good either to British supremacy or to the Indian people. Evil and peril to both is the only dismal outlook. On the other hand, a number of Native States, according to the noble views and successful work of Lords Salisbury and Iddesleigh, will contribute vastly both to the gain and glory of the British people, to vast expansion of trade, and to the prosperity and affection of the Indian hundreds of millions of the human race.

If India is thus strengthened in prosperity, and patriotically satisfied in British supremacy, I cannot feel the least fear of Russia ever dreaming of invading India. Without any military help from England, and without any large European army, India will be all sufficient in itself to repel any invasion, and to maintain British supremacy for her own and Britain's sake.

I hope earnestly that this Commission will, as Sir Louis Mallet has urged, grapple with the disease of the evil results of the present system of expenditure, instead of, like other past Commissions and Committees, keeping to the habit of merely palliating symptoms. I do not much intervene in examining details of departmental expenditure, such examination at proper intervals, as used to be the case in the time of the Company, serves the important purpose of keeping the Government up to mark in care of expenditure. But unless the whole Government is put on a natural basis, all examinations of details of departmental expenditures will be only so much "palliating with symptoms," and will bring no permanent good and strength either to the Indian people or to the British supremacy.

I offer to be cross-examined on all my representations.

As before, I shall send a copy of this to every member of the Commission.

Yours truly,

DADABHAI NAOROJI.

VI.

Cambridge Lodge,
West Hill Road,
Southfields, S.W.

31st January, 1897.

DEAR LORD WELBY,—I request you kindly to put before the Commission this, my sixth, representation on the subjects of our enquiry.

Nobody can more appreciate the benefits of the British connexion than I do. Education in particular, appreciation of, and desire for, British political institutions, law and order, freedom of speech and public meeting, and several important social reforms. All these are the glory of England and gratitude of India. I am most sincerely ready to accord my gratitude for any benefit which Britain can rightly claim.

But, while looking at one side, justice demands that we look at the other side also. And the main object of this Commission is to see the other side of the system of the administration and management of expenditure and right apportionment.

It must be remembered that while education and law and order have been beneficial to the Indians of British India they were also most essential to the very existence of the British in India. Only that while the benefits have been to both Britain and British India, the cost has been *all* exacted from the Indians.

The British Empire in India is built up entirely with the money of India, and, in great measure, by the blood of India. Besides this, hundreds of millions, or, more probably, several thousands of millions (besides what is consumed in India itself by Europeans and their careers of life) of money, which Britain has unceasingly, and ever increasingly, drawn from British Indians, and is still drawing, has materially helped to make Britain the greatest, the richest, and most glorious country in the world—benefitting her material condition so much that, even when there is a general and loud cry of depression in agriculture, etc., the Chancellor of the Exchequer is rejoicing that his income tax is marvellously increasing; while British India in its turn is reduced to "extreme poverty" and helotry.

Will the India Office be good enough to give us a Return of the enormous wealth which Britain has drawn out of India during the past century and a half, calculated with ordinary British commercial 5 per cent. compound interest, leave alone the 9 per cent. ordinary commercial rate of interest of British India? What a tale will that Return tell! The India Office must have all the records of the India House as well as its own.

I give a few figures that are available to me. The best test of this drain from British India is (1) that portion of produce exported out of British India for which nothing whatever has returned to her in any shape, either of merchandise or treasure; (2) the profits of her whole exports which she never got; (3) that portion of the exports which belongs to the Native States, and which the Native States get back, with their due profits, are incuded in the total imports, and are therefore not included in the "net exports." For No. (1) I have the following authoritative figures for only 45 years (1849-50 to 1894-5, "Statistical Abstract of British India," No. 30, 1895, p. 299). Will the India Office supply previous figures?

This table shows that British India sent out, or exported, of her produce to the extent of £526,740,000, for which she has not received back a single farthing's worth of any kind of material return. Besides this loss or drain of actual produce, there is (No. 2) the further drain of the profits on an export of £2,851,000,000, which, taken at only 10 per cent., will be another £285,000,000—which British India has not received—subject to the deduction of portion of (No. 3), viz., the profits of the Native States. To this has to be added the profits which Indian foreigners (*i.e.*, the capitalists of Native States) make in British India, and carry away to their own States. Freight and marine insurance premiums have to be taken into account, for whether for exports from, or imports into, India, these items are always paid in England. It is necessary to know how these two items are dealt with in the Returns of the so-called trade of British India. In ordinary circumstances, one may not complain if a foreigner came and made his profits on a fair and equal footing with the people of British India. But British India is not allowed such fair and equal footing.

First, the unrighteous and despotic system of Government prevents British India from enjoying its own produce or resources, and renders it capital-less and helpless. Then, foreign capitalists come in and complete the disaster, sinking the people to the condition of their hewers of wood and drawers of water. The enormous resources of India are all at the disposal and command of these foreigners.

In understanding correctly the tables to which I refer, it must be borne in mind that all the loans made to India form a part of the imports, and are already paid for and included in that portion of the exports which is equal to the total imports, the "net exports" in the table being, *after* allowing for *all* imports, including loans. Otherwise, if these loans were deducted from the imports, the "net exports" will be so much larger. The position of the exploitation by the foreign capitalists is still worse than I have already represented. Not only do they exploit and make profits with their own capital, but they draw even their capital from the taxation of the poor people themselves. The following words of Sir James Westland in the telegram of the *Times* of 18th December last will explain what I mean.

"Sir J. Westland then explained how closely connected the Money Market of India was with the Government balances, almost as the available capital employed in commerce practically being in those balances. . . . . A crore and a half which under normal conditions would have been at head quarters in Calcutta and Bombay and been placed at the disposal of the mercantile community for trading purposes."

The Bank of Bengal and Chamber of Commerce "pressed the Government to take up the question of the paper currency reserve as urgently as possible, and pass a Bill without delay to afford relief to commerce." So, the European merchants, bankers, etc., may have Indian taxes at their disposal, the profits of which they may take away to their own country! The poor wretched taxpayers must not only find money for an unrighteous system of Government expenditure but must also supply capital to exploit their own resources.

The reference to this Commission is to enquire into expenditure and apportionment. I am fully convinced, and my representations fully prove it, that if the system of the administration and management of expenditure and the apportionment were based on principles of righteousness honesty, honour, and unselfishness, the political peculiarities of India are such as would produce an abiding attachment and connexion between the two countries, which will not merely be of much benefit to British India but of vastly more benefit to the British themselves than at present. Hence, my extreme desire that the connexion should continue, and I can say truly that, in a spirit of loyalty both to India and to the British Empire, I have devoted my life to strengthening this connexion. I feel it therefore my duty (though a painful one) to point out candidly the causes which, in my opinion, have weakened, and are weakening more and more, this connexion, and, unless checked, threaten to destroy it.

I. The un-English autocratic and despotic system of administration, under which the Indian people are not given the slightest voice in the management of their own expenditure. It is not creditable to the British character that they should refuse to a loyal and law-abiding people that voice in their own affairs which they value so much for themselves.

II. The unrighteous "bleeding" of India, under which the masses have been reduced to such "extreme poverty" that the failure of one harvest causes millions upon millions to die from hunger, and scores of millions are living on "scanty subsistence." What Oriental despotism or Russian despotism in Russia can produce a more deplorable result?

III. The breach or evasion by subterfuges of solemn pledges and proclamations, issued by her Majesty and the British nation, and the flouting of such Acts and Resolutions of Parliament as are favourable to Indians. Such proceedings destroy the confidence of the Indian people in the justice of British rule. To sum up, these and other errors in administration have had the effect of inflicting upon India the triple evil of depriving the people of Wealth, Work, and Wisdom, and making the British Indians, as the ultimate result, "extremely poor," unemployed (their services which are their property in their own country, being plundered from them) and degradingly deteriorated and debased, crushing out of them their very humanhood.

Before I proceed further, let me clear up a strange confusion of ideas about prosperous British India and poverty-stricken British India. This confusion of ideas arises from this circumstance. My remarks are for British India only.

In reality there are two Indias—one the prosperous, the other poverty-stricken.

(1) The prosperous India is the India of the British and other foreigners. They exploit India as officials, non-officials, capitalists, in a variety of ways, and carry away enormous wealth to their own country. To them India is, of course, rich and prosperous. The more they can carry away, the richer and more prosperous India is to them. These British and other foreigners cannot understand and realise why India can be called "extremely poor," when they can make their life careers; they can draw so much wealth from it and enrich their own country. It seldom occurs to them, if at all, what all that means to the Indians themselves.

(2) The second India is the India of the Indians—the poverty-stricken India. This India, "bled" and exploited in every way of their wealth, of their services, of their land, labour, and all resources by the foreigners, helpless and voiceless, governed by the arbitrary law and argument of force, and with injustice and unrighteousness—this India of the Indians becomes the "poorest" country in the world, after one hundred and fifty years of British rule, to the disgrace of the British name. The greater the drain the greater the impoverishment, resulting in all the scourges of war, famine and pestilence. Lord Salisbury's words face us at every turn, "Injustice will bring down the mightiest to ruin." If this distinction of the "prosperous India" of the slave-holders and the "poverty-stricken India" of the slaves be carefully borne in mind, a great deal of the controversy on this point will be saved. Britain can, by a righteous system, make both Indias prosperous. The great pity is that the Indian authorities do not or would not see it. They are blinded by selfishness—to find careers for "our boys."

To any appeals the ears of the British Indian authorities are deaf. The only thing that an Indian can do is to appeal to the British *people*. I must explain. I have no complaint against the British people. The Sovereign, the British people, and Parliament, have all in one direction done their duty by laying down the true and righteous principles of dealing with India. But their desires and biddings are made futile by their servants, the Indian authorities, in both countries. For these reasons my only resource is to appeal to the British people and to this Commission to cause the orders of her Majesty and of Parliament to be carried out.

It is not needful for me to repeat my views, which I have given in my five previous representations, which have been in the hands of the Commission from nine to fifteen months, and in which I have dealt with both the injustice and the evils, and the remedy of the present system of expenditure and apportionment, and it remains for the Commission to cross-examine me on all the six representations.

I would add here a few more remarks arising from some of the evidence and other circumstances.

The Indians are repeatedly told, and in this Commission several times, that Indians are partners in the British Empire and must share the burdens of the Empire. Then I propose a simple test. For instance, supposing that the expenditure of the total Navy of the Empire is, say, £20,000,000, and as partners in the Empire you ask British India to pay £10,000,000, more or less, British India, as partner, would be ready to pay, and therefore, as partner, must have her share in the employment of British Indians, and in every other benefit of the service to the extent of her contribution. Take the Army. Suppose the expenditure of the total Army of the Empire is, say, £40,000,000. Now, you may ask £20,000,000, or more or less, to be contributed by British India. Then, as partners, India must claim, and must have, every employment and benefit of that service to the extent of her contribution. If, on the other hand, you force the helpless and voiceless British India to pay, but not to receive, a return to the extent of the payment, then your treatment is the unrighteous wicked treatment of the slave-master over British India as a slave. In short, if British India is to be treated as a partner in the Empire, it must follow that to whatever extent (be it a farthing or a hundred millions) British India contributes to the expenses of any department, to that extent the British Indians must have a share in the services and benefits of that department—whether civil, military, naval or any other; then only will British India be the "integral part" of, or partner in, the Empire. If there be honour and righteousness on the side of the British, then this is the right solution of the rights and duties of British India and of both the references to this Commission. Then will the Empire become a true Empire with an honest partnership, and not a false Empire and an untrue partnership. This is the main, principal question the Commission has to clear up. This will fully show the true nature and solution of both the expenditure and apportionment. I appeal to the British people. When I have been personally observing, during forty years, how the British people are always on the side of the helpless and the oppressed; how, at present, they are exerting every nerve, and lavishing money, to save the thousands of Armenians, then I cannot believe that the same people will refuse to see into the system of expenditure adopted by their own servants, by which not merely some thousands or hundred thousands suffer, but by which millions of their own fellow-subjects perish in a drought, and scores of millions live underfed, on scanty subsistence, from one end of the year to the other. The so-called Famine Relief Fund is nothing more or less than a mere subterfuge of taxing the starving to save the dying. This fund does not rain from heaven, nor does the British Exchequer give it. If the Government spend, say £5,000,000, on the present famine they will simply squeeze it out of the poverty-stricken surviving taxpayers, who would in turn become the victims of the next drought.

The British people stand charged with the blood of the perishing millions and the starvation of scores of millions, not because they desire so, but because the authorities to whom they have committed the trust betray that trust and administer expenditure in a manner based upon selfishness and political hypocrisy, and most disastrous to the people. There is an Indian saying: "Pray strike on the back, but don't strike on the belly."

Under the Native despot the people keep and enjoy what they produce, though at times they suffer some violence on the back. Under the British Indian despot the man is at peace, there is no violence; his substance is drained away, unseen, peaceably and subtly—he starves in peace and perishes in peace, with law and order! I wonder how the English people would like such a fate! I say, therefore, to the British people, by all means help the poor Armenians, but I appeal to you to look home also, and save the hundreds of millions of your own fellow-subjects, from whom you have taken thousands of millions of wealth, and obtained also your

Indian Empire, entirely at their cost and mainly with their blood, with great careers for thousands of yourselves at our cost and destruction.

The great question is not merely how to meet a famine when it occurs—by taxing the poor people—but how to prevent the occurrence of the famine. As long as the present unrighteous system will prevail there will be no end of the scourges of India. We are thankful for the benefit of the knowledge of "Western civilisation." But what we need is the deeds of *Western righteousness and honour* to stop the famine and to advance the prosperity of both countries. With relation to the present famine I have to make one or two remarks.

For the famine of 1878, the British help amounted to the magnificent sum of about, I think, £700,000. On the other hand the British public have to remember that they have been drawing, by the unrighteous system of the authorities, every year 30 to 40, or more times, £700,000, from poor India; or say from the time of the last famine they have drawn from India, and added to their own wealth, some £400,000,000 or more (leaving alone what they have been draining for a century and a half), and if they now give even £4,000,000 or £5,000,000 in the present distress, it will be but 1 or 2 per cent. of what they have obtained from India during the last eighteen years. It is a duty of the British people to give in abundance from the great, great abundance they have received. As far as the poor people of India are concerned, they will receive whatever you would give with deep gratitude in their dire extremity.

The second fact is, what the British people will readily and early give will have a double blessing. They will in the first instance save so many lives, and in the next place save the poor survivors from so much taxation, which otherwise the Government would exact every farthing of, for whatever Government would spend from the revenue. The novel loud and vain boast of the Government of India having resources to meet the famine simply means this, that every farthing of the whole famine expenditure (bad or good) by the Government, will be, by their despotic power, squeezed out of the wretched people themselves by taxation in which they have not the slightest voice. Never was there a false trumpet blown than the boast of the Government to be able to cope with the famine "with its own resources." Of course the resources of despotism are inexhaustible, for who can prevent it from taxing as much as it likes? It is a wonder to me that they do not feel ashamed of talking of "their own resources," when it all means so much more squeezing of a squeezed and helpless people. And especially when they not only, Shylock-like, take the whole pound of their large salaries, but also the ounce of blood of their illegal and immoral exchange compensation!

Amongst the most favourite excuses of the Anglo-Indians is, that the extreme poverty of the people and the disasters of famines are owing to increase of population. I have dealt with this subject in my third representation, and I want to say a few words more. The point to which I want to draw attention here is, that Anglo-Indians, official or non-official of every kind, are not at all competent to pronounce any judgment upon the causes of poverty and disasters of famines. For they themselves are the accused, as the cause of all the evils, and they cannot be judges to try themselves. Their own deep interest is concerned in it. Let them withdraw their hand from India's throat, and then see whether the increase in population is not an addition to its strength and production instead of British-made famines and poverty. Then it will also be seen that the hundreds of millions of British India, instead of being afflicted with all sorts of evils, will become your best customers and give you a *true* trade—more than your present trade with the whole world.

I now refer to a strange sign of the times. By an irony of fate, and as an indication of the future, and after 150 years of British connexion and rule, Russia—to whom the Anglo-Indians always point as a threat—offers generous sympathy and aid to starving and dying British subjects. I do not pretend to know Russia's mind, but any one can see what the effect of this, aided by the emissaries, might be on India. "See how kind and generous the Russians are, and give us help." It will be further pointed out, "See, not only are the Russians sympathetic with you, but their great Emperor himself has published in his book words of condemnation of the rule which sucks away your lifeblood." The *Times* of 10th December last, in its leader on the Russo-Chinese Treaty, says:—"Russia, we may be sure, will pursue her own policy and promote her own interests." "Russia is bent upon developing her vast Asiatic Empire." But the blind Indian authorities would not see that England would not have any chance to hold her own in India without the true (not lip-loyal) attachment of the Indian people. Is it possible for any sane man to think that any one nation can hold another in slavery and yet expect loyal devotion and attachment from it? It is not nature, not human nature. It has never happened and will never happen. Righteousness alone can exalt and be enduring. Events are moving fast. The time is come when the question must be speedily answered, whether India is to be a real partner and strength to England, or a slave and a weakness to England—as it has hitherto been. How much of the future destiny of the British Empire and India depends upon this, a man of an unbiassed mind can think for himself. India forms five-sixths of the population of the British Empire.

I put one question, which I have often put, and which is always ignored or evaded. Suppose the British people were subjected to the same despotic treatment of expenditure by some foreign people, as India is by the British Indian authorities, would the British people stand it a single day without rebelling against it? No, certainly not; and yet, can the British people think it righteous and just to treat the Indians as the Indian authorities do—as mere helpless and voiceless slaves. Macaulay has truly said that

"that would indeed be a doting wisdom which, in order that India might remain a dependency, would make it a useless and costly dependency, which would keep a hundred millions (now 225,000,000) from being our customers in order that they might continue to be our slaves."

The question of remedy I have already dealt with in my fifth representation, and I would not have said more here. But as the *Times* of 8th December last, in its article on "Indian Affairs," confirms, by actual facts and events, the wisdom and statesmanship of Lords Salisbury and Iddesleigh in their one great work of righteous and wise policy, I desire to quote a few words. Fortunately, it is the very Mysore State to which this righteous and wise act was done. The *Times* says:—

"The account which Sir Sheshadri Iyer rendered to it of his last year's stewardship is one of increasing revenue, reduced taxation, expenditure firmly kept in hand, reproductive public works, and a large expansion of cultivation, of mining and of industrial undertakings. The result is a surplus which goes to swell the previous accumulations from the same source."

Can the present system of British administration and management of the expenditure ever produce such results? Never. A dozen Gladstones will not succeed.

Continuous and increasing "bleeding" can only reduce strength and kill. The *Times*' article concludes with the words:—

"A narrative such as Sir Sheshadri Iyer was able to give to the Representative Assembly of Mysore makes us realise the growth of capital in the Native States, and opens up new prospects of industrial undertakings and railway construction in India on a silver basis."

Can this be said of British India? No. I shall quote one other extract.

"One of the Bombay Chiefs, after some experience of railway-making in his own and adjoining territories, struck out a new departure at the beginning of the present year. He conceived the idea of public loans to be issued for railway construction by one Feudatory Prince to another on the guarantee of the revenues of the borrowing State. The first transaction in which this principle is completely carried out was a loan of two million rupees by H.H. Sir Bhagvat Sinhji, the ruler of Gondal, to H.H. Jasvant Sinhji, the ruler of Jamnagar on the 8th of January, 1896."

Now, anybody who knows Jamnagar, knows that with ordinary good management it will not be long before that State is in a possition to pay off its debts, just as the good management of Mysore was able to do, and the good management of Gondal has enabled its ruler to lend such an amount. This loan by Gondal, it must be remembered, is in addition to building its own railway in its own territory from its own revenue, without any loan, or help, or additional taxation.

No one can rejoice more than myself that Native States which adopt ordinary good management go on increasing in prosperity in strong contrast with the system of the British management of expenditure. This is fully confirmatory of the words of Lords Salisbury and Iddesleigh as to what should be done for British India's prosperity. I have quoted these words in my fifth representation. And some of them are worth quoting here once more. Lord Salisbury said:—

"The general concurrence of opinion of those who know India best is that a number of well-governed small Native States are in the highest degree advantageous to the development of the political and moral condition of the people of India. . . . But I think the existence of a well-governed Native State is a real benefit, not only to the stability of our rule, but because more than anything it raises the self-respect of the Natives, and forms an ideal to which the popular feelings aspire."

Referring to the several phases of the British rule, he sums up that they produce an amount of inefficiency which, when reinforced by natural causes and circumstances, creates a terrible amount of misery. It might also be noted that the richest provinces and most important seaports are now British. So the people of British India should be much more prosperous than those living in the inferior districts left to Native Chiefs. Yet in British India is the "terrible amount of misery," after a rule of 150 years by the most highly-trumpeted and most highly paid services. Lord Iddesleigh not only agreed with the best course indicated by Lord Salisbury, but actually put it fully into operation with the confidence that the course he took would "at once afford a guarantee for the good government of the people, and for the security of British rights and interests." And after an experience of fifteen years, the writer in the *Times* is able to express such highly favourable opinion as I have quoted above.

Another favourite argument of some Anglo-Indians is the want of capacity of the Indians. In the evidence last year this was referred to once or twice. There is a paper of mine in the Journals of the East India Association on that subject, but I do not want to trouble the Commission with it. It is the old trick of the tyrant not to give you the opportunity of fair trial, and to condemn you off-hand as incapable. The Indians are put to the iniquitous handicap to come over to this country for the civil services in their own country, and from the Army and Navy they are entirely excluded from the commissioned ranks; and all this in complete violation of the most sacred pledges and Acts of Parliament. I will not, however, trouble the Commission with any further remarks on this all-important subject. It is enough for me to put before the Commission the article in the *Times* of 5th October last on Indian affairs as the latest honest expression of a well-known Anglo-Indian, as there have been many already from time to time from other Anglo-Indians. I put this article as an appendix.

In question 13,353, Lord Wolseley said "there never was an India until we made it"; and in question 12,796, Sir Ralph

Knox says, "My own view is that England has made India what she is." I acknowledge the correctness of these statements, viz., an India to be exploited by foreigners, and the most wretched, the poorest, the helpless, without the slightest voice in her own expenditure, perishing by millions in a drought, and starving by scores of millions; in short, "bleeding" at every pore and a helotry for England. It is not England of the English people who have made India what she is. It is the British Indian authorities who have made her what she is.

And now I shall give some account of the process by which this deplorable result was begun to be achieved. I give the character of the process in authoritative words—words of the Court of Directors, the Bengal Government, and Lord Clive—disinterred and exposed by the Committee of 1772.

First I shall give a few words of the Court of Directors:—

"A scene of most cruel oppression" (8/2/1764). "That they have been guilty of violating treaties, of great oppression and a combination to enrich themselves" (Court of Directors' Letter, 26/4/1765). "The infidelity, rapaciousness, and misbehaviour of our servants in general." "Every Englishman throughout the country . . . . exercising his power to the oppression of the helpless Native." "We have the strongest sense of the deplorable state . . . . from the corruption and rapacity of our servants, and the universal depravity of manners throughout the settlement," "by a scene of the most tyrannic and oppressive conduct that ever was known in any age or country" (17/5/1766).

Now, a few words of Lord Clive and Bengal letters:—

"Rapacity and luxury." "It is no wonder that the lust of riches should readily embrace the proffered means of its gratification, or that the instruments of your power should avail themselves of their authority, and proceed even to extortion in those cases where simple corruption could not keep pace with their rapacity." "Luxury, corruption, avarice, and rapacity" "to stem that torrent of luxury, corruption and licentiousness," "the depravity of the Settlement," "shameful oppression and flagrant corruption," "grievous exactions and oppressions." "The most flagrant oppressions by members of the Board." "An administration so notoriously corrupt and meanly venal throughout every department," "which, if enquired into, will produce discoveries which cannot bear the light . . . . but may bring disgrace upon this nation, and at the same time, blast the reputation of great and good families."

Such were the first relations between England and India, and the manner in which India was being made what she is.

Change came—corruption and oppression were replaced

by high salaries. It is so easy and agreeable to give one's own countrymen high salaries at other people's expense—the drain remains going on heavier and heavier. What the drain in the last century was generally estimated at—something like three or five millions a year—has now become, perhaps, ten times as much. Would the India Office be good enough to give a correct statement?

Adding insult to injury, the Indians have often flaunted in their face the loans made to them, which are perhaps not one twentieth of what is taken away from the wretched country, and which further drains the country in the shape of profits and interest. And the capitalists also are supposed to benefit us by using us as hewers of wood and drawers of water, and taking away from the country the profits of the resources of that country, and thus we lose our own wealth, services, and experience, helplessly; and yet we are told by some we are getting immensely prosperous. May the British people never meet our fate!

After I had finished the above I attended the meeting at the Mansion House. I do not in any way blame the speakers; but what a humiliating confession it was about the treatment of India by England. The only wonder is that those who made this confession did not seem to be conscious of its humiliation and unrighteousness. On the contrary, they took it with a complacency as if it was a merit of the Indian authorities. But Nature spoke the truth of the great wrong through them. Here is a people, who if they pride themselves—and justly pride—upon anything, it is their love of liberty, their determination to submit to no despotic master, who beheaded one king and banished another to preserve and maintain their government, with the voice of the people themselves, who sing that Britain shall never be a slave, whose fundamental boast is that they regard "taxation without representation is tyranny," and that they would resist any such tyranny to a man. These people, it is confessed from a platform in the very centre of the struggle for liberty, proclaimed with a *naïveté* and unctuousness that they deliberately in India deprived the hundreds of millions of people of this very right of humanhood for which they are so proud for themselves, that they reduced the people of India from humanhood to beasts of burden, depriving them of every voice whatsoever in their own affairs, and that they deliberately chose to govern them as the worst despots—the foreign despots for whom Macaulay has said that "the heaviest of all yokes is the yoke of the stranger." And it is this yoke of the worst despotism they imposed upon India, with all its most horrible evils of exploitation and all the scourges of this world. A Briton would not be a slave, but he would make hundreds of millions of others his slaves!—the greatest crime that any one nation can commit against another. And yet these Anglo-Indians are so callous to their own British instincts and character, that they proclaimed from the platform, with every complacency, that they had deliberately committed the unhumanising wrong, without feeling the least blush of shame, and to the disgrace and humiliation of their own nation, the British people, though the British people never desired such un-English unrighteousness towards the people of India; on the contrary, they always desired and proclaimed, by the most solemn pledges and Acts of Parliament, that the Indians shall be British citizens, with all the rights and duties of British citizenship, exactly like those which the British people themselves enjoy. Never was there a more condemnatory confession than in those speeches, that with the results of the terrible famine and plague they were bringing out more and more the bitter fruits of their unrighteous system in the administration of expenditure in the deaths of millions by famine and in the starvation of scores of millions.

The other day an Anglo-Indian military officer, talking about the immigration of the persecuted Jews in this country, held forth with the greatest indignation why these wretched Jews should come to this country and deprive our poor workingmen of their bread. Little did he think at the time that he himself was an immigrant forced upon the Indian people by a despotic rule, and was depriving them, not of the bread of one person, but perhaps of hundreds, or thousands, of the poor workingmen of India.

I felt thankful from the bottom of my heart to the Lord Mayor for that meeting. It brought out two things—a satisfactory assurance to the Indian people that the British people are feeling for their distress, and are willing to help; and a lesson to the British people which they ought to take to heart, and for which they should do their duty, that their servants have deliberately adopted an un-English and unrighteous course, and deprived hundreds of millions of human beings of the very thing which the British people value most above all things in the world—their own voice in their own affairs; their highest glory above all other nationalities in the world. They call us fellow-citizens, and they must make their word a reality, instead of what it is at present, an untruth and a romance—simply a relationship of slaveholder and slave.

I shall sum up my six representations by reading before the Commission a brief note of my propositions at the commencement of my examination, leaving the Commission to cross-examine me afterwards. I shall also lay before the Commission certain other papers bearing upon our enquiry.

Yours truly,

DADABHAI NAOROJI.

APPENDIX.

[From the *Times*, October 5, 1896.]

INDIAN AFFAIRS.

PRINCE RANJITSINHJI AND MR. CHATTERJI.

THE head of English cricket for the year, and the head of the India Civil Service competition for the year are both Hindus. Mr. Chatterji's achievement is not less remarkable in the arena of intellectual athletics than is Prince Ranjitsinhji's in the world of sport. Probably no career open to Englishmen exerts a more powerful attraction on the clever youth of our public schools and Universities than the India Civil Service, and the competition for its appointments has been elaborated into the most searching test that the wit of examiners can devise. The distinguished academic careers of many of the sixty-one gentlemen who follow Mr. Chatterji in the list show the class of rivals among whom he has won the first place. As Prince Ranjitsinhji is not only head of English cricket for 1896, but also head by performances of exceptional brilliancy, so Mr. Chatterji is *facile princeps* in the great intellectual struggle, with a long interval between himself and the next man.

There is a certain fitness that these young Hindus should be representatives of the two ancient castes which from time immemorial ruled India. Prince Ranjitsinhji belongs to the Rajput, literally "Royal-born," or military caste that supplied the hereditary soldier families of Hindustan. Mr. Chatterji springs of what is regarded by his countrymen as a more august lineage. With an unbroken and a verified descent from one of the five Brahmans who, according to the tradition which in India passes for history, brought sacred rites into the lower valleys of the Ganges from the north twelve hundred years ago, his family forms one of a close confederacy which has furnished, during ten centuries, the intellectual force in Bengal. Indians of the high descents to which Mr. Chatterji and Prince Ranjitsinhji belong have hitherto been infrequent visitors to England. Their caste-rules long stood in the way of their crossing "the black-water," and although this infraction of ancient custom may now be condoned by penance on their return, the great majority of Indians in Great Britain are still derived from races or classes holding a lower position in the Indian social scale. The young hero of the cricket-field represents a stock whose one pursuit during ages has been the practice of the manly virtues and of war. The head of the India Civil Service examination represents a caste whose functions during an equal period have been the art of government and the acquisition of learning. Prince Ranjitsinhji is a Rajput of Western India. Mr. Chatterji is a Brahman of its most easterly province, Bengal.

The service which Prince Ranjitsinhji has performed for India is not that he has proved one of his race to be capable of the highest achievement in our national sport, but that he has made the fact known to the whole British people. The few Englishmen who know the Indians well, readily admit that the Rajputs are brave and athletic and the Brahmans clever at learning. But to the masses of our countrymen who pay gate-money, Prince Ranjitsinhji's performances amount to a new discovery of India. It brings home to them the fact that among our fellow-subjects in Asia, those fellow-subjects whose very hundreds of millions turn them into numerical abstractions, there are men who can take the lead in the national sport which all Englishmen love and more or less understand. Prince Ranjitsinhji's victory has enabled the average Englishman to realise India, and has made him respect Indians to a degree that no other triumph could have secured. But it merely is the crest of the wave of a movement which has long been going on in India, and which is there producing striking results. That movement is from the old pursuits of the East to the new pursuits of the West. Half a century ago the standards of excellence in India remained little affected by modern influences. To become learned in the Veda was still the highest aim of a Brahman; to ride about at the head of his little household guard was still the ambition of a Rajput chief. To take part in a public game of football would have been as far beneath the dignity of a Rajput prince as the study of anatomy would have been degrading to a Brahman. The recent successes of Prince Ranjitsinhji and Mr. Chatterji give emphasis in England to a change which has for some time been well understood in India—a change from the old pursuits of the high castes and from their old standards of excellence to the new pursuits and the new standards of excellence which Englishmen carry with them to whatever country they go. At first it seemed that the change was a mere matter of imitation. But the change has long advanced beyond the imitative stage. Prince Ranjitsinhji's playing is distinguished above all things by its originality, *verve*, and personal resource. The long interval between

Mr. Chatterji and the next man to him on the list indicates a not less remarkable capacity.

Their successes do not stand alone. Among the most interesting features at the British Association this year was the paper on Electrical Waves by Professor J. C. Bose. This gentleman, an M.A. of Cambridge, Doctor of Science of London, and a graduate of the Calcutta University, had already won the attention of the scientific world by his strikingly original researches on the polarisation of the electric ray. His later papers on the Determination of the Indices of Electric Refraction and of the Wave-Length of Electric Radiation were published, with high tributes, by the Royal Society. Lord Kelvin declared himself "literally filled with wonder and admiration for so much success in these difficult and novel experimental problems." The originality of the achievement is enhanced by the fact that Dr. Bose had to do the work in addition to his incessant duties as Professor of Physical Science in Calcutta and with apparatus and appliances which in this country would be deemed altogether inadequate. He had to construct for himself his instruments as he went along. The paper which was read before the British Association the other day "On a Complete Apparatus for the Study of the Properties of Electric Waves" forms the outcome of this two-fold line of labour—construction and research. Professor Bose is not only an example of the change from the old philosophical and *a priori* pursuits of learned Indians to the experimental science of the West, but he has also persuaded the Government to recognise that change. He has been deputed to visit the chief laboratories in Europe, with a view to forming a well-equipped laboratory in Calcutta for physical and electrical work. The position which Professor Bose has attained among British men of science, while himself still in the first energies of manhood, is as significant as the successes of Prince Ranjitsinhji and Mr. Chatterji in their widely diverse fields of effort.

Perhaps an even more striking example of the new departure is to be found in the case of Lieutenant S. C. Biswas, who distinguished himself so honourably during the late insurrection in Brazil. As first lieutenant of an infantry regiment he was told off, on the night of the great bombardment, after the fire had gone on for six hours, to seize or silence a battery. Advancing with his company he seems to have fallen into a sort of trap, and was called on to surrender on pain of instant destruction. "Comrades," he shouted to his men, "you will see how a son of the sacred land of Hindustan can throw himself on those guns. Follow!" Somehow he got in between the fire, the artillerymen were cut down, and the cannons captured. Such is the narrative as given by a Brazilian writer last March. Lieutenant Biswas, like Mr. Chatterji and Professor Bose, was a Bengali. Their successes, like that of Prince Ranjitsinhji, mean that in India the old order is giving place to the new, and that Indians seem likely to win high places for themselves in the new world of practical achievement, as their fathers held a high place, from Alexander the Great onwards, in the old world of abstract thought.

VII.

Washington House,
72, Anerley Park, S.E.
November 3rd, 1897.

DEAR LORD WELBY,—I now give my statement on the Admission of Natives to the Covenanted Civil Service in India, as promised by me at the meeting of the Commission on 21st July last, and request you to place it before the Commission. I shall send a copy to the members.

If required, I shall give any further statement I can on any particular point that may require to be more elucidated. I shall be willing to be cross-examined if required.

The first deliberate and practical action was taken by Parliament in the year 1833.

All aspects of the whole question of all services were then fully discussed by eminent men; and a Committee of the House made searching enquiry into the whole subject.

I give below extracts from what was said on that occasion, and a definite conclusion was adopted.

I am obliged to give some of the extracts at length, because it must be clearly seen on what statesmanlike and farseeing grounds this conclusion was arrived at.

The italics all through are mine, except when I say that they are in the original.

East India Company's Charter,
Hansard, Vol. XIX, Third Series, p. 169.
July 5th, 1833.

The MARQUIS OF LANSDOWNE: "But he should be taking a very narrow view of this question, and one utterly inadequate to the great importance of the subject, which involved in it the happiness or misery of 100,000,000 of human beings, were he not to call the attention of their lordships *to the bearing which this question and to the influence which this arrangement must exercise upon the future destinies of that vast mass of people.* He was sure that their lordships would feel, as he indeed felt, that their only justification before God and Providence for the great and unprecedented dominion which they exercised in India was in the happiness which they communicated to the subjects under their rule, and in proving to the world at large and to the inhabitants of Hindustan that the inheritance of Akbar (the wisest and most beneficent of Mahomedan Princes) had not fallen into unworthy or degenerate hands. Hence it was important that when the dominion of India was transferred from the East India Company to the King's Government they should have the benefit of the experience of the most enlightened councillors, not only on the financial condition of our Empire in the East but also on the character of its inhabitants. He stated confidently, after referring to the evidence given by persons eminently calculated to estimate what the character of the people of India was, that they must, as a first step to their improved social condition, be admitted to a larger share in the administration of their local affairs. On that point their lordships had the testimony of a series of successful experiments and the evidence of the most unexceptionable witnesses who had gone at a mature period of their life and with much natural and acquired knowledge to visit the East. Among the crowd of witnesses which he could call to the improvable condition of the Hindu character he would select only two; but those two were well calculated to form a correct judgment, and fortunately contemplated Indian society from very different points of view. Those two witnesses were Sir Thomas Monro and Bishop Heber. He could not conceive any two persons more eminently calculated to form an accurate opinion upon human character, and particularly upon that of the Hindu tribes. They were both highly distinguished for talent and integrity, yet they were placed in situations from which they might have easily come to the formation of different opinions—one of them being conversant with the affairs of the East from his childhood and familiarised by long habit with the working of the system, and the other being a refined Christian philosopher and scholar going out to the East late in life, and applying in India the knowledge which he had acquired here to form an estimate of the character of its inhabitants. He held in his hand the testimony of each of those able men, as extracted from their different published works, and with the permission of the House he would read a few words from both. Sir T. Monro, in speaking of the Hindu character, said: 'Unless we suppose that they are inferior to us in natural talent, which there is no reason to believe, it is much more likely that they will be duly qualified for their employments than Europeans for theirs—because the field of selection is so much greater in the one than in the other. We have a whole nation from which to make our choice of Natives, but in order to make choice of Europeans we have only the small body of the Company's Covenanted servants. No conceit more wild and absurd than this was ever engendered in the darkest ages: for what is in every age and every country the great stimulus to the pursuit of knowledge but the prospect of fame or wealth or power? Or what is even the use of great attainments if they are not to be devoted to their noblest purpose, the service of the community, by employing those who possess them according to their respective qualifications in the various duties of the public administration of the country? Our books alone will do little or nothing; dry, simple literature will never improve the character of a nation. To produce this effect it must open the road to wealth and honour and public employment. Without the prospect of such reward no attainments in science will ever raise the character of a people.' That was the sound practical opinion of Sir T. Monro, founded on his experience acquired in every part of India, in every department of the public service. Bishop Heber during his extensive journey of charity and religion through India, to which he at length fell a martyr, used these remarkable expressions: 'Of the natural disposition of the Hindu I still see abundant reason to think highly, and Mr. Bayley and Mr. Melville both agreed with me that they are constitutionally kind-hearted, industrious, sober, and peaceable; at the same time that they show themselves on proper occasions a manly and courageous people.' And again: 'They are decidedly by nature a mild, pleasing, and intelligent race, sober, parsimonious, and, where an object is held out to them, most industrious and persevering.' Their lordships were therefore justified in coming to the same conclusion—a conclusion to which, indeed, they must come if they only considered the acts of this people in past ages—if they only looked at the monuments of gratitude and piety which they had erected to their benefactors and friends—for to India, if to any country, the observation of the poet applied :—

> 'Sunt hic etiam sua præmia laudi,
> Sunt lacrymæ verum, et mentem mortalia tangunt.'

But, however much civilisation had been obscured in those regions, whatever inroads foreign conquest and domestic superstition had made upon their moral habits, it was undeniable that they had still materials left for improving and ameliorating their condition; and their lordships would be remiss in the performance of the high duties which devolved upon them if they did not secure to the numerous Natives of Hindustan the ample development of all their mental endowments and moral qualifications. *It was a part of the new system which he had to propose to their lordships that to every office in India every Native, of whatsoever caste, sect, or religion, should by law be equally admissible, and he hoped that Government would seriously endeavour to give the fullest effect to this arrangement, which would be as beneficial to the people themselves as it would be advantageous to the economical reforms which were now in progress in different parts of India.*"

. . . . .

(*Page* 174, *July 5th*, 1833.)—"And without being at all too sanguine as to the result of the following up those principles without calculating upon any extension of territory through them, he was confident *that the strength of the Government would be increased by the happiness of the people over whom it presided, and by the attachment of those nations to it.*"

Vol. XIX., Third Series, p, 191.
July 5th, 1833.

Lord Ellenborough: "He felt deeply interested in the prosperity of India, and when he was a Minister of the Crown, filling an office peculiarly connected with that country, he had always considered it his paramount duty to do all in his power to promote that prosperity. He was as anxious as any of his Majesty's Ministers could be to raise the moral character of the Native population of India. He trusted that the time would eventually come, though he never expected to see it, when the Natives of India could, with advantage to the country and with honour to themselves, fill even the highest situations there. He looked forward to the arrival of such a period, though he considered it far distant from the present day; and he proposed, by the reduction of taxation, which was the only way to benefit the lower classes in India, to elevate them ultimately in the scale of society, so as to fit them for admission to offices of power and trust. To attempt to precipitate the arrival of such a state of society as that he had been describing was the surest way to defeat the object in view. He never, however, looked forward to a period when all offices in India would be placed in the hands of Natives. No man in his senses would propose to place the political and military power in India in the hands of the Natives.

"The Marquess of Lansdowne observed that what the Government proposed was that all offices in India should be by law open to the Natives of that country.

"Lord Ellenborough said such was precisely the proposition of Government, but our very existence in India depended upon the exclusion of the Natives from military and political power in that country. We were there in a situation not of our own seeking, in a situation from which we could not recede without producing bloodshed from one end of India to the other. We had won the Empire of India by the sword, and we must preserve it by the same means, doing at the same time everything that was consistent with our existence there for the good of the people."

Macaulay fully answers Lord Ellenborough.

Vol. XIX, Third Series, p. 533.
July 10th, 1833.

Mr. MACAULAY: "I have detained the House so long, Sir, that I will defer what I had to say in some parts of this measure—important parts, indeed, but far less important as I think than those to which I have adverted, till we are in Committee. There is, however, one part of the Bill on which, after what has recently passed elsewhere, I feel myself irresistibly impelled to say a few words. *I allude to that wise, that benevolent, that noble clause, which enacts that no Native of our Indian Empire shall, by reason of his colour, his descent, or his religion, be incapable of holding office.* At the risk of being called by that nickname which is regarded as the most opprobrious of all nicknames by men of selfish hearts and contracted minds—at the risk of being called a philosopher—*I must say that, to the last day of my life, I shall be proud of having been one of those who assisted in the framing of the Bill which contains that clause.* We are told that the time can never come when the Natives of India can be admitted to high civil and military office. We are told that this is the condition on which we hold our power. We are told that we are bound to confer on our subjects—every benefit which they are capable of enjoying?—no—which it is in our power to confer on them?—no—but which we can confer on them without hazard to our own domination. *Against that proposition I solemnly protest as inconsistent alike with sound policy and sound morality.*

"I am far, very far, from wishing to proceed hastily in this most delicate matter. I feel that, for the good of India itself, the admission of Natives to high office must be effected by slow degrees. But that when the fulness of time is come, when the interest of India requires the change, we ought to refuse to make that change lest we should endanger our own power—this is a doctrine which I cannot think of without indignation. Governments, like men, may buy existence too dear. '*Propter vitam vivendi perdere causas,*' *is a despicable policy either in individuals or in States. In the present case, such a policy would be not only despicable, but absurd.* The mere extent of empire is not necessarily an advantage. To many Governments it has been cumbersome; to some it has been fatal. It will be allowed by every statesman of our time that the prosperity of a community is made up of the prosperity of those who compose the community, and that it *is the most childish ambition to covet dominion which adds to no man's comfort or security.* To the great trading nation, to the great manufacturing nation, no progress which any portion of the human race can make in knowledge, in taste for the conveniences of life, or in the wealth by which those conveniences are produced, can be matter of indifference. It is scarcely possible to calculate the benefits which we might derive from the diffusion of European civilisation among the vast population of the East. *It would be, on the most selfish view of the case, far better for us that the people of India were well governed and independent of us, than ill-governed and subject to us*—that they were ruled by their own kings, but wearing our broad cloth, and working with our cutlery, than that they were performing their salaams to English Collectors and English magistrates, but were too ignorant to value, or too poor to buy, English manufactures. To trade with civilised men is infinitely more profitable than to govern savages. *That would indeed be a doting wisdom, which, in order that India might remain a dependency, would keep it a useless and costly dependency—which would keep a hundred millions of men from being our customers in order that they might continue to be our slaves.*

"It was, as Bernier tells us, the practice of the miserable tyrants whom he found in India, when they dreaded the capacity and spirit of some distinguished subject, and yet could not venture to murder him, to administer to him a daily dose of the pousta, a preparation of opium, the effect of which was in a few months to destroy all the bodily and mental powers of the wretch who was drugged with it, and to turn him into a helpless idiot. *That detestable artifice, more horrible than assassination itself*, was worthy of those who employed it. *It is no model for the English nation. We shall never consent to administer the pousta to a whole community—to stupefy and paralyse a great people, whom God has committed to our charge, for the wretched purpose of rendering them more amenable to our control.* What is that power worth which is founded on vice, on ignorance, and on misery — which we can hold only by violating the most sacred duties which as governors we owe to the governed—which as a people blessed with far more than an ordinary measure of political liberty and of intellectual light, we owe to a race debased by three thousand years of despotism and priestcraft? *We are free, we are civilised to little purpose, if we grudge to any portion of the human race an equal measure of freedom and civilisation.*

"Are we to keep the people of India ignorant in order that we may keep them submissive? Or do we think that we can give them knowledge without awakening ambition? Or do we mean to awaken ambition and to provide it with no legitimate vent? Who will answer any of these questions in the affirmative? Yet one of them must be answered in the affirmative by every person who maintains that we ought permanently to exclude the Natives from high office. *I have no fears. The path of duty is plain before us: and it is also the path of wisdom, of national prosperity, of national honour.*

"The destinies of our Indian Empire are covered with thick darkness. It is difficult to form any conjecture as to the fate reserved for a State which resembles no other in history, and which forms by itself a separate class of political phenomena. The laws which regulate its growth and its decay are still unknown to us. It may be that the public mind of India may expand under our system till it has outgrown that system; that by good government we may educate our subjects into a capacity for better government, that, having become instructed in European knowledge, they may, in some future age, demand European institutions. Whether such a day will ever come I know not. *But never will I attempt to avert or to retard it. Whenever it comes, it will be the proudest day in English history.* To have found a great people sunk in the lowest depths of slavery and superstition, to have so ruled them as to have made them desirous and capable of all the privileges of citizens would indeed be a title to *glory all our own.* The sceptre may pass away from us. Unforeseen accidents may derange our most profound schemes of policy. Victory may be inconstant to our arms. *But there are triumphs which are followed by no reverses. There is an empire exempt from all natural causes of decay. Those triumphs are the pacific triumphs of reason over barbarism; that empire is the imperishable empire of our arts and our morals, our literature, and our law.*"

Vol. XIX, Third Series, p. 536.

July 10th, 1833.

Mr. WYNN: "In nothing, however, more unreservedly did he agree with the hon. member than in the sentiments which he so forcibly impressed on the House at the close of his speech. *He had been convinced, ever since he was first connected with the affairs of India, that the only principle on which that Empire could justly or wisely or advantageously be administered was that of admitting the Natives to a participation in the government, and allowing them to hold every office the duties of which they were competent to discharge.* That principle had been supported by the authority of Sir Thomas Monro, and of the ablest functionaries in India, and been resisted with no small pertinacity and prejudice. It had been urged that the Natives were undeserving of trust, that no dependence could be placed on their integrity, whatever might be their talents and capacity, which no one disputed. Instances were adduced of their corruption and venality—*but were they not the result of our conduct towards them?* Duties of importance devolved upon them without any adequate remuneration either in rank or salary. There was no reward or promotion for fidelity; and why then complain of peculation and bribery. *We made vices and then punished them; we reduced men to slavery and then reproached them with the faults of slaves.*"

Vol. XIX, Third Series, p. 547.
July 10th, 1833.

Mr. CHARLES GRANT, in replying, said "he would advert very briefly to some of the suggestions which had been offered in the course of this debate. Before doing so, he must first embrace the opportunity of expressing not what he felt, for language could not express it, but of making an attempt to convey to the House his sympathy with it in its admiration of the speech of his hon. and learned friend the member for Leeds—a speech which, he would venture to assert, had never been exceeded within those walls for the development of statesmanlike policy and practical good sense. It exhibited all that was noble in oratory, all that was sublime, he had almost said, in poetry—all that was truly great, exalted, and virtuous in human nature. If the House at large felt a deep interest in this magnificent display it might judge of what were his emotions when he perceived in the hands of his hon. friend the great principles he had propounded to the House glowing with fresh colours and arrayed in all the beauty of truth.

. . . .

"If one circumstance more than another could give him satisfaction it was that the main principle of this Bill had received the approbation of the House, and that the House was now legislating for India and the people of India on the great and just principle that in doing so the interests of the people of India should be principally consulted, and that all other interests of wealth, of commerce, and of revenue, should be as nothing compared with the paramount obligation imposed upon the legislature of promoting the welfare and prosperity of that great Empire which Providence had placed in our hands.

. . . . .

"Convinced as he was of the necessity of admitting Europeans to India, he would not consent to remove a single restriction on their admission unless it was consistent with the interests of the Natives. Provide for their protection and then throw open wide the doors of those magnificent regions and admit British subjects there—not as aliens, not as culprits, but as friends. In spite of the differences between the two peoples, in spite of the difference of their religions, there was a sympathy which he was persuaded would unite them, and he looked forward with hope and eagerness to the *rich harvest of blessings which he trusted would flow from the present measure.*"

Page 624, *July 12th*, 1833.

MR. WYNN: "He could not subscribe to the perfection of *the* system that had hitherto prevailed in India; for he could not forget that the Natives and half-castes were excluded from all employment in situations where they could be more effective than Europeans and at a much smaller cost. *The principle of employing those persons he considered to be essential to the good government of India*, and be could not applaud that system which had been founded on a violation of that principle."

Vol. XX., Third Series, p. 323.
August 5th, 1833.

DUKE OF WELLINGTON: "Then with respect to the clause declaring the Natives to be eligible to all situations. Why was that declaration made in the face of a regulation preventing its being carried into effect? It was a mere deception. It might, to a considerable extent, be applicable in the capitals of the Presidencies; but, in the interior, as appeared by the evidence of Mr. Elphinstone, and by that of every respectable authority, it was impracticable. He certainly thought that it was advisable to admit the Natives to certain inferior civil and other offices; but the higher ones must as yet be closed against them, if our Empire in India was to be maintained."

After such exhaustive consideration from all political, imperial, and social aspects, the following, "that wise, that benevolent, that noble clause," was deliberately enacted by the Parliament of this country—worthy of the righteousness, justice, and noble instincts of the British people in the true British spirit.

3 and 4 William IV., cap. 85. 1833.

"That no Native of the said territories, nor any natural-born subject of his Majesty resident therein, shall, by reason only of his religion, place of birth, descent, colour, or any of them, be disabled from holding any place, office, or employment under the said Company."

Ret. C—2376, 1879, p. 13.

"The Court of Directors interpreted this Act in an explaining despatch in the following words:—'The Court conceive this section to mean that *there shall be no governing caste in British India;* that whatever other tests of qualification may be adopted, distinction of race or religion shall not be of the number; that no subject of the King, whether of Indian or British or mixed descent, shall be excluded from the posts usually conferred on Uncovenanted servants in India, *or from the Covenanted Service itself,* provided he be otherwise eligible.'"

After this explanation by the Court of Directors, how did they behave?

During the twenty years of their Charter, to the year 1853, they made the Act and their own explanation a complete dead letter. They did not at all take any steps to give the slightest opportunity to Indians for a single appointment to the Covenanted Civil Service, to which my statement chiefly refers; though the British people and Parliament are no party to this unfaithfulness, and never meant that the Act should remain a sham and delusion.

Twenty years passed, and the revision of the Company's Charter again came before Parliament in 1853; and if anything was more insisted on and bewailed than another, it was the neglect of the authorities to give effect to the Act of 1833. The principles of 1833 were more emphatically insisted on. I would just give a few extracts from the speeches of some of the most eminent statesmen in the debate on the Charter.

Hansard, Vol. 120, p. 865.
April 19th, 1852.

Mr. Golbeurn: "Sir Thomas Monro had said—There is one great question to which we should look in all our arrangements, namely, what is to be the final result of our government on the character of the people, and whether that character will be raised or lowered. Are we to be satisfied with merely securing our power and protecting the inhabitants, leaving them to sink gradually in character lower than at present, or are we to endeavour to raise their character? It ought undoubtedly to be our aim to raise the minds of the Natives, and to take care that whenever our connexion with India shall cease, it shall not appear that the only fruit of our dominion had been to leave the people more abject than when we found them. It would certainly be more desirable we should be expelled from the country altogether, than that our system of government should be such an abasement of a whole people."

Hansard, Vol. 121, p. 496.
May 11th, 1852.

Lord MONTEAGLE, in presenting a petition to the House of Lords, said: "But a clause recommended or supported as he believed by the high authority of Lord William Bentinck was made part of the last Charter Act of the 3rd and 4th William IV, and affirmed the principle of an opposite policy. It was to the following effect: . . . . Yet notwithstanding his authority, notwithstanding likewise the result of the experiment tried and the spirit of the clause he had cited, there had been a practical exclusion of them from all 'Covenanted Services,' as they were called, from the passing of the last Charter up to the present time."

Hansard, Vol. 127, p. 1,184.
June 3rd, 1853.

Mr. BRIGHT: "Another subject requiring close attention on the part of Parliament was the employment of the Natives of India in the service of the Government. The right hon. member for Edinburgh (Mr. Macaulay), in proposing the India Bill of 1833 had dwelt on one of its clauses, which provided that neither colour nor caste nor religion nor place of birth should be a bar to the employment of persons by the Government; whereas, as matter of fact, from that time to this no person in India had been so employed who might not have been equally employed before that clause was enacted; and from the statement of the right hon. gentleman the President of the Board of Control, that it was proposed to keep up the Covenanted Service system, it was clear that this most objectionable and most offensive state of things was to continue. Mr. Cameron, a gentleman thoroughly versed in the subject, as fourth Member of Council in India, President of the Indian Law Commission, and of the Council of Education for Bengal—what did he say on this point? He said: 'The statute of 1833 made the Natives of India *eligible to all offices* under the Company. But during the twenty years that have since elapsed not one of the Natives has been appointed to any offices except such as they were eligible to before the statute.'"

Hansard, Vol. 128, p. 759. 1853.

MACAULAY said: "In my opinion we shall not secure or prolong our dominion in India by attempting to exclude the Natives of that country from a share in its government" (*Contemporary Review*, June, 1883, p. 803).

Hansard, Vol. 128, p. 986.
June 30th, 1853.

MR. RICH: "But if the case as to the Native military was a strong one, it was much stronger as to civilians. It had been admitted that ninety-five per cent. of the administration of justice was discharged by Native judges. Thus they had the work, the hard work; but the places of honour and emolument were reserved for the Covenanted Service—the friends and relatives of the directors. Was it just that the whole work, the heat and labour of the day, should be borne by Natives and all the prizes reserved for Europeans? Was it politic to continue such a system? They might turn up the whites of their eyes and exclaim at American persistence in slavery. There the hard work was done by the negro whilst the control and enjoyment of profit and power were for the American. Was ours different in India? What did Mill lay down? European control — Native agency. And what was the translation of that? *White power, black slavery.* Was this just, or was it wise? Mill said it was necessary in order to obtain respect from the Natives. But he (Mr. Rich) had yet to learn that injustice was the parent of respect. Real respect grew out of common service, common emulation, and common rights impartially upheld. We must underpin our Empire by such principles, or some fine morning it would crumble beneath our feet. So long as he had a voice in that House it should be raised in favour of admitting our Native fellow subjects in India to all places to which their abilities and conduct should entitle them to rise."

Hansard, Vol. 129, p. 581.
July 21st, 1853.

Mr. MONCTON MILNES: "Objectionable as he believed many parts of the Bill were, he considered this was the most objectionable portion, and from it very unhappy consequences might arise. When the Natives of India heard it proclaimed that they had a right to enter the service of the Company, they would by their own intelligence and ability render themselves qualified for that service, if they only had the means of doing so. Then one of the two consequences would follow. They would either find their way into the service, or else the Company would have arrayed against them a spirit of discontent on the part of the whole people of India, the result of which it would be difficult to foresee. He did not see on what principles of justice, if they once admitted the principle of open competition, they could say to the Natives of India they had not a perfect right to enter the service."

Hansard, Vol. 129, p. 665.
July 22nd, 1853.

Mr. J. G. PHILLIMORE quotes Lord William Bentinck: "*The bane of our system* is not solely that the Civil Administration is entirely in the hands of foreigners, but the holders of this monopoly, the patrons of these foreign agents, are those who exercise its directing power at home; that this directing power is exclusively paid by patronage, and that the value of the patronage depends exactly upon the degree in which all the honours and emoluments of the State are engrossed by their clients to the exclusion of the Natives. There exists in consequence, on the part of the home authorities, an interest in the Administration precisely similar to what formerly prevailed as to commerce, *and directly opposed to the welfare of India*."

Though open competition was introduced, the monopoly of the Europeans and the injustice and injury to the Indians was allowed to continue by refusing to the Indians simultaneous examinations in India as the only method of justice to them, as will be seen further on.

Mr. Rich and Lord Stanley (the late Lord Derby) then emphatically put their fingers upon this black plague-spot in the system of British rule.

Hansard, Vol. 129, p. 682.
July 22nd, 1853.

Mr. RICH raised the question whether or not the Natives were to be admitted to *the Company's Covenanted Service.* He said: "As regarded employment in the public service, the Natives were placed in a worse position by the present Bill than they were before. The intention of the Act of 1833 was to open the services to the Natives; and surely now, when our Indian Empire was more secure than it was at that time, it was not wise to deviate from such a line of policy. His object was that all offices in India should be effectively opened to Natives, and therefore he would not require them to come over to this country for examination, as such a condition would necessarily entail on Natives of India great expense, expose them to the risk of losing caste, and thereby operate as a bar against their obtaining the advantages held out to all other of her Majesty's subjects. The course of education through which the youth of India at present went at the established colleges in that country afforded the most satisfactory proof of their efficiency for discharging the duties of office. . . . .

"This was not just or wise, and would infallibly lead to a most dangerous agitation, by which in a few years that *which would now be accepted as a boon would be wrested from the Legislature as a right.* They had opened the commerce of India in spite of the croakers of the day. *Let them now open the posts of government to the Natives, and they would have a more happy and contented people.*"

Hansard, Vol. 129, p. 684.
July 22nd, 1853.

Lord STANLEY: "He could not refrain from expressing his conviction that, in refusing to carry on examinations in India as well as in England—a thing that was easily praticable—the Government were, in fact, negativing that which they declared to be one of the principal objects of their Bill, and confining the Civil Service, as heretofore, to Englishmen. *That result was unjust, and he believed it would be most pernicious.*"

Hansard, Vol. 129, p. 784.
July 25th, 1853.

Lord STANLEY: "Let them suppose, for instance, that instead of holding those examinations here in London, that they were to be held in Calcutta. Well, how many Englishmen would go out there—or how many would send out their sons, perhaps to spend two or three years in the country on the chance of obtaining an appointment! *Nevertheless, that was exactly the course proposed to be adopted towards the Natives of India.*"

Hansard, Vol. 129, p. 778.
July 25th, 1853.

Mr. BRIGHT said: "That the motion now before the Committee involved the question which had been raised before during these discussions, but which had never been fairly met by the President of the Board of Control, namely, whether the clause in the Act of 1833, which had been so often alluded to, had not up to this time been altogether a nullity. If any doubt had been entertained with respect to the object of that clause, it would be removed by reference to the answers given by the then President of the Board of Control to the hon. member for Montrose and to the speech of the right hon. gentleman the present member for Edinburgh (Mr. Macaulay), in both of which it was distinctly declared that the object was to break down the barriers which were supposed to exist to the admission of the Natives as well as Europeans to high offices in India. And yet there was the best authority for saying that nothing whatever had been done in consequence of that clause. He (Mr. Bright) did not know of a single case where a Native of India had been admitted to any office since that time, more distinguished or more highly paid than he would have been competent to fill had that clause been not passed."

Hansard, Vol. 129, p. 787.
July 25th, 1853.

Mr. MONCTON MILNES said: "He thought the Bill was highly objectionable in this respect that while it pretended to lay down the generous principle that no condition of colour, creed or caste was to be regarded as a disqualification for office, it hampered the principle with such regulations and modifications as would render it all but impossible for the

Natives to avail themselves of it. The Bill in this respect was a delusion and would prove a source of chronic and permanent discontent to the people of India."

Hansard, Vol. 129, p. 788.
July 25th, 1853.

Mr. J. G. PHILLIMORE said: "He also feared that the Bill would prove delusive, and that although it professed to do justice to the Natives the *spirit of monopoly would still blight the hopes and break the spirits of the Indian people. While such a state of things continued India would be attached to this country by no bond of affection*, but would be retained by the power of the Army and the terror of the sword. He implored of the Committee *not to allow such an Empire to be governed in the miserable spirit of monopoly and exclusion.*"

Will the present statesmen ever learn this truth? Is it a wonder that the British people are losing the affections of the Indian people?

Hansard, Vol. 129, p. 1,335.
August 5th, 1853.

Earl GRANVILLE: "I, for one, speaking individually, have never felt the slightest alarm at Natives, well-qualified and fitted for public employments, *being employed in any branch of the public service of India.*"

Thus began the second chapter of this melancholy history with the continuation of the same spirit of selfishness which had characterised the previous twenty years, with the clear knowledge of the gross injustice to the Indians by not allowing them the same facility as was allowed to English youths, by simultaneous examinations in India and England. This injustice continued till the second chapter ended in the Mutiny of 1857, and the rule passed from the Company to the Crown.

The third chapter from that time began again with the revival of great hopes—that, however unfortunate and deplorable the Mutiny was, one great good sprang from that evil. The conscience of the British people was awakened to all previous injustice and dishonour brought upon them by their servants, and to a sense of their own duty. A new era opened, brighter, far brighter, than even that of the Act of 1833.

Not only was the Act of 1833 allowed to continue a living reality, at least in word, but in directing the mode of future services the Act of 1858 left it comprehensively open to adopt any plan demanded by justice. It did not indicate in the slightest degree prevention or exclusion of Indians from *any* service or from simultaneous examinations in India and England, or of any mode of admission of Indians into the Covenanted Civil Service, or of doing equal justice to all her Majesty's natural-born subjects. I shall show further on the interpretation by the Civil Service Commissioners themselves.

The sections of the Act of 1858 are as follows:—

1.—21-22 Vic., Cap. 106, "An Act for the better Government of India" (2nd August, 1858). Section 32 provides that:—

"With all convenient speed after the passing of this Act, regulations shall be made by the Secretary of State in Council, with the advice and assistance of the Commissioners for the time being acting in execution of her Majesty's Order in Council of Twenty-first *May*, One thousand, eight hundred, and fifty-five, 'for regulating the admission of persons to the Civil Service of the Crown,' for admitting all persons being natural-born subjects of her Majesty (and of such age and qualification as may be prescribed in this behalf) who may be desirous of becoming candidates for appointment to the Civil Services of *India* to be examined as candidates accordingly, and for prescribing the branches of knowledge in which such candidates shall be examined, and generally for regulating and conducting such examinations under the superintendence of the said last-mentioned Commissioners, or of the persons for the time being entrusted with the carrying out of such regulations as may be from time to time established by her Majesty for examination, certificate, or other test of fitness in relation to appointments to junior situations in the Civil Services of the Crown, and the candidates who may be certified by the said Commissioners or other persons as aforesaid to be entitled under such regulations shall be recommended for appointment according to the order of their proficiency as shown by such examinations, and such persons only as shall have been so certified as aforesaid shall be appointed or admitted to the Civil Services of *India* by the Secretary of State in Council: Provided always, that all regulations to be made by the said Secretary of State in

Council under this Act shall be laid before Parliament within fourteen days after the making thereof, if Parliament be sitting, and, if Parliament be not sitting, then within fourteen days after the next meeting thereof."

2.—The same Act, Cap. 106, Sect. 34, provides:—

"With all convenient speed after the commencement of this Act, regulations shall be made for admitting any persons *being natural-born subjects of her Majesty* (and of such age and qualifications as may be prescribed in this behalf) who may be desirous of becoming candidates for cadetships in the Engineers and in the Artillery, to be examined as candidates accordingly, and for prescribing the branches of knowledge in which such candidates shall be examined, and generally for regulating and conducting such examinations."

Though this Section does not impose any disability on an Indian—for it provides for "any persons being natural-born subjects of her Majesty"—yet an Indian is totally excluded from such examination. As I have already placed before the Commission my correspondence with the War Office, I need not say more.

3.—Sections 35 and 36 provide:—

"Not less than one-tenth of the whole number of persons to be recommended in any year for military cadetships (other than cadetships in the Engineers and Artillery) shall be selected according to such regulations as the Secretary of State in Council may from time to time make in this behalf from among the sons of persons who have served in India in the military or civil services of her Majesty, or of the East India Company."

"Except as aforesaid, all persons to be recommended for military cadetships shall be nominated by the Secretary of State and Members of Council, so that out of seventeen nominations the Secretary of State shall have two and each Member of Council shall have one; but no person so nominated shall be recommended unless the nomination be approved of by the Secretary of State in Council."

In these sections also there is no exclusion of Indians.

But the Sovereign and the people did not rest even by such comprehensive enactment by Parliament. They explicitly emphasised and removed any possible doubt with regard to the free and equal treatment of all her Majesty's natural-born subjects without any distinction of race, colour, or creed.

Thus, on the 1st November, 1858, followed the great and glorious Proclamation by the Sovereign on behalf of the British people: our complete "great charter" of our national and political rights of British citizenship and of perfect equality in all the services of the Sovereign—a proclamation the like of which had never been proclaimed in the history of the world under similar circumstances.

Here are the special clauses of that Proclamation:—

"We hold ourselves bound to the Natives of our Indian territories by the *same obligations of duty which bind us to all our other subjects*, and those obligations, by the blessing of Almighty God, we shall *faithfully and conscientiously* fulfil."

"And it is our further will that, so far as may be, our subjects, of whatever race or creed, be freely and impartially admitted to offices in our service, the duties of which they may be qualified, by their education, ability, and integrity, duly to discharge.

"*In their prosperity will be our strength, in their contentment our security, and in their gratitude our best reward. And may the God of all Power grant to us, and to those in authority under us, strength to carry out these our wishes for the good of our people.*"

Such was the noblest Proclamation of 1858. What more could we ask, and what bonds of gratitude and affection, and what vast benefits to both countries, were expected to tie us to the connexion with Britain by a loyal and honourable fulfilment of it?

Yes, I was in Bombay when this glad—I may almost say divine—message to India was proclaimed there to a surging crowd. What rejoicings, what fireworks, illuminations, and the roar of cannon! What joy ran through the length and breadth of India, of a second and firm emancipation, of a new British political life, forgetting and forgiving all the past evil and hoping for a better future! What were the feelings of the people! How deep loyalty and faith in Britain was rekindled! It was said over and over again: Let this Proclamation be faithfully and conscientiously fulfilled, and England may rest secure and in strength upon the gratitude and contentment of the people—as the Proclamation had closed its last words of prayer.

Now, when I look back to-day to that day of joy, how I feel how all this was doomed to disappointment, with the

E E

addition of some even worse features, of dishonour, injustice, and selfishness. However, I must proceed with the sad tale.

Not long after her Majesty's Proclamation of 1858, a Committee was appointed by the Secretary of State for India of the following members of his own Council: Sir J. P. Willoughby, Mr. Mangles, Mr. Arbuthnot, Mr. Macnaghten, and Sir Erskine Perry, all Anglo-Indians. This Committee made its report on 20th January, 1860, from which I give the following extracts on the subject of the pledge of the Act of 1833:—

"2. We are in the first place *unanimously* of opinion that it is not only just, but expedient, that the Natives of India shall be employed in the administration of India to as large an extent as possible consistently with the maintenance of British supremacy, and have considered whether any increased facilities can be given in this direction.

"3. It is true that, even at present, no positive disqualification exists. By Act 3 and 4 Wm. IV, cap. 85, sec. 87, it is enacted 'that no Native of the said territories nor any natural-born subject of his Majesty resident therein shall, by reason only of his religion, place of birth, descent, colour, or any of them, he disabled from holding any place, office, or employment under the said Company.' It is obvious, therefore, that when the competitive system was adopted, it could not have been intended to exclude Natives of India from the Civil Service of India.

"4. Practically, however, they are excluded. The law declares them eligible, but the difficulties opposed to a Native leaving India and residing in England for a time, are so great, that, as a general rule, it is almost impossible for a Native successfully to compete at the periodical examinations held in England. *Were this inequality removed, we should no longer be exposed to the charge of keeping promise to the ear and breaking it to the hope.*

"5. Two modes have been suggested by which the object in view might be attained. The first is, by alloting a certain portion of the total number of appointments declared in each year to be competed for in India by Natives, and by all other natural-born subjects of her Majesty resident in India. The second is to hold simultaneously two examinations, one in England and one in India, both being, as far as practicable, identical in their nature, and those who compete in both countries being finally classified in one list, according to merit, by the Civil Service Commissioners. The Committee have *no hesitation in giving the preference to the second scheme*, as being the *fairest*, and the most in accordance with the principles of a general competition for a common object.

"6. In order to aid them in carrying out a scheme of this nature, the Committee have consulted the Civil Service Commission, and, through the favour of Sir Edward Ryan, they have obtained a very able paper, in which the advantages and disadvantages of either plan are fully and lucidly discussed. They would solicit your careful consideration of this document, and will only, in conclusion, add that, in the event of either of the plans being adopted, it will be requisite to provide for the second examination of successful competitors in India, as nearly as possible resembling that now required in England. The Civil Service Commissioners do not anticipate much difficulty in arranging for this. The Committee, however, are decidedly of opinion that the examination papers on which the competition is to proceed in India and England should be identical; but they think, in justice to the Natives, that three colloquial Oriental languages should be added to the three modern European languages, so as to give the candidates the opportunity of selection."

I asked the India Office to give me a copy of the "very able paper" of the Civil Service Commission above referred to. The India Office refused to give it to me. I was allowed to see it in the India Office, and I then asked to be allowed to take a copy of it myself there and then. This even was refused to me. I ask this Commission that this Report be obtained and be added here.

The above forms a part of the Report, the other part being a consideration of the advantages and disadvantages of an "exclusive" Covenanted Civil Service. With this latter part I have nothing to do here. The first part quoted above about the admission of Natives into the Covenanted Civil Service was never as far as I know published.

It is a significant fact that the Report of the public Service Commission on the two subjects of the so-called "Statutory" Service and simultaneous examinations being in accordance with (what I believe and will show further on) the determined foregone conclusions of the Government of

India and the Secretary of State, was published and is being repeatedly used by Government in favour of their own proceedings, while the Report of 1860 of the Committee of five Members of Council of the Secretary of State for India was not only never published by Government as far as I know, but even suppressed in the Return made in 1879 on "Civil Service" (Return [C. 2376] 1879). Even the Public Service Commission has not given, I think, the Report of 1860.

No action was taken on this part of the Report of 1860. This Report was made thirty-seven years ago, and even so early as then it was considered, and strongly recommended, that simultaneous examinations was the only way of redeeming the honour of England and of doing justice to India. The Report was suppressed and put aside, as it did not suit the views of the Secretary of State for India, who himself had appointed the Committee.

Thus the new stage of the Proclamation of 1858, with all the hopes and joy it had inspired, began so early as 1860 to be a grievous disappointment and a dead letter, just as dead as the Act of 1833.

The next stage in this sad story is again a revival of hope and joy in a small instalment of justice by a partial fulfilment of all the pledges of 1833 and 1858. This was a bright spot in the dark history of this question, and the name of Sir Stafford Northcote will never be effaced from our hearts.

Sad to say, it was to be again darkened with a disappointment of a worse character than ever before. On August 13th, 1867, the East India Association considered the following memorial proposed by me, and adopted it, for submission to Sir Stafford Northcote (Lord Iddesleigh), the then Secretary of State for India :—

"We, the members of the East India Association, beg respectfully to submit that the time has come when it is desirable to admit the Natives of India to a larger share in the administration of India than hitherto.

"To you, Sir, it is quite unnecessary to point out the justice, necessity, and importance of this step, as in the debate in Parliament, on May 24th last, you have pointed out this so emphatically and clearly that it is enough for us to quote your own noble and statesmanlike sentiments. You said: 'Nothing could be more wonderful than our Empire in India; but we ought to consider on what conditions we hold it and how our predecessors held it. The greatness of the Mogul Empire depended upon the liberal policy that was pursued by men like Akbar availing themselves of Hindu talent and assistance and identifying themselves as far as possible with the people of the country. He thought that they ought to take a lesson from such a circumstance, and if they were to do their duty towards India they could only discharge that duty by obtaining the assistance and counsel of all who were great and good in that country. It would be absurd in them to say that there was not a large fund of statesmanship and ability in the Indian character' (*Times* of May 25th, 1867).

"With these friendly and just sentiments towards the people of India we fully concur, and therefore instead of trespassing any more upon your time, we beg to lay before you our views as to the best mode of accomplishing the object.

"We think that the competitive examination for a portion of the appointments to the Indian Civil Service should be held in India, under such rules and arrangements as you may think proper. What portion of the appointments should be thus competed for in India we cannot do better than leave to your own judgment. After the selection is made in India, by the first examination, we think it essential that the selected candidates be required to come to England to pass their further examinations with the selected candidates of this country.

"In the same spirit, and with kindred objects in view for the general good of India, we would ask you to extend your kind encouragement to Native youths of promise and ability to come to England for the completion of their education. We believe that if scholarships tenable for five years in this country were to be annually awarded by competitive examination in India to Native candidates between the ages of fifteen and seventeen, some would compete successfully in England for the Indian Civil Service, while others would return in various professions to India, and where by degrees they would form an enlightened and unprejudiced class, exercising a great and beneficial influence on Native society, and constituting a link between the masses of the people and their English rulers.[1]

[1] This clause was an addition proposed by Sir Herbert Edwards.

"In laying before you this memorial we feel assured, and we trust that you will also agree with us, that this measure, which has now become necessary by the advancement of education in India, will promote and strengthen the loyalty of the Natives of India to the British rule, while it will also be a satisfaction to the British people to have thus by one more instance practically proved its desire to advance the condition of their Indian fellow-subjects, and to act justly by them.

"We need not point out to you, Sir, how great an encouragement these examinations in India will be to education. The great prizes of the appointment will naturally increase vastly the desire for education among the people."

A deputation waited on Sir Stafford Northcote on 21st August, 1867, to present the petition. In the course of the conversation, Colonel Sykes explained the objects; and after some further conversation Sir Stafford Northcote said:—

"He had the question under consideration, and had conversed with Sir Herbert Edwards and others on it, and Sir Herbert had furnished him with a paper on it. Two plans were suggested—the one proposed that appointments should be assigned for competition in India, the other that scholarships should be given to enable Natives to come to finish their education in England. The first would manifestly be the most convenient for the Natives themselves; but it was urged in favour of the second that it would secure a more enterprising class than the first—men with more backbone—and he admitted the force of that. Moreover, he quite saw the advantage to India of a more efficient class which had had an English training. He took a very great interest in the matter, and was inclined to approve both proposals. He was corresponding with Sir J. Lawrence and the Indian Government on the subject" (*Journal of the East India Association*, Vol. I., pp. 126-7).

In 1868 Sir Stafford Northcote, in paragraph 3 of his despatch, Revenue No. 10, of 8th of February, 1868, said as below:—

"This is a step in the right direction, of which I cordially approve, but it appears to me that there is room for carrying out the principle to a considerable extent in the regulation provinces also. The Legislature has determined that the more important and responsible appointments in those provinces shall be administered exclusively by those who are now admitted to the public service solely by competition; but there is a large class of appointments in the regulation as well as in the non-regulation provinces, some of them scarcely less honourable and lucrative than those reserved by law for the Covenanted Civil Service, to which Natives of India have certainly a preferential claim, but which, as you seem to admit, have up to this time been too exclusively conferred upon Europeans. *These persons, however competent, not having entered the service by the prescribed channel, can have no claim upon the patronage of the Government, none, at least, that ought to be allowed to override the inherent rights of the Natives of the country; and therefore, while all due consideration should be shown to well-deserving incumbents, both as regards their present position and their promotion, there can be no valid reason why the class of appointments which they now hold should not be filled, in future, by Natives of ability and high character.*"

I only note this here as what Sir Stafford Northcote had prescribed and instructed the Government of India for the Uncovenanted Services, but which instructions have also been made a dead letter as usual—I do not in this statement discuss this branch of the subject, viz., the Uncovenanted Service, except for some short reference to some subsequent grievous events. I content myself with an expression of the Duke of Argyll on what Sir Erskine Perry describes in his "Memorandum" addressed to Lord Salisbury on 9th December, 1876, as "the vicious practice, supposed to be rapidly growing up in India, of appointing Englishmen to all the well paid Uncovenanted offices." The Duke of Argyll in his despatch (10th March, 1870, Financial) said: "The principle which her Majesty's Government steadily kept in view throughout the discussion on these furlough rules is, that the Uncovenanted Service should be principally reserved for the Natives of the country, and that superior appointments, which require English training and experience, should be made as heretofore in England. And they look with great disfavour on the system which appears to be growing up in India of appointing Englishmen in India to situations that ought only as a rule to be filled by civilians by open competition."

All such instructions, as usual, are thwarted by what Lord Lytton calls "subterfuges" and great ingenuity.

While Sir Stafford Northcote was considering, maturing, and preparing to bring into action the petition of the East India Association, Mr. Fawcett raised the subject in the House of Commons. Referring to simultaneous examinations for the Covenanted Service, he said :—

Hansard, Vol. 191, pp. 1,839-40.
May 8th, 1868.

"There would be no difficulty in carrying out this plan. . . . . His proposal was that there should be examinations at Calcutta, Madras and Bombay, that there should be the same papers and the same tests as in London, and the successful candidates, whether English or Native, should spend two years in this country. To this he had reason to believe, from memorials he had received from Calcutta and Bombay, the Natives would not object, though they naturally objected to coming over to England in the first instance without any guarantee of success. . . . All they aske for was to be subjected to precisely the same trial as the English. . . . . With reference to their alleged inferiority of character he had asked what would be the effect on English character if we, having been subjected, were debarred from all but the meanest offices of the State. Our civilisation and our literature would be destroyed. Nothing would save us from debasement. It was an indisputable fact that many Natives competent to govern a Province were fulfilling the humblest duties at salaries less than was received by the youngest member of the Indian Civil Service. Lord Metcalf had well said that the bane of our system was that the advantages were reaped by one class and the work was done by another. . . . . Sir Bartle Frere, in one of his despatches, said he had been much struck with the fact that the ablest exponents of English policy and our best coadjutors in adapting that policy to the wants of the various nations occupying Indian soil were to be found among the Natives who had received a high-class English education."

Hansard, Vol. 191, p. 1843.
May 8th, 1868.

Mr. Fawcett moved : "That this House whilst cordially approving of the system of open competition for appointments in the East India Civil Service, is of opinion that the people of India have not a fair chance of competing for these appointments, as long as the examinations are held nowhere but in London; this House would therefore deem it desirable that simultaneously with the examination in London, the same examination should be held in Calcutta, Bombay and Madras." I may here remark that at this time and till 1876 the Report of the five Councillors of the India Office of 1860, which I have given before, was not known to anybody outside, and Mr. Fawcett could not have known anything about it.

In the same speech from which a passage is extracted in the Memorial of the East India Association, Sir Stafford Northcote has said: "The English Government must necessarily labour under great disadvantages, and *we should endeavour* as far as possible to develop the system of Native government, to bring out Native talent and statesmanship, and to enlist in the cause of government all that was great and good in them."

The outcome of the petition of the East India Association, Mr. Fawcett's motion, and Sir Stafford Northcote's favourable reception of the petition, was that Sir Stafford Northcote introduced a clause in his Bill entitled "the Governor-General of India Bill" to grant the first prayer of the petition; and the Governor-General, Lord Lawrence, published a Resolution on 30th June, 1868, to grant the second prayer of the Memorial, and some scholarships were actually commenced to be given. But by a strange fatality that pursues everything in the interests of the Indians, the scholarships were soon abolished.

I do not enter into any details of this incident, as it affects only in an indirect manner and to a very small extent the question I am considering, viz., the admission of Indians in the Covenanted Civil Service.

I revert to the clause introduced by Sir Stafford Northcote in 1868. As this clause will come further on in the course of correspondence, I do not repeat it here.

This clause was subsequently passed in 1870, under the Duke of Argyll as Secretary of State, who communicated it to the Government of India by a despatch of 31st March, 1870. The Government of India being dilatory, as it is generally the misfortune of Indian interests, the Duke of Argyll in his despatch of 18th April, 1872, reminded the

Government of India about the rules required by the Act, as follows:—

"Referring to the 6th section of 33rd Victoria, cap. 3, I desire to be informed whether your Excellency in Council has prescribed the rules which that Act contemplates for the regulation of the admission of Natives to appointments *in the Covenanted Civil Service* who have not been admitted to that service in accordance with the provisions of the 32nd section of the 21st and 22nd Victoria, cap. 106."

The dilatoriness of the Government of India continuing, the Duke of Argyll again reminded the Governor-General of India in a despatch of 22nd October, 1872:—

"I have not received any subsequent communication from your Excellency's Government on the subject, and therefore conclude that nothing has been done, although I addressed your Government on the subject on 18th April last."

These two reminders were not known to the public until a Return was made in 1879 [C—2,376].

Three years passed after the enactment of the clause, and the public not knowing of anything having been done, the East India Association felt it necessary to complain to the Duke of Argyll on the subject.

The following is the correspondence between the East India Association and Mr. Grant Duff in 1873, giving his Grace's speech, and a brief account of the events from 1867 to 1873:—

"EAST INDIA ASSOCIATION,
"20, Great George Street, Westminster, London.
"*September*, 1873.

"*To* M. E. GRANT DUFF, Esq., M.P., *Under-Secretary of State for India, India Office*.

"SIR,—By the direction of the Council of the East India Association, I have to request you to submit this letter for the kind consideration of his Grace the Secretary of State for India.

"On the 21st August, 1867, this Association applied to Sir Stafford Northcote, the then Secretary of State for India, asking that the competitive examination for a portion of the appointments to the Indian Civil Service should be held in India, under such rules and arrangements as he might think proper, and expressing an opinion that, after the selection had been made in India by the first examination, it was essential that the selected candidates should be required to come to England to pass their further examinations with the selected candidates for this country.

"Sir Stafford Northcote soon after introduced a clause in the Bill he submitted to Parliament, entitled 'The Governor-General of India Bill.'

"The enactment of this Bill continued in abeyance, until, under the auspices of his Grace the present Secretary of State, it became law on the 25th March, 1870, as 'East India (Laws and Regulations) Act.' Moving the second reading of the Bill on the 11th March, 1869, his Grace, in commenting upon clause 6, in a candid and generous manner made an unreserved acknowledgment of past failures of promises, non-fulfilment of duty, and held out hopes of the future complete fulfilment to an adequate extent, as follows:—

"'I now come to a clause—the 6th—which is one of very great importance involving some modification in our practice, and in the principles of our legislation *as regards the Civil Service in India.* Its object is to set free the hands of the Governor-General, under such restrictions and regulations as may be agreed to by the Government at home, *to select, for the Covenanted Service of India, Natives of that country,* although they may not have gone through the competitive examination in this country. It may be asked how far this provision is consistent with the measures adopted by Parliament for securing efficiency in that service; but there is a previous and, in my opinion, a much more important question which I trust will be considered—how far this provision is essential to enable us to perform our duties and fulfil our pledges and professions towards the people of India . . . . .

"'With regard, however, *to the employment of Natives in the government of their country in the Covenanted Service* formerly of the Company, and now of the Crown, I must say that we have not fulfilled our duty, or the promises and engagements which we have made.

"'In the Act of 1833 this declaration was solemnly put forth by the Parliament of England: "And be it enacted that no Native of the said territories, nor any natural-born subject of his Majesty resident therein, shall, by reason only of his religion, place of birth, descent, colour, or any of them, be disabled from holding any place, office, or employment under the said Company."

"'Now, I well remember that in the debates in this House in 1853, when the renewal of the Charter was under the consideration of Lord Aberdeen's Government, my late noble friend Lord Monteagle complained, and I think with great force, that while professing to open every office of profit and employment under the Company or the Crown to the Natives of India, we practically excluded them by laying down regulations as to fitness which we knew Natives could never fulfil. If the only door of admission to the Civil Service of India is a competitive examination carried on in London, what chance or what possibility is there of Natives of India acquiring that fair share in the administration of their own country which their education and abilities would enable them to fulfil, and therefore entitle them to possess? I have always felt that the regulations laid down for the competitive examination rendered nugatory the declaration of the Act of 1833; and so strongly has this been felt of late years by the Government of India that various suggestions have been made to remedy the evil. One of the very last—which, however, has not yet been finally sanctioned at home, and respecting which I must say there are serious doubts—has been suggested by Sir John Lawrence, who is now about to approach our shores, and who is certainly one of the most distinguished men who have ever wielded the destinies of our Indian Empire. The palliative which he proposes is that nine scholarships—nine scholarships for a Government of upwards of 180,000,000 of people!—should be annually at the disposal for certain Natives, selected partly by competition and partly with reference to their social rank and position, and that these nine scholars should be sent home with a salary of £200 a year each, to compete with the whole force of the British population seeking admission through the competitive examinations. Now, in the first place, I would point out the utter inadequacy of the scheme to the ends of the case. To speak of nine scholarships distributed over the whole of India as any fulfilment of our pledges or obligations to the Natives would be a farce. I will not go into details of the scheme, as they are still under consideration; but I think it is by no means expedient to lay down as a principle that it is wholly useless to require Natives seeking employment in our Civil Service to see something of English society and manners. It is true that in the new schools and colleges they pass most distinguished examinations, and as far as books can teach them, are familiar with the history and constitution of this country; but there are some offices with regard to which it would be a most important, if not an essential, qualification that the young men appointed to them should have seen something of the actual working of the English constitution, and should have been impressed by its working, as any one must be who resides for any time in this great political society. Under any new regulations which may be made under this clause, it will, therefore, be expedient to provide that Natives appointed to certain places shall have some personal knowledge of the working of English institutions. I would, however, by no means make this a general condition, for there are many places in the Covenanted Service of India for which Natives are perfectly competent, without the necessity of visiting this country; and I believe that by competitive examinations conducted at Calcutta, or even by pure selection, it will be quite possible for the Indian Government to secure able, excellent, and efficient administrators.'

"The clause thus introduced, in a manner worthy of an English generous-minded nobleman, and passed into law, is as follows:—

"'6. Whereas it is expedient that additional facilities should be given *for the employment of Natives of India, of proved merit and ability, in the Civil Service of her Majesty in India*, be it enacted that nothing in the "Act for the Government of India," twenty-one and twenty-two Victoria, chapter one hundred and six, or in the "Act to confirm certain appointments in India, and to amend the law concerning the Civil Service there," twenty-four and twenty-five Victoria, chapter fifty-four, or in any other Act of Parliament, or other law now in force in India, shall restrain the authorities in India by whom appointments are or may be made to offices, places, and employments *in the Civil Service of her Majesty in India*, from appointing any Native of India to any such office, place, or employment, although such Native shall not have been admitted to the said Civil Service of India in manner in section thirty-two of the first-mentioned Act provided, but subject to such rules as may be from time to time prescribed by the Governor-General in Council, and sanctioned by the Secretary of State in Council, with the concurrence of a majority of members present ; and that, for the purpose of this Act, the words "Natives of India" shall include any person born and domiciled within the dominions of her Majesty in India, of parents habitually resident in India, and not established there for temporary purposes only ; and that it shall be lawful for the Governor-General in Council to define and limit from time to time the qualification of Natives of India thus expressed ; provided that every resolution made by him for such purpose shall be subject to the sanction of the Secretary of State in Council, and shall not have force until it has been laid for thirty days before both Houses of Parliament.'

"It is now more than three years since this clause has been passed, but the Council regret to find that no steps have apparently yet been taken by his Excellency the Viceroy to frame the rules required by it, so that the Natives may obtain the due fulfilment of the liberal promise made by his Grace.

"The Natives complain that, had the enactment referred to the interests of the English community, no such long and unreasonable delay would have taken place, but effect would have been given to the Act as quickly as possible, *and they further express a fear that this promise may also be a dead-letter.*[1]

"The Council, however, fully hope that further loss of time will not be allowed to take place in promulgating the rules required by the Act. The Natives, after the noble and generous language used by his Grace, naturally expect that they will not be again doomed to disappointment, and most anxiously look forward to the promulgation of the rules—to give them, in some *systematic* manner, 'that fair share in the administration of their own country which their education and abilities would enable them to fulfil, and therefore entitle them to possess,' not only as a political justice, but also as a national necessity, for the advancement of the material and moral condition of the country.

"I remain, Sir, your obedient Servant,

"W. C. PALMER, Capt.

"*Acting Honorary Secretary of the East India Association.*"

[1] To our misfortune and to the dishonour of the authorities, it has been made a dead letter.

"India Office, London,
October 10th, 1873.

"SIR,—I am directed by the Secretary of State for India in Council to acknowledge the receipt of your letter of the 2nd October, relative to the provisions of the 33rd Victoria cap. 3, section 6; and to inform you that the subject is understood to be under the consideration of the Government of India, the attention of which has been twice called to it.

"2. The Duke of Argyll in Council will send a copy of your letter to the Government of India, and again request the early attention of that authority to that subject.

"I am, Sir, your obedient Servant,
"(Sd.) M. E. GRANT DUFF.

"*The* ACTING HONORARY SECRETARY,
East India Association."

Such is the candid confession of non-performance of duty and non-fulfilment of solemn pledges for thirty-six years, and the renewed pledge to make amends for past failures and provide adequate admission for the future for at least some share in the administration of our own country. The inadequacy is clearly shown by the ridicule of nine scholarships for 180,000,000 souls, and the proposal to adopt means for the abolition of the monopoly of Europeans. When was this confession and this new pledge made? It was to pass the 6th clause of Act 33 Vic., cap. 3. The clause was passed on 25th March, 1870, one year after the above speech was made, and nearly three years after it was first proposed. Twice did Sir C. Wingfield ask questions in the House of Commons, and no satisfactory reply was given. At last the East India Association addressed the letter which I have given above to the India Office, and from the reply it will be seen how slow our Indian authorities had been, so as to draw three reminders from the Secretary of State.

With regard to the remark in the letter as to the complaint of the Natives that, "had the enactment referred to the interests of the English community, no such long and unreasonable delay would have taken place," I need simply point to the fact of the manner in which the Coopers Hill College was proposed and carried out promptly and with no difficulty raised, as is always raised against Indian interests.

In 1879 the India Office made a Return [C—2,376] on the ("Civil Service"). In this Return, after the despatch of the Secretary of State for India of 22nd October, 1872, no information is given till the Government of India's despatch of May 2nd, 1878.

In this Return, as I have said already, the Report of the Committee of the five members of the Council of the Secretary of State of 1860, recommending that simultaneous examinations was the only fair way of redeeming the honour of the British name and doing justice to the Indians, was suppressed. There is a despatch of the Government of India of 1874, which Sir E. Perry in his memorandum describes as follows:—

"Nearly two years afterwards (20th August, No. 31 of 1874) the Government of India replied to this despatch, transmitting rules, but noticing very jejunely the principal question raised by his Grace. Rules were finally suggested for adoption by the Secretary of State, those originally transmitted being deemed by him, under legal advice, to place too narrow a construction on the statute" (Public Despatch to India, No. 131 of 20th of August, 1874).

These documents also have no place in the Return. Who knows what other inconvenient documents also may have not appeared. This is always the difficulty in Indian matters for Indian interests. The public can never know the whole truth. The Government put forward only such information as they like, and the public is left in the dark, so as not to be in a position to judge rightly. The way of the Indian authorities is first to ignore any Act or Resolution of Parliament or Report of any Committee or Commission in favour of Indian interests. If that is not enough, then to delay replies. If that does not answer, then openly resist, and by their persistence carry their own point unless a strong Secretary of State prevents it. But, unfortunately, to expect a strong and just Secretary of State on behalf of Indian interests is a rare good fortune of India, because he changes so often and is mostly in the hands of the Anglo-Indian members of his Council and other Anglo-Indian officials of the India Offie. If any Committee or Commission really want to know the whole truth, they must do what the Committee of 1772 did—to have *every* document on the subject under consideration to be produced before them.

What an exposure that Committee of 1772 made of the most outrageous, most corrupt, and most tyrannical misconduct of the Government and officials of the day.

I may also mention that the despatch of the Duke of Argyll (10 March, 1870, Financial), to which I have already referred, has also not been given in the Return.

Of course, I am not surprised at these suppressions. It is our fate, and the usual ways of a despotic régime. But why I mention this is that the public are misled and are unable to know the true state of a case in which Indian interests are involved; the public cannot evolve these suppressions from their inner consciousness.

And still the outside public and the non-official witnesses are sometimes blamed for not supplying criticisms on the statements made by the officials of Government!

Again, there is the despatch of Lord Salisbury of 10th February, 1876, not given in the Return. Sir E. Perry, referring to this despatch, says: "Lord Salisbury decided the matter once for all in his despatch of 10th February, 1876, Financial, in which he quoted the Duke of Argyll's despatch of 1870 *(Supra)*, and after stating that he concurred in the views thus expressed, he proceeded to lay down precise rules by which the appointment of Englishmen in India to the higher Uncovenanted offices should in future be restricted." Now I cannot say whether all these suppressed documents were satisfactory or not, or whether they are published in some other place; but when the India Office omits such information in a Return on the subject itself, what are we to do? And if we criticise upon imperfect information, the authorities come down upon us denouncing us in all sorts of ways for our wrong statements, exaggerations, inaccuracies, and what not.

The next despatch that the Return gives is that of the Government of India of 2nd May, 1878. It was in connexion with this despatch that Lord Lytton wrote a note dated 30th May. In this note he had the courage to expose the whole character of the conduct of Indian authorities in both countries since the passing of the Act of 1833, denouncing that conduct as consisting of deliberate, transparent subterfuges, and dishonourable, as making promises to the ear and breaking them to the hope. Here are Lord Lytton's own words, referring to the Act of 1833:—

"The Act of Parliament is so undefined, and indefinite

obligations on the part of the Government of India towards its Native subjects are so obviously dangerous, that no sooner was the Act passed than the Government *began to devise means for practically evading the fulfilment of it.* Under the terms of the Act which are studied and laid to heart by that increasing class of educated Natives whose development the Government encourages, without being able to satisfy the aspirations of its existing members, every such Native if once admitted to Government employment in posts previously reserved to the Covenanted Service is entitled to expect and claim appointment in the fair course of promotion to the highest post in that service.

"We all know that these claims and expectations never can or will be fulfilled. We have had to choose between prohibiting them and cheating them: and we have chosen the least straightforward course. The application to Natives of the competitive examination system as conducted in England, and the recent reduction in the age at which candidates can compete, are all so many deliberate and transparent subterfuges for stultifying the Act and reducing it to a dead letter. Since I am writing confidentially I do not hesitate to say that both the Governments of England and of India appear to me, up to the present moment, unable to answer satisfactorily the charge of having taken every means in their power of breaking to the heart the words of promise they had uttered to the ear."

I admire the English candour and courage with which this humiliating confession is made. But I protest that so far as the people, the Parliament and the Sovereign are concerned, it is an injustice to them to put the dishonour and the disgrace of subterfuges to their charge. It is a libel upon the statesmen of 1833, that they said so many deliberate falsehoods intentionally when they contended for the justification of the clause for equality in such noble and generous and English spirit and terms. It is a gross libel on the Sovereign and the people of this country that the Proclamation of 1858, so solemnly promulgated, calling God to witness and to help, was all hypocrisy, an intentional mockery and delusion. I protest against this assumption. The truth I believe to be is that the Sovereign, the Parliament and the people of this country sincerely meant what they said—but that their servants, the executive authorities in both countries, uncontrollable and free to follow their own devices in their original spirit of selfishness and oppression with which they commenced their rule in India, frustrated the highest and noblest desires of the Sovereign and the people by "deliberate and transparent subterfuges to attain their own selfish ends"—which on one occasion an Anglo-Indian very *naïvely* confessed in these remarkable words. In a debate at the Society of Arts, 19th February, 1892, upon Siam, Sir Charles Crossthwaite said: "The real question was who was to get the trade with them, and how we could make the most of them so as to find fresh markets for our goods and *also employment for those superfluous articles of the present day*, OUR BOYS." So the whole reason of the existence of the world is market for British capitalists and employment for "*our boys.*"

In India this greed for the monopolising of profits of trade, and of the employment of "our boys," is the chief key to the system of all the actions of an unsympathetic, selfish rule as it is at present made by the executive authorities. Not that it need be so. A righteous system can be adopted, as many a statesman has declared, by which both England and India may be blessed and benefited, and for which purpose the Indians have been crying all along in the wilderness. Let the saddle of the present evil system be on the right horse. The Sovereign, the Parliament and the people have done all that could be desired. The only misfortune is that they do not see to their noble wishes and orders being carried out, and leave their servants to "bleed" India of all that is most dear and necessary to the human existence and advancement—wealth, wisdom and work—material and moral prosperity. Reverting to Lord Lytton's true confession, that the executives have "cheated" and "subterfuged," frustrated and dishonoured all Acts and resolutions of Parliament and the most solemn Proclamations of the Sovereign, one would think that after such confessions some amends will be made by a more honourable course. Far from it. This despatch of 2nd May, 1878, will remain one of the darkest sections in this sad story, instead of any contrition or reparation for the past evil.

What did the Government propose in this despatch? To destroy everything that is dearest to the Indian heart—his two great Charters of 1833 and 1858, the Act of a partial justice of 1870—to murder in cold blood the whole political existence of equality of Indians as British citizens which—at least by law, if not by deed or action of the authorities—they possessed, and make them the *Pariahs* of the high public service.

Mark! by the Act of 1870, the Indians were to have a distinct proportion of appointments (which was fixed by the Government of India to be about one-fifth, or about 7 every year) in the *Covenanted Civil Service*—which meant that in the course of 25 to 30 years, the duration of the service of each person, there would gradually be about 180 to 200 Indians admitted into the Covenanted Civil Service. This was a most bitter pill for the Anglo-Indians, official and non-official, to swallow. The Government resorted to every subterfuge to ignore and with passive resistance to make the Act a dead letter. This not succeeding, they deliberately proposed to throw aside all Acts, Resolutions, and Proclamations—all pledges and laws of equality—and to establish a "close Native Civil Service;" that is to say, to deprive the Natives once and for ever of any claim to the whole higher Covenanted Services, and *by law* be shut up in a lazaretto of a miserable close service.

And what was to be *this close* service? Not even to the extent to which the Act of 1870 led to the hope of the share in the Covenanted Civil Service—but only to propose to assign certain fixed appointments now held by the Covenanted Service, and to rob the Uncovenanted Service of some of their appointments to cast them into this service; that is to say, in reality to make a "pariah" service of a small number of Covenanted Service employments—about 90 or so (the Uncovenanted being already the Indian's own)—in place of what the Act of 1870 would have entitled them, to the extent of 180 or more, and to be eligible to the *whole* Covenanted Service employments; and what is still worse, and exhibits the inner spirit, that even this miserable so-called "close" service was not to be entirely reserved for the Indians, but, as I understand, a door is left open for Europeans also to get into it. And still more, the Government of India so mercilessly wanted to put the badge and stamp of inferiority and exclusion upon the Indians at large and rob them of their only consolation, their only hope and charter, that they already possessed by law and by pledges, of equality of British citizenship with the British subjects of this country. But there is something still worse: the Government coolly proposed not only not to give them simultaneous examinations in India, but to deprive them even of the right they now possess of competing for the Covenanted Service in this country itself.

Were the Government of India gone mad? The Government of India said, in cold blood, that "the ordinary Covenanted Civil Service should no longer be open to Natives;" thus proposing insidiously that the Acts of 1833 and 1870 and the Proclamation should be thrown to the winds. So these Acts and the Proclamations of the Sovereign upon which hangs all our devoted loyalty, all our hopes and aspirations (though in all conscience most mercilessly disregarded) all that is at all good and great in the British name in India, all that is to be swept away by a new un-British and tyrannical legislation! The whole despatch is so distressful, so full of false blandishments, that I cannot venture to say anything more about it. The wonder is that on the one hand Lord Lytton exposes the "subterfuges" and dishonour of the Executive, and himself and his colleagues sign such a despatch of 2nd May, 1878. And what is still more curious is this; about seventeen months before this despatch, on 1st January, 1877, at the Delhi Assemblage, on the assumption of the title of Empress of India, Lord Lytton on behalf of her Majesty said :—

"But you the Natives of India, whatever your race and whatever your creed, have a recognised claim to share *largely* with your English fellow-subjects according to your capacity for the task, in the administry of the country you inhabit. *This claim is founded on the highest justice.* It has been repeatedly affirmed by British and Indian statesmen and by the legislation of the Imperial Parliament. It is recognised by the Government of India as binding on its honour and consistent with all the aims of its policy;" and all such "highest justice" and all this "binding on honour" ended in this extraordinary despatch of 2nd May, 1878! It is the most dismal page in the whole melancholy affair about the Covenanted Service.

But the further misfortune is that since the despatch of 2nd May, 1878, the whole heart and soul of the Government is directed in the spirit of the despatch, and though they have not attempted to alter legislation, they have by persistence and devices most ingeniously carried out their own object, and made the Acts of 1833 and 1870, and the great Proclamations, mere shams and delusions. With trumpet tongues they have proclaimed to the world that the miserable "*close* service" was an extraordinary and generous concession, when in reality we are plundered of what we already possessed by the Act of 1870, and our political position is reduced to the condition of political pariahs.

I do not enter here into a discussion of the un-English and subtle procedure by which we are deprived of the so-called "statutory service," which had secured for us no less than a complete and free admission into the whole Covenanted Civil Service, to the number which had been at the time considered for a beginning as a fair proportion of about one-sixth or one-fifth of the total number of this service.

There is one other important reason why I do not pursue any more the criticisms upon this despatch. The Secretary of State himself found it impossible to swallow it, summarily disposed of its fallacies, hollowness, brushed it aside, and insisted upon carrying out the Act of 1870.

Now before going further, I have to request the Commission to bear in mind that the Government of India had, by this despatch, most earnestly and laboriously committed themselves to a "close Native service," and it will be seen that they bided their time and left no stone unturned, by any means whatever, to attain ultimately their object.

As I have said above, Lord Cranbrook, the then Secretary of State, would not swallow the preposterous despatch, and put down his foot against such openly violating all honourable and solemn pledges of the Sovereign and Acts of Parliament.

Lord Cranbrook in his despatch of 7th November, 1878, said in reply:—

"6. But your proposal of a close Native service with a limited class of high appointments attached to it, and your suggestions that the Covenanted Civil Service should no longer be open to Natives, involve an application to Parliament which would have no prospect of success, and which I certainly would not undertake. Your lordship has yourself observed that no scheme would have a chance of sanction which included legislation for the purpose of repealing the clause in the Act of 1833 above quoted, and the obstacles which would be presented against any attempt to exclude Natives from public competition for the Civil Service would be little less formidable.

"10. It is, therefore, quite competent to your lordship's Government to appoint every year to the Civil Service of India any such number of Natives as may be determined upon, and the number of Covenanted civilians sent out from this country will have to be proportionately decreased. The appointments should in the first instance be only probationary, so as to give ample time for testing the merit and ability of the candidates.

"11. It appears to me that the advantages of such a simple scheme will be obvious:—

"(i) It will undoubtedly be much more popular with the Natives, as it will place them on a footing of social equality with the Covenanted civilian;

"(ii) Inasmuch as it will exclude no civilian at present in India from any office which he has a moral claim to expect, it will avoid any clashing with the vested interests of the Civil Service;

"(iii) It will avoid the necessity of any enhancement of salaries of Uncovenanted officers which is now proposed, not because such enhancement is necessary, but from the necessity of creating a class of well-paid appointments to form sufficient prizes for a close Native service;

"And lastly, it pursues the same system of official training which has proved so eminently successful in India."

Thus foiled in the monstrous attempt to inflict upon the Indians the most serious political disaster, the Government of India whined and lay low to wait their opportunity, and as compelled, and with bad grace, made the required rules one year after the despatch of 2nd May, 1878.

With their despatch of 1st May, 1879, the Government of India sent the rules, and explained in para. 8 of the despatch the proportion of Indians they proposed to select: "the proposed statutory rules, in brief, provide that a proportion not exceeding one-sixth of all the recruits added to the Civil Service in any one year shall be Natives selected in India by the local Governments."

I give here the rules proposed:

"No. 18.

"RULES for the APPOINTMENT of NATIVES of INDIA to offices ordinarily held by members of her Majesty's Covenanted Civil Service in India.

"In exercise of the power conferred by the Statute 33 Vict., cap. 3, section 6, the Governor-General in Council has been pleased to make the following rules, which have been sanctioned by the Secretary of State in Council with the concurrence of a majority of members present:—

"I.—Each Local Government may nominate persons who are Natives of India within the meaning of the said Act, for employment in her Majesty's Covenanted Civil Service in India within the territories subordinate to such Government. Such nominations shall be made not later than the first day of October in each year. No person shall be nominated for employment in the said service after he has attained the age of twenty-five years, except on grounds of merit and ability proved in the service of Government, or in the practice of a profession.

"II.—Nominations under the foregoing rule shall, if approved by the Governor-General in Council, be provisionally sanctioned by him. The total number of nominations so sanctioned in any year shall not exceed one-fifth of the total number of recruits appointed by her Majesty's Secretary of State to the said service in such year; provided that the total number of such nominations sanctioned in each of the years 1879, 1880, and 1881 may exceed the said proportion by two. On sanction being given by the Governor-General in Council, the nominee shall be admitted on probation to employment in the said service; such admission may be confirmed by the Governor-General in Council, but shall not be so confirmed until the Local Government shall have reported to the Governor-General in Council that the probationer has acquitted himself satisfactorily during a period of not less than two years from the date of his admission, and that he has, unless specially exempted by the Governor-General in Council, passed such examinations as may from time to time be prescribed by the Local Government subject to the approval of the Governor-General in Council. In case of persons admitted under these rules after they have attained the age of twenty-five years, the Governor-General in Council may confirm their admission without requiring them to serve for any period of probation.

"III.—Persons admitted under these rules to employment in the said service shall not, without the previous sanction of the Governor-General in Council in each case, be appointed to any of the undermentioned offices, namely:—

"Members of a Board of Revenue.

"Secretaries to the several Governments and Administrations in India.

"Chief Magisterial, or Chief Revenue, Officers of Districts.

"Commissioners of Division, or of Revenue.

"IV.—Persons admitted under these rules to employment in the said service shall ordinarily be appointed only to offices in the province wherein they were first admitted. But the Governor-General in Council may transfer from one province to another a person finally admitted to employment in the said service.

"V.—Any person admitted under these rules may, with the previous sanction of the Governor-General in Council, be declared by the Local Government to be disqualified for further employment in the said service."

Two comments suggest themselves with regard to these rules—when read with the light that the Government of India's whole heart was in the "close Native service"—and that, therefore, to carry out loyally the Act of 1870 was naturally against their grain.

At the very beginning they began to nibble at the Statute of 1870 and proposed in Rule III. not to put Natives on the same footing with Europeans with regard to all high offices. On this unworthy device I need not comment, as the Secretary of State himself struck out this Rule III. without much ceremony.

Now, whether intentionally or unintentionally, the rules had been so framed that had the Government of India sat down to devise the most effective means of bringing discredit and failure on the service under the Act of 1870, they could not have done better or worse than these rules. These Indian civilians were to be the colleagues of and to do the duties with the best educated and severely tested (educationally, physically, and morally) English youths. Particular care was taken not to prescribe any systematic compulsory rules for such high test and for obtaining recruits worthy of being included in such a highly trained service as the Covenanted Civil Service, of which these Indians were to be an integral part and in which service they were to be exactly on the same footing as English civilians. This was the crux and spirit of the whole matter; the rules simply made the matter one of patronage and back-door influence. It needs no stretch of the imagination to see that such a course could lead only to one result, as it has always done, viz., failure. It was absurd to expect that such Indian civilians could prove as successful and efficient as the English civilians so well prepared. This was the first covert blow given by the Government of India at the very birth of the operation of the Act of 1870, and unfortunately Lord Cranbrook did not see this ingenious device.

The Commission can hardly realise the intensity of the gratitude of the Indians to Sir Stafford Northcote for proposing, and the Duke of Argyll for passing, the clause in the Act of 1870, and not less intense was their gratitude to Lord Cranbrook and to Sir Erskine Perry who co-operated with him, for the determination with which Lord Cranbrook overcame all strenuous opposition and the blandishments of the Government of India of their own good will and justice to the Indians; and he compelled that Government to give effect to the Act of 1870.

The clause was at last given effect to, though with great reluctance and under compulsion, after ten long years. This is generally the case. For all Indian interests the officials always require long and most careful and most mature consideration, till by lapse of time the question dies. Under Lord Cranbrook this clause had better fortune, but only to end in utter and more bitter disappointment to the Indians, and to add one more dishonour to the British name. The first appointments under the clause, though after a delay of ten years, again infused a new life of loyalty and hope in the justice of the British people, throughout the length and breadth of India. It was a small instalment, but it was a practical instalment, and the first instalment of actual justice. And it was enough, for an ever disappointed and unjustly treated people, to rejoice, and more so for the future hope of more justice and of righteous rule, little foreseeing to what bitter disappointment they were to be doomed in the course of the next ten years! The first appointments were made under the rules in 1880. Now we come to the next melancholy stage.

The immediate development of the compulsion on the Government of India to carry out the clause of 1870—coupled with the fear of the possible effect of the despatch of Sir Stafford Northcote of 8th February, 1868, to restrict employment of Europeans to those only who pass the examination here, and to insist upon the inherent rights of the Indians to all appointments—was to produce a sullenness of feeling and great vexation among the Anglo-Indian body generally (with, of course, honourable and noble exceptions).

I do not enter, as I have already said, upon the latter question of the Uncovenanted Service. I mention it here simply because it added to the anger of the Anglo-Indians against the noble policy of men like Sir Stafford Northcote. I confine myself to the said story about the admission of Indians in the Covenanted Civil Service.

Well, the so-called "statutory" service was launched in 1880. It was called by a distinctive name "statutory" as if the whole Covenanted Service was not also a "statutory" service, and as if the clause of 1870 was not simply for full admission into the whole Covenanted Service. But what is in a name? The Government of India knew the value of creating and giving a distinct name to the service so that they may with greater ease kill it as a separate service; and at last, kill it they did. The Anglo-Indians, official and non-official, were full charged with sullenness and anger, and with the spark of the "Ilbert Bill" the conflagration burst out.

Here I may point out how shrewdly Lord Salisbury, while fully approving the clause of 1870, had prophesied the coming storm. On the debate on the clause in 1870, Lord Salisbury had said:—

"Another most important matter is the admission of Natives to employments under the Government of India. I think the plan of the noble duke contained in this Bill is, I believe, the most satisfactory solution of a very difficult question." And after so fully accepting the clause, he said: "One of the most serious dangers you have to guard against is the possibility of *jealousy* arising from the introduction of Natives into the service."

Owing to this jealousy ten years elapsed before any action was taken on the Act of 1870, and that even *under compulsion* by Lord Cranbrook. Before three years after this effect was given to the clause, Lord Salisbury's prophecy was fulfilled. Explosion burst out over the Ilbert Bill.

I cannot enter here into the various phases of the excitement on that occasion, the bitter war that raged for some time against Indian interests. I content myself with some extracts from the expression of Lord Hartington (the Duke of Devonshire) upon the subject. It clearly proves the action of the *jealousy* of the Anglo-Indians. Lord Hartington said (speech, House of Commons, August 23, 1883):—

"It may by some be thought sufficient to say, that the Anglo-Indian, whatever may be his merits, and no doubt they are great, is not a person who is distinguished by an exceptionally calm judgment."

Hansard, Vol. 283, p. 1818.
August 23rd, 1883.

"I could quote passages in letters in the Indian papers in which it is admitted that the agitation was directed against the policy of the Home Government in providing appointments for Native civilians while there are many Europeans without appointments. . . . . I believe that the cause of the prevalent excitement is to be found, not in this measure, but in the general course of policy that has been pursued both by this Government and the late Government. It has been the policy of Governments for some years past to impress upon the Government of India the desirability of obtaining the assistance of the Native population as far as possible in the government of that country. Over and over again that policy has been inculcated from home. In 1879 a resolution was passed which limited appointments of the value of Rs. 200 a month to officers of the army and to Natives. That restriction has been rigidly enforced, and has met with *all kinds of opposition from non-official classes of Europeans, who think that all the appointments must be reserved for them.* The same spirit was shown when it was determined that admission to the Engineering College at Roorki should be confined to Natives. . . . . Agitation of the same character has been seen before when there was just as little foundation for it. Lord Macaulay, Lord Canning, and other Anglo-Indian statesmen experienced the same kind of opposition from Anglo-Indians; but all these reproaches have recoiled, not against the statesmen with regard to whom they were uttered, but against the persons uttering them themselves. . . . .

"There is a further reason, in my opinion, why this policy should be adopted, and that is that it is not wise to educate the people of India, to introduce among them your civilisation and your progress and your literature, and at the same time to tell them they shall never have any chance of taking any part or share in the administration of the affairs of their country, except by their getting rid in the first instance of their Europeans rulers. Surely it would not be wise to tell a patriotic Native of India that. . . . .

"Whatever difference of opinion there may be, there can, in my opinion, be very little doubt that India is insufficiently governed at the present time. I believe there are many districts in India in which the number of officials is altogether insufficient, and that is owing to the fact that the Indian revenue would not bear the strain if a sufficient number of Europeans were appointed. The Government of India cannot afford to spend more than they do in the administration of the country, *and if the country is to be better governed that can only be done by the employment of the best and most intelligent of the Natives in the service.*"

It was on this occasion that Lord Salisbury made the confession that all the pledges, proclamations, and Acts to which Lord Northbrook had referred was all "political hypocrisy." The reasons which Lord Salisbury assigned were not accurate, but I cannot strike off into a new controversy now. It is enough for me to say that, as I have already said, I protest against placing this "hypocrisy" at the door of the people, Parliament, and Sovereign of this country. It lies on the head of the servants, the executives in both countries. It is they who would ruin the Empire by their "hypocrisy" and selfishness.

At last, however, the agitation of the Ilbert Bill subsided. The eruption of the volcano of the Anglo-Indian hearts stopped, but the anger and vexation continued boiling within as the cause of the explosion still remained. And the Government of India were biding their time to carry out that most un-English scheme of the despatch of 2nd May, 1879, to create a *pariah* lazaretto to consign these *pariah* thereto.

Owing to the persistence of Lord Cranbrook the appointments under the Act of 1870 had begun in 1880, and continued to be made, *i.e.*, about six or seven Indians continued to be admitted in the Covenanted Civil Service. The main cause of the explosion having continued, and the Government of India having set its heart upon its own scheme, a new departure and development now arose. The question at the bottom was how to knock the "statutory service" on the head, and put down effectively the cry for simultaneous examinations. The explosion under the excuse of the Ilbert Bill did not effect that object, and so, according to Lord Lytton's confession of the general conduct of the Executive, something else should be done.

We now enter upon the next stage of this sad story. I shall place some facts and any fair-minded Englishman will be able to draw his own conclusions. Before I do so certain preliminary explanation is necessary.

In India, when the authorities are decided upon certain views which are not likely to be readily accepted by the public, a Commission or Committee comes into existence. The members are mostly officials or ex-officials—English or Indians. Some non-officials, English or Indians or both, are sometimes thrown in, selected by the Government itself. It is a well understood thing that in all matters officials are bound always to take and support the Government views. The ex-officials are understood to be bound by gratitude to do the same. If anyone takes an independent line, either in a Commission or Committee, or in his own official capacity, and displeases the Government, I cannot undertake to say with instances what happens.

Perhaps some Anglo-Indians themselves may feel the sense of duty to supply some instances from their own experience. Almost by accident an instance has just come back before me in the *Champion*, of Bombay, and which gives the incident almost in the author's (Mr. Robert H. Elliot) words: "Mr. Geddes came before the Finance Committee (1871-74), and that the members thought it well worth examining him is evidenced by the fact that he was examined at very great length. Here was a chance for Duff: he thought he would do a very clever thing, and as Mr. Geddes had introduced into his financial pamphlet some views of rather a novel description, and had, besides, made use of some rather out-of-the-way illustrations, this gave a good opportunity for putting questions in such a way as was calculated to cast ridicule on Mr. Geddes, and depreciate the value of the important points he had brought out. But this was far from being all. It was intimated pretty plainly to Mr. Geddes that his opinions ought to be in harmony with the Government he served, and here Mr. Geddes said that he certainly ought to be in harmony with the Government if there was any spirit of harmony in it. Mr. Geddes was clearly not to be put down, and Duff thought he would try something more severe. 'You hold an appointment in the Government, do you not?' 'Yes,' said Mr. Geddes. 'And do you expect to return to that post?' asked Duff. 'Now, my dear John,' continues the author, 'you will not find that question in the report, for the simple reason that it was ordered to be expunged.'" Would some Anglo-Indian kindly give us some information of what afterwards became of Mr. Geddes? I would not trouble the Commission with my own treatment before the same Committee, which was anything but fair, because, like Mr. Geddes, I had something novel to say. I would only add that an important and pointed evidence of Lord Lawrence, on the wretchedness and extreme poverty of India, was also suppressed in the Report.

The officials have therefore to bear in mind to be in harmony with Government or think of their posts—and I suppose the ex-officials have also to bear in mind that there is such a thing as pension.

Here is one more instance. When Mr. Hyndman published his "Bankruptcy of India," Mr. Caird at once wrote to the *Times* contradicting him. The India Office soon after sent him to preside over the Famine Commission. He, though at first much prejudiced by Anglo-Indian views, and going to bless the Government, returned cursing. He made a report on the condition of India, and that being contrary to official views, O! how Government laboured to discredit him!

Lastly, Commissions or Committees report what they like. If they are in the expected harmony with Government, all is well. But anything which Government does not want or is contrary to its views is brushed aside. Reports of Commissions must be in harmony with the views of the Government. If not, so much the worse for the Commissioners; and this is what has actually happened with the Public Service Commission, which I am now going to touch upon as the next stage in this sad history of the fate of Indians for services in their own country.

When I came here in 1886, I paid a visit to Lord Kimberley, the Secretary of State for India. I had been favoured with more than an hour's conversation, mainly on the two topics of "statutory service" and simultaneous examinations, and I found him a *determined*, decided opponent to both, and completely, to our misfortune, saturated with Anglo-Indian views—not seeming to realise at all the Indian side. He urged to me all the Anglo-Indian stock arguments, and I saw what he was really aiming at—the very thing which Lord Cranbrook had summarily rejected—the scheme of the Government of India of the despatch of 2nd May, 1878, the close service.

From that interview I saw clearly what the "Public Service Commission" was for—that the abolition of the "statutory" service, the suppression of the cry for simultaneous examinations, and the adoption of the scheme of 2nd May, 1878, were determined, foregone conclusions.

Soon after my conversation with Lord Kimberley, I happened to be on the same boat with Sir Charles Turner on my way to Bombay. Sir Charles Turner was going out by appointment by Lord Kimberley to join the Public Service Commission. I at once prepared a short memorandum, and gave it to him. Afterwards, in the course of the conversation, he told me that he had certain instructions from Lord Kimberley. Sir Charles Turner, of course, could not tell me, whatever they may have been. But I could not help forming my own conclusions from what I had myself learnt from Lord Kimberley himself in my conversation with him. Sir Charles Aitchison was the President of the Commission, and he, as Lieutenant-Governor of the Punjab, made a representation to the Commission, in which he expressed his clear opposition to the simultaneous examinations. About the "statutory" service he had already most strongly objected to, two years before the appointment of the

Commission, in a very inaccurate and hasty argument and on very imperfect information. In a country like India, governed under a despotism, where, under present circumstances, service under and favour of Government is to many the all in all, what effect must the declaration of the head of the province, and the well-known decided views of the Government itself, produce upon the invited witnesses—not only official, but non-official also—can hardly be realised by Englishmen, who have their government in their own hands.

The third important member's—Sir Charles Crossthwaite—view, as I have already indicated, seemed the anxiety about "our boys."

There were among the members of the Commission—

8 European officials,
1 Indian official,
3 Indian ex-officials,
1 Non-official European, the General Secretary of the Behar Indigo Planters' Association. It would be worth while to know what share the planters had taken in the Ilbert Bill agitation.
1 Eurasian,
2 Indian non-officials, one of whom, I think, never attended the Commission till it met for Report.

Mr. Kazi Shahabu-din, before he joined the Commission, distinctly told me that he was dead against both questions, "statutory" and simultaneous. It was all very good, he said to me, to *talk* of eternal principles and justice and all that, but he was determined not to allow the Hindus to advance. The views of Sir Syad Ahmad Khan were no secret as being against simultaneous examinations and statutory service. I am informed that Mr. Nuhlkar and Mr. Mudliar were sorry for their action in joining in the Report, and Mr. Romesh Chandra Mitra has, I think, expressed some repudiation of his connexion with the Report of the Commission. The Rájá of Bhinga only joined the Commission at the Report.

Our misfortune was, as I saw at that time, the three Hindu members did not, I think, fully realise how a death blow was being struck at the future political and administrative advance and aspirations of the Indians; and how, by an insidious and subtle stroke all pledges and Acts of Parliament, and Proclamations—the very breath of our political life—the hope and anchor of our aspirations and advance were being undermined and swept away. I have also already pointed out the *determination* of the Government of India since their letter of 2nd May, 1878, not only to stop further advance, but even to take away what they, the Indians, already had.

I was a witness before this Commission. I fully expected that as I was considered one of the chief complainants in these matters, I would be severely examined and turned inside out. But the Commission, to my surprise, carried on with me more of an academical debate than a serious practical examination, and seemed wishful to get rid of me quickly, so much so, that I was forced to request that a Memorandum which I had placed before them should be added to my evidence on several points.

I may here explain that simultaneous examinations was by far the most important matter, and, if granted, would have dispensed with the necessity of the "statutory" service. The chief fight was for simultaneous examinations.

First, as far as the "statutory" service is concerned, here is the extraordinary result. In the instructions, the object of the Commission was stated, "broadly speaking," "to devise a scheme which may reasonably be hoped to possess the necessary elements of *finality*, and to do *full justice* to the claims of the Natives of India *to higher and more extensive* employment in the public service"; and in this the Governor-General in Council fully and cordially agreed.

This was the promise, and what is the performance? The admission of one-sixth Indians into the Covenanted Service we already possessed by law—and in operation. We were already eligible to all Uncovenanted Services. Full justice, and still higher and more extensive employment were promised—and what did we actually get? We were deprived of what we already by law (of 1870) possessed; and instead of giving us "full justice" it deprived us of all our hopes and aspirations to be admitted to an equality of employment with British officials; and we were coolly, mercilessly, despotically, and illegally consigned to a small pariah service, open to Europeans also—which had been *already schemed and firmly determined upon ten years before* in the despatch of 2nd May, 1878—in utter and dishonourable violation of the Acts of 1833 and 1870, and three gracious Proclamations. This is the way in which the Public Service

Commission has carried out its object to devise a scheme to possess elements of finality and to do full justice to the claims of the Natives to *higher* and *more extensive* employment in the public service.

Now, with regard to simultaneous examinations, the conduct of the Public Service Commission seems to be still more extraordinary. Why they actually reported as far as I can see, in opposition to the weight of evidence, I cannot understand. Mr. William Digby has analysed the evidence in a letter to Lord Cross, of 8th May, 1889, and I append that part of his letter. I asked the Secretary of State to inform me whether Mr. Digby's analysis was correct or not, but the information was not given me.

There is again a curious coincidence between the action of Lord Lytton and Lord Dufferin which I may intervene here.

Of Lord Lytton I have already mentioned about the contrast between his speech at the Delhi Durbar in January, 1877, and his action in the despatch of 2nd May, 1878.

On 4th October, 1886, was started the Public Service Commission, and in the beginning of the very next year, 1887, on the occasion of the Jubilee, Lord Dufferin said in his Jubilee speech :—

"Wide and broad, indeed, are the new fields in which the Government of India is called upon to labour, but no longer as aforetime need it labour alone. Within the period we are reviewing education has done its work, and we are surrounded on all sides by Native gentlemen of great attainments and intelligence, from whose hearty, loyal, and honest co-operation we may hope to derive the greatest benefit. In fact, to an administration so peculiarly situated as ours, *their advice, assistance, and solidarity are essential to the successful exercise of its functions.* Nor do I regard with any other feelings than those of approval and good-will their natural ambition to be more extensively associated with their English rulers in the administration of their own domestic affairs." At the same time the Empress of India thus emphasises her great Proclamation of 1858 :—

"It had always been, and will always be, her earnest desire to maintain unswervingly the principles laid down in the Proclamation published on her assumption of the direct control of the Government of India."

And these two declarations of hope and justice came to what end? Within two years, as I have already said, Lord Cross, with a ruthless hand, snatched away from us the small instalment of justice which Sir S. Northcote had done to us, consigned us to a small "pariah service," and destroyed virtually all our charters and aspirations.

I now come to the last dark section of this sad chapter, which also shows that, to our misfortune, we have had nothing but bitter disappointments—since 1833—nothing but "subterfuges" and "political hypocrisy" up to the present day.

Propose anything for the benefit of Europeans and it is done at once. The Royal Engineering College at Coopers Hill and the Exchange compensation allowance are two notorious instances, the latter especially heartless and despotic. The Government of India has distinctly admitted that the compensation is illegal. It knew also that it would be a heartless act towards the poverty stricken people of India. But of course, when European interests are concerned, legality and heart go to the winds; despotism and force are the only law and argument. Here is another curious incident connected both with examinations and Europeans.

As I have already placed before the Commission my papers on the entire exclusion of Indians from military and naval examinations, either here or in India, I will not say anything more. The curious incident is this:—

The War Office would not admit Indians to examinations even in this country, and on no account simultaneously in India. But they allowed Europeans to be examined directly in India. St. George College, Massoori, examined its boys. A boy named Roderick O'Connor qualified for Sandhurst from the college in 1893. Two boys named Herbert Roddy and Edwin Roddy had also passed from that college.

On 2nd June, 1893, the House of Commons passed the resolution to have simultaneous examinations in England and India for all the services for which the examinations are at present held in England alone.[1]

[1] "All open competitive examinations heretofore held in England alone for appointments to the Civil Services of India shall henceforth be held simultaneously both in India and England, such examinations in both countries being identical in their nature, and all who compete being finally classified in one list according to merit."

Had such a Resolution been passed for any other department of State it would have never dared to offer resistance to it. But with unfortunate India the case is quite different.

The Resolution of 2nd June, 1893, having been carried, the Under-Secretary of State for India (Mr. Russell) said (*Hansard*, vol. 17, p. 1035): "It may be in the recollection of the House that in my official capacity it was my duty earlier in the Session to oppose a Resolution in favour of simultaneous examinations. But the House of Commons thought differently from the Government. *That once done* I need hardly say that *there is no disposition on the part of the Secretary of State for India or myself to thwart or defeat the effect of the vote of the House of Commons* on that Resolution.

"We have consulted the Government of India, and have asked them as *to the way* in which the resolution of the House *can best be carried out*. It is a matter too important to be carried out without the advice of the Indian Government, and at present impossible to state explicitly what will be done." Now the Commission will observe that the Government of India was to be consulted as to *the way* in which the Resolution was to *be best carried out, and not as to whether it was to be carried out or not nor to thwart or defeat it.* What did the Prime Minister (Mr. Gladstone) say:—

"The question is a very important one, and has received the careful consideration of Government. They have determined that the Resolution of the House should be referred to the Government of India without delay, and that there should be a prompt and careful examination of the subject by that Government, who *are instructed* to say in *what mode* in their opinion, and under what conditions and limitations the Resolution *could be carried into effect*." It must be observed again that the Government of India were to be instructed to say *by what mode the Resolution could be carried into effect*.

After such declarations by two important officials what did the Secretary of State do?

Did he loyally confine himself to these declarations? We know that Lord Kimberley (who was then the Secretary of State) was dead against simultaneous examinations. He knew full well that the Government of India was well known to the world *to be as dead against any such interest of the Indians.* Sir James Peile in his minute even said as much. And yet in a very clever way the Indian Office adds a sentence to its despatch, virtually telling the Government of India to resist altogether.

The last sentence added to the despatch was :—

"3. I will only point out that it is indispensable that an adequate number of the members of the Civil Service shall always be Europeans and that no scheme would be admissible which does not fulfil that essential condition."

And further, that there should remain no doubt of the real intention of this sentence, six members of the Council wrote vehement minutes emphatically indicating that the Government of India should resist—not obey the instruction as to what mode should be adopted to carry out the Resolution. And thus, knowing full well what the Government of India's views were, knowing also that the Resolution was passed *notwithstanding the opposition of the Government;* knowing also that Mr. Russell had distinctly told the House of the acceptance by the Government of what the House decided, and promising on behalf of the Secretary of State, as well as himself, *not to thwart or defeat the Resolution*, Lord Kimberley sent the Indian lamb back to the Government wolf, as if the Resolution of the House was not of the slightest consequence, and the Governments here and in India were supreme and above the House of Commons. They had always done this for two-thirds of a century to every Act or Resolution of Parliament, or the Sovereign's Proclamations.

With such open suggestion and encouragement from the Secretary of State and his councillors, and with their own firm determination not to allow the advancement of the Natives by simultaneous examination — even having only lately snatched away from the hands of the Indians the little instalment of justice that was made by Sir Stafford Northcote and the Duke of Argyll, and was approved by Lord Salisbury—what could be expected in reply to such a despatch. Of course, the Government of India resisted with a will, tooth and nail, as they had always done.

At first, the Government of Madras was one for justice. And then, in the vicious circle in which all Indian interests are usually cleverly entangled, the Government here made that very resistance of the Indian Government a subterfuge and excuse for itself—that as the Government of India refuses they could not carry out the resolution! And the

House of Commons had, as usual on Indian matters, one more disregard and insult.

And thus was one more disappointment—the bitterest of all the 64 years of disappointments the people of India have suffered. And yet there are men who raise up their hands in wonder that there should be any dissatisfaction among the Indians, when they themselves are the very creators of this discontent and great suffering.

I have referred to Lord Kimberley's actions, which showed how he was actuated from the very beginning. Now even *before* the despatch was sent to India, Lord Kimberley himself showed his full hand and let the Government of India know, by anticipation, his entire resistance to the Resolution within nine days of the passing of the Resolution on 2nd June, 1893, and ten days *before* the despatch was sent to India. He said (dinner to Lord Roberts by the Lord Mayor—*Times*, 13th June, 1893) :—

"There is one point upon which I imagine, whatever may be our party politics in this country, we are all united; that we are resolutely determined to maintain our supremacy over our Indian Empire. That I conceive is a matter about which we have only one opinion, and let me tell you that that supremacy rests upon three distinct bases. One of those bases, and a very important one, is the loyalty and good-will of the Native Princes and population over whom we rule. Next, and not less important, is the maintenance of our *European* Civil Service, upon which rests the foundation of our administration in India. . . . . Last, not because it is the least, but because I wish to give it the greatest prominence, we rest also upon the magnificent European force which we maintain in that country, and the splendid army of Native auxiliaries by which that force is supported. . . . . Let us firmly and calmly maintain our position in that country; let us be thoroughly armed as to our frontier defences, and then I believe we may trust to the old vigour of the people of this country, come what may, to support our supremacy in that great Empire."

Now, if it was as he said, there was only one opinion and such resolute determination, why on earth was all the fuss and expense of a Public Service Commission made? If European service was a resolute determination, was it not strange to have the subject of simultaneous examinations taken up at all by the Commission on grounds of *reason*, when it was a resolute, despotic, foregone conclusion? And why was the statutory service disturbed when it had been settled by Northcote, Argyll, and Salisbury and Parliament as a solution of compromise?

Now, we must see a little further what Lord Kimberley's speech means. It says, "One of those bases, and a very important one, is the loyalty and good-will of the Native Princes and population over whom we rule." Now, the authorities both in England and India do everything possible to destroy that very loyalty and good will, or, as it is often called, contentment, which these authorities profess to depend upon. I cannot say anything here about the Native Princes. But what about the good-will of the Native population! Is it productive of loyalty and good-will (will a Briton be similarly content) to tell the Indians, "you will be kept down with the iron heel upon your neck of European services—military and civil—in order to maintain our power over you, to defend ourselves against Russian invasion, and thereby maintain our position in Europe, to increase our territory in the East, and to violate all our most solemn pledges. And all this at *your* cost, and mostly with your blood, just as the Empire itself has been built up. We have the power and for our benefit; and you put your Parliament and your Proclamations into your pocket." Queer way of producing contentment and loyalty!

This is a strange superiority over the despotic old Indian system! It is seldom a matter of the slightest thought to our authorities as to who should pay for these European services and for the outside wars, and what the consequences are of the "bleeding."

In connexion with India generally, the Englishman (with some noble exceptions) deteriorates from a lover of liberty to a lover of despotism, without the slightest regard as to how the Indians are affected and bled. He suddenly becomes a superior, infallible being, and demands that what he does is right, and should never be questioned. (Mr. Gladstone truly called the "argument and law of force" as the law and argument of the present Anglo-Indian rule.) "Our boys" is his interest. The "boys" of others may go to the dogs, perish or be degraded for what he cares.

This is what the Anglo-Indian spirit of power, selfishness,

and despotism (strange products of the highest civilisation) speaks through the mouth of the heads. How this spirit, if continued, will recoil on this country itself, there cannot be for Englishman themselves much difficulty to understand.

My remarks about Lord Kimberley are made with much pain. He is one of the best Englishmen I have ever met with. But our misfortune is this. Secretaries of State (with few exceptions) being not much conversant with or students of the true Indian affairs, place themselves in the hands of Anglo-Indians. If, fortunately, one turns out capable of understanding the just claim of the Indians and does something, some successor under the everlasting influence of permanent officials subverts the justice done, and the Indian interests perish with all their dire consequences. A Sir Stafford Northcote gives, a Lord Cross snatches away.

It will be seen that the very claim now put forward by the Indian authorities of having done a great favour by the "Provincial Service" is misleading and not justified. On the contrary we are deprived of what we already possessed by an Act of Parliament (1870) of admission into the *full Covenanted* Civil Service to the extent of about 180 or 200 appointments, while what is given to us with much trumpeting is a miserable "close pariah service" of about 95 Covenanted specific appointments, and that even not confined to Indians, but open to Europeans also, and so devised that no regular admission (as far as I know) on some organised system and tests is adopted, and I understand it to be said that some twenty or thirty years will elapse before the scheme will come into some regular operation. Can there be a greater blow and injustice to the Indians and a greater discredit to the authorities? But what is worst of all is that insidious efforts are made to undermine and destroy all our charters of equal British citizenship with the people of this country.

Lord Kimberley's speech in support of the present system is the best justification of what Macaulay had said that "the heaviest of all yokes is the yoke of the stranger." If this speech meant anything, it meant that the British yoke over India should be as heavy a foreign yoke as could be made. For he does not say a word that if England employs the European Agency for its own sake he should think it just that England should pay for it, or, at least, the greater portion or half of it. Any such act of justice does not seem to occur to the Anglo-Indian "Masters." India alone must bleed for whatever the Master wills. And Britain cares not as it has nothing to pay. Worse still, the masters do not seem to care what deterioration of character and capacity is caused to the Indians.

As to the fitness and integrity of the Indians in any kind of situation—military or civil—there is now no room for controversy, even though they have not had a fair trial they have shown integrity, pluck, industry, courage and culture, to a degree of which the British people may well be proud, as being the authors of it. I have already touched upon the point of fitness in one of the statements.

About loyalty. In the despatch of 8th June, 1880, the Government of India itself said, "To the minds of at least the educated among the people of India—and the number is rapidly increasing—any idea of the subversion of British power is *abhorrent* from the consciousness that it must result in the wildest anarchy and confusion."

The fact is that because India asks and hopes for *British* rule on *British* principles, and not un-British rule on un-British principles of pure despotism aggravated by the worst evils of a foreign domination, that the educated are devotedly loyal, and regard their efforts for this purpose as their highest and best patriotism. Nothing can be more natural and sensible.

SUMMARY.

In 1833 a noble clause was passed by Parliament—everything that the Indians could desire. Had the Executives loyally and faithfully carried out that clause, India would have been in the course of more than sixty years a prosperous and contented and deeply loyal country, and a strength and a benefit to the British Empire to an extent hardly to be conceived or realised at present, when, by an opposite course, India is afflicted with all the horrors and misery to which humanity can possibly be exposed. After 1833, twenty years passed but nothing done. Fresh efforts were made in Parliament to put the Indians on the same footing as British subjects, by simultaneous examinations in this country and India. Stanley, Bright, Rich and others protested to no purpose; the violation of the Act of 1833 continued.

Then came the great and glorious Proclamation of the Queen in 1858, and a new bright hope to the Indians; but not fulfilled up to the present day. In 1860 a Committee of five members of the Council of the Secretary of State pointed out the dishonour of the British name, and reported that simultaneous examinations were the best method to do justice to the Act of 1833—to no purpose; the Report was suppressed and the public knew nothing about it. In 1867 the East India Association petitioned for the admission into the Covenanted Civil Service of a small proportion of Indians. Sir Stafford Northcote admitted the justice of the prayer, and proposed a clause to give a partial fulfilment of the Act of 1833. The Duke of Argyll passed it. Lord Salisbury approved of it, but pointed out how the jealousy of the Anglo-Indians would wreck it—a prophecy which was not long to be fulfilled.

The Government of India resisted tooth and nail, and made some outrageous proposals in the despatch of 2nd May, 1878. It was then that Lord Lytton, in a minute, admitted the ignoble policy of subterfuges and dishonour upon which the Executives had all along acted since 1833.

A strong and justly inclined Secretary (Lord Cranbrook) persisted, brushed aside all resistance and plausibilities, and compelled the Government of India to give effect to the clause. The Government of India, with bad grace and very reluctantly, made the rules—cleverly drawn up to throw discredit upon the service—the worst part was rejected by Lord Cranbrook; but an insidious device remained, and the appointments were begun to be made. The Anglo-Indians boiled with rage, and the explosion on the Ilbert Bill was the open declaration of war. Lord Salisbury on that occasion confessed that the conduct of the Executive all along was merely "political hypocrisy."

The agitation subsided, but the appointments having remained to be continued the boiling under the crater continued, and, instead of exploding, the Government resorted to other devices and gained their settled object with a vengeance—the report of the Public Service Commission confirmed the foregone conclusions against the Statutory Service and simultaneous examinations.

The statutory service of full eligibility and of about 200 employments in the course of thirty years in the whole

Covenanted Service was abolished, and the wretched scheme of May 2nd, 1878, established instead.

The whole position has been thrown back worse than it ever was before.

A Conservative (Sir Stafford Northcote) proposed, and a Liberal (Duke of Argyll) passed the Act of 1870 to do some justice. A Conservative (Lord Cranbrook) insisted upon carrying it out. A Liberal (Lord Kimberley) began to undermine it, and another Conservative (Lord Cross) gave it the death blow—though, to the humiliation of the House of Commons, the Act remains on the Statute Book. What faith can the Indians have on any Act of Parliament? To-day something given, to-morrow snatched away; Acts and Resolutions of Parliament and Proclamations notwithstanding.

Once more Parliament did justice and passed the Resolution, in 1893, for simultaneous examinations, to share the same grievous fate as all its former enactments. And the Indian Executive thus stands proclaimed the supreme power over the heads of all—Parliament, People, and Sovereign.

The whole force and object of the two references to our Commission is to reply to Sir Henry Fowler's most important challenge, and that reply mainly depends upon the consideration of the way in which the clauses in the Acts of 1833 and 1870 and the Proclamations are dealt with.

Sir Henry Fowler's challenge is this: "The question I wish to consider is, whether that Government, with all its machinery as now existing in India, has, or has not, promoted the general prosperity of the people of India, and whether India is better or worse off by being a province of the British Crown; that is the test."

I may here give a few extracts as bearing upon the subject and its results. I am obliged to repeat a few that I have already cited in my previous statements.

Sir William Hunter has said: "You cannot work with imported labour as cheaply as you can with Native labour, and I regard the more extended employment of the Natives not only as an act of justice but *as a financial necessity*. . . . I believe that it will be impossible to deny them a larger share in the administration. . . . The appointments of a few Natives annually to the Covenanted Civil Service will not solve the problem. . . . If we are to govern the Indian people efficiently and cheaply we must govern them *by means of themselves* and pay for the administration at the market rates of Native labour. . . . Good work thus commenced has assumed such dimensions under the Queen s Government of India that it can no longer be carried on, *or even supervised, by imported labour* from England, except at a cost which India cannot sustain."

. . . . .

"I do not believe that a people numbering one-sixth of the whole inhabitants of the globe, and whose aspirations have been nourished from their earliest youth on the strong food of English liberty, can be permanently denied a voice in the government of the country."

Lord Salisbury has said: "But it would be a great evil if the result of our dominion was that the Natives of India who were capable of government should be absolutely and hopelessly excluded from such a career."

Now that it is emphatically declared that all professions of equality of British citizenship were only so much hypocrisy—that India must be bled of its wealth, work, and wisdom, that it must exist only for the maintenance of British rule by its blood, its money, and its slavery—England and India are face to face, and England ought to declare what, in the name of civilisation, justice, honour, and all that is righteous England means to do for the future. The principles of the statesmen of 1833 were: "Be just and fear not;" the principles of the present statesmen appear to be: "Fear and be unjust." Let India know which of the two is to be her future fate. However mighty a Power may be, justice and righteousness are mightier far than all the mightiness of brute force. Macaulay has said: "Of all forms of tyranny I believe that the worst is that of a nation over a nation." And he has also said: "The end of government is the happiness of the people." Has the end of Indian government been such, or all a "terrible misery," as Lord Salisbury has truly characterised it? Let the question be honestly answered.

The statesmen of 1833 accepted that "the righteous are as bold as a lion." But the authorities seem to have always forgotten it or ignored it; and political cowardice has been more before their eyes.

Lord Salisbury has said many more truths, but I have mentioned them before.

Mr. Gladstone has said:—

"It is the predominance of that moral force for which I heartily pray in the deliberations of this House, and the conduct of our whole public policy, for I am convinced that upon that predominance depends that which should be the first object of all our desires as it is of all our *daily official prayers*, namely, that union of heart and sentiment which constitutes the two bases of strength at home, and therefore both of strength and good fame throughout the civilised world."

Again: "There can be no more melancholy, and in the last result, no more degrading spectacle upon earth than the spectacle of oppression, or of wrong in whatever form, inflicted by the deliberate Act of a nation upon another nation. . . . .

"But on the other hand there can be no nobler spectacle than that which we think is now dawning upon us, the spectacle of a nation deliberately set on the removal of injustice, deliberately determined to break—not through terror, and not in haste, but under the sole influence of duty and honour—determined to break with whatever remains still existing of an evil tradition, and determined in that way at once to pay a debt of justice, and to consult by a bold, wise and good Act, its own interest and its own honour."

These extracts refer to Ireland. They apply with ten times the force to India.

With regard to India, he has fully admitted that there the law and argument of England was "the law and argument of force." Lord Randolph Churchill realised the true position of the evil of foreign domination of England in India under the present system. He said:—

"The position of India in relation to taxation and the sources of the public revenues is very peculiar, not merely from the habits of the people, and their strong aversion to change, which is more specially exhibited to new forms of taxation, *but likewise from the character of the government, which is in the hands of foreigners, who hold all the principal administrative offices and form so large a part of the Army*. The impatience of the new taxation which will have to be borne wholly as a consequence of *the foreign rule imposed on the country*, and virtually to meet additions to charges arising outside of the country, would *constitute a political danger*, the real magnitude of which, it is to be feared, is not at all appreciated by persons who have no knowledge of or concern in the Government of India, but what those responsible for that Government have long regarded *as of the most serious order*."

The East India Company, in their petition against change of government, said :—

"That your petitioners cannot contemplate without dismay the doctrine now widely promulgated that India should be administered with an especial view to the benefit of the English who reside there; or that in its administration *any advantage should be sought for her Majesty's subjects of European birth*, except that which they will necessarily derive from their superiority of intelligence, and from the increased prosperity of the people, the improvement of the productive resources of the country and the extension of commercial intercourse."

The course, however, during the administration by the Crown, has been to regard the interests of Europeans as the most important and paramount, and generally every action is based upon that principle, with little concern or thought what that meant to the people of India at large.

Everything for the benefit of Indian interests is the romance, and everything for the benefit of the British and "cruel and crushing tribute" from Indians is the reality.

The edifice of the British rule rests at present upon the sandy foundation of Asiatic despotism, injustice, and all the evils of a foreign domination, as some of the best English statesmen have frequently declared; and the more this edifice is made heavier by additions to these evils, as is continuously being done, by violation of pledges and exclusion of Indians from serving in their own country, with all its natural evil consequences, the greater, the more devastating and complete, I am grieved to foresee, will be the ultimate crash.

The question of remedy I have already dealt with in one of my representations to the Commission.

In a letter in the *Times* of September 28 last, Bishop Tugwell quotes an extract from the *Times* with regard to the African races. How much more forcibly does it apply to India, to whom the people of England mostly owe the formation and maintenance of the British Indian Empire, and who for their reward receive "terrible misery" and "bleeding."

The *Times* says :—

"The time has long passed away when we were content to justify our rule by the strong hand alone. We should no longer hold our great tropical possessions with an easy conscience did we not feel convinced that our tenure of them is for the advantage, not of ourselves only, but of the subject peoples."

Can a fair-minded, honest Englishman say that he has this easy conscience with regard to India, after the wars, famine and pestilence which have been devastating that ill-fated country, after a British rule of a century and a half?

Macaulay has said, in 1833 :—

"'*Propter vitam vivendi perdere causas*' is a despicable policy either in individuals or States. In the present case such a policy would not only be despicable but absurd."

After describing from Bernier the practice of miserable tyrants of poisoning a dreaded subject, he says :—

"That detestable artifice, more horrible than assassination itself, was worthy of those who employed it. It is no model for the English nation. We shall never consent to administer the pousta to a whole community — to stupefy and paralyse a great people—whom God has committed to our charge, for the wretched purpose of rendering them more amenable to our control."

Lord Hartington said in 1883 :—

"It is not wise to educate the people of India, to introduce among them your civilisation and your progress and your literature, and at the same time to tell them they shall never have any chance of taking any part or share in the administration of the affairs of their country, except by their getting rid in the first instance of their European rulers. Surely it would not be wise to tell a patriotic Native of India that."

This naturally suggests the question of the future of India with regard to Russia. This is rather a wide subject, and somewhat indirectly connected with this statement. But I may say here that there are, in my thinking, certain features in the Indian rule of great plausibility, which the Russians, by their emissaries, will urge upon the mind of the masses of the Indians, when they are in any spirit of discontent, with great effect against the English. Nor need I enter on the speculation whether Russia would be able to make a lodging in India. These are matters which every Englishman is bound to consider calmly. The English people and Parliament should not wait to consider them till it is too late. My whole fear is, that if the British people allow things to drift on in the present evil system, the disaster may come to both countries when it is *too late* to prevent or repair it.

My whole earnest anxiety is that righteous means may be adopted by which the connexion between the two countries may be strengthened with great blessings and benefits to both countries. I speak freely, because I feel strongly that it is a thousand pities that a connexion that *can* be made great and good to both countries is blindly being undermined and destroyed with detriment to both. My previous statements have clearly shown that. The whole question of the *blessing* or *curse* of the connexion of England and India upon both countries rests mainly upon the honourable and loyal fulfilment of the Act of 1833 and the Proclamation of 1858, or upon the dishonour of the non-fulfilment of them: "Righteousness alone will exalt a nation;" "Injustice will bring down the mightiest to ruin."

I conclude with my earnest hope and prayer that our Commission will pronounce clearly upon all the vital questions involved in their two references on which I have submitted my views.

One last word of agony. With the dire calamities with which we have been overwhelmed, and in the midst of the greatest jubilation in the world, in which we took our hearty share, in spite of those calamities, we have not, as far as I know, got the word of our greatest hope and consolation —a repetition of the most gracious Proclamation of 1858, of equality of British citizenship, which we received on the assumption of the Imperial title and on the Jubilee; nor of anything of its application.

Yours truly,

DADABHAI NAOROJI.

APPENDIX.

Extract from Mr. William Digby's letter of 8th May, 1889, to Lord Cross.

I.—SIMULTANEOUS EXAMINATIONS IN INDIA AND IN ENGLAND.

In asking for the examinations for the Covenanted Civil Service to be held simultaneously in India and in England, solely on the grounds of equal justice to the Indian and English subjects of the Queen-Empress, the people of India are simply taking up the position provided for them by the Special Committee of the India Office which sat and reported in 1860. That Committee recommended, as being only fair, the holding, "simultaneously, two examinations, one in England and one in India, both being, as far as practicable, identical in their nature." They further recommended that "those who compete in both countries should be finally classified in one list, according to merit, by the Civil Service Commissioners." "Were this inequality removed," added the Committee, "we should no longer be exposed to the charge of keeping promise to the ear and breaking it to the hope." The proposal for simultaneous examinations had its genesis in your lordship's office, those who proposed it were English officials, and, in asking for its adoption, Indians are merely acting upon the sense of justice of Englishmen highly experienced in Indian affairs.[1] It will be obvious, therefore, that such a claim as is put forward is compatible with perfect loyalty to the maintenance of the connexion between England and India. The Committee, as will be seen on reference to their Report, were not unanimous in all their conclusions, but on the point I have referred to there was perfect unanimity.

On the question of simultaneous examinations, the Public Service Commission reported, in brief, as follows: "That it

[1] The members of the Committee were: Mr. J. P. Willoughby, Sir Erskine Perry, Sir W. H. Arbuthnot, Mr. Ross D. Mangles, and Mr. E. Macnaghten.

is inexpedient to hold an examination in India for the Covenanted Civil Service simultaneously with the examination in London" ("Summary of Conclusions and Recommendations," para. 128, p. 140). I refer in this letter to the summary rather than to the detailed statements in the Report, as I do not at present wish to contest each statement in paragraph 60. Should, however, such an examination become necessary, a criticism in detail of the observations made by the Commissioners cannot, in view of what follows, be less condemnatory than the remarks to be made upon the summary.

The recommendation of the Commissioners, my lord, on the question of simultaneous examinations is against the weight of evidence taken by them. An analysis of the opinions expressed by the witnesses and of the witnesses themselves reveals the most startling results. Evidently the Commission has not examined the evidence, or taken it into due consideration. There are, too, certain grave incidents in connexion with the manner in which this portion of the evidence was obtained, and the foregone conclusion to which at least one highly-placed member of the Commission had committed himself, as render it more than ever improbable that the Report of the Commission can be held to be deserving of your lordship's confidence or commendation, and which wholly militate against legislation being undertaken to give the recommendations, or some of them, the force of law.

I will take the witnesses examined Presidency by Presidency and Province by Province, and show in what direction the balance of testimony lies.

1.—BENGAL.

Total number of witnesses examined . .	—	—	195
For simultaneous examinations . .	—	143	
Against " " . .	—	35	
Majority for	108	—	
Neutral or doubtful	—	17——	195

2.—MADRAS.

Total number of witnesses examined . .	—	—	100
For simultaneous examinations . .	—	63	
Against " " . .	—	25	
Majority for	38	—	
Neutral or doubtful	—	12——	100

3.—BOMBAY.

Total number of witnesses examined . .	—	—	112
For simultaneous examinations . .	—	64	
Against " " . .	—	38	
Majority for	26	—	
Neutral or doubtful	—	10——112	

4.—NORTH-WEST PROVINCES AND OUDH.

Total number of witnesses examined . .	—	—	68
For simultaneous examinations . .	—	31	
Against " " . .	—	29	
Majority for	2	—	
Neutral or doubtful	—	8—— 68	

5.—THE PUNJAB.

Total number of witnesses examined . .	—	—	80
For simultaneous examinations . .	—	36	
Against " " . .	—	26	
Majority for	10	—	
Neutral or doubtful	—	18—— 80	

6.—CENTRAL PROVINCES.

Total number of witnesses examined . .	—	—	42
For simultaneous examinations . .	—	24	
Against " " . .	—	10	
Majority for	14	—	
Neutral or doubtful	—	8—— 42	

SUMMARY.

Province.	For.	Against.	Doubtful.
1. Bengal	143	35	17
2. Madras	63	25	12
3. Bombay	64	38	10
4. North-West Provinces and Oudh .	31	29	8
5. The Punjab	36	26	18
6. Central Provinces	24	10	8
TOTALS	361	163	73

Majority for . . . . . . 198, or 68·8 per cent.
" over Against and Doubtful, 125, or 60·4 "

Of the 361 in favour it may be remarked, 49 or 13·5 per cent. were Europeans not from any one part of the Empire, but from all parts of India.

In their Report the Commissioners have not published any statistical information of the kind given above. To obtain it the evidence of every witness, whether his evidence were oral or written, has been examined.

The case against the Report, however, is only imperfectly shown even in the statement submitted in the above tabulated particulars. A closer analysis reveals much of great interest and of the highest value. What is revealed increases one's wonder that, in face of the evidence they took, and in view of the instructions they received, the Commissioners could have reported in the sense they adopted. An examination of the following figures will well repay any time bestowed upon them.

I.—BENGAL.

Class of Witness.	Europeans. For.	Europeans. Ag.	Europeans. Dbtfl.	Indians. For.	Indians. Ag.	Indians. Dbtfl.
1. Covenanted Civilians	6	14	2	4	—	—
2. Statutory ,,	—	—	—	3	—	1
3. Uncovenanted Service:						
a. Judicial and Executive	—	2	1	22	5	1
b. Educational Department	3	3	—	9	—	2
c. Others	—	3	—	1	1	1
4. General Public:						
a. Barristers, Vakils, & Solicitors	1	2	1	39	1	1
b. Zemindars	—	—	—	20	1	—
c. Merchants	—	—	3	2	—	—
d. Others	1	2	2	8	1	—
5. English Newspapers	2	—	—	5	—	—
6. Vernacular ,,	—	—	—	10	—	—
7. Associations and Societies	—	—	—	6	—	—
8. Secretary, Government of India, and High Court Judges	—	—	2	1	—	—
Totals	13	26	11	130	9	6

An examination in detail of the facts summarised above shows that

(1) among Europeans the Hon. H. J. Reynolds, C.S.I., Mr. H. J. S. Cotton, Mr. H. M. Kisch, Mr. H. Beveridge, and Mr. C. B. Garret, all civilians of high position, Mr. A. O. Hume, C.B., a retired official of great experience, long service, and almost unequalled knowledge of the country and the people, and

(2) Sir A. W. Croft, K.C.I.E., Director of Public Instruction for Bengal, and Mr. C. H. Tawney, M.A., Principal of the Presidency College, Calcutta, among Educationalists,

were in favour of simultaneous examinations. Of the Indian figures it may be stated that in Class 3*a* against the proposal two of the witnesses were Mahomedans, in Class 4*a* the solitary individual was a Mahomedan, and in Class 4*d* the same thing is true, with this difference, that the witness was a gentleman holding a high position in a Native Indian State, being Secretary to the Council of his Highness the Nizam of Hyderabad. As much is made of Mahomedan opposition to simultaneous examinations, it may be added here that the principal Moslem officials of Hyderabad were examined—one at Calcutta, one at Madras, others at Bombay. I think it is due that I should state in detail the Indian witnesses in Bengal who gave evidence in favour of simultaneous examinations: a scrutiny of their names and of the positions they hold will unmistakably show that the leading men of wealth, attainments and position—alike in the professions, in commerce and in society, are heartily in favour of their countrymen being permitted, by a first examination in India, to compete for the highest places in the gift of the Government of India. They, who have most to lose, are not afraid of ill consequences following. Nearly all that is eminent, learned, energetic, and loyal in Bengal, is to be found represented in the following list. A more remarkable consensus of opinion than is afforded in this list could not be obtained in regard to any matter of high importance in any country. I lay the more stress upon the testimony of Bengal for this, probably sufficient, reason. In the Lower Provinces alone in the Empire is there, on any large scale, private property in land. Lord Cornwallis's Permanent Settlement and the creation of a large body of Zemindars have, in Bengal, called a wealthy class into existence. If anywhere in India, it is in Bengal that men are most interested in the maintenance of a strong, efficient, and stable administration. Elsewhere in the Empire the ryotwari system of land tenure does not admit of the growth, on any extensive scale, of a wealthy and cultured class connected with the land. Yet it is in Bengal, where, as I have already said, men have most to lose, that there is the heartiest support, from Hindus and Mahomedans alike, of the proposal for holding simultaneous examinations in England and in India. To anyone acquainted with the personnel of Indian Society in Bengal, the names of the Maharaja Jotendro Mohun Tagore, K.C.S.I., the Maharaja of Durbhunga, Babu Joykissen Mukerji, Kumar Nil Krishna Deb, Nawab Wilayat Ali Khan Bahadur, among Zemindars; Rajah Durga Churn Laha among Merchants, himself the Prince of Indian Merchants; the Hon. C. M. Ghose, High Court, Calcutta, the Hon. Dr. Mohendro Lal Sircar, C.I.E., Nawab Abdul Latif Bahadur, C.I.E. (whose weight and influence with a large section of his community it is impossible to over-rate), among Judicial officers; the thirty-nine barristers, vakils, and solicitors mentioned in Class IV*a.*, and the gentlemen whose names are given in all the other classes, will be held to represent the flower of wealth, culture, influence, and weighty good sense among seventy millions of people. Of one hundred and forty-four witnesses examined in Bengal—

129 were for Simultaneous Examinations,
9 ,, against,
6 ,, doubtful.

That the British Indian Association should have given evidence in favour of the change is, from the point of view of security, of great importance. Its action is as if the Carlton, the Junior Carlton, the St. Stephen's and the Constitutional Clubs of London were to make a deliverance to the Government of the day on some important matter. Whatever might be said of such a deliverance it could not be called revolutionary. Considering that Bengal has a third of the whole of the inhabitants of British India within its borders, that Hindu witnesses were ten to one in favour, that nearly one half of Indian Mahomedans live in this Presidency and that of fourteen witnesses of this faith examined,

10 were for Simultaneous Examinations, and only
4 ,, against,

the testimony is of so remarkable and so weighty a character as to unprejudiced minds, I submit, to be irresistible. To scorn, or set aside on insufficient grounds, such a representation is to invite discontent.

Of Europeans who were examined in Bengal, it is true, there were forty-three against to fourteen in favour. It would be invidious for me to set names on either side against one another, but if this were permissible the force of experience and authority would clearly tell in favour of the smaller numbers. The list of Indians is as follows :—

BENGAL.

Indians in Favour of Simultaneous Examinations.

Class I.—Covenanted Civil Service.

Con. No.	No. in Rept.	
1	11	Brojo Nath De, Esq., C.S., Joint Magistrate, Hughli.
2	16	K. G. Gupta, Esq., C.S., Barrister-at-Law, Joint Magistrate and Deputy Collector, Nuddeah.
3	47	B. L. Gupta, Esq., C.S., Officiating District and Session Judge, Furridpore.
4	49	Romesh Chunder Dutt, Esq., Joint Magistrate and Deputy Collector, Bakhergunje.

Total of Class I. 4

CLASS II.—THE STATUTORY CIVIL SERVICE.

Con. No.	No. in Rept.	
1	45	Bu. Ambica Churn, Sen., Assistant Magistrate and Collector, Shahabad.
2	23*s*	Bu. Nunda Kumar Bose, Statutory Civil Service.
3	28*s*	Bu. Surjya Kumar Agasti, Statutory Civil Service.

Total of Class II. . . . 3

CLASS III*a*.—UNCOVENANTED SERVICE, JUDICIAL AND EXECUTIVE.

1	6	Bu. Brojendro Kumar Seal, B.L., District Judge, Bankurah, and Assistant Session Judge, Burdwan.
2	38	Hon. Moulvi Abdul Jubbar, Member of the Bengal Legislative Council, Deputy Magistrate, 24 Perguns.
3	44	Bu. Obhoy Chunder Dos, Deputy Magistrate and Deputy Collector, 24 Perguns.
4	51	Sarat Chunder Banerji, Esq., M.A., B.L., Extra Assistant Commissioner, Kamrup, Assam.
5	53	Lalla Hukum Chand, M.A., Registrar, High Court, Hyderabad.
6	75	Maulvi Abdul Bari, a member of the Subordinate Judicial Service.
7	76	Bu. Girish Chunder Choudhury, First Subordinate Judge, Patna.
8	82	Bu. Durgagoti Banerji, Deputy Magistrate and Deputy Collector.
9	83	Bu. Srinath Roy, Fourth Judge of the Small Cause Court, Calcutta.
10	85	Bu. Tariny Churn Ghose, Deputy Collector.
11	86	Bu. Rajendra Nath Mitter, Deputy Collector.
12	92	Bu. Chundi Churn Sen, Munsiff, Krishnagar.
13	94	Bu. Bhola Ram Mullick, Third Grade Subordinate Judge, and Judge Small Causes Court, Pubna.
14	114	Bu. Anundo Chunder Sen, Deputy Collector.
15	116	Akhay Kumar Sen, Deputy Magistrate Fourth Grade, and Personal Assistant to the Commissioner.
16	117	Bu. Bani Madhub Mitter, Subordinate Judge, Dacca.
17	128	Bu. Mohendro Nath Mitter, Judge Small Causes Court, Dacca and Munshigunje.
18	143	Bu. Kunjo Lal Banerji, late Second Judge, Calcutta Court of Small Causes.
19	147	Bu. Issur Chunder Mitter, of the Subordinate Executive Service.
20	155	Rai Ram Shunker Sen Bahadur, Retired Deputy Magistrate.
21	162	Bu. Kali Charan Ghose, Deputy Collector.
22	5*s*	Rai S. C. Banerji, Extra Assistant Commissioner, Assam.

Total of Class IIIa . . . 22

CLASS III*b*.—EDUCATIONAL DEPARTMENT.

1	17	Rev. Lal Behari De, Professor, Hughli College.
2	124	Maulvi Abdul Khair Mahomed Sadiq, Superintendent Dacca Madrissa.

Con. No.	No. in Rept.	
3	125	Bu. Jagat Bundhu Laha, Headmaster, Dacca Normal School.
4	127	Bu. Iswar Chunder Bose, Headmaster, Collegiate School, Dacca.
5	135	Bu. Shoshee Bhushun Dutt, Assistant Professor, Dacca College.
6	146	Bu. Chunder Mohun Ghose, Teacher of Anatomy in the Campbell Medical School.
7	149	Bu. Radhica Prasanna Mukerji, Acting Inspector of Schools, Presidency Circle.
8	151	Dr. P. K. Roy, Professor, Presidency College, Calcutta.
9	18s	Bu. Bhudeb Mukerji, Inspector of Schools (Retired).
		Total of Class IIIb . . . 9

CLASS III*c*.—UNCOVENANTED SERVICE—UNCLASSIFIED.

1	93	Bu. Abinash Chunder Bose, Treasurer, Accountant General's Office, Bengal.
		Total of Class IIIc . . . 1

CLASS IV*a*.—BARRISTERS, VAKILS, AND SOLICITORS.

1	10	Hon. Kali Nath Mitter, Member Bengal Legislative Council, Attorney High Court.
2	29	Bu. Girija Bhushan Mukerji, B.A., B.L., Pleader, High Court.
3	32	Bu. Mohesh Chunder Choudhury, Vakil, High Court.
4	40	M. N. Ghose, Esq., Barrister-at-Law, High Court, Calcutta.
5	42	Monomohun Ghose, Esq., Barrister-at-Law, High Court, Calcutta.
6	43	Bu. Rash Behari Ghose, LL.D., Pleader, High Court, Member Bengal Legislative Council.
7	59	Saraf-ud-din, Esq., Barrister-at-Law.
8	64	Bu. Guru Proshad Sen, Pleader, High Court, practising at Patna.
9	65	Maulvi Khuda Baksh, Government Pleader, Patna.
10	66	Bu. Bisseshwur Sing, Pleader of the District Judge's Court, Shahabad.
11	73	Bu. Bhup Sen Sing, Pleader, High Court.
12	74	Bu. Jodu Nath Sahai, Pleader, High Court.
13	77	Bu. Chutturbhuj Sahai, Pleader, District Court, Patna.
14	78	Bu. Joy Prokash Lal, Pleader, and Dewan Dumraon, Raj.
15	79	Bu. Basant Kumar Bose, Vakil, High Court.
16	80	Bu. Debendro Chunder Ghose, Pleader, High Court.
17	88	Bu. Jadub Prosonno Shome, Pleader, District Court, Allahabad.
18	89	Bu. Upendra Chandra Mitter, Vakil, High Court.
19	95	Bu. Jibun Krishna Ghose, Pleader, Judges Court, Alipore.
20	97	Bu. Kali Nath Mukerji, Pleader, High Court.
21	100	Bu. Annada Prosad Banerji, Government Pleader, High Court.

Con. No.	No. in Rept.	
22	102	Bu. Ambica Churn Bose, Pleader, High Court.
23	103	Bu. Ishur Chunder Chuckerburty, Pleader, High Court.
24	105	Bu. Girish Chunder Choudhury, Pleader, High Court.
25	106	Bu. Okhil Chunder Sen, Pleader, High Court.
26	107	Saligram Sing, Pleader, High Court.
27	108	Bu. Trailakya Nath Mitter, Pleader, High Court, President Serampore Municipality.
28	111	Bu. Ashutosh Biswas, Pleader, High Court.
29	113	Bu. Dina Nath Dhur, Government Pleader, District Court, Dacca.
30	120	Bu. Rojoni Nath Bose, Vakil, High Court.
31	123	Bu. Rajani Kanto Choudhuri, Pleader, District Judge's Court, Calcutta.
32	126	Bu. Trailakya Nath Bose, Pleader, High Court.
33	133	Bu. Anundo Chunder Ray, Pleader, District Court.
34	134	Bu. Surrat Chunder Gupta, Pleader, Judge's Court; elected Chairman of the Local Board, and a Member of the District Board of Dacca.
35	138	Bu. Gobind Chunder Das, Pleader of the Dacca Judge's Court and High Court.
36	140	Bu. Keshub Chunder Acherji, Pleader, Judge's Court, Mymensing, *Zemindar*, Member of the Local Board, etc.
37	156	Bu. Mritunjoy Roy, a Pleader of the High Court.
38	163	Bu. Durga Mohun Das, Pleader, High Court.
39	205	Hon. Rao Saheb Vishva Nath Naryan Mandelik, C.S.I., Additional Member of the Council of the Viceroy, Government Pleader, High Court, Bombay.

Total of Class IVa . . 39

CLASS IV*b*.—*ZEMINDARS*.

1	28	His Highness Maharajah Sir Luchmeshwar Sing Bahadur, K.C.I.E., of Durbhanga.
2	41	Bu. Joy Kissen Mukerji, *Zemindar*, 24 Pergunnahs.
3	58	Nawab Wilayat Ali Khan Bahadur, Patna.
4	60	Maulvi Syad Fuzl Imam, *Zemindar*, Vice-President, Patna Municipality, Member of the District Board.
5	62	Rai Joy Kissen, Patna.
6	70	Rajah Rameshwar Sing Bahadur, younger brother of the Maharaja of Durbhanga.
7	84	Bu. Charu Chunder Mitter, *Zemindar* in Allahabad and Hughli, Senior Vice-Chairman, Allahabad Municipality.
8	109	Maulvi Fuzl-ul-Rahman, Vice-Chairman Nattore Municipality, *Zemindar* in Rajshaye.
9	118	Khajah Mahommed Ashgar, Vice-Chairman of the District Board of Dacca.
10	130	Bu. Radha Balhab Choudhury, *Zemindar* and Honorary Magistrate, Vice-Chairman, Municipal Board, Sherepore Town.
11	139	Bu. Madan Mohun Bysack, Merchant and *Zemindar*, Dacca.

Con. No.	No. in Rept.	
12	144	Bu. Binode Behary Roy, eldest son of Bu. Chuckhun Lal Roy, of Chagdigi, *Zemindar*.
13	148	Bu. Jogendro Chunder Ghose, *Zemindar*.
14	152	Roy Jogendro Nath Choudhury, *Zemindar*, Taki.
15	158	Kumar Nil Krishna Deb, of the Shobhabazar Deb family.
16	160	Rai Jodu Nath Bahadur, *Zemindar*, in the district of Nuddea.
17	161	Bu. Tara Prosad Mukerji, *Zemindar*, Chairman of the Revelgunje Municipality.
18	166	Bu. Hem Chunder Ghose, *Zemindar*, Hughli.
19	11s	Maharajah Sir Jotendro Mohun Tagore, K.C.S.I.
20	12s	Bu. Abhoy Churn Goho, *Zemindar*, Banian, etc., etc.
		Total of Class IVb . . . 20

CLASS IV*c*.—MERCHANTS.

1	22	Rajah Durga Churn Laha, Merchant, Calcutta.
2	110	Bairamji Nusserwanji, Esq., Merchant, Calcutta.
		Total of Class IVc . . . 2

CLASS IV*d*.—GENERAL PUBLIC, UNCLASSIFIED.

1	26	Hon. Dr. Mohendro Lal Sircar, C.I.E., Hon. Presidency Magistrate, Calcutta, Member of the Bengal Legislative Council, Calcutta.
2	48	Nawab Abdul Lutif Bahadur, C.I.E.
3	87	Bu. Dhirendra Nath Pal, Private Gentleman, Jessore.
4	90	Bu. Ashutosh Mukerji, B.A., etc., etc.
5	96	Bu. Chunder Sekhur Gupta, Government Pensioner.
6	99	Bu. Nilkanto Chatterji, M.A.
7	154	Dr. Annada Prosad Kastgiri.
8	159	Pundit Jadubeshwur Tarka Ratna, Tole Pundit in Rangpore.
		Total of Class IVd . . . 8

CLASS V.—ENGLISH NEWSPAPERS.

1	5	Bu. Norendro Nath Sen, Editor, *Indian Mirror*.
2	12	Bu. Surendro Nath Banerji, Editor, *Bengali*.
3	104	Bu. Moti Lal Ghose, on the staff of the *Amrita Bazar Patrika*.
4	119	Bu. Shoshi Bhushun Roy, Editor, *Dacca Gazette*.
		Total of Class V . . . 4

CLASS VI.—VERNACULAR NEWSPAPERS.

1	122	Bu. Kali Prosonno Ghose, Manager of the estate of Raja Rajendro Narain Roy Chowdhury, aud Editor of a literary journal.
2	129	Bu. Obhoy Churn Nag, Editor of the *Charu Varta*, and a Pleader in the Judges Court, Mymensing.
3	150	Pundit Sadanada Misra, Editor of the *Sarshudhanidhi*.
4	157	Bu. Akhoy Kumar Sircar, Editor of the *Nobo Bibhakar* and *Sadharani*.

Con. No.	No. in Rept.	
5	165	Bu. Krishna Kumar Mitter, Editor of the *Sanjibani* newspaper.
6	7s	Bu. Prokash Nath Mullick, Editor, *Samay* newspaper, Calcutta.
7	19s	Editor, *Prajabundhu* newspaper.
8	21s	Editor, *Bangabashi* newspaper.
9	25s	Editor, *Sansodhini* newspaper.
10	27s	Bu. Bani Madhub Datta, Editor, *Dainik* newspaper.
		Total of Class VI . . . 10

CLASS VII.—ASSOCIATIONS AND SOCIETIES.

1	136	Bu. Satish Chunder Ghosh, Honorary Secretary and Delegate of the Parjoar Association.
2	142	Bu. Janendro Nath Bose, Delegate of the Sripur Hitashadhini Sabha, and Taki Hitakari Sabha, Professor of Ripon College.
3	145	Bu. Hari Nath Sen, Delegate of the Baraset Association, Sub-Inspector of Schools.
4	153	Bu. Kishory Mohun Ganguly, Delegate of the Shibpore Ratepayers Association.
		Total of Class VII . . . 4

CLASS VIII.—HIGH COURT JUDGES, ETC.

1	46	Honourable Chunder Madhub Ghose, Judge, High Court, Bengal.
		Total of Class VIII . . 1

The authorities who would lightly set aside such an expression of opinion would incur a most serious risk. The very significant fact is elicited by this examination of evidence that, as I have already remarked, there are actually ten Mahomedan witnesses in favour of simultaneous examinations against four who object to them; two are neutral. Thus, in the largest province in the Empire, where nearly half the Mahomedans in British India are located, there are twice as many Mahomedan witnesses in favour than there are against! This circumstance robs the following sentence from the Report of much of its value:—"Under the second [*i.e.*, evidence 'given by others who feel that, in the present circumstances of the country, important classes of the community are practically debarred from success in examinations designed mainly as tests of educational fitness'] may be included the majority of the witnesses belonging to the Mahomedan community." (Paragraph 60 of Commissioners' Report.) The statement is technically correct, but in its essentials is strangely misleading. As I shall shortly have occasion to show the evidence of Mahomedan witnesses was taken in a manner which causes grave suspicion as to perfect fairness. For example, fifteen Mahomedan gentlemen were considered sufficient to express the opinions and views of twenty-three millions of Bengal Mahomedans; fifteen (the same number) were thought necessary to perform a similar duty for six millions in the Punjab, while sixteen were called in the North-Western Provinces, where there are less than twelve millions of Moslems.[1] Fairly dealt with, and all the considerations taken into account, the utterance of the Commissioners respecting Mahomedan evidence which I have quoted is scarcely fair, inasmuch as it deals with a set of facts differing in important particulars, in each Presidency or Province. The mere enumeration of figures in such a case would be gravely misleading. Yet this is what the Commission appears to have done.

The tables in regard to the other Presidencies and Provinces I give without comment. The details, however, are at your lordship's service should they be desired. Those details are omitted solely from a wish not to make this communication too long. An examination of them shows me that what I have said of Bengal might be said of the other parts of the Empire.

2.—MADRAS.

Class of Witness.	Europeans.			Indians.		
	For	Ag.	Neu.	For	Ag.	Neu.
1. Covenanted Civil Service	3	2	3	—	—	—
1a. Military Officers in Civil Employ	1	—	—	—	—	—
2. Statutory Civil Service	—	—	—	1	1	—
3. Uncovenanted Service:						
a. Judicial and Executive	1	1	—	13	—	—
b. Educational Department	1	5	2	3	1	1
c. Unclassified	2	1	—	4	5	—
4. General Public:						
a. Barristers, Vakils & Solicitors	—	—	5	10	—	—
b. Zemindars	—	—	—	—	—	—
c. Merchants	—	—	—	1	—	—
d. Unclassified	1	1	—	8	5	—
5. English Newspapers	—	—	—	2	—	—
6. Vernacular ,,	—	—	—	2	—	—
7. Associations and Societies	—	—	—	7	2	—
8. Members of Council and High Court Judges	—	1	1	3	—	—
Totals	9	11	11	54	14	1

[1] The Population figures are taken from the Census Returns of 1881.—Wm. D.

3.—BOMBAY.

Class of Witness.	Europeans. For	Ag.	Neu.	Indians. For	Ag.	Neu.
1. Covenanted Civil Service	5	16	—	2	—	—
1a. Conservator of Forests	—	—	1	—	—	—
2. Statutory Civil Service	—	—	—	2	1	—
3. Uncovenanted Service:						
a. Judicial and Executive	—	3	1	9	4	—
b. Educational Department	3	4	1	5	2	1
c. Unclassified	—	—	—	1	—	—
4. General Public:						
a. Barristers, Vakils, & Solicitors	—	—	1	7	1	—
b. Zemindars	—	—	—	—	—	—
c. Merchants	—	—	—	—	1	—
d. Unclassified	—	—	1	11	3	2
5. English Newspapers	1	—	—	3	—	—
6. Vernacular ,,	—	—	—	5	—	—
7. Associations and Societies	2	—	—	6	2	—
8. Members of Council and High Court Judges	—	—	2	2	1	—
Totals	11	23	7	53	15	3

4.—NORTH-WESTERN PROVINCES AND OUDH.

Class of Witness.	Europeans. For	Ag.	Neu.	Indians. For	Ag.	Neu.
1. Covenanted Civil Service	1	8	3	—	1	—
2. Statutory Civil Service	—	—	—	1	1	—
3. Uncovenanted Service:						
a. Judicial and Executive	1	—	1	4	7	—
b. Educational Department	—	1	1	—	—	—
c. Unclassified	—	—	—	—	—	—
4. General Public:						
a. Barristers, Vakils, & Solicitors	3	1	1	4	1	1
b. Zemindars	—	—	—	9	3	—
c. Merchants	—	—	—	—	—	—
d. Unclassified	—	—	—	1	2	—
5. English Newspapers	—	—	—	—	—	—
6. Vernacular ,,	—	—	—	—	1	—
7. Associations and Societies	1	—	—	5	2	—
8. Members of Council and High Court Judges	—	1	1	1	—	—
Totals	6	11	7	25	18	1

5.—THE PUNJAB.

Class of Witness.	Europeans. For	Ag.	Neu.	Indians. For	Ag.	Neu.
1. Covenanted Civil Service	1	9	2	—	—	—
1a. Military Officers in Civil Employ	—	2	—	—	—	—
2. Statutory Civil Service	—	—	—	4	1	—
3. Uncovenanted Service:						
a. Judicial and Executive	2	3	—	10	2	2
b. Educational Department	3	—	—	1	2	—
c. Unclassified	—	—	—	—	—	1
Carried forward	6	14	2	15	5	3

Class of Witness.	Europeans.			Indians.		
	For	Ag.	Neu.	For	Ag.	Neu.
Brought forward . .	6	14	2	15	5	3
4. General Public:						
a. Barristers, Vakils, & Solicitors.	—	1	—	3	—	2
b. Zemindars.	—	—	—	—	—	1
c. Merchants.	—	—	—	—	—	—
d. Unclassified	—	—	—	2	1	6
5. English Newspapers . . .	—	—	—	—	—	1
6. Vernacular ,, ...	—	—	—	3	1	2
7. Associations and Societies . .	—	—	—	7	4	—
8. Members of Council and High Court Judges	—	—	1	—	—	—
Totals	6	15	3	30	11	15

6.—CENTRAL PROVINCES.

Class of Witness.	Europeans.			Indians.		
	For	Ag.	Neu.	For	Ag.	Neu.
1. Covenanted Civil Service . .	1	2	3	—	—	—
2. Statutory Civil Service . . .	—	—	—	—	—	1
3. Uncovenanted Service:						
a. Judicial and Executive . .	—	—	3	5	5	—
b. Educational Department . .	—	2	—	1	—	—
c. Unclassified	—	—	—	—	—	—
4. General Public:						
a. Barristers, Vakils, & Solicitors.	2	—	—	4	—	1
b. Zemindars.	—	—	—	2	—	—
c. Merchants.	—	—	—	—	—	—
d. Unclassified	—	—	—	3	—	—
5. English Newspapers . . .	—	—	—	1	—	—
6. Vernacular ,, ...	—	—	—	2	—	—
7. Associations and Societies . .	—	—	—	3	1	—
8. Members of Council, and High Court Judges	—	—	—	—	—	—
Totals	3	4	6	21	6	2

SUMMARY OF TABLES.

EUROPEANS.

PRESIDENCY OR PROVINCE.	1. Covenanted Civil Service.		1a. Special Officers.		2. Statutory.		3a. Uncov. Service Judicial and Executive.		3b. Educational.		3c. Uncov. Service. Unclassified.		4a. General Public. Barristers, etc.		4b. Zemindars.		4c. Merchants.		4d. General Public. Unclassified.		5. English Newspapers.		6. Vernacular News-papers.		7. Associations and Societies.		8. Members of Council and High Court Judges.	
	For	Ag.	For	Ag.	For	Ag.	For	Ag.	For	Ag.	For	Ag.	For	Ag.	For	Ag.	For	Ag.	For	Ag.	For	Ag.	For	Ag.	For	Ag.	For	Ag.
1. Bengal	6	14	0	0	0	0	0	2	3	3	0	3	1	2	0	0	0	0	1	2	3	0	0	0	0	0	0	0
2. Madras	3	2	1	0	0	0	1	1	1	5	2	1	0	0	0	0	0	0	1	1	0	0	0	0	0	0	0	1
3. Bombay	5	16	0	0	0	0	0	3	3	4	0	0	0	0	0	0	0	0	0	0	1	0	0	0	2	0	0	0
4. N.-W. Provs. and Oudh	1	8	0	0	0	0	1	0	0	1	0	0	3	1	0	0	0	0	0	0	0	0	0	0	1	0	0	1
5. The Punjab	1	9	0	2	0	0	2	3	3	0	0	0	0	1	0	0	0	0	0	0	0	0	0	0	0	0	0	0
6. Central Provinces	1	2	0	0	0	0	0	0	0	2	0	0	2	0	0	0	0	0	0	0	0	0	0	0	0	0	0	0
Totals	17	51	1	2	0	0	4	9	10	15	2	4	6	4	0	0	0	0	2	3	4	0	0	0	3	0	0	2

Europeans: For 49
" Against 90

Total 139

INDIANS.

Presidency or Province.	1. Covenanted Civil Service.		1a. Special Officers.		2. Statutory Civil Service.		3a. Uncov. Service. Judicial and Executive.		3b. Educational Department.		3c. Uncov. Service. Unclassified.		4a. General Public. Barristers, Vakils, etc.		4b. Zemindars.		4c. Merchants.		4d. General Public. Unclassified.		5. English Newspapers.		6. Vernacular Newspapers.		7. Associations and Societies.		8. Members of Council and High Court Judges.	
	For	Ag.	For	Ag.	For	Ag.	For	Ag.	For	Ag.	For	Ag.	For	Ag.	For	Ag.	For	Ag.	For	Ag.	For	Ag.	For	Ag.	For	Ag.	For	Ag.
1. Bengal	4	0	0	0	3	0	22	5	9	0	1	1	39	1	20	1	2	0	8	1	4	0	10	0	6	0	1	0
2. Madras	0	0	0	0	1	1	13	0	3	0	4	5	10	0	0	0	1	0	8	5	2	0	2	0	7	2	3	0
3. Bombay	2	0	0	0	2	1	9	4	5	2	1	0	7	1	0	0	0	1	11	3	3	0	5	0	6	2	2	1
4. N.-W. Provs. and Oudh	0	1	0	0	1	1	4	7	0	0	0	0	4	1	9	3	0	0	1	2	0	0	0	1	5	2	1	0
5. The Punjab	0	0	0	0	4	2	10	2	1	2	0	0	3	0	0	0	0	0	2	1	0	0	3	1	7	4	0	0
6. Central Provinces	0	0	0	0	0	0	5	5	1	0	0	0	4	0	2	0	0	0	3	0	1	0	2	0	3	1	0	0
Totals	6	1	0	0	11	5	63	23	19	4	6	6	67	3	31	4	3	1	33	12	10	0	22	2	34	11	7	1

	For	Against	Total
European Witnesses	49;	90;	139
Indian "	312;	73;	385
	361	163	524

The Summary shows, as might have been expected, a decided preponderance of opinion among European Covenanted Civilians and Special Officers against simultaneous examinations. The numbers are 18 for, 55 against, or three to one against. It is surprising, all things considered, there should have been so many Europeans in favour of a proposal which, while it will do nothing to weaken but much to strengthen the connexion of India with England, will certainly, when carried out, lessen the number of Europeans employed in India. When the examination of these tables is farther proceeded with, and the Uncovenanted and non-official Europeans[1] are taken into account, the great disparity of numbers largely passes away. While there is still a majority of Europeans against, it is comparatively small; the numbers are nearly equal, being 31 for, 37 against. When these numbers are set opposite to those of Indians on both sides, the result is, I venture to submit, overwhelming in its significance.

FOR OR AGAINST SIMULTANEOUS EXAMINATIONS.

EUROPEANS.

	FOR.	AGAINST.
Covenanted Officials	18	53
Uncovenanted and non-Officials . .	31	37
Totals . . .	49	90

INDIANS.

	FOR.	AGAINST.
Covenanted Officials	17	6
Uncovenanted and non-Officials . .	295	67
Totals . . .	312	73

Thus, while of European witnesses there are considerably less than two to one against, of Indians, including the disproportionate "cloud of witnesses" of the Mahomedan faith introduced in Madras, the North-West Provinces, and the Punjab, there are more than four to one for. From the tables given on pp. 467-468 *supra* it will have been seen that there is not a part of the Empire in which the majority of witnesses, European and Indian counted together, were not in favour of simultaneous examinations. It should not be forgotten that four-fifths of the witnesses examined were

[1] I group these together, as, under the scheme of the Commissioners, it is intended they shall have the same privileges as Indians in regard to entrance into the Provincial Service.—WM. D.

summoned as being persons whose opinions were of special value. Here it may be well to set out the names of the Europeans who gave evidence in favour. They are as follows :—

Hon. H. J. Reynolds, C.S.I.
Sir A. W. Croft, K.C.I.E.
H. Beveridge, C.S.
C. H. Tawney, M.A.
H. J. S. Cotton, C.S.
C. B. Garret, C.S.
H. M. Kisch, C.S.
A. O. Hume, C.B.
F. J. Rowe
J. Kemp
Hon. P. O'Sullivan
J. H. Garstin, C.S.I.
H. E. Stokes, C.S.
E. Gibson, C.S.
J. H. H. Ellis
J. R. Upshon
Col. T. G. Clarke
H. G. Turner, C.S.
Hon. F. Brandt
G. Maddox
W. Wordsworth
G. W. Forrest
G. Geary
Hon. Justice West
J. Monteath, C.S.
Sir W. Wedderburn, Bart.
J. Clarke
A. Cotterell Tupp, C.S.
W. C. Nibbet
F. C. Lewis, M.A.
Col. Holroyd
Carr Stephen, C.S.
J. Sime, M.A.
G. Lewis, B.A.
W. Coldstream, C.S.
C. S. Arthur Wixon
J. P. Goodridge, C.S.
F. W. Dillon
A. Ewbank
F. Wyer
W. M. Elliott
Rev. D. Mackenzie, M.A., D.D.

RECORD OF EVIDENCE ACCORDING TO NATIONALITY.

PRESIDENCY OR PROVINCE.	EUROPEANS		HINDUS.		PARSEES.		MAHOMEDANS.		POPULATION.	
	For	Ag.	For	Ag.	For	Ag.	For	Ag.	Hindus.	Mahomedans.
1. Bengal . . .	14	26	118	5	1	—	10	4	45,452,806	22,704,724
2. Madras . . .	9	11	54	5	—	—	—	9	28,497,666	1,933,571
3. Bombay . .	11	23	27	6	20	3	6	6	17,834,985	3,774,360
4. N.-W. Provinces and Oudh .	6	11	21	6	—	1	4	11	38,555,121	6,162,900
5. Punjab . . .	6	15	23	2	—	—	7	9	9,252,295	11,662,434
6. Central Provs. .	3	4	21	2	—	—	—	4	8,703,110	285,687
Totals . .	49	90	264	26	21	4	27	43	148,295,983	46,523,676

The record of evidence according to Nationality shows that Europeans and Mahomedans are in a majority, adverse, the proportions curiously being nearly the same—in both cases less than two to one against. The Hindus were ten to one in favour, the Parsees five to one. Such an expression of race opinion should, I submit, have been ascertained by the Commission, should have been mentioned in the Report, and due weight should have been given to it in the recommendations made. There are one hundred and fifty millions of Hindus in British India; representatives of the various Hindu races by ten to one are in favour of a particular course; there are fifty millions of Mahomedans, less than two are against this particular course to one in favour. All are Indians, all are Indian subjects of the Queen-Empress. They work cordially together in the everyday affairs of the Empire. They are good neighbours. Their numbers ought to be counted together. In the United Kingdom Scottish votes are not separated from English votes. Carry out this fair principle in the present instance, and it will be found the Indian votes are four to one in favour. Nevertheless, the Commission—whose Report, of course, should be according to the evidence [otherwise, why trouble about taking evidence?] makes recommendations in a contrary sense, declaring there was no consensus of opinion. A Report built upon such shifting sand cannot possibly stand.

Among those, in the above enumeration, designated Neutral or Doubtful, it is only fair to the cause I am urging that I should state, are some who make suggestions which if acted upon, would find place in the Covenanted Service for a large proportion of Indians. For example:—

Mr. Larminie, Commissioner, Dacca Division, "Some posts should be reserved exclusively for Europeans—the rest for Indians."

Mr. Elliott, Public Prosecutor, Cuddapah, would give one-fourth of appointments to Indians.

Hon. M. Melvill, C.S.I., Member of Council, Bombay, would give one-fourth of appointments to Indians.

A. Ewbank, Esq., Principal of the Patna College, proposes the Statutory Service should be enlarged and recruited by nomination followed by real examination, till it reaches a third of the Civil Service.

F. Wyer, Esq., Civil Service, Collector and Magistrate, Dacca, objects on account of practical difficulties in the examination, advocates equal apportionment of appointments on political grounds, the Indian appointments again divided according to the religions of India.

Honourable P. O'Sullivan, Barrister-at-Law, Advocate-General, Madras—"If it is found to be practicable, this [simultaneous examinations] might be done."

W. M. Elliot, Esq., Pleader and Public Prosecutor, Cuddapah, Madras—If an apportionment of appointments be made, he has no objection to a simultaneous examination; he would give one-fourth of the apportionment.

Rev. D. Mackenzie, M.A., D.D., Principal, Free General Assembly's Institution, Bombay, wants the service to be recruited considerably by graduates.

It may, further, be remarked that the majority of the objections expressed to simultaneous examinations was owing to what is called the present insufficient educational advantages in India. No attempt seems to have been made by Sir Charles Aitchison or by Sir Charles Turner (they took the lead in examining on this point) to bring out the undoubted fact that—given the examinations in India the teaching standard would, in time, necessarily be raised to the requisite height and fulness. All the consequential benefits were likewise ignored. That advancement all along the line, in every walk of life, advancement in which the backward classes would share, must result, and every profession in India incidentally gain, were wholly ignored. Equally was it ignored that an immense impetus would be given to the provision of educational facilities by Indians themselves, the Government thereby, in a measure, being relieved of a portion of the burden of higher education. Again, when it was so frequently tacitly assumed that Indians were not fitted for high administrative and executive posts, no one asked the obvious question how this could be known or how the difficulties in the way of overcoming it, if it existed, could be conquered until a trial was made. As a matter of fact, so far as trial has been made and Indians have been appointed to positions of responsibility, it is freely acknowledged that they have satisfied all expectations and have discharged their duties with ability and integrity. What the Duke of Argyll has called the still more important point than that of efficiency even, namely, how the pledges of the British monarch and legislature and British statesmen as to equality of treatment could be fulfilled, was completely ignored. No more valuable branch of enquiry than this can be imagined, if equity is to mark our rule in India. The loss to Europeans of some places in the Covenanted Service is as nothing compared to our reputation for good faith. "I would sacrifice Gwalior or any frontier of India ten times," said the Duke of Wellington in 1802, "in order to preserve our character for scrupulous good faith." Very little, if anything, was done by the Commissioners in the putting of questions calculated to elicit favourable observations on this branch of the enquiry, while it is not going too far to say that the tendency of the examination was to elicit objections.

How to some extent this came about, and how it was that the clear and emphatic preponderance of evidence in favour of simultaneous examinations seems never to have struck the Commissioners, would be hard of understanding, were it not that the Proceedings of the Commission itself afford an answer, to which answer it is with no little regret I now find myself compelled to ask your lordship's attention.

Copies of Correspondence between the War Office and Mr. Dadabhai Naoroji.

VIII.

Cambridge Lodge,
West Hill Road, S.W.
5th June, 1896.

SIR,—I find from the Paper of the "Examinations held under the direction of the Civil Service Commissioners," that I have to apply to you for a copy of "the Regulations respecting examinations for admission to the Royal Military College, Sandhurst, and the Royal Military Academy, Woolwich, and of the Regulations respecting the examinations of Militia and University Candidates for Commissions in the Army." May I request you to furnish me with a copy of these Regulations?

I remain, yours faithfully,
DADABHAI NAOROJI.

The Military Secretary,
War Office.

Forwarded with the Military Secretary's compliments.

War Office,
London, S.W.
6th June, 1896.

Cambridge Lodge,
West Hill Road, S.W.
8th June, 1896.

DEAR SIR,—I am much obliged to you for so promptly sending me the four pamphlets of Regulations.

In the paper of the Civil Service Commissioners to which I referred in my last letter I find under the heading "General Notices," among the qualifications of Candidates, Section 4, as follows:—

"4. *Nationality.*—A person born in a foreign country who

can prove that his father or his paternal grandfather was born in British Dominions, is, if he has not expatriated himself under the Naturalisation Act of 1870, admissible as a natural born British subject to all open competitions which he is in other respects qualified to enter, except those for Student Interpreterships."

I do not find this qualification of "Nationality" mentioned in the pamphlets you have been good enough to send me. You will oblige me much by informing me whether I am right in understanding that the qualifications given under "General Notices" by the Civil Service Commissioners apply to the Army examinations, and that they include Indians as being born in "British Dominions" and being thus "natural born British subjects."

Yours truly,
DADABHAI NAOROJI.

The Military Secretary,
War Office,
London, S.W.

War Office,
Pall Mall, S.W.
10th June, 1896.

SIR,—I am directed by the Secretary of State for War to acknowledge the receipt of your letter of the 8th instant, and to acquaint you in reply that candidates for commissions in the British Army must be of pure European descent, and are also required to be British born or naturalised British subjects.

I am, Sir, your obedient Servant,
COLERIDGE GROVE, M.S.

Dadabhai Naoroji, Esq.,
Cambridge Lodge,
West Hill Road, S.W.

Cambridge Lodge,
West Hill Road, S.W.
14th June, 1896.

SIR,—I am much obliged for your letter of the 10th inst., informing me that "candidates for commissions in the British

Army must be of pure European descent, and are also required to be British born or naturalised British subjects."

I shall feel further obliged if you would kindly inform me by what Act of Parliament is this limit laid down for the candidates, to the exclusion of other British subjects of her Majesty of other descent and born in her Majesty's British dominions, such as British India and the colonies.

I remain, your obedient Servant,

DADABHAI NAOROJI.

The Under-Secretary of State,
War Office,
Pall Mall, London, S.W.

100/Candidates/1681.

War Office,
Pall Mall, S.W.
25th June, 1896.

SIR,—With reference to your further letter of the 14th instant, I am directed by the Secretary of State for War to acquaint you that the conditions for admission to the Army are not laid down by Act of Parliament but by regulation, and that the regulations are to the effect already conveyed to you.

I am, Sir, your obedient Servant,

COLERIDGE GROVE, Mil. Sec.

Dadabhai Naoroji, Esq.,
Cambridge Lodge,
West Hill Road, S.W.

Cambridge Lodge,
West Hill Road, S.W.
26th June, 1896.

SIR,—I am much obliged by your letter of 25th inst. (100/Candidates/1681) explaining that "the conditions for admission to the Army are not laid down by Act of Parliament but by regulation."

I shall feel much obliged by your informing me that if these conditions are not laid down by Act of Parliament then by what other authority are they laid down? May I also request you kindly to supply me with a copy of such authority and of the regulations in which these conditions are specified ?

I remain, your obedient Servant,

DADABHAI NAOROJI.

The Under-Secretary of State,
War Office,
Pall Mall, London, S.W.

100/Candidates/1685.

War Office,
Pall Mall, S.W.
6th July, 1896.

SIR,—With reference to your letter of the 26th ultimo, I am directed by the Secretary of State for War to transmit to you a copy of the Sandhurst Regulations, and also a copy of the Form of Particulars which is sent to all candidates who apply for examination for admission to the Royal Military College.

I am, Sir, your obedient Servant,

COLERIDGE GROVE, Mil. Sec.

Dadabhai Naoroji, Esq.,
Cambridge Lodge,
West Hill Road, S.W.

Cambridge Lodge,
West Hill Road, Wandsworth, S.W.
8th July, 1896.

SIR,—I have received your letter of 6th inst. (100/Candidates/1685) for which I thank you.

I am sorry I did not make my meaning clear.

You said in your letter of 25th ult. (100/Candidates/1681) "that the conditions for admission to the Army are not laid down by Act of Parliament, but by Regulation."

Now what I desire to know is this. I have always understood that the only constitutional authority or power for laying down all such conditions is Parliament, while you say that these conditions are not laid down by an Act of Parliament. Then, what other constitutional authority has the power and has laid down these conditions according to which the Regulations are made? The Regulations you have been good enough to send me, but what I want to know is the name of the constitutional body or power by whose authority such a law is made.

I am, your obedient Servant,

DADABHAI NAOROJI.

The Under-Secretary of State,
War Office,
Pall Mall, London, S.W.

100/Candidates/1689.

War Office,
Pall Mall, S.W.
18th July, 1896.

SIR,—With reference to your letter of the 8th instant, and previous correspondence, I am directed by the Marquis of Lansdowne to acquaint you that the conditions for admission to the commissioned ranks of the Army are laid down by regulations made by the Secretary of State for War, under the authority of her Majesty the Queen, as signified by Article I. of the Royal Warrant for the Pay, Appointment, Promotion, and Non-effective Pay of the Army.

I am to add that this exhausts all the information I am able to afford you on the subject of your enquiry.

I am, Sir, your obedient Servant,

COLERIDGE GROVE, M.S.

D. Naoroji, Esq.,
Cambridge Lodge,
West Hill Road, Wandsworth, S.W.

Cambridge Lodge,
West Hill Road, Wandsworth, S.W.
19th July, 1896.

SIR,—I am much obliged for the information you have been good enough to send me in your letter (100/Candidates 1689) of 18th inst., viz., "that the conditions for admission to the commissioned ranks of the Army are laid down by Regulations made by the Secretary of State for War under the authority of her Majesty the Queen, as signified by

Article I of the Royal Warrant for the Pay, Appointment, Promotion and Non-effective Pay of the Army."

May I request you to inform me where I can get a copy of this "Royal Warrant," or to furnish me with a copy?

I remain, your obedient Servant,

DADABHAI NAOROJI.

The Under-Secretary of State,
War Office,
Pall Mall, London, S.W.

100/Candidates/1692.

War Office,
Pall Mall, S.W.
23rd July, 1896.

SIR,—I am directed by the Secretary of State for War to acknowledge the receipt of your letter of the 19th instant, and to acquaint you in reply that a copy of the Royal Warrant can be obtained from Messrs. Eyre and Spottiswoode, East Harding Street, Fleet Street, E.C.

I am, Sir, your obedient Servant,

COLERIDGE GROVE, M.S.

D. Naoroji, Esq.,
Cambridge Lodge,
West Hill Road, Wandsworth, S.W.

Cambridge Lodge,
West Hill Road, Southfields, S.W.
7th August, 1896.

SIR,—I thank you for your letter of 23rd ult. (100/Candidates/1692), and I have obtained a copy of the Royal Warrant from Messrs. Eyre and Spottiswoode.

In your letter of 10th June last you were good enough to acquaint me "that candidates for commissions in the British Army must be of pure European descent, and are also required to be British-born or naturalised British subjects." In your letter of 18th July last (100/Candidates/1689) you inform me "that the conditions for admission to the commissioned ranks of the Army are laid down by regulations made by the Secretary of State for War under the authority her Majesty the Queen as signified by Article I. of the

Royal Warrant for the Pay, Appointment, Promotion, and Non-effective Pay of the Army."

I need not say how very much obliged I feel to the Secretary of State for War for all your replies, and I now beg further indulgence and favour of his lordship to give me some further explanation on the matter that I need.

In "Article I.—First Appointments," I do not find a word to exclude British subjects like the Indian-British subjects. The candidates are required to be "persons duly qualified under regulations approved by our Secretary of State."

Now I cannot suppose that any such regulations can be made constitutionally under the Warrant by the Secretary of State as would supersede any Act of Parliament or any Proclamations of her Majesty the Queen; but that such regulations can only be made in accordance with Acts of Parliament and Proclamations of the Sovereign. I desire to know whether I am right.

Under this Section I. of the Warrant there is in clause 1A: "To a duly qualified candidate from a university." In the regulations for such candidates certain British universities are specified. There are Indian-British subjects who have graduated and are graduating almost every year in some of these universities. There is not a word to exclude such graduates; this would show that the Warrant did not mean to exclude Indians. Under clause 3 there is: "By open competition." Here again no exclusion is made by the Warrant of British-Indian subjects.

And it stands to reason that it could not be otherwise. The Act of Parliament of 1833 enacted "that no Native of the said territory (meaning India), nor any natural born subject of his Majesty resident therein, shall, by reason only of his religion, place of birth, descent, or any of them, be disabled from holding any place, office, or employment under the said Company."

Now all the powers, duties, and responsibilities of the Company are transferred to the Queen by another Act of Parliament of 1858, and the entire exclusion of the considerations of religion, place of birth and descent, has remained as binding now as it was by the Act of 1833 for any place, office, or employment under her Majesty. Not only did Parliament not repeal or amend the clause of the Act of 1833, but in far more emphatic and explicit terms the

Sovereign issued a Proclamation, strongly and explicitly confirming, and in the most solemn manner pledging before God and man, with an invocation of the blessing of God, placing her Indian subjects on exactly the same footing as all her Majesty's other subjects, in these clear words:—

"We hold ourselves bound to the Natives of our Indian territory by the same obligations of duty which bind us to all our other subjects; and these obligations, by the blessing of Almighty God, we shall faithfully and conscientiously fulfil."

"And it is our further will that, so far as may be, our subjects of whatever race or creed, be freely and impartially admitted to offices in our service, the duties of which they may be qualified by their education, ability, and integrity duly to discharge."

"In their prosperity will be our strength, in their contentment our security, and in their gratitude our best reward. And may the God of all power grant to us and to those in authority under us strength to carry out these our wishes for the good of our people."

Nothing can be clearer than that British Indian subjects are most solemnly and honourably pledged to be exactly like all other British subjects.

In 1887 on the occasion of the Great Jubilee, the Queen and Empress of India again confirmed her Proclamation of 1858 in these clear words:—

"It had always been, and will always be her earnest desire to maintain unswervingly the principles laid down in the Proclamation published on her assumption of the direct control of the government of India."

I do not see, therefore, how it is possible that the Queen would intend in this Warrant anything contrary not only to Acts of Parliament but to her own most gracious and explicit Proclamations of 1858 and 1887. That our gracious Sovereign and the British people, whose voice and desire she represents, could have been anything but sincere in her Proclamations cannot be admitted for a moment, and it is impossible to believe that her Majesty's Warrant could have had the least intention of stultifying and superseding Acts of Parliament and falsifying her Majesty's own great Proclamations, so seriously made to the world on two great and historical occasions.

There is this further indication. I find that in the spirit

of and in accordance with the Acts of 1833 and 1858 and the Proclamations of 1858 and 1887—all the Civil Services of the United Kingdom in every department—Civil, Military, and Naval—are open to the British Indian subjects. There are no doubt some flaws in the rules and their execution, which I cannot refer to in this letter; but the fact is there, that all the Civil Services of the United Kingdom are open to the Indian British subjects to the same extent as to any other British subjects: such as the British people.

There is one other explanation I feel necessary to ask as to the qualifications stated in your letter of June 10—that the Candidates "must be of pure European descent, and are also required to be British-born or naturalised British subjects."

This would mean that a Turk or a Russian, or a Bulgarian, or a Spaniard, or any other of European descent can have the qualification of admission by being only naturalised; while natural-*born* subjects of her Majesty's own British dominions, and even after publicly pledged to be exactly like other British subjects, are to be excluded as only mere helots. Even those born in the Colonies would appear to be thus excluded.

You will easily see how puzzled I feel at your letter of June 10 last, and I shall feel exceedingly obliged to the Secretary of State for War to give me the necessary explanations.

I remain, your obedient Servant,

DADABHAI NAOROJI.

The Under-Secretary of State,
War Office,
Pall Mall, London, S.W.

Cambridge Lodge,
West Hill Road, Southfields, S.W.
31st August, 1896.

SIR,—I hope you have received my letter of 7th inst., and shall feel obliged to have the explanation I have requested for.

I remain, your obedient Servant,

DADABHAI NAOROJI.

The Under-Secretary of State,
War Office,
Pall Mall, London, S.W.

No. 100/Candidates/1709.

War Office,
London, S.W.
22nd September, 1896.

SIR,—I am directed by the Secretary of State for War to acknowledge the receipt of your letter of the 31st ultimo, and to express his regret that a reply to your former letter, dated 7th August, has unavoidably been delayed. The subject will receive the Marquis of Lansdowne's consideration on his return to this office, when a further communication will be made to you.

I am, Sir, your obedient Servant,
G. LAWSON.

D. Naoroji, Esq.,
Cambridge Lodge,
West Hill Road, Southfields, S.W.

Cambridge Lodge,
West Hill Road, Southfields, S.W.
10th December, 1896.

SIR,—Referring to your letter No. 100/Candidates/1709. May I request the favour of the Secretary of State for War for a reply to my letter of 7th August last?

I remain, yours faithfully,
DADABHAI NAOROJI.

The Under-Secretary,
War Office,
London, S.W.

100/Candidates/1703.

War Office,
London, S.W.
21st December, 1896.

SIR,—With reference to previous correspondence, I am directed by the Secretary of State for War to say that your letter of the 7th August last has received his fullest consideration. I am to acquaint you that in the regulations which govern the admission of candidates to the Army it is clearly laid down that only such candidates as are considered "in all respects suitable to hold a commission in the Army" are eligible. It has been decided that pure European descent is an essential qualification.

I am further to add that there is nothing whatever, either in the Queen's Proclamation or in the regulations for the admission of university candidates to which you have referred, which could have the effect of obliging the military authorities to grant commissions in the Army to candidates who are not considered suitable.

I have the honour to be, Sir,
Your obedient Servant,
ARTHUR HALIBURTON.

D. Naoroji, Esq.

Cambridge Lodge,
West Hill Road, Southfields, S.W.
28th December, 1896.

SIR,—I have received your letter of 21st inst. (100/Candidates/1703).

It appears from your reply that my letter of 7th August last has been misunderstood. Perhaps I have not been clear enough. I briefly recapitulate our correspondence.

I first asked you to furnish me with a copy of the Regulations. You kindly sent me four pamphlets. I read the pamphlets and wrote to you. After quoting the 4th section, under "General Notices" of the paper of the Civil Service Commissioners on the question of the "Nationality" of the candidates, I pointed out that I had not found the qualification of "Nationality" mentioned at all in the pamphlets, and asked whether I was right in understanding that the qualifications given under "General Notices" by the Civil Service Commissioners, applied to the Army examinations, and that they included Indians, as being born in "British dominions" and being thus natural born British subjects.

To this you replied "that candidates for commissions in the British Army must be of pure European descent, and are also required to be British-born or naturalized British subjects." I thereupon naturally asked you to inform me by what Act of Parliament was this limit laid down for the candidates to the exclusion of other British subjects of her Majesty of other descent and born in her Majesty's British dominions, such as British India and the Colonies. To this you replied that "the conditions for admission to the Army are not laid down by Act of Parliament but by Regulation, and that the Regulations are to the effect already conveyed to you."

I then asked: "I have always understood that the only constitutional authority or power for laying down all such conditions is Parliament, and you say that these conditions are not laid down by Act of Parliament. Then what other constitutional authority has the power and has laid down these conditions, according to which the Regulations are made. What I want to know is the name of the constitutional body or power by whose authority such a law is made." You replied: "That the conditions of admission to the commissioned ranks of the Army are laid down by Regulations made by the Secretary of State for War, under the authority of her Majesty the Queen, as signified by Article I of the Royal Warrant for the Pay, Appointment, Promotion, and Non-effective Pay of the Army."

I requested, and you kindly informed me, where I could get a copy of the Warrant. I obtained it and then wrote my letter of 7th August last, to which your letter under acknowledgment is the reply. I pointed out in my letter that "In Article I, First Appointments, I do not find a word to exclude British subjects like the Indian British subjects. The candidates are required to be persons duly qualified under Regulations approved by the Secretary of State." In thus pointing out that the Royal Warrant had not in any way authorised to make any regulations to exclude British Indian subjects, I further said: "Now I cannot suppose that any such regulations can be made constitutionally under the Warrant by the Secretary of State as would supersede any Act of Parliament, or any Proclamations of her Majesty the Queen, but that such regulations can only be made in accordance with Acts of Parliament and Proclamations of the Sovereign. I desire to know whether I am right." To this the Secretary of State for War has not been pleased to give any reply in your present letter: I beg to ask it again.

For further confirmation of my view, that the Royal Warrant upon which the Regulations are said to be based does not in any way authorise the exclusion of Indian subjects from becoming candidates for commissions in the Army, I cited two points from the Warrant itself: (1) "About the eligibility as candidates of graduates of some of the universities, in which no exclusion is made for British Indian graduates of those universities"; and (2) of "Open competition." I shall deal with point (1) further on when I shall deal with your present letter. On point (2) of "Open competition" laid down in the Queen's Warrant itself, the Secretary of State has not been pleased to give any explanation. I beg for it again. After expressing my views that the Warrant gave no authority to exclude Indians, I endeavoured to show that it stood to reason that the Queen's Warrant could not and would not make any such exclusion. I cited the solemn pledges and actions of both her Majesty and Parliament, and said that "it was impossible to believe that her Majesty's Warrant could have had the least intention of stultifying and superseding Acts of Parliament and falsifying her Majesty's own great Proclamations so seriously made to the world on two great and historical occasions." To this there is no reply, and I beg again the Secretary of State's attention to this part of my letter of 7th August last, and to explain how and by whom could such Acts and Proclamations be superseded and disregarded.

In your letter under reply, you say: "It has been decided that pure European descent is an essential qualification." But you do not say *who* has so decided. Parliament has not so decided, her Majesty has not so decided. Who is this mysterious great potentate, superior to the Queen, and superior to Parliament, who had the authority to decide contrary to the express desire and decisions of the Queen, the Parliament, and the British people, represented by them?

You further say, "that in the Regulations which govern the admission of candidates to the Army, it is clearly laid down that only such candidates as are considered in all respects suitable to hold a commission in the Army are eligible."

First of all, the Regulations have no authority to exclude the Indians as I have already explained. Next, even according to your extract, it does not at all follow that the British Indians are excluded. If any of them offer to show themselves and can show themselves "in all respects suitable to hold a commission" by submitting themselves to all the tests and conditions which are required from candidates, they are also eligible. What, then, had anyone the right to exclude

Indians altogether, contrary to the authoritative decisions of her Majesty and Parliament? Can any man in his senses believe that out of 225,000,000 of British Indians you will not get a few thousands who are "in all respects suitable to hold a commission in the Army" if fair and honest trial is allowed to them as candidates? Parliament does not believe so—her Majesty does not believe so.

Referring to the second paragraph of your present letter, I never said anything of "obliging the military authorities to grant a commission in the Army to anyone not considered suitable." My question is not for the "unsuitable" graduates, but for those who offer to prove themselves to be "suitable" under the *same* conditions as are required from any other candidates. The Royal Warrant does not exclude any section of the graduates of the specified universities. Unauthorised Regulations are of no force.

My last enquiry in my letter of 7th August last has also not been replied to. How is it that a Turk, or a Russian, or any of European descent can by mere naturalization become a candidate; and a British Indian subject, born in her Majesty's own dominions, and to whom equality is pledged in every honourable and binding manner should be excluded?

I fully trust that the Secretary of State would be good enough to reply to all my enquiries.

The only authoritative rational explanations I have met with are:—

1. Lord Salisbury's direct and significant words, "India must be bled," and that "all talk of pledges, equality, etc., was political hypocrisy."

2. Lord Lytton has explicitly said with regard to the actions of the authorities that they were "so many deliberate and transparent subterfuges for stultifying the Act and reducing it to a dead letter." He further says, "I do not hesitate to say that both the Governments of England and India appear to me up to the present moment unable to answer satisfactorily the charge of having taken every means in their power of breaking to the heart the words of promise they had uttered to the ear."

3. A committee of five Members of the Council of the India Office declared as far back as 1860 that the British were exposed to the charge of "keeping promise to the ear and breaking it to the hope."

I respectfully ask whether the action of the War Office making arbitrary and unauthorised Regulations to exclude the British Indians from the commissions in the Army falls under the above explanations or whether there is any other satisfactory explanation.

I once more sincerely trust that the Secretary of State will be pleased to reply to all my questions.

I remain, your obedient Servant,

DADABHAI NAOROJI.

The Under-Secretary of State,
War Office,
London, S.W.

100/Candidates/1745.

War Office,
London, S.W.
25th January, 1897.

SIR,—I am directed to acknowledge the receipt of your letter of the 28th ultimo, and to express the regret of the Secretary of State for War that my letter of the 21st idem did not impart to you the full information it was intended to convey.

In reference to the doubts which you apparently entertain as to the authority under which the Regulations for admission to the Army are made, I am to call your attention to the preamble of the "Royal Warrant for Pay, Promotion, etc.," from which you will learn that such Warrant has the express sanction of her Majesty the Queen, and that the Secretary of State for War is appointed by her Majesty to be "the sole administrator and interpreter" thereof, and "empowered to issue such detailed instructions in reference thereto as he may from time to time deem necessary."

The detailed instructions governing the grant of commissions in the Army are made by the Secretary of State under the above authority, and are, as you are already aware, to be found in paragraph 1 of the Regulations for admission to the Royal Military College, Sandhurst, and to the Royal Military Academy, Woolwich, when read in conjunction with Appendix I. to those Regulations.

I am, Sir, your obedient Servant,

D. Naoroji, Esq. ARTHUR HALIBURTON.

Cambridge Lodge,
West Hill Road, Southfields, S.W.
26th January, 1897.

SIR,—I have received your letter of 25th inst. (No. 100/ Candidates/1745).

I am sorry to trouble the Secretary of State again because my enquiry remains just as much unanswered as before. In my letter of 7th August last my very first question is this :—

"Now I cannot suppose that any such regulations can be made constitutionally under the Warrant by the Secretary of State as would supersede any Act of Parliament or any Proclamation of her Majesty the Queen; but that such regulations can only be made in accordance with Acts of Parliament and Proclamations of the Sovereign. I desire to know whether I am right."

To this question I have yet received no reply. If I am right, then the Secretary of State has no right or powers to exercise such absolute power as he claims in your present letter. No executive officer has any despotic powers to make any regulations which can at all contravene any Act of Parliament or Proclamation of the Queen sanctioned by Parliament. I, therefore, submit that the Secretary of State has no power or authority whatever to exclude British-Indian subjects.

The Secretary of State by claiming such powers as your letter assumes, exposes her Majesty and Parliament to the charge of un-English hypocrisy, *i.e.*, that her Majesty on the one hand proclaims to the world repeatedly that British-Indian subjects are exactly like the British subjects, and on the other hand stultifies and breaks her own pledges by giving to the Secretary of State authority to disregard her Proclamations. The same charge will apply to Parliament for allowing such a thing. I anticipated this in my letter of 7th August last, when I said, after citing the Acts and Proclamations :—

"That our Gracious Sovereign and the British people, whose voice and desires she represents, could have been anything but sincere in her Proclamations cannot be admitted for a moment, and it is impossible to believe that her Majesty's Warrant could have had the least intention of stultifying and superseding Acts of Parliament and falsifying her Majesty's own great Proclamations, so seriously made before the world on two great and historical occasions."

The fact is that the Warrant gives no such power or authority to make any regulations contrary to Acts or Proclamations. Every power given to any executive officer is subordinate to and restricted by Acts of Parliament and Proclamations of the Queen, unless the Secretary of State means to attribute to her Majesty and Parliament mean political hypocrisy. I therefore ask again my very first question in my letter of 7th August last, which I have quoted above, and in this letter I restrict myself to that question.

I am, your obedient Servant,

DADABHAI NAOROJI.

The Under-Secretary of State,
War Office, London, S.W.

Cambridge Lodge,
West Hill Road, Southfields, S.W.
12th May, 1897.

SIR,—I shall feel much obliged by being favoured with the reply to my letter of 26th January, 1897.

I am, your obedient Servant,

DADABHAI NAOROJI.

The Under-Secretary of State,
War Office, London, S.W.

100/Candidates/1786.

War Office,
London, S.W.
25th May, 1897.

SIR,—With reference to your letter of the 12th inst., requesting that a reply may be sent to your letter of the 26th January last, I am directed by the Secretary of State for War to acquaint you that he has nothing to add to the various communications which have been already made to you relative to candidates for commissions in the British Army.

I am, Sir, your obedient Servant,

ARTHUR HALIBURTON.

Dadabhai Naoroji, Esq.,
Cambridge Lodge,
West Hill Road, Southfields, S.W.

Washington House,
72, Anerley Park, S.E.
16th January, 1900.

SIR,—Referring to your letter of 10th June, 1896, in which you inform me that "candidates for commissions in the British Army must be of pure European descent, and are also required to be British born or naturalized British subjects," I have to request you to kindly inform me whether any alteration has been made in the rule above cited; if so, kindly inform what it is.

Yours obediently,
DADABHAI NAOROJI.

The Under-Secretary of State,
War Office,
Pall Mall, S.W.

No. 100/Candidates/2097.

War Office,
London, S.W.
23rd January, 1900.

SIR,—I am directed by the Secretary of State for War to acknowledge the receipt of your letter of the 16th inst., and to acquaint you in reply that no change has been made in the regulations which require that candidates for commissions in the British Army must be of pure European descent, and must also be British born or naturalized British subjects.

I have the honour to be, etc., etc.,
G. FLEETWOOD WILSON.

Dadabhai Naoroji, Esq.,
Washington House,
72, Anerley Park, S.E.

Copies of Correspondence between the Admiralty and Mr. Dadabhai Naoroji.

IX.

Cambridge Lodge,
West Hill Road, S.W.
5th June, 1896.

SIR,—I find in the paper for "Examinations held under the direction of the Civil Service Commissioners," which the Secretary has been good enough to supply me, that I have to apply to you for a copy of the Regulations for "Examinations for the Navy."

May I request you to supply me with a copy of these Regulations?

I remain, yours faithfully,
DADABHAI NAOROJI.

Secretary,
Admiralty,
London, S.W.

N.

Admiralty,
8th June, 1896.

SIR,—I have received and laid before My Lords Commissioners of the Admiralty your letter of the 5th instant, and in forwarding a copy of the Regulations for entering the Royal Navy as an assistant clerk, etc., I am to acquaint you that the power of nominating candidates is vested in the hands of the First Lord of the Admiralty, to whose private secretary all applications for nominations should be addressed.

The regulations for the entry of surgeons and engineers are to follow.

I am, Sir, your obedient Servant,
EVAN MACGREGOR.

Dadabhai Naoroji, Esq.,
Cambridge Lodge, West Hill Road, S.W.

Cambridge Lodge,
West Hill Road, S.W.
14th June, 1896.

SIR,—I am much obliged for your letter of 8th inst. (N.), enclosing papers for examinations in connexion with the Navy.

In the paper of Civil Service Commissioners to which I referred in my last letter I find under the heading "General Notices," among the qualifications of candidates, Section 4, as follows:—

"4.—NATIONALITY: A person born in a foreign country who can prove that his father or his paternal grandfather was born in British Dominions is, if he has not expatriated himself under the Naturalization Act of 1870, admissible as a natural-born British subject to all open competitions; which he is in other respects qualified to enter, except those for Student Interpreterships."

I do not find this qualification of "nationality" mentioned in the papers you have been good enough to send me. You will oblige me much by informing me whether I am right in understanding that the qualifications given under "General Notices" by the Civil Service Commissioners apply to the examinations for the Navy, and that therefore Indians of British India are included as being born in "British Dominions," and being thus "natural-born British subjects."

I remain, your obedient Servant,
DADABHAI NAOROJI.

The Secretary,
Admiralty,
London, S.W.

N. Admiralty,
6th July, 1896.

SIR,—In reply to your letter of the 14th ultimo, relative to the qualifications as regards nationality of candidates for entry in the Royal Navy, I am commanded by my Lords Commissioners of the Admiralty to acquaint you that appointments in the Civil Service, which are under the Regulations of the Civil Service Commissioners, are subject to the terms of the paragraph respecting nationality in the "General Notices" of the Civil Service Commissioners, to which you refer in your letter, but appointments in the Royal Navy are not governed by these Regulations.

I am, Sir, your obedient Servant,

R. D. AWDRY.

Dadabhai Naoroji, Esq.,
Cambridge Lodge, West Hill Road, S.W.

Cambridge Lodge,
West Hill Road, Wandsworth, S.W.
9th July, 1896.

SIR,—I beg to acknowledge with thanks the receipt of your letter of 6th inst. (N.) informing me "that appointments in the Civil Service, which are under the Regulations of the Civil Service Commissioners, are subject to the terms of the paragraph respecting Nationality in the 'General Notices' of the Civil Service Commissioners to which you refer in your letter, but appointments in the Royal Navy are not governed by these Regulations."

I have therefore to request you to oblige me further by informing me by what Regulations these appointments to the Royal Navy are governed, and according to what Act of Parliament are any regulations laid down with regard to the nationality of the candidates for the Royal Navy.

I am, Sir, your obedient Servant,

DADABHAI NAOROJI.

The Secretary,
Admiralty, Whitehall, S.W.

N. Admiralty,
16th July, 1896.

SIR,—In reply to your letter of the 9th instant.

I am commanded by my Lords Commissioners of the Admiralty to acquaint you that appointments to the Royal Navy are not governed by Act of Parliament, but by Regulations laid down by the Lords Commissioners of the Admiralty in virtue of the powers conferred on them by Patent.

I am, Sir, your obedient Servant,

EVAN MACGREGOR.

Dadabhai Naoroji, Esq.,
Cambridge Lodge,
West Hill Road, Wandsworth, S.W.

Cambridge Lodge,
West Hill Road, Wandsworth, S.W.
17th July, 1896.

SIR,—I have received your letter of the 16th inst. (N.) and thank you for informing me that appointments to the Royal Navy are governed by Regulations laid down by the Lords Commissioners of the Admiralty in virtue of the Powers conferred on them by Patent.

May I request you to inform me where I can get a copy of this "Patent" or to furnish me with a copy?

I remain, your obedient Servant,
DADABHAI NAOROJI.

The Secretary,
Admiralty, Whitehall, London, S.W.

N. Admiralty,
25th July, 1896.

SIR,—In reply to your letter of the 17th instant, I am commanded by my Lords Commissioners of the Admiralty to acquaint you that the Patent of the Board of Admiralty will be found in the report of the Royal Commission upon the Administration of the Army and the Navy, Parliamentary Paper C-5979 of 1890.

I am, Sir, your obedient Servant,
EVAN MACGREGOR.

Dadabhai Naoroji, Esq.,
Cambridge Lodge,
West Hill Road, Wandsworth, S.W.

Cambridge Lodge,
West Hill Road, Southfields, S.W.
8th August, 1896.

SIR,—I thank you for your letter of 25th ult. (N). I have obtained copy of Parliamentary Paper C-5979 of 1890.

In my letter of 14th June last I requested you to inform me "whether I am right in understanding that the qualifications given under 'General Notices' by the Civil Service Commissioners apply to the Examinations for the Navy, and that therefore Indians of British India are included, as being born in 'British dominions' and being thus 'natural-born British subjects.'"

To this you did not favour me with a direct reply, but in your reply of (N) 6th ult., you informed me that "appointments in the Royal Navy are not governed by these Regulations." In your letter (N.) of 16th ult. you informed me "that appointments to the Royal Navy are not governed by Act of Parliament, but by Regulations laid down by the Lords Commissioners of the Admiralty in virtue of the powers conferred on them by Patent."

I may here offer my sincere thanks for all the replies you have sent me, to the Lords Commissioners of the Admiralty; and I now beg further indulgence and favour to give me some further explanations on the matter that I need.

I have seen the Patent in the Return above mentioned, and I find nothing therein to exclude the British Indian subjects from the cadetships in the Navy.

And it stands to reason that it could not be otherwise. I cannot suppose that under the British Constitutional Government any Patent would be issued, or any Regulation would be made by any Department, in supersession or invalidation of any Act of Parliament, or any public Proclamations of the Queen; and the Patent very properly does not seem to do anything of the kind.

The Act of Parliament of 1833 enacted that no Native of the said territory (meaning India), nor any natural-born subject of his Majesty resident therein, shall, by reason only of his religion, place of birth or descent, or any of them, be disabled from holding any place, office or employment under the said Company.

Now, all the powers, duties and responsibilities of the Company are transferred to the Queen by another Act of Parliament of 1858, and the entire exclusion of the considerations of religion, place of birth or descent, has remained as binding now as it was by the Act of 1833, for any place, office or employment under her Majesty. Not only did Parliament not repeal or amend the clause of the Act of 1833, but in far more emphatic and explicit terms the Sovereign issued a Proclamation, strongly and explicitly confirming, and in the most solemn manner pledging before God and man, with an invocation of the blessing of God, placing her Indian subjects on exactly the same footing as all her Majesty's other subjects, in these clear words :—

"We hold ourselves bound to the Natives of our Indian territory by the same obligations of duty which bind us to all our other subjects; and these obligations by the blessing of Almighty God we shall faithfully and conscientiously fulfil."

"And it is our further will that so far as may be, our subjects, of whatever race or creed, be freely and impartially admitted to offices in our service the duties of which they may be qualified by their education, ability and integrity duly to discharge."

"In their prosperity will be our strength, in their contentment our security, and in their gratitude our best reward. And may the God of all power grant to us, and to those in authority under us, strength to carry out these our wishes for the good of our people."

Nothing can be clearer than that British-Indian subjects are most solemnly and honourably pledged to be exactly like all other British subjects.

In 1887, on the occasion of the Great Jubilee, the Queen and Empress of India again confirmed her Proclamation of 1858 in these clear words :—

"It had always been, and will always be, her earnest desire to maintain unswervingly the principles laid down in the Proclamation published on her assumption of the direct control of the government of India."

I do not see, therefore, how it is possible that the Queen would intend in this Patent anything contrary not only to Acts of Parliament but to her own most gracious and explicit Proclamations of 1858 and 1887. That our gracious Sovereign and the British people, whose will and desire she represents, could have been anything but sincere in her Proclamations cannot be admitted for a moment, and it is impossible to believe that her Majesty's Patent could have had the least intention of stultifying and superseding Acts of Parliament and falsifying her Majesty's own great Proclamations so seriously made to the world on two great and historical occasions.

There is this further indication. I find that in the spirit of and in accordance with the Acts of 1833 and 1858 and the Proclamations of 1858 and 1887 all the Civil Services of the United Kingdom in every department—civil, military, and naval—are open to the British-Indian subjects. There are, no doubt, some flaws in the rules and their execution which I cannot refer to in this letter; but the fact is there, that all the Civil Services of the United Kingdom are open to the British-Indian subjects to the same extent as to any other British subjects.

You yourself have been good enough to point out to me in your letter (N., 6th July last) "that appointments in the Civil Service, which are under the regulations of the Civil Service Commissioners, are subject to the terms of the paragraph respecting nationality in the 'General Notices' of the Civil Service Commissioners to which you refer in your letter."

I shall, therefore, be much obliged by informing me that the cadetships in the Navy are as open to British-Indian subjects as they are to all other British subjects of her Majesty. If not I shall be thankful for an explanation for the exclusion of British-Indian subjects, contrary to Acts of Parliament, confirmed and proclaimed by two great Proclamations of her Majesty the Queen.

I remain, your obedient Servant,

DADABHAI NAOROJI.

The Secretary,
Admiralty,
Whitehall, London, S.W.

N. Admiralty, S.W.

10*th August*, 1896.

SIR,—I have laid before My Lords Commissioners of the Admiralty your letter of the 8th inst. respecting Naval cadetships for British-Indian subjects.

I am, Sir, your obedient Servant,

EVAN MACGREGOR.

Dadabhai Naoroji, Esq.,
Cambridge Lodge,
West Hill Road, Southfields, S.W.

Admiralty, Whitehall.

13*th August*, 1896.

SIR,—I have received and read your letter of the 8th inst.

I must demur to your arguments and conclusions; but after all the discussion between us is only academical, as no application for a cadetship for a Native of India has been made to me during my tenure of office, nor is any one now before me.

If there were I should, in accordance with the practice of my predecessors, and with the unlimited right which I possess to exercise an unfettered choice, select such boys among the whole of the applicants as seemed most likely to me from their antecedents, their surroundings, their physical attributes and other considerations, to become the most efficient officers, with the greatest prospect of being successful in leading and governing British seamen.

That is the responsibility which rests upon me, and which I should do my best to discharge.

I am, yours very faithfully,

GEORGE J. GOSCHEN.

Cambridge Lodge,

West Hill Road, Southfields, S.W.

16th August, 1896.

SIR,—I feel exceedingly thankful for your reply of 13th inst. As I do not know the reasons of your demur to my arguments and conclusions, I cannot say anything about it.

It is not a mere academical matter. It is of the most vital importance to the Indians, and I may say to England also. Honest fulfilment, or non-fulfilment of the pledges of the Acts and Proclamations, makes all the difference between Indians' British Citizenship and British Slavery, between prosperity and "bleeding" poverty, between the blessing and the curse of British Rule, between honour and dishonour of the British name, between the loyalty and disloyalty of the Indians, and between the stability and instability of the British Indian Empire which in reality is mainly the British Empire.

But your kind and straight letter makes it unnecessary for me to say anything more upon this matter. Your letter shows, if I understand it rightly, that the Indian-British subjects are not to be excluded from the Navy on account of their nationality, race or creed, but that their applications will be fairly and honestly treated for fitness as those of any British-born subjects.

That no application has been hitherto made is owing to the firm belief among the Indians that they are excluded on account of their nationality, not only from all the higher ranks but even from the lower ranks of seamen, stoker, etc. One venturesome Parsee (Mr. Pirozshaw Dorabji) however, notwithstanding this belief, prepared himself at Hull, to make himself fit for a sea life and for a stokership—and applied to the Admiralty for employment as stoker. I have not the papers before me and I write from memory. But you will be able to verify by seeing the correspondence that has taken place. I think no objection was taken as to his fitness, but the final reply was, I think, that Europeans were preferred, or something to that effect.

Further the Admiralty asks from India a contribution of £100,000 per year, but it does not seem to see, that if India is a partner in the Empire and not a slave, the Indians ought in all fairness to have a return in the employment of the Indians to the extent of the amount of their share. This incident further confirms the belief that the Admiralty does not mean to treat India fairly as a partner and as entitled to a fair share in the Imperial Services in proportion to their part. This incident, I mention simply in illustration. It is a large and very important subject, and I do not think it would be appropriate for me to intrude it in this correspondence.

As the misapprehension of exclusion is removed by your kind letter, I would request your further consideration with regard to one point in connexion therewith. Your assurance needs some clear statement as to what qualifications will be considered necessary for fitness. You will, I have no doubt, at once see this need. The Indians are unfairly and heavily handicapped under present arrangements, by not being able to apply on spot for first appointments, as the people of the United Kingdom are; and before the Indians come over all the distance from India to England, under several difficulties, they must be able to see whether they possess the necessary qualifications and can calculate upon fair chances of success.

For instance, with regard to the different Civil Services of both the United Kingdom and India, the necessary qualifications are laid down; and even handicapped as the Indians are with the necessity of coming over here, they know what to expect; just the same for Law, Medicine, Universities, Colleges, Engineering or other professions.

They will abide by whatever the standards and kinds of qualifications there may be for any employment. All that is needed is that they should know before leaving India what will be required of them for admission.

I am, yours very faithfully,

DADABHAI NAOROJI.

Rt. Hon. G. J. Goschen,
First Lord of the Admiralty.

Admiralty, Whitehall,
24th August, 1896.

Sir,—In reply to your letter of the 16th inst., I feel bound to say that I think you have failed to appreciate the drift of my letter, or to draw the natural inferences from it.

I called the discussion of the general arguments from Proclamations, etc., "academical" as regards the point of the admission of Indian-born boys as cadets into the Naval Service, because no one has a right to a nomination, the selection of candidates resting entirely with the First Lord of the Admiralty.

A discussion therefore as to *rights* becomes "academical."

I further explained how my choice would be guided by my wish to secure officers who would be best qualified to govern British seamen. I must frankly say that I was under the impression that the words I used would lead you to infer that preference would be given to those of British parentage.

I cannot for one moment admit that the, to my mind, very small contribution of India to the cost of the Navy, viz., £100,000 or so, towards a total expenditure of some £22,000,000, establishes any kind of claim to admission to the ranks of the Navy. It is a contribution in respect of protection given, and nothing else.

Generally speaking, the Regulations of the Navy in respect to the parentage of those who are to be admitted to the various ranks approximate to those of the Army and have been in force for many years.

I am, Sir, yours very faithfully,

GEORGE J. GOSCHEN.

Cambridge Lodge,
West Hill Road, Southfields, S.W.
28th August, 1896.

SIR,—I have received your letter of 24th inst.

I shall not at present say anything about the academical discussion. Nor is the present correspondence fit to discuss the important question of the exaction of £100,000 from India without any voice of the Indians. Small or large amount is not material. Whether India is partner or slave in the Empire—that is the question. But that discussion must rest at present. I had mentioned this simply as an illustrative incident about the belief in India that the British Indians were absolutely excluded, on account of their nationality, no matter however qualified they may be. And after all your present letter shows that the belief was well founded.

In your first letter of 13th inst. you directed my attention to the fact that no application had been made by an Indian. Then you pointed out (if such an application were made) that you would follow the practice of your predecessors, and with the unlimited right which you possessed to exercise an unfettered choice, you would select such boys among *the whole*[1] of the applicants as seemed most likely to you from their antecedents, their surroundings, their physical attributes and other considerations to secure the most efficient officers with the greatest prospect of being successful in leading and governing British seamen. You did not say what the practice of your predecessors was. You said only what you would do. You stated the qualifications about the *whole* of the applicants, but not a word about entire disqualification of Indians on account of their nationality alone, though this reply was to my questions, which were distinctly directed, as follows, to that particular point of "nationality."

First.—In my letter of 14th June last, I asked:—

"I do not find this qualification of 'Nationality' mentioned in the papers you have been good enough to send me. You will oblige me much by informing me whether I am right in understanding that the qualifications given under 'General Notices' by the Civil Service Commissioners apply to the examinations for the Navy, and that therefore Indians of British India are included as being born in British

[1] Italics are mine.

dominions and being thus natural-born British subjects." The qualification especially referred to by me was clearly mentioned to be that of "Nationality."

To this my first enquiry you did not favour me with a direct reply.

Second.—In my letter of 8th inst. I again as pointedly made my enquiry as follows: "I shall therefore be much obliged by informing me that the cadetships in the Navy are as open to British-Indian subjects as they are to all other British subjects of her Majesty."

In your reply of 13th inst. to this enquiry, there was not a word said that Indians were positively excluded as Indians. On the contrary, as I have stated above, you laid all stress upon qualifications for fitness. If Indians were disqualified by their "Nationality," the reply of 13th inst. had no meaning—as laying stress upon qualifications of fitness, unlimited right of selection, unfettered choice, etc., etc.

Your present letter of 24th inst. is again as puzzling. You say that "no one has a right to a 'nomination.'" I did not ask or claim any such right, any more than any other British subject had.

You say "the selection of candidates rests entirely with the First Lord of the Admiralty." But really this must be certainly on some definite principles, and founded upon and ordered by some constitutional authority (which has not been pointed out in your letter), and not on the mere absolute whim or the despotic will of the First Lord, as if he were an Oriental despot. But what is still stranger is, that if an Indian is excluded because he is an Indian, and if the First Lord has positively determined not to consider any Indian application, what was the good of telling the Indian that he would consider the *whole* of the applicants. You say: "I further explained how my choice would be guided by my wish to secure officers who would be best qualified to govern British seamen." This shows that it was certain qualifications you wanted in each individual applicant, and not a decided exclusion of an Indian if he possessed the qualifications. But if you left yourself no choice, and would give no consideration to an Indian applicant, what was the good of telling him about how your choice was to be guided?

You say: "I frankly say that I was under the impression that the words I used would lead you to infer that preference would be given to those of British parentage." "Preference" would mean that if there were an Indian and a British applicant of equal merits "preference" would be given to the British. But even of the "preference" of British parentage there was no clear indication in your letter of 13th inst. But even supposing that such an inference was possible, then if the Indian was wholly and absolutely excluded as an Indian "preference" is only an idle word and means nothing.

Thus you will see that the matter is still left vague in your present letter of 24th inst.

I again put the question directly.

Is the Indian to be excluded on the ground of his nationality or not? It is desirable that such a vital matter to above two hundreds of millions of British subjects should not rest on mere misleading and vague "drifts," "inferences," or "impressions," but must be clear in statement.

In the last sentence of your letter, where there is something like a clear statement, though under cover, the matter is still left vague. You say: "Generally speaking the Regulations of the Navy in respect of the parentage of those who are to be admitted to the various ranks approximate to those of the Army and have been in force for many years." A wrong does not become a right by being enforced.

However, you have not favoured me as to what these Regulations of the Army are, and your words "*generally* speaking" and "approximate" still leave a certain vagueness as if the Regulations of the Navy and Army were not quite alike.

I have a reply from the War Office. That reply, however unconstitutional and unauthorised, un-British and dishonourable to solemn pledges it appears to me, is at least direct and clear and not left to mere impressions or inferences. This reply is "that candidates for commissions in the British Army must be of pure European descent, and are also required to be British-born or naturalized British subjects."

Now I request you kindly to inform me whether in the Navy also there is exactly, as above, the same absolute and complete exclusion of British Indians as in the Army, so that the matter may be dealt with in its true character. If the exclusion in the Navy is exactly like that in the Army then all that is said about "preference," "qualification," "exercise of unlimited right of selection," "fitness," "no applications had been received from Indians," and leaving matters to "drifts," "impressions," and "inferences" would appear to be mere excuse and of no good or use.

Kindly make the matter clear, whatever it may be.

I am informed that there were or are some Japanese in the Navy. I do not know whether this is true. If it is so I would be obliged to be informed what their position was or is.

I remain, yours very faithfully,

DADABHAI NAOROJI.

Rt. Hon. G. J. Goschen,
First Lord of the Admiralty,
Whitehall, S.W.

Cambridge Lodge,
West Hill Road, Southfields, S.W.
5th December, 1896.

SIR,—I have addressed a letter to you on the 28th August last.

I shall feel obliged for reply to it.

I remain, yours faithfully,

DADABHAI NAOROJI.

Rt. Hon. G. J. Goschen,
First Lord of the Admiralty,
Whitehall, S.W.

Admiralty, Whitehall.
8th December, 1896.

SIR,—In reply to your letter of the 28th August allow me to say in all courtesy that you seem to me to be endeavouring to create a grievance—while none, to my knowledge, has existed hitherto—by your efforts to draw from me an unnecessary declaration.

I have nothing to add to my previous letters—which appear to me to be perfectly intelligible to anyone who wishes to understand them—beyond pointing out to you, in reply to one of your questions, that the regulations which govern admission to various branches in the Navy and Army are accessible to the public, and will furnish you with the means of testing the statements I made to you with regard to them.

I regret that I cannot undertake to continue this correspondence.

I am, Sir, yours very faithfully,

GEORGE J. GOSCHEN.

Cambridge Lodge,
West Hill Road, Southfields, S.W.
10th December, 1896.

SIR,—I have received your letter of the 8th inst., and I am very sorry I am forced to trouble you again. I am not going into any argument upon your letter. But there seems to me some misunderstanding, and I shall feel much obliged by its being cleared up by you. The question is simply this, and to which the War Office has given a direct reply: Is the Navy open to British-Indian subjects, as it is open to the inhabitants of the United Kingdom; or is it not—the regulations being the same for all?

The reason for a reply is twofold. The Indians then will know whether they should apply or not at all. Secondly, it is necessary for me that, as a witness before the Royal Commission on Indian Expenditure, I should reply with correct knowledge of facts.

There are other points of great importance connected with the Navy in its relations with India, but I should not trouble you at present with these.

I remain, yours faithfully,

DADABHAI NAOROJI.

Rt. Hon. G. J. Goschen,
First Lord of the Admiralty,
Whitehall.

Admiralty, Whitehall,
15th December, 1896.

SIR,—Mr. Goschen desires me to acknowledge the receipt of your letter of the 10th inst., and in reply to point out that your original questions related to the admission of Indian subjects as Commissioned Officers in H.M. Navy, and Mr. Goschen's answers have been directed to that point.

You now ask generally whether the Navy is open to

British-Indian subjects, as it is open to the inhabitants of the United Kingdom. To this his answer is in the negative.

I remain, Sir, yours faithfully,

W. GRAHAM GREENE.

Dadabhai Naoroji, Esq.

Cambridge Lodge,
West Hill Road, Southfields, S.W.
16th December, 1896.

SIR,—I am very much obliged for your direct reply in the "negative" to my question in yesterday's letter. But I am sorry to find that you have yet left doubtful whether in your "negative" the question of "the admission of Indian subjects as Commissioned Officers in H.M.'s Navy" is included. I shall be thankful to have this cleared up, as the War Office has done. You are aware that the chief object of my enquiry was about the admission of Indian subjects as Commissioned Officers in H.M.'s Navy.

I remain, yours faithfully,

DADABHAI NAOROJI.

Rt. Hon. G. J. Goschen,
First Lord of the Admiralty,
Whitehall.

Admiralty, Whitehall.
18th December, 1896.

SIR,—Mr. Goschen having informed you in his letter of the 8th December that he could not undertake to continue the correspondence on the subject of the admission of Indian subjects as Commissioned Officers in H.M. Navy, only consented to reply to your letter of the 10th December inasmuch as your further enquiry was directed to the Navy as a whole.

Having answered this question, Mr. Goschen must again decline to renew the correspondence on a subject which he considers to have been definitely closed.

I remain, Sir, yours faithfully,

W. GRAHAM GREENE.

Dadabhai Naoroji, Esq.

Cambridge Lodge,
West Hill Road, Southfields, S.W.
19th December, 1896.

SIR,—I have received your letter of yesterday that our correspondence on the subject of the fact of the admission of Indian subjects as Commissioned Officers in her Majesty's Navy is definitely closed.

Now that hereafter you may not blame me again as you have done before about the interpretations of your impressions, inferences, etc., it is necessary for me, as I have no doubt you yourself in justice will admit, to state unambiguously what I understand as the end of our correspondence. The end is that every British-Indian subject, on account of his nationality, is entirely excluded and disqualified to be admitted as Commissioned Officer in H.M.'s Navy.

This point being ended, I have now to ask your considerate attention to my letter of 8th August last.

In the last paragraph of that letter I have said: "I shall therefore be much obliged by informing me that the cadetships in the Navy are as open to British-Indian subjects as they are to all other British subjects of her Majesty."

To this part of my enquiry you have now closed the correspondence as stated above, *i.e.*, in the "negative."

There remains now the second part of my enquiry, and for which I crave your reply. I said next in the same paragraph:—

"If not I shall be thankful for an explanation for the exclusion of British-Indian subjects, contrary to Acts of Parliament confirmed and proclaimed by two great Proclamations of her Majesty the Queen."

I shall feel very much obliged indeed for a clear explanation of this second, new question.

I remain, Sir, yours faithfully,

DADABHAI NAOROJI.

Rt. Hon. G. J. Goschen,
First Lord of the Admiralty,
Whitehall.

TABLE, &c., SHOWING EXPENDITURE ON WARS BEYOND THE INDIAN FRONTIERS.

(Extracted from Colonel Hanna's "Backwards and Forwards.")

STATEMENT SHOWING APPROXIMATE COST OF THE FORWARD POLICY ON THE NORTH-WEST FRONTIER UP TO 1896, INCLUDING THE AFGHAN WAR OF 1878-79-80.

	Rupees.	
I.—The Afghan War	223,110,000[1]	Sir Evelyn Baring, Financial Member of the Viceroy's Council.
II.—Military Railways on the North-West Frontier since the War.	163,967,910[2]	Administrative Reports on Railways in India.
III.—Beluchistan Agency since the War. Government Allotment, Rs. 865,600 per annum, for sixteen years.	13,849,600	*Moral and Material Progress of India*, 1893-94, p. 157.
IV.—Special Grants to Beluchistan Agency— Reservoir in Pishin . . . . Rs. 261,240 Quetta Water Works . . . 499,000 Buildings at Quetta 374,000	1,134,240	Financial Statements— 1889-90, p. 15, par. 31. 1891-92, p. 23, par. 16. 1892-93, p. 32, par. 84.
V.—Lease of Quetta District, and subsidy in lieu of right to collect tolls in the Bolan Pass since 1883.	715,000	*Progress and Condition of India*, 1891-92, p. 15.
VI.—Preparations for War with Russia in 1885 . .	22,880,710	Official Estimate. Return, dated India Office, 8th June, 1894.

VII.—Special Defence Works on Frontier and Rawal Pindi.	30,000,000[3]	Approximate.
VIII.—Military Roads on North-West Frontier; expended principally on the Dera Ghazi Khan and Pishin road.	2,000,000[4]	Financial Statement—1888-89, p. 10.
IX.—Afghan Boundary Commissions	1,700,000	Financial Statements — 1885-86, p. 22, par. 52; 1894-95, p. 27, par 118.
X.—Permanent Increase of Indian Army in 1885-6— A. 10,753 British Troops . Rs. 95,809,200 B. 19,220 Native Troops . 65,924,600 C. Deferred Pay of above British Troops . . . 553,000	162,286,800	Official Estimate. Return, dated India Office, 8th June, 1894.
XI.—Increase in the Native Pension Establishment, due to the Afghan War, Waziri and Chitral Campaigns, and other Expeditions on North-West Frontier.	18,591,300	Approximate.
XII.—Cost to Government of Imperial Service Troops .	1,400,000	*Progress and Condition of India*, 1894-5, p. 169.

[1] Five millions sterling were contributed by the English Exchequer to the War Expenses.

[2] Provision is made in the Budget Estimate for 1896-97 for a further sum of Rs. 4,954,000 to be expended on these useless railways.

[3] "A large sum has been spent on defences and military establishments at Quetta, including an advanced position covering the place, strategic roads, and defences for various bridges, tunnels, etc., on the Sind-Pishin Railway. . . . . An entrenched position has been formed at Rawal Pindi, and a defensive post at Multan."—"Indian Finance Statement for 1896-97."

[4] This sum only represents a small portion of the money expended on military roads in Beluchistan and other places beyond the Indus, as large sums are annually disbursed by both the military and civil departments in building new roads and maintaining the old ones.

STATEMENT SHOWING APPROXIMATE COST OF THE FORWARD POLICY ON THE NORTH-WEST FRONTIER UP TO 1896, INCLUDING THE AFGHAN WAR OF 1878-79-80.—*Continued.*

		Rupees.	
XIII.—Re-establishment and Maintenance of British Agency at Gilgit—			
A. For three years, at the rate of Rs. 50,000 a year . . .	Rs.150,000		*Blue Book, Chitral*, p. 20.
B. For four years at the rate of Rs. 200,000 a year . . .	800,000		Financial Statements— 1893-94, p. 7, par 11.
C. Special Grant	90,000	3,005,500	1894-95, p 21, par 83.
D. "	481,500		1893-94, p. 7, par 11.
E. Transport	784,000		1893-94, p. 13, par 24.
F. "	300,000		1894-95, p. 28, par 121.
G. "	400,000		
XIV.—Re-occupation of the Kuram Valley in 1892-93, at Rs. 450,000, per annum for three years.		1,350,000	Financial Statement—1893-94, p. 7, par. 11.
XV.—Grants for so-called Mobilisation—			Financial Statements—
A. 1889	Rs. 2,035,000		1889-90, p. 24, par 57.
B. 1890	600,000	5,385,000[1]	1890-91, p. 8. par. 12.
C. 1891	2,134,000		1892-93, p. 8, par. 13.
D. 1892	616,000		1892-93, p. 32, par. 84.
XVI.—Additional Transport Animals, Remounts, and Mules—			Financial Statements—
A. 1891	Rs. 1,321,000		1892-93, p. 8, par. 13.
B. 1893	267,000	1,825,000[2]	1894-95, p. 6, par. 9.
C. 1894	237,000		1894-95, p. 28, par. 121.
XVII.—Rise in price of food, forage, and increase of number of animals to be fed—			Financial Statements—
A. 1889	Rs. 795,000		1889-90, p. 24, par 57.
B. 1892	1,500,000	3,485,000	1893-94, p. 7, par. 11.
C. 1893	700,000		1893-94, p. 27, par. 63.
D. 1894	490,000		1894-95, p. 28, par. 121.

Item		Rupees	Authority
XVIII.—Expeditions on North-West Frontier since 1888-89 .		5,075,680	Official Estimate. Return, dated, India Office, 8th June, 1894.
XIX.—Minor operations (not scheduled) since 1884-85 . .		3,239,100	Official Estimate.
XX.—Waziri Campaign, including cost of Delimitation Commission, Fortified Post and Tochi Cantonments.		3,824,000	Financial Statements— 1895-96, p. 15, par. 50, and p. 56, par. 200. 1896-97, p. 34, par. 132.
XXI.—Chitral Campaign, including occupation of Chitral during past and present year.		21,500,000	Financial Statement—1896-97, p. 7, par. 11, and footnote.
XXII.—Khyber Rifles raised after the War		1,398,240	*Progress and Condition of India*, 1891-92, p. 17.
XXIII.—Subsidies—			
A. Amir of Afghanistan since the War . .	Rs. 21,000,000	22,857,400	13 years at 12 lakhs, 3 at 18 lakhs.
B. Khyberies Afghanistan since the War . .	1,400,640		*Progress and Condition of India*, 1891-92, p. 17.
C. Ruler of Chitral and his brothers	60,000		*Chitral Blue Book*, pp. 9 and 13.
D. Gomal Chiefs since 1890	296,760		*Progress and Condition of India*, 1891-92, p. 17.
E. Other small Chiefs on N.-W. Frontier . .	100,000		*Progress and Condition of India*, 1891-92, pp. 16 and 18.
Total Rupees		714,580,480	

[1] Provision is made in the Budget Estimate for 1896-97, for Rs. 4,949,000, "for preparations for mobilisation of the Field Army."

[2] The maintenance of the Transport Branch of the Commissariat Department cost, in 1893-94, no less than Rs. 3,408,140; yet, in the following year, it broke down when called upon to provide carriage for the Division of 15,000 men mobilised for the relief of Chitral.

COST OF THE FORWARD POLICY.

[*Extract from Colonel Hanna's "Backwards and Forwards," Chap. III.*]

1. The above table contains the official confession of the cost of the Forward Policy to the people of India, a confession that is very far from telling the whole tale of cruel exactions and dangerous waste which is the true history of that policy.

2. Take, for instance, the first item in that table, the cost of the Afghan War—Rs. 223,110,000—and see how it expands in the light of Major Evelyn Baring's admission, in his Financial Statement of the year 1882-83, that "it cannot be doubted that a great deal of the expenditure debited to the ordinary (military) account really belongs to the war," and that money spent "by reason of it"—the war—"was set down among civil charges." In proof of this latter assertion he adduced the fact that the Punjab Northern State Railway, the construction of which had to be hurried on for the purpose of moving up troops and supplies, cost, on that account, considerably more than it otherwise would have done, and yet not a rupee of this enhanced price was debited to war expenditure;[1] but he made no mention of the large sums spent, during the three years the war lasted, by the political officers in buying the services or the neutrality of the tribesmen, either individually or collectively, along the three lines of advance, nor yet of the cost of those political officers themselves, taken from their Indian appointments, yet still drawing their pay from the Civil List, though both these forms of expenditure were due to the war.

3. There is nothing to surprise us in these deceptive classifications: they are the natural outcome of the desire to minimise the cost of a policy which runs counter to the wishes and interests of the people who have to pay for it; and they are as common as they are natural, vitiating the official figures for all the frontier expeditions and minor operations, just as much as they falsify those of the Afghan War. One proof of this, but that a very glaring one, must suffice.

4. During a period of ten years—from 1885 to 1895—great activity prevailed all along our frontier, from Quetta to Gilgit, from Sikkim to Burma, the expeditions and operations on its North-West section alone admittedly absorbing Rs. 52,569,500. In reality they cost considerably more.

5. In the Financial Statement for the year 1888-89, Rs. 2,035,000 were set down to mobilization—an entirely new item of expenditure—which was thus explained and defended by Sir David Barbour, then the Financial Member of Council: "The Rs. 2,035,000 on account of mobilization is intended to meet the cost of purchasing transport animals, provisions, and equipment, so that, in case of need, an army corps may be in a position to take the field promptly. This is one of those precautions which in the present day of scientific warfare cannot be neglected. *The greater portion of the cost will be incurred once and for all, and will not recur.*"[2] The Rs. 2,035,000 proved insufficient for the purpose in view, and the Financial Statement for 1890-91 contained a further provision of Rs. 600,000, "to complete the arrangements and preparations to facilitate mobilization."

[1] Indian Financial Statement for 1882-83.

[2] *Ib.*, 1889-90, page 24, par. 57.

6. To people of my views, the need of providing for the mobilization of an army corps, *for service across the frontier*, was not apparent; but we derived a certain amount of comfort from the assurance that the process, unnecessary as we thought it, and expensive as it certainly was, had been completed, and we noted with satisfaction the absence of the word *mobilization* from the Financial Statement for the year 1891-92. All the greater, therefore, were our disappointment and astonishment when, in the course of the same year, a revised estimate was made public, in which besides Rs. 800,000 "sanctioned during the year for additional transport mules," and Rs. 521,000 "for remounts and ordnance mules,"[1] Rs. 2,134,000 were set down as "*Expenditure in India in preparations to facilitate mobilization;*" whilst the Financial Statement for 1892-93 placed Rs. 616,000 to the account of "*Measures intended to facilitate the speedy mobilization of the army.*"

7. Now, if Rs. 2,635,000 was an adequate provision for the mobilization of an army corps—there was never any talk of mobilizing two—what became of the transport, provisions, and equipment bought with that money? There can be but one answer to the question—it had all disappeared, used up in frontier expeditions and minor operations; and so far as transport is concerned, we have the clearest proof that the Rs. 2,750,000 nominally devoted to mobilization in 1891-92 and 1892-93, went the same way, for when in the spring of 1895 a single division—minus the greater part of its cavalry and its horse and field artillery—was ordered on active service, it was found that there were only 7,482 Government mules available, and the military authorities, after buying or hiring every baggage animal that they could lay hands on, were reduced to the necessity of borrowing the transport service of the Jaipur and Gwalior Imperial Service Troops, and depriving a number of our own regiments of their regimental baggage ponies.[2]

8. In the current year Rs. 4,949,000 have again been devoted to the mobilization of a field army, and Sir James Westland has promised the Indian taxpayers that Rs. 4,348,000 of that amount "*will be non-recurring, initial expenditure.*" Can he, I wonder, ever have read his predecessor's similar assurance? The sum is large, nevertheless it is absolutely certain that if, in the course of the next two or three years, India should become involved in "scientific warfare," she would find herself utterly destitute of the means of prosecuting it, unless indeed her Government had meanwhile put a stop to the expeditions and operations which are perpetually frittering away her resources of all kinds, but more especially her supply of transport cattle.

9. It is worth noting that this habit of concealing the true cost

[1] See Table of Costs, XVI A, 1891, Rs. 1,321,000 (Rs. 800,000 + 521,000).

[2] Sir Henry Brackenbury, Military Member of the Viceroy's Council, in his remarks on the military expenditure in 1895-96, mentions that "no less than 40,000 transport animals were employed with the Chitral Relief Force." As regards camels, he said: "We were dependent entirely upon hired camels, or upon camels purchased expressly for the campaign. . . But the number which could be hired was extremely small, and at the very outset the Government was obliged to have recourse to purchase. . . . . *The camels purchased by Government have for the most part so broken down in health that it has been found impracticable to retain any but a very small number of them for future use.*"

of past expeditions and operations is closely allied to that tendency to under-estimate the probable expense of each new phase of the expansion fever, to which we owe the most stupendous financial blunder on record—the estimating of the total net cost of the Afghan War at £5,752,000 in February, 1880, and the revision of that estimate in June of the same year by rather more than £9,000,000! The £15,000,000 at which the cost of the war was then placed, rose in October to £15,777,000, and when the accounts were made up at the close of the financial year—March, 1881—this sum was found to have fallen short of the monies already expended by £828,000, whilst war expenditure still showed no sign of coming to an end![1]

10. The story is so old a one that there has been time for most of us to forget it, but we all know that it has repeated itself in still more startling form, though on a smaller scale, *à propos* of that campaign which so unpleasantly laid bare the deficiencies of Indian transport arrangements, and the untrustworthiness of Indian Budgets.

11. The first estimate for the Chitral Expedition amounted only to Rs. 1,500,000; the sum actually spent upon it, to Rs. 17,647,000, or nearly twelve times more than that estimate; whilst, according to Sir James Westland, "it has left us a legacy of permanent expenditure in the occupation of Chitral and of its communications, which has involved in 1895-96 an expenditure of Rs. 1,022,000, and will involve in 1896-97 an expenditure of Rs. 2,317,000 . . . . irrespective of the Political Expenditure, which comes to Rs. 200,000 in 1895-96 and Rs. 220,000 in 1896-97; . . . . also of Military Works Expenditure, Rs. 216,000 in 1896-97."[2]

[1] Indian Financial Statement for 1881-82.
[2] *Ib.*, 1895-97.

X.

INDIAN CURRENCY.

The following letter was printed in the *Times* of June 3, 1898:

To the Editor of the "Times."

Sir,—You will kindly allow me to express my views on the subject of the Indian currency.

1. Fall or rise in exchange does not in itself (other circumstances being the same) matter in true international trade, which adjusts itself automatically to the requirements of exchange. I would illustrate this. I desire, for instance, to lay out £1,000 for sending a quantity of piece goods to India. I calculate the price of the manufacturer, exchange, whatever it may be, 1s., 2s., or 3s. per rupee, freight, insurance, commission, etc., and see whether the price in India would pay me a fair profit. If I think it would I enter into the transaction, sell my bill to an East India bank, and take the usual commercial chances of supply, demand, etc., when the goods arrive in India. I give this illustration in its simplest form of the general character of commercial transactions between this country and India. There are variations of the method of these transactions, but into them I do not enter at present, to avoid confusion. The main principle is the same.

2. Closing the mints or introducing a gold standard does not and cannot save a single farthing to the Indian taxpayers in their remittances for "home charges" to this country. The reason is simple. Suppose we take roundly £20,000,000 sterling in gold to be the amount of the "home charges." The Indian taxpayers have to send as much produce to this country as is necessary to buy £20,000,000 sterling, not an ounce less, no matter whatever may be the rupee, or whatever the standard—gold or silver—in India, England must receive £20,000,000 in gold or produce worth £20,000,000 in gold.

3. Closing of the mints and thereby raising the true rupee worth, at present about 11d. in gold, to a false rupee to be worth about 16d. in gold is a covert exaction of 45 per cent. more taxation (besides producing other effects which I do not mention) from the Indian taxpayers. The reason is again simple. Suppose a rayat has to pay Rs. 10 for land tax. This rupee means a fixed quantity of silver stamped with the mint stamp, and is truly worth at present only about 11d. of gold. By closing the mints this rupee is forced up to the worth of 16d. of gold, and the rayat is compelled to find this high-priced false rupee of 16d. of gold, or, in other words, to sell 45 per cent. more of his produce to get this false rupee, the Government thus getting 45 per cent. more taxation than it is entitled to, even according to its own "despotic" legislation.

4. The introduction of a gold standard, while it will not save a single farthing or a single ounce of produce to the Indian taxpayer in his payment of "home charges," as explained above, will simply add more to his already existing grievous burdens (and injure him in other ways which I avoid mentioning here), to the extent of the heavy cost of the alteration.

I have thus put forth four simple clear propositions. It is necessary for your other correspondents to consider whether these propositions are true or not. If once these fundamental issues or premises are settled further discussion will have a sound basis to go upon. At present the whole controversy is based upon the assumption that closing of mints or introduction of a gold standard will produce to the Indian taxpayers an enormous saving in their remittances for "home charges." This, I say, is a mere fiction of the imagination and an unfortunate delusion.

I avoid also entering on the question of the remedy. It is useless to talk about the remedy before making a true diagnosis of the real character of the disease.

After the above four simple propositions are settled I shall, with your permission, express my views about the real disease and its remedy.

I may here take the opportunity of saying that the constitution of the present Currency Committee is utterly unsatisfactory, as it does not contain any representative of the Indian taxpayers.

I remain, yours truly,

DADABHAI NAOROJI.

Washington House, 72, Anerley Park, S.E.
May 29, 1898.

I.—STATEMENT SUBMITTED TO THE INDIAN CURRENCY COMMITTEE OF 1898.

Washington House,
72, Anerley Park, S.E.
July 30, 1898.

MY DEAR SIR WILLIAM WEDDERBURN,—In accordance with the reply of the 5th inst. from the Currency Committee to your letter saying "they will, however, be glad to accord their best consideration to any written communication which you may desire to lay before them," I send you this statement, which you would be good enough to forward to them.

2. I may add that I am willing to submit to any cross-examination that may be considered necessary to test the correctness of my views, or to ask me other questions. You know that I have been in business in the City for twenty-five

years as a merchant, and also as a commission agent; I have dealt with almost every kind of export and import between England and India. I have seen some commercial and monetary crises, including that of "the Black Friday," when I think Messrs. Overend Gurney and Co. closed their doors.

3. Fall or rise in exchange does not in itself (other circumstances remaining the same) matter in true international trade, which adjusts itself automatically to the requirements of exchange. To establish this proposition by a detailed explanation of the mode of operations of Indian trade, I attach as Appendix A some letters which I wrote to the *Times* and the *Daily News* in 1886.

4. Closing the mints or introducing a gold standard does not and cannot save a single farthing to the Indian taxpayers in their remittance for "Home Charges" to this country. The reason is simple. Suppose we take roundly £20,000,000 sterling to be the amount of the "Home Charges." The Indian taxpayers have to send as much produce to this country as is necessary to buy £20,000,000, not an ounce less, no matter whatever may be the rupee or whatever the standard (gold or silver) in India. England must receive £20,000,000 in gold, or produce worth £20,000,000. The only way in which relief can come to the Indian taxpayers in these remittances is the rise in the prices of the Indian merchandise in this country, and not by any juggling with the currency laws of India.

5. The Government of India, in their despatch to the Secretary of State (Simla, November 9, 1878), themselves admit this in so many words:—

"66. Now, it is plain that so long as the amount of the so-called tribute is not changed the quantity of merchandise necessary to pay it will not change either, excepting by reason of a change of its value in the foreign country to which it goes." (C 4868, 1886, p. 25.)

6. Closing of the mints, and thereby raising the true rupee, worth at present about 11d. in gold, to a false rupee to be worth 16d. in gold, is a covert exaction of about 45 per cent. more taxation all round from the Indian taxpayers, and at the same time of increasing the salaries of officials and other payments in India by Government to the same extent, and giving generally the advantage to creditors over debtors, the former being generally well-to-do, and the latter the

poorer classes, especially in the case of the money-lenders and the rayats.

7. The real and full effect of the closing of the mints must be examined by *itself*, irrespective of the effect of other factors. First of all, the closing of the mints was illegal, dishonourable, and a despotic act. It is a violation of all taxation Acts, by which there was always a distinct contract between the Government and the taxpayers based upon the fundamental principle of sound currency—*i.e.*, of a certain definite rupee. And what is that fundamental principle upon which the currency, both of this country and of India, is based? The former is upon what is called the gold standard, and the latter the silver standard. Take this country first.

8. Here the whole currency is based upon a sovereign—a fixed unit of a certain quantity of gold, whatever its relative exchangeable value may be with all other commodities. A sovereign is nothing more or less than, or anything else but, 123.274 grains of gold of a certain fineness, with a stamp upon it, certifying to the world that it is what it professes to be, and that no restriction whatsoever was to be placed either on the market of gold or on the coining of gold. Any person may present 123.274 grains of gold, of standard fineness with the mintage (which, I think, is three halfpence on an ounce),[1] and ask for a sovereign and will get it. It is not buying or selling gold; Government simply having fixed a unit of currency measure, stamps the unit that it is the proper unit. I should be surprised if Government here should even think of interfering with this unrestricted sale and coinage of gold, as the foundation of the sound currency of this country. The sovereign is the standard by which every other commodity, including silver, is measured in its exchangeable value, just as a foot is a standard measure of length, a gallon of liquid. The taxpayer's contract with the Government is that he is to pay in such unrestricted sovereigns, and every taxation law lays down the payment in such sovereigns.

9. Similarly about India—substitute 180 grains of standard silver, with 2 per cent. for mintage for a rupee, in place of 123.274 grains of gold, with three halfpence for every ounce of gold coined, for a sovereign, and all the above remarks apply word for word to the case of India, except that I should

[1] I understand that there is no charge now. (Coinage Act of 1870, Sec. 8.)

not be surprised at the Indian authorities playing any pranks, regardless of consequences to the Indian people, as long as they are considered favourable to the "interests," and are to be made at the cost of the Indians.

10. This is the true rupee—180 grains of standard silver at its market value, with nearly 4 grains more for mintage, is convertible into a rupee without any restriction either on the silver market or on the free coining of silver. It is in this true rupee that the taxpayer is legally bound to pay his taxes. Any interference with the fundamental principle and law of the rupee is illegal, immoral, or dishonourable.

11. Now comes the false rupee. The true rupee, in its relation to gold at the present market value of silver of 184 grains, is worth, say, about 11d. of gold. Government intervenes, abuses its power or duty to coin silver unrestrictedly, makes the rupee scarce and false, and forces it up to the value of 16d. of gold, or about 269 grains of silver (including mintage), which the rupee does not contain. And the taxpayer is compelled, by what Mr. Gladstone called "the argument and law of force," to pay his tax in this false rupee, under the false pretence of using the word "rupee" when this "rupee" is not one rupee but nearly one and a half rupee.

12. Let us now take the factor of closing the mints by *itself.* Suppose I go into the market with my produce to buy 184 grains of standard silver for which I am asked one maund of rice. I go to the mint and ask to coin this into a rupee which I have to pay to the Sircar for my tax. If I get the rupee, then it is all right. But no, the mint refuses to coin. It virtually tells me, "Bring 269 grains of silver (*i.e.*, worth 16d. of gold) and you will get a rupee." I go into the market to get the rupee. The man who has the rupee tells me, "If you give me 269 grains of silver, or as much produce as would buy 269 grains of silver, I would give you the rupee." What alternative remains for me but to give as much of my rice, about 1½ maunds, to get this false "rupee," instead of only one maund to get the true rupee which I can get in the *same market* and at the *same time?* This is altogether independent of whatever the *actual* price of commodities may be.

13. If the actual price of rice does not show this fall, owing to the disguise of the false "rupee," it is not that the closing of the mints has not produced this decline, but that

other fortunate factors have influenced the price, whose benefit is robbed away from me by the Government by the covert device of the closing of the mints. Otherwise I would have received so much higher price for my produce than the actual price. The loss, therefore, to me is all the same, as I was forced to pay in my produce for 269 grains of silver to get the false "rupee" instead of at the *same moment* paying for 184 grains of silver to get the true rupee. These two different prices in merchandise for the false and the true rupee are demanded, as I have said above, at the *same time*, and in the same market, *i.e.*, the price of the false rupee, 45 per cent. higher than that of the true rupee, entirely irrespective of any general market rise or fall of price at any same time. If the actual price of rice be 1½ maunds for the false rupee, the price at the *same time* will be one maund for the true rupee, or for 184 grains of silver.

14. To test this in another way. Let us take some commodity in the country itself upon which the factor of the closing of the mints produces its full effect in the actual market, and which is not materially affected by other commercial factors, which operate generally upon the general merchandise. Such a commodity in India is gold. It is affected, not in merely foreign exchange or international relations, but in *India itself* as a commodity, like every other commodity. Say, I have a sovereign, and I want to sell it for rupees in India itself—not for exchange to foreign parts. If the "rupee" were the honest, true rupee of the market value of 184 grains of silver, I should get 22 such rupees for my sovereign, but at the false value of the "rupee," *i.e.*, the market value 269 grains of silver, I actually get only 15 "rupees." This is the actual price of gold in India, a decline in the proportion of the false inflation of the false "rupee." This is the case with every commodity, as can be tested by offering produce for the true rupee of 184 grains of silver, and for the false rupee or 269 grains of silver at the *same time* and in the *same market.*

15. In addition to the higher taxation thus inflicted on the Indian taxpayers, by an irony of fate, the very "interests" (bankers, merchants, planters, foreign capitalists of all kinds, etc.) for whose behalf, besides that of Government itself, all this dislocation of currency was made, are now loudest in their cry for all the mischief caused also to them, and yet the

authorities in both countries remain blind and infatuated enough not to learn even by experience, and persist in a mischievous course.

16. In the Treasury letter of 24th November, 1879 (c. 4868, 1886, p. 31) to the India Office, my Lords say:—

"1. The proposal appears to be open to those objections to a token currency which have long been recognised by all civilised nations, viz.: That instead of being automatic, it must be 'managed' by the Government, and that any such management not only fails to keep a token currency at par, but exposes the Government which undertakes it to very serious difficulties and temptations.

17. "2. It appears to my Lords, that the Government of India, in making the present proposal, lay themselves open to the same criticisms as are made upon Governments which have depreciated their currencies. In general, the object of such Governments has been to diminish the amount they have to pay to their creditors. In the present case, the object of the Indian Government appears to be to *increase the amount they have to receive from their taxpayers*. My Lords fail to see any real difference in the character of the two transactions.

18. ". . . . If, on the other hand, it is the case that the value of the rupee has fallen in India, and that it will be raised in India by the operation of the proposed plan, that plan is open to the objection that *it alters every contract and every fixed payment* in India.

19. "This proposal is, in fact, contrary to the essential and well-established principle of the currency law of this country, which regards the current standard coin as a piece of a given metal of a certain weight and fineness, and which condemns as futile and mischievous every attempt to go behind this simple definition.

20. "It is perfectly true as stated in the despatch (paragraph 41), that the "very essence of all laws relating to the currency has been to give fixity to the standard of value as far as it is possible," but it is no less true that, according to the principles which govern our currency system, the best and surest way, and, indeed, the only tried and known way, of giving this fixity is to adhere to the above definition of current standard coin. A pound is a given quantity of gold, a rupee is a given quantity of silver; and any attempt to give those

terms a different meaning is condemned by experience and authority.

21. "3. If the present state of exchange be due to the depreciation of silver, the Government scheme, if it succeeds, may relieve :—

(1) The Indian Government from the inconvenience of a nominal re-adjustment of taxation in order to meet the loss by exchange on the home remittances :

(2) Civil servants and other Englishmen who are serving or working in India, and who desire to remit money to England :

(3) Englishmen who have money placed or invested in India which they wish to remit to England. *But this relief will be given at the expense of the Indian taxpayer*, and with the effect of increasing every debt or fixed payment in India, including debts due by *ryots to money lenders ;* while its effect will be materially qualified, so far as the Government are concerned, by *the enhancement of the public obligations in India, which have been contracted on a silver basis.* . . . .

22. "If, then, a case has been made out, which my Lords do not admit, for an alteration of the currency law of India, the particular alteration which the Government of India propose could not, in the opinion of the Treasury, be entertained until the doubts and objections which have suggested themselves to my Lords are answered and removed. These objections are founded on principles which have been long and ably discussed, and which are now generally admitted by statesmen and by writers of accepted authority to lie at the root of the currency system.

23. "It is no light matter to accept innovations which must sap and undermine that system, and my Lords have therefore felt it their duty plainly—though they hope not inconsistently with the respect due to the Government of India—to express their conviction that the plan which had been referred to them for their observations is one which *ought not to be sanctioned* by her Majesty's Government or by the Secretary of State." (Italics are mine.)

24. Can condemnation be more complete and convincing?

25. The introduction of a gold standard, while it will not save a single farthing or a single ounce of produce to the Indian taxpayer in his payment of "Home Charges," as already explained, will simply add more to his already exist-

ing grievous burdens to the extent of the heavy cost of the alteration, and injure him, Heaven knows in what other ways, as the events of the past five years have shown.

26. The whole basis of the action of the Government is, and was, the assumption that, as fall in exchange will necessitate increased burden of taxation, the closing of the mints and introduction of a gold standard will save the Indian taxpayer from any such additional burden of taxation which would otherwise arise enormously in the remittance of "Home Charges," and that it is imperatively necessary to establish a stable ratio between gold and silver. That the anxiety of the Government about increased burdens of taxation and its political dangers, and that to save the people from the former and the Government from the latter, were the professed motives of all the present currency laws, would be clear from Government's own despatches.

27. In order not to encumber the statement here with the extracts from those despatches, I give them as Appendix B.

28. Both these objects, viz., saving people from additional taxation, and thereby Government from political danger, by the present proposals, and past currency legislation, are pure delusions. The Government might as well have tried to stop the action of gravitation, as to try against a natural law, that while gold and silver should fluctuate in value in relation to and like all other commodities, yet between themselves they could be made to keep up a fixed ratio, or to try to make a rupee which may be only worth 11d. or even 6d. of gold, become worth 16d. of gold, unless Government have found the philosopher's stone or have attained the divine power of creating something out of nothing.

29. It is not that the Government of India did not know this, or were not told this from the highest authority and others, and in distinct and emphatic terms. Of this I have already given (see *supra* 16 to 23 paras.) extracts from the despatch of the Treasury, of November 24th, 1879.

30. Notwithstanding the clear and emphatic views of the Treasury expressing "their conviction that the plan which had been referred to them for their observations is one which *ought not to be sanctioned by her Majesty's Government, or by the Secretary of State*," the Government of India and the India Office again opened the subject in another form.

31. Lord Randolph Churchill wrote to the Treasury on

January 26th, 1886, and forwarded on March 17th, 1886, a letter from the Government of India dated February 2nd, 1886 (c. 4868, 1886, pp. 3-5). To avoid repetition, I would not take extracts from these letters, as the reply of the Treasury embodies their views.

32. This reply of the Treasury is dated May 31st, 1886 (signed Henry H. Fowler):—"6. As a result of this review of the inconveniences caused by the depression in the value of silver, the Government of India express their opinion . . . . Yet there remains one thing which is not beyond the possibility of human control, and that is 'the establishment of a fixed ratio between gold and silver.' The proposition thus stated as an undoubted axiom is, however, one of the most disputable and disputed points in economic science. My Lords may, in passing, compare with this statement the declaration recorded by Mr. Goschen, Mr. Gibbs, and Sir Thomas Seccombe as the representatives of her Majesty's Government at the International Monetary Conference of 1878, that 'the establishment of a fixed ratio between gold and silver was utterly impracticable.'"

33. "The Indian Government further express their belief (paragraph 7) that it is possible to 'secure a stable ratio between gold and silver,' and that 'a serious responsibility will rest both on the Government of India and on her Majesty's Government if they neglect any legitimate means to bring about this result.' It would, however, have been more satisfactory if the Indian Government had undertaken to explain the grounds of their confidence that a stable ratio between gold and silver can be established, and the methods by which this is to be accomplished. . . . ."

34. "8. In December, 1878, Lord Cranbrook, then Secretary of State for India, forwarded to the then Chancellor of the Exchequer (Sir Stafford Northcote), without any expression of opinion, two despatches from the Government of India, containing certain proposed remedies for the evils arising out of the depression in the value of silver which were then in full force. In the only one of those despatches to which reference need here be made, after *unfavourable* reference to previous suggestions—(1) that a gold standard and gold currency should be introduced into India; and (2) that the weight of silver in the rupee should be increased, it was proposed to limit the free coinage of silver at the

Indian mints. The intention of this change was to introduce into India a gold standard, while retaining its native silver currency, the ratio between the currency unit (the rupee) and the standard (the sovereign) being fixed arbitrarily by the Government. The means for attaining this end are worked out in the despatch with great elaboration of detail." (Italics are mine.)

35. "9. This despatch and its proposals were submitted by Lord Cranbrook, on behalf of the Indian Government, and Sir Stafford Northcote, as Chancellor of the Exchequer, to a Committee consisting of Sir Louis Mallet, Mr. Edward Stanhope, M.P., Sir Thomas Seccombe, Mr. (now Sir Thomas) Farrer, Mr. (now Sir Reginald) Welby, Mr. Giffen, and Mr. Arthur Balfour, M.P. These gentlemen reported, on the 30th April, 1879—'That having examined the proposals contained in the despatch, they were unanimously of opinion that they could not recommend them for the sanction of her Majesty's Government.'

36. "10. Subsequently, on the 24th November, 1879, the Treasury replied in detail to the proposals of the Indian Government. In the first part of that letter, which summarises the case as stated in the despatch, I am to call the particular attention of the Secretary of State to the following passages, which seem to apply with equal force to the present situation :—

37. "'My Lords need not point out that a change of the Currency Laws is one of the most difficult tasks which a Government can undertake, and that it is most unadvisable to legislate hastily and under the influence of the pressure of the moment, or of an apprehension of uncertain consequences, upon a subject so complicated in itself and so important to every individual of the community, in its bearing upon the transactions and obligations of daily life.

38. "'It is not proved that increase or re-adjustment of taxation must necessarily be the consequence of matters remaining as they are, for nothing is said about reduction of expenditure, and equilibrium between income and expenditure may be regained by economy of expenditure as well as by increase of taxation. Further, the cost of increase of salaries may be met, or at least reduced, by a careful revision of establishments. . . .

39. "'A perusal of the despatch leads to the conclusion

that the Government of India are especially anxious to put an end to the competition of silver against their own bills as a means of remittance to India. But my Lords must ask whether this would be more than a transfer of their own burden to other shoulders; if so, who would eventually bear the loss, and what would be the effect on the credit of the Government and on the commerce of India?'"

40. The letter then further quotes the paragraphs, which I have already given before, pointing out that the relief wished for by the Government "will be given at the expense of the Indian taxpayer."—(*Supra*, par. 21.)

41. "The Treasury find no reason stated in the despatch of the Government of India in the present year, which induces them to dissent from the conclusions thus sent forth on the authority of Sir Stafford Northcote as to the results of any attempt artificially to enhance the gold price of silver. . .

42. "'13 . . . . It has been the policy of this country to emancipate commercial transactions as far as possible from legal control, and to impose no unnecessary restrictions upon the interchange of commodities. To fix the relative value of gold and silver by law would be to enter upon a course directly at variance with this principle, and would be regarded as an arbitrary interference with a natural law, not justified by any present necessity.'

43. ". . . . The observation of the Treasury in 1879, 'that nothing is said about reduction of expenditure,' seems to apply still more strongly to the existing situation, and it may be safely concluded that the control of its expenditure is far more within the reach of a Government than is the regulation of the market value of the precious metals" (c. 4868, 1886, p. 12).

44. Before proceeding further I may in passing point out that in 1876 the Government of India itself was against their present proposals, and, as my Lords of the Treasury say, they have urged no sound reasons to alter those views. I have not got the Government of India's despatch of 1876, but I quote from that of November 9, 1878 (c. 4868), 1886, p. 18.

45. "3. The despatch above referred to (October 13th, 1876) discussed in some detail. . . . The general result, however, was to point out that the adoption of a gold standard with a gold currency that should replace the existing

silver would be so costly as to be impracticable, and would otherwise be open to objection; . . . .

46. "4. The despatch notices also, *but only to reject it*, the proposal that the Indian standard of value, and with it the exchange value of the rupee, might be raised by limiting the coining of silver in the future and by adopting a gold standard without a gold currency." (The italics are mine.)

47. The Government of India, in their reply of February 9, 1877, to a resolution of the Bengal Chamber of Commerce passed by them on July 15, 1876, said:—

"8. The value of no substance can serve as a standard measure of value unless its use as the material of legal tender currency is freely admitted. If, therefore, the free coinage of silver on fixed conditions were disallowed in India silver would no longer be the standard of value of India, but another standard would be substituted, namely, the monopoly value of the existing stock of rupees tempered by any additions made to it by the Government or illicitly. If no such conditions were made the value of the rupee will gradually but surely rise."

48. "9. The stamp of a properly regulated mint, such as the Indian Mints, adds nothing except the cost of manufacture and seigniorage to the value of the metal on which it is impressed, but only certifies to its weight and purity."

49. "10. A sound system of currency must be automatic or self-regulating. No civilised Government can undertake to determine from time to time by how much the legal-tender currency should be increased or decreased, nor would it be justified in leaving the community without a fixed metallic standard of value even for a short time. It is a mistake to suppose that any European nation has rejected silver as a standard of value without substituting gold" (c. 7060, II, 1893, p. 337. Petition of the Indian Association to the House of Commons).

50. And yet the Government forgot its "civilisation" and its "sound system," and inflicted upon poor India the penalty of its folly by the troubles of the past five years, and what is worse still, they want to persist in the same mischief.

51. Reverting to the above replies of the Treasury, after such complete condemnation by the Treasury of the proposals of the Government of India, the Indian authorities fought shy of the Treasury, and, after inditing a meaningless despatch

to keep up appearances, left the Treasury severely alone, as far as I know, and adopted their own usual means to have their own way to rush into their own foregone, crude, and thoughtless legislation. The only wonder is that the Committee of 1893, while knowing all this, and seeing all the pitfalls and serious consequences of the proposals, allowed the Indian Government to have their own way, in the face of the emphatic rejection by the Treasury of these proposals.

52. To me the proceedings of the Indian authorities are nothing surprising. Whenever they make up their mind to do a thing they would do it—be the opposition what it may—be it of Parliament itself. Resolutions or statutes of Parliament, or condemnation by the Treasury, are to them nothing. The usual process in such cases is to appoint a Commission or a Committee, put in Members, and have witnesses of their own choice, leaving, if possible, just a small margin for appearance of independence. Generally, they get their own foregone conclusions. If by some happy chance the Commission decided anything against their view, so much the worse for the Commission. The Report is pigeon-holed, never to see the light of day, or to ignore such part as is not agreeable. If thwarted (as in this instance by the Treasury), the Government keep quiet for a time, wait for more favourable opportunities, and are at it again, taking better care against another mishap.

53. Thus they took their own usual course, which has, as was clearly predicted at the time, launched us on the present sea of troubles.

54. What is stranger still is, that after the Treasury so distinctly condemned these proposals, they did not care to see that any contemplated rash and crude legislation was not inflicted on the Indian taxpayers. The fact seems to be that India is the vile body upon which any quacks may perform any vivisection, and try any cruel, crude, or rash experiments. What matters what is done to it? The Treasury, *i.e.*, the English taxpayer, has not to suffer in any way. India is our helot, she can be forced to pay everything. But they forget Lord Salisbury's *eternal* words—"Injustice will bring down the mightiest to ruin."

55. The next natural question is—Why is it that fall in exchange should cause grievous troubles to India and not to any other self-governing, silver using country? What is the

real disease which creates all the never-ceasing pains of India? The reply is given by Lord Salisbury in four words, "India must be bled" under a system of "political hypocrisy." As long as this is the fate of India under an un-British system of government, no jugglery, no loud professions of benevolence, no device of raising a rupee to what it is not worth, will cure India's sad fate and "terrible misery" (Lord Salisbury's words).

56. I shall let the authorities themselves speak about the real cause of India's troubles. Lord Salisbury's view I have given above. The following extracts explain this view more explicitly and how it is effected. First, Lord Salisbury has explained that "the injury is exaggerated in the case of India, where so much of the revenue is exported without a direct equivalent."

57. And the literature of this very controversy itself supplied a clear explanation. Lord Randolph Churchill, as Secretary of State for India, explains how the "bleeding" and the drain of revenue is effected, and indicates also the final retribution—just as Lord Salisbury does, as already quoted by me. Lord Randolph Churchill, in his despatch to the Treasury of January 26th, 1886 (c. 4,868) 1886, p. 4, says:—first—

58. "It need hardly be said that it is in consequence of the large *obligatory payments* which the Government of India has to make in England in gold currency that the fall in the exchange value of the rupee affects the public finances." (Italics are mine.)

59. And next he hits the nail on the head, and gives concisely and unmistakeably the real evil from which all India's woes flow.

60. He says:—" The position of India in relation to taxation and the sources of the public revenues is very peculiar, not merely from the habits of the people, and their strong aversion to change, which is more specially exhibited to new forms of taxation, but likewise *from the character of the Government, which is in the hands of foreigners, who hold all the principal administrative offices and form so large a part of the Army.* The impatience of new taxation, which would have to be borne *wholly as a consequence of the foreign rule imposed on the country, and virtually to meet additions to charges arising outside of the country*, would constitute a *political danger*, the real magnitude

of which, it is to be feared, is not at all appreciated by persons who have no knowledge of, or concern in, the government of India, but which those responsible for that Government have long regarded as of the most serious order." (The italics are mine.)

61. Here, then, is the real disease—"*the character of the Government, which is in the hands of foreigners*, who hold all the principal administrative offices, and form so large a part of the Army"—"the taxation which would have to be borne *wholly as a consequence of the foreign rule* imposed on the country, and virtually to meet additions to charges arising outside of the country."

62. And it is remarkable that this was prophesied more than a hundred years ago by the highest Indian authority of the day.

Sir John Shore, in his famous minute in 1787 (Parliamentary Return 377 of 1812, para. 132), says:—

63. "Whatever allowance we may make for the increased industry of the subjects of the State owing to the enhanced demand for the produce of it (supposing the demand to be enhanced), there is reason to conclude that the benefits are more than counterbalanced by *evils inseparable from the system of a remote foreign dominion*." (Italics are mine.)

64. These *evils of the system of a remote foreign dominion* must be faced by the British rulers before it is "too late." No jugglery of currency, or loud professions of benevolence, or the hundred and one subterfuges to which Indian authorities resort, will ever cure these evils—or put British rule on a solid and safe foundation and relieve the Indian people of all these national, political and moral degradations and debasement, and economic and material destruction. Give India true *British* rule in place of the present *un-British* rule, and both England and India will be blessed and prosperous.

65. Now, with regard to the immediate position—What is to be done now? Retrace the false step of 1893, taken in spite of the clear warnings of the Treasury and others, and against the "law of Nature." The opening of the mints to the unrestricted coining of silver will correct all the mischievous results that have flowed from the closing of the mints. And further, the true remedy, as pointed out by the Treasury, is a reduction of expenditure and readjustment of establishments.

66. It never occurs to the Indian authorities in both countries that the high salaries of officials may be reduced, say a third, and, as repeatedly urged by many a right-thinking man, Native agency should be substituted—except for the highest control—for the foreign agency, and that Britain should contribute its fair share of the expenditure, to the extent to which such expenditure is incurred for *its own purposes* and *benefits*, such as the European services and Imperial wars, etc. Of course, anybody can understand that it is hard for officials to cut their own salaries, and let the Indians to come by their own, or ask the British people to contribute a fair share. But this is the only remedy both for the preservation of English rule and for the prosperity of both England and India.

67. The opening of the mints will have immediate important effects. (1.) The stringency of the money market and the consequent dislocation of trade will be remedied. (2.) The poor taxpayer will have to submit to such additional taxation only (after careful and earnest reduction of expenditure and avoiding of suicidal and unnecessary wars) as will be absolutely necessary to meet the deficit caused by the natural fall of exchange, instead of a concealed enormous enhancement of the *whole* taxation of the country, under the disguise and by the creation of a false "rupee" by closing the mints, to the extent of the difference between the value of the true and false rupee (may be between 6d. and 16d., or nearly three times as much).

The Indian authorities must take the advice which the Treasury has given, and restore the currency law to its original purity and soundness.

68. The second proposal for a gold standard (with partial or full quantity of gold) must be abandoned. The Government of India have themselves condemned the proposal, as already stated, paragraph 45. What does it mean? It is most inopportune at present. It means that all the proportionate small quantity of silver that is in British India, and the proportionately large quantity that is in the Native States, must be forcibly (not by any natural economic cause but by the despotism of the State) deprived of a large portion of its present value by throwing a large quantity of it in the market, and buy a large quantity of gold at a still higher proportion of value by the large additional demand created by it. All this

loss in cheapening silver, and dearer gold to be squeezed out of the poor, wretched, famished ryot of India.

69. The conversion of silver into gold standard cannot be carried out without great cost (see paragraph 45), which will be the highest cruelty and tyranny to inflict upon the "bloodless" and miserable and helpless people of India, and especially this infliction to be made on the false assumption that it will give relief from the burden of the remittances for "Home Charges," when it will do nothing of the kind, as stated by Government itself.

70. The step is not at all necessary for any economic purpose except that it will be a convenience to the foreign exploiter, official and non-official. A gold currency without gold (paragraph 46) and with an unrestricted silver currency is a delusion rejected by Government itself, and forcibly impressed by the Treasury.

71. I do sincerely hope and trust that this and all such heartlessness towards, and un-British treatment of, the wretched people of India will become a thing of the past, and a true *British* rule may bring blessing and prosperity to both Britain and India.

72. I beg to give in Appendix C. a statement of December 11th, 1892, which I had submitted to the Currency Committee in 1892, from which it will be seen that I had then pointed out the objections to the proposals. I also beg to refer the Committee to my evidence before the same Committee on December 17th, 1892 (c. 7060, II, 1893, p. 106).

73. There are several other more or less minor questions. Suppose a ryot is paying Rs. 10, what will be taken from him in gold? Will it be at the rate at which the intrinsic value of the silver is at the time (at present 11d. may be 6d.), or will demand be made at the present false value of 1s. 4d., or even in the despotic power, at the rate of 2s., *i.e.*, £1 of the Rs. 10?

74. When gold currency is introduced what salary will be paid to the officials at 11d. or 6d. of whatever the market value of the rupee may be, or at 16d., or even 24d., of the despotic value of the "rupee," for every rupee of the salary—a rupee of 180 grains of silver. In other words, will it be £25 at 6d., or about £46 at 11d., or about £66 at 16d., or £100 at 24d. for a present salary of Rs. 1,000, of a rupee of 180 grains?

75. There is the foreign merchant or capitalist of every kind always wanting to save himself in his trade-risks at the cost of the taxpayer, besides using to no small extent, or to the extent of the deposits of revenue in the banks, the revenues of the taxpayers, as his capital for his trade, and besides what is brought back to India, out of the "bleeding" of India as his, the foreign capitalist's capital. Is Government going to inflict oppression upon the Indian taxpayer whenever these "interests" raise a cry and agitation for their selfish ends? Merchants and all sorts of foreign capitalistic exploiters and speculators must be left to themselves. It is no business of the State to interfere in their behalf at the cost of the Indian taxpayers; they know their business; they are able, and ought to be left to take care of themselves. They exploit the country with the Indians' revenue and "bleeding." That is bad enough in all conscience—the profits are theirs, and the losses must be also theirs, and not an additional infliction upon the Indian taxpayers.

76. The Government here dare not play such pranks with the taxpayers. In India the Government only thinks of the foreign "interests" (official and non-official) first, and of the subjects afterwards, if it ever thinks of the subjects at all when foreign "interests" are concerned.

77. Lord Mayo has truly said: "I have only one object in all I do. I believe we have not done our duty to the people of the land. Millions have been spent on the conquering race which might have been spent in enriching and in elevating the children of the soil. We have done much, but we can do a great deal more. It is, however, impossible, unless we spend less on the 'interests' and more on the people."

78. On another occasion he said: "We must take into account the inhabitants of the country—the welfare of the people of India is our primary object. If we are not here for their good, we ought not to be here at all."—The *Hindu* of 4th May, 1898. Sir W. Hunter's "Life of Mayo."

79. This is exactly the whole truth. It is the "interests" alone that the present selfish system and spirit of Government care for—and though that is some profit to England it is most destructive to India. If, according to the noble words of Lord Mayo, the *people's* true welfare were made the object, England itself will be vastly more benefited than it is at

present, and India will also be benefited and will bless the name of England, instead of cursing it as she now begins to do—shut your eyes to it as much as you like. Do as Lord Mayo says, and all difficulties of trade, taxation, finances, currency, famine, plague, unnecessary wars, and last, but not least, of *poverty and disaffection* will vanish. The past has been bad, "bleeding, and degrading"; let the future be good yet—prospering and elevating. India then will be quite able to pay as much as may be necessary for healthy government, and *all necessary* progress.

80. In the above remarkable and true words of Lord Mayo, you have the cause of all India's woes and evils, and all England's political dangers of "the most serious order," as well as the proper remedy for them. Will this Currency Committee rise to its duty and patriotism?

Yours truly,

DADABHAI NAOROJI.

Sir William Wedderburn,
Chairman of the British Committee of
The Indian National Congress,
84, Palace Chambers, Westminster, S.W.

APPENDIX A.—INDIAN EXCHANGES.

From the TIMES, *September 9th*, 1886.

SIR,—I hope you will kindly allow me to make a few observations upon Indian exchanges. I shall first describe the mode of operation of an export transaction from India. In order to trace the effect of the exchange only, I take all other circumstances to remain the same—*i.e.*, any other circumstances, such as of supply and demand, etc., which affect prices.

I take an illustration in its simplest form. Suppose I lay out Rs. 10,000 to export 100 bales of cotton to England. I then calculate, taking exchange into consideration, what price in England will enable me to get back my Rs. 10,000, together with a fair profit—say, 10 per cent.—making altogether Rs. 11,000. Suppose I take exchange at 2s. per rupee, and find that 6d. per lb. will bring back to me in remittance as much silver as would make up Rs. 11,000, I then instruct my agent in England to sell with a limit of 6d. per lb., and to remit the proceeds in silver, this being the simplest form of the transaction. The result of the transaction, if it turned out as intended, will be that the cotton sold at 6d. per lb. will bring back to me Rs. 11,000, and the transaction will be completed.

Now, I take a transaction when exchange is 1s. 4d. instead of 2s. per rupee. I lay out Rs. 10,000 for 100 bales of cotton, all other circumstances remaining the same, I calculate that I can get back my Rs. 10,000, and 10 per cent. profit, or Rs. 11,000 altogether, if my cotton were sold at 4d. per lb. Then I instruct my agent for a limit of 4d., which, being obtained, and silver being remitted to me at the reduced price, I get back my Rs. 11,000.

The impression of many persons seems to be that, just as I received 6d. per pound when exchange was 2s. per rupee, I get 6d. also when exchange is only 1s. 4d. per rupee, and that, silver being so much lower, I actually get Rs. 16,500, instead of only Rs. 11,000. This, however, is not the actual state of the case, as I have explained above. When exchange is at 2s. per rupee, and I get 6d. per lb. for my cotton, I do not get 6d. per lb. when exchange is only 1s. 4d. per rupee, but I get only 4d. per lb.; in either case the whole operation is that I laid out Rs. 10,000 and received back Rs. 11,000. When exchange is 2s. I get 6d. of gold; when exchange is 1s. 4d. I do not get 6d. of gold but 4d. of gold, making my return of silver, at the lower price, of the same amount in either case—viz., Rs. 11,000.

I explain the same phenomenon in another form, to show that such alone is the case, and no other is possible. Supposing that, according to the impression of many, my cotton could be sold at 6d. per lb. when exchange is only 1s. 4d.—that is to say, that I can receive Rs. 16,500 back for my lay-out of Rs. 10,000, why my neighbour would be only too glad to undersell me and be satisfied with 40 per cent. profit in place of my 50 per cent. profit, and another will be but too happy and satisfied with 20 per cent., and so on till, with the usual competition, the price will come down to the natural and usual level of profits.

The fact is no merchant in his senses ever dreams that he would get the same price of 6d. per lb. irrespective of the exchange being either 2s. or 1s. 4d. Like freight, insurance, and other charges, he takes into consideration the rate of exchange, and settles at what price his cotton should be sold in order that he should get back his lay-out with the usual profit. This is what he expects, and he gains more or less according as the state of the market is affected by other causes, such as larger supply or demand, or further variation in exchange during the pendency of the transaction.

Taking, therefore, all other circumstances to remain the same, and the exchange remaining the same during the period of the completion of the transaction, the effect of the difference in the exchange at any two different rates is that when exchange is lower you get so much less gold in proportion, so that in the completion of the transaction you get back in either case your cost and usual profit. In the cases I have supposed above, when exchange is 2s. and price is 6d. per lb., then when exchange is 1s. 4d. the price obtained or expected is 4d. per lb., in both cases there is the return of Rs. 11,000 against a cost of Rs. 10,000.

I stop here, hoping that some one of your numerous readers will point out if I have made any mistake. It is very important in matters of such complicated nature as mercantile transactions that the first premises or fundamental facts be clearly laid down. If this is done a correct conclusion will not be difficult to be arrived at. I have, therefore, confined myself to simple facts. If what I have said above is admitted, I shall next explain the operation of imports into India, and then consider in what way India is actually affected by the fall in exchange or in the value of silver.

Yours faithfully,

National Liberal Club,
September 2nd.

DADABHAI NAOROJI.

From the TIMES, *September 13th*, 1886.

SIR,—Mr. Dadabhai Naoroji, in his letter to you on this subject, seems to enunciate the proposition that because he gets 6d. per lb. for cotton when exchange is 2s. per rupee, therefore he will get 4d. per lb. when exchange is 1s. 4d. But it is not so. As a matter of fact, when exchange was 2s. per rupee the price of cotton was about 3d. per lb., and now with exchange at 1s. 5d. it is about 4d. per lb. The subject is not elucidated by imaginary *data*.

Yours respectfully,
R. L.

London, *September 9th*.

From the TIMES, *September 13th*, 1886.

SIR,—Allow me to point out that the account given by Mr. Dadabhai Naoroji, in the letter published in your columns of the 9th inst., of the effect on commercial transactions between India and England of a fall in the exchange value of the rupee is scarcely an adequate one.

Mr. Dadabhai Naoroji's contention is twofold—first, that the commercial profit on an article of merchandise such as cotton is independent of the rate of exchange, and, secondly, that this is due to the fact that a fall in the rate of exchange is accompanied by a proportionate fall in the gold price of cotton in England.

The first of these contentions is so far correct that, although a sudden fall in exchange will, under ordinary circumstances, temporarily raise the exporter's profit above the normal level, competition will always come into play to bring it back to that level.

The second of Mr. Dadabhai Naoroji's contentions appears, however, to be based on a partial apprehension of the facts. When Mr. Dadabhai Naoroji talks of instructing his agent for a certain limit, he means, of course, that he instructs his agent not to sell below that limit. His agent, if he is a man of business, sells at the best price he can get consistently with his instructions, and this price is determined, not by the rate of exchange, but by the whole of the conditions affecting the market at the moment.

Other things being equal, the instant effect of a sudden fall in exchange is to increase the exporter's margin of profit. Competition, as your correspondent points out, immediately sets in to reduce profit to its normal level. But in what way is it that competition operates to produce this effect? Surely by inducing an increase of supply. Other things being equal, it is in virtue of such an increase of supply alone that the price of the cotton in London can be lowered.

Now, increase of supply in London implies, as its correlate, increase of demand in India; and increase of demand in India implies, other things being equal, increase of price in India. In other words, equilibrium is attained, not, as your correspondent would have it, through a fall of the selling price in England proportionate to the fall in exchange, but through a fall of the selling price in England less than proportional to the fall in exchange combined with a rise of the buying price in India less than inversely proportional to the fall in exchange.

I am, Sir, your obedient Servant,

Streatham Common. JAMES W. FURRELL.

From the TIMES, *September 16th*, 1886.

SIR,—In reply to "R. L.'s" letter in the *Times* of yesterday, I may first explain that I made no reference to actual prices in the market, as such prices are the resultant of many influences—supply, demand, bulling and bearing speculations, present stocks and future prospects of supply, every day's telegraphic news from all parts of the world, political complications, Bank rate of interest, and various other small and temporary influences. I therefore explain again that what I am considering at present is the effect of only the fall and rise in exchange, leaving all other circumstances that affect prices as uninfluenced or unaltered.

"R. L." says:—"As a matter of fact, when exchange was 2s. per rupee, the price of cotton was about 3d. per lb., and now, with the exchange at 1s. 5d., it is about 4d. per lb." I do not find this to be a fact. Even were it fact it would not matter at all, as all other circumstances of supply, demand, etc., have to be taken into account therewith. But what "R. L." states does not appear to be a fact. I shall confine myself to cotton, though I could give similar decline in other principal commodities.

Exchange began to decline about the time when Germany demonetised its silver, about 1873. The Statistical Abstract of the United Kingdom, 33rd number, gives the "average price" of raw cotton as follows:—

—	1873.	1874.	1875.	1876.	1877.	1878.	1879.
Per cwt. £ . . .	4·01	3·62	3·47	3·02	2·93	2·80	2·76
—	1880.	1881.	1882.	1883.	1884.	1885.	—
Per cwt. £ . . .	2·94	2·92	2·93	2·91	2·85	2·86	—

This shows a fall of nearly 30 per cent.

Now Mr. Furrell's letter. He is right in supposing that the shipper's instructions mean not to sell below the limit. I have been a merchant and an agent in the City for some 25 years, and, knowing full well what my shipper meant, I sold at the best price I could get. He is also right in saying that the price is determined by the whole of the conditions affecting the market at the moment, and that is just the reason why, as I have said above, I did not refer to actual prices. So far we agree, but Mr. Furrell's fallacy begins in this sentence: "Other things being equal, the instant effect of a sudden fall in exchange is to increase the exporter's margin of profit." Here he first forgets the "whole of the conditions" to which he referred in the previous paragraph, as determining the price at any moment, and next he forgets that the increase of the margin takes place in the case of those exporters only who have already entered into their transactions, and those transactions at the moment are uncompleted, so far as the remittances of the proceeds are concerned. But those exporters who have yet to begin their transactions have no such increase in their margin of profit, as they have not yet had any transaction or margin of profit, pending or existing. I took the simplest instance of an exporter entering into a transaction at a particular rate of exchange, and described the process of the operation of that transaction from its initiation, as far as exchange alone was concerned, independent of "the whole of the conditions." And then I further explained that any fluctuation in exchange during the pendency of the transacton was the exporter's further chance of profit or loss. But I may go further, and now explain that even in the case of transactions already entered into, the fluctuations in exchange do not affect the exporter in the bulk of the trade. The bulk of the shipments from India are drawn against, and as soon as this is done, the exporter has no further interest at all in any subsequent fluctuations in exchange, beyond his little margin above the amount of his bill, and thus it will be seen that in most cases there is no instant effect to increase the exporter's margin of profit.

Yours faithfully,

National Liberal Club, DADABHAI NAOROJI.
September 14th.

From the TIMES, *September 20th*, 1886.

SIR,—Mr. Dadabhai Naoroji, in his letter in the *Times* of this morning, while finding in my previous communication a "fallacy" which has no place in it, leaves altogether untouched the point really at issue between us.

After stating that the price of an article of Indian export depends, not on the rate of exchange only, but on the whole of the conditions affecting the market at the moment, I proceeded to treat the question on the basis taken up by your correspondent, and to consider the effect of the rate of exchange apart from all other conditions.

"*Other things being equal,*" I remarked, "the *instant* effect of a sudden fall in exchange is to increase the exporter's margin of profit."

Mr. Dadabhai Naoroji quotes this sentence correctly enough, but in criticising it he entirely ignores the force of the words that I have italicised. He says I first forget the "whole of the conditions" referred to in the previous paragraph, the fact being that by the words "other things being equal," I expressly exclude these conditions.

I next, your correspondent adds, forget that the increased margin of profit affects only transactions begun but not completed, while leaving unaffected the transactions not yet begun. How the "instant" effect of a sudden fall in exchange could apply to transactions not begun is not very obvious.

There was the less room for misunderstanding that I went on to say that, under ordinary circumstances, competitiou at once came into play to reduce profit to its normal level.

The fact is Mr. Dadabhai Naoroji and myself are in agreement except on one point, to which he makes no reference in the letter under reply.

He contends that competition operates by reducing prices in England proportionally to the fall in exchange. I contend that competition operates by concurrently reducing prices in England, and raising them in India.

I am, Sir, your obedient Servant,

Streatham Common, JAMES W. FURRELL.
September 15th.

From the TIMES, *September 27th*, 1886.

SIR,—Mr. Furrell's letter, published in the *Times* of to-day, concludes:—"The fact is Mr. Dadabhai Naoroji and myself are in agreement except on one point, to which he makes no reference in the letter under reply. He contends that competition operates by reducing prices in England proportionally to the fall in exchange. I contend that competition operates by concurrently reducing prices in England and raising them in India."

Now what Mr. Furrell says in his first letter is this:—"Competition, as your correspondent points out, immediately sets in to reduce profit to its normal level. But in what way is it that competition operates to produce this effect?" And then he answers himself by begging the whole question:—"Surely by inducing an increase of supply." And he goes on, "Other things being equal" (though he does not allow among the "other things" supply to remain equal), "it is in virtue of such an increase of supply alone that the price of the cotton in London can be lowered."

Now, as an independent fact, an increase of supply may, no doubt, lower prices. But it is not in virtue of an increase of supply alone that prices can be lowered in London. What I am pointing out is, how the competition and the lower price are the direct result of lower exchange or higher value of gold only, without any increase of supply being at all induced or made, and any rise in price being caused in India. The fact simply is that, because gold is of higher value, cotton is sold at as much less gold as would suffice to bring back to the exporter his actual outlay and profit. Or, putting it in another way, the manufacturer of England may send his order direct to India to buy at the silver price there, and pay his gold for it at the rate of exchange, without a single ounce of additional supply or any increase in price in India being necessitated.

What I mean, then, is simply this. To treat the subject in its simplest form, I take every other circumstance—*i.e.*, supply, demand, etc.—to remain the same, and consider the effect of exchange only, and I show that from this simple cause—viz., the lower exchange only—if price be 6d. when exchange is 2s., the price will be 4d. when exchange is 1s. 4d., irrespective of or without causing any increase whatever in the supply or in the price in India.

Yours faithfully,

National Liberal Club, DADABHAI NAOROJI.
September 20th.

From the DAILY NEWS, *September 24th*, 1886.

SIR,—I now state the mode of operation of an import transaction into India. Taking all other circumstances to remain the same, suppose I am willing to lay out Rs. 10,000 for importing, say, 50 bales of grey shirtings—supposing that 2s. per rupee be the exchange—I find that I shall have to pay 6s. per piece in order that, at the market price in India, I should be able to realise Rs. 11,000 on the sale. Now, when exchange goes down to 1s. 4d., I see that, unless I am able to buy in England at 4s. a piece (instead of 6s.), either I cannot send the indent from India or the market price must rise in India as much as I may have to pay more than 4s. in England. Under the ordinary operation of economic laws, it is not necessary that I should be obliged to pay more than 4s. per piece in England. Gold having appreciated here—in other words, prices of all commodities having proportionately fallen—the cost of production to the manufacturer will be so much *less* gold. What cost him 6s. in gold before now costs him only 4s. in gold, and he is able to sell to me at 4s. for what he formerly charged 6s., the value of 4s. now being equal to that of the 6s. before, and I am able to sell at the same number of rupees now in India as I did before when exchange was 2s. per rupee, and the price of the shirting was 6s. per piece. Suppose in England the produce of a farm is worth £100, and that the landlord, the tenant, or farmer, and the labourers divided it equally, or £33⅓ each. Now, suppose gold having risen, the same produce is worth only £75. The share of each should then be £25, which, at its higher value or purchasing power is equal to the former £33⅓. But the landlord thinks he must still have his £33⅓, and the wage-earners ask for the same quantity of gold as before, and a struggle arises. But whatever the struggle between them (into the merits of which I need not enter here) the produce fetches £75 only (equal in value to the former £100). The manufacturer thus gets his raw produce, whether home or foreign, at the depreciated price. The manufacturer also has his difficulty with the item of wages, which, if not proportionately reduced according to the rise in gold, prevents the cost of the manufactured article being fully reduced. But the market price of the article falls in accordance with the appreciation of gold, and the indentor from India gets what he wants at such reduced gold price. Articles produced in limited quantities or of reputed makers, or of some specialities, may and do command their own prices, and Indian importers may be, or are, obliged to pay some higher price for the same; but for the great bulk of the articles of trade the Indian importer has not to pay generally much more than he did before, except so far as any fluctuations in exchange during the course of the transaction may necessitate any higher or lower payment. All other circumstances remaining the same, the indentor from India pays more or less gold according to the state of the exchange, paying less gold when gold is high or exchange and silver low, or paying more gold when gold is low and exchange or silver high; the result being that the importer pays the same amount of silver whether exchange is low or high. He lays out his Rs. 10,000 and gets the goods in England at such varying prices in gold, according to exchange, as enable him to get Rs. 11,000 on sale in India.

To sum up, for the bulk of the trade, other circumstances remaining the same, India does not get for her exports more silver for her produce, but less gold at lower exchange; and she does not pay for her imports more silver, but less gold at lower exchange. In actual operation the result, of course, is not quite so rigid. Various influences affect the course of the market. What I mean is, that taking the simple element of appreciation of gold and fall in silver or exchange, the course of trade is not much affected in prices in India. Were India concerned merely in the fall in exchange and nothing else, that would not have mattered much to her, beyond making the owners of gold so much richer in proportion to the fall in silver, as compared with gold, and introducing an additional element of the chances of profit or loss, in the fluctuations in the rate of exchange during the pendency of the transactions. But even in that case, the exporting merchant protects himself from this risk by selling his bills against his produce to the Indian Banks, whereby the rate of exchange for his transaction is fixed. The proceeds of his produce have to pay a certain sterling amount to the bank here. As far as the banks are concerned, they are dealers in money. For every bill that they buy in India in order to receive money in this country they sell also in India a bill to pay in this country. The two operations are entered into at same time at different rates of exchange, and the difference of the rate is their profit of the day, all selling and buying transactions covering each other. Those exporters who do not draw against their produce or shipment, and wait for returns from England, undertake the additional chance of loss or gain of the fluctuation of exchange, just as they take the chance of loss or gain from fluctuations in price from other causes. The importer of goods into India is not so well able to protect himself against the fluctuations of exchange when he cannot buy ready-made goods, and must wait for some time for the execution of his order by the manufacturer. But by telegraphic communications and by selling bills forward here much protection is secured. Upon the whole, as I have said above, fall in exchange would not matter much to India if her trade alone were concerned. She can control her wants by taking more or less. But the direction in which India really suffers, and suffers disastrously, from the fall in exchange or silver is a different one. I shall state my views upon that subject in my next.

Yours faithfully,

National Liberal Club. DADABHAI NAOROJI.

From the DAILY NEWS, *September 28th*, 1886.

SIR,—I would give a few details of the transactions of trade between England and India to make the effect of fluctuations in exchange a little clearer. Resuming the illustration of my first letter, of Rs. 10,000 laid out for 100 bales of cotton, I first take the case in which the exporter does not draw against his shipment, but waits for remittance of proceeds of sale from England. Suppose he has based his transaction on an exchange of 1s. 4d. per rupee to sell at 4d. per lb. to get back his Rs. 11,000. Suppose, before the cotton is sold exchange falls to 1s. 2d. This fall in exchange (all other things remaining the same) lowers the price to 3½d. per lb., and suppose the cotton is so sold. To the exporter this fall will make no difference, as though his cotton sold at ½d. less, he gets the difference made up by the lower exchange of 2d., and thus gets the same amount of silver as he had calculated on. The same will be the result if exchange rose and price rose with it. Though he will get more gold from the rise in price, he will get as much less silver owing to the rise in exchange, the result being the original amount of silver. Suppose again that exchange falls or rises after the cotton is sold, but before the proceeds are converted into silver, by the purchase of silver or bill of exchange. In that case, if the exchange falls, it is so much profit to the exporter, as he will get more silver for the gold already secured by the sale when exchange was higher; and if exchange rises he loses, as he gets so much less silver at the higher exchange. Next I take the transaction in which the exporter draws against his cotton, so that he gets his silver back at once from the bank that buys his draft at the exchange he has calculated on, and undertakes that the bank shall have a fixed amount of gold paid to it in England out of the proceeds of the sale. In other words, the exporter converts his outlay from silver into gold—*i.e.*, instead of Rs. 10,000 in silver it is now fixed to a certain amount in gold to be paid to the bank in England.

Now, suppose exchange falls before the cotton is sold. With the fall in exchange there is a corresponding fall in price, and the exporter realises so much less gold. But as he has already engaged to pay a fixed amount of gold to the Bank on the basis of a higher exchange, he suffers as much loss as the proceeds are shorter than the amount of the draft. A fall in exchange in such a case is a loss and not a profit to the exporter. In that case, it is the rise in exchange before produce is sold that is profitable to the exporter. Next, suppose that exchange rises or falls after the cotton is sold, that would not matter to the exporter at all, because he has not to receive any remittance, but the gold of the proceeds is to be given away to the Bank, excepting only such surplus or deficit that the proceeds may leave after the payment to the Bank. It will be seen from the above that in the two different kinds of operations—viz., clear shipments and draft shipments, the results from the fluctuations of exchange are entirely the reverse of each other. In the second case, in which the shipment is drawn against, and which forms the bulk of the actual export transactions, a fall in exchange before the goods are sold is a loss, and not profit, to the shipper. In considering, therefore, the result of the fall in exchange, it is necessary to bear in mind whether the particular transaction is a free shipment or a draft shipment, for in each case the result is quite different. And as the bulk of the export trade of India is of draft shipments, the result of a fall in exchange is a risk of loss, and not a chance of profit. The shipper who draws against his shipment does not desire a fall in exchange, but a rise, before his goods are sold; for such rise, by raising the price, will give him so much more gold to leave a balance in his favour after paying the Bank the amount of gold already contracted for and fixed by the draft. The surplus gold will go back to him as so much more profit than he had calculated upon. The general idea that a fall in exchange is somehow or other always a gain to the exporter of produce from India, is not correct. As shown above, in the case of shipments against which bills are drawn (and which is the case with most of the export business), a fall in exchange before the cotton is sold is actually adverse and a loss to the exporter. Once exchange becomes settled, subject only to the usual small trade fluctuations, it is no matter at all whether a rupee is 2s. or 1s. The price of produce will adapt itself to the relations of gold and silver, and the exporter will get back only his outlay and usual profit, whatever the exchange may be.

In the case of imports into India, in a certain way the importer is able to be free from any risk of the fall in exchange. He telegraphs his order to his agent here to buy at a certain price at a certain exchange. The agent manages, if the market allows it, to buy at the limit, and sell a bill at the same time at the required exchange. If the goods are ready made, the agent sells his bill at once. If there is delay in the manufacturing of the goods, he sells the bill forward, so that when the goods are ready the Bank engages to buy the bill at the stipulated rate of exchange, no matter whether the rate of the day is the same or more or less. As in the case of the exporter, it is also the same with the importer, that when exchange is normally settled it does not matter to him whether it is 2s. or 1s. per rupee. The price and the trade adjust themselves, and settle down into a normal condition, according to the relation between gold and silver. As a further elucidation of the fact that fall in exchange brings down proportionally a fall in the price of the produce exported from India, I may mention that if the holders of cotton in England did not sell their cotton in accordance with the relation between gold and silver, or in other words according to exchange, the cotton manufacturers can send their orders to Bombay to buy there at the silver price, and then pay in gold according to the exchange—*i.e.*, remit from England silver or bank bills according to the price of silver or rate of exchange. The manufacturers in England know every day what the prices are in India, and can, and often do, buy there by telegram as readily as in Liverpool or London. As this letter has already become long enough, I postpone the consideration of the actual and permanent injury to India caused by the fall from 2s. per rupee to my next letter.

Yours faithfully,

National Liberal Club, DADABHAI NAOROJI.
September 24th.

APPENDIX B.

1. Government of India to Secretary of State, November 9th, 1878:—

"12. . . . And bearing in mind the necessary fixity of much of the existing taxation, the difficulty of finding new sources of revenue. and the dissatisfaction caused by all increases of taxation, even by those for which there is the most urgent necessity, it is indisputable that the political inconvenience of this gradually increasing burden is extremely great, aggravated as it further is by the uncertainty of its amount and the impossibility of foreseeing its fluctuations, which may at any moment become the cause of the most grave financial embarrassment."—(C. 4,868, 1886, p. 19.)

2. Now is it not very strange that the necessity of avoiding additional taxation is met by laying on as heavy a taxation as possible in the covert way of creating a false rupee?

3. "74. To this might further be added that the political risks of the present time, and the prospects they create of necessary additional taxation, which, if our proposals were adopted, might be avoided wholly or to a great extent, or even be met by reduction of taxation, add force to the argument that if these changes are to be made, there would be special political advantage in making them now."—(P. 26.)

4. Now this beats everything. While by proposing the device of closing the mints, and giving a false value to the rupee, they are

actually increasing the burden of taxation to the extent of the false increase of the value of the rupee, the Government, with an extraordinary *naivete*, say that their proposals will "*even be met by reduction of taxation!*" The Government of India has beaten itself!

5. India Office to Treasury January 26th, 1886:—

"It is not, however, upon the large amount of the charge that Lord Randolph Churchill is desirous of dwelling, so much as upon the extreme difficulty in which the Government of India is placed in regulating its finances, and the dangers that attend a position in which any sudden fall in the exchange may require the increased charge caused thereby to be met by additional taxation."—(C. 4,868, 1886, p. 4.)

6. "The imposition of additional taxation has always been a matter of much anxiety to the Indian Government, and the greatest objection has always been evinced to imposing such taxation in forms to which the people are unaccustomed, or to frequent changes, or to measures which give rise to fears of possible further changes and additional taxes."—(P. 4.) Is it for this reason that this covert way was discovered to impose heavy additional taxation?

7. Government of India to the Secretary of State for India, February 2nd, 1886:—

"Speaking generally, the period of financial pressure to which we refer may be said to have extended from 1873-74 to 1880-81, and to have involved increased taxation, large reductions in public works expenditure, and a heavy addition to the gold debt held in England."—(C. 4,868, 1886, p. 6.)

8. "This state of affairs would be an evil of the greatest magnitude in any country in the world; in a country such as India it is pregnant with danger."—(P. 7.)

And so the Government of India aggravate this state!

9. "If a stable ratio between gold and silver cannot be secured we must continue to add to the gold debt of India, though we are fully aware of the objections to borrowing largely in England in a time of peace, and view with apprehension the additional burden which will be imposed on India when borrowing in England ceases, and the remittances from India must be increased in order to pay the interest charge on an increased gold debt."—(P. 8.)

Is that the reason why Government goes on increasing this debt with a light heart?

10. The words used by Lord Lytton's Government in a despatch dated November 9th, 1878, might be applied almost literally to the circumstances of the present day.

11. "At the present time when political events may throw upon India new burdens of unusual magnitude, the position of our Government in relation to this question assumes a character of extreme gravity. Whether, if such demands upon us arise, they would require us to have resort to increased taxation to provide additional resources for the service of the year, or to loans to meet sudden or unusual charges, or, as may be more probable, to a combination of the two, the anxiety that will attend our financial administration must be very great; and if the holders of silver should under any combination of circumstances, throw any considerable quantity on the market, as is at all events possible, the consequences to India might be financially disastrous. How a sudden call to supply by taxation a million or more to provide for

further loss by exchange, and one or two millions for war charges could be met, we are at a loss to know; yet that such demands might arise no one can say is so improbable as to remove them from a serious claim on our attention. The prospects of a loan in such a case would not be much more satisfactory. Any temporary relief obtained by borrowing in England would be more than compensated by the increased burdens created in the future, and the necessary tendency of things would be to go from bad to worse." (P. 10.)

12. So it appears that this "extreme gravity," "the anxiety," and going "from bad to worse" were the reasons why wars of Imperial interest were undertaken, and why the increasing burdens are going on! And why it is now decided that India and India alone should bear every burden?

13. Lord Randolph Churchill, in his letter to the Treasury of January 26th, 1886, says:—"It is not, however, upon the large amount of the charge that Lord Randolph Churchill is desirous of dwelling so much as upon the extreme difficulty in which the Government of India is placed in regulating its finances and the dangers that attend a position in which any sudden fall in exchange may require the increased charge caused thereby to be met by additional taxation."

14. These extracts are sufficient to show the anxiety of the Government for increasing burdens on the people, and political danger to Government; and the beauty of the whole thing is, that they have done and are doing the very things which they proclaimed loudly should not be done: increased both taxation with a light heart and political danger with a vengeance!

15. I shall add what was said on the passing of the Bill in 1893:—

(C. 7,098, 1893, p. 15.)

In the Legislative Council of June 26th, 1893, the Hon. Mr. Mackay, who was perhaps one of the most active persons in bringing about this legislation, said:—

"I am completely in accord with the provisions of the Bill just introduced by the Hon. Sir David Barbour, and with the greatest deference I venture to congratulate your Excellency on having succeeded in bringing forward a measure which will have the effect, not only of restoring the finances of the country to a satisfactory condition, but which will also impart to trade and commercial transactions that legitimate amount of certainty of which they have been deprived for the past twenty years. The measure at the same time relieves the country of that dread of additional and seriously disturbing taxation which has been weighing upon it for some time past."

His Excellency the President said (p. 18):—

16. "I think, then, that I may sum up this part of the case by saying that it has now been established almost beyond controversy that to leave matters as they were meant for the Government of India hopeless financial confusion; for the commerce of India a constant and ruinous impediment; for the taxpayers of India the prospect of heavy and unpopular burdens; for the consumers of commodities a rise in the prices of the principal necessaries of life; and for the country, as a whole, a fatal and stunting arrestation of its development (p. 20)." . . . . "We earnestly hope that our

proposals may be fruitful of good, that the commerce of India may be relieved from an impediment which has retarded its progress, that the Government of India may be enabled to meet its obligations without adding to the burdens of the taxpayer; and that capital will flow more freely into this country without the adventitious stimulus which we have hitherto been unable to refuse. We trust, finally, that in process of time sufficient reserves of gold may be accumulated to enable us to render our gold standard effective, and thereby to complete the great change towards which we are taking the first steps to-day. Time only can show whether all these hopes will be fulfilled or be disappointed."

17. Vain, unfortunate hope! A Currency Committee is sitting again. What was said by the Treasury and others has come to pass, and all the glowing prophecies of the Indian authorities, based upon clear fallacies, have been falsified—and yet persistence in the same course!

APPENDIX C.

INDIA, July 1st, 1893.—THE CURRENCY QUESTION.

Statement Submitted by Mr. Dadabhai Naoroji to the Currency Committee.

The questions of exchange and currency in connexion with India have, unlike those questions in other countries, two different branches, and it is very important to keep them distinctly in mind.

(1) Political. (2) Commercial.

(1) The political aspect entails upon British India the compulsory remittance of about £16,000,000 to this country every year (which will now be £19,000,000, as no more railway capital will be forthcoming to be used here instead of drawing on India). I am not discussing here the righteousness or otherwise of this state of affairs. It is the loss caused by the fall in exchange in the remittances of these (now) £19,000,000 which is the point under consideration. Otherwise the question of exchange would have no significance, as I have shown in my letters to the *Times* in September, 1886.

The proposal to introduce a gold currency into India is based on the argument that it would save all present loss to the people of India from the fall in exchange. It will do nothing of the kind. It will simply inflict greater loss and hardship on the wretched Indian taxpayer. I explain.

The Indian taxpayer, at the time when exchange was 2s. per rupee, was sending produce to England worth 16 crores of rupees to meet the payment of £16,000,000. Now, taking exchange, say roundly 1s. per rupee, he has to send produce worth 38 crores of rupees to meet the (present) remittance of £19,000,000—or at a double rate. To avoid the confusion of ideas that prevails through the present controversy, I would eliminate silver altogether from the problem and put it in another form—that when one rupee was equal to 2s. the Indian taxpayer sent, say, one million tons of produce to meet the £19,000,000 of Home Charges—when a rupee is 1s. he has to send two million tons of produce to meet the same demand. Whether the currency be gold or silver or copper or lead will not be of the slightest consequence. The Indian taxpayer will have to send to this country as much produce, and not one ounce less, as would purchase £19,000,000—the only difference in the quantity of produce to be sent will depend solely on the rise or fall in gold. Only there will be on the poor taxpayer this additional infliction—that he will be saddled with the heavy cost of the conversion of the currency in gold; and gold becoming so much more in demand will still further rise, and the taxpayer will have to send so much more produce to meet the additional rise in the value of gold. All talk of saving to the Indian the present loss by fall in exchange is pure imagination.

Again, suppose a ryot is paying Rs. 10 as land tax. When gold currency is introduced, what will Government take from him in place of Rs. 10? Will Government demand at the supposed rate of 1s. per rupee—*i.e.*, ten shillings only—or will Government demand arbitrarily in its despotic power at the rate of the fictitious value of a rupee as two shillings and will take £1, or any amount at any higher rate above the intrinsic value of the rupee? Taking the gross revenue comprehensively, the total gross revenue is Rs. 850,000,000, what will Government take from the taxpayer when gold currency is introduced? Will it take at the present supposed rate of 1s. per rupee, viz., £42,500,000, or will it arbitrarily impose a double revenue at the rate of 2s. per rupee, so that from his present poor produce the taxpayer must sell double the produce to meet the demands of Government. If the latter, what a precious benefit will this be to the Indian taxpayer from the gold currency!

When gold currency is introduced what salary will be paid to the European official? Suppose he has a salary of Rs. 1,000 per month, will Government give him at the rate of 1s. per rupee *i.e.*, £50, and will the official accept £50 for the Rs. 1,000? Is no all the present strong agitation of the Anglo-Indian a clear reply that he will do nothing of the kind, but will continue his agitation till he gets £100 or something near it for his Rs. 1,000: or in other words get his salary doubled at a stroke, at the expense of the starving ryot? And has not Government already shown that it will yield to such agitation, and will be readily "liberal" to European demands at the sacrifice of the Indians? It has already yielded to the demands of the Uncovenanted Europeans and has given them a fixed exchange of 1s. 9d. per rupee for their furlough, no matter whether exchange is 1s. or even less, say 6d. Now the whole European service is agitating to get them 1s. 9d. or some other high fixed exchange, even to the extent of half their salary. Do these Anglo-Indians really want to exact from the starving ryot such high exchange when the rupee is worth perhaps a shilling or even sixpence? Who will pay this difference? Of course an arbitrary Government may oppress a people as much as they like, but will the British people and Parliament allow such a thing?

On the top of all this comes the merchant with his agitation for the gold currency, that he may be saved, at the sacrifice of the ryot, from his risks of trade. The profits of trade are for his pocket, but risks of a commercial disturbance must be met by the ryot! The poverty-stricken ryot must protect the well-to-do-trader! God save India!

I do not need to trouble the Committee with any further

remarks as to the effect of the introduction of a gold currency on the condition of the people, who, according to Lord Lawrence's testimony, are living on scanty subsistence, and who, according to Lord Cromer, are already "extremely poor." Our friends the Anglo-Indians have to bear in mind that they are taking already from the mouths of the poor Indian about Rs. 150,000,000 or more every year as salaries, allowances, pensions, etc., to the so much deprivation of the provision of the children of the soil. Will they never understand or consider this, and what evil that means to India?

A word about the proposal to stop free coinage of silver. Now we know that a trade, internal or external, especially internal, requires abundant currency in a country like India; the curtailment of the coinage of the rupee will dislocate and cripple the free action of the trade of the country, especially internally, and will inflict serious injury and create some new complications. Secondly, the rupee, being thus artificially raised to a fictitious value by being made scarce, will depress the price of produce, and the ryot will be obliged to part with more of his poor produce to meet the demands of Government. Will this be a benefit to him? Further, by this restriction on coinage the wretched Indian taxpayer will not be relieved of a single ounce of produce in his forced remittances for the Home Charges of £19,000,000—in gold. Whatever the exchangeable value of gold is in relation to produce will have to be paid by the poor ryot, be the forced artificial exchange or the fictitious value of the rupee what it may. By restricting the coinage of silver—the price of silver in relation to produce being artificially enhanced—the taxpayer will have to pay the salary of all the European and other officials in such higher priced rupee, with so much more produce to part with! which, in short, will in effect be a far heavier burden, by increasing the *whole* salary of the officials of all the services, both Indians and Europeans, at so much the greater sacrifice of the wretched ryot.

The agitation for stopping coinage of silver or introducing gold currency, far from relieving the Indian taxpayer from the present loss by fall in exchange, which in all conscience is very heavy indeed, will actually inflict greater injury upon the helpless fellows. All attempts at artificial tampering with currency will, besides injuring the people, recoil upon the perpetrators of the mischief. They can no more raise the value of silver fictitiously than they can suspend gravitation.

The evil of the present loss from exchange does not arise from the fall in exchange, but from the unfortunate unnatural political and economic condition of British India. Were there no compulsory remittances to this country (any ordinary *free* transactions of business or loans between two countries not mattering beyond the usual risks of business), there would be no evil or embarrassing loss to Government such as we are considering. The excessive European services are the cause of all such calamity upon the Indians. Any other silver-using country—for instance, China—has no problem like that which at present embarrasses the British Indian Government.

(2). Coming to the second branch of the question, viz., the effect of the fall in exchange on international trade (for it is in such trade or business only that exchange is concerned), the best thing I can do is to give below the letter I wrote to the *Times* in September, 1886, and some other letters (I have inserted those letters, which I need not repeat here). Of the letters to the *Times* that paper was pleased to write approvingly in one of its leaders.[1] Further, I have made, in the statement, some remarks as to the action of the United States in endeavouring futilely to stop the silver storm, instead of allowing it to run its course. This I need not give here.

The step which the Government has now taken will, I am afraid, produce much mischief, and inflict great injury on the taxpayer, crushingly heavy loaded as he already is. The utmost that the Government might have done would have been, as I was afraid they were determined to do, to give some fixed exchange to the officials for their remittances to this country—to as much as half the salary. This would have been bad enough, but the course the Government have adopted, and for which there was no great necessity, will, I fear, prove far more injurious.

II.—STATEMENT SUBMITTED TO THE INDIAN CURRENCY COMMITTEE OF 1898.

Washington House,
72, Anerley Park, S.E.
October 20th, 1898.

DEAR SIR WILLIAM,—Since my letter of 28th July last, I have perused the Blue Book of the evidence given before the Currency Committee, and I feel it necessary to make a further statement.

"BRITISH INDIA."

2. These words are often used in a very misleading and confusing manner. I give below an extract from a statement which I have submitted to "the Royal Commission on Indian Expenditure and Apportionment of Charges," which I hope will place the matter in a clearer light.

3. "Before I proceed further let me clear up a strange confusion of ideas about prosperous British India and poverty stricken British India. This confusion of ideas arises from this circumstance. My remarks are for British India only.

4. "In reality there are two Indias—one the prosperous, the other poverty-stricken.

[1] The *Times*, January 26th, 1889:—"We observe with pleasure that Lord Cross says nothing on the bounty alleged to be enjoyed by the Indian wheat grower through the fall in the value of silver. This piece of nonsense has been again and again exposed in the letters of our correspondents, and never more clearly and forcibly than by Mr. Dadabhai Naoroji."

"(1) The prosperous India is the India of the British and other foreigners. They exploit India as officials, non-officials, capitalists, in a variety of ways, and carry away enormous wealth to their own country. To them India is, of course, rich and prosperous. The more they can carry away, the richer and more prosperous India is to them. These British and other foreigners cannot understand and realise why India can be called 'extremely poor,' when they can make their life careers; they can draw so much wealth from it and enrich their own country. It seldom occurs to them, if at all, what all that means to the Indians themselves.

"(2) The second India is the India of the Indians—the poverty-stricken India. This India, 'bled' and exploited in every way of their wealth, of their services, of their land, labour, and all resources by the foreigners; helpless and voiceless, governed by the arbitrary law and argument of force, and with injustice and unrighteousness—this India of the Indians becomes the 'poorest' country in the world, after one hundred and fifty years of British rule, to the disgrace of the British name. The greater the drain, the greater the impoverishment, resulting in all the scourges of war, famine, and pestilence. Lord Salisbury's words face us at every turn: 'Injustice will bring down the mightiest to ruin.' If this distinction of the 'prosperous India' of the slave-holders, and the 'poverty-stricken India' of the slaves be carefully borne in mind, a great deal of the controversy on this point will be saved. Britain can, by a righteous system, make both Indias prosperous. The great pity is that the Indian authorities do not or would not see it. They are blinded by selfishness—to find careers for our 'boys.'"—(Letter to LORD WELBY, dated 31st January, 1897.)

5. This state of affairs arises from the evil system of an un-British foreign dominion, as predicted by Sir John Shore in 1787. This evil makes the action of the British trader and capitalist an exploitation which otherwise, under ordinary circumstances, under *true* British system, would be legitimate trade and investment.

6. Almost throughout the Blue Book the thing chiefly considered is the requirements and benefits of "The Foreign Prosperous British India." "Indian's India" chiefly comes in only for the consideration as to how to tax the Indians in order to meet the requirements and benefits of the British

official bleeders and non-official exploiters. Earnestly and repeatedly are questions put and answers given how additional taxation should be raised—*not how to probe the evil and to find the true remedy.*

7. The main scope and direction of the evidence is as if India were a country and property of the Anglo-Indians, and British traders and capitalists; as if, therefore, their wants and requirements, and the means of enabling them to carry away as much wealth as they possibly can to England, were the chief object; and as if to consider the land, resources, and labour of India as only the instruments for the above purpose.

"INDEBTEDNESS OF INDIA."

8. This expression is repeatedly brought out for the self-satisfaction and justification of the exploitation. Let us examine how this particular phenomenon is brought about.

9. The process is this: The total amount of "Home Charges" is £15,795,836 (Statistical Abstract for 1896-7, p. 106 [c. 9,036], 1898). Out of this I deduct fully: Railways, £5,790,567, and Stores Department, £951,700. In deducting these two items I do not mean that I admit the necessity of doing so entirely, but that I want to avoid any controversy at this stage upon what are called "Public Works Loans" made by England, and Government Stores. The remainder, after making the above deduction, is £9,053,569 = Rs. 199,178,518, at 11d. per rupee, about Rs. 22 per £1, about which is the present legitimate rate for the true rupee, and which, with much more, though under disguise, the Indian taxpayer is actually forced to pay. Taking, roughly, Rs. 200,000,000, every pie of it is drawn from the people of British India and becomes an addition to the capital or wealth of England, and is altogether spent in England every year.

10. Next, the European services are paid in India every year (at Rs. 1,000 and upwards per annum, not including lower salaries) about Rs. 94,679,627 (including a small amount of pensions paid to Eurasians not separately given). (Parl. Ret. 192 of 1892.) I do not know whether this amount includes the payments made for and to European soldiers in India. I think not. If so, this has to be added to the above amount. To it has also to be added, I think, the illegal exchange compensation which is allowed to Europeans,

thereby out-Shylocking Shylock himself by not only taking the pound of flesh, but an ounce of blood also. Almost the whole of this amount of Rs. 94,679,627, say, roughly, Rs. 95,000,000, plus soldiers' payments and exchange compensation, is a loss to the people of British India, excepting, in a way, a small portion which goes to the domestic servants, house-owners, etc. But these amounts would have gone all the same to these domestics, etc., even though Indians had been in the place of the Europeans. The services rendered by such domestics, etc., being consumed by others than the children of the soil, are so far a loss to the country.

11. But I do not propose to argue this point here. I allow for the present this expenditure in British India by the European officials as not forming a part of the loss by the drain. I think it is generally claimed by the Anglo-Indians that such expenditure in India by European officials is about, on an average, half of the salaries and emoluments paid to them in India, and that the other half is about the amount which is remitted to England for families and the savings. Taking, therefore, this half of Rs. 94,679,627=Rs. 47,339,813, and adding this amount to Rs. 200,000,000 (paragraph 9), the total is, roughly, Rs. 250,000,000 every year; probably more if the two additions mentioned above of European soldiers' payments and exchange compensations were made. This enormous amount of annual political drain causes what Sir George Wingate very properly calls a "cruel and crushing tribute." Never could India have suffered such a cruel fate in all its history or existence.

12. The first step, therefore, towards the so-called "indebtedness" is that British India is "bled" every year to the amount of about Rs. 250,000,000 clean out of the country, and this enormous wealth is year after year poured into England. Will the India Office be good enough to make a return of the enormous wealth which England has drained out of India during its whole connexion?

13. Now, the second stage in the process of the manufacture of "indebtedness" is that out of this enormous wealth drawn away from India—sufficient and far more than sufficient to build thousands of miles of railways and every possible public works, and to meet every possible requirement of good government and progress, to the highest prosperity and civilisation—out of this enormous drain a small portion

is taken back to India as "British capital," when it is nothing of the kind, and by means of the so-called "British capital" all Indian resources of land and labour are further exploited by "British" (?) capitalists of every kind. All the profits made thereon are so much more wealth drawn away from India and brought to England.

14. Further, the foreign exploiters are not satisfied with the small portion of "Indian wealth" which they take back to India as their own capital, but they insist upon being further helped from the very current revenues of the country. So voracious are these exploiters that they clamour against Government for not putting its whole revenue at their disposal in the Presidency banks, instead of keeping a portion in the Treasury. Thus there is at first a political "bleeding," which is the foundation evil, and in its train and by its help comes the so-called "commercial" or capitalistic exploitation.

15. Thus is manufactured that complacent "indebtedness" in the name of which the bleeding and exploitation are unceasingly and ever-increasingly carried on, and which is so pleasant, so profitable, and so nice an excuse to the Anglo-Indian and "British capitalist's" heart.

16. In reality there is not a single farthing of "indebtedness" from India to England. It is England that is under a very vast material and moral debt to India. Of the latter —moral debt—I cannot speak much here, though it is no less enormous and grievous than the former.

17. Besides the sum of Rs. 400,000,000 now drained from India (paragraph 24) every year, (1) the British Indian Empire is built up at the *entire* expense of India, and mainly with Indian blood. Even now Indian blood is contributing in extending the British Empire and benefits in other parts of the world. And what a reward—a helotry! (2) Not only this, but in addition to the cost of building up the whole Indian Empire England has taken away from India an amount of wealth since its connexion with India which, with ordinary commercial compound interest, will amount to thousands and thousands of millions sterling.

18. It may be asked whether I mean that I do not want British capitalists to go and trade or employ their capital in India? I mean nothing of the kind. By all means let them do so. Under ordinary circumstances India will hail it, as any other country may do. But let it be with their own

capital. Let them bring their own capital, and make upon it as much profit as they can, with India's blessing upon it. What I mean is that they should not first "plunder" India, leaving it wretched and helpless, then bring back a portion of "plundered" India's wealth as their *own*, exploit therewith India's resources of land and labour, carry away the profits, and leave the Indians mere hewers of wood and drawers of water—mere slaves, in worse plight than even that in which the slaves of the Southern States of America were.

19. If England can understand her true interests—political, moral, economic, or material—if she would hold back her hand from India's throat, and let India enjoy its *own* resources, England can make India prosperous, and, as a necessary consequence, can derive from India far, far greater benefit, with India's blessing, than what she derives at present with India's curse of the scourges of war, and pestilence, and famine, and of an ever-increasing poverty.

20. The word "indebtedness" must be taken at its correct interpretation. It is simply "bleeding" and exploitation, or what Mr. Bright indirectly characterised "plunder."

"Balance of Trade in India's Favour," and "Excess of Exports over Imports as a Benefit to India."

21. What is balance of trade in its true sense? Say a country exports £100,000,000 worth of its produce. It gets back in imports, say, £80,000,000 worth of other countries' merchandise. The remaining balance of £20,000,000 of the original exports, and, say, 10 per cent. of profits, or £10,000,000—altogether £30,000,000—has *to be received*. This £30,000,000 is called balance of trade in favour of that country. And when that country actually receives this balance of £30,000,000, either in the shape of bullion or merchandise, then its account is said to be squared or settled.

22. I have not included in this trade account any true borrowing or lending. Such borrowing or lending can be considered by itself. A country's borrowing is included in its imports, and the interest it pays is a part of its exports. This loan account between any two independent countries can be estimated and allowed for. And that in no way affects the *bonâ fide* balance of trade. If India be allowed to and can *get* its true "balance of trade" it would be only too happy to

make any legitimate borrowing or lending with any country, with benefit to both.

23. But such is *not* India's condition. What is India's actual condition? What is its so-called "balance of trade," of which much mistaken or wrong view is taken in the evidence? Be it first remembered, as I have already explained under the heading of "indebtedness," that what is called India's debt is nothing of the kind, but simply and solely a part of its own wealth taken away from it.

24. Let us see what the amount is (C. 9,036, 1898, p. 277). Taking the last five years as an illustration, the total net exports for 1892-3 to 1896-7 are Rs. 1,314,600,000. The total exports for the same period are Rs. 5,688,000,000; taking 10 per cent. profits thereon, will be Rs. 568,800,000. Therefore the total excess of net exports, plus profits, would be Rs. 1,883,400,000. Then, again, the so-called "loans" from this country are included in imports, the net exports must be increased to that extent. The addition to commercial debt in this country after 1891-2 to 1896-7 is £6,479,000 (C. 9,036, 1898, p. 130), or, say, £6,500,000, which, at the average rate of exchange of the same years (p. 131), about 1s. 2d. per rupee, or nearly Rs. 17 per £1, is equal to Rs. 110,500,000. So that the total of net exports (excluding loans from imports) and profits will be Rs. 1,883,400,000 plus 110,500,000 equal to Rs. 1,993,900,000, or about roundly Rs. 2,000,000,000. During the five years the average per year will be about Rs. 400,000,000. Now, to call this a "balance of trade in favour of India" is the grossest abuse of language. It is neither any "trade" nor "balance of trade." It is simply and solely the *remittances* of the official bleeding and the exploitation of the non-official capitalists. Not a *pie* of this tremendous amount—Rs. 400,000,000 every year—will India ever see back as its *own*: while in true balance of trade the whole of this amount should go back to India as its *own*.

25. No wonder Sir William Harcourt's heart rejoiced at the leaps and bounds with which the income-tax increased year after year in this country. In his speech on the occasion of his famous Budget he rejoiced at the increasing income-tax, never seeming to dream how much of it was drawn from the "bleeding" drain from India.

26. With what self-satisfied benevolence have examiners and witnesses talked of the great benefit they were conferring

upon India by making every effort to increase the excess of exports in order to enable poor India to meet her "indebtedness." Such is the Indian myth! But what is the reality? To increase the net exports as much as possible means to increase the remittance of the bleeding and exploitations of every year of which not a farthing is to return to India as its *own*. Extraordinary, how ingeniously matters can be and are represented, or rather misrepresented, and the public here entirely misled!

SURPLUSES AND SOLVENCY.

27. There never have been and never will be true surpluses or solvency of British India as long as the present evil system of government lasts. What is a surplus of the finance of any country? Suppose that in England you raise £100,000,000 of revenue. Suppose £95,000,000 are spent and £5,000,000 remain in hand at the end of the year, and this £5,000,000 is called surplus, and that the Government, if it does not impose any additional taxation or does not borrow, is solvent. Now, the essential condition of this surplus is that the whole of the £95,000,000 has returned to the tax-paying people themselves in a variety of ways, and continues to be part and parcel of the wealth of the country. And the remaining £5,000,000 will also go back to the people and remain a part of the wealth of the country.

28. But what is the case with India? It is nothing of the kind. Suppose Rs. 1,000,000,000 are raised as revenue. Suppose Rs. 950,000,000 are spent, leaving Rs. 50,000,000 in hand at the end of the year. Now, are these Rs. 50,000,000 a surplus? No. The Rs. 950,000,000 have not all returned to the people and have not remained as part of India's *own* wealth. Some Rs. 250,000,000 (see paragraph 12) are drained clean out of the country by foreigners, never to return to India. Till these Rs. 250,000,000 are returned to India as its own, which they never are, and which is a dead loss, to talk of the surplus of Rs. 50,000,000 is another gross abuse of language. Instead of Rs. 50,000,000 surplus there is a pure deficit or rather entire loss of Rs. 250,000,000. And such perpetual losses are pure bankruptcy.

29. I repeat, that there never has been and never will be any surplus in India as long as, from every year's revenue, there is a clean drain, which at present is at the rate of about

Rs. 250,000,000. In this country all that is raised as revenue returns to the country, just as all water evaporating from the ocean returns to the ocean. And England's ocean of wealth remains as full as ever, as far as revenue is concerned. India's ocean, on the contrary, must go on evaporating and drying every year more and more.

30. The only reason why the Indian Government does not go into bankruptcy—bankrupt though it always is—is that it can, by its despotism, squeeze out more and more from the helpless taxpayer, without mercy or without any let or hindrance. And if at any time it feels fear at the possible exasperation of the people at the enormity, it quietly borrows and adds to the permanent burden of the people without the slightest compunction or concern. Of course the Government of India can never become bankrupt till retribution comes and the whole ends in disaster.

31. I have referred in the above consideration to the official bleeding only, but when to this is added the further exploitation of the land (meaning all the resources) and labour of the country, which I have already described, the idea of surplus or solvency, or of any addition to the wealth or prosperity of the *people* (however much it may be of the Europeans) becomes supremely ridiculous and absurd.

Import of Bullion and Hoarding.

32. Reference is frequently made to this matter. I think the best thing I can do is to give an extract from my reply to Sir Grant Duff:—

Westminster Review, November, 1887.

33. "Sir Grant Duff refers to the absorption of gold and silver and to hoarding. What are the facts about British India? In my 'Poverty of India' I have treated the subject at some length. The total amount (after deducting the exports from imports) retained by India during a period of eighty-four years (1801 to 1884), including the exceptionally large imports during the American War, is £455,761,385. This is for *all* India. The population at present is 254,000,000. I may take the average of eighty-four years roughly—say, 200,000,000. This gives 45s. 6d. per head for the whole eighty-four years, or 6½d. per head per annum. Even if I took the average population as 180,000,000, the amount per

head for the eighty-four years would be 50s., or 7d. per head per annum. Of the United Kingdom I cannot get returns before 1858. The total amount of treasure retained by the United Kingdom (after deducting exports from imports) is, for twenty-seven years from 1858 to 1884, £86,194,937. Taking an average of 31,000,000 of population for twenty-seven years, the amount retained for these twenty-seven years is 55s. 7d. per head, or very nearly 2s. 1d. per head per annum; while in India for more than three times the same period the amount is only 45s. 6d. per head, or 6½d. per head per annum. France has retained from 1861 to 1880 (Mulhall's Dictionary) £208,000,000, and taking the population, say 37,000,000, that gives 112s. per head in twenty years, or 5s. 7d. per head per annum.

34. "Sir Grant Duff ought to consider that the large amount of bullion is to be distributed over a vast country and a vast population, nearly equal to five-sixths of the population of the whole of Europe; and when the whole population is considered what a wretched amount is this of gold and silver—viz., 6½d. per head per annum—received for all possible wants! India does not produce any gold or silver. To compare it with Europe: Europe retained in ten years, 1871-1880 (Mulhall, 'Progress of the World,' 1880), £327,000,000 for an average population of about 300,000,000, or 21s. 10d. per head, or 2s. 2d. per head per annum. India during the same ten years retained £65,774,252 for an average population of, say, 245,000,000; so that the whole amount retained for the ten years is about 5s. 4d., or only 6½d. per head per annum, against 21s. 10d. and 2s. 2d. respectively of Europe. This means that India retained only one-fourth of what Europe retained per head per annum during these ten years. It must be further remembered that there is no such vast system of cheques, clearing-houses, etc., in India as plays so important a part in England and other countries of Europe. Wretched as the provision of 6½d. per head per annum is for *all* wants—political, social, commercial, etc.—there is something far worse behind for British India. All the gold and silver that I have shown above as retained by India is not for British India only, but for the Native States, the frontier territories, and the European population; and then the remainder is for the Native population of British India. We must have official information about

these four divisions before we can form a correct estimate of what British India retains. The Native States, as I have said before, have no foreign drain except the small amount of tribute of about £700,000. Some frontier territories receive something instead of paying any tribute. These States therefore receive back for the exports of their merchandise, and for the ordinary trade profits on such exports, full returns in imports of merchandise and treasure, and this treasure taken away by the Native States and frontier territories forms not a small portion of what is imported into India. It must also be considered how much metal is necessary every year for waste of coin and metal, and for the wants of circulating currency. When Government can give us all such information, it will be found that precious little remains for British India beyond what it is compelled to import for its absolute wants. I hope England does not mean to say that Englishmen or Englishwomen may sport as much as they like in ornaments or personal trinkets or jewellery, but that the wretch of a Native of British India, their fellow-subject, has no business or right to put a few shillings' worth of trinkets on his wife's or daughter's person —or that Natives must simply live the lives of brutes, subsist on their 'scanty subsistence,' and thank their stars that they have that much.

35. "I will now try to give some indication of what bullion British India actually retains. Mr. Harrison gave his evidence before the Parliamentary Committee of 1871-74, that about £1,000,000 of fresh coinage was more than sufficient to supply the waste of coin or metal. Is it too much to assume that in the very widespread and minute distribution, over a vast surface and a vast population, of small trinkets or ornaments of silver, and their rough use, another million may be required to supply waste and loss? If only a pennyworth per head per annum be so wanted, it would make a million sterling. Next, how much goes to the Natives States and the frontier territories? Here are a few significant official figures as an indication: The 'Report of the external land trade and railway-borne trade of the Bombay Presidency for 1884-85' (p. 2) says of Rajputana and Central India :—'13. The imports from the external blocks being greater than the exports to them, the balance of trade due by the Presidency to the other provinces amounts to

Rs. 12,01,05,912, as appears from the above table and the following.' I take the Native States from the table referred to.

EXCESS OF IMPORTS IN BOMBAY PRESIDENCY.

From	Rajputana and Central India . .	Rs. 5,55,46,753
,,	Berar	1,48,91,355
,,	Hyderabad	8,67,688
	Total. . . .	Rs. 7,13,05,796

Or £7,130,579. This means that these Native States have exported so much more merchandise than they have imported. Thereupon the Report remarks thus:—'The greatest balance is in favour of Rajputana and Central India, caused by the import of opium from that block. Next to it is that of the Central Provinces. It is presumed that these balances are paid back *mainly in cash*' (the italics are mine). This, then, is the way the treasure goes; and poor British India gets all the abuse—insult added to injury. Its candle burns not only at both ends, but at all parts."

36. Far from any important quantity or any quantity of bullion going to British India as "balance of trade," Rs. 400,000,000 worth of British India's wealth at present goes clean out of the country every year never to return to it as its *own*.

BENEFITS DERIVED FROM CHEAP SILVER.—A LOW RUPEE AND LOW EXCHANGE PROMOTES AND DEVELOPS EXPORTS.

37. That there is some temporary advantage from low exchange to silver-using countries over gold-using countries, I have already explained in my letter to the *Daily News* of September 24th, 1886 (Appendix A of my letter already submitted). But in British India this little advantage is of not much avail to the poor people. What becomes of it when they must perforce lose every year, never to return to them, Rs. 400,000,000 of wealth out of their miserable total produce, leaving them so much more poor and miserable? It is idle to talk of the people of British India deriving benefit from low exchange or from anything as long as these tremendous bleedings and the exploitation go on.

PRICES AND WAGES.

38. The above remarks apply equally to prices and wages. How on earth, under such drain, can there be any healthy

increase of prices or wages arising from true prosperity? Before the Royal Commission on Indian Expenditure and Apportionment, a member having asserted that there was general rise of prices, Mr. Jacob, as official witness, confirmed the statement. Thereupon I prepared some questions, took the paper to Mr. Jacob, and gave it to him to enable him to prepare the replies. And, what was my surprise when he told me that the subject was not of his department, and he would not answer the questions, though he did not hesitate to say that there was a general rise of prices! If of any use I shall produce the questions before the Committee. But, first of all, there are no reliable statistics sufficient to draw any correct conclusions; and conclusions of any value cannot be drawn about any one factor from prices or wages which are the results of many factors.

39. I would not lengthen this statement by noting several other points in the Blue-book, but conclude by repeating what Sir John Shore has said more than a hundred years ago (in 1787). His words were true then, are true to this day, and will remain true in future if the evil pointed out by him continues. He said: "Whatever allowance we may make for the increased industry of the subjects of the State, owing to the enhanced demand for the produce of it (supposing the demand to be enhanced) there is reason to conclude that the benefits are more than counterbalanced by evils inseparable from the system of a remote foreign dominion."

40. This evil system must be altered, or, as I have said before (paragraph 5), what, under natural circumstances, would in any country be legitimate trade and investments by British people become, under this evil system of an un-British rule, cruel exploitation. Unless the evil is remedied, there is no hope for British India, and disaster both for England and India is the only look out.

41. Let England pay fairly and honestly her share of expenditure incurred for her own interests, and end the bleeding by a careful consideration of the following words of the Duke of Devonshire, as Secretary of State for India, spoken in 1883: "There can, in my opinion, be very little doubt that India is insufficiently governed. . . . . If the country is to be better governed, that can only be done by the employment of the best and most intelligent of the Natives in the service." And the best means of attaining

this object is to give honourable fulfilment to the Resolution passed by the House of Commons in June, 1893, about simultaneous examinations.

42. Unless Acts and Resolutions of Parliament and Royal Proclamations are honourably fulfilled, and a righteous Government, worthy of the English character and promises and professions is established, no currency or financial jugglery, or "political hypocrisy," or any "subterfuges," or un-British despotic ruling will avail or remedy the ever-growing and various evils that *must* constantly flow from an unrighteous system.

43. Lord Salisbury's eternal words stare us in the face: "Injustice will bring down the mightiest to ruin."

Yours truly,

DADABHAI NAOROJI.

Sir William Wedderburn, M.P.,
Chairman of the British Committee of
The Indian National Congress,
84, Palace Chambers, Westminster, S.W.

The following brochure was published by the India Reform Society in 1853 and reprinted in 1899.

INDIA REFORM. No. IX.—The State and Government of India under its Native Rulers.

INDIA REFORM SOCIETY, 1853.

On Saturday, the 12th of March, a Meeting of the Friends of India was held in Charles Street, St. James's Square, with a view of bringing public opinion to bear on the Imperial Parliament in the case of India so as to obtain due attention to the complaints and claims of the inhabitants of that vast Empire. H. D. Seymour, Esq., M.P., having been called to the chair, the following Resolutions were agreed to by the meeting :—

1. That the character of the alterations to be effected in the constitution of our Indian Government at the termination of the East India Company's Charter Act, on the 30th of April, 1854, is a question which demands the most ample and serious consideration.

2. That although Committees of both Houses of Parliament have been appointed, in conformity with the practice on each preceding renewal of the Charter Act, for the purpose of investigating the nature and the results of our Indian Administration, those Committees have been appointed on the present occasion at a period so much later than usual, that the interval of time remaining before the expiration of the existing powers of the East India Company is too short to permit the possibility of collecting such evidence as would show what alterations are required in our Indian Government.

3. That the enquiry now being prosecuted by Committees of the Legislature will be altogether unsatisfactory if it be confined to the evidence of officials and of servants of the East India Company, and conducted and terminated without reference to the petitions and wishes of the more intelligent of the Natives of India.

4. That it is the duty of the friends of India to insist upon a temporary Act to continue the present Government of India for a period not exceeding three years, so that time may be given for such full enquiry and deliberation as will enable

Parliament within that period to legislate permanently for the future administration of our Indian Empire.

5. That in order to obtain such a measure, this meeting constitutes itself an "Indian Reform Society," and names the undermentioned gentlemen as a Committee.

T. Barnes, Esq., M.P.
J. Bell, Esq., M.P.
W. Biggs, Esq., M.P.
J. F. B. Blackett, Esq., M.P.
G Bowyer, Esq., M.P.
J. Bright, Esq., M.P.
F. C. Brown, Esq.
H. A. Bruce, Esq., M.P.
Lieut.-Col. J. M. Caulfield, M.P.
J. Cheetham, Esq., M.P.
W. H. Clarke, Esq.
J. Crook, Esq., M.P.
J. Dickinson, Jun., Esq.
M. G. Fielden, Esq., M.P.
Lieut.-Gen. Sir J. F. Fitzgerald, K.C.B., M.P.
W. R. S. Fitzgerald, Esq., M.P.
M. Forster, Esq.
R. Gardner, Esq., M.P.
Right Hon. T. M. Gibson, M.P.
Viscount Goderich, M.P.
G. Hadfield, Esq., M.P.
W. Harcourt, Esq.
L. Heyworth, Esq., M P.
C. Hindley, Esq., M.P.
T. Hunt, Esq.
E. J. Hutchins, Esq., M.P.
P. F. C. Johnstone, Esq.
M. Lewin, Esq.
F. Lucas, Esq., M.P.
T. McCullagh, Esq.
E. Miall, Esq., M.P.
G. H. Moore, Esq., M.P.
B. Oliveira, Esq., M.P.
A. J. Otway, Esq., M.P.
G. M. W. Peacocke, Esq., M.P.
Apsley Pellatt, Esq., M.P.
J. Pilkington, Esq., M.P.
J. G. Phillimore, Esq., M.P.
T. Phinn, Esq., M.P.
H. Reeve, Esq.
W. Scholefield, Esq., M.P.
H. D. Seymour, Esq., M.P.
W. D. Seymour, Esq., M.P.
J. B. Smith, Esq., M.P.
J. Sullivan, Esq.
G. Thompson, Esq., M.P.
F. Warren, Esq.
J. A. Wise, Esq., M.P.

Correspondence on all matters connected with the Society to be addressed to the Hon. Secretary, by whom subscriptions will be received in aid of its object.

John Dickinson, Jun., *Hon. Sec.*

Committee Rooms, Clarence Chambers, 12, Haymarket.

April 12th, 1853.

NOTE BY DADABHAI NAOROJI.

March, 1899.

Whatever may be the merits or demerits of "The State and Government of India under its Native Rulers," one thing is certain, that the greatest evil of the present un-British system of British rule in India did not exist under the Native rulers—viz., the unceasing and ever-increasing "bleeding" and drain of India by "the evils inseparable from the system of a remote foreign dominion" (Sir John Shore, 1787), and by inflicting upon India every burden of expenditure incurred even for the interests of Britain itself. This evil is further aggravated by what Lord Salisbury calls "political hypocrisy," or by what Lord Lytton calls "deliberate and transparent subterfuges," producing what Lord Salisbury calls "terrible misery," or what Lord Cromer calls "extreme poverty," or what Lord Lawrence described as "that the mass of the people live on scanty subsistence."

The British Indian Empire is formed and maintained entirely by Indian money and mainly by Indian blood, and, moreover, Britain has drawn thousands of millions of pounds besides.

Any fair-minded Englishman, after making himself acquainted with all the *realities*, instead of the Anglo-Indian *romance*, of the present un-British system (notwithstanding much good done to and gratefully acknowledged by the Indians), will come to the conclusion that in the material and economic condition of India the existing system has been the greatest curse with which India has been ever afflicted.

This deplorable state of affairs cannot go on, and, as several eminent Englishmen have repeatedly foretold, it must end in disaster. "It carries with it," said Sir John Malcolm, "its nemesis, the seeds of the destruction of the Empire itself." "Injustice," said Lord Salisbury, "shall bring down the mightiest to ruin."

There is no justification of British rule in India, if it is to be an un-British despotism, with all the crushing additional evils of a *foreign* despotism; for, as Macaulay says, "The heaviest of all yokes is the yoke of the stranger." It has been repeatedly said by eminent Englishmen that—using Lord Mayo's words—"The welfare of the people of India is our primary object. If we are not here for their good, *we ought not to be here at all*."

The despotism of former rulers is no justification for the bleeding despotism of the British rulers.

Washington House,
72, Anerley Park, London, S.E.

INDIA REFORM, 1853.

The State and Government of India under its Native Rulers.

We threaten to appropriate the territories of the Native Princes, our allies, upon the strength mainly of our own virtues and of their vices. All Native Governments, we say, are bad: all Native Governors are tyrants and sensualists. Their subjects are groaning under oppression, and we are bound to relieve them; all who wear turbans are worthless—all who wear hats are worthy. There was no good government in India until the advent of the Anglo-Saxon; it is the Anglo-Saxon who has taught the Indian the arts of civil life, and who shows him what government ought to be. The ruins of the tombs and temples of ancient Greece and Rome are worthy of all admiration; they are proofs of the genius and taste of the people who created them; the more magnificent ruins of ancient India are monuments only of ostentation and selfishness. "I contemplated those ruins," said Lord Ellenborough, "with admiration of our predecessors, and with humiliation at our own shortcomings." "You might as well be humiliated by the sight of the Pyramids," was the retort of Lord Aberdeen.

What is deserving of all praise in the West is not praiseworthy in the East. When we see great works of utility and ornament in the West we pronounce them to be evidence of prosperous and tranquil Governments; but similar works in the East seem to lead us to a different judgment. At this moment we are dependent for millions of our revenue upon magnificent works of irrigation, constructed by our predecessors; the country is strewn with the remains of similar works. We pass them without notice and dwell upon our own comparatively puny efforts at imitation.

We found the people of India, it is said, abject, degraded, false to the very core. Mussulman dominion had called into full activity all the bad qualities which Hinduism has in itself a fatal tendency to generate. The most indolent and selfish of our own Governors have been models of benevolence and beneficence when compared with the greatest of the Native Sovereigns. The luxurious selfishness of the Moghul Emperors depressed and enfeebled the people. Their predecessors were either unscrupulous tyrants or indolent debauchees. Nor were their successors, the Ghilji Sovereigns, any better.

Having the command of the public press in this country, and the sympathy of the public mind with us, it is an easy task thus to exalt ourselves at the expense of our predecessors. We tell our own story, and our testimony is unimpeachable, but if we find anything favourable related of those who have preceded us the accounts we pronounce to be suspicious. We contrast the Moghul conquests of the fourteenth century with the "victorious, mild and merciful progress of the British arms in the East in the nineteenth." But, if our object was a fair one, we should contrast the Mussulman invasion of Hindostan with the contemporaneous Norman invasion of England—the characters of the Mussulman Sovereigns with their contemporaries in the West—their Indian wars of the fourteenth century with our French wars, or with the Crusades—the effect of the Mahomedan conquest upon the characters of the Hindoo, with the effect of the Norman conquest upon the Anglo-Saxon, when "to be called an Englishman was considered as a reproach—when those who were appointed to administer justice were the fountains of all iniquity—when magistrates, whose duty it was to pronounce righteous judgments were the most cruel of all tyrants, and greater plunderers than common thieves and robbers";—when the great men were inflamed with such a rage of money that they cared not by what means it was acquired; when the licentiousness was so great that a Princess of Scotland found "it necessary to wear a religious habit in order to preserve her person from violation."[1]

The history of the Mahomedan dynasties in India is full, it is said, of lamentable instances of the cruelty and rapacity of the early conquerors, not without precedent, however, in contemporary Christian history; for when Jerusalem was taken by the first Crusaders, at the end of the eleventh century, the garrison, consisting of 40,000 men, "was put to the sword without distinction; arms protected not the brave, nor

[1] Henry of Huntingdon, Anglo-Saxon Chronicle, and Eadmon.

submission the timid; no age or sex received mercy; infants perished by the same sword that pierced their mothers. The streets of Jerusalem were covered with heaps of slain, and the shrieks of agony and despair resounded from every house." When Louis VII. of France, in the twelfth century, "made himself master of the town of Vitri, he ordered it to be set on fire; in consequence of this inhuman order, 1,300 persons who had taken refuge, perished in the flames." In England, at the same time, under our Stephen, war "was carried on with so much fury, that the land was left uncultivated, and the instruments of husbandry were destroyed or abandoned," and the result of our French wars in the fourteenth century was a state of things "more horrible and destructive than was ever experienced in any age or country." The insatiable cruelty of the Mahomedan conquerors, it is said, stands recorded upon more undeniable authority than the insatiable benevolence of the Mahomedan conquerors. We have abundant testimony of the cruelty of contemporary Christian conquerors; have we any evidence of their benevolence?

As attempts are thus systematically made, in bulky volumes, to run down the character of Native Governments and Native Sovereigns, in order that we may have a fair pretext for seizing upon their possessions, it becomes necessary to show that we have a Christian Roland for every Native Oliver; that if the Mussulman conquerors of India were cruel and rapacious, they were matched by their Christian contemporaries. It is much our fashion to compare India in the fifteenth and sixteenth centuries with England in the nineteenth, and to pique ourselves upon the result. "When we compare other countries with England," said a sagacious observer,[1] "we usually speak of England as she now is, we scarcely ever think of going back beyond the Reformation, and we are apt to regard every foreign country as ignorant and uncivilised, whose state of improvement does not in some degree approximate to our own, even though it should be higher than our own was at no distant period." It would be almost as fair to compare India in the sixteenth with England in the nineteenth century, as it would be to compare the two countries in the first centuries of the Christian era, when India was at the top of civilisation, and England at the bottom. India had gradually declined in civilisation from

[1] Sir Thomas Munro.

the date of the invasion of Alexander up to the time of the first Mussulman conquest; but we have abundant testimony to prove that, at that date, and for centuries before it, her people enjoyed a high degree of prosperity, which continued to the breaking up of the Moghul Empire early in the eighteenth century.

THE STATE OF INDIA AT THE TIME OF GREEK INVASION.

"All the descriptions of the parts of India visited by the Greeks," Mr. Elphinstone tells us, "give the idea of a country teeming with population, and enjoying the highest degree of prosperity." There were 1,500 cities between the Hydaspes and the Hyphasis. Palilothra was eight miles long, and one and a half broad, defended by a deep ditch and high rampart, with 570 towers and 164 gates. The numerous commercial cities and posts for foreign trade, which are mentioned in the Periplus, attest the progress of the Indians in a department which more than any other shows the advanced condition of a nation. Arrian mentions with admiration that all the Indians were free. The army was in constant pay during war and peace; the arms and horses were supplied by the State; they never ravaged the country. The Greeks speak of the bravery of the Indian armies opposed to them as superior to that of other nations with whom they had to contend in Asia. They spoke of the police as excellent. In the camp of Sandracotus, consisting of 400,000 men, the sums stolen did not amount to more than about £3 daily. Justice was administered by the King and his assessors. The revenue was derived from the land, which was said to belong to the King; it amounted to one-fourth of the produce. The fields were all measured, and the water carefully distributed for irrigation; taxes were imposed upon trade, and an income-tax levied from merchants and traders. Royal roads are spoken of by Strabo, and milestones; the war-chariots were drawn by horses in time of war, and by oxen on a march. The arts, though simple, were far from being in a rude state. Gold, gems, silks, and ornaments were in all families; the professions mentioned show all that is necessary to civilised life. The number of grains, spices, etc., which were grown afford proofs that the country was in a high state of cultivation. "Their institutions were less rude, their conduct to their enemies more humane, their general learning much more considerable, and in the knowledge of the being and nature of God they were already in possession of a light which was but faintly perceived, even by the loftiest intellects in the best days of Athens."[1]

In the time of Asoca, a Hindoo Sovereign, who reigned some centuries before the Christian era, his edict columns bear testimony to the extent of his dominions, and the civilised character of his government, since they contain orders "for establishing hospitals and dispensaries throughout his Empire, as well as for planting trees and digging wells along the public highways;" and 56 B.C. another Hindoo sovereign, Vicramaditya, is represented to have been a powerful monarch, who ruled a civilised and populous country.

Writers, both Hindoo and Mussulman, unite in bearing testimony to the state of prosperity in which India was found at the time of the first Mahommedan conquest. They dwell with admiration on the extent and magnificence of the capital of the kingdom of Canouj, and of the inexhaustible riches of the Temple of Somnath.

Many of the Sovereigns of each of the Mussulman dynasties were men of extraordinary character. The prudence, activity, and enterprise of Mahommed of Ghuzni, and his encouragement of literature and the arts, were conspicuous: "he showed so much munificence to individuals of eminence that his capital exhibited a greater assemblage of literary genius than any other monarch in Asia has ever been able to produce. If rapacious in acquiring wealth, he was unrivalled in the judgment and grandeur with which he knew how to expend it."

His four immediate successors were patrons of literature and the arts, and acceptable to their subjects as good governors. Can we say as much for their contemporaries, William the Norman and his descendants, in the twelfth and thirteenth centuries? It is generally supposed that the conquest of India by the Mahommedans was an easy task, but history tells us that none of the Hindoo principalities fell without a severe struggle; that some of them were never subdued, but remain substantive States at this moment; and that Shahab-ûd-Deen, the first founder of the Mahommedan

[1] Elphinstone's "History of India," vol. i.

Empire in India, towards the end of the twelfth century, was signally defeated by the Rajpoot Sovereign of Delhi.[1]

One of his successors, Kootub-ûd-Deen, who erected the Kootub Minar, "the highest column in the world," and near it a mosque, which for grandeur of design and elegance of execution was equal to anything in India, was generally beloved for the frankness and generosity of his disposition, and left a permanent reputation as a just and virtuous ruler.

"Sultana Rezia was endowed," says the historian Ferishta, "with every princely virtue, and those who scrutinise her actions the most severely will find in her no fault" but "that she was a woman." She evinced all the qualities of a just and able sovereign. History does not make quite such favourable mention of our King John, or of Philip of France, her contemporaries. Julal-ûd-Deen, of the same dynasty, was celebrated for his clemency, his magnanimity, and love of literature.

The Hindoo kingdoms of Carnata and Tellingana were re-established about the middle of the fourteenth century. The first, with its capital, Bijanuggur, "attained to a pitch of power and splendour not perhaps surpassed by any previous Hindoo dynasty"; and such was the mutual estimation between the Hindoo and Mussulman sovereigns of the Deccan that inter-marriages took place between them, Hindoos were in high command in the Mussulman army, and Mussulmans in the Hindoo, and one Rajah of Bijanuggur built a mosque for his Mahommedan subjects.[2] In the reign of Mahomed Toglak, A.D. 1351, there was an admirably regulated horse and foot post from the frontier to the capital. That capital, Delhi, is described as a most magnificent city, its mosques and walls without an equal upon the earth.

The public works of his successor, Feroz Shah, consisted of 50 dams across rivers to promote irrigation, 40 mosques and 30 colleges, 100 caravanseries, 30 reservoirs, 100 hospitals, 100 public baths, 150 bridges, besides many other edifices for pleasure and ornament; and, above all, the canal from the point in the Jumna where it leaves the mountains of Carnal to Hansi and Hissar, a work which has been partially restored by the British Government. The historian of this monarch expatiates on the happy

[1] Elphinstone's "History of India," vol. i., pp. 547-696; vol. ii., p. 90.
[2] Elphinstone, vol. ii., p. 203.

state of the ryots under his government, on the goodness of their houses and furniture, and the general use of gold and silver ornaments amongst their women. He says, amongst other things, that every ryot had a good bedstead and a neat garden. He is said to be a writer not much to be trusted; but the general state of the country must no dou , have been flourishing, for Milo de Conti, an Italian traveller, who visited India about A.D. 1420, speaks highly of what he saw in Guzerat, and found the banks of the Ganges covered with towns amidst beautiful gardens and orchards. He passed four famous cities before he reached Maarazia, which he describes as a powerful city, filled with gold, silver, and precious stones. His accounts are corroborated by those of Barbora and Bartema, who travelled in the early part of the sixteenth century. The former in particular describes Cambay as a remarkably well-built city, situated in a beautiful and fertile country, filled with merchants of all nations, and with artisans and manufacturers like those of Flanders. Cæsar Frederic gives a similar account of Guzerat, and Ibn Batuta, who travelled during the anarchy and oppression of Mohammed Tagluk's reign, in the middle of the fifteenth century, when insurrections were reigning in most parts of the country, enumerates many large and populous towns and cities, and gives a high impression of the state in which the country must have been before it fell into disorder.

Abdurizag, an ambassador from the grandson of Tamerlane, visited the South of India in 1442, and concurs with other observers in giving the impression of a prosperous country. The kingdom of Candeish was at this time in a high state of prosperity under its own kings; the numerous stone embankments by which the streams were rendered applicable to irrigation are equal to anything in India as works of industry and ability.

Baber, the first sovereign of the Moghul dynasty, although he regards Hindostan with the same dislike that Europeans still feel, speaks of it as a rich and noble country, and expresses his astonishment at the swarming population and the innumerable workmen of every kind and profession. Besides the ordinary business of his kingdom, he was constantly occupied with making aqueducts, reservoirs, and other improvements, as well as in introducing new fruits, and other productions of remote countries. His son, Humayon, whose character was free from vices and violent passions, was defeated, and obliged to fly from Hindostan, by Shir Shah, who is described as a prince of consummate prudence and ability, "whose measures were as wise as benevolent," and who, notwithstanding his constant activity in the field, during a short reign had brought his territories into the highest order, and introduced many improvements into his civil government. "He made a high road extending for four months' journey from Bengal to the Western Rhotas near the Indus, with caravanserais at every stage, and wells at every mile and a half. There was an Imam and Muezzim at every mosque, and provisions for the poor at every caravanserai, with attendants of proper castes for Hindoos as well as for Mussulmans. The road was planted with rows of trees for shade, and in many places was in the state described when the author saw it, after it had stood for eighty-two years."[1]

It is almost superfluous to dwell upon the character of the celebrated Akbar, who was equally great in the cabinet and in the field, and renowned for his learning, toleration, liberality, clemency, courage, temperance, industry, and largeness of mind. But it is to his internal policy that Akbar owes his place in that highest order of princes whose reigns have been a blessing to mankind.[2] He forbade trials by ordeal, and marriages before the age of puberty, and the slaughter of animals for sacrifice. He also permitted widows to marry a second time, contrary to Hindoo law. Above all, he positively prohibited the burning of Hindoo widows against their will. He employed his Hindoo subjects equally with Mahommedans, abolished the capitation tax on infidels, as well as all taxes on pilgrims, and positively prohibited the making slaves of persons taken in war. He perfected the financial reforms which had been commenced in those provinces by Shir Shah. He remeasured all the lands capable of cultivation within the Empire; ascertained the produce of each begah;[3] determined the proportion to be paid to the public; and commuted it for a fixed money rent, giving the cultivator the option of paying in kind if he thought the money rate too high. He abolished at the same time a vast

[1] Elphinstone's History, vol. ii, p. 151.
[2] *Ib.*, p. 280.
[3] More than half an acre

number of vexatious taxes and fees to officers. The result of these wise measures was to reduce the amount of the public demand considerably. His instructions to his revenue officers have come down to us, and show his anxiety for the liberal administration of his system, and for the ease and comfort of his subjects. The tone of his instructions to his judicial officers was "just and benevolent;" he enjoined them to be sparing in capital punishments, and, unless in cases of dangerous sedition, to inflict none until he had received the Emperor's confirmation. He forbade mutilation or other cruelty as the accompaniment of capital punishment. He reformed and new modelled his army, paying his troops in cash from the treasury, instead of by assignments on the revenue. Besides fortifications and other public works he erected many magnificent buildings, which are described and eulogised by Bishop Heber. System and method were introduced into every part of the public service, and the whole of his establishments present "an astonishing picture of magnificence and good order, where unwieldy numbers are managed without disturbance, and economy is attended to in the midst of profusion."

Akbar appears with as much simplicity as dignity. European witnesses describe him as "affable and majestical, merciful and severe, temperate in diet, sparing in sleep, skilful in making guns, casting ordnance, and mechanical arts, curiously industrious, affable to the vulgar, loved and feared of his own, terrible to his enemies." Can we say as much for his great contemporaries—Elizabeth of England, or Henry the Fourth of France?

The Italian traveller, Pietro del Valle, who wrote in the last year of the reign of Jehanger, Akbar's son, A.D. 1623, bears this testimony to the character of that Prince, and to the condition of the people under his rule: "Generally all live much after a genteel way, and they do it securely, as well because the king does not prosecute his subjects with false accusations nor deprive them of anything when he sees them live splendidly and with the appearance of riches (as is often done in other Mahommedan countries), as because the Indians are inclined to those vanities."

But the reign of Shah Jehan, the grandson of Akbar, was the most prosperous ever known in India. His own dominions enjoyed almost uninterrupted tranquillity and good government; and, although Sir Thomas Roe was struck with astonishment at the profusion of wealth which was displayed when he visited the Emperor in his camp in 1615, in which at least two acres were covered with silk, gold carpets and hangings, as rich as velvet embossed with gold and precious stones could make them, yet we have the testimony of Tavernier that he who caused the celebrated peacock throne to be constructed, who, at the festival of his accession, scattered amongst the bystanders money and precious things equal to his own weight, "reigned not so much as a king over his subjects, but rather as a father over his family." His vigilance over his internal government was unremitting, and for the order and arrangement of his territory, and the good administration of every department of the State, no Prince that ever reigned in India could he compared to Shah Jehan.

All his vast undertakings were managed with so much economy that, after defraying the expenses of his great expedition to Candahar, his wars in Balk, and other heavy charges, and maintaining a regular army of 200,000 horse, Shah Jehan left a treasure which some reckoned at near six, others at twenty-four millions in coin, besides his vast accumulations in wrought gold and silver and in jewels.

His treatment of his people was beneficent and paternal, and his liberal sentiments towards those around him cannot be better shown than by the confidence which he so generously reposed in his sons.[1]

So stable was the foundation upon which this prosperity rested that the Empire continued to be in a flourishing condition for a large portion of the long, intolerant, and oppressive reign of Aurungzebe; and, notwithstanding the misgovernment which followed in the next thirty years, under a series of weak and wicked Princes, and the commotions which attended the breaking up of the Empire, the enormous wealth which Nadir Shah was enabled to carry away with him when he quitted Delhi in 1739 is proof that the country was still in a comparatively prosperous condition.

Among many distinguished Princes of the Deccan in the fifteenth and sixteenth centuries Mulik Amber, the Regent of Bijapore, holds a distinguished place both as a warrior and a statesman. He is described to have been a man of uncommon genius. He made his regency respected at home

[1] Elphinstone, vol. ii, p. 399.

and abroad. He abolished revenue-farming; substituted a fixed money assessment for a payment in kind, and revived the village establishments where they had fallen into decay. By such means the country soon became thriving and prosperous, and although his expenditure was liberal his finances were abundant. For upwards of twenty years he was the bulwark of his country against foreign conquest. Though almost constantly engaged in war, this great man found leisure to cultivate the arts of peace. He founded the city of Kirkee, built several splendid palaces, and introduced a system of internal administration which has left his name in every village far more venerated as a ruler than renowned as a general.[1]

Of the character of the Hindoo Sovereigns who were the contemporaries of the Mussulman Emperors in the fourteenth and fifteenth centuries we know nothing, but we know that their territories had attained to a pitch of power and splendour which had not been surpassed by their ancestors. We know also that the principal administrators of the Mussulman dynasties, with rare exceptions, were Hindoos—that they were entrusted with the command of armies, and with the regulation of the finances.

The "robber," Sevajee, who entered upon the scene in the latter part of the sixteenth century, and who shook the Moghul Empire to its foundation during the reign of Aurungzebe, was an able as well as a skilful general. His civil government was regular, and he was vigorous in exacting from his provincial and his village officers obedience to the rules which he laid down for the protection of the people. His enemies bear witness to his anxiety to mitigate the evils of war by humane regulations, which were strictly enforced. Altogether this robber hero has left a character which has never since been equalled or ever approached by any of his countrymen. None, however, of his military successes raise so high an idea of his talents as the spirit of his domestic administration,[2] and the effect of these appear to have been permanent for nearly eighty years after his death, viz., in 1758. We have the following interesting account of the state of the Mahratta Territory from the pen of Anquetil du Perron :—

"On February 14, 1758, I set out from Mahé for Goa, in

[1] Grant Duff, vol. i, pp. 94-6.
[2] Grant Duff's "History of the Mahrattas," vol. ii.

order to proceed to Surat, and, in all my routes, I took care to keep specimens of the money of all the States I passed through, so that I have examples of every coin that is current from Cape Cormorin to Delhi.

"From Surat, I passed the Ghats, the 27th of March the same year, about ten in the morning, and when I entered the country of the Mahrattas, I thought myself in the midst of the simplicity and happiness of the golden age where nature was yet unchanged, and war and misery were unknown. The people were cheerful, vigorous, and in high health, and unbounded hospitality was a universal virtue: every door was open, and friends, neighbours, and strangers, were alike welcome to whatever they found. When I came within seven miles of Aurungabad, I went to see the celebrated pagoda of Ellora."[1]

Sevajee had several worthy successors; amongst them were the Peishwahs, Ballajee Wiswanath, and his son Bajee Rao Bullal. This latter is said to have united the enterprise, and vigour, and hardihood of a Mahratta Chief with the polished manners, sagacity and address which frequently distinguished the Brahmins of the Concan. He had the head to plan and the hand to execute. To assiduous industry, and minute observation, he superadded a power of discrimination that brought him to fix his mind to points of political importance. He was a man of uncommon eloquence, penetration, and vigour, simple in his habits, enterprising and skilful as a military leader, and at all times partaking of the fare and sharing the privations of the meanest horseman.

His successor, Ballajee Rao, was a man of considerable political sagacity, of polished manners, and of great address; though indolent and voluptuous, he was generous and charitable, kind to his relations and dependents, and an enemy to external violence; amidst the distractions of war, he devoted much of his time to the civil administration of his territory; in his reign the condition of the whole Mahratta population was much ameliorated, the system of farming the revenues was abolished, the ordinary tribunals of civil justice were improved, and the Mahratta peasantry "have ever since blessed the days of Nana Laish Peishwah."[2] Although the

[1] Extracted from page 376 of the *Gentleman's Magazine* of 1762, headed "Brief Account of a Voyage to India, by M. Anquetil du Perron."

[2] Grant Duff's "History of the Mahrattas," vol. ii., p. 160.

military talents of Mahdoo Rao, who succeeded him, were conspicuous, yet his character as a sovereign is entitled to far higher praise. "He is deservedly celebrated for his firm support of the weak against the oppressive—of the poor against the rich—and, as far as the construction of society admitted—for his equity to all." He prevented his revenue officers from abusing their authority by vigilant superintendence, and by readily listening to the complaints of the common cultivators, and at that time, the Mahratta country, in proportion to its fertility, was more thriving than any other part of India. The preference shown in promoting officers who could boast of hereditary rights encouraged patriotism and applied national feeling to purposes of good government. Mahdoo Rao was assisted in his government by his minister, "the celebrated Rám," Ram Shastree, a pure and upright judge, whose conduct would have been considered admirable under any circumstances. The benefits which he conferred on his countrymen were principally by example. The weight and soundness of his opinions were universally acknowledged during his life, and the decisions of the Punchayets which gave decrees in his time are still considered precedents. His conduct and unwearied zeal had a wonderful effect in improving the people of all ranks; he was a pattern to the well disposed; the greatest man who did wrong stood in awe of Ram Shastree, and although persons possessed of rank and riches did, in several instances, try to corrupt him, none dared to repeat the experiment, or to impeach his integrity. His habits were simple in the extreme; it was a rule with him to keep nothing more in his house than sufficed for the day's consumption.[1] And such was his stirling virtue and stern sense of justice, that when asked by Ragonauth Rao what atonement he could make for his participation in the murder of his nephew, the Peishwah Nasrain Rao, the brother and immediate successor of Madhoo Rao: "The sacrifice of your own life," was the reply of the virtuous and undaunted Shastree; "for your future life cannot be passed in amendment, neither you nor your government can prosper; and for my own part, I will neither accept employment nor enter Poonah whilst you preside in the administration." He kept his word, and retired to a sequestered village near Waee.[2]

[1] Grant Duff, vol. ii., p. 208.
[2] *Ibid.*, p. 250.

The murdered Nasrain Rao, a youth of eighteen, was affectionate to his relations, kind to his domestics, and all but his enemies loved him.

The celebrated Hyder Ali was the contemporary and antagonist of Madhoo Rao, by whom he was more than once signally defeated; but Hyder turned these failures to account, and, like the Czar Peter, "submitted to be worsted that he might learn to be superior." By usurpation from his sovereign, the Rajah of Mysore, and by subsequent conquests, he made himself master of a territory 400 miles in length from north to south, and near 300 miles in breadth from east to west, with a population of many millions, an army of 300,000 men, and a revenue computed to amount to £5,000,000. Although almost constantly engaged in war, the improvement of his country and the strictest executive administration formed the constant objects of his care. The manufacturer and the merchant prospered in every part of his dominions; cultivation increased, new manufactures were established, and wealth flowed into the kingdom. Against negligence or malversation he was inexorable, the officers of revenue fulfilled their duty with fear and trembling; the slightest defalcation was summarily punished. He had his eye upon every corner of his own dominions, and in every Court of India. The minutest circumstance of detail was known to him; not a movement in the remotest corner could escape him; not a murmur or intention of his neighbours but flew to him. His secretaries successively read to him the whole correspondence of the day, and although unable to write himself, he dictated in few words the substance of the answer to be given, which was immediately written, read to him, and dispatched. He possessed the happy secret of uniting minuteness of detail with the utmost latitude of thought and enterprise. As his perseverance and dispatch of business were only equalled by his pointedness of information, so his conciseness and decision in the executive departments of a great government are probably unprecedented in the annals of man.[1]

He bequeathed to his son, Tippoo Sultan, an overflowing treasury, which he had filled; a powerful Empire, which he had created; an army of 300,000 men, that he had formed,

[1] For this character of Hyder, see Colonel Fullarton's "View of the Interests of India," and Wilke's "History of India," vol. ii.

disciplined, and inured to conquest; and a territory which, as contemporary historians and eye-witnesses assure us, had in no way deteriorated under the sway of his successor.

"When a person, travelling through a strange country, finds it well cultivated, populous with industrious inhabitants, cities newly founded, commerce extending, towns increasing, and everything flourishing, so as to indicate happiness, he will naturally conclude it to be under a form of government congenial to the minds of the people. This is a picture of Tippoo's country, and this is our conclusion respecting its government. It has fallen to our lot to tarry some time in Tippoo's dominions, and to travel through them as much, if not more, than any other officer in the field during the war; and we have reason to suppose his subjects to be as happy as those of any other sovereign; for we do not recollect of any complaints or murmurings among them; although, had causes existed, no time would have been more favourable for their utterance, because the enemies of Tippoo were in power and would have been gratified by any aspersion of his character. The inhabitants of the conquered countries submitted with apparent resignation to the direction of their conquerors; but by no means as if relieved from an oppressive yoke in their former government; on the contrary, no sooner did an opportunity offer than they scouted their new masters and gladly returned to their loyalty again."[1] "Whether from the operation of the system established by Hyder, from the principles which Tippoo adopted for his own conduct, or from his dominions having suffered little by invasion for many years, or from the effect of these several causes united, his country was found everywhere full of inhabitants and apparently cultivated to the utmost extent of which the soil was capable, while the discipline and fidelity of his troops in the field until their last overthrow were testimonies, equally strong, of the excellent regulations which existed in his army. His government, though strict and arbitrary, was the despotism of a strict and able sovereign, who nourishes, not oppresses, the subjects who are to be the means of his future aggrandisement, and his cruelties were, in general, inflicted only on those whom he considered as his enemies."[2]

It would be a great mistake, however, to suppose that all

[1] Moore's "Narrative of the War with Tippoo Sultan," p. 201.
[2] Dirom's "Narrative," p. 249.

this prosperity was created either by Hyder or his son. Their sway, which did not last for half a century, was too short for such a work. The foundation of it was laid by the ancient Hindoo dynasty which preceded them—the constructors of the magnificent canals by which Mysore is intersected, and which insures to the people certain and prodigal returns from its fertile soil.[1]

The British Government and their great rival, Hyder Ali, appeared on the political stage of India nearly at the same moment, and in the year that Hyder established his sway over Mysore, by usurpation from its legitimate sovereign, Bengal—the brightest jewel in the Imperial Crown of the Moghuls—came into our possession. Although still suffering from the scourge of a recent Mahratta invasion, Clive described the new acquisition as a country "of inexhaustible riches,"[2] and one that could not fail to make its new masters the richest corporation in the world. "In spite," says Mr. Macaulay, "of the Mussulman despot and of the Mahratta freebooter Bengal was known through the East as the Garden of Eden—as the rich kingdom. Its population multiplied exceedingly; distant provinces were nourished from the overflowing of its granaries; and the noble ladies of London and Paris were clothed in the delicate produce of its looms." From another authority[3] we have an account of the people of Bengal under its Native sovereigns, which we should be disposed to regard as fabulous if it did not come from one who had been long resident in the country, and who spoke from an intimate acquaintance with his subject. "In truth (says Mr. Holwell), it would be almost cruelty to molest this happy people; for in this district are the only vestiges of the beauty, purity, piety, regularity, equity, and strictness of the

[1] "The watercourses in Mysore, in magnitude rather resembling navigable canals, which, issuing from the embankments, are conducted with admirable skill along the slope of the hills, and occasionally across ravines, with a fall barely sufficient for the flow of the water, fertilise the whole of the intermediate space between their course and the river. These works are of great antiquity, the last in order of time, which supplies Seringapatam, having been completed in the year 1690 by Sheik Deo Raj Ovdaar, to whom the country is also indebted for some of its most useful civil regulations."—Wilke's "Mysore," vol. ii.

[2] "Life of Clive."

[3] "The enormous amount of capital in the hands of individuals at this time may be inferred from the fact that in the Mahratta invasion of 1742 the banking firm of Juggat Sett, of Moorshedabad—then the capital of Bengal—was plundered to the extent of two and a half millions sterling." —Duff's "History of the Mahrattas," vol. ii, page 12.

ancient Hindostan Government. Here the property, as well as the liberty of the people, are inviolate. Here no robberies are heard of, either public or private. The traveller, either with or without merchandise, becomes the immediate care of the Government, which allots him guards, without any expense, to conduct him from stage to stage ; and these are accountable for the safety and accommodatian of his person and effects. At the end of the first stage he is delivered over, with certain benevolent formalities, to the guards of the next, who, after interrogating the traveller as to the usage he had received in his journey, dismissed the first guard with a written certificate of their behaviour and a receipt for the traveller and his effects, which certificate and receipt are returnable to the commanding officer of the first stage, who registers the same and regularly reports it to the Rajah.

"In this form the traveller is passed through the country; and if he only passes he is not suffered to be at any expense for food, accommodation, or carriage for his merchandise or baggage; but it is otherwise if he is permitted to make any residence in one place above three days, unless occasioned by sickness, or any unavoidable accident. If anything is lost in this district, for instance a bag of money or other valuables, the person who finds it hangs it on the next tree, and gives notice to the nearest chowkey, or place of guard; the officer of which orders immediate publication of the same by beat of tomtom, or drum."[1]

"By the prudent administration of a system of sound policy and humanity, the rich province of Dacca was cultivated in every part, and abounded in everything requisite for the comfort and gratification of its inhabitants. Justice was administered with impartiality, and the conduct of its administrators, Gholab Aly Khan and Jeswunt Roy, gained great credit to their principal, Sarferaz Khan. Jeswunt Roy had been educated under the Nawab Aly Khan, whose example he emulated in purity, integrity, and indefatigable attention to business; and in framing his arrangements for the government of the province, he studied to render them conducive to the general ease and happiness of the people; he abolished all monopolies, and the imposts which had been laid upon the grain."[2]

[1] Holwell's Tracts upon India.
[2] Stewart's "History of Bengal," p. 430.

Such was the State of Bengal, when Alivardy Khan, the predecessor of Surajah Dowlah—of "Black Hole" memory—a nominal Lieutenant of the King of Delhi, assumed its government. Under his rule, notwithstanding many serious defects in his character, and some black deeds, the country was considerably improved. Many of his relations and friends, whom he employed in affairs of trust, were men of great abilities and merit. If guilty of negligence or oppression, he never failed to dismiss them; merit and good conduct were the only sure passports to his favour. He looked upon all his subjects as creatures of the same God, and placed Hindoos upon an equality with Mussulmans, choosing Hindoos for his Ministers, and nominating them to high military command as well as to civil situations of importance. It is not surprising, therefore, that the Hindoos served him and his family with exemplary zeal and fidelity. During his reign the revenues derived from the province, instead of being drawn to the distant treasury of Delhi, were spent on the spot. This was an incalculable advantage, and one cause of that prosperity which the people enjoyed under his reign, "when peace, plenty, and good order everywhere prevailed, and the profound and universal tranquillity was never disturbed, except by the occasional insurrection of a refractory Zemindar at some remote corner of a province."[1]

But in less than ten years after Bengal had become subject to British rule a great and sudden change had come over the land.

"Every ship (Mr. Macaulay tells us) from Bengal had for some time brought alarming tidings. The internal misgovernment of the province had reached such a pitch that it could go no further. What, indeed, was to be expected from a body of public servants exposed to temptation such that, as Clive once said, flesh and blood could not bear it, armed with irresistible power, and responsible only to the corrupt, turbulent, distracted, ill-informed Company, situated at such a distance that the average interval between the sending of a dispatch and the receipt of an answer was above a year and a half! Accordingly, during the five years which followed the departure of Clive from Bengal, the misgovernment of the English was carried to a point such as seemed hardly compatible with the very existence of society. The Roman

[1] Stewart's "History of Bengal." Asiatic Annual Register.

proconsul, who, in a year or two, squeezed out of a province the means of rearing marble palaces and baths on the shores of Campania, of drinking from amber, of feasting on singing birds, of exhibiting armies of gladiators and flocks of camelopards; the Spanish viceroy, who, leaving behind him the curses of Mexico or Lima, entered Madrid with a long train of gilded coaches, and of sumpter-horses, trapped and shod with silver, were now outdone. Cruelty, indeed, properly so-called, was not among the vices of the servants of the Company. But cruelty itself could hardly have produced greater evils than sprang from their unprincipled eagerness to be rich. They pulled down their creature, Meer Jaffer; they set up in his place another Nabob named Meer Cossim.

"But Meer Cossim had parts and a will; and, though sufficiently inclined to oppress his subjects himself, he could not bear to see them ground to the dust by oppressions which yielded him no profit—nay, which destroyed his revenue in the very source. The English accordingly pulled down Meer Cossim, and set up Meer Jaffer again; and Meer Cossim, after revenging himself by a massacre surpassing in atrocity that of the Black Hole, fled to the dominions of the Nabob of Oude. At every one of these revolutions the new Prince divided among his foreign masters whatever could be scraped together in the treasury of his fallen predecessor. The immense population of his dominions was given up as a prey to those who had made him a Sovereign, and who could unmake him. The servants of the Company obtained, not for their employers, but for themselves, a monopoly of almost the whole internal trade. They forced the Natives to buy dear and to sell cheap. They insulted with impunity the tribunals, the police, and the fiscal authorities of the country. They covered with their protection a set of Native dependents who ranged through the provinces, spreading desolation and terror wherever they appeared; every servant of a British factor was armed with all the power of the Company. Enormous fortunes were thus rapidly accumulated at Calcutta, while thirty millions of human beings were reduced to the extremity of wretchedness. They had been accustomed to live under tyranny, but never under tyranny like this. They found the little finger of the company thicker than the loins of Surajah Dowlah. Under their old masters they had at least one resource; when the evil became insupportable, the people rose and pulled down the Government. But the English Government was not to be shaken off. That Government, oppressive as the most oppressive form of barbarian despotism, was strong with all the strength of civilisation."[1]

"I can only say," writes Clive, "that such a scene of anarchy, corruption, and extortion was never seen or heard of in any country but Bengal; the three provinces of Bengal, Behar, and Orissa, producing a revenue of £3,000,000 sterling, have been under the absolute management of the Company's servants ever since Meer Jaffer's restoration to the Soobahship; and they have, both civil and military, exacted and levied contributions from every man of power and consequence, from the Nabob down to the lowest Zemindar. The trade has been carried on by free merchants, acting as gomastahs to the Company's servants, who, under the sanction of their names, have committed actions which make the name of the English stink in the nostrils of a Gentoo and a Mussulman; and the Company's servants have interfered with the revenues of the Nabob, turned out and put in the officers of the Government at their pleasure, and made everyone pay for their preferment."[2]

A severe famine followed upon this misgovernment, so that it is not surprising to find the Governor-General, Lord Cornwallis, twenty years afterwards, describing Bengal as a country that was hastening to decay. These are his words: "I am sorry to be obliged to say that agriculture and commerce have for many years been gradually declining; and that at present, excepting the class of Shroffs and Banyans, who reside almost entirely in great towns, the inhabitants of these provinces were advancing hastily to a general state of poverty and wretchedness. In this description I must even include almost every Zemindar in the Company's territories; which, though it may have been partly occasioned by their own indolence and extravagance, I am afraid must also be in a great measure attributed to the defects of our former system of mismanagement."

Nor was it in our own territory alone that the evil of our misrule was felt. It spread into the dominions of our allies. From our first connexion with the Nabob of Oude, his

[1] Macaulay's Essay on Lord Clive.
[2] Malcolm's "Life of Clive," vol. ii.

kingdom was made a carcass for the British to prey upon. "I fear," said Mr. Hastings,[1] when still vested with the supreme rule over India, and describing a state of things which he had been a party in producing, "I fear that our encroaching spirit, and the insolence with which it has been exerted, has caused our alliance to be as much dreaded by all the powers of Hindostan as our arms. Our encroaching spirit, and the uncontrolled and even protected licentiousness of individuals, have done more injury to our national reputation than our arms and the credit of our strength has raised it. Every person in India dreads a connexion with us, which they see attended with mortifying humiliation to those who have availed themselves of it." And as a signal example of this feeling, and of measures which awakened it, he adduces our dealings with the Nabob of Oude.

Before those dealings commenced, Oude, says the historian Mill, was in a high state of prosperity, it yielded, without pressure upon the people, a clear income of three millions, but by quartering, not only an army of soldiers, but a host of civilians upon him, we soon reduced the Nabob to a state of the bitterest distress and his country to poverty; so that after bearing the burthen for some years, he found his income reduced to half its former amount. In nine years, unjustifiable extortions, to the amount of thirty-four lacs of rupees (£340,000) per annum, "had been practised on that dependent province.[2] The numbers, influence, and enormous amount of the salaries, pensions, and encroachments of the Company's Service, civil and military, in the Vizier's service, said Mr. Hastings, have become an intolerable burthen upon the revenue and authority of his Excellency, and exposed us to the enmity and resentment of the whole country, by excluding the Native servants and adherents of the Vizier from the rewards of their services and attachment. I am afraid that few men would understand me if I were to ask by what right or policy we levied a tax on the Nabob Vizier, for the benefit of patronised individuals, and fewer still if I question the right or policy of imposing upon him an army for his protection, which he could not pay, and which he does not want; with what expression of features

[1] Gleig's "Life of W. Hastings," vol. ii.

[2] Mill's "History of India," vol. v., p. 316.

could I tell him to his face, 'You do not want it but you shall pay for it'? The first was a scandal to our Goverment, for every Englishman in Oude was possessed of an independent and sovereign authority. They learned, and taught others, to claim the revenue of lacs as their right, though they could gamble away more than two lacs (I allude to a known fact) at a sitting."[1] Mr. Hastings did not content himself with this exposure of events which had occured under his own administration. He withdrew a portion of that army which the Nabob "did not want, but for which he was obliged to pay," but this burden was fastened upon him again with additions by Mr. Hastings' successor, Lord Cornwallis, in spite of the Nabob's earnest deprecations. Having gradually increased our demands under the name of subsidy from £250,000 to £700,000 per annum, Lord Teignmouth further increased it, and Lord Wellesley, under a threat of seizing upon the whole in 1801 extorted a surrender from the Nabob of one half of his dominions, valued at £1,300,000 of annual revenue, in satisfaction of a demand which we had imposed upon him of £700,000. But our exactions did not stop here; between the years 1815 and 1825, we extracted more than four millions under the name of loans from the Nabob, or, "as they might be more justly described," says the Governor-General, Lord W. Bentinck, "unwilling contributions extorted by fear of our power:"[2] for which we gave him the empty title of King, and a territory entirely unproductive, little better than a wilderness.[3]

This is a brief history of our dealings with Oude, not penned by those who have suffered from them, but by the doers themselves. It is based upon facts that are upon our records, and is therefore indisputable. If Oude, then, is now misgoverned—if its people are impoverished and oppressed—who is to blame—the Native Sovereigns, or those who have thus trampled upon the Native Sovereigns? Let Englishmen—now that the great question of India is before them—decide upon this question; and let them not be drawn away from its merits by an appeal to the personal character of some of the chief actors in this drama.

Lord Cornwallis was indisputably a just man, Lord Teign-

[1] "Life of W. Hastings," vol. ii., p. 458.
[2] Minute, July 30, 1831.
[3] Bishop Heber's "Travels," vol. ii., pp. 81-87.

mouth a religious man, and Lord Wellesley a great man; nevertheless, there was nothing wise or great, just or religious, in their treatment of their helpless allies, the Sovereign Princes of Oude.

We have seen that when the Governor-General, Lord Cornwallis, was pronouncing the Kingdom of Bengal to be in a state of rapid decay, the Kingdom of Mysore, under the rule of Tippoo, was upon the evidence of eye-witnesses in a state of high prosperity; that its prosperity had in no way diminished many years afterwards under the regency of Poorneah, we have, amongst many others, the testimony of the great Duke, who, speaking from his own observation, pronounced the government of Mysore to be in every respect entitled to applause, and, as a mark of his approbation and esteem, made the Dewan Poorneah a present of his picture.[1]

"Every trait," says the British Resident of that day,[2] "in the character of Poorneah marks him as an extraordinary man. . . . To a mind of singular vigour he added an extensive acquaintance with the resources of the country, and an intimate knowledge of characters. The revenue of Mysore has been raised to its present amount by the superior management of Poorneah; by his attention to the repair of tanks and watercourses, and the construction of roads and bridges: by the encouragement which he has given to strangers to resort to and settle in Mysore, and his general endeavours to improve the agriculture of the country and the situation of the people under the Government of the Rajah."[3]

Contemporary with Poorneah, and in no ways inferior to him, was Nana Furnawese, who for a quarter of a century administered the territory of the Peishwah, during the minority of Bajee Rao. "To attempt a character of this great statesman would be to detail a history of Mahratta politics for the last twenty-five years, during which he discharged the duties of Minister with abilities unequalled. During the long and important period of his administration, by the force and energy of his single mind, he held together his vast Empire—composed of members whose interests were as opposite as the most anomalous elements—and by the

[1] Colonel Wilkes.
[2] Duke of Wellington's Despatches, vol. I.
[3] Official Report on Mysore, 1805; Asiatic Annual Register, 1805.

versatility of his genius, the wisdom and firmness and moderation of his government, he excited this mass of incongruities to one mutual and common effort. With that wise and foreseeing policy which, strong in its own resources, equally rejects the extremes of confidence and despair, he supplied from the fertility of unexhausted genius an expedient for every possible event."[1]

The state of the territory which has been so long administered by this distinguished man was visited not many years after by the late Sir John Malcolm, who thus describes its condition:—

"It has not happened to me ever to see countries better cultivated, and more abounding in all produce of the soil, as well as in commercial wealth, than the southern Mahratta districts, when I accompanied the present Duke of Wellington to that country in the year 1803. I particularly here allude to those large tracts near the borders of the Kistnah. Poonah, the capital of the Peishwah, was a very wealthy and a thriving commercial town, and there was as much cultivation in the Deccan as it was possible an arid and unfruitful country could admit."[2]

And of another large portion of the Mahratta territory, Malwa, now and formerly under the sovereignty of the Holkar family, and of the character of some of its rulers, we have the same favourable testimony from the same distinguished witness:—

"With respect to Malwa, I saw it in a state of ruin, caused by the occupancy for a period of more than half-a-century of that fine country by the Mahratta armies, the Pindarries, and, indeed, the assembled predatory hordes of all India. Yet, even at that period, I was perfectly surprised at the difference that exists between a distant view of such countries and a nearer examination of their actual condition. I had ample means afforded to me as the person appointed to occupy that territory, and to conduct its civil, military, and political administration, to learn all that the records of Government could teach, and to obtain from other sources full information of this country; and I certainly entered upon my duties with the complete conviction that commerce would be unknown, and that credit could not exist in a province

[1] Asiatic Annual Register, vol. v., p. 70; Miscellaneous Extracts.
[2] Evidence before Committee of Commons, 1833, p. 41.

which had long possessed, from its position, the transit trade between the rich provinces of Western India and the whole of the North-West Provinces of Hindostan, as well as the more eastern ones of Saugor and Bundlecund. I found, to my surprise, that in correspondence with the first commercial and moneyed men of Rajpootana, Bundlecund, and Hindostan, as well as with those of Guzerat, dealings in money to a large amount had continually taken place at Oogein and other cities, where soucars or bankers of character and credit were in a flourishing state, and that goods to a great amount had not only continually passed through the province, but that the insurance offices which exist through all parts of India, and include the principal moneyed men, had never stopped their operations, though premiums rose, at a period of danger, to a high amount. The Native Government of Malwa, when tranquillity was established through our arms, wanted nothing but that which the attachment of the Natives of India to their soil soon supplied them with, a return of the inhabitants. And I do not believe that in that country the introduction of our direct rule could have contributed more, nor indeed so much, to the prosperity of the commercial and agricultural interests as the re-establishment of the efficient rule of its former Princes and chiefs, who, though protected from attack, are quite free in their internal administration from our interference. With respect to the southern Mahratta districts, of whose prosperity I have before spoken, if I refer, as I must, to their condition before the last few years of Bajee Row's misrule, I do not think that either their commercial or agricultural interests are likely to be improved under our rule, except in that greatest of blessings, exemption from wars which, while under our protection, they equally enjoy, and I must unhesitatingly state that the provinces belonging to the family of 'Putwurden,' and some other chiefs on the banks of the Kistna, present a greater agricultural and commercial prosperity than almost any I know in India. I refer this to their system of administration, which, though there may be at periods exactions, is, on the whole, mild and paternal; to the knowledge and almost devotion of the Hindoos to all agricultural pursuits; to their better understanding, or, at least, better practice than us in many parts of the administration, particularly in raising towns and villages to prosperity from the encouragement given to moneyed men, and to the introduction of capital; and, above all, to Jagheerdars (Kandownos) residing on their estates, and these provinces being administered by men of rank, who live and die on the soil, and are usually succeeded in office by their sons or near relatives. If these men exact money at times in an arbitrary manner, all their expenditure, as well as all they receive, is limited to their own provinces; but, above all causes which promote prosperity, is the invariable support given to the village and other Native institutions, and to the employment, far beyond what our system admits, of all classes of the population."[1]

"The success of Allia Baee in the internal administration of her dominions was altogether wonderful. . . . . The undisturbed internal tranquillity of the country was even more remarkable than its exemption from foreign attack. This was equally produced by her manner of treating the peaceable as well as the more turbulent and predatory classes; she was indulgent to the former, and although strict and severe, just and considerate towards the latter. . . . . The fond object of her life was to promote the prosperity of all around her; she rejoiced, we are told, when she saw bankers, merchants, farmers, and cultivators rise to affluence, and so far from deeming their increased wealth a ground of exaction, she considered it a legitimate claim of increased favour and protection. . . . . There would be no end to a minute detail of the measures of her internal policy. It is sufficient to observe she has become by general suffrage the model of good government in Malwa. . . . . She built several forts, and at that of Jaum constructed a road with great labour and cost over the Vindhya range, where it is almost perpendicular. . . . . Among the Princes of her own nation it would have been looked upon as sacrilege to have become her enemy, or indeed not to have defended her against any hostile attempt. She was considered by all in the same light. The Nizam of the Deccan and Tippoo Sultan held her in the same respect as the Peishwah, and Mahomedans joined with the Hindoos in prayer for her long life and prosperity.

"In the most sober view that can be taken of her character, she certainly appears within her limited sphere to have been one of the purest and most exemplary rulers that ever existed, and she affords a striking example of the

[1] Sir John Malcolm.

practical benefit a mind may receive from preferring worldly duties under a deep sense of responsibility to its Creator."[1]

Equally favourable testimony to the condition of the dominions of the Rajah of Berar, another member of the great Mahratta confederacy, was given by eye-witnesses :—

"The thriving condition of the province, indicated by the appearance of its capital (says a European traveller) and confirmed by that of the districts which we subsequently traversed, demands from me a tribute of praise to the ancient Princes of the country. Without the benefit of navigation (for the 'Nerbudda' is not here navigable) and without much inland commerce, but under the fostering hand of a race of good Princes, a numerous people tilled a fertile country, and still preserve in the neatness of their homes, in the number and magnificence of their temples, their ponds, and other public works; in the size of their towns, and in the frequency of their plantations, the undoubted signs of enviable prosperity. The whole merit may be safely ascribed to the former government, for the praise of good administration is rarely merited by Mahratta chieftains, and it is sufficient applause to say that the Chief of Saugor in twenty years, and the Rajah of Berar in four, have not much impaired the prosperity which they found."[2]

"We now," says another traveller in Berar, "continued our journey through a fine champaign country, abundantly watered with rivulets that issue from the neighbouring mountains. It was entirely free from jungle, full of villages, and beautifully varied with tufts of trees and pools of water. It is more easy to conceive than express the delight we experienced in changing the difficulties of the former part of the journey. The Mahratta Government being well established in this part of the route, we experienced very civil and hospitable treatment, and found plenty of every kind of grain, which this highly-cultivated country produced at a very cheap rate;" and although inland commerce derives very little encouragement from the Government, which pays no attention to the public roads, yet the whole exports in

[1] Malcolm's "History of Central India," vol. 1, pp. 176, 195.

[2] Journey from Mirzapore to Nagpore in 1798, by a Member of the Asiatic Society. Asiatic Annual Register, vol. 8; Miscellaneous Tracts p. 32.

seasons of plenty are said to employ a hundred thousand bullocks.[1]

From the Mahratta we pass to the Rajpoot States; and here again we bring the evidence of an eye-witness to bear upon their condition :—

"As compared with the cultivation of the King of Oude's dominions, it has always struck me that there was a marked superiority in the appearance of the British territory. At the same time, it is but fair to state that I have beheld small independent States, governed by Hindoo Rajahs, where the cultivation appeared superior to that of the Company's provinces, and where the independent aid of the peasantry announced a greater security of rights. In the year 1810, when a large force marched beyond the British territory, the division halted for nearly two months within the dominion of the Rajah of Tihree, the flourishing condition of which excited the admiration of the whole army."[2]

"In passing through the Rampore territory,[3] we could not fail to notice the high state of cultivation to which it has attained, when compared with the surrounding country; scarcely a spot of land is neglected : and although the season was by no means favourable, the whole district seems to be covered with an abundant harvest. As we have no reason to conclude from the description we had received of the present Regent that this state of prosperity had been produced by any personal exertions on his part, we were solicitous to trace its source, and to discover whether, in the nature of the tenures, the mode of arrangement or otherwise, there were any peculiar circumstances which it might be useful for us to advert to in the course of executing the duty entrusted to us. The management of the Nawab Fyz-oolah Khan is celebrated throughout the country. It was the management of an enlightened and liberal landlord, who devoted his time and attention and employed his own capital in promoting the prosperity of his country. When works of magnitude were required, which could not be accomplished by the efforts of the individual, the means of undertaking them were supplied by his bounty. Watercourses were constructed, the rivulets were sometimes made to overflow and fertilise the adjacent

[1] Miscellaneous Tracts, Asiatic Annual Register, vol. ii, p. 166.
[2] White's "State of British India," 1822.
[3] Report from Commissions upon the North-West Provinces, 1808.

districts, and the paternal care of a popular chief was constantly exerted to afford protection to his subjects, to stimulate their exertions, to direct their labours to useful objects, and to promote by every means the success of the undertaking.

"If the comparison for the same territory be made between the management of the Rohillas and that of our own government, *it is painful to think that the balance of advantage is clearly in favour of the former.* After seven years' possession of the country, it appears by the report that the revenue has increased only by two lacs of rupees, or £20,000. The papers laid before Parliament show that in twenty years which have since elapsed, the collective revenues of Rohilcund, and the other districts forming the ceded provinces of Oude, had actually declined £200,000 per annum.

"We could not fail, however, to observe the singular difference which the application of greater capital and greater industry is capable of producing in the state of contiguous lands. While the surrounding country seemed to have been visited by a desolating calamity, the lands of the Rajahs Diaram and Bugwaut Sing, under every disadvantage of season were covered with crops produced by a better husbandry, or by greater labour. It should here be explained that the neighbouring lands alluded to in the report *consisted of British territory, already five years in our occupation.*"[1]

And even after all the abuse that has been lavished upon Oude and upon its sovereigns, we find upon unexceptionable testimony that neither the state of the country nor the character of its sovereigns is so black as it is represented by our own officials.

"I was pleased and surprised (says Bishop Heber),[2] after all I had heard of Oude, to find the country so completely under the plough, since, were the oppression as great as is sometimes stated, I cannot think that we should witness so considerable a population and so much industry; yet that sufficient anarchy and misrule exists, the events of yesterday afforded sufficient reason for supposing.

"We found invariable civility, and good-natured people backing their carts and elephants to make room for us, and displaying, on the whole, a far greater spirit of hospitality

[1] Appendix to Political Report, 1882, pp. 36-37.
[2] Bishop Heber's "Journal," vol. ii, pp. 77-79.

and accommodation than ten foreigners would have met with in London.

"The present king is fond of literary and philosophical pursuits.

"Saadat Ali, himself a man of talent and acquirements, fond of business, and well qualified for it, but, in his latter days, unhappily addicted to drunkenness, left him a country, with six millions of people, a fertile soil, a most compact position, and upwards of two millions of ready money in the treasury, with a well regulated system of finance, a peasantry tolerably well contented, no army to maintain, except for police or parade, and everything likely to produce an auspicious reign.

"I can bear witness certainly to the truth of the king's statement, that his territories are really in a far better state of cultivation than I had expected to find them. From Lucknow to Sandee, where I am now writing, the country is as populous and well cultivated as most of the Company's provinces. I cannot, therefore, but suspect that the misfortunes and anarchy of Oude are somewhat overrated."—P. 89.

"He was fond of study, and in all points of oriental philology and philosophy is really reckoned a learned man, besides having a strong taste in its mechanics and chemistry.

"Like our James I., he is said to be naturally just and kind-hearted; and with all those who have access to him he is extremely popular. No single act of violence and oppression has ever been ascribed to him, or supposed to be perpetrated with his knowledge; and his errors have been a want of economy in his expenses, a want of accessibility to his subjects, a blind confidence in favourites, and, as will be seen, an unfortunate, though not very unnatural, attachment to different points of etiquette and prerogative." He is described by Lord Hastings as a Sovereign admirable for uprightness, humanity, and mild elevation.

The same high authority testifies to the prosperous condition of the State of Bhurtpore under the Native Sovereigns:

"The country, though still bare of wood, has more scattered trees than we had seen for many days back; and notwithstanding that the soil is sandy, and only irrigated from wells, it is one of the best cultivated and watered tracts which I have seen in India. The crops of corn now on the ground were really beautiful; that of cotton, though gone by, showed marks of having been a very good one. What is a sure proof of wealth, I saw several sugar mills, and large pieces of ground where the cane had just been cleared; and, contrary to the usual habits of India, where the cultivators keep as far as they can from the highway, to avoid the various molestations to which they are exposed from thieves and travellers, there was often a narrow pathway winding through the green wheat and mustard crops, and even this was crossed continually by the channels which conveyed water to the furrows.

"The population did not seem great; but the villages which we saw were apparently in good condition and repair, and the whole afforded so pleasing a picture of industry, and was so much superior to anything which I had been led to expect in Rajpootana, of *which I had seen in the Company's territories* since leaving the southern parts of Rohilcund, that I was led to suppose that either the Rajah of Bhurtpore was an extremely exemplary and parental governor, or that the system of management adopted in the British provinces was in some way or other less favourable to the improvement and happiness of the country than some of the Native States."[1]

To the high character of Pertab Sing—the first Rajah of Sattara—as a ruler, and to the prosperous condition of his territory, we have the emphatic testimony of the British Government itself:—

"We have been highly gratified by the information, from time to time transmitted to us by our Government, on the subject of your Highness's exemplary fulfilment of the duties of that elevated situation in which it has pleased Providence to place you.

"A course of conduct so suitable to your Highness's exalted station, and so well calculated to promote the prosperity of your dominions, and the happiness of your people, as that which you have wisely and uniformly pursued, while it reflects the highest honour on your own character, has imparted to our minds the feelings of unqualified satisfaction and pleasure. The liberality also which you have displayed in executing, at your own cost, various public works of great utility, and which has so greatly raised your reputation in the eyes of the Princes and people of India,

[1] Bishop Heber's "Journal," vol. ii, p. 361.

gives you an additional claim to our approbation, respect, and applause.

"Impressed with these sentiments the Court of Directors of the East India Company have unanimously resolved to transmit to you a sword, which will be presented to you through the Government of Bombay, and which we trust you will receive with satisfaction, as a token of their high esteem and regard."[1]

And whilst thus congratulating this Rajah on the prosperity of his dominions, and the happiness of his people, the condition of some thirty millions of Native British subjects, who have been under British rule for almost a century, is thus described by an unimpeachable witness[2]:—

"No one has ever attempted to contradict the fact that the condition of the Bengal peasantry is almost as wretched and degraded as it is possible to conceive, living in the most miserable hovels, scarcely fit for a dog kennel, covered with tattered rags, and unable, in too many instances, to procure more than a single meal a day for himself and family. The Bengal ryot knows nothing of the most ordinary comforts of life. We speak without exaggeration when we affirm that if the real condition of those who raise the harvest, which yields between three and four millions a year, was fully known, it would make the ears of one who heard thereof tingle."

Now, one of two things: either the British Government found the people of Bengal in this appalling state, or they have been reduced to this state under British rule. If this was their normal state, what has the British Government been doing for a century that they have not extricated them from it?—or if they have sunk into this state, what has that Government to say for itself in extenuation of such a result? We have seen it admitted by the Governor-General Lord Cornwallis that in his time—that is, sixty years ago—the "people were advancing hastily to a state of poverty and wretchedness." We have it upon record, that almost immediately after our acquisition of Bengal, the Government, instead of being the "richest corporation in the world," as promised by Clive, were without a shilling in their treasury.[3] From the times of Akbar down to the government of Meer

[1] Letter of the Court of Directors, Par. Pa. A.D. 1843. No. 569, p. 1268.
[2] Dr. Marshman, *Friend of India*, April 1st, 1852.
[3] Vansittart's Narrative of Events in Bengal.

Jaffer, A.D. 1837, the annual amount of revenue, and the modes of levying it, continued with little variation. But in order to raise the sum which he had engaged to pay us after his elevation, and the annual tribute which he was at the same time bound to pay the King of Delhi, he raised the assessment upon the lands, and multiplied exactions. We continued these extra cesses, and from 1765 to 1790 our revenue system was one of constant changes and experiments, heavy arrears were outstanding, and the country was represented as already exhausted and impoverished.

. . . .

"A new progeny [said the Governor-General, Lord Hastings] has grown up under our hand; and the principal features which show themselves in a generation thus formed beneath the shade of our regulations are a spirit of litigation which our judicial establishments cannot meet and a morality certainly deteriorated. If in the system, or the practical execution of it, we should be found to have relaxed many ties of moral or religious restraint, or the conduct of individuals to have destroyed the influence of former institutions without substituting any check in their place—to have given loose to the most froward passions of human nature, and deprived the wholesome contact of public opinion and private censure, we shall be forced to acknowledge that our regulations have been productive of a state of things which imperiously calls on us to provide an immediate remedy for so serious a mischief."[1]

This was the judgment of a Governor-General upon the effect produced by our judicial regulations upon the character of the people; and with respect to the protection of person and property, we have it stated upon competent authority,[2] that it is at this moment just as it has been for the last fifty years, viz., so bad that no man of property within a circle of sixty or seventy miles round Calcutta "can retire to rest with the certainty that he shall not be robbed of it again before morning;" and yet, with all this evidence before us, evidence that, notwithstanding our best intentions, "our administration," as the Governor-General Lord W. Bentinck admitted, "had in all its branches, revenue, judicial, and police, been a failure." We boast of progress—of Indian progress!

[1] Lord Hastings' Minute, in Parliamentary Papers, 1827, p. 157.
[2] *Friend of India*, 28th August, 1851.

The object of these pages is to show, on behalf of those who cannot answer for themselves, that they are neither so black, nor we so white, as we paint them and ourselves—that their government and institutions were neither so defective, nor ours so perfect, as we assert them to have been; and that the "History of Indian Progress," which we create in bulky volumes, only means, after all, that the Christian Indian government of the nineteenth century is better than the Mahomedan and Hindoo governments of the fifteenth and sixteenth centuries. This is the extent of our pretensions, and we can only support this claim by depreciating the characters and doings of our predecessors, and exaggerating our own, and after all leaving it much in doubt whether the balance is really in our favour.

SOME FURTHER OPINIONS ON THE SUBJECT OF NATIVE RULERS AND BRITISH RULE.

By Dadabhai Naoroji.

March, 1899.

The Court of Directors, in their letter to Bengal of February 8th, 1764, say:[1]—

"One great source of the disputes . . . . appears evidently to have taken its rise from the unwarrantable and licentious manner of carrying on the private trade of the Company's servants, their goomastas etc. . . . .

"Your deliberations on the inland trade have laid open to us a scene of most cruel oppression. . . . ."

Lord Clive's letter to Thomas Rous, Esq., dated at Madras, April 17th, 1765, says:—

"The confusion we behold, what does it arise from? Rapacity and luxury. . . . ."

The Court of Directors' letter to Bengal, April 26th, 1765:—

"That they (the English in Bengal) have been guilty of violating treaties, of great oppression, and a combination to enrich themselves."

On September 30th, 1765, Lord Clive wrote to the Court of Directors:—

"It is no wonder that the lust of riches should readily embrace

1 Parliamentary Report of Committee, of May, 1772, vol. iii, pp. 294, etc.

the proffered means of its gratification, or that the instruments of your power should avail themselves of their authority, and proceed even to extortion in those cases where simple corruption could not keep pace with their rapacity. Examples of this sort set by superiors could not fail of being followed in a proportionate degree by inferiors; the evil was contagious and spread among the civil and military, down to the writer, the ensign, and the free merchant. . . . . All is not safe, danger still subsists from your formidable enemies within—luxury, corruption, avarice, rapacity."

The Bengal letter of September 30th, 1765, to the Court of Directors :—

"The opportunity of acquiring immense fortunes was too inviting to be neglected and the temptation too powerful to be resisted . . . . this indulgence (to receive presents) has certainly been extended to the most shameful oppression and flagrant corruption . . . . together with the recent proofs before us of notorious and avowed corruption . . . . and the numberless complaints made of grievous exactions and oppressions. . . ."

Court of Directors' letter to Bengal, December 24th, 1765:—

"Your deliberations in the inland trade have laid open to us a scene of most cruel oppression."

Bengal letter of January 31st, 1766, to the Court of Directors :—

". . . . for we must observe, although with much regret, that the misconduct of individuals hath rendered the English name so odious. . . . It was firmly our intention to avoid further retrospection of the conduct of our administration, so notoriously corrupt and meanly venal throughout every department."

Letter of the Court of Directors to Bengal, May 17th, 1766 :—

". . . . We have the strongest sense of the deplorable state . . . . from the corruption and rapacity of our servants, and the universal depravity of manners throughout the settlement . . . . think the vast fortunes acquired . . . . by a scene of the *most tyrannic* and *oppressive conduct that ever was known in any age or country*." [Italics are mine.]

Lord CLIVE'S letter to GEORGE DUDLEY, Esq., dated Calcutta, September 8th, 1766 :—

"But retrospection into actions which have been buried in oblivion for so many years; which if inquired into, may produce discoveries which cannot bear the light . . . . but may bring disgrace upon the nation, and at the same time blast the reputation of great and good families."

SIR THOMAS MUNRO.

"It would be more desirable that we should be expelled from the country altogether, than that the result of our system of government should be such an abasement of a whole people."[1]

[1] India Reform Tracts, Tract vi., p. 112.

"But even if we could be secured against every internal commotion, and could retain the country quietly in subjection, I doubt much if *the condition of the people would be better than under their Native Princes.*" [Italics are mine.]

"The consequence, therefore, of the conquest of India by the British arms, would be in place of raising *to debase the whole people.* There is, perhaps, no example of any conquest in which the Natives have been so completely excluded from all share of the government of their country as British India. Among all the disorders of the Native States, the field is open to every man to raise himself, and hence among them there is a spirit of emulation, of restless enterprise, and independence far preferable to the servility of our Indian subjects."

In a minute, dated December 31, 1824, he wrote:—

"It is not enough that we confer on the natives the benefits of just laws and of moderate taxation, unless we endeavour to raise their character; but under a foreign Government there are so many causes which tend to depress it, that it is not easy to prevent it from sinking. It is an old observation that he who loses his liberty loses half his virtue. This is true of nations as well as of individuals. To have no property scarcely degrades more in one case than in the other to have property at the disposal of a foreign Government in which we have no share. The enslaved nation loses the privileges of a nation, as the slave does those of a free man; it loses the privilege of taxing itself, of making its own laws, of having any share in their administration or in the general government of the country. . . . . It is not the arbitrary power of a national sovereign, but subjection to a foreign one, that destroys national character and extinguishes national spirit. When a people cease to have a national character to maintain, they lose the mainspring of whatever is laudable both in public and in private life, and the private sinks with the public character."—(*Indian Spectator*, February 19th, 1899.)

Mill's "History of India," by J. Wilson, vol. vi, p. 671 (India Reform Tracts, Tract ii, p. 3), thus describes the effect of the system of the British rule:—

"It is an exhausting drain upon the resources of the country, the issue of which is replaced by no reflux; it is an extraction of the life-blood from the veins of national industry, which no subsequent introduction of nourishment is furnished to restore."

Mr. Montgomery Martin writes ("Eastern India, 1838," vol. i, p. xii):—

"The annual drain of £3,000,000 on British India has amounted in thirty years, at 12 per cent. (the usual Indian rate) compound interest, to the enormous sum of £723,900,000 sterling. . . . So constant and accumulating a drain, even in England, would soon impoverish her. How severe, then, must be its effects on India, where the wage of a labourer is from twopence to threepence a day! Were the hundred millions of British subjects in India converted into a *consuming* population, what a market would be presented for British capital, skill and industry!"

What, then, must be the condition now, when the drain is getting perhaps ten times larger, and a large amount besides is eaten in the country itself by others than the people. Even an ocean would be dried up if a portion of its evaporation did not always return to it as rain or river. If interest were added to the drain, what an enormous loss would it be!

Mr. FREDERICK JOHN SHORE, of the Bengal Civil Service says (1837):—

"But the halcyon days of India are over; she has been drained of a large proportion of the wealth she once possessed, and her energies have been cramped by a sordid system of misrule to which the interest of millions have been sacrificed for the benefit of the few. The gradual impoverishment of the people and country, under the mode of rule established by the British Government, has. . . ." "The grinding extortions of the English Government have effected the impoverishment of the country and people to an extent almost unparalleled. . . ."

"The fundamental principle of the English had been to make the whole Indian Nation subservient in every possible way to the interest and benefit of themselves. . . . Had the welfare of the people been our object a very different course would have been adopted, and very different results would have followed; for, again and again, I repeat it, there is nothing in the circumstance itself, of our being foreigners of different colour and faith, that should occasion the people to hate us. We may thank ourselves for having made their feelings towards us what they are."

SIR GEORGE WINGATE (1859):—

"Such is the nature of the tribute we have so long exacted from India. . . . From this explanation some faint conception may be formed of the cruel crushing effect of the tribute upon India. . . ." "The Indian tribute, whether weighed in the scale of justice or viewed in the light of our interests, will be found at variance with humanity, with common sense, and with the received maxims of political science."

LORD SALISBURY.

On January 22nd, 1867, Lord Salisbury (then Lord Cranborne and Secretary of State for India) said (*Hansard*, vol. 185, p. 839):—

"But there are other considerations, and I think the hon. gentleman (Sir Henry Rawlinson) stated them very fairly and eloquently. I do not myself see our way at present to employing very largely the Natives of India in the regions under our immediate control. *But it would be a great evil if the result of our dominion was that the Natives of India who were capable of government should be absolutely and hopelessly excluded from such a career.* The great advantage of the existence of Native States is that they afford an outlet for statesmanlike capacity such as has been alluded to. I need not dwell upon the consideration to which the hon. gentleman so eloquently referred, but I think *that the existence of a well-governed*

Native State is a real benefit, not only to the stability of our rule, but because, more than anything, it raises the self-respect of the Natives and forms an ideal to which the popular feelings aspire."

On May 24th, 1867, Lord IDDESLEIGH (then Sir Stafford Northcote and Secretary of State for India) said (*Hansard*, vol. 187, p. 1,068) :—

"*Our Indian policy should be founded on a broad basis. There might be difficulties ; but what we had to aim at was to establish a system of Native States which might maintain themselves in a satisfactory relation*, keeping the virtues of Natives States, and getting rid, as far as possible, of their disadvantages. We must look to the great *natural* advantages which the government of a Native State must *necessarily* have. Under the English system there were advantages which would probably never be under Native Administration—regularity, love of law and order and justice."

Had Lord Iddesleigh lived he would have with pleasure seen that the advantages he refers to are being attained in the Native States. Lord Iddesleigh proceeds :—

"But Native Administration had the advantage in *sympathy between the governors and the governed.* Governors were able to appreciate and understand the prejudices and wishes of the governed; especially in the case of Hindu States the religious feelings of the people were enlisted in favour of their governors instead of being aroused against us.[1] He had been told by gentlemen from India that nothing impressed them more than walking the streets of some Indian town, they looked up at the houses on each side and asked themselves, 'what do we really know of these people—of their modes of thought, their feelings, their prejudices—and at what great disadvantage, in consequence, do we administer the government ?' The English Government must necessarily labour under great disadvantages,[2] and *we should endeavour as far as possible to develop the system of Native government to bring out Native talent and statesmanship, and to enlist in the cause of government all that was great and good in them.* Nothing could be more wonderful than our Empire in India ; but we ought to consider on what conditions we hold it and how our predecessors held it. The greatness of the Mogul Empire depended on the liberal policy that was pursued by men like the great Emperor Akbar and his successors availing themselves of Hindu talent and assistance, and identifying themselves as far as possible with the people of the country. They ought to take a lesson from such circumstances. *If they were to do their duty towards India they could only discharge that duty by obtaining assistance and counsel of all who are great and good in that country.* It would be absurd in them to say that there was not a large fund of statesmanship and ability in the Indian character. They really must not be too proud. They were always ready to speak of the English Government as so infinitely superior to anything in the way of Indian Government. But if the Natives of India were disposed

[1] The same can be said about the Muhammadans and other people.

[2] The greatest of them is the economic evil which Lord Salisbury has truly called the bleeding of the country.

to be equally critical, it would be possible for them to find out weak places in the harness of the English administration. The system in India was one of great complexity. It was a system of checks and counter-checks, and very often great abuses failed to be controlled from want of a proper knowledge of and sympathy with the Natives." [The italics are mine.]

On the same day Lord SALISBURY, supporting Lord Iddesleigh, said (*Hansard*, vol. 187, p. 1073):—

"*The general concurrence of opinion of those who know India best is that a number of well-governed small Native States are in the highest degree advantageous to the development of the political and moral condition of the people of India.* The hon. gentleman (Mr. Laing) arguing in the strong official line seems to take the view that everything is right in British territory and everything dark in Native territory. Though he can cite the case of Oudh, I venture to doubt if it could be established as a general view of India as it exists at present. If Oudh is to be quoted against Native Government, the Report of the Orissa Famine, which will be presented in a few days, will be found to be another and far more terrible instance to be quoted against English rule. *The British Government has never been guilty of the violence and illegality of Native Sovereigns. But it has faults of its own, which, though they are far more guiltless in intention, are more terrible in effect.* Its tendency to routine; its listless, heavy heedlessness, sometimes the result of its elaborate organisation; a fear of responsibility, an extreme centralisation—all these results traceable to causes for which no man is culpable, *produce an amount of inefficiency which, when reinforced by natural causes and circumstances, creates a terrible amount of misery.* All these things must be taken into consideration when you compare our elaborate and artificial system of government with the more rough and ready system of India. In cases of emergency, unless you have men of peculiar character on the spot, the simple form of Oriental government will produce effects more satisfactory than the more elaborate system of English rule. I am not by this denying that our mission in India is to reduce to order, to civilise and develop the Native Governments we find there.[1] But I demur to that wholesale condemnation of a system of government which will be utterly intolerable on our own soil, but which has grown up amongst the people subjected to it. It has a fitness and congeniality for them impossible for us adequately to realise, but which compensate them to an enormous degree for the material evils which its rudeness in a great many cases produces. I may mention as an instance what was told me by Sir George Clerk, a distinguished member of the Council of India, respecting the Province of Kathiawar, in which the English and Native Governments are very much intermixed. There are no broad lines of frontier there, and a man can easily leap over the hedge from the Native into the English jurisdiction. Sir George Clerk told me that the Natives having little to carry with them were continually in the habit of migrating from the English into

[1] This is being actually done. Every effort is being made to bring the administration of the Native States to the level of the organisation of the British system—which is not a little to the credit of the British Government.

the Native jurisdiction but that he never heard of an instance of a Native leaving his own to go into the English jurisdiction. [The italics are mine.]

In the above extract Lord Salisbury says that "the inefficiency reinforced by natural causes and circumstances creates a terrible amount of misery." These natural causes and circumstances which create the terrible amount of misery are pointed out by Lord Salisbury himself, as Secretary of State for India, in a Minute (29/4/75). He says "the injury is exaggerated in the case of India, where so much of the revenue is exported without a direct equivalent." And this is so because, as he says, "As India must be bled;" so that he truly shows that though under the British rule there is no personal violence, the present un-British system of the administration of expenditure cannot but create and does "*create a terrible amount of misery.*"

Mr. BRIGHT (speech in the Manchester Town Hall, December 11th, 1877):—

"I say a Government (British) like that has some fatal defect, which at some distant time must bring disaster and humiliation to the Government and to the people on whose behalf it rules."

Lord LYTTON, Viceroy (1878):—

"No sooner was the act (1833) passed than the Government began to devise means for practically evading the fulfilment of it. . . . . We have had to choose between prohibiting them and cheating them, and we have chosen the least straightforward course . . . . are all so many deliberate and transparent subterfuges for stultifying the Act and reducing it to a dead letter . . . . having taken every means in their power of breaking to the heart the words of promise they had uttered to the ear."

The SECRETARY OF STATE FOR INDIA (Lord RANDOLPH CHURCHILL), in his despatch of January 26th, 1886, to the Treasury, makes this remarkable admission about the consequences of the present "character of the Government," of the foreign rule of Britain over India:—

"The position of India in relation to taxation and the sources of the public revenues is very peculiar, not merely from the habits of the people and their strong aversion to change, which is more especially exhibited to new forms of taxation, but likewise *from the character of the Government*, which is in the hands of foreigners, who hold all the principal administrative offices, and form so large a part of the army. The impatience of new taxation, which would have to be borne *wholly as a consequence of the foreign rule imposed on the country* and virtually to meet additions to charges arising outside of the country, would constitute a political danger the real magnitude of which, it is to be feared, is not at all appreciated by persons who have no knowledge of or concern in the government of India, but which those responsible for that government have long regarded as of the *most serious order*." [The italics are mine.]

Sir W. HUNTER, in his "Imperial Gazetteer," says about Bhavnagar in connexion with Kathiawad :—

"Bhavnagar has taken the lead in the material development of her resources, and is the first State in India which constructed a railway at her own expense and risk."

I may say that Gondal did the same in conjunction with Bhavnagar, and Baroda had done that long before. In handing over the rule of Gondal to the Prince on the completion of his minority, Major Nutt, the British Administrator, and in charge of the State at the time, says with just pride and pleasure, in reference to the increase of revenue from £80,000 in 1870 to £120,000 in 1884 :—

"One point of special interest in this matter is, *that the increase in revenue has not occasioned any hardship to Gondal subjects.* On the contrary, never were the people generally—high and low, rich and poor—in a greater state of social prosperity than they are now." [The italics are mine.]

The Bombay Government has considered this "highly satisfactory."

At the installation of the late Chief of Bhavnagar, Mr. Peile (now Sir James Peile), the Political Agent, describes the State as being then "with flourishing finances and much good work in progress. Of financial matters I need say little; you have no debts, and your treasury is full." When will British Indian financiers be able to speak with the same pride, pleasure, and satisfaction? "No debt, full treasury, good work in progress, increase of revenue, with increase of social prosperity, for high and low, rich and poor." Will this ever be in British India under the present policy? No. There will be only ever-increasing poverty.

THE INSTANCE OF THE NATIVE STATE OF MYSORE.

Of the work of the late Mahárájá from 1881 till his death at the end of 1894, it would be enough to give a very brief statement from the Address of the Dewan to the Representative Assembly held at Mysore on October 1st, 1895, on the results of the late Mahárájá's administration during nearly fourteen years of his reign, as nearly as possible in the Dewan's words. The Mahárájá was invested with power on

March 25th, 1881. Just previous to it (under British administration) the State had encountered a most disastrous famine, by which a fifth of the population had been swept away, and the State had run into a debt of 80 lakhs of rupees to the British Government. The cash balance had become reduced to a figure insufficient for the ordinary requirements of the administration. Every source of revenue was at its lowest, and the severe retrenchments which followed had left every department of State in an enfeebled condition. Such was the beginning. It began with liabilities exceeding the assets by 30¾ lakhs, and with an annual income less than the annual expenditure by 1¼ lakhs. Comparing 1880-1 with 1894-5, the annual revenue rose from 103 to 180 lakhs, of 75·24 per cent., and after spending on a large and liberal scale on all works and purposes of public utility, the net assets amounted to over 176 lakhs in 1894-5, in lieu of the net liability of 30¾ lakhs with which his Highness's reign began in 1881:—

	Rs.
In 1881 the balance of State Funds was . .	24,07,438
Capital outlay on State Railways	25,19,198
Against a liability to the British Government of .	80,00,000

Leaving a balance of liability of Rs. 30¾ lakhs.

ON JUNE 30TH, 1895.

ASSETS—		
(1) Balance of State Funds . . .		1,27,23,615
(2) Investment on account of Railway Loan Repayment Fund . .		27,81,500
(3) Capital Outlay on Mysore Harihar Railways		1,48,03,306
(4) Capital Outlay on other Railway .		41,33,390
(5) Unexpended portion of Capital borrowed for Mysore-Harihar Railway (with British Government) .		15,79,495
		3,60,21,306
LIABILITIES—		
(1) Local Railway Loan	Rs. 20,00,000	
(2) English Railway Loan	1,63,82,801	
		1,83,82,801
Net assets		Rs.1,76,38,505
ADD OTHER ASSETS—		
Capital outlay on original Irrigation Works .	Rs.99,08,935	

Besides the above *expenditure from current revenue*, there is the subsidy to the British Government of about Rs.25,00,000 a year, or a total of about Rs. 3,70,00,000 in the fifteen years from 1880-1 to 1894-5, and the Mahárájá's civil list of about Rs. 1,80,00,000 during the fifteen years, also paid from the *current revenue.* And all this together with increase in expenditure in every department. Under the circumstances above described, the administration at the start of his Highness's reign was necessarily very highly centralised. The Dewan, or the Executive Administrative Head, had the direct control, without the intervention of Departmental Heads of all the principal departments, such as the Land Revenue, Forests, Excise, Mining, Police, Education, Mujroyi, Legislative. As the finances improved, and as Department after Department was put into good working order and showed signs of expansion, separate Heads of Departments were appointed, for Forests and Police in 1885, for Excise in 1889, for Mujroyi in 1891, and for Mining in 1894. His Highness was able to resolve upon the appointment of a separate Land Revenue Commissioner only in the latter part of 1894. Improvements were made in other Departments — Local and Municipal Funds, Legislation, Education, etc. There are no wails which unfortunately the Finance Ministers of British India are obliged to raise, year after year, of fall in Exchange, over-burdening taxation, etc., etc.

And all the above good results are side by side with an increase of population of 18·34 per cent. in the ten years from 1881 to 1891, and there is reason to believe that during the last four years the ratio of increase was even higher. During the fourteen years the rate of mortality is estimated to have declined 6·7 per mille.

But there is still the most important and satisfactory feature to come, viz., that all this financial prosperity was secured not by resort to new taxation in any form or shape. In the very nature of things the present system of administration and management of Indian expenditure in British India cannot ever produce such results, even though a Gladstone undertook the work. Such is the result of good administration in a Native State at the very beginning. What splendid prospect is in store for the future if, as heretofore, it is allowed to develop itself to the level of the British system with its own Native Services, and not bled as poor British India is by the infliction of European Services, which are bleeding India to death.

Sir Wm. Hunter's "Life of Lord Mayo."

Lord Mayo says:—

"I believe we have not done our duty to the people of this land. Millions have been spent on the conquering race *which might have been spent in enriching and in elevating the children of the soil.* We have done much, but we can do a great deal more. It is, however, impossible unless we spend less on the 'interests' and 'more on the people.'

"We must first take into account the inhabitants of the country. *The welfare of the people of India is our primary object. If we are not here for their good, we ought not to be here at all.*"

"The heaviest of all yokes," says Macaulay, "is the yoke of the stranger."

The existing system of British Rule is an un-British, debasing, destructive, despotic and impoverishing Rule. A righteous Rule based on true British principles will be a great blessing both to England and India.

Dadabhai Naoroji.

A SELECTION FROM ADDRESSES.

[*Reprinted from* INDIA, *November 18th, 1898.*]

MR. DADABHAI NAOROJI AT MANCHESTER.

A CORDIAL RECEPTION.

[FROM A SPECIAL CORRESPONDENT.]

A largely attended public meeting was held under the auspices of the East Manchester Liberal Association, in the Chorlton Town Hall, Manchester, on Monday evening last, to hear addresses from Mr. Dadabhai Naoroji (on India) and Mr. Alfred Mond, the Liberal candidate for South Salford. The chair was taken by Councillor A. H. Scott, and there were upon the platform most of the Liberal leaders in the East Manchester Division.

After the Chairman's opening speech,

Mr. DADABHAI NAOROJI rose amidst loud cheers to address the meeting. He said the Chairman's speech had struck several important keynotes. He was there that evening—and he hoped to be in the neighbourhood for a week to come—(cheers)—with the object of creating a clear understanding between Lancashire and India. They might properly ask what credentials he had to speak upon that important subject. The best credential he could present was that his life's career had been passed in this country, as a man of business, having business in part with Lancashire. He claimed to know something about Lancashire's wishes. On the other hand he was well acquainted with the wants of his own country and with the relations of India to this country. The question of those relations was most important to both. England was a great country having great questions to deal with ; but he challenged anyone to stand up and say that there was any subject of greater importance to England than India. It was necessary they should understand each other clearly. Were the interests of India and those of Lancashire hostile, or were they identical ? Was the good of India associated with the good of England ? and was the good of Lancashire mixed up with the good of India ? That was the question they had to examine. Lancashire was the birth-place of

Free Trade. They demanded, and very properly, that India should remain a Free Trade country—and India was, perhaps, the greatest Free Trade country in the world. The question then was—What was their present connexion ? What were their commercial relations ? India had been a dependent of this country now for a century and a half. Had England developed a commercial connexion with the country which was satisfactory to them ? Take a few facts. The exports of British and Irish produce to the whole of the world were valued at £300,000,000. What was India's share ? Despite the fact that the colonies were for the most part Protectionist, we exported to the Canadian Dominion 30s. per head of the population ; to Australia something like 155s. per head ; to the Cape of Good Hope and Natal 45s. per head ; whilst to British India we exported hardly eighteenpence per head per annum. Was that to be the result of our 150 years' rule in India, looking at it from the view of British interests alone ? To foreign countries English exports greatly exceeded 1s. 6d. per head. The United States took something like 8s. only per head per annum of British products. Out of their £300,000,000 worth of British exports hardly £30,000,000 went to India ; and of that £30,000,000 the produce of Lancashire would hardly exceed £20,000,000. Had they, then, an interest or not in developing the capacity of the Indians to be able to buy their goods to the extent which would be satisfactory to them ? What would that extent be ? First they must remember that India consisted of two portions, namely, British India and the Native States. If statistics could be given it would be found that out of what was called British Indian trade there was a large portion that belonged to the Native States. For that they could not take credit. The Native States took a large portion of the produce they sent to India ; and, taking British India by itself, they would find that their exports hardly amounted to 1s. per head per annum. Was this a thing to be satisfied with ? The people of India, be it remembered, had been civilised for thousands of years ; they knew what the enjoyments and the requirements of civilisation were ; and if they were in a position to buy £1 worth of British products per head per annum it would equal the amount of British exports to the whole world at the present time. (Hear, hear.) The English were doing their best to find new markets. Let

India be placed in such an economic position that she could take English goods to the extent of only £1 per head per annum and they would be utterly unable to supply all her wants. The word "unemployed" would vanish from the English dictionary. (Cheers.) He asked them then to consider very carefully—why was it, notwithstanding our complete communication with India and our control there, that there was constant friction between India and Lancashire—India thinking that Lancashire is treating her uujustly, and Lancashire thinking that India ought not to have any advantage in the matter of trade? But the interests of both were identical. Why then should India not be in a better position? Upon whom did the responsibility rest? It was one of the purposes for which he was there that night to try and answer that question. He exhorted Englishmen for their own sake, as well as for the sake of India, to consider it. Why should there be such evils, after 150 years of British rule, as famines, pestilences, and war? Certainly India must expect something better than that which was its condition before the English occupation. Had that been realised? (A Voice: "Yes.") He hoped the gentleman who had said "yes" would put aside his present notions and reconsider the matter. (Hear, hear.) If he took the trouble to study the subject—(A Voice: "I have lived in your country")—yes (continued Mr. Naoroji), you have lived in my country, and I am glad to hear it. It is our misfortune, however, that so many English gentlemen have lived in India as if they had never seen it. (Hear, hear, and cheers.) They go about with their eyes shut, indifferent to the real question—What are the interests of the Indians themselves? Their whole heart is concentrated on one thing—how to benefit themselves—(hear, hear)—without any regard to the circumstances in which the Natives of India are placed. (Loud cheers.) It is the evil groove in which they are moving, and I implore this meeting not to be misled by these gentlemen who fail to see what they ought to see, and who come home and try to mislead the public here by representations which are anything but true. (Cheers.) I do not speak with indignation or anger; I am speaking the bare truth; and it is most important that the British should be informed and should judge for themselves, and not be misled by those who have made it their interest to exploit India as if India had been created by God for that simple object. (Cheers.) Proceeding, Mr. Naoroji said Englishmen usually went to India in two capacities—first, as officials to rule over the Indian people; secondly, as merchants and capitalists. Both classes had only one idea—in the one case it was how to get all the best places in the administration for themselves—and, they were sometimes candid enough to say, "for our boys"—in the other it was how to benefit themselves without caring very much what happened to the people among whom they lived. (Hear, hear.) It was said by one of England's noblest citizens, whose name would always elicit among the Indians, as well as among Englishmen, the most grateful applause, Mr. John Bright—(cheers)—"You can govern India if you like for the good of England; but the good of England must come through the channels of the good of India." (Loud cheers.) Let them consider whether such was not the case. Mr. Bright put the whole case in a nutshell. He said further: "There are but two modes of gaining anything by our connexion with India; the one is by plundering the people of India and the other by trading with them. I prefer it by trading with them. But in order that England may become rich by trading with India, India itself must become rich." He (Mr. Naoroji) knew that the feeling of the British people was not that England should benefit from India by plunder. (Cheers.) He could say that in all sincerity—he knew it thoroughly well. Belief in that one thing had enabled him to keep up the struggle against all odds, during the last quarter of a century upon this question. (Hear, hear.) If the British people would take the matter into their own hand and not allow themselves to be misled by their friends the Anglo-Indians, a better state of things would speedily be brought about. Already he was pleased to think that there were numbers who recognised that India was not being dealt with as it ought to be. Lancashire was most interested in this question, and if they were once agreed that their interests lay in the good of both and not in the good of one, they would understand the question much more easily, because then they would be going on lines which were clear before them. Mr. Bright well understood that the Indians, unless they had the means, could never buy the products of Lancashire. The evil they had to combat lay in the adoption of the principle which Lord Salisbury once laid down, namely, that the principle on which India was to be governed was that

India must be bled. That was the foundation of the system of British rule; it had existed for 150 years more or less. Were the English people to rest satisfied with it? If so there was an end of the matter. The only result must be, as Lord Hartington once put it, that the Indian people must wish to get rid of it. That would be the natural consequence of the system. Lord Salisbury's justification of it was a great reflection upon the British character. The British people did not deserve it. Political hypocrisy lay at the root of the system of government. Lord Lytton when Viceroy caused a minute to be issued in which it was distinctly acknowledged that the policy of the British Government was a policy of deliberate and transparent subterfuges. Not only so but a committee of members of the India Office at the close of the Mutiny—about the year 1860—who met to consider the question of British policy, laid it down distinctly that you are open to the charge of breaking promises deliberately made. He had told the meeting the principle on which the system of government was based, and the means adopted to carry it out. Now for the result. One of the results was that a large volume of wealth was withdrawn from India year after year, which meant the impoverishment of the country. The economic condition of India, therefore, was that a continual bleeding took place, and the inevitable consequence of that was the most terrible misery. It did not require any scientific elucidation—any man of common sense could tell that a country from which the stream of wealth constantly flowed, and never returned, must gradually lose vigour and life. The English nation would not submit to it for a single moment. They could not complain, therefore, that the Indian people protested against it. It was a system which, if continued, must some day end in disaster both to England and to India. (Hear, hear.) What then was their position? The loss to India was a treble loss. There was the loss of wealth, the loss of employment—Native Indians being left out of the higher offices—and the moral loss involved in the loss of capacity. One thing the British had done: they had educated the people of India, and that was a blessing for which they were grateful. As long as ignorance was bliss they said nothing; now they had learnt what it was to be a nation—what it was to be a prosperous nation—how England had built up her prosperity—for which, indeed, she owed a great deal to India. Had the British people ever properly considered that question? They had taught the people of India what the condition of a people ought to be; they had taught them patriotism; they had given them a new political life, and they then said to them: "You are our fellow-subjects; you are partners in the Empire, and we want to treat you on righteous and equitable terms." Unfortunately, however, all this was mere romance; the reality was that the governing class—those to whose care they were consigned—knew only one thing and that was how to benefit themselves. Now that was a kind of relationship which could not last long. The Indian people suffered morally far more grievously even than they did economically. They had the knowledge that they were capable of doing this or that, but they were not permitted—they must remain simple helots. That was a grievous thing—he meant the loss of employment—the loss of capacity as human beings, with its inevitable consequence, the sinking lower and lower in the scale of humanity. Were they to thank the English nation for that? As men of common sense, who knew their own interests, they must see that the system of government in India ought to be such as would benefit the Indian people as well as themselves. Such, however, is not the system at present, and it must be changed. It was proclaimed repeatedly: "You, the people of India, are our partners; you must take a share in the responsibilities of Empire." But the partnership seemed to be an extraordinary one. Would any two gentlemen present, he would like to know, enter into such a partnership—the one providing the capital and the other taking all the profit? (Laughter and cheers.) He thought Lancashire men would not endorse such a principle in their own business. Take, for instance, the recent war on the North-West frontier. Why did they enter upon that war? It was because they wanted to save the Empire from Russian aggression. Would anybody say, then, that England had no interest in that war? Was it all the interest of India? Yet India must pay every farthing of the cost. They must shed their blood and bear the expense also, not the smallest share being borne by the British Treasury. After the last Afghan War Mr. Gladstone—(cheers)—took up the cudgels and along with Mr. Fawcett succeeded in getting Parliament to agree that the expense should be shared by the English nation. Their reasons were simple. The British entered upon that war essentially for Imperial purposes. And what was more, the Indians themselves were not consulted in any way whatever. They had no voice in it. The only argument and law known to them was the argument and law of force. Well, Mr. Gladstone, soon after he came into power, carried out, though in the face of much opposition, the principle he had enunciated, and succeeded in getting one-fourth of the cost of the war debited to the Imperial treasury. He gave India five millions. That was the extent to which they were relieved, and he did not think it was worthy of the English people, grateful as they were for it. It, however, admitted the principle; it became a precedent; and it was the more encouraging because the British people did not object to it. It had their approval; and even now when the question was mooted the English Press endorsed that principle — the principle of the Imperial Government bearing a part of the cost of warlike operations undertaken for Imperial purposes. Under the present Government, however—owing, should they say, to the tribes or the cleverness of their Anglo-Indian friends?—the old system had been reverted to. When it came to a question of payment, suddenly it was found that India was most prosperous—capable of supplying everything—and wanted no charitable aid from this country. He asked the English people, was this honourable? Was it just? It was, however, but an incident of the situation—a surface evil. The fundamental evil was this—they had a civil and military service in India which inflicted upon the country this treble loss—loss of wealth, loss of employment, and the moral loss, loss of capacity. The result was they could not have that trade with India which Mr. Bright, in the passage quoted, regarded as so essential. Mr. Bright said England should derive benefit from India not by plunder but by trade England was now deriving benefit by plunder. Then came the great question of honour. Did the British people make promises and break them? Was it creditable to us as a nation that a man in the position of Lord Salisbury should be obliged to confess that we carried on the administration of India by a system of political hypocrisy? He implored his hearers to make this matter their careful study—if not for the Indians' sake yet for their own. England did not derive the benefit she might from India. If she would put India in the position of being able to buy English goods to the extent of £1 per head, which was not a very large amount, they would, in such circumstances, be enabled to export as much to India as they now did to the whole world. Was there not, then, sufficient ground for the charges he made against the English administration—first, political hypocrisy, the non-fulfilment of promises? Acts of Parliament, Proclamations by the Queen, all went for nothing. Was that a character worthy of the British name? It was for the British people themselves to take the question up, to study it thoroughly and to adopt a system by which both India and England might be benefited. Then would English rule in India rest upon the affection as well as the self-interest of the Indian people, because they would not like the superior hand of Britain to be removed. If the Indian people from such notions thought the British rule ought to continue, they could then defy half a dozen Russias; they could raise a force in India sufficient to drive back Russia to St. Petersburg. Even now they were carrying on wars all over the world, and India supplied them with a reserve of force, and if they had the backing of the Indian people themselves they could defy all Europe, because India was as large as Europe, and able to cope with Europe single-handed. (Cheers.) This should be his last word: Don't be misled by the misrepresentations of that section of the community which had a monopoly of power and pelf, and did not want to lose it. The interest of the two peoples was to be united, and if the Indians believed—as they did—that British supremacy was a great good for them, for their regeneration, for their material and moral development, then they could easily believe that India would be thoroughly loyal. It was not merely loyalty; it was to their own self-interest that they should remain related to Britain; but if the old bad principle of government was to continue—the principle that India must be bled in order that the Anglo-Indians should be able to make fortunes for themselves—then, as any child might tell them, their relations must some day break. That the Indians certainly did not desire; but if ever the time came when they were disaffected the fault would not be theirs, but that of the British alone. The educated portion of the people knew well wherein lay the interest of India. They understood that if they could have really British rule instead of that un-British rule by which they were governed to-day, the result would be a blessing to both of them. (Loud cheers.)

The meeting was afterwards addressed by Mr. Alfred Mond, and others; and Mr. Naoroji was cordially thanked for his most instructive and interesting address.

[Reprinted from INDIA, *June 2nd, 1899.]*

THE CONDITION OF INDIA.

ADDRESS BY MR. DADABHAI NAOROJI.

[FROM OUR OWN REPORTER.]

On Sunday last, May 29, the "Sunday Afternoon Conference" which is held from week to week at Westbourne Park Chapel, London, for the consideration of various subjects of religious or social interest and importance was devoted to the Indian question, Mr. Dadabhai Naoroji delivering an address on the present political and economic condition of India.

There was a very large attendance, which included a fair proportion of Indian gentlemen.

The chair was taken by Mr. Wallis Chapman, who, in introducing Mr. Naoroji, said there were few more responsible duties imposed on the English people than that of the government of India. They were consequently the more indebted to Mr. Naoroji for his willingness to give them the benefit of the knowledge which he had obtained during a lifetime of devotion to the cause of his and their Indian fellow-subjects.

Mr. Naoroji, who was received with cheers, said it was clear that any subject which was thought worthy of consideration on such a day and in such a place must be regarded as a grave one, and a question affecting the weal or woe of three hundred millions of people surely came within that category. Moreover, the action of the English nation in regard to the people of India was of as vital importance to themselves as it was to India, and it was not even of less vital consequence to the whole human race. For a new element had lately come into existence in the councils of the nations. A country which had hitherto confined itself, under its Monroe doctrine, to its own continent was now coming forward to share in what was called the Imperialism of the world, and the question had already arisen which course that country should follow. The

American people would unquestionably look to the government of India by the British people to see whether that government was a model for them to follow or an evil example which they should avoid, and on that account the relations between England and India were becoming more and more important to the whole human race, irrespective of the interests of those great countries. Consequently it was the duty of every voter in Great Britain to know what his responsibilities were and what the condition of India had been during the century and a half of regular British administration. He would deal first with the political condition of India at the present moment, and would regard it in its two aspects—the legislative and the executive. There existed Legislative Councils in India, and it was generally believed that those councils gave to the Indian people something like what they in England enjoyed in the way of representative government, and that by those means the people of India had some voice in their own government. This was simply a romance. The reality was that the Legislative Council was constituted in such a way as to give to the Government a complete and positive majority. The three or four Indians who had seats upon it might say what they like, but what the Government of India declared was to become law did invariably become the law of the country. To take, for instance, the question of expenditure—when a Budget was brought forward in the House of Commons members went on contesting it, item by item, for six months—they saw that their constituents' interests were properly protected, and that the Government took no advantage of their power. Of course, in the British Parliament also the majority had the final word; but, whereas in that case that majority was subject to the people and could be turned out by them, in the Indian legislative councils the majority, instead of being given by the people, was managed and manipulated by the Government itself. But matters were even worse than this. The expenditure of the revenues was one of the most important points in the political condition of any country, but in India there was no such thing as a legislative Budget. The representative members had no right to propose any resolution or go to any division upon any item concerned in the Budget, which was passed simply and solely according to the despotic will of a despotic Government. The

Natives of India had not the slightest voice in the expenditure of the Indian revenues, and the idea that they had was the first delusion on the part of the voters of England which he wished to correct. It would be seen in what an absurd position the so-called Native representatives of India were placed. In the expenditure of the revenue they had, as he had explained, not the least voice, but when the time came for the imposition of taxes they were quite welcome to impose what taxation they could upon their countrymen. Yet if they did impose additional taxes these countrymen blamed them, while if, on the other hand, they resisted any particular Bill of taxation the Government officials turned round and said, "These Indians seem to think it possible to govern a country without revenue," and this they made an argument against the capacity of the Natives to take an adequate part in the government of their country. The Legislative Council was simply and solely, he declared, a delusion and a farce, and its working constituted a worse despotism than was ever exercised by any Native ruler even in the old days. An Oriental despot, when he misgoverned, acted, so to speak, like a butcher, and people were astounded and horrified; this new despotism of civilisation rather resembled a murder effected by a clever but unscrupulous surgeon who drew all the blood from his victim while leaving scarcely a scar upon the skin. Moreover, if under Oriental despotism the results to the individual were serious, they at least were not so terrible to the country. A particular victim was no doubt often despoiled of his fortune, bnt some favourite benefited, and the money at least remained in the country; whereas the British—or rather un-British—system of despotism took away year by year a greater portion of the wealth of India, with the result that at the present day the Indians under British rule were the very poorest people in the world. And it was not as if there were any necessity that this should be the case. British statesmen had in the past recognised that by a different and more righteous system of government the situation of both India and England might be vastly improved, and that the latter might make ten times more money out of India by benefiting the latter country than was at present drawn from her destruction and impoverishment. With regard to the executive portion of the Government of India, they found most emphatically realised the old saying that taxation without representation was tyranny. But he did not wish to suggest for a moment that it was the desire of the British people that this state of things should continue. On the contrary, he was so absolutely convinced that the British people did not wish that India should go on being governed on wicked lines, for they had done all they could—all save one thing—to secure that the Government of India should be carried on upon lines of righteousness. After the terrible exposures of British mis-government in and before the days of Warren Hastings the British people made a firm stand and strongly declared that India should not be subjected to such treatment any longer, with the result that in 1833 the British Government openly and decidedly stated that the Government of India should be a righteous one, and that the people of India should be treated in the same manner as the people of Great Britain. That, by the way, was the era of emancipations, among others of that which had enabled him to stand before an English constituency and, by obtaining their suffrages, to go to the House of Commons to plead his country's cause. (Hear, hear.) However, all the great statesmen of the time to which he referred declared with one voice that the Bill must pass, no matter what the consequences might be, and it did pass, its general effect being that no Native of India should by virtue of his religion or descent be disabled from holding any place, office, or employment under the Company. It might be asked what more than that the Indian people wanted, and he replied that they wanted nothing more—except that the British people should carry into effect honourably the Act they had passed. In 1853 there was a revision of the Act, when Lord Stanley of that day—the late Earl of Derby—Mr. Bright and other true Britons protested that the measure was completely and wholly a dead letter. But the Government of India and the Indian authorities nevertheless continued to act upon the one principle that the Indian Services were their monopoly, not to be encroached upon by any other persons, and the representations of Lord Stanley and Mr. Bright were not listened to. Then came the Mutiny, upon which he did not wish to touch beyond saying that if it was anyone's fault it was the fault of the British Government and their Indian Governor-General. However, it was for the most part Indians who, even in the Mutiny, saved the British Empire in India. Lord George Hamilton talked glibly of the manner in which the British Empire had been built up by the expenditure of British treasure and the spilling of British blood. Well, much of the blood spilt in building up the Empire had been Indian blood, while with regard to treasure the British people had not spent a single farthing in creating or upholding it so far as the Indian portion of it was concerned. They had, on the contrary, constrained the wretched Indian Natives to contribute the whole cost, and were still drawing from India year by year millions upon millions to the still greater impoverishment and destruction of the Indian people. That, however, was somewhat by the way. After the Mutiny, when British power was re-established, the true British spirit was at once aroused, and once more the generous declaration went forth in the shape of a Proclamation from the Throne. "We hold ourselves bound to the Natives of our Indian territory," the Proclamation ran, "by the same obligations of duty which bind ourselves to our other subjects, and those obligations, by the blessing of Almighty God, we shall faithfully and conscientiously fulfil. And it is our further will that, so far as may be, our subjects, of whatever race or creed, shall be freely and impartially admitted to offices in our service, the duties which they may be qualified by their education, ability, and integrity duly to discharge. . . . . In their prosperity will be our strength, in their contentment our security, and in their gratitude our best reward. And may the God of all Power grant to us and those in authority under us strength to carry out these our wishes for the good of our people." But did the British people feel that in the impoverishment of India they could be strong or that they could be secure while India, far from being content, was terribly suffering? As to their reward he would not say at that moment what cause there was for gratitude or how much of it prevailed, but he would repeat that even putting matters on the very low platform of selfishness, the British nation would derive ten times more profit from India than was the case at present if they would only alter their treatment. (Hear, hear.) Similar proclamations had been issued since—when the Queen was declared Empress of India and at the Jubilee, but all these solemn obligations and Acts of Parliament had been and were being scattered to the winds in order that Anglo-Indian officials might keep in their hands the monopoly of Indian Government and might provide for their boys. (Hear, hear.) What were the economic consequences of this state of things? They were summed up in the declaration of Lord Salisbury himself that India must be "bled," and was the principle on which the whole present system of Indian government was based. Lord Salisbury coolly and deliberately, in the memorandum to which he referred, admitted that India was injured by the drain that was constantly going on in the way of the exportation of so much revenue without any direct equivalent, and went on to say that as the great mass of the people, the agricultural community, had no more blood remaining in them, the lancet should be applied to those parts where the blood was congested or at least sufficient. He had said enough, he thought, to show how the unhappy Indian Natives were regarded by Anglo-Indian officials. The lot of the former, indeed, was somewhat worse than that of the slaves in America in old days, for the masters had an interest in keeping them alive, if only that they had a money value. But if an Indian died, or if a million died, there was another or there were a million others ready to take his or their places and to be the slaves of British officials in their turn. Who, he asked in conclusion, was responsible for all this? The British people might ask: "What more can we do? We have declared that India shall be governed upon righteous lines." Yes, but their servants have not obeyed their instructions, and theirs was the responsibility and upon their heads was the blood of the millions who were starving year by year. For their own sakes, as well as for the sake of the Indian people, it was time that they awoke. They were so taken up at present by the extension of their Empire that they little dreamed of a day which might come at any moment when their existing Empire might suffer an upheaval and explosion which would shatter it to pieces. He held out no threats, but that would be the natural consequence of an iniquitous and unjust system of government, as had been declared by Lord Salisbury when he said that injustice would bring down the mightiest kingdom. (Applause.)

Subsequently a series of questions were put to Mr. Naoroji, who answered them in considerable detail. He declared that famines were far less harmful in the feudatory States than in that part of India which was under direct British rule, because those States lost nothing by their subjection to Great Britain except the small tribute paid yearly, and were consequently improving their position every day, and were enabled to establish a reserve fund and Treasury balances, out of which the people could be helped in time of need. For these feudatory States he admitted that British supremacy was a blessing. The average annual income of the Natives of India per head had, he said in answer to another question, been estimated by the present Lord Cromer as not more than twenty-seven rupees, but his own belief was that, at the present rate of exchange, it was not more than 25s. Let them contrast that with the average annual income per head of the people of Great Britain, which was estimated at £41.

A vote of thanks to Mr. Naoroji was moved by Miss Annie Lee-Brown, secretary of the local Women's Liberal Association, and seconded by Mr. Martin Wood, late of Bombay, who said the best method in which those present could express their thanks would be to study the subject and bring to bear such influence as they possessed with a view to remedying the condition of things of which they had heard.

The vote was heartily carried, and Mr. Naoroji having briefly returned thanks the meeting concluded.

[*Reprinted from* INDIA, *July 6th, 1900.*]

MR. DADABHAI NAOROJI AT WALTHAMSTOW.

"INDIA MUST BE BLED."

[FROM OUR OWN REPORTER.]

Mr. Dadabhai Naoroji addressed a meeting held on Sunday last, July 1st, at the United Methodist Free Church, Markhouse Road, Walthamstow, in aid of the Indian Famine Relief Fund. Mr. Peter Troughton occupied the chair.

The Chairman, in opening the proceedings, said the Indian famine was a subject of very great interest to all Englishmen, and he was sure they would all gladly welcome some authentic information on the subject. He would therefore ask Mr. Dadabhai Naoroji to start his speech right away. (Applause.)

Mr. Dadabhai Naoroji, who was received with cheers, said: Mr. Chairman, I feel exceedingly pleased at having to address so large a meeting of English ladies and gentlemen. I assure you it is a great consolation to me that English people are willing to hear what Indians have to say. I will make bold to speak fully and heartily, in order that you may know the truth. I will take as a text the following true words: "As India must be bled." These words were delivered by a Secretary of State for India, Lord Salisbury himself. I don't mention them as any complaint against Lord Salisbury. On the contrary, I give him credit for saying the truth. I want to impress upon you what these important words mean. Let us clearly understand what is meant by bleeding a nation. It is perfectly true that when government is carried on people must pay taxes. But there is a great difference between taxing a people and bleeding a people. You in England pay something like fifty shillings, or more now, of taxes per head per annum. We in India pay only three to four shillings per head per annum. From this you may conclude that we must be the most lightly-taxed people in the world. That is not the case, however; our burden is nearly twice as heavy as yours. The taxes you pay in this country go from the hands of the taxpayers into the hands of the Government, from which they flow back into the country again in various shapes, fertilising trade and returning to the people themselves. There is no diminution of your wealth; your taxes simply change hands. Whatever you give out you must get back. Any deficit means so much loss of strength. Supposing you pay a hundred million pounds every year, and the Government uses that money in such a way that part only returns to you, the other part going out of the country. In that case you are being bled, part of your life is going away. Suppose out of the hundred million pounds only eighty million pounds return to you in the shape of salaries, commerce, or manufactures. You will have lost twenty million pounds. Next year you will be so much the weaker; and so on each year. This is the difference between taxing people and bleeding people. Suppose a body of Frenchmen were your rulers, and that out of the hundred million pounds of taxes they took ten to twenty million pounds each year; you would then be said to be bleeding. The nation would then be losing a portion of its life. How is India bled? I supposed your own case with Frenchmen as your rulers. We Indians are governed by you. You manage our expenditure and our taxes in such a way that while we pay a hundred million pounds of taxation this hundred million never returns to us intact. Only about eighty million returns to us. There is a continual bleeding of about twenty millions annually from the revenues. Ever since you obtained territorial jurisdiction and power in India, in the middle of the last century, Englishmen and other Europeans that went to India have treated that country in the most oppressive way. I will quote a few words of the Court of Directors at the time to show this. "The vast fortunes acquired in the inland trade have been obtained by the most oppressive conduct that ever was known in any country or age." The most oppressive means were adopted in order to bring away from the country enormous quantities of wealth. How was the Indian Empire obtained by you? It has been generally said that you have won it by the sword, and that you will keep it by the sword. The people who say this do not know what they are talking about. They also forget that you may lose "it by force." You have not won the Indian

Empire by the sword. During these hundred and fifty years you have carried on wars by which this great Empire has been built up it has cost hundreds of millions of money. Have you paid a single farthing of it? You have made the Indians pay every farthing. You have formed this great British Empire at our expense, and you will hear what reward we have received from you. The European army in India at any time was comparatively insignificant. In the time of the Indian Mutiny you had only forty thousand troops there. It was the two hundred thousand Indian troops that shed their blood and fought your battles and that gave you this magnificent Empire. It is at India's cost and blood that this Empire has been formed and maintained up to the present day. It is in consequence of the tremendous cost of these wars and because of the millions on millions you draw from us year by year that India is so completely exhausted and bled. It is no wonder that the time has come when India is bleeding to death. You have brought India to this condition by the constant drain upon the wealth of that country. I ask any one of you whether it is possible for any nation on the face of the earth to live under these conditions. Take your own nation. If you were subjected to such a process of exhaustion for years, you would come down yourselves to the condition in which India now finds herself. How then is this drain made? You impose upon us an immense European military and civil service, you draw from us a heavy taxation. But in the disbursement and the disposal of that taxation we have not the slightest voice. I ask anyone here to stand up and say that he would be satisfied if, having to pay a heavy taxation, he had no voice in the government of the country. We have not the slightest voice. The Indian Government are the masters of all our resources, and they may do what they like with them. We have simply to submit and be bled. I hope I have made it quite clear to you, that the words of Lord Salisbury which I have quoted are most significant; that the words are true and most appropriate when applied to India. It is the principle on which the system of British government has been carried on during these 150 years. What has been the consequence? I shall again quote from Lord Salisbury. He says: "That as India must be bled the lancet should be directed to the parts where the blood is congested, or at least sufficient, not to those parts already feeble from the want of it." Lord Salisbury declared that the agricultural population, the largest portion of the population of India, was feeble from the want of blood. This was said twenty-five years ago; and that blood has been more and more drawn upon during the past quarter of a century. The result is that they have bled to death; and why? A large proportion of our resources and wealth is clean carried away never to return to us. That is the process of bleeding. Lord Salisbury himself says: "So much of the revenue is exported without a direct equivalent." I ask any one of you whether there is any great mystery in these dire famines and plagues? No other country exhausted as India has been exhausted by an evil system of government would have stood it half the time. It is extraordinary that the loyalty of the Indians who are bled by you is still so great. The reason of it is that among the Hindoos it is one of their most cherished and religious duties that they should give obedience and loyalty to the powers that govern them. And they have been loyal to that sentiment, and you have derived the benefit of it. It is a true and genuine loyalty. But do not expect that that loyalty cannot fail, that it will continue in the same condition in which it is at the present time. It is for the British to rouse themselves and to open their minds, and to think whether they are doing their duty in India. The theory maintained by statesmen is that India is governed for the benefit of India. They say that they do not derive any benefit from the taxation. But this is erroneous. The reality is that India, up to the present day, has been governed so as to bring about the impoverishment of the people. I ask you whether this is to continue. Is it necessary that, for your benefit, we must be destroyed? Is it a natural consequence, is it a necessary consequence? Not at all. If it were British rule and not un-British rule which governed us England would be benefited ten times more than it is. (Cheers.) You could benefit yourselves a great deal more than you are doing if your Executive Government did not persist in their evil system, by which you derive some benefit, but by which we are destroyed. I say let the British public thoroughly understand this question, that by destroying us you will ultimately destroy yourselves. Mr. Bright knew this, and this is an extract from one of his speeches. He said, or to the effect: By all means seek your own benefit and your own good in connexion with India; but you cannot derive any good except by doing good to India. If you do good to India you will do good to yourselves. He said there were two ways of doing good to yourselves, either by plunder or by trade. And he said he would prefer trade. Now, I will explain how it would benefit you. At the present time you are exporting to the whole world something like three hundred millions worth of your produce a year. Here is a country under your control with a population of three hundred millions of human souls, not savages of Africa. Here is India, with a perfectly free trade entirely under your control, and what do you send out to her? Only eighteen pence per year per head. If you could send goods to the extent of £1 per head per annum India would be a market for your whole commerce. If such were the case you would draw immense wealth from India besides benefiting the people. I say that if the British public do not rouse themselves the blood of every man that dies there will lie on their head. You may prosper for a time, but a time must come when you must suffer the retribution that comes from this evil system of government. What I quoted to you from Lord Salisbury explains the real condition of India. It is not the first time that English statesmen have declared this as absolutely as Lord Salisbury has done. During the whole century Englishmen and statesmen of conscience and thought have time after time declared the same thing, that India is being exhausted and drained, and that India must ultimately die. Our misery is owing to this exhaustion. You are drawing year by year thirty millions of our wealth from us in various ways. The Government of India's resources simply mean that the Government is despotic and that it can put any tax it chooses on the people. Is it too much to ask that when we are reduced by famine and plague you should pay for these dire calamities? You are bound in justice and in common duty to humanity to pay the cost of these dire calamities with which we are afflicted. I will conclude with Lord Salisbury's other true words: "Injustice will bring down the mightiest to ruin." (Great applause.)

At the conclusion of Mr. Dadabhai Naoroji's address a collection was made on behalf of the famine relief fund, and the meeting ended, as it had begun, with devotional exercises.

[*Reprinted from* INDIA, *July 27th, 1900.*]

MR. NAOROJI AT PLUMSTEAD.

[FROM OUR OWN REPORTER.]

On Saturday, July 21st, Mr. Dádabhai Naoroji addressed the delegates of the Metropolitan Radical Federation, at a meeting held at the Plumstead Radical Club, under the presidency of Mr. James Jeffrey, L.C.C. There was a fairly large attendance.

Mr. Naoroji, who was heartily cheered, took the following resolution as the text of his speech :—

"RESOLVED :

"Considering that Britain has appropriated thousands of millions of India's wealth for building up and maintaining her British Indian Empire, and for directly drawing vast wealth to herself; that she is continuing to drain about £30,000,000 of India's wealth every year unceasingly in a variety of ways; and that she has thereby reduced the bulk of the Indian population to extreme poverty, destitution, and degradation; it is therefore her bounden duty in common justice and humanity to pay from her own exchequer the costs of all famines and diseases caused by such impoverishment.

"That, therefore, for the present famine and diseases the British Exchequer should pay the whole cost of both saving life and restoring the stricken people to their normal industrial condition and wants, instead of further oppressing and crushing the Indian people themselves to find these costs directly or by loan under the deceptive pretext or disguise of what is called 'the resources of the Government of India,' which simply means squeezing the wretched people themselves.

"That it is most humiliating and discreditable to the British name that other countries should be appealed to or should have to come to Britain's help for relief of Britain's own subjects, and after and by her un-British rule of about 150 years.

"And that for the further prevention of famines and plagues, and to restore prosperity to the Indian people, as well as for benefiting vastly the masses of the British people also, measures must be adopted to put an end to the exhausting and impoverishing bleeding, by dealing with justice for all expenditures for British interests, and by honourably carrying out the true and declared policy and solemn pledges of the British people, Parliament, and Sovereign, by the Act 1833 and her Majesty's Proclamations of 1858, 1877, and 1887."

Dealing with the first part of the resolution, he said it was a pure matter of fact that Great Britain, during the whole period of her connexion with India, had never spent a single farthing of British money on the Eastern Empire. All the great wars which had been engaged in had been paid for by the Indians themselves, and it was India, or rather its Natives, who had given this noble heritage to the British Empire. Indians had also shed their blood in order to maintain and extend that Empire. Up to the time of the Indian Mutiny the British Army there never exceeded 40,000 men, while its average strength was from 15,000 to 20,000 men. But the Indian Army of 200,000 was placed at the service of the Empire; it was maintained by India, and it shed its blood for India. Surely these facts required no comment. But that was not all. From the time when Great Britain first obtained territorial jurisdiction in India down to the present day it had drawn millions upon millions sterling from that Empire. Great Britain had appropriated this Indian wealth, thereby reducing the population to extreme poverty. At the beginning of the century only about 3 millions a year was drawn from India, but now the amount taken away was officially admitted to be about 30 millions sterling annually. This was an open sore, and no country could withstand being bled unceasingly in this manner. (Hear, hear.) As he had said the result had been to reduce the bulk of the Indian population to extreme poverty, destitution, and degradation; and, to use the terms of his resolution, it was "Great Britain's bounden duty, in common justice and humanity, to pay from her own Exchequer the costs of all famines and diseases caused by such impoverishment." There could only be one ending to this continual bleeding of India. Famine was following upon famine; each visitation was becoming more disastrous, and the present was the most disastrous of the whole century. For from thirty to forty years he had been as one crying in the wilderness against this terrible treatment. He had realised, and he had endeavoured to make the people realise, that a country thus drained must in the end die. Great Britain owed a debt to these poor, wretched, dying people. (Hear, hear.) The British people, through their policy, were the cause of the misery which now prevailed, and the least they could do surely was to try and help the Natives of India in their time of terrible distress. The great idea of the Indian Government appeared to be not to let the English taxpayer have any trouble or annoyance in connexion with India. The rulers of that Empire seemed to think that the moment the English taxpayer was called upon to contribute a farthing for the maintenance of India, he would demand to know the reason why India had been treated in the manner she had been. They were well aware, too, that no good reason could be shown for such treatment. Let him give one illustration of the unwisdom of maintaining a running sore. Thirty years ago France and Germany had a deadly struggle. France was beaten and had to pay dearly for it. A heavy burden was imposed upon her, a severe wound was inflicted. But in process of time it healed. France paid her debt, the account was closed, and she became as prosperous as ever. Why was not an endeavour made to treat India in the same way? Why, having once drawn from her enormous sums of money, was not the account closed and the Natives of India allowed to reap the benefit of the wealth which their country produced? No. The policy was to keep the wound running day after day and month after month, and they might rely upon it that until the bleeding was stopped India would have no chance of prosperity. It surely was the duty of the British Exchequer, seeing that their policy was responsible for the present famine and disease, to pay the whole cost of saving life and of restoring the stricken people to their normal industrial condition instead of further oppressing and crushing the Indian people themselves by compelling them to find these costs directly or by loan under the deceptive pretext or disguise of what is called "the resources of the Government of India," which simply meant squeezing the wretched people themselves. The term "resources of the Government of India" was a most deceptive one. They had often been told that India had not exhausted her borrowing powers. But what were the facts? The Government of India consisted of Europeans. The Indians had not the slightest voice in the expenditure of a single farthing. They had only to pay, and, before any portion of the taxation exacted from them could be used for the benefit of India, 200,000,000 of rupees were annually devoted to the payment of salaries and pensions of Europeans who constituted the Government of India. The population of England paid 50s.

per head per annum in the form of taxation. The people of India did not even pay 5s. per head; yet, strange to say, they were crushed by a heavier burden of taxation than were the English. The incidence and heaviness of taxation did not depend upon the amount; it depended upon the capacity to bear it; and the fact was that, while English taxation represented from 6 per cent. to 8 per cent. of the taxpayers' income, the taxation in India represented 14 or 15 per cent. They all knew how hard it was for a man earning £1 per week to give 1s. out of it. It was far more easy for a man with an income of £1,000 a year to give away £100; and hence it was that the people of India, in their wretchedness and impoverishment, felt so heavily the taxation imposed upon them. Was it not most humiliating and discreditable to the British name that other countries should be appealed to to come to Britain's help for the relief of Britain's own subjects after they had been under British rule for a period of 150 years? British rule was supposed to confer great blessings upon the Indian race. But what had been the results of it? Millions of the people were dying of famine and disease, and scores of millions from year's end to year's end never knew what it was to have a full meal! As had been well said it was a shame that our own fellow-subjects should starve while the British Empire was the greatest and richest in the world. In treating India as they were doing they were killing the bird that laid the golden eggs. They were deriving great benefits from India, but those benefits carried with them losses to the Indian people. If they would only treat India honestly, if they would act as honourable Englishmen and fulfil their pledges to India, they would be able to gain ten times as much benefit from India, and those benefits would then carry with them the blessings of the Indian people. More than that, how was the wealth now withdrawn from India distributed? It went into the pockets of the capitalists and the higher classes. It did not benefit the working men of Great Britain. He had no desire to appeal to their selfishness, but he was bound to point out the economic fact that the doing of evil reflected upon all who had a share in it. Now, in England the production represented something like £40 per head per annum. They exported goods to the whole world, and the amount of exports was placed at three hundred millions sterling per annum. Upon those exports rested the question of their employment. Their own colonies had slammed the door of protection in their face, European countries had also adopted protective tariffs; so, too, had the United States of America, and yet, notwithstanding this fact, Great Britain annually exported produce to the value of three hundred millions sterling. India was the only place where they had perfect freedom of trade, entirely under their own control. But what proportion of the British exports went into that country? Only about twenty-five million sterling. Why was it that such a small amount was exported to India? Simply because the process of bleeding had been carried on to such an extent that the people had literally no money left with which to buy British produce. Now if, instead of treating the Natives of India in this cruel and barbarous fashion, they were to deal with them honestly, what would be the result? Let them remember that the Indians were not a race of savages. Two thousand years ago they were the most highly civilised nation in the world. And what sort of people were the Natives of England when at that period they were discovered by Cæsar? (A laugh.) Now, the Indians know how to enjoy the good things of this world, and if they were only allowed to benefit by what they produced they would be able to buy the manufactures of Great Britain. The Government were willing to massacre savages in South Africa in order to find markets for British goods, whereas if they would only develop the resources of India with her three hundred millions of population, they would find ample outlet for British trade, and there would soon cease to be any unemployed in Great Britain. Thus if they would only adopt an honest policy to India they would benefit ten times to the extent they now did. Nemesis always followed upon unrighteousness, and, as Lord Salisbury once said, "Injustice will bring the mightiest of the earth to ruin." He did not see why England should be an exception to that rule. British rule had given the people security of life and property; but of what value to them was a life which meant death by starvation or disease, or of what good was property when it was only produced for the benefit of Great Britain? The fact was that Indian Natives were mere helots. They were worse than American slaves, for the latter were at least taken care of by their masters, whose property they were. All the Indian people asked was that this country should faithfully carry out the terms of the Queen's Proclamation of 1858 which promised that "Our subjects, of whatever race or creed, be freely and impartially admitted to offices in our service, the duties of which they may be qualified to discharge." Hitherto the policy of Great Britain had been in distinct contravention of Parliamentary pledges and of the Queen's Proclamation. The romance was that British rule was a blessing to India; the reality was that it was destroying India, and they might depend upon it that the destruction of India must ultimately be followed by the destruction of Great Britain. Let them alter their policy before it was too late. He very much feared that the present famine would be followed by another famine next year, because the land had become so dry. Things were going from worse to worse, and it behoved the people of Great Britain to arouse themselves, and in the interests of humanity and common justice to adopt such a policy in India as would enable the people to develop the enormous wealth of that country and to enjoy the fruits of their own country. (Loud cheers.)

The resolution was then put to the meeting and unanimously approved, and the chairman was authorised to sign and forward to the Prime Minister a petition embodying its provisions.

[*Reprinted from* INDIA, *November 30th, 1900.*]

MR. DADABHAI NAOROJI AT KENNINGTON.

INTERESTING DEBATE ON THE INDIAN FAMINE.

The subject set down for discussion at the weekly meeting, last Saturday, of the St. John's Literary and Debating Society, Kennington, was "The Indian Famine; Its Causes and Remedy." The chair was occupied by the Rev. H. G. G. Mackenzie, and the principal speaker was Mr. Dadabhai Naoroji. There was a large attendance of members, and among the visitors were Messrs. G. K. Singh, Mukerji, and T. S. Naidu.

In opening the proceedings the chairman commented on the fearful and appalling ignorance which prevailed in this country on Indian affairs and expressed the pleasure they had in welcoming one who was able to speak with so much authority on the subject which they had to debate that evening. (Hear, hear.)

Mr. Naoroji, who was received with cheers, said that although he proposed to confine himself that evening to the discussion of the causes of the Indian Famine and the remedy it must not be supposed for one moment that he desired to ignore, in the slightest degree, the good which India had reaped from her connexion with England—(hear, hear)—indeed the very fact that he was on that occasion addressing an English audience and pointing out the faults associated with British rule was in itself the best compliment he could pay to that rule in India. It was not necessary that he should attempt to describe the horrors of the famine. The descriptions of the misery and tortures suffered by millions of the Indian people, which had already appeared in the English Press, must have sufficiently lacerated their hearts. He would go direct, therefore, to the causes of the famine.

When the British people first obtained territorial power in India, bad seeds were unfortunately sown. The Company went there solely for the sake of profit, greed was at the bottom of everything they did, and the result was that corruption, oppression, and rapacity became rampant. That was the state of things at the very beginning of our political connexion with India, as was fully proved by reports of the Court of Directors of the East India Company. One of those reports set forth that vast fortunes acquired in the Indian trade had been obtained largely by tyranny and oppression. One result was that there was a heavy drain of wealth from India, and the Europeans who went out there were so anxious to acquire riches that they did not wait until they had earned or deserved them, but they seized them in defiance of all economic principles. That was one cause of India's trouble.

Again, in the formation of the Indian Empire there had occurred many wars which had entailed enormous expenditure. Probably the cost of them had gone into hundreds of millions, and towards this the British people had not contributed a single farthing. Everything expended upon the formation of the British Empire in India had been exacted from the Indian people and, in addition to that, the Natives had shed their blood freely—and to a much greater extent than Englishmen—in order to insure the maintenance of the British supremacy. Year by year the burden upon India had steadily increased, and the three millions which was annually exacted at the beginning of the present century had now grown to 25 or 30 millions. The worst of it was that India was afforded no chance of recuperation. She was suffering from a running wound which was slowly but surely sapping her vitality, and he ventured to assert that if Great Britain, now the richest country in the world, were to be subjected to similar treatment, she would as certainly fall into a state of impoverishment such as now afflicted her Eastern dependency.

It might be asked were not the famines due to droughts? His answer was in the negative. India was able to grow any quantity of food. Her resources in that respect were inexhaustible, and when famines had occurred in the past—before she was subjected to the continual drain of her wealth—the population were able to withstand them because they had stores of grain upon which they could fall back. But nowadays they were unable to accumulate such stores. Immediately the grain was grown it had to be sold in order to provide the taxation of the country, and the people were therefore not in a position to cope with famine. Indeed, the

English little knew the actual conditions under which the Indian Natives existed. A large proportion of the population was in a normal state of starvation. The people were always underfed, even in good years, and consequently, when bad years came, they the more readily succumbed. No doubt, thanks to the assistance which had been sent from this country, many thousands of lives had been saved. But for what? The people had been reduced to living skeletons; they had lost all stamina, and they would fall easy victims to disease. Now, if England failed to produce a single ear of corn in any one year there would not of necessity arise a famine, for the nations of the world would at once pour into the country stores of food which the people would be able to buy. But the difficulty of India was that the Natives had no money with which to buy food should their crops fail, and hence it was that these disastrous famines arose. India was being made to bleed at every pore, her agricultural population —the vast mass of the people—had become weak for want of blood, and their poverty was accentuated by the fact that much of her produce was sent out of the country without anything being received in return for it.

Now he came to the remedy. It was to be found in two words and two words alone—"honour" and "justice." There was not the slightest necessity that India should suffer in order that England might gain. If only the right policy were adopted India could be made prosperous, and at the same time England would reap ten times the benefit she now had from the connexion. She would gain the blessings and the gratitude of the people in lieu of their curses and their blood. What ought to be the British policy in India had been laid down in terms which gave the greatest satisfaction to the Natives of India. From 1833 onwards it had been stated in official document after official document—in Act of Parliament and in Royal Proclamation—that the Natives should have perfect equality with British citizens, and should not be debarred by reason of their origin or place of birth from holding any place or office for which by education they were fitted. (Cheers.) But, unfortunately, these solemnly-made promises had never been fulfilled. The people were still kept under a bad system of government. They had no voice in the expenditure of the money exacted from them in the form of taxes. The Queen, in her Proclamation after the

Indian Mutiny, promised that the Natives should be freely and impartially admitted to offices, "the duties of which they might be qualified by their education, ability, and integrity to discharge." But that promise had not been fulfilled, and therein was to be found Great Britain's dishonour. The promise was renewed when her Majesty assumed the title of Empress of India. It was reiterated on the occasion of her Jubilee. But it had ever been a case of promise to the ear which was broken to the hope. Even Lord Salisbury had described it as a "political hypocrisy," while Lord Lytton had asserted that "every transparent subterfuge had been resorted to" in order to avoid giving effect to it. One of the remedies which he put forward as essential for curing India's troubles was the abolition of this particular piece of British dishonour. Let Great Britain honourably fulfil her pledges in this respect and he believed that they would witness in India an amount of prosperity beyond conception.

Next he came to the question of justice. Surely when there were two partners in an undertaking it was only just that each should contribute to the cost of carrying it on. It was not fair that one should bear the whole burden and the other reap the sole benefit. Yet that was characteristic of the partnership between England and India. Whatever expenditure was incurred in the government of India, whatever outlay was involved in the maintenance of British rule there, the whole cost had had to be defrayed by India. He would not deny the necessity of maintaining European civil and military services there, but he did contend that, inasmuch as the main purpose of those services was to uphold British rule and to keep out the Russians, the cost of them ought at least to be equally divided instead of being wholly exacted from India. Why, he would like to know, should India have to pay the cost of maintaining the India Office in London, and why should she provide the salary of the Secretary of State for India? The same principle was not applied to the British Colonies; there was a Secretary of State for the Colonies, and there was a Colonial Office, but the Colonies were not called upon to contribute one farthing of the cost involved. Again, why should India pay the whole cost of carrying on the wars on the North-West frontier, the object of which was to keep the Russians at a distance? Certainly Mr. Gladstone gave them an instalment of justice in regard to the war of 1878-80 when he made a grant from the Imperial Exchequer of five million sterling towards defraying the total expenditure of twenty millions. But even that did not go far enough, for why should a wealthy country like England pay only one-fourth and a poor wretched country like India contribute three-fourths of the cost of a war waged for the promotion of purely Imperial interests? If only England were to treat India more fairly in regard to financial matters, and if this continual drain of Indian wealth were to be put a stop to, not only would the Natives of India be placed in a better position to withstand famine but they would be able and willing to purchase British manufactures, and an enormous impetus would thereby be given to British trade with India. The small amount of trade we now did with India as compared with other parts of the world was remarkable, and if only that country were enabled to be prosperous England would find her hands full in supplying Indian trade demands, and the unemployed would soon become an extinct class. If India were treated with honour and justice the result would be the disappearance of famine and destitution and the re-appearance of prosperity, accompanied by still greater prosperity for England.

A very interesting debate followed, several of the speakers urging that the lecturer had not shown a sufficient recognition of the benefits of British rule, and of the generosity of the British people in periods of distress. It was suggested that the Indian people were partly to blame for their condition because they relied too much on agriculture and had no manufacturing industries.

In the course of the discussion Mr. Mukerji insisted that loyalty was ingrained in the Native mind. It was part and parcel of their religion, and they were always grateful for services done on their behalf. When the Prince of Wales visited India he had a magnificent reception, but it was a noteworthy fact that when Lord Ripon left their shores still greater crowds of Natives assembled to do him honour, because they knew he had endeavoured to rule them justly, notwithstanding the discouragement with which he met at the hands of the Europeans there.

Mr. Singh also joined in the discussion and said it had been asked whether India would have been better off under Russian rule. His reply was that two wrongs did not make a right. (Hear, hear.) A suggestion had been thrown out as to whether there had been an adequate recognition on the part of the people of India of generous response to the various appeals for funds to cope with various famines. He thought the best reply to that was to be found in the readiness with which the people of India had volunteered their services to fight for Great Britain in South Africa and in China in the day of her need. (Cheers.) He complained, however, that no matter how well fitted a Native might prove to be to hold public office in India, he was unfairly debarred from rising to positions—especially in the Army—which were open to Europeans, some of whom were now cheering Mr. Kruger in France.

Mr. Naoroji, replying on the whole debate, said no speaker had attempted to dispute his assertion that Indian resources had been exhausted by British policy—which was thus responsible for the famines. It had been suggested that India should look more to manufacturing industries and be less dependent upon agriculture. But it seemed to be forgotten that the Indian industries had been destroyed by the British policy. India was originally noted for her industries. Venice and other ancient cities acquired great wealth through their trade with India, but Great Britain had deprived them of their life blood, and they could no longer carry on their industries because they had no means wherewith to maintain them. One of the speakers had stated that India was more prosperous now than before she came under British rule. To the eye that was so. But really it was not the case. They must remember that there were now two Indias—British India which was flourishing, and the India of the Indians which was not prosperous. He thought he had been able to show that England's policy had had might and not right as its foundation. There was no ground for charging India with ingratitude and disloyalty if she resented the violation of the solemn pledges to treat her people justly; and he warned them that the three hundred millions of Indian Natives were now beginning to understand the position and might be tempted, unless something was done to ameliorate their condition, to use force in order to destroy force. They were not discussing what Russia might do under similar circumstances. He admitted that if Russia took India to-morrow the Natives would fall from the frying pan into the fire. They were undoubtedly now in the frying pan, but surely Great Britain was not entitled to justify the breaking of honourable pledges by simply suggesting that Russia might do worse. England had taught India one very important lesson, viz., that the ruler was for the people, but the people were not for the ruler. He reiterated his friend's statement that loyalty was part and parcel of the Indian religion, which enjoined that the king should be father to the people and that the people should be children to the king, and finally he tendered hearty thanks for the sympathetic hearing which had been accorded to him.

A vote of thanks to the Rev. chairman brought the pro ceedings to a close.

INDEX.